MARYLAND'S
BLUE & GRAY

MARYLAND'S
BLUE & GRAY

A Border State's Union and Confederate Junior Officer Corps

Kevin Conley Ruffner

Louisiana State University Press   *Baton Rouge and London*

Designer: Michele Myatt Quinn
Typeface: Goudy
Typesetter: Impressions Book and Journal Services, Inc.
Printer and binder: Thomson-Shore, Inc.

Grateful acknowledgment is made for permission to reproduce excerpts from unpublished
materials in the following collections and depositories: Special Collections, Alderman
Library, University of Virginia, Charlottesville; Erick Davis Collection, in the possession
of Tom Clemens; George M. Emack Collection, in the possession of William A. Tidwell;
Manuscripts Division, Maryland Historical Society Library; Special Collections, William
R. Perkins Library, Duke University.

Portions of Chapters 5 and 6 were first published, in somewhat different form, as "Lost
in the Lost Cause: The 1st Maryland Infantry Regiment (C.S.)," *Maryland Historical Magazine*, XC (1995), 424–45.

Chapter 7 was first published, in somewhat different form, as "'More Trouble Than a
Brigade': Harry Gilmor's 2d Maryland Cavalry in the Shenandoah Valley," *Maryland Historical Magazine*, LXXXIX (1994), 388–411.

Library of Congress Cataloging-in-Publication Data
Ruffner, Kevin Conley.
    Maryland's Blue and Gray : a Border State's Union and Confederate
Junior Officer Corps / Kevin Conley Ruffner.
        p.   cm.
    Includes bibliographical references and index.
    ISBN 0-8071-2135-5 (cloth : alk. paper)
    1. Maryland—History—Civil War, 1861–1865.   2. United States.
Army—Officers—History—19th century.   3. United States. Army—
History—Civil War, 1861–1865.   4. Confederate States of America.
Army—Officers.   5. Soldiers—Maryland—History—19th century.
I. Title.
E512.4.R84   1997
973.7'452—dc21   97-7078
                                                                        CIP

Contents

Acknowledgments   xi

Abbreviations Used in Notes   xv

INTRODUCTION: A COLLECTIVE BIOGRAPHY
    OF MARYLAND'S JUNIOR CIVIL WAR OFFICERS   1

1   AN AGE OF UNCERTAINTY   14

2   MARYLAND OCCUPIED   34

3   RALLY AROUND THE FLAG   56

4   RUNNING THE BLOCKADE   76

5   MARYLAND'S HIGH TIDE   92

6   THE SHATTERED VISION   120

7   DEATH THROES OF THE MARYLAND LINE   179

8   UNCERTAIN YANKEES   212

9   THE MARYLAND BRIGADE'S DESPAIR   234

10   MARYLAND REDEEMED   260

CONCLUSION   280

Appendix: Roster of Union and
    Confederate Junior Officers   291

Bibliography   389

Index   415

Illustrations

Maps

Maryland at the Time of the Civil War   15
Baltimore in 1860   24

Photographs   *following page 150*

Members of the Maryland Guard Battalion
Bradley T. Johnson
Arnold Elzey
George H. Steuart
Edward R. Dorsey
Wilson C. Nicholas
William I. Rasin
George E. Emack
William H. Murray
Joseph Forrest
Henrietta Forrest
William W. Goldsborough
Camp St. Mary's of the Maryland Line
Christopher C. Callan
Harry Gilmor
John D. Imboden
James L. Clark
John R. Kenly
Thomas S. J. Johnson
Maurice Albaugh

Peter Bernard Wilhelm Heine
John W. Wilson
David L. Stanton
Isaiah Lightner
Edward M. Mobley
Edward Y. Goldsborough
George W. Shriver
James R. Hosmer

Tables

1. Union Military Organizations Raised in Maryland   8
2. Confederate Military Organizations from Maryland   11
3. Years of Birth of Confederate Officers from Maryland   42
4. Occupations of Confederate Officers from Maryland   44
5. Schools Attended by Confederate Officers from Maryland   46
6. Geographic Origins of the Maryland Brigade   64
7. Years of Birth of Union Officers from Maryland   66
8. Places of Birth of Union Officers from Maryland   67
9. Occupations of Union Officers from Maryland   68

Acknowledgments

J ust as no general fights a battle alone, no author writes his own book
alone. I am indebted to many people for assistance, advice, and support
during the several years that this manuscript developed into its present
form. I am both proud and sad to have been one of Marcus Cunliffe's last
students at George Washington University before his death in 1990. This
eminent historian's unique insights into American culture and the American military are reflected not only in his many works but, I hope, to some
degree in this book, as he suggested that I take a look at a border state
and its role during the Civil War.

I also wish to thank Robert Harris Walker, Jr., at George Washington
University, for his help with the manuscript in its early stages, at a time
when I faced mobilization during Operation Desert Storm. James O. Hor-
ton, also of George Washington University, and Michael P. Musick offered many fine suggestions based on their knowledge of American social
history and, in Mike's case, on an intimate familiarity with the Official
Records at the National Archives. Mike always manages to find something new on the dusty shelves at the National Archives. Ross M. Kimmel, at the Maryland Department of Natural Resources, provided considerable help with Confederate Maryland sources, and Joseph P. Reidy
of Howard University lent insight into the role of black Marylanders.
B. Franklin Cooling, the well-known Civil War historian, has long supported my interest in the Civil War. Iva Beatty of George Washington
University's Student Services helped with preparation of early versions
of the manuscript.

The researcher into Civil War history accrues a mighty debt to various
individuals and institutions. At the Maryland Historical Society, Robert
J. Brugger, Mary Ellen Hayward, Ernest L. Scott, Jr., Robert I. Cottom,
Jr., Angela S. Anthony, Jeff D. Goldman, and Jessica M. Pigza aided me

in many ways during my forays to Baltimore. Richard J. Sommers, David Keough, Pamela Cheney, and Randy W. Hackenberg helped me tap the valuable Civil War manuscript and photograph collections at the United States Army Military History Institute at Carlisle Barracks. The Museum of the Confederacy in Richmond also offers a wealth of information on Confederate military history. Guy R. Swanson, Corrine P. Hudgins, and Eva-Maria Ahladas assisted me in obtaining copies of records and photographs. John R. Sellers made research at the Manuscripts Division of the Library of Congress much more user-friendly with his practical guide. Other helpful archivists, editors, historians, and librarians include Jane F. Levey, of the Historical Society of Washington, D.C.; Michael Plunkett and Ervin L. Jordan, Jr., of the University of Virginia; Diane B. Jacob at the Virginia Military Institute; Lawrence H. McDonald and Michael Meier, at the National Archives; Robert K. Krick, at the Fredericksburg and Spotsylvania National Military Park; Christopher Calkins, at the Petersburg National Battlefield; Dennis E. Frye, formerly of the Harpers Ferry National Historical Park; and Ben Primer, of Princeton University.

I would also like to thank Edward L. Ayers, John D. Chapla, Tom Clemens, Robert J. Driver, Jr., Joseph T. Glatthaar, Harold E. Howard, Perry D. Jamieson, S. Roger Keller, William J. Miller, Brigadier General William A. Tidwell, USAR (Ret.), and Daniel C. Toomey for their assistance with various research questions regarding Maryland's role in the Civil War. The descendants of Maryland's officers were also very helpful. In the course of my research, I had the good fortune to meet Mrs. Margaret K. Fresco, one of the living legends of St. Marys County, whose grandfather, Joseph Forrest, organized the 4th Maryland Battery (C.S.). David Callan likewise provided me with considerable information about his forefather, Christopher C. Callan, who remains one of the most unusual officers to have served in the Maryland Line. Other descendants, P. James Kurapka, Charles L. Mobley, Jr., and George Rich, also provided genealogical information.

The Phoebe R. Jacobsen Conference on Maryland History, sponsored by the Maryland State Archives, allowed me an opportunity to discuss my research in 1991. My thanks to Edward C. Papenfuse and Gregory A. Stiverson for their invitation and encouragement.

Thomas W. Steptoe of Charles Town, West Virginia, himself the descendant of Confederate officers, hosted me at his cabin in the Blue Ridge Mountains for several weeks. His generous hospitality enabled me to fin-

ish writing this study at a point where time was of the essence. My gratitude to Tom and his wife Sharon for taking in a stranger and treating
him well.

Stephen D. Oltmann of Fairfax, Virginia, produced the maps of Maryland and Baltimore with very little guidance and in record time. They
enhance the value of the text by showing the geographic complexities of
Maryland in 1860 and 1861.

I cannot forget to extend thanks to Louisiana State University Press
for not only accepting my manuscript for publication but also for cheer-
fully assisting me in all of the steps toward that goal. I am especially
pleased to have worked with Margaret Dalrymple, John Easterly, Catherine Landry, and the freelance editor Trudie Calvert. The anonymous
reader provided many rays of hope when I had grown weary of marketing
the manuscript.

Just as Professor Cunliffe did not live to see this book, unfortunately,
three grandchildren of Confederate soldiers also did not see its publication. I would like to remember my grandmother, Gatewood H. Sharood,
for all of her love and support over the years as I pursued my interest in
history. T. C. Greever and Elizabeth H. Coiner both graciously shared
with me their time and wonderful family holdings in my studies of the
Confederacy.

Finally, my interest in the Civil War originates with my parents, Bob
and Peggy Ruffner, who have trooped with me over many battlefields and
who nurtured my interest. My wife, Sonja, patiently accepted my spend-
ing more time at archives and libraries than at home. I hope that this
book will be a small token of my appreciation for her sacrifices.

Abbreviations Used in Notes

CGSO   Compiled Service Records of Confederate Generals and Staff Officers
CSR   Compiled Service Records
GUAAR   Georgetown University Archives Alumni Records
LAIG   Letters Received by the Confederate Adjutant and Inspector General
LC   Library of Congress
LSOW   Letters Received by the Confederate Secretary of War
MHS   Maryland Historical Society Library
MSA   Maryland State Archives
NA   National Archives
RG   Record Group
SHSP   *Southern Historical Society Papers*
USAMHI   United States Army Military History Institute

MARYLAND'S
BLUE & GRAY

Introduction:
A Collective Biography of Maryland's
Junior Civil War Officers

The military man in the United States during the first half of the nineteenth century has been characterized by a modern historian as fitting into one of three models: the Quaker, the Rifleman, and the Chevalier. Marcus Cunliffe, in his book *Soldiers and Civilians: The Martial Spirit in America, 1775–1865*, notes that men of the Quaker model resented the trappings of military pageantry and the waste of war. Perhaps the most durable of the three models in American society, Quakerism was centered in the North and had little opportunity to spread into the South or the frontier West.[1]

In contrast, the Rifleman model was represented in all sections of the United States. The Rifleman, with a long and honorable lineage, drew from the nation's rural yeomanry who left home and farm "at a minute's notice" to defend liberty. Yet this same figure became easily bored with military routine and derived satisfaction from continual action, quick victory, and a speedy return to civilian life. The Rifleman, writes Cunliffe, was "a mixture of the genial and the brutal, the callous and the sentimental, of patriotism and patrioteering, he is the prime type of a nation which is 'martial but unmilitary.'"[2]

The third model, the Chevalier, is generally associated with the gentry of the South, although military men of this type were also found throughout the North and in the frontier areas of the United States. Cunliffe describes the Chevalier as a "mounted gentleman, the symbol of authority, the conscious heir of a gracious tradition. . . . His code of honor antedates the spirit of nationalistic warfare." The Chevalier, by all ac-

1. Marcus Cunliffe, *Soldiers and Civilians: The Martial Spirit in America, 1775–1865* (Boston, 1968), 412–23.
2. *Ibid.*, 417.

counts, was out of date in America, where, as Alexis de Tocqueville observed, "it is strange to see with what feverish ardour the Americans pursue their own welfare; and to watch the vague dread that constantly torments them lest they should not have chosen the shortest path which may lead to it." Despite the seeming anachronism of the Chevalier, the model symbolized the subdued ambitions of Americans who devoured the romantic novels of Sir Walter Scott.[3]

The Quaker, Rifleman, and Chevalier models partially capture the spirit of militarism in Maryland in 1861. Although the Mason-Dixon line marked the boundary between Yankee North and Dixie South, the actual separation was far less defined in Maryland. That state exhibited traits of both North and South. Maryland's large immigrant and free black populations set it apart from the tobacco and cotton kingdoms of the Deep South. A large urban metropolis, Baltimore, served as a center for industrial and commercial development. The city's natural harbor and good rail transportation facilities linked Maryland with the North and West and tied the state to the world's markets. Maryland maintained its traditional tobacco base while expanding into other agricultural products. Maryland in 1860 was still very much a slave state, which bound its fortune to that of the South and distinguished it from its northern neighbors.

In many ways, the civil war fought in Maryland in the years 1861 to 1865 was a microcosm of the war that afflicted the entire nation. In few states did the war have more impact on families and the social and political order. The upheaval that occurred there has been studied primarily for its ramifications on politics and race relations. Jean H. Baker's *Ambivalent Americans: The Know-Nothing Party in Maryland* and *The Politics of Continuity: Maryland Political Parties from 1858 to 1870* provide good analyses of the disruption of Maryland's political order in the middle period. William J. Evitts also studied party activity in Maryland in the decade preceding the war in *A Matter of Allegiances: Maryland from 1850 to 1861*. Baker's and Evitts' works provide fascinating details on the political cauldron bubbling over in Maryland and the vulnerability of the

3. *Ibid.*, 422; Alexis de Tocqueville, *Democracy in America*, trans. Henry Reeve (2 vols.; New York, 1961), II, 161; the influence of the Romantic Age on American militarism in both the North and South is noted by Cunliffe, *Soldiers and Civilians*, 348, and in Gerald F. Linderman, *Embattled Courage: The Experience of Combat in the American Civil War* (New York, 1987), 15–16.

various parties as the debate over slavery overwhelmed all other issues. Charles Branch Clark also studied the war's impact on the state's political structure in *Politics in Maryland During the Civil War*. Gary Lawson Browne's *Baltimore in the Nation, 1789–1861* looks at the development of Maryland's largest city and its unique role in the state. Another study examines the social-political-economic framework of slavery in Maryland and the effects of the war on the status quo. Barbara Jeanne Fields's *Slavery and Freedom on the Middle Ground: Maryland During the Nineteenth Century* is the most recent examination of the role of free blacks and slaves in the war that destroyed slavery as an institution in Maryland.[4]

Maryland acted with great reluctance after the surrender of Fort Sumter and attempted to remain neutral in the face of inevitable conflict between North and South. Many prosecessionist Marylanders and equally ardent Unionists, however, opposed taking the middle road. The federal government urgently needed to keep Maryland in the Union to ensure the security of the capital at Washington, D.C. The movement of federal troops through Baltimore brought upheaval and bloodshed although there was little open resistance when Union forces ultimately occupied the state. Union and Confederate leaders recognized the state's military and political importance, and several major battles and campaigns took place on Maryland's soil.

Although Baker, Clark, Evitts, Fields, and other historians have discussed various aspects of Maryland's role in the war, there has been little study of the state's white population. Our knowledge of the reaction of Marylanders to the secession crisis and the internecine conflict is drawn from a few accounts published by aging veterans decades after the war. Henry Kyd Douglas' *I Rode with Stonewall: The War Experiences of the Youngest Member of Jackson's Staff*, Randolph H. McKim's *A Soldier's Rec-*

---

4. Jean H. Baker, *Ambivalent Americans: The Know-Nothing Party in Maryland* (Baltimore, 1977), and *The Politics of Continuity: Maryland Political Parties from 1858 to 1870* (Baltimore, 1973); William J. Evitts, *A Matter of Allegiances: Maryland from 1850 to 1861* (Baltimore, 1974); Charles Branch Clark, *Politics in Maryland During the Civil War* (Chestertown, 1952); Gary Lawson Browne, *Baltimore in the Nation, 1789–1861* (Chapel Hill, 1980); Barbara Jeanne Fields, *Slavery and Freedom on the Middle Ground: Maryland During the Nineteenth Century* (New Haven, 1985). An exception to the dearth of study of nonpolitical or slave issues in Civil War Maryland is Richard R. Duncan, "The Social and Economic Impact of the Civil War on Maryland" (Ph.D. dissertation, Ohio State University, 1963).

ollections, McHenry Howard's *Recollections of a Maryland Confederate Soldier and Staff Officer Under Johnston, Jackson, and Lee*, W. W. Goldsborough's *The Maryland Line in the Confederate Army, 1861–1865*, Harry Gilmor's *Four Years in the Saddle*, George W. Booth's *Personal Reminiscences of a Maryland Soldier in the War Between the States, 1861–1865*, and Bradley T. Johnson's volume, *Maryland*, in *Confederate Military History* all present a version of the war colored by sentimentality and distance from the actual events. These works reflect the viewpoints of Marylanders who served in the Confederate army. Union Marylanders wrote little about their experiences after the war, which gives the erroneous impression that Maryland made little contribution to the northern war effort.[5]

As a result of this imbalance in the literature, Maryland is seen as an occupied state that supported the Union cause only under duress. Modern Civil War students commonly regard Maryland Confederates as the prime examples of Cunliffe's Chevalier model, while Union Marylanders barely meet the definition of the Rifleman model. One of most fervent Confederate Marylanders, Brig. Gen. Bradley T. Johnson, wrote in 1899:

> The first forces raised for the Union in Maryland were, with the exception of the First regiment, mainly composed of foreigners, aliens by birth and aliens to the institutions, ideals and motives that for nine generations had formed the character of Marylanders. They were good men, but not Marylanders. They were devoted to the Union, but they had no conception of the force and duty of "courage and chivalry." The Confederate Mary-

5. Henry Kyd Douglas, *I Rode with Stonewall: The War Experiences of the Youngest Member of Jackson's Staff* (Chapel Hill, 1940); Randolph H. McKim, *A Soldier's Recollections: Leaves from the Diary of a Young Confederate* (New York, 1910); McHenry Howard, *Recollections of a Maryland Confederate Soldier and Staff Officer Under Johnston, Jackson, and Lee* (1914; rpr. Dayton, 1975); W. W. Goldsborough, *The Maryland Line in the Confederate Army* (1869, 1900; rpr. Port Washington, 1972); Harry Gilmor, *Four Years in the Saddle* (1866; rpr. Baltimore, 1987); George Wilson Booth, *Personal Reminiscences of a Maryland Soldier in the War Between the States, 1861–1865* (1898; rpr. Gaithersburg, 1986); and Bradley T. Johnson, *Maryland*, Vol. II of *Confederate Military History*, ed. Clement A. Evans (1899; rpr. Wilmington, 1987). Primary sources regarding Union soldiers from Maryland are exceedingly scarce. The best overall reference guide to Union Marylanders is L. Allison Wilmer, J. H. Jarrett, and George W. F. Vernon, *History and Roster of Maryland Volunteers, War of 1861–5* (2 vols.; 1898; rpr. Westminster, 1987 and 1990). The best single regimental history of a U.S. Maryland unit is Charles Camper and J. W. Kirkley, *Historical Record of the First Maryland Infantry* (1871; rpr. Baltimore, 1990). Other Union military histories include Frederick W. Wild, *Memoirs and History of Capt. F. W. Alexander's Baltimore Battery* (Baltimore, 1912), and C. Armour Newcomer, *Cole's Cavalry; or, Three Years in the Saddle in the Shenandoah Valley* (Baltimore, 1895).

landers, on the other hand, embodied the faith and pride of the State. Not a historic family of Maryland but was represented in the Maryland Line.[6]

Johnson's description of his fellow Maryland Confederates is echoed by other veterans who wore Maryland gray. Their Union counterparts are relegated to the lower-caste status of draftees, substitutes, or "Dutchmen" (German-born immigrants). This image has persisted to this day without any substantial revision or review by Civil War historians.[7]

The divisiveness of the war that sundered families in the 1860s etched a deep scar on Maryland's psyche. Yet the state has received little attention from such prominent Civil War historians as Bell Irvin Wiley, James I. Robertson, Jr., Gerald F. Linderman, Reid Mitchell, James M. McPherson, Bruce Catton, or Douglas Southall Freeman. Wiley's masterful volumes, *The Life of Johnny Reb* and *The Life of Billy Yank,* provide reams of information on the lives and experiences of Confederate and Union soldiers. Wiley's analysis of the backgrounds and motives of Civil War soldiers has set the standard that other students in the field strive to match. Yet it is disappointing that Wiley made little reference, beyond the basic sources, to the peculiar dilemma that Maryland men faced during the war.[8]

6. Johnson, *Maryland*, 98.

7. For examples of modern-day perceptions, see Daniel D. Hartzler, *Marylanders in the Confederacy* (Silver Spring, 1986), 2; Harry Wright Newman, *Maryland and the Confederacy* (Annapolis, 1976), 258–59; and Thomas V. Huntsberry and Joanne M. Huntsberry, *Maryland in the Civil War*, vol. I (Baltimore, 1985). Two recent works contribute to the photographic and illustrative record of the war in Maryland: Robert I. Cottom, Jr., and Mary Ellen Hayward, *Maryland in the Civil War: A House Divided* (Baltimore, 1994), and Daniel D. Hartzler, *A Band of Brothers: Photographic Epilogue to Marylanders in the Confederacy* (N.p., 1992).

8. Bell I. Wiley, *The Life of Johnny Reb: The Common Soldier of the Confederacy* (1980; rpr. Baton Rouge, 1994), and *The Life of Billy Yank: The Common Soldier of the Union* (1980; rpr. Baton Rouge, 1994). James I. Robertson, Jr., *Soldiers Blue and Gray* (Columbia, 1988), updates Wiley's work with further research and sources. Linderman, *Embattled Courage*, looks at the values that Civil War soldiers held at the beginning of the war and how the experience of combat changed them. Reid Mitchell, *Civil War Soldiers: Their Expectations and Experiences* (New York, 1988), also seeks to find the meaning of military service for Americans in the Civil War; Mitchell's second book, *The Vacant Chair: The Northern Soldier Leaves Home* (New York, 1993), explores the relationship between home and family on Union soldiers. James M. McPherson's *What They Fought For, 1861–1865* (Baton Rouge, 1994) is an introduction to his upcoming major work on this topic. Bruce Catton and Douglas Southall Freeman are the preeminent historians of the two major armies in the eastern theater; see Catton, *The Army of the Potomac* (3 vols.; New York,

Maryland was the most important of the border states in 1861 because of its proximity to Washington, D.C., and the new Confederate capital at Richmond, Virginia. The events leading up to the outbreak of war and the role of the border states (Maryland, Delaware, Kentucky, Tennessee, Missouri, and western Virginia) have been of great interest over the years. The actual conduct of the war and its impact on border state residents have drawn less attention. Michael Fellman's *Inside War: The Guerrilla Conflict in Missouri During the American Civil War* is the first in-depth study of the horror unleashed on one border state before, during, and after the Civil War. Other modern historians have used Tennessee as an example of the divided nature of a border state. Fred A. Bailey, for example, studied postwar Tennessee veteran surveys to ascertain the attitudes and experiences of Confederate officers and men.[9] The "new social history" of the past twenty-five years has broadened the horizons of military history and allows for a greater range of study.[10]

1951–53), and Freeman, *Lee's Lieutenants: A Study of Command* (3 vols.; New York, 1942–44).

9. Michael Fellman, *Inside War: The Guerrilla Conflict in Missouri During the American Civil War* (New York, 1989); William E. Parrish, *Turbulent Partnership: Missouri and the Union, 1861–1865* (Columbia, 1963); E. Merton Coulter, *The Civil War and Readjustment in Kentucky* (1926; rpr. Gloucester, 1966); William C. Wright, *The Secession Movement in the Middle Atlantic States* (Rutherford, 1973); Daniel W. Crofts, *Reluctant Confederates: Upper South Unionists in the Secession Crisis* (Chapel Hill, 1989); Stephen V. Ash, *Middle Tennessee Society Transformed, 1860–1870: War and Peace in the Upper South* (Baton Rouge, 1988); Edward Conrad Smith, *The Borderland in the Civil War* (1927; rpr. Freeport, 1969); Gustavus W. Dyer and John Trotwood Moore, eds., *The Tennessee Civil War Veterans Questionnaires* (5 vols.; Easley, 1985); Fred A. Bailey, *Class and Tennessee's Confederate Generation* (Chapel Hill, 1987); Fred A. Bailey, "Class and Tennessee's Confederate Generation," *Journal of Southern History*, LI (1985), 31–60.

10. For a more complete analysis of the uses of social history in the study of the military, see John Keegan, *The Face of Battle* (New York, 1976); Peter Kartsen, ed., *The Military in America: From the Colonial Period to the Present* (rev. ed.; New York, 1986); Edward M. Coffman, "The New American Military History," *Military Affairs*, XLVIII (1984), 1–5; Richard H. Kohn, "The Social History of the American Soldier: A Review and Prospectus for Research," *American Historical Review*, LXXXVI (1981), 553–67; Peter Karsten, "The 'New' American Military History: A Map of the Territory, Explored and Unexplored," *American Quarterly*, XXXVI (1984), 389–418; Benjamin Franklin Cooling, "Toward a More Useable Past: A Modest Plea for a Newer Typology of Military History," *Military Affairs*, LII (1988), 29–31. An especially interesting discussion of social history and the Civil War is found in Maris A. Vinovskis, "Have Social Historians Lost the Civil War? Some Preliminary Demographic Speculations," *Journal of American History*, LXXVI

Maryland's Blue and Gray: A Border State's Union and Confederate Junior Officer Corps is a prosopography, or collective biography, of the men from Maryland who served as captains and lieutenants in the Union Army of the Potomac and the Confederate Army of Northern Virginia. Representing varying segments of Maryland's antebellum society, these men provide a unique opportunity to study the backgrounds, motivations, and experiences of a particular group who fought in the nation's bloodiest war. A collective biography of this nature will enable the modern student to compare and contrast those Marylanders who supported the North with those who espoused the southern cause. Our comprehension of the reasons why friends, family members, and neighbors took up arms against one another will be enhanced by this detailed examination of a select group of Maryland Civil War officers.[11]

Although students of the war debate the exact number of Marylanders who served in the Union and Confederate forces, estimates range up to sixty thousand Marylanders in the northern ranks and as many as twenty-five thousand in Confederate service. These figures, however, must be approached with caution. Maryland raised twenty infantry and four cavalry regiments for Union service as well as six artillery batteries. Additionally, the state offered smaller infantry and cavalry units and several regiments of United States Colored Troops (USCT). Maryland furnished a total of forty-two units of various sizes to the federal government during the Civil War (see Table 1).

Maryland did not officially raise any troops for Confederate service; however, exiles from the state organized one infantry regiment, one infantry battalion, two cavalry battalions, and four batteries of artillery that fought under the Maryland streamer. Confederate Marylanders also served

---

(1989), 34–58; see also Vinovskis, ed., *Toward a Social History of the American Civil War* (New York, 1990).

11. For examples of other collective biographies, see Larry J. Daniel, *Soldiering in the Army of Tennessee: A Portrait of Life in a Confederate Army* (Chapel Hill, 1991); Edward M. Coffman, *The Old Army: A Portrait of the American Army in Peacetime, 1784–1898* (New York, 1986); J. C. A. Stagg, "Enlisted Men in the United States Army, 1812–1815: A Preliminary Survey," *William and Mary Quarterly*, XLIII (1986), 615–45; Fred Anderson, *A People's Army: Massachusetts Soldiers and Society in the Seven Years' War* (Chapel Hill, 1984); Charles Royster, *A Revolutionary People at War: The Continental Army and American Character, 1775–1783* (Chapel Hill, 1979); and Joseph Allen Frank and George A. Reaves, *"Seeing the Elephant": Raw Recruits at the Battle of Shiloh* (Westport, 1989).

Table 1. Union Military Organizations Raised in Maryland

Unit	Date Organized	Date Mustered Out
1st Inf. Regt.	May, 1861	July, 1865
2nd Inf. Regt.	September, 1861	July, 1865
3rd Inf. Regt.	August, 1861–May, 1862	July, 1865
4th Inf. Regt.	July–August, 1862	May, 1865
5th Inf. Regt.	September, 1861	September, 1865
6th Inf. Regt.	August–September, 1862	June, 1865
7th Inf. Regt.	July–August, 1862	May, 1865
8th Inf. Regt.	August, 1862–April, 1863	May, 1865
9th Inf. Regt. (6 Months)	June–July, 1863	February, 1864
10th Inf. Regt. (6 Months)	June–July, 1863	January, 1864
11th Inf. Regt. (100 Days)	June, 1864	October, 1864
11th Inf. Regt. (1 Year)	October, 1864	June, 1865
Consolidated with 1st Regt., Eastern Shore Inf., February, 1865.		
12th Inf. Regt. (100 Days)	July, 1864	November, 1864
13th Inf. Regt.	March, 1865	May, 1865
Formed from 1st Regt., Potomac Home Brigade Inf., March–April, 1865.		
1st Regt., Eastern Shore Inf.	September, 1861	February, 1865
Consolidated with 11th Inf. Regt. (1 Year), February, 1865.		
2nd Regt., Eastern Shore Inf.	October–December, 1861	January, 1865
Consolidated with 1st Regt., Eastern Shore Inf., January, 1865.		
1st Regt., Potomac Home Brigade Inf.	August–December, 1861	August–December, 1864
Formed basis of 13th Inf. Regt., March–April, 1865.		

2nd Regt., Potomac Home Brigade Inf.	August–October, 1861	May, 1865
3rd Regt., Potomac Home Brigade Inf.	October, 1861–May, 1862	May, 1865
Purnell Legion Inf.	October–December, 1861	October, 1864
Patapsco Guards, Independent Co. of Inf.	September, 1861	August, 1865
1st Cav. Regt.	August, 1861–June, 1862	August, 1865
1st Regt., Potomac Home Brigade Cav. (Cole's cav.)	August–November, 1861	June, 1865
2nd Cav. Regt. (6 Months)	July–August, 1863	January–February, 1864
3rd Cav. Regt.	August, 1863–January, 1864	September, 1865
Purnell Legion, Cav. Battalion	October, 1861–September, 1862	November, 1864

Consolidated with 8th Infantry Regiment, November, 1864.

Smith's Independent Co. of Cav.	October, 1862	June, 1865
Btry. A, Light Art. (Rigby's)	August–September, 1861	March, 1865

Consolidated with Btry. B.

Btry. B, Light Art. (Snow's)	September–October, 1861	July, 1865

Consolidated with Btry. A, March, 1865.

Btry. D, Light Art.	November, 1864	June, 1865
Baltimore Btry., Light Art. (Alexander's)	August, 1862	June, 1865
Btry. A (Second), Light Art. (Junior Art.) (6 Months)	July, 1863	January, 1864

(cont.)

Table 1 (cont.)

Unit	Date Organized	Date Mustered Out
Btry. B (Second), Light Art. (Eagle Art.) (6 Months)	July, 1863	January, 1864
4th U.S. Colored Troops (USCT)	July–September, 1863	May, 1866
7th USCT	September–November, 1863	November, 1866
9th USCT	November, 1863	November, 1866
19th USCT	December, 1863	January, 1867
30th USCT	February–March, 1864	December, 1865
39th USCT	March, 1864	December, 1865

Source: Compiled from Wilmer, Jarrett, and Vernon, *History and Roster of Maryland Volunteers, War of 1861–65.*

in numerous military organizations raised by other southern states and were often not recognized as Maryland soldiers (see Table 2).[12]

In this book I discuss Maryland's junior officer corps as a whole but focus on those men who served with the two rival armies in the Virginia theater of operations. Marylanders who served as army lieutenants and captains in western campaigns, Union officers from the state assigned to the USCT regiments in the Army of the Potomac, Maryland junior of-

12. The number of men from Maryland who served in the Union and Confederate armies is the subject of much discussion. The oft-quoted figure of sixty thousand Union Marylanders is derived from Wilmer, Jarrett, and Vernon, *History and Roster*, 6–8. An estimate of Union and Confederate Marylanders is found in Hartzler, *Marylanders in the Confederacy*, 1–2. For the most recent discussion of exactly how many Marylanders served in the opposing armies, see Brice M. Clagett's book review of Daniel Carroll Toomey's *Index to the Roster of the Maryland Volunteers, 1861–1865* (Harmons, 1986), in *Maryland Historical Magazine*, LXXXII (1987), 320–21. Further questions are raised in Clagett's letter to the editor in the spring, 1996, issue of *Maryland Historical Magazine*, 116–17, and Ruffner's response in the summer, 1996, issue, 245–48.

Table 2. Confederate Military Organizations from Maryland

Unit	Date Organized	Date Mustered Out
1st Inf. Regt.	June, 1861	August, 1862
2nd Inf. Battalion	September, 1862	April, 1865
1st Cav. Battalion	November, 1862	April, 1865
2nd Cav. Battalion (Gilmor's battalion)	May–June, 1863	April, 1865
1st Art. Btry. (Maryland Art.)	July, 1861	April, 1865
2nd Art. Btry. (Baltimore Light Art.)	September, 1861	April, 1865
3rd Art. Btry. (Latrobe Art.)	January, 1862	April, 1865
4th Art. Btry. (Chesapeake Art.)	January, 1862	April, 1865

Other Confederate Units Containing Marylanders

Co. G, 1st South Carolina Inf. Regt.
1st South Carolina Regular Heavy Art. Battalion
15th South Carolina Heavy Art. Battalion
Cos. E and F, 1st Virginia Inf. Regt.
Co. N, 2nd Regt. Virginia State Reserves
2nd Co. D, 3rd Regt. Virginia Inf. Local Defense Troops
Co. H, 7th Virginia Inf. Regt.
Co. B, 9th Virginia Inf. Regt.
Co. G, 13th Virginia Inf. Regt.
Co. B, 21st Virginia Inf. Regt.
Co. E, 30th Virginia Battalion Sharpshooters
Co. E, 44th Virginia Inf. Regt.
2nd Co. H, 47th Virginia Inf. Regt.
2nd Co. K, 1st Virginia Cav. Regt.
Co. G, 7th Virginia Cav. Regt.
Co. F, 12th Virginia Cav. Regt.
Co. M, 23rd Virginia Cav. Regt.
Co. A, 24th Battalion Virginia Partisan Rangers
35th Virginia Cav. Battalion
43rd Battalion, Virginia Partisan Rangers
McNeill's Rangers
Breathed's Battery, Stuart Horse Art.
2nd Co. C, 19th Virginia Heavy Art. Battalion

Sources: Compiled from Goldsborough, *The Maryland Line in the Confederate Army,* and Wallace, *A Guide to Virginia Military Organizations, 1861–1865.*

ficers in either the U.S. or C.S. navy or marine corps, and officers who served primarily in a staff or support function (chaplains, quartermasters, ordnance officers, and surgeons) lie outside the parameters of this work.

The 365 junior officers who served in the Union Army of Potomac's Maryland Brigade (composed of the 1st, 4th, 7th, and 8th infantry regiments) and the Confederate Army of Northern Virginia's Maryland Line (1st Maryland Infantry Regiment, 2nd Infantry Battalion, 1st and 2nd cavalry battalions, and 1st, 2nd, and 4th artillery batteries) form the basis for this study. I have made an extensive review of the military and civilian careers of these men in an attempt to provide an in-depth analysis of a sizeable segment of Maryland's officer population (see Appendix). Using the written words of these men, in the form of excerpts from letters, diaries, memoirs, and official papers, I hope to give the modern reader clear insight into the lives of a heretofore often overlooked Civil War soldiery.

The Maryland Line included virtually every junior officer who served in a Maryland Confederate unit in the eastern theater during the four years of war. The only state organization not discussed in this work is the 3rd Maryland Battery (C.S.), which spent the entire war in the West. Men in the Union's Maryland Brigade, the largest unit from the state to serve with the Army of the Potomac, came from throughout the state, especially from Baltimore and western Maryland. The fact that the four regiments of the Maryland Brigade remained in the service until Appomattox (as opposed to the two Eastern Shore regiments and the Potomac Home Brigade regiments) made these officers a better group to study. The Union sample, unlike the Confederate, does not contain any artillery or cavalry officers because the Maryland Brigade was, almost exclusively, an infantry organization.

This examination of men who held company-grade positions in Maryland units during the Civil War is more than an organizational history. I look at the social and economic background of the officers, including birthplace, age, occupation, ethnicity, religion, residence or regional identification, education, wealth, and slaveholding status. I also discuss their reactions to secession and abolitionism, and their political beliefs as expressed during the war with regard to local elections, the 1864 presidential campaign, emancipation of Maryland slaves in 1864, and faith in Unionist principles and the southern ideal of states' rights. I examine why, how, where, and when these men joined the army and became officers and their reaction to army life and professional development as leaders on the battlefield and in camp. I explore the impact of casualties, promotions, resignations, and discipline and morale problems on the officer corps. The personal relationships of the men are of particular concern with regard to Confederate officers who had to leave their families. Also of interest are their reactions to the conduct of the war in Maryland: suspension of habeas corpus; suppression of civil rights, and the invasion of Maryland by southern troops. Finally, I consider relations between Maryland officers and the Union and Confederate military hierarchy, and their dealings with northern and southern society, and with subordinate soldiers.

Maryland's Blue and Gray integrates military and social history to elucidate the makeup, influences, goals, and experiences of a portion of nineteenth-century Maryland society. In essence, this work attempts to discover the cultural similarities between Union and Confederate Marylanders and the irreconcilable differences that brought them into mortal conflict.

·1·

An Age of Uncertainty

In the mid-nineteenth century, John Pendleton Kennedy, a wealthy Maryland politician and socialite, disgustedly wrote: "Nothing can be more contemptible than the state politics and management of Maryland. We have not a man in public service above mediocrity, and the whole machinery of our politics is moved by the smallest, narrowest, most ignorant and corrupt men in the State. . . . The result," Kennedy added, "is something even below a shaky mediocrity in every department of affairs." Kennedy's observations summed up the popular perception that the state lacked natural leadership and that America was on the verge of losing its distinctive national character.[1]

In an age of uncertainty, Maryland shared concerns felt throughout the nation over rapid industrialization, slavery, immigration, urbanization, and the shifting of political loyalties. The growing sectionalism that affected the United States existed in microcosm in Maryland. The state was not a single entity; geography divided its political, social, and economic interests. The division of Maryland into three, sometimes categorized as four, regions deeply affected the development of the state and its outlook when war came in 1861[2] (see Map 1).

Founded in 1634 as a refuge for English Roman Catholics in the New World, Maryland developed a Chesapeake culture based on the cultivation and exportation of tobacco. From its small, Catholic-oriented base

1. Evitts, *A Matter of Allegiances*, 46; Baker, *Ambivalent Americans*, 57–58; Baker, *Politics of Continuity*, 15–16. For more information on Kennedy's role in 1860–61, see Stefan Nesenhöner, "Maintaining the Center: John Pendleton Kennedy, the Border States, and the Secession Crisis," *Maryland Historical Magazine*, LXXXIX (1994), 413–26.

2. A discussion of the state's regions is found in Evitts, *A Matter of Allegiances*, 5–13; Baker, *Ambivalent Americans*, 7–18; Baker, *Politics of Continuity*, 6–13; Fields, *Slavery and Freedom*, 6–22.

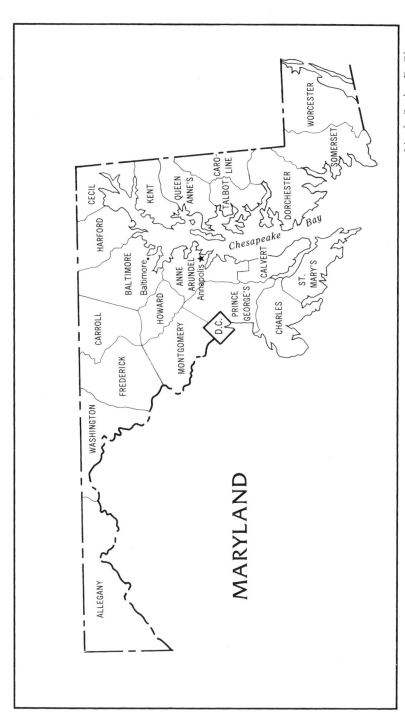

MARYLAND

Maryland Counties at the Time of the Civil War

Map by Stephen D. Oltmann

in southern Maryland where the Potomac River joins Chesapeake Bay, immigrants from all backgrounds moved up the bay and settled along its many tributaries. At the same time, primarily German-speaking settlers moved southward from Pennsylvania and occupied the fertile valleys nestled along the Catoctin Mountains in the west.[3]

The settlement patterns of the seventeenth and eighteenth centuries shaped the sectional divisions of nineteenth-century Maryland. The counties of St. Marys, Charles, Calvert, Prince Georges, Montgomery, and Anne Arundel composed the heart of southern Maryland. The oldest of the state's four regions, southern Maryland remained embedded in the old system of tobacco production and slave labor. During the decades following the first census enumeration in 1790, population growth in southern Maryland stagnated. The region had 109,308 white and black residents in 1850, representing less than 20 percent of the state's total population.[4]

Numbers do not accurately portray the decline of southern Maryland. The cradle of the state had become a backwater although it still exercised political power beyond its small population. The drop in the white population was particularly significant: southern Maryland lost 10 percent of its white residents between 1790 and 1850. Only 12 percent of all whites in the state lived in the region. This loss was attributed to the weakening hold of tobacco on the state's economy. In St. Marys County alone, tobacco production dropped by nearly 40 percent between 1840 and 1850. By 1859, tobacco accounted for only 14 percent of Maryland's overall agricultural production. Fluctuations in the world market and the exhaustion of soil throughout Maryland spurred the downward spiral in tobacco production. Many whites, in consequence, abandoned southern Maryland for Kentucky and other developing areas in the Southwest.[5]

As tobacco declined in southern Maryland, the region also fell behind in other indicators of progress. Industrial development sidestepped the area as did urban growth. The nation's capital in Washington, D.C., had little impact on population growth or economic investment in sur-

3. For a recent history of the state, see Robert J. Brugger, *Maryland: A Middle Temperament, 1634–1980* (Baltimore, 1988).

4. Fields, *Slavery and Freedom*, 8–13.

5. For a discussion of the decline of tobacco in Maryland, see Avery O. Craven, *Soil Exhaustion as a Factor in the Agricultural History of Virginia and Maryland, 1606–1860* (1925; rpr. Gloucester, 1965); Fields, *Slavery and Freedom*, 5, 13; Baker, *Ambivalent Americans*, 9.

rounding southern Maryland. In 1860, Prince Georges County had only twelve manufacturing establishments while neighboring Charles County counted five. Similarly, Annapolis, the only town in the region (with the exception of the District of Columbia), was stagnating. In the eyes of one observer, the state capital had "degenerated into one of the most dreary, dull, and monotonous places in the state."[6]

The landowners of southern Maryland were not impervious to the changes that threatened their way of life. The 1860 census revealed a dichotomy that split even southern Maryland. Prince Georges County ranked fourth among the top five counties in the state for the highest farm cash value, whereas Charles County ranked in the bottom three counties. Farmers in Montgomery County, for example, fearing the dev-astation they had witnessed over the past decade, organized the Old Club in Sandy Spring in 1844 to improve agricultural practices and output. The use of Peruvian guano as well as gypsum and manure as fertilizer revitalized fields throughout southern Maryland that had been exhausted by tobacco. Planters also learned to diversify crops and to plow better. An optimistic farmer boasted in 1859 that "there is no such thing as worn-out land; that expression conveys a falsehood; it is a very practical thing, with a moderate degree of intelligence and no very large means, to restore these lands to any degree of fertility they have ever possessed. This lesson has been well learned in Maryland. . . . We have tried all the alternatives, we have been 'down hill' and many have been 'West,' and have abandoned both one and the other for 'improvement' and know that is the best thing." Southern Maryland farmers took this advice to heart; within a ten-year period the number of bushels of wheat and corn raised in three counties doubled.[7]

The institution of slavery remained viable in southern Maryland de-

6. U.S. Census Bureau, *Manufactures of the United States in 1860; Compiled from the Original Returns of the Eighth Census* (Washington, D.C., 1865), 228; Evitts, *A Matter of Allegiances,* 10; Harold W. Hurst, "The Northernmost Southern Town: A Sketch of Pre–Civil War Annapolis," *Maryland Historical Magazine,* LXXVI (1981), 240–49.

7. U.S. Census Bureau, *Agriculture in the United States in 1860; Compiled from the Original Returns of the Eighth Census* (Washington, D.C., 1864), 72–73; Roger Brooke Farquhar, *Historic Montgomery County, Maryland: Old Homes and History* (Baltimore, 1952), 37–39; Craven, *Soil Exhaustion,* 158–59; Baker, *Ambivalent Americans,* 9; Vivian Wiser, "Improving Maryland's Agriculture, 1840–1860," *Maryland Historical Magazine,* LXIV (1969), 105–32.

spite the loss of many white families and the downturn in the tobacco economy. The number of slaves in the six-county area fluctuated only slightly from 1790 to 1860, when there were nearly 46,000 black men, women, and children in bondage. The experience in southern Maryland proved that "slavery fitted as well into the improved farming . . . as it did into the destructive work" of the one-crop system. Indeed, "it was upon the larger plantations, where capital and a careful division of labor could be practiced, that the most rapid recovery took place and the greatest advances were made." The 4,524 slave owners in southern Maryland in 1860 owned an average of ten slaves each. This figure is misleading, however, because the bulk of slave owners possessed just one slave and the median slaveholding pattern statewide was three slaves. Prince Georges County claimed the most slaves and slave owners in the region, followed by Charles County. Calvert County had the least investment in slavery with only 4,609 slaves and 528 masters. Slavery in southern Maryland continued to be productive in terms of labor and resale value. Twelve percent of the slave population of Anne Arundel and Prince Georges counties were sold in the 1830s, and the slave trade picked up as slavery spread into Texas.[8]

In the main, the region's decline was gradual, not noticeably affecting the daily rhythm of life for southern Maryland's gentry. One woman cast an idyllic portrait of her godmother's house in Prince Georges County:

> Life at Beechwood was lived in an inflexible routine, because in the minds of master and mistress, what *had been* must *continue* to be; there was just no other way. On the farm, the day started before the cock crowed and it ended after he had gone to roost. In the big house there seemed, from sun to sun, nothing for which to hurry; except for occasional social calls made and received, which in general were well planned and timed, quarterly and at that time important shopping trips to Baltimore; a Cotillion now and then or an eagerly anticipated "party," given at one or another of the

8. U.S. Census Bureau, *Agriculture*, 231; Craven, *Soil Exhaustion*, 163; Fields, *Slavery and Freedom*, 24–25. For an examination of one county during this period, see Donald J. McCauley, "The Limits of Change in the Tobacco South: An Economic and Social Analysis of Prince George's County, Maryland, 1840–1860" (M.A. thesis, University of Maryland, n.d.). For a comparison of slaveholding patterns in Charles County and Baltimore city, see Lawrence H. McDonald, "Prelude to Emancipation: The Failure of the Great Reaction in Maryland, 1831–1860" (Ph.D. dissertation, University of Maryland, 1974). A discussion of Maryland slavery is also found in Robert William Fogel and Stanley L. Engerman, *Time on the Cross: The Economics of American Negro Slavery* (Boston, 1974), 53, 55, 221–22.

hospitable county homes, each *tomorrow* was expected to be just another *today*.[9]

Life in southern Maryland revolved around the home with occasional interruptions for jousting tournaments, oyster feasts, church meetings, and picnics. The six counties from the tip of Point Lookout on the Chesapeake Bay to the western fringes of Montgomery County represented traditional southern values and the southern economy. Politically, the region shifted as the second American party system disintegrated. From 1836 to 1848, the six counties were considered safe for the Whig party's presidential and gubernatorial candidates. Whiggery in southern Maryland adhered less to the principles of internal improvements and commercial development than to its descent from the state's Federalists. These men "tended to see themselves as upper class, and they regarded Democrats as 'locofoco' and parvenu." The party maintained the region's political strength against other sections of the state, primarily western Maryland and Baltimore.[10]

The coalition of an aristocratic, planter-class Whiggery with commercially oriented Whigs elsewhere in the state began to crumble in 1850. The Compromise of 1850 caused the first chinks in the Whig hold over Maryland. The party fractured into northern and southern branches and lost its national organization. The Democrats also badly damaged the Whigs in Maryland by seizing constitutional reform as a popular issue. Agitation over the state's 1776 constitution had stirred in Maryland since 1820 because it disproportionately favored southern Maryland. This region enjoyed political status far beyond its number of voters as compared with the other sections of the state. The original constitution restricted the number of elections in the state and shared power between southern Maryland and the Eastern Shore. In 1836, the state adopted several amendments which made the governor's office an elected position and reapportioned representation in the legislature to resemble the population distribution more closely.[11]

In 1847, Maryland elected a Democratic governor who promised action

9. Effie Gwynn Bowie, *Across the Years in Prince George's County: A Genealogical and Biographical History of Some Prince George's County, Maryland, and Allied Families* (Richmond, 1947), 13.

10. Evitts, *A Matter of Allegiances*, 10, 22. For more on party loyalties in Maryland, see W. Wayne Smith, "Jacksonian Democracy on the Chesapeake: Class, Kinship and Politics," *Maryland Historical Magazine* LXIII (1968), 55–67.

11. Evitts, *A Matter of Allegiances*, 31–39.

on the issue of constitutional reform. Whigs statewide naturally opposed reform, and opposition was centered in southern Maryland. The Whigs, however, could not suppress the call for a constitutional convention in 1850 because the Democrats manipulated the issue and maintained control of the governor's seat. From that point on, the constitutional convention seemed to drag. "Instead of a convention of men acting under an exalted sense of great responsibility," one observer thundered, "we have seen . . . a constant display of factious opposition, originating in sectional interest and party prejudices." The new constitution greatly expanded the appointive powers of the governor and opened some county and state positions for election. The dissatisfaction felt by many of the state's voters over the constitutional convention simultaneously weakened the Whig party while creating interest in the state's political system as a whole.[12]

The events of 1850–1851 altered political power and allegiances in Maryland, a shift that continued throughout the decade. Other regions of the state also felt the impact of these political changes as well as ongoing radical social and economic development. The Eastern Shore of Maryland, the narrow peninsula bounded by the Chesapeake Bay on the west and the Atlantic Ocean on the east, witnessed an increase in its white population after 1790 but a drastic decline in slaveholding. Unlike southern Maryland, the area epitomized a slave society where the one-crop system, tobacco, was no longer viable. As a result, landowners readily took up truck farming, which required less labor. Excess slaves were sold to other areas of the state or country or were manumitted. The number of slaves in the eight-county region in 1850 dropped by nearly a third from the first census count in 1790. The free black population on the Eastern Shore simultaneously rose 534 percent, almost matching the number of slaves in the region.[13]

The Eastern Shore was a land of contrasts in 1860. Isolated from the mainland, it developed a distinctive sense of identity which was occasionally expressed in the desire to separate from the state and unite with neighboring Delaware.[14] Although the region had fewer slaves, Talbot

12. Ibid., 40–42.

13. Fields, *Slavery and Freedom*, 13.

14. During the 1851 Constitutional Convention, Thomas Hicks, later governor of the state during the secession crisis, openly favored an amendment allowing sections of the state to leave and form new bonds. See Baker, *Ambivalent Americans*, 14; Baker, *Politics of Continuity*, 8–9.

County was the home of the state's wealthiest slave owner and is remembered today as the birthplace of the great black abolitionist Frederick Douglass. The shift to other farm products did not improve the standard of living on the Eastern Shore. Caroline County ranked at the bottom in the cash value of its farms in 1860, and many whites worried about the tremendous increase in the free black population.[15] The lack of reliable land transportation on the Eastern Shore led many voters to support Whig policies throughout the 1840s, yet not in as solid a block as southern Maryland. Moreover, the constitution of 1851 diluted the hold that the Eastern Shore shared with southern Maryland as power shifted to the state's third and largest region.

Western Maryland had two components. Northern Maryland was centered along the fall line and encompassed the counties of Carroll, Frederick, Howard, Baltimore, and Harford.[16] Western Maryland also included the state's mountainous counties, Washington and Allegany. Both sections gained in population and economic development in the first half of the nineteenth century. Western Maryland had nearly 70 percent of the state's total white population in 1850, nearly half of its free blacks, and less than 20 percent of its slaves. This growth was concentrated in the region's two extremities. The eastern edge of the region witnessed more than 400 percent growth in Baltimore city and county, while the western portion, centered in Allegany County, saw its population jump to over 20,000 residents in 1850 from a mere 4,500 in 1790.[17]

Industrial development and internal improvements fueled western Maryland's growth. The construction of the Baltimore and Ohio Railroad, the Chesapeake and Ohio Canal, and the National Turnpike opened the region to coal mining in the west and allowed the export of grain from the hinterland counties of Frederick and Carroll to the port at Baltimore. Towns such as Frederick, Westminster, Boonsboro, Williamsport, and Cumberland sprang up virtually overnight along the major thoroughfares, accommodating travelers and serving as local markets for county farmers.

15. U.S. Census Bureau, *Agriculture,* 72–73, 231.

16. Montgomery and Cecil counties are occasionally listed in northern Maryland. For the purposes of this study, however, Montgomery County is included in southern Maryland while Cecil County belongs to the Eastern Shore. Both counties shared similarities with two regions.

17. Fields, *Slavery and Freedom,* 10–13. For a discussion of the development of Allegany County, see Katherine A. Harvey, *The Best-Dressed Miners: Life and Labor in the Maryland Coal Region* (Ithaca, 1969).

Three of the state's top five farm counties in cash value were located in western Maryland. The one county that ranked at the bottom of this list, Allegany, made up for the poverty of its soil by exporting the coal that lay beneath it.[18]

The numerous settlers of German origin in western Maryland had little need for slaves on their farms because agricultural production focused primarily on grain and corn. The seven-county region had approximately fourteen thousand slaves in 1860; the average holding was four slaves. Slaves as property or as a workforce were a minor factor in western Maryland. Whiggery had less attachment in western Maryland than might be expected considering the region's interest in internal improvements. Jacksonian Democracy, with its assertion of the "common man," attracted many of the region's farmers and laborers. Western Maryland Whigs contained Democratic power until 1850, when constitutional reform overwhelmed the Whig coalition. The schism that affected the Whig party in western Maryland was particularly severe and cast a shadow over the fortunes of the entire party for the next presidential election in 1852.[19]

In the meantime, winds of change blew through the state's fourth region. Baltimore ranked as the third largest city in the United States in 1860 with 212,418 residents throughout its twenty wards. The city's growth over the past seventy years had been phenomenal—Baltimore had only 13,000 residents in 1790. By 1860 the size and diversity of the city's population as well as its peculiar economic interests qualified it as its own region although the city still had much in common with western Maryland. Originally shipping only Maryland tobacco and grain, the city expanded its exports to include coal from western Maryland and textiles and other finished products from the state's mills. Baltimore's industrial output far surpassed that of any other city in the South, and it had 1,100 manufacturing establishments by 1860. The Baltimore and Ohio Railroad linked the city with the state's interior while other railroad networks tied it with Pennsylvania and the District of Columbia.[20]

18. Evitts, *A Matter of Allegiances*, 11–12; U.S. Census Bureau, *Agriculture*, 72–73; Baker, *Ambivalent Americans*, 22. For life in western Maryland, see Ella E. Clark, ed., "Life on the C&O Canal," *Maryland Historical Magazine*, LV (1960), 82–122.

19. U.S. Census Bureau, *Agriculture*, 231; Evitts, *A Matter of Allegiances*, 23.

20. U.S. Census Bureau, *Population of the United States in 1860; Compiled from the Original Returns of the Eighth Census* (Washington, D.C., 1864), 210–13; U.S. Census Bureau, *Manufactures*, 228; Fields, *Slavery and Freedom*, 41–44; Evitts, *A Matter of Allegiances*, 12–14; Baker, *Politics of Continuity*, 12.

Between 1830 and 1850, 130,000 immigrants landed at the city's port. Some of the newly arrived passengers took advantage of Maryland's good transportation system to move further into the interior of the United States, but many opted to remain in Baltimore, where job opportunities were readily available. By 1860, the city had 52,000 foreign-born residents, of whom the vast majority were German or Irish. Immigrants formed nearly 25 percent of the city's population and 28 percent of the white population. Crowding into the city, the immigrants displaced native whites and slave and free blacks in both the housing and job markets. Although they lived in every ward of the city, foreigners congregated in Baltimore's first, second, and eighth wards. The nearly 70 percent of the state's total foreign-born population who lived in Baltimore aroused suspicions among native citizens throughout the state. And the failure of many immigrants to speak English or practice the Protestant faith caused Americans to fear their new neighbors. Party hacks immediately enrolled the new immigrants as Democrats, which heightened the worries of native Whigs.[21]

Blacks occupied a unique status in the state's largest city. There were only 2,218 slaves and 1,296 slave owners in Baltimore in 1860; the city's 25,000 free blacks far outnumbered its slaves. The richest ward, the eleventh, had the highest number of slaves with a total assessed value of nearly $41,000 in 1853. Free blacks were scattered throughout each ward, although they were found primarily in the eleventh, fifteenth, and seventeenth wards. Competition with native and immigrant whites resulted in declining numbers of working free blacks and slaves in the city, which in turn caused a loss in the total black population. M. Ray Della, Jr., noted that among the complications brought about by immigration in Baltimore during the 1850s, was the competition of native middle- to low-class whites with immigrants and with Negroes, who had previously held semi-skilled and skilled jobs. Because there were now enough whites to perform the semiskilled jobs, Negroes were no longer needed. Upper-class whites thus had to face increased competition between their hired-out slaves and

21. Fields, *Slavery and Freedom*, 44; U.S. Census Bureau, *Population*, 215; M. Ray Della, Jr., "An Analysis of Baltimore's Population in the 1850's," *Maryland Historical Magazine*, LXVIII (1973), 23; Jorg Echterncamp, "Emerging Ethnicity: The German Experience in Antebellum Baltimore," *Maryland Historical Magazine*, LXXXVI (1991), 1–22; Baker, *Ambivalent Americans*, 22; Mark T. Arisumi, "The Irish as Southern Democrats: The Political Persuasions of the Catholic Irish Immigrants in Baltimore, 1850–1865" (M.A. thesis, University of Maryland, 1988); Evitts, *A Matter of Allegiances*, 68–73.

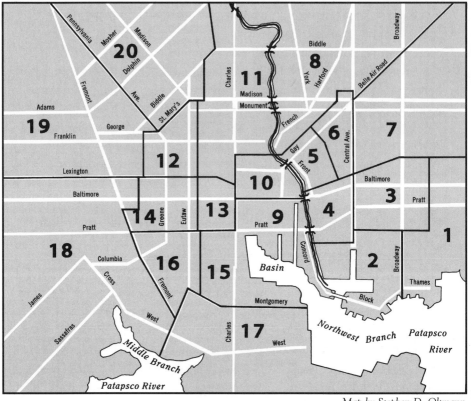

Baltimore in 1860

Map by Stephen D. Oltmann

the whites and free blacks. Free Negroes competed with everyone else, including other free blacks, but had the least chance for survival because they were the only element of the labor force that was completely expendable and almost without defense.[22]

The social turmoil in Baltimore in the 1850s contributed to the city's political turbulence, and Baltimore politics grew increasingly rowdy and less statesmanlike as the decade progressed. The 1851 constitution opened state and local governments to the scrutiny of the general public, resulting in increased political patronage and corruption throughout the state. The reforms of the constitution, however, only slightly altered Baltimore's representation in the General Assembly at the beginning of the 1852 presidential campaign.[23]

The Whigs held their national convention in Baltimore and, after much rancor, nominated Mexican War hero General Winfield Scott; but he alienated many Maryland Whigs, who believed he did not fully support the Compromise of 1850. Many Whigs in southern Maryland and the Eastern Shore believed the compromise was the only way to bind the North and South and prevent dissolution over slavery. These men regarded federal and state adherence to the Fugitive Slave Act as the linchpin for the preservation of sectional harmony. Scott's defeat marked the demise of the Whig party both nationally and in Maryland. For the first time, the Democrats won a presidential campaign in Maryland. The loss was particularly keen in western Maryland, where the party had been racked by discord over reform. Whig support for Scott in other areas of the state could not prevent Democratic victory.[24]

With the Whig party in shambles, Marylanders from all walks of life felt at a loss in coping with the sudden changes that swept the state. The uncertainty of these changes played on the nerves of Maryland's voters. Some, like Kennedy, opposed the scoundrels who got elected for personal gain. Other Marylanders worried about the flood of foreigners that swamped Baltimore and many of the smaller towns in western Maryland. During the summer of 1853, many Marylanders turned to prohibition as a form of social control and then to nativism. Temperance proved short-

22. U.S. Census Bureau, *Population*, 210–13; U.S. Census Bureau, *Agriculture*, 231; Della, "Analysis of Baltimore's Population," 21, 32.

23. Evitts, *A Matter of Allegiances*, 39–41; Fields, *Slavery and Freedom*, 20–21.

24. Evitts, *A Matter of Allegiances*, 48–53.

lived, but nativism blossomed into a major political party in Maryland in the mid-1850s.[25]

Fearing immigrants and Roman Catholics, nativists banded together in secret clubs, vowing to preserve the American ideals. Presenting a united front as the Order of the Star-Spangled Banner, they entered the public arena in 1853. They were quickly dubbed "Know-Nothings" for the rites of their order and were still political unknowns a year later. By October, 1854, the Know-Nothings (who adopted the official name "American party") won their first major election when they captured the mayoralty of Baltimore and began their meteoric rise to power.[26]

The Know-Nothings adopted the outward forms of the regular parties and abandoned requirements for membership in the secret order. The Know-Nothing party appealed to a wide spectrum of Maryland society, but lower- to middle-class native-born Protestants from Baltimore or other towns formed the party's core. The new party members came from the dying Whig party, as well as some former Democrats threatened by the situation in Baltimore. The city, formerly the center of Maryland's Democracy, became the stronghold of Know-Nothingism, while southern Maryland, the bastion of Whiggery, turned to the new Democratic party. The Democratic party emerged in southern Maryland because many Catholics in that region resented the rhetoric of the American party. Likewise, slaveholders in the state's oldest section (many of whom were Catholic) feared the increasingly abolitionist tone of many former national Whigs and of the nativists and were lured to the Democratic party, which adamantly supported the rights of southern slave owners. The elite segment of Baltimore's population in the eleventh ward also voted Democratic for many of the same reasons expressed by southern Marylanders.[27]

The Know-Nothings valiantly tried to avoid the issue of slavery, instead questioning whether natives or foreigners should govern. The mystique of the Know-Nothings generated considerable interest in the young party, both in Maryland and nationally. During the 1855 elections, the party swept into power in Baltimore's city council, took the statehouse at Annapolis, and dominated Maryland's seats in the U.S. House of Rep-

25. Evitts, *A Matter of Allegiances*, 54, 59–67; Baker, *Ambivalent Americans*, 7–8, 19.

26. Baker, *Ambivalent Americans*, 30; Evitts, *A Matter of Allegiances*, 64–67.

27. Baker, *Ambivalent Americans*, 142, 145–47; Evitts, *A Matter of Allegiances*, 80–88; Douglas Bowers, "Ideology and Political Parties in Maryland, 1851–1856," *Maryland Historical Magazine*, LXIV (1969), 197–217.

resentatives. Its obsession with retaining office forced the party to abandon its xenophobic and anti-Catholic roots while adopting an unspecific platform based on Unionism. Moreover, the party accepted the spoils system and the politics of violence that attracted gangs of working-class whites to intimidate voters on election day. The tradition of election violence in Baltimore was not new, and the Know-Nothings incorporated a system of clubs centered on volunteer fire companies just as the Democrats organized clubs for new immigrants.[28]

The streets of Baltimore became a battlefield between Know-Nothing clubs such as the Rip Raps, Plug Uglies, and Blood Tubs, who battled Democratic clubs with similar colorful titles. The 1856 presidential election validated the strength of the Know-Nothing party in Maryland even though its candidate, Millard Fillmore, suffered a national defeat. The election's violence in Baltimore and statewide scandal reflected intense party rivalry and the breakdown of the electoral system. Police protection in the city was notoriously weak, and the violence was often random as much as politically directed. During this period of urban unrest, according to Jean Baker, "the uses of violence were too rewarding for political leaders, too therapeutic for participants, and too institutionalized for society to stop."[29]

Eventually, the Democrats manipulated violence at the polls to their political benefit. The governor of the state, Democrat Thomas W. Ligon, admonished the Know-Nothing party for fraudulent practices during the 1857 congressional elections. He accomplished little because the American party controlled the General Assembly. For the next year and a half, political activity tapered off as the Know-Nothings enjoyed their supremacy. The incumbent Know-Nothing mayor of Baltimore, Thomas Swann, easily won reelection in 1858 because the Democrats could not front a candidate. The intimidation employed by the American party during this election disgusted Baltimoreans, who organized the City Reform Association in early November, 1858, to clean up the election process in the city.[30]

28. Baker, *Ambivalent Americans*, 49–50, 121–24; Evitts, *A Matter of Allegiances*, 89. The role of the volunteer fire companies and violence is discussed in Amy Sophia Greenberg, "Mayhem in Mobtown: Firefighting in Antebellum Baltimore," *Maryland Historical Magazine*, XC (1995), 164–79.

29. Baker, *Ambivalent Americans*, 129–34.

30. *Ibid.*, 99–100; J. Thomas Scharf, *History of Maryland from the Earliest Period to the*

The reformers called for the appointment of trustworthy judges to over-see polling and the establishment of a strong police force. The Know-Nothings mobilized their forces to meet the reform challenge. A mammoth rally at Mt. Vernon Square in Baltimore was a show of strength for the Know-Nothings, who gathered under their new symbol, an awl—a worker's tool used by club members to stab opponents at the polls. Banners proclaimed the might of the Know-Nothings, one reading "Reform move-ment, Reform man, if you can vote, I'll be damned." As expected, the city elections of 1859 provided scenes worthy of a war, and the Know-Nothings bloodily defeated the reformers in Baltimore in conjunction with corrupt judges, policemen, and gangs who declared themselves "pre-pared to carry the election . . . by wholesale murder."[31]

The Democrats incorporated the reform spirit as a means of reasserting political power in the state. The 1859 elections revealed the power of reform in areas outside the city as the Democrats regained seats in Con-gress and took control of the state legislature. When the General As-sembly convened in Annapolis in early 1860, the Democrats refused to seat any members of the American party elected through fraudulent prac-tices. The House of Delegates also adopted the resolutions of the City Reform Association regarding the organization of the Baltimore police, election procedures, and jury selection. The Know-Nothings were thus stripped of their stranglehold on Baltimore, which effectively killed the party in Maryland. By that time, Know-Nothingism had already dissolved on the national level under the weight of the slave question. Slavery overshadowed all other issues in the American political arena by 1860 to the great detriment of the regular parties.[32]

John Brown's seizure of the U.S. arsenal at Harpers Ferry, Virginia, just across the Potomac River from Maryland, on October 16, 1859, attracted immediate attention in the state. The violence that plagued Kansas and Missouri over the expansion of slavery now struck home, and white Mary-landers feared a Negro insurrection. The presence of the nation's largest free black population increased concern among whites, who feared they would be murdered in their sleep. A bill in the legislature to prohibit manumission and to regulate the employment of free blacks marked a step

Present Day (3 vols.; 1879; rpr. Hatboro, 1967), III, 255–62; Evitts, *A Matter of Allegiances,* 119–23.

31. Baker, *Ambivalent Americans,* 54–55; Evitts, *A Matter of Allegiances,* 123; "Address of the Central Reform Committee" in Scharf, *History of Maryland,* III, 275–76.

32. Baker, *Ambivalent Americans,* 152; Evitts, *A Matter of Allegiances,* 128–33.

toward tighter control of the Negro population. The Jacobs Bill, however, failed when presented for a public referendum in the fall of 1860 because it was too harsh and threatened to upset the delicate balance that white employers had arranged over the years regarding slave and free black labor.[33]

John Brown's raid revealed the confusion of white Marylanders as to their state's status within the nation. Constituents humiliated Congressman Henry Winter Davis, a former Whig and most recently a Know-Nothing, when he supported a northerner for Speaker of the House of Representatives. Meanwhile, Marylanders passed declarations favoring the rights of the south as a part of the Union. Such actions marked Maryland's course throughout the secession crisis. Marylanders could not decide whether they were northern or southern.[34]

A visitor arriving in Baltimore in 1860 immediately sensed the state's identity crisis: "Baltimore had Northern characteristics of finance and commerce which greatly resembled Philadelphia, New York or Boston, but culturally and socially Baltimore had Southern ties which were most evident." The existence of slavery further complicated the dilemma. Historically, the state was part of the Chesapeake Bay society, which linked it closely to Virginia. Industrialism and the transportation revolution, however, bonded the state with the North and West. Pennsylvania contributed the largest group of native whites born outside the state, outnumbering the second largest group, from Virginia, 18,457 to 7,560.[35]

This same visitor would have been impressed by the southern feeling and hospitality evident in Baltimore. Despite the city's enormous growth, the inner city had few slums, and its residential dispersion more closely resembled that of Richmond and Norfolk than New York or Philadelphia. Baltimore, the first and largest city that travelers encountered after crossing the Mason-Dixon line, retained a unique status among America's metropolitan areas at midcentury.[36]

The 1860 presidential election highlighted Maryland's role as a border

33. Baker, *Politics of Continuity*, 28; Evitts, *A Matter of Allegiances*, 123–28, 136–37; Fields, *Slavery and Freedom*, 76–85.

34. Baker, *Politics of Continuity*, 29–30; Evitts, *A Matter of Allegiances*, 135–38.

35. Quotation from Della, "Analysis of Baltimore's Population," 20; U.S. Census Bureau, *Population*, 215; Jane N. Garrett, "Philadelphia and Baltimore, 1790–1840: A Study of Intra-Regional Unity," *Maryland Historical Magazine*, LV (1960), 1–13.

36. Patricia C. Click, *The Spirit of the Times: Amusements in Nineteenth-Century Baltimore, Norfolk, and Richmond* (Charlottesville, 1989), 9–11.

state. The campaign was essentially a fight between two candidates, John C. Breckinridge of Kentucky, representing the radical wing of southern Democrats, and John Bell of Tennessee, of the Constitutional Union party. The "Black Republican," Abraham Lincoln, had little support in the state, and his former rival in Illinois, Stephen A. Douglas, played a minor role. Bell's Constitutional Union party appealed to the compromise spirit that still existed in Maryland and called for increased loyalty to the Union. Breckinridge claimed to represent the true Democratic party in Maryland and called for federal recognition of the right to expand slavery into the territories. The difference between the two leading contenders was, as one Maryland paper claimed, "between 'Bell and the Union' or 'Breckinridge and Disunion!'"[37]

The state's vote separated along sectional lines and loyalties formed in the 1850s. The heart of Breckinridge's support lay in Baltimore City, Charles, Prince Georges, and St. Marys counties in southern Maryland and Talbot and Worcester counties on the Eastern Shore. Breckinridge's victory in Baltimore resulted from the city's denunciation of the Know-Nothings, who had become entangled with Bell's Constitutional Union party. That party attracted a wide following of former Whigs and some Americans although Bell clearly rejected nativism. The Constitutional Union party enjoyed widespread support in all sections. Bell's critical defeat in Baltimore meant that he lost Maryland's electoral vote by less than 1 percent. The Democratic sweep in Baltimore in November, 1860, also obliterated the remnants of Know-Nothingism; the city had elected a reform mayor and council the previous month. The two other presidential candidates, Lincoln and Douglas, made a faint showing, primarily in the far reaches of western Maryland.[38]

The election of 1860 did not resolve Maryland's dilemma between loyalty to the Union and fidelity to southern brotherhood. Rather, Lincoln's election heightened tensions between the two sections, which exploded when South Carolina seceded on December 20. One by one, the

37. Baker, *Politics of Continuity*, 35–45; Evitts, *A Matter of Allegiances*, 141–51. Both the Democratic and the Constitutional Union parties held their 1860 national conventions in Baltimore; see Betty Dix Greeman, "The Democratic Convention of 1860: Prelude to Secession," *Maryland Historical Magazine*, LXVII (1972), 225–53; Donald Walter Curl, "The Baltimore Convention of the Constitutional Union Party," *Maryland Historical Magazine*, LXVII (1972), 254–77.

38. Baker, *Politics of Continuity*, 30, 43–44; Evitts, *A Matter of Allegiances*, 145–50.

states of the Deep South followed suit, and by February, 1861, eight states had withdrawn from the Union. Bombarded with pleas and advice from the South, Maryland took faint steps to prepare for its own secession. Meetings were held throughout the state supporting one side or the other while the governor, Thomas H. Hicks, who had belonged to every major party in Maryland politics, disregarded calls for a special session of the General Assembly. Because it was an off-year for the legislature, Hicks did not convene the heavily southern Maryland/Eastern Shore–dominated assembly, an act for which he was roundly castigated.[39]

The majority of Marylanders still supported peaceful means to preserve the Union and prevent war. A group of citizens in Kent County reflected the interests of that community, stating that "the honor and rights of Maryland are suspended in a balance, and they are afraid the scales are not held by hands which would give a just weight in these days of bargain and sale. They are afraid that the 'masterly inactivity' of their Governor, and the timidity of his partizans may lead them unwillingly into an alliance repugnant to their feelings, sentiments, sympathies, and material interests. They wish to exercise the right of freemen in this contest between freemen, and Abolitionism." The committee of "representatives, as well as the possessors, of a large slave-holding and landed interest" in Kent County approved resolutions calling for a state convention to be held in Baltimore and cited their desire to see "some satisfactory adjustment which will be acceptable to the North and the South."[40]

The committee rejected the notion that they desired only secession. Judge Ezekiel F. Chambers, a member of the group, discussed his views on secession and the convention: "I look upon it as the greatest curse that has befallen the country, involving horrors which no imagination has yet conceived the extent of. 'Tis to avoid this very curse that he [Chambers] desired to have a Convention—a Convention of conservative men— Union-loving men—men who could by authority of the people of the State actively urge conciliation." Judge Chambers and the committee resolved that, barring a peaceful settlement, secession remained the only course of action left for Maryland: "If then, the North shall refuse this and shall continue to deprive us of our property and when we attempt to

39. Baker, *Politics of Continuity*, 47–48; Evitts, *A Matter of Allegiances*, 154–57, 161–65.

40. Evitts, *A Matter of Allegiances*, 165–67; Walter J. Kirby and Lanetta W. Parks, *Roll Call: The Civil War in Kent County* (Silver Spring, 1985), 128–33.

reclaim it, meet us, as they have done with denunciations and abusive language, with violence and mobs and as has actually occurred with death, how can we remain in the Union with such a North? Impossible! every instinct of human nature, every dictate of prudence, every demand of patriotism forbid it."[41]

The organizing committee for the state convention met in Baltimore in mid-February with Judge Chambers as chairman. After passing resolutions, the committee adjourned until the following month, at which time it appointed "a committee of well known and influential gentlemen, to wait upon the Virginia convention . . . and urge that body to recommend a border State convention." Maryland's latent Unionism prevented any more drastic action, but secession talk affected the state's commercial affairs. Marylanders actively supported the Crittenden Compromise, which proposed that slavery be recognized in the U.S. Constitution, and sent delegates to the Washington Peace Conference in February. The failure of both compromise efforts effectively closed formal efforts to reach a peaceful solution to the crisis.[42]

Abraham Lincoln's passage through Baltimore en route to his inauguration in Washington, D.C., served as a poor introduction for the president-elect. Lincoln, a minority president, had received only 1,211 votes in the entire state of Maryland. Fearing assassination, he secretly made his way through the city during the late hours of February 22 and arrived at the nation's capital without fanfare. Lincoln's behavior damaged his already strained image in the border state and fueled the ridicule of pro-southern Marylanders.[43]

On March 4, Lincoln took the oath of office as the nation's sixteenth president. For Marylanders who stood in the crowd at the East Front of the U.S. Capitol, the future was fraught with uncertainty as the nation's first Republican president gave his address. Within six weeks, Marylanders, who had long vacillated over their state's role in "this age of wild and reckless fanaticism," were forced to decide whether their loyalties lay

41. Kirby and Parks, *Roll Call*, 132.

42. Scharf, *History of Maryland*, III, 373–74, 379–83, 399; Baker, *Politics of Continuity*, 52; Evitts, *A Matter of Allegiances*, 159–60, 164–66.

43. Evitts, *A Matter of Allegiances*, 172–75; Norma Cuthbert, ed., *Lincoln and the Baltimore Plot, 1861* (San Marino, 1949); Adalbert John Volck, a Baltimore draftsman, lambasted Lincoln for sneaking into Washington. See Hermann Warner Williams, Jr., *The Civil War: The Artists' Record* (Meriden, 1961), 23.

with the new Confederate States of America or with the old United States.[44]

The decade preceding the breakup of the Union set the stage for the Civil War in Maryland. The colonial settlement of Maryland formed the blueprint for the state's sectionalism in the nineteenth century, and there were growing social, political, and economic differences after 1850. Southern Maryland and the Eastern Shore were vastly different from the northern and western parts of the state. Baltimore served as the middle ground for the state's discordant elements, where Maryland's agricultural, slave-based southern way of life clashed with the entrepreneurial spirit of the North and its emphasis on heavy foreign immigration and free labor. The two worlds, distinct in most of the United States, coexisted within Maryland's narrow boundaries. Just as these separate spheres were drawn into national conflict in 1861, so they erupted among Maryland's fractured societies.

The men who served as officers in Maryland's Union and Confederate regiments came of age during this traumatic period in American history. The events of the 1850s impressed Maryland's future officers with the failure of compromise and the disintegration of their familiar world. They grew hardened in the belief that war remained the only means to bridge the enormous gulf between the two spheres. This war, which utterly disrupted their lives and carved a theater of operations from their home, partially resulted from the turmoil that preceded it in the border state of Maryland.

44. Evitts, *A Matter of Allegiances*, 77.

·2·

MARYLAND OCCUPIED

The attack on federal troops at Fort Sumter in Charleston Harbor by South Carolina secessionists on April 12, 1861, ignited the war that few Marylanders wanted. With the departure of the Upper South states, the federal government could ill afford to let Maryland slip into Confederate hands. Control of the state by the Union army was fundamental to the security of Washington, D.C., and the importance of the state's railroads soon forced Marylanders, however ambivalent they were about the war's causes, to choose sides. Abraham Lincoln's call for volunteers on April 15 to put down the rebellion meant that federal troops had to pass through the state to secure the nation's capital.[1]

The first large contingent of Union soldiers, about two thousand men from Massachusetts and Pennsylvania, entered Baltimore by train on April 19 and encountered a large, hostile crowd. Transferring from the President Street terminus of the Philadelphia, Wilmington, and Baltimore Railroad to cars at the Baltimore and Ohio's Camden Street Station to continue the trip to Washington, the 6th Massachusetts Regiment was attacked by howling mobs. Fighting raged in the streets of Baltimore until it was quelled by the mayor and police chief. The Massachusetts unit, those "miserable cravens" as one prominent Maryland Confederate later called them, lost an estimated forty-two killed and wounded during the violence while twelve Baltimoreans died and scores were injured.[2]

1. Evitts, A Matter of Allegiances, 175–91.
2. Ibid., 175–80; Harold R. Manakee, Maryland in the Civil War (Baltimore, 1961), 30–38; Matthew Ellenberger, "Whigs in the Streets? Baltimore Republicanism in the Spring of 1861," Maryland Historical Magazine, LXXXVI (1991), 23–38; Charles B. Clark, "Baltimore and the Attack on the Sixth Massachusetts Regiment, April 19, 1861," Maryland Historical Magazine, LVI (1961), 39–71; Charles McHenry Howard, "Baltimore and

The Baltimore "riots" made headlines in newspapers across the country, and partisans on both sides either condemned the action of the mobs or saw the riots as blood shed in the defense of southern liberty. The real motivation and background of the crowd has been a subject of some interest over the years. A large portion of the crowd were "wharf rats," men who frequented the docks and were always ready for a fight. Many, however, were honest citizens drawn to the commotion and aroused at the sight of troops passing through the city.[3]

An 1859 graduate of Georgetown College and a Baltimore City attorney, Francis X. Ward, led the charge on the Massachusetts militia. When he grabbed their flag, Ward was struck in the hips by a bullet that passed through him, then killed another citizen. Ward survived his injury and later served as a second lieutenant and adjutant of the 1st Maryland Infantry Regiment (C.S.).[4]

George W. Booth, who in a month's time would be a first lieutenant in the 1st Maryland Infantry (C.S.), also participated in the violence that spring day. When a Massachusetts militiaman dropped his weapon, Booth saw Edward W. Beatty, a customs officer at the port, pick it up. Firing the rifle at the northerners, Beatty turned to the crowd for ammunition, which Booth provided. Beatty later served in Booth's company until his death in battle in 1862. Beatty's twenty-one-year-old son, also named Edward, received a commission in 1862 as an officer in the 1st Maryland Cavalry Battalion (C.S.).[5]

James Ryder Randall read about the tumult in Baltimore in the New Orleans *Delta*. Randall, a native of Baltimore and a teacher in Louisiana, was shocked to read of the civilian casualties. Among the list of the wounded, Randall found the name of his old Georgetown College room-

the Crisis of 1861," *Maryland Historical Magazine*, XLI (1946), 257–81; George W. Brown, *Baltimore and the Nineteenth of April, 1861* (Baltimore, 1881); Bradley T. Johnson, "Memoir of First Maryland Regiment," *SHSP*, IX (1881), 347; Frank Towers, ed., "Military Waif: A Sidelight in the Baltimore Riot of 19 April 1861," *Maryland Historical Magazine*, LXXXIX (1994), 427–46; Scharf, *History of Maryland*, III, 403–409; James M. McPherson, *Battle Cry of Freedom: The Civil War Era* (New York, 1988), 286–87.

3. Evitts, *A Matter of Allegiances*, 184.

4. Johnson, *Maryland*, 431–33; Francis X. Ward file, GUAAR; *The Biographical Cyclopedia of Representative Men of Maryland and the District of Columbia* (2 vols.; Baltimore, 1879), I, 251–52.

5. Booth, *Personal Reminiscences*, 6–8; Goldsborough, *Maryland Line*, 53.

mate, Francis X. Ward. Unable to contain his sorrow, Randall hurriedly composed a poem expressing his indignation at Maryland's subjugation. Three days later the poem was published in Louisiana and, soon thereafter, put to music as "Maryland, My Maryland!" Ward's blood "that flecked the streets of Baltimore" served to rally prosouthern Maryland sympathizers to the Confederate banner.[6]

The pace of events picked up quickly in Maryland after the fighting in Baltimore. Sporadic outbursts of violence continued to upset the city as residents on both sides of the issue attacked one another. The city's mayor, George W. Brown, and Governor Thomas H. Hicks appealed for reason. Hicks exclaimed, "I am a Marylander, and I love my State, and I love the Union, but I will suffer my right arm to be torn from my body before I will raise it to strike a sister state." The state's elected officials dispatched a committee to visit President Lincoln in Washington to demand that no more federal troops pass through Baltimore.[7]

The chief executive replied that though it was necessary to reinforce Washington, "I make no point of bringing them *through* Baltimore. . . . By this, a collision of the people of Baltimore will be avoided, unless they [Marylanders] go out of their way to seek it." Lincoln added, "I hope you will exert your influence to prevent this."[8]

In a letter to a group representing the Young Men's Christian Association of Baltimore, Lincoln resented their appeal for "peace on any terms." The president condemned the attitude of these Marylanders when "the rebels attack Fort Sumter, and your citizens attack troops sent to the defense of the Government, and the lives and property in Washington, and yet you would have me break my oath and surrender the Government without a blow." Lincoln clearly stated his duties and intention regarding Maryland:

> I have no desire to invade the South; but I must have troops to defend this Capital. Geographically it lies surrounded by the soil of Maryland; and mathematically the necessity exists that they [federal troops] should come over her territory. Our men are not moles, and can't dig under the earth; they are not birds, and can't fly through the air. There is no way but to

6. Manakee, *Maryland in the Civil War*, 44–46.

7. *Ibid.*, 39–43; Scharf, *History of Maryland*, III, 409–10; Evitts, *A Matter of Allegiances*, 181.

8. Roy P. Basler, ed., *The Collected Works of Abraham Lincoln* (8 vols.; New Brunswick, 1953), IV, 340–41.

march across, and that they must do. But in doing this there is no need of collision. Keep your rowdies in Baltimore, and there will be no bloodshed. Go home and tell your people that if they will not attack us, we will not attack them; but if they do attack us, we will return it, and that severely.[9]

To give greater impact to his message to President Lincoln, Governor Hicks reportedly ordered two companies of militia to march from the city and burn railroad bridges leading into Baltimore from the North. The police chief of Baltimore, George P. Kane, did not feel that enough was being done to secure his city, and he actively sought the aid of other prosouthern Marylanders. In a telegram to Bradley T. Johnson of Frederick, Kane excitedly requested him to "bring your men by the first train and we will arrange with the railroad afterwards. Streets red with Maryland blood; send expresses over the mountains of Maryland and Virginia for the riflemen to come without delay. Fresh hordes will be down on us tomorrow. We will fight them and whip them or die." Johnson, a graduate of Princeton College and a Frederick lawyer and politician, departed immediately and arrived in Baltimore with his company on April 20. Within a few weeks, Johnson would play an instrumental role in organizing Maryland's first regiment for the Confederacy. Three other units from outlying areas of Baltimore followed Johnson's Frederick company, including the Pikesville Forest Rangers, commanded by Wilson Carey Nicholas. Nicholas, a future officer of the 1st Maryland Infantry (C.S.), occupied the federal arsenal at Pikesville.[10]

The following day, April 21, Baltimoreans prepared for the onslaught of federal troops then encamped at Cockeysville but rumored to be moving on the city. Ad hoc groups of men formed the Volunteer Ununiformed Corps after the city government hastily authorized the expenditure of $500,000 for its defense. A graduate of the United States Military Academy, Isaac R. Trimble, was appointed to command these new units expected to engage the enemy that same day. Reinforcements such as the Howard County Dragoons under George Ridgely Gaither, Jr., poured into Baltimore while other volunteer units and militia forces patrolled the city's suburbs. Frank A. Bond, a young farmer from Anne Arundel County, seized Annapolis Junction, disrupting rail and telegraph

9. *Ibid.*, 341–42.

10. Scharf, *History of Maryland*, III, 413–14; Johnson, *Maryland*, 22–23; Johnson, "Memoir of First Maryland Regiment," 347–48; Evitts, *A Matter of Allegiances*, 181–82.

lines between Baltimore and Washington. Nicholas N. Snowden, an 1843 graduate of Georgetown College and resident of Laurel, likewise deployed his men on the Annapolis-Washington road and cut communications there.[11]

The Lincoln government carefully balanced the need to protect the capital with the desire to keep Maryland in the Union. Lincoln accepted the mayor's request that federal troops not pass through Baltimore and withdrew the force from Cockeysville. General Winfield Scott devised alternative routes for northern forces to move to Washington without going through Maryland's largest urban area. Benjamin Butler, in one of his first acts as a Union general, shipped his units to Annapolis and then moved them southward. This proved to be a temporary measure because the threat to Washington grew each day that Union troops did not control Maryland.

The Baltimore and Ohio Railroad became the key to Maryland's security. The line ran from Baltimore toward Frederick, into western Virginia, then back into Maryland, near Cumberland. The railroad, under the presidency of John W. Garrett, carried vital agricultural and industrial products and was the primary means of transportation between the east and west. General Scott knew that Washington could never be safe unless federal troops held this rail line. By late April, the Baltimore and Ohio served as a conduit for Confederate supplies and personnel from Baltimore to Harpers Ferry, where Virginia troops had captured the arsenal and established a garrison. The southern hold on Harpers Ferry, at the critical junction of the Potomac and Shenandoah rivers, not only threatened Maryland but potentially severed the railroad and the nearby Chesapeake and Ohio Canal.[12]

11. Scharf, *History of Maryland*, III, 416–18.

12. General Butler recognized the importance of the railroad and requested advice on what to do about the movement of supplies to Confederate forces at Harpers Ferry. Regarding Maryland's Confederate forces, Butler wrote to General Winfield Scott on May 6, 1861, about his fear that local troops might oppose the passage of the U.S. troops through Baltimore and suggesting that rebel cavalry commanders Capt. William H. Dorsey and Capt. George R. Gaither be arrested. See U.S. War Department, *The War of the Rebellion: A Compilation of the Official Records of the Union and Confederate Armies* (128 vols.; Washington, D.C., 1880–1901), Ser. I, Vol. II, 623–24. For a discussion of the Civil War along the Chesapeake and Ohio Canal, see Walter S. Sanderlin, "A House Divided: The Conflict of Loyalties on the Chesapeake and Ohio Canal, 1861–1865," *Maryland Historical Magazine*, XLI (1946), 257–81.

On April 22, Governor Hicks finally called the state legislature into session to meet in Frederick on the twenty-sixth to "deliberate and consider of the condition of the State, and take such measures as in their wisdom they may deem fit to maintain peace, order and security within our limits." Hicks's call for the legislature to convene in western Maryland, within miles of Confederate forces at Harpers Ferry, encouraged southerners to believe that Maryland's secession was imminent. Hicks, a slave owner, however, changed the site of the special session from Annapolis to Frederick because federal troops now occupied the state capital (he later claimed that the site was moved because Frederick had a greater pro-Union population).[13]

On April 27 the state senate stated its recognition that many Marylanders thought it would commit the state to secession. The senators unanimously declared that "all such fears are without just foundation. We know that we have no constitutional authority to take such action. You need not fear that there is a possibility that we will do so." In a space of a few days, the Maryland legislature dashed the hopes of prosouthern Marylanders when the House of Delegates also refused to adopt an ordinance of secession. One historian has concluded that despite the excitement generated by the Baltimore massacre, "Unionism ... was always uppermost in Maryland."[14]

Bradley T. Johnson roundly criticized the state legislature and particularly Governor Hicks when, as a Confederate colonel in late 1862, he wrote about the activities of the previous spring. Johnson claimed that a "small body of influential, honorable, and sincere members were opposed to *hasty action*. They dallied and delayed and lost a *week*. A *week* in war, never to be recovered. A *week* in Revolution—a century in the tranquil current of civil affairs."[15]

13. Scharf, *History of Maryland*, III, 424; Evitts, *A Matter of Allegiances*, 187–88. The delegates are described in Ralph A. Wooster, "The Membership of the Maryland Legislature of 1861," *Maryland Historical Magazine*, LVI (1961), 94 102.

14. Scharf, *History of Maryland*, III, 425; Evitts, *A Matter of Allegiances*, 190. Two recent books examine Maryland's southern perspective in the spring of 1861: Lawrence M. Denton, *A Southern Star for Maryland: Maryland and the Secession Crisis, 1860–1861* (Baltimore, 1995), and Bart Rhett Talbert, *Maryland: The South's First Casualty* (Berryville, 1995). Robert Schoeberlein, "Baltimore in 1861: A Case Study of Southern Unionism" (M.A. thesis, University of Maryland, Baltimore County, 1994), also examines the role of Baltimore during this critical period.

15. Johnson, "Memoir of First Maryland Regiment," 348.

The state's failure to join the Confederacy bitterly hurt prosouthern Marylanders, who faced exile in Virginia if they were to realize their dreams of an independent Maryland. On May 5, General Butler moved his command to Relay House, a junction that controlled the passage of the Baltimore and Ohio Railroad between Frederick and the railroad's namesake, thus effectively ending any threat to the railroad or to Washington. In a well-planned and executed maneuver, Butler then occupied Baltimore during the evening of May 13 and the early morning hours of the fourteenth. Union troops seized Federal Hill, overlooking downtown Baltimore, and easily suppressed any attempts by city residents to support the rebellion.[16]

The federal occupation of Baltimore ended the state's attempts to maintain any semblance of neutrality. The Confederacy's failure to incorporate Maryland and the other border states was the South's first major setback in its struggle for independence. Maryland's failure to join the Confederacy meant that the war would be fought mainly in Virginia and the defense of Richmond would be a primary factor in Confederate military planning. Nevertheless, Marylanders, whether they liked it or not, now lived in a "seat of war" and would endure four years of constant military activity and occupation.[17]

The 146 men who served as junior officers in the Maryland Line during the four years of the war came from diverse backgrounds.[18] The oldest known officer was forty-nine years old in 1861; the youngest was only fifteen when Union troops moved into Maryland. Nicholas Burke, a Baltimore city bailiff and son of a War of 1812 colonel from Maryland, was the oldest Confederate officer and, probably because of his advanced age, had a brief military career. In contrast, the youngest serving officer, Francis W. "Polk" Burke (no known relationship to Nicholas Burke), first appeared as an enlisted man in 1862, when he was captured by the enemy. He later served as a second lieutenant in the 2nd Maryland Cavalry Battalion (C.S.). The year of birth for 108 men has been discerned and shows that the average year of birth was 1835. The largest number of Maryland

16. Scharf, *History of Maryland*, III, 421–24.

17. McPherson, *Battle Cry of Freedom*, 306–307; Allan Nevins, *The Improvised War, 1861–1862* (New York, 1959), 146–47, Vol. I of Nevins, *The War for the Union*, 4 vols.

18. Unless specifically cited, all information on the Maryland Confederate junior officers is derived from the roster in the Appendix. The Notes on the Roster provide details on the compilation of this material.

officers in the Confederate army were born between 1838 and 1841 (see Table 3).

Maryland's Confederate officers were overwhelmingly natives of the state, among ninety-eight of these men, eighty-seven, or 89 percent, hailed from Maryland. Eight of the remaining eleven officers were born in neighboring Virginia or in the District of Columbia. One officer, Wilson C. Nicholas, was born in 1836 at the Brooklyn Navy Yard in New York, where his father, a career U.S. Navy officer, was stationed. The place of birth was purely accidental because Nicholas came from a distinguished Virginia family and his grandfather, a Virginia governor, was a friend of Thomas Jefferson.[19] There were only two men of foreign birth in the ranks of Maryland's junior officer corps. Christopher C. Callan, born in Ireland in 1837, spent most of his life in Georgetown, District of Columbia. William Smyth, a clerk living in Baltimore's National Hotel in 1860, reported to the census enumerator that year that his place of birth was Ireland.

A survey of the residences of these men at the outbreak of the war provides some insight into the support the South enjoyed in Maryland. Thirty-nine, or 30 percent, of 130 officers with known residences at the time of their enlistment or appointment came from the city of Baltimore. Six of the officers, the largest number of men whose ward has been identified, lived in the eleventh ward, the city's richest area. None of the officers of the Maryland Line are known to have resided in the city's immigrant wards, the Irish eighth or the German first and second wards.[20] Southern Maryland provided the second largest contingent of Confederate officers with 35 men. They were almost equally divided among the region's six counties; Prince Georges County provided 10 officers whereas only 4 came from Montgomery County. No officers came from Calvert County.

Western Maryland provided twenty-five officers, the majority from Baltimore and Frederick counties, in the units raised by the state for the Confederate army. The Eastern Shore had the lowest number of officers serving in the Maryland Line although it was still a respectable eighteen, or 13.8 percent of all officers with known residences. Somerset and Dor-

19. Johnson, *Maryland*, 363–65; *Genealogy and Biography of Leading Families of the City of Baltimore and Baltimore County, Maryland* (New York, 1897), 71.

20. Joseph Garonzik, "The Racial and Ethnic Make-up of Baltimore's Neighborhoods, 1850–70," *Maryland Historical Magazine*, LXXI (1976), 392–402.

Table 3. Years of Birth of Confederate Officers from Maryland

Year of Birth	Number	Year of Birth	Number
1812	1	1834	5
1820	2	1835	6
1821	1	1836	7
1822	1	1837	4
1824	2	1838	14
1826	3	1839	10
1827	2	1840	8
1828	3	1841	12
1830	3	1842	6
1831	5	1843	3
1832	2	1844	3
1833	4	1846	1
Unknown	38		

Sources: Compiled Service Records; 1860 Census; Genealogical Sources.

chester counties contributed five officers each. Seven officers lived in Washington, D.C., at the time of the war while another six men lived in various parts of the country. Three of these men lived in Virginia, and the remainder were scattered across the nation. Frederick Y. Dabney, for example, was the son of a Hinds County, Mississippi, judge. Dabney himself was a civil engineer with the Southern Railroad in Mississippi upon his assignment to the 1st Maryland Battery.

Many of the Marylanders who served as officers in the Confederate army had seen the world before taking up arms. James R. Herbert left his home in Woodstock, Howard County, at the age of thirteen to go to sea. After crossing the Atlantic, Herbert was one of two members of his ship's crew to survive a cholera epidemic. Considering himself lucky, Herbert settled down to a mercantile life in Baltimore until the war came. Alexander McK. Pittman joined William Walker's filibuster attempt in Nicaragua at the age of twenty. He lost an arm there in April, 1855, and later returned to Baltimore. William Independence Rasin, born in Kent County in 1842, moved to St. Louis at an early age following the death of his father. When he was fifteen, Rasin established his own business at Fort Leavenworth, Kansas, and witnessed much of the violence in that territory when free-soilers and slavery proponents battled for control. Francis X. Ward received an appointment as secretary to the United States legation in Costa Rica following his graduation from Georgetown College. Serving only a few months, Ward resigned after John Brown's raid and returned to his home in Baltimore to study law and to wait for his state's decision regarding secession.[21]

Maryland's Confederate lieutenants and captains came from a well-to-do background when they joined the army (see Table 4). A survey of eighty-seven officers whose prewar occupations are known reveals that 62 percent came from the professional or semiprofessional categories (proprietors, clerks, and businessmen). The fifteen clerks in Maryland's Confederate officer corps formed the largest single component in the two categories, followed by students and lawyers. This is not surprising given the concentration of men from Baltimore, although professionals and semiprofessionals were found statewide. Twenty-six men made their living from agriculture in 1860–1861; 30 percent of the Confederate junior officer corps from Maryland. As expected, these men came from regions of the state outside of Baltimore. Four of twenty-six were considered planters, but only one man worked as a farmhand.[22]

The smallest group of officers, seven men, or just 8 percent, made their living as skilled workers. One of these men, John W. Torsch, was a twenty-seven-year-old Baltimore engraver who had worked with several large New York journals before the war and had returned to his native city to open his own studio. A full-page advertisement in the 1860 Baltimore city directory stated that Torsch, a "Designer and Engraver on Wood," maintained an office at 117 Baltimore Street. "His long experience," the notice claimed, "in New York, Boston and Philadelphia Establishments has imparted to him facilities not possessed by any similar Artist in Baltimore, and it is with the utmost confidence that he invites the public to an examination of his specimens."[23]

As a group, Maryland's Confederate junior officer corps belonged to a

---

21. Johnson, *Maryland,* 296–97, 382–95, 431–33; *Biographical Cyclopedia,* II, 708–709, I, 251–52; Statement of Alexander McK. Pittman, RG 94, Records of the Adjutant General's Office, Case Files of Investigations by Levi C. Turner and Lafayette C. Baker, 1861–66, M797, NA (hereafter referred to as Turner-Baker Files); obituary of Rasin in *Confederate Veteran,* XXIV (1916), 466; Ward File, GUAAR.

22. Occupational categories adopted from Baker, *Ambivalent Americans,* 145.

23. John W. Woods, *Woods' Baltimore City Directory, Containing a Corrected Engraved Map of the City* (Baltimore, 1860), 63.

Table 4. Occupations of Confederate Officers from Maryland

	Number		*Number*
Apprentice tailor	1	Medical doctor	1
Architect	1	Merchant	7
Bookkeeper	2	Planter	4
Butcher	1	Railroad employee	1
City bailiff	1	Railroad worker/farmer	1
Clerk	15	Salesman	1
Engineer	3	Stonecutter	1
Engraver	1	Student	11
Farmer	20	Teacher	1
Farmhand	1	Tinner	1
Farm manager	1	U.S.M.A. cadet	1
Lawyer	9	V.M.I. cadet	1

Sources: Compiled Service Records; 1860 Census; Genealogical Sources.

distinctive occupational level in the antebellum period, most of them in the highest strata of Maryland's urban and rural professions. No officers were listed as belonging to the unskilled workforce.

The officers had an average real and personal estate value of $1,086 and $1,502, respectively, according to the 1860 census. This value, of course, is subject to variance because the majority of officers, like most households in the state, did not report any wealth.[24] Joseph Forrest of Oakville in St. Marys County was the richest man to serve as a junior officer in the Maryland Line. The son of a War of 1812 general, Forrest attended Georgetown College in the 1830s but did not graduate. A planter in his native county, Forrest owned two plantations that had a combined value of $114,650 in 1860. Finding "himself largely indebted to various creditors, and to an amount nearly equal to the value of his real estate," Forrest took his family and fifty-six slaves from Maryland to Texas at the opening of the war. He later returned to Virginia and organized the Chesapeake Artillery in 1862.[25]

24. Baker, *Ambivalent Americans*, 62–64, 142, 179–80.
25. GUAAR; 1860 Census for St. Marys County, Maryland; interview with Margaret K. Fresco of Ridge, Maryland, a granddaughter of Captain Forrest, November 9, 1990. Forrest's petition for a presidential pardon is in RG 94, Records of the Adjutant General's

As might be expected given the occupational and economic levels of Maryland Confederate officers, the educational background of these men proved very high by the standards of the nineteenth century. Thirteen men, including one cadet each at the Virginia Military Institute at Lexington, Virginia, and the United States Military Academy at West Point, New York, were enrolled as students in 1860–1861. In addition, more than two dozen officers had attended or completed degrees at such institutions as Georgetown College, the University of Virginia, Dickinson College, Princeton College, St. John's College, Oxford College, Jefferson College, and Yale College. Other officers received their education in the Baltimore city public schools, Charlotte Hall, West River Classical Institute, Bel Air Academy, Snow Hill Academy, and Hallowell College in Alexandria, Virginia (see Table 5). None of the Confederate officers were listed by the 1860 census or in military service records as illiterate.[26]

Determining the religious affiliation of these officers has proven a difficult task without extensive analysis of church and parish records throughout the state. Maryland had a substantial Catholic population concentrated in southern Maryland, Baltimore city, and areas of western Maryland. A rough count of Maryland's officer ranks reveals seventeen Catholics, nearly 12 percent of all officers. This estimate matches the proportion of Maryland Catholics in the 1850 census. Given the heavy immigration of Catholics to the state during the decade preceding the Civil War, it is likely that other Catholics served as officers in the Confederate Maryland Line.[27]

It has not been possible to identify the number of Protestants who served as officers in the Maryland Line. Of all Marylanders affiliated with a Protestant denomination before the war, 60 percent were Methodists; thus it is reasonable to assume that this percentage was also reflected in the Confederate junior officer corps. The Episcopal church also had adherents in Maryland from the days when the colony shifted from its Catholic orientation. One Episcopalian, James R. Herbert, served in both the 1st Maryland Infantry (C.S.) and the 2nd Maryland Infantry Battalion

Office, Pardon Petitions and Related Papers Submitted in Response to President Andrew Johnson's Amnesty Proclamation of May 29, 1865, M1003, NA (hereafter cited as Amnesty Papers).

26. The best source showing the educational background of Confederate soldiers from Maryland at a single institution is James S. Ruby, ed., *Blue and Gray: Georgetown University and the Civil War* (Washington, D.C., 1961).

27. Evitts, *A Matter of Allegiances*, 64.

Table 5. Schools Attended by
Confederate Officers from Maryland

	Number
Baltimore city schools	2
Bel Air Academy	1
Charlotte Hall Academy and Jefferson College	1
Charlotte Hall Academy and Princeton College	1
Charlotte Hall Academy and St. John's College	1
Charlotte Hall Academy, St. John's College, and Georgetown College	1
Charlotte Hall Academy and University of Virginia	1
Georgetown College	12
Hallowell College	1
Oxford College	1
Snow Hill Academy, University of Virginia, and Princeton College	1
University of Maryland Medical School	1
Washington College and University of Virginia	1
West River Classical Institute	1
West River Classical Institute and Dickinson College	1
Yale College	1

Sources: Compiled Service Records; 1860 Census; Genealogical Sources.

(C.S.). No doubt other Episcopalians served in the Maryland Line. At least one officer, Wilson C. Nicholas, professed not to belong to any organized church.[28] A search has not revealed any Jewish officers among the 146 Confederate company-grade officers in the Maryland Line.

Many of Maryland's junior officers came from distinguished families in the Chesapeake Bay region whose ancestry dated to the founding of Maryland and Virginia. Prominent Maryland family names such as Contee, Snowden, Digges, Edelin, Howard, and Nicholas were represented among the Maryland Line's officers. R. Snowden Andrews, the son of an Irish-born U.S. Army officer and a mother who claimed an extensive Maryland lineage, organized the 1st Maryland Battery in 1861. Eugene Digges of Charles County descended from Virginia's first governor. Digges, an 1857 graduate of Georgetown College and a law student in New York, received

28. Baker, *Ambivalent Americans,* 138; *Genealogy and Biography,* 71.

his commission as second lieutenant in the 1st Maryland Infantry (C.S.). Joseph K. Roberts, Jr., was the great-nephew of the governor of Maryland in the 1820s and the son of a Prince Georges County lawyer. After joining the 1st Maryland Cavalry (C.S.) as a private, Roberts was promoted to second lieutenant in 1863. John Grason, an officer in the 4th Maryland Battery, also hailed from a well-connected family and was the son of a Maryland governor. Fielder Cross Slingluff, a lieutenant in the 1st Maryland Cavalry Battalion, came from a German Dunker family that settled in Baltimore after the American Revolution. By the time of the war, the Slingluff family had made its mark in banking and mercantile interests.[29]

The Maryland Line was truly a "band of brothers." At least three pairs of brothers served as officers in the Maryland Line; Clapham and William H. Murray of the 1st and 2nd Maryland Infantry (C.S.) are the most notable example. Other officers no doubt also had brothers serving as enlisted men in the Maryland Line or in other Confederate units. William I. Rasin fought with the 1st Maryland Cavalry (C.S.) while his brother served as a sergeant, later lieutenant, in the Virginia artillery. Second Lieut. Thomas H. Tolson of the 2nd Maryland Infantry (C.S.) had a brother in the same company. Many officers also had relatives in Confederate service. William W. Goldsborough's cousin Bradley T. Johnson also commanded the Maryland Line. Captain William F. Dement of the 1st Maryland Battery had five cousins in the Confederate army.

Just as Marylanders served with family members for the Confederacy, these officers sometimes had to fight against loved ones. Among the 146 captains and lieutenants in the Maryland Line, no cases have been found of brothers in gray fighting brothers in blue, although two Confederate officers had fathers who served in the Union military. R. Snowden Andrews supported the South while his father, a Regular Army officer and hero of the Mexican War, remained loyal. The older Andrews went on to become the paymaster general of the entire Union army. The father of Capt. Nicholas of the 1st Maryland Infantry (C.S.), Capt. John S. Nicholas, did not resign from the U.S. Navy at the commencement of the war and continued to serve under the "old flag." Occasionally, family members would meet on the same battlefield wearing different uniforms.

29. Johnson, *Maryland*, 186–87, 395–97; GUAAR files on Digges and Roberts; Bowie, *Across the Years*, 752; Roberts obituary in the Baltimore *Sun*, October 2–3, 1888; J. Thomas Scharf, *History of Baltimore City and County* (Philadelphia, 1881), 852–53.

Charles E. Goldsborough was an assistant surgeon with the 5th Maryland Infantry (U.S.) when he was wounded at Winchester in 1863. The doctor fell into hands of the 2nd Maryland Infantry (C.S.), his cousin William W. Goldsborough's unit.[30]

The decision to join the Confederate army was not an easy one for many Marylanders. Fighting for the Confederacy meant that Marylanders had to leave home and family, often exposing wives and children to the wrath of pro-Union neighbors or to the repression of occupying Union forces. Confederate Marylanders sacrificed their rights as citizens and forfeited their property. William F. Dement, for example, had his property in Charles County confiscated by Union troops and had to petition for its return after the war.[31]

During the course of the four years of war, Confederate Marylanders fought Union Marylanders on the same battlefield on several occasions. In some cases, soldiers from Maryland served in the Confederate army against the wishes of their families. The division of families was a harsh result of the war and one that struck Maryland's border state residents more heavily than most parts of the nation.

What motivated these men to leave Maryland for an uncertain destiny? Noah Dixon Walker, the son of a wealthy Baltimore clothier, was offered $250,000 by his father to sail to England, where he could do as he pleased with the money. Walker, twenty-seven years old at the outbreak of the war, had just returned from a grand tour of Europe when he learned of the crisis facing Maryland. He refused to obey his father and instead left Baltimore for the new Confederate capital, where he joined the Richmond Zouaves, Company E of the 44th Virginia Infantry Regiment. Elected second lieutenant, Walker finally wrote his father in early 1863 to explain his action:

At the beginning of the present revolution which has separated the Northern from the Southern states, and given birth to the Confederate government, I perceived that it was a struggle between Liberty, on the one side, and Tyranny on the other. I believed that Abraham Lincoln had been placed in power by an insane political faction, upon the ruins of our once sacred Constitution, and that he and his party, to possess and hold the

30. Hartzler, *Marylanders in the Confederacy*, 41.
31. William F. Dement file, Amnesty Papers.

political power of the country, would perpetrate any act, however outrageous, to continue their unconstitutional authority.

Walker concluded that "the accuracy of these opinions, formed at the inception of the revolution, have been fully proved and confirmed by subsequent events."[32]

In a series of fascinating letters to Francis G. Wood, a former Princeton College friend then in New York, McHenry Howard of Baltimore explained his views of Maryland's position during the secession crisis. At the time of the 1860 presidential election, Howard, a future Confederate officer, noted that "I live just between the North and the South, hearing both sides of the question and *feeling* both sides. Secondly Maryland is one of the border states, which now suffer most from the wrongs complained of by the South, and whose condition and prospects would be most vitally affected in case of disunion." The young man continued, "I do not believe that a State has the right to secede, but that when every constitutional mode of obtaining redress is exhausted and when the evil is of a sufficient magnitude, there always remains underneath every constitution and every government that last right of revolution." Regarding the slavery question, Howard emphatically declared, "I would to God [wish] that a slave had never set his foot on the soil of this country. I hope most earnestly for its ultimate extinction, but I do most earnestly contend that you of the North must leave us to settle it for ourselves, there must be no outside force, it is unjust & it retards the very object which it seeks."[33]

Wood, in a reply in early 1861, admitted that he had been too preoccupied with business matters to be overly concerned with political issues. He wrote that "Abraham Lincoln passed through here [Utica, New York] this morning and I went to see him. I could not get within thirty rods of him, but was agreeably disappointed in his personal appearance." Regarding secession, Wood admitted that "perhaps after all Mac the dissolution of the Union, had better be made now—certainly if this slavery question is to be the touch stone in our political battles. I am tired of it.

32. Noah Dixon Walker Papers, MS 1455, Manuscripts Division, MHS; "Noah Dixon Walker to his Father Noah Walker," *Maryland Historical Magazine*, XXX (1935), 363–65.

33. McHenry Howard to "Dear Frank" in November (exact date not given), Charles Howard Papers, MS 469.4, Manuscripts Division, MHS.

In the first place not one man in a thousand with us knows any thing about it except by hearsay and in the abstract."[34]

Howard's next letter on May 17 found him preparing to leave Baltimore to join a volunteer company in Virginia. Howard appealed to his friend not to "join in the illegal, mad and ruinous movement which is now precipitating the North upon the South, for disguise as you will it is nothing less. Eleven States have seceded with unparalleled unanimity from the Union. They desire nothing more than to live at peace and govern themselves. In Heaven's name why not let them depart in peace, why must brothers blood be shed by brothers lances in the most enlightened country and the most enlightened and Christian age?" Howard thought that the "outbreak of April 19th was not a return to mob law as Northern papers say. The roughs are unionists. It resulted from the irrepressible indignation of the people at seeing armed men pass over our soil to subjugate our brethren of the South." In a final letter to Wood on May 18, Howard closed by saying that he would not be able to attend the June reunion at Princeton. "I hope to see you some of these days when we shall again have Peace, blessed Peace which like health we do not appreciate until we have lost it and which when lost it is equally hard to regain." Shortly after writing his last letter to Wood, Howard enlisted as a sergeant in the 1st Maryland Infantry (C.S.) and later received his commission.[35]

Other Marylanders echoed the same sentiments as Walker and Howard. Randolph Harrison McKim grew up at Belvidere, an estate in Baltimore, and favored the Confederacy over the objections of his parents. At his departure, young McKim said, "Well, father, I comfort myself with the promise, 'When my father and my mother forsake me, then the Lord will take me up.'" On the eve of the Battle of First Manassas, nineteen-year-old McKim, a graduate of the University of Virginia and an enlisted man in the 1st Maryland Infantry (C.S.), wrote his mother:

> It grieved me to the quick to find that you are still in ignorance of my real position in Virginia now, and I confess I almost felt self-reproached when you said that you were perfectly satisfied with my promise not to join the Southern Army "without my father's consent." . . . I say then in justifica-

34. Francis G. Wood to "Dear Howard," February 18, 1861, *ibid.*
35. McHenry Howard to "Dear Frank," May 17, 18, 1861, *ibid.*

tion of my course that I could not get home safely to get advice, and I felt very hopeful that papa, as most other Union men in Baltimore, had changed his sentiments when he found that the government means to establish a despotism and call it by the sacred name of Union. I do not now believe, after learning that I am disappointed to a great extent in this expected change so far, that papa will not finally cease to support what he has believed a free and righteous government, when he finds beyond contradiction that Lincoln has overthrown the government of our forefathers and abolished every principle of the Declaration of Independence.[36]

Henry Kyd Douglas, a native of Virginia but a resident of Washington County, Maryland, considered slavery a "curse to the people of the Middle States." Born in 1840, Douglas had met John Brown when the radical abolitionist lived near the young man's home at Ferry Hill Place across the Potomac River from Shepherdstown, Virginia (now West Virginia). Douglas also witnessed Brown's capture at Harpers Ferry after the latter's abortive attempt to incite a slave insurrection and was present at his trial at the Jefferson County courthouse in Charles Town. After graduating from Franklin and Marshall College in Pennsylvania in 1859 and from law school in 1860, Douglas moved to St. Louis, Missouri, to practice law. When Virginia seceded in the spring of 1861, Douglas immediately returned home and enlisted in a Virginia infantry company raised in the neighborhood of Shepherdstown.[37]

Even after a year of war, many Marylanders still harbored strong feelings about the division of the nation. Samuel T. McCullough, a young lawyer from Annapolis, summed up his reason for joining the Confederate cause in 1862 in a letter to his father:

> When I left home I was undecided as to which course I would pursue. Since, however, we have been down here, we have upon consultation decided upon taking a step which will for a long time separate your son from you all, and perhaps forever. . . . The "*Cause of the South*" has always you know had my heartfelt sympathies. I have determined to give them my active support. I am fully impressed with the danger & discomfort that attend the step but I have resolved to take it. Wherever in life (*as now*) duty—*imperative duty* & mere convenience incline to two essentially & radically different courses, I shall never hesitate which to follow. Such is

36. McKim, *Soldier's Recollections*, 9, 30–31.
37. Douglas, *I Rode with Stonewall*, 3.

now the case duty I feel as well as a feeling, & self-respect impel me to a step which will banish me from a home of comfort & plenty, a home where I have never received aught but kindness & friendly offices.[38]

The majority of Maryland's Confederate lieutenants and captains had no prior military experience beyond service in the militia or in antebellum volunteer units. Most were as green as the men they commanded. George W. Booth summed up his feelings about war, which were shared by other novice officers: "My earliest predilections were of a martial character. As a boy, the story of the deeds of soldier and sailor were to me of the most engrossing interest, and the display of heroism which attended the long struggle of the Revolutionary period, the war of 1812, and later, that with Mexico were read and reread with an ardor that almost approached worship."[39]

Maryland had a fairly well-organized militia system in place before the war, which, unlike those in many states, had remained in place during the long years of peace. The 5th and 53rd Maryland Regiments were composed of the militia of the city of Baltimore and had seen service during the 1835 Bank Riots and again during the 1857 Baltimore and Ohio Railroad strike. Throughout the Know-Nothing domination of the city, the militia was caught in a power struggle between the city's mayor and the state governor that resulted in the militia's loss of strength and prestige. This malaise effectively ceased after John Brown's seizure of Harpers Ferry. Five companies from Baltimore, in conjunction with Frederick militiamen, rushed to the scene and assisted in the capture of the abolitionist.[40]

The action at Harpers Ferry inspired state residents to reconsider the militia's condition and its ability to defend Maryland. Not satisfied with

38. Samuel T. McCullough to his father, August 13, 1862, in Jedediah Hotchkiss Papers (# 2822), Special Collections, Alderman Library, University of Virginia, Charlottesville.

39. Booth, *Personal Reminiscences*, 5.

40. For a general history of militia activities before the war, see James H. Fitzgerald Brewer, *History of the 175th Infantry (Fifth Maryland)* (Baltimore, 1955), 112–33, and Joseph M. Balkoski, *The Maryland National Guard: A History of Maryland's Military Forces, 1634–1991* (Baltimore, 1991). For the militia's role at Harpers Ferry, see Gregory A. Stiverson, ed., *"In Readiness to Do Every Duty Assigned": The Frederick Militia and John Brown's Raid on Harper's Ferry, October 17–18, 1859* (Annapolis, 1991).

the present system, 226 Baltimore residents volunteered to serve in a new organization, the Maryland Guard, in December, 1859. The organization's constitution called for the election of an executive committee (composed of the commandant, secretary, treasurer, and one representative for every ten members), and new members had to be nominated and voted on before being accepted. Members agreed to serve for a period of three months "for drill and instruction, and mutually pledge their word of honor as gentlemen to conform to the . . . rules & regulations." Membership cost an initial fifty cents to join with monthly dues of twenty-five cents. Fines for absence without leave from the weekly meetings were assessed at twenty-five cents; misconduct during drill cost from ten cents to one dollar.[41]

The formation of the Maryland Guard did not completely satisfy the concerns of Marylanders about the militia. Capt. W. C. Pennington offered a resolution in January, 1861, protesting the state government's neglect of the militia. He requested that nonmembers of the Maryland Guard be permitted to drill with the unit so they could obtain some military knowledge. The Maryland Guard successfully attracted members in part because of its colorful uniforms and precision drill.[42]

By April, 1861, the 53rd Maryland Regiment contained the Maryland Guard Battalion with six companies and three companies of the Independent Greys Battalion. As the state reached a fever point that spring, more volunteer companies sprang up virtually overnight. In St. Marys County, for example, a local paper reported that the news of Fort Sumter was received wildly: "We have never witnessed an excitement more general and intense than has prevailed in our midst. . . . It indicates in the most unmistakable manner that the sympathies of our people are exclusively with the South." A few days later, men in the county gathered to purchase arms for volunteers.[43]

41. Maryland Guard Constitution and Membership Roster, MS 566, Manuscripts Division, MHS.

42. Maryland Guard Record Book, MS 2165, *ibid.* For a description of the Maryland Guard in 1861, see Howard, *Recollections,* 9–15.

43. Newspaper clippings from the Baltimore *Telegram* assembled by Samuel Z. Ammen entitled "Maryland Troops in the Confederate Army from Original Sources" (original scrapbook in possession of Elden E. Billings, copy furnished by Ross M. Kimmel), 9; Robert E. T. Pogue, *Yesterday in Old St. Mary's County* (New York, 1968), 165. For volunteer

At least nineteen future officers in the Confederate Maryland Line served for some time in the militia or volunteer companies from Baltimore, and more served in the outlying areas of the state. These men thus received a modicum of training and experience that proved valuable when war came.[44]

A few men in the officer ranks possessed greater knowledge of the military profession. Several future Confederate officers had prewar aspirations to serve as officers in the Regular Army. Edmund Barry was an officer in the Mexican War and on the frontier, where he learned both Spanish and Indian warfare. In his application for a Regular Army commission in 1855, Barry was held to be "a fine scholar, he is one of the best educated men in the Army—either among officers or men." To add extra weight to his appointment, Barry's father was "one of our best Citizens of Balto. & one of our strongest political friends." William H. Murray, prominent in Baltimore's Maryland Guard, also applied for a commission in 1857 but did not receive a formal appointment in the U.S. Army. Weeks before the April riots in Baltimore, Anthony Kennedy (the brother of John Pendleton Kennedy) nominated Robert Carter Smith, the son and grandson of distinguished Marylanders, for appointment in the U.S. military. Kennedy thought that Smith's appointment could help smooth tense relationships between Maryland and the new administration. He noted that "Mr. R. C. Smith is a young gentleman of fine character & attainments and by the reverses of fortune, without any fault of his own is now compelled to look around him for new means of support, his education, his antecedents and his pride of character would fully justify you in conferring such an appointment."[45]

---

companies raised in another Maryland county at this time, see Frederic Emory, *Queen Anne's County, Maryland: Its Early History and Development* (Baltimore, 1950), 495–98. Rosters of the various companies raised in Baltimore city in April–May, 1861, are found in RG 109, War Department Collection of Confederate Records, Muster and Pay Rolls for Maryland Units, NA.

44. The importance of the militia and volunteer system in the South, especially the Upper South, is highlighted in Richard M. McMurray, *Two Great Rebel Armies: An Essay in Confederate Military History* (Chapel Hill, 1989), 97–98. The men identified as belonging to Baltimore's militia or volunteer companies before the war are Booth, Brown, Bussey, Cross, Deppish, Dorsey, Herbert, Hough, Howard (William K.), Marriott, Mullan, Murray brothers, O'Brien, Smith (R. C.), Tormey, Torsch, Walters, and Ward.

45. RG 107, Records of the Office of the Secretary of War, Applications for Appointment in the Regular Army, 1854–61: Maryland, NA. Of the approximately ninety men

For the most part, Confederate Marylanders went to war to defend civil liberties and the right of individual states to choose their destiny. Slavery was a minor motivation for the taking up of arms. Only two officers from Baltimore listed in the 1860 census were possible slave owners, although five of the city's Confederate officers employed servants, both white and black, in their households.[46] Maryland's slaveholders had little to gain from sectional conflict, and even officers serving in the Confederate army from Maryland expressed a lack of confidence in the "peculiar institution." These men were clearly not of the fire-eating persuasion, just as their Maryland brothers in blue shared little enthusiasm for abolitionism.

---

requesting appointment in the Regular Army in this time period, six later served as officers in the Confederate Maryland Line.

46. The 1860 Slave Census for Baltimore city shows that Edward Dorsey owned three slaves in the fourth ward and William Hough owned one slave in the eleventh. It is possible that these are not the same men who later served in the Confederate army. Five Confederate officers (Andrews, Beatty, Bonn, Cushing, and Hough) employed a total of six white servants, six mulatto servants, and five black servants at the time of the 1860 enumeration.

·3·

Rally Around the Flag

Union Marylanders exhibited little fervor at the outbreak of the conflict. Indeed, Maryland's support of the Union wavered in the spring of 1861. At first glance, the state appeared as a seething cauldron of secessionist sentiment beginning to bubble over with the Baltimore riots in April. More than anything else, Marylanders were confused during the heady spring days. As Baltimoreans prepared to meet the influx of troops from the North, John G. Johannes mobilized his company of the Baltimore City Guard Battalion to defend the city. Johannes and his men began destroying rail lines leading into Baltimore. Ironically, Johannes later served throughout the war as a Union officer.[1]

The same night that Johannes' City Guard commenced burning the Northern Central Railroad bridges at Melvale, Relay House, and Cockeysville, John W. Wilson's Baltimore County volunteer company, the Union Rifles, mobilized at Cockeysville to repulse attempts to cut the city's links with the North. While Wilson's volunteers were guarding the Big Gunpowder Bridge, a group of armed men approached them. The leader of the band asked to speak with Wilson, and after several minutes of conversation, Wilson exclaimed, "The city of Baltimore could not raise money enough to hire me to do such a thing!" The pro-Union man returned to his troops and loudly asked: "Will you stick to me boys? These men say Governor Hicks has ordered them to come up here and offer me five hundred dollars to burn Big Gunpowder Bridge. If they do it, they will walk over my dead body first." Through his resolute stand, Wilson, a native of Lancaster County, Pennsylvania, prevented the destruction of the crucial transportation link.[2]

1. Scharf, *History of Maryland*, III, 413; Evitts, *A Matter of Allegiances*, 185.
2. Camper and Kirkley, *Historical Record*, 252–53.

Edward M. Mobley, the sheriff of Washington County in western Maryland, told Governor Hicks on April 22 of secessionist efforts in that part of the state: "Virginia troops searching houses in Maryland on Saturday near Harper's Ferry for arms. I appealed to General Harper, commander, to recall them, which he promised if Northern troops are forbidden." Exasperated, Mobley asked the governor: "What is to be done with Southern? What steps shall I take?" Although he was unable to stop the Confederate activities, they strengthened Mobley's personal loyalty to the federal government. Elected as sheriff on the Union ticket in 1859, Mobley, a carriage maker, later raised a company of northern volunteers from Washington County and also recruited his son for military service.[3]

Maryland's flirtation with secession proved short-lived. The arrival of northern troops stabilized Unionist sentiment in the state. Important economic and social ties with the North were recalled, and Governor Hicks managed to subdue the secessionist impulse of the legislature. "The high tide of Southern sentiment," Jean H. Baker writes, "had receded and left the state on Union ground."[4]

Preservation of the Union was the greatest single motivation for Marylanders who supported the northern cause. Relatively few Union junior officers from Maryland owned slaves or had any ties to the peculiar institution. With the exception of Unionists from the Eastern Shore, slavery was an alien way of life.[5] This did not mean, however, that Union Marylanders were rabid abolitionists. The contrary seems to be true because many white Marylanders loathed the Negro as competition in a state with

3. *Official Records*, Ser. I, Vol. II, 589. Unless specifically cited, all information on the Maryland Union junior officers is derived from the roster in the Appendix. The Notes on the Roster explain how it was compiled. See also RG 94, Records of the Adjutant General's Office, Compiled Service Records of Volunteer Union Soldiers Who Served in Organizations from the State of Maryland, M384, NA, and RG 15, Records of the Veterans Administration, Pension Applications of Maryland Union Officers (hereafter respectively referred to as CSR and Pension Records and the name of the officer).

4. Baker, *Politics of Continuity*, 54.

5. A survey of slaveholders from Baltimore city reveals that only one Union junior officer in the Maryland Brigade from that city may have owned any slaves in 1860 (Baltimore City 1860 Slave Census). For a discussion of the slaveholders in one Union Maryland regiment, see "Union Soldier Slave Owners," *Confederate Veteran*, VII (1899), 408. An interesting analysis of the reasons why northerners went to war in 1861 is found in Earl J. Hess, *Liberty, Virtue, and Progress: Northerners and Their War for the Union* (New York, 1988).

one of the nation's largest free black populations. The brother of a Union officer wrote from Fort Monroe in Virginia in 1862 that "I like the place very well for a change, but for one thing it is awful, that is the confounded Negroes they dont do anything but lay about they live in houses built on purpose for them & live better than the white people who live in huts underground. The Negroes are very saucy. One gave me some impudence & I started after him but he got away to[o] quick. I can't stand negro impertinence any where."[6]

The Emancipation Proclamation changed the war's purpose from a struggle to maintain the Union to one of freeing the slaves. One future Maryland officer protested in a letter to his father in late January, 1863, that the "Administration has forgotten the cause the War was for. I have not if they have. I think it was for the Restoration of the Union and not abolishing Slavery which it has come to if it had been I would have not been in the Army this day." When the Union army recruited Negroes as soldiers, the War Department appointed whites to command the United States Colored Troops. Many white officers and enlisted men in northern volunteer regiments sought appointment in Negro units because they believed in freedom for blacks. Yet only one junior officer from the Union Maryland Brigade later commanded black troops. Similarly, a survey of over two dozen company-grade officers in Maryland's six black regiments reveals that none of these men came from the state. For most Union Marylanders, the war did not revolve around the slave question.[7]

One Marylander living in Ohio wrote his family after Lincoln's election emphasizing the importance of America's unique form of government: "War, Secession, and South Carlina is in every ones Mouth the Subject is discused on every corner and lane truley the little cotton state oncest in the course of her ill spent life time has caused herself to be notised. But I hope the South will pause and take one sober thought before the

6. A discussion of the white fear of free blacks is found in Baker, *Politics of Continuity*, 104–105. William H. Moffett to father, August 5, 1862, in Edwin W. Moffett Papers, MS 1373, Manuscripts Division, MHS.

7. Edwin W. Moffett to father, January 20, 1863, Moffett Papers; Joseph T. Glatthaar, *Forged in Battle: The Civil War Alliance of Black Soldiers and White Officers* (New York, 1990), 39–41. For a discussion of emancipation in Maryland, see Charles Lewis Wagandt, *The Mighty Revolution: Negro Emancipation in Maryland, 1862–1864* (Baltimore, 1964); John W. Blassingame, "The Recruitment of Negro Troops in Maryland," *Maryland Historical Magazine*, LVIII (1963), 20–29.

break of this glorious Union for ever; for the people here as a general thing are willing to make almost any concession to preserve the Union."[8]

Jacob Engelbrecht of Frederick, a friend of many federal officers from that town, recounted the dissolution of the Union. When the news of Lincoln's election arrived, Engelbrecht wrote in his diary that "the South carolineans & Allabamaens were ready to seceed from the Union of the U. States and at this time they are making wonderful preparations to leave this glorious Union." Engelbrecht added, "For my own part I say go as quick as you please . . . the sooner they go the better for the piece & quiet of our Country." On December 21, 1860, just a day after South Carolina voted to secede, Englebrecht wrote, "Thank you Gentlemen, you have been dominaring long enough, and I hope you will stay out of the Union."[9]

One Carroll County resident summed up his feelings about the problems facing the nation in 1861: "How anyone can compare the revolution down South with the glorious one in which our forefathers rebelled against a government whose very oppressions planted them in America, I am unable to conceive." F. A. Shriver told his cousin, "This tyrannical Lincoln, as you think, is only trying to save us and our nation from eternal ruin."[10]

Throughout the spring of 1861, some Marylanders grew increasingly frustrated as one southern state after the other left the Union. Engelbrecht commented in early April that he desired that "Uncle Sam (or rather now Uncle Abe) will give the seceding boys a good sound drubbing. The Constitution and the laws must be sustained." Other Marylanders, such as Amos Fleagel in Ohio, were more restrained: "But of course there are some few Zelous followers on old abe who talk of going down South and whip the little cotton State one morning before Breekfast and then if the rest of the South says beens to whip them till noon and then come home and eat there Suppers on there own fair fields of freedom; But this you know is easier said then done."[11]

8. Amos Fleageal to sister and brother, n.d., in Flegeal Family Papers, Harrisburg Civil War Round Table Collection, USAMHI.

9. Dieter Cunz, "The Maryland Germans in the Civil War," *Maryland Historical Magazine*, XXXVI (1941), 398–400.

10. Frederic Shriver Klein, ed., *Just South of Gettysburg: Carroll County, Maryland, in the Civil War* (Westminster, 1963), 20.

11. Cunz, "Maryland Germans," 400; Amos Flegeal to sister and brother, n.d., in

With the state securely under federal control by mid-May, 1861, few, if any, Marylanders encountered difficulties in joining the Union army. The state slowly responded to President Lincoln's call for volunteers on April 15; Governor Hicks did not even issue a similar proclamation until a month later. Unsettled conditions in Maryland prevented any effective organization of military units by Unionists during the spring. A handful of companies, such as Captain Wilson's Union Rifles, managed to "show the flag" during the Baltimore crisis although few attempts were made to raise Union regiments in the state until after General Butler subdued Baltimore.[12]

The initial presidential proclamation of April 15 called for four regiments of 3,123 Maryland volunteers to serve for ninety days. Two days later, Governor Hicks wrote President Lincoln to clarify that the state militia would serve only within the state's boundaries. Secretary of War Simon Cameron responded that same day, confirming that "the troops called for from Maryland are destined for the protection of the Federal capital and the public property of the United States within the limits of the State of Maryland, and it is not intended to remove them beyond those limits except for the defense of this District." On May 14, the governor issued his call for three-month volunteers and appointed John R. Kenly, a Baltimore lawyer, Mexican War veteran, and prominent militia officer, to organize the Maryland regiments. Three days later, the secretary of war told the governor that three-month men were no longer being accepted for service and that troops were now wanted for three years.[13]

On May 6, Kenly and John C. McConnell, a city real estate agent, opened a recruiting office in downtown Baltimore and within ten days enough men signed up to fill four infantry companies. By the end of the

---

Flegeal Family Papers. For further discussion of Unionism in Maryland, see Carl M. Frasure, "Union Sentiment in Maryland, 1859–1861," *Maryland Historical Magazine*, XXIV (1929), 210–24.

12. Charles B. Clark, "Recruitment of Union Troops in Maryland, 1861–1865," *Maryland Historical Magazine*, LIII (1958), 153; Edward Quinn, "Recruitment and Enlistment in Maryland During the Civil War" (M.A. thesis, Catholic University of America, 1943); Millard Les Callette, "A Study of the Recruitment of the Union Army in Maryland" (M.A. thesis, Johns Hopkins University, 1954).

13. *Official Records*, Ser. I, Vol. I, 80, 199, 210; Camper and Kirkley, *Historical Record*, 2–6.

month, Kenly had a full regiment of ten infantry companies, which went into federal service at Relay House as the 1st Maryland Infantry Regiment (U.S.). While being trained, armed, and equipped, Kenly's men suppressed potential southern sympathizers in Baltimore. Two companies, under the command of Capts. Benjamin H. Schley of Frederick and Francis G. F. Waltemeyer of Baltimore, arrested the city's police chief and several officers on the night of June 26 and imprisoned them at Fort McHenry. The following day, Major General Nathaniel P. Banks, commanding the Department of Annapolis, ordered Col. Kenly to assume duties as the provost marshal of Baltimore.[14]

Upon receiving the news of the arrest of Kane and the appointment of Col. Kenly, the Baltimore police commissioners disbanded the police department. The officers and men of the 1st Maryland Infantry (U.S.) were now the only armed force in Baltimore to maintain law and order as well as to prevent insurrection by rebel sympathizers. Kenly immediately formed a new police force made up of "Union citizens" who replaced the old force and arrested the police commissioners for their treasonous behavior. Kenly's prompt action averted any real trouble in Baltimore and kept the city in the firm grip of the federal government. By mid-July, the Maryland colonel returned to the task of preparing his regiment for active service. Kenly and his men had performed their police duties so effectively that Maj. Gen. John A. Dix, commander of Baltimore, reported in October, "The city has never been so free from disorder, disturbance, and crime as it has been during the last sixty days, and during the whole time not a single soldier has been employed in aid of police."[15]

As recruiting picked up during the summer and fall of 1861, Maryland organized other units for service. The 2nd and 5th Maryland Infantry Regiments (U.S.) were mustered into service in September from men recruited in Baltimore and surrounding counties. The 3rd Maryland Infantry Regiment (U.S.) originally drew its men from Baltimore and in early 1862 added several companies from western Maryland. John C. McConnell received a commission as captain of Company A, 1st Maryland Infantry (U.S.), but resigned in August to take command of the new regiment. Two other units, the German Rifles and the Baltimore (or Dix's) Light Infantry, also formed in 1861, but they failed to recruit enough men

14. Camper and Kirkley, *Historical Record*, 6, 12–18.
15. *Ibid.*; Scharf, *History of Maryland*, III, 435–39; *Official Records*, Ser. I, Vol. II, 624.

and subsequently consolidated with the 3rd Maryland Infantry (U.S.) in the spring of 1862.[16]

Recruiting drives were held throughout the state, although the number of enlistments proved disappointing and, according to one prosouthern Baltimore paper, an "up-hill business."[17] Four regiments of infantry came from western Maryland, primarily Allegany and Washington counties, in late 1861 and early 1862. The western companies and units from the Baltimore area assembled as the 1st, 2nd, 3rd, and 4th regiments of the Potomac Home Brigade Infantry, assigned to protect the upper region of the state. A battalion of cavalry was also raised in Frederick and Cumberland and designated as the 1st Battalion, Potomac Home Brigade Cavalry, better known as Cole's Cavalry for its commander, Capt. (later Col.) Henry A. Cole.

The Eastern Shore counties organized two regiments for home defense in 1861. The citizens of Chestertown appealed to the governor on August 24 for arms because "the battle of Manassas has evidently increased secessionism in our State." The Unionists wrote that "the State of Maryland can without question be kept in the Union if the conservative men are properly organized and armed. A large majority of her people have the good sense to see that the interests of our State are inseparably blended with the Union, but such has been the fraudulent and violent spirit and course of the secessionists that upon the occasion of another outbreak similar to that of Baltimore the Union men would be again overawed unless they were properly armed, and thus prepared to meet rebellion face to face."[18]

In early September, the War Department agreed to arm and equip units from the Eastern Shore for local defense on the same grounds as those raised in western Maryland. These units would remain on duty in Maryland "unless special necessity shall require their presence elsewhere."[19]

The postmaster of Baltimore, George W. Purnell, organized the Purnell Legion in the fall of 1861. Drawing on the popular early war concept of a classical Roman legion, the Purnell Legion originally had nine infantry

16. Brief histories of all Maryland Union regiments are found in Wilmer, Jarrett, and Vernon, *History and Roster*.

17. Clark, "Recruitment of Union Troops," 154.

18. *Official Records*, Ser. I, Vol. I, 463; Kirby and Parks, *Roll Call*, 134–35.

19. *Official Records*, Ser. I, Vol. I, 338–39, 482–83.

companies, two cavalry companies, and two batteries of artillery. The nightmare of providing supplies for such a diverse unit and the difficulties of command and control led to the abandonment of the legion after a few months of combat. The Purnell Legion was then divided into an infantry regiment, a cavalry battalion, and two independent batteries, commanded by Capts. Alonzo Snow and John W. Woolcot.[20]

A hodgepodge of other Maryland units entered Union service during the first months of the war. The 1st Maryland Cavalry Regiment (U.S.), for example, had companies from Baltimore, western Maryland, Pennsylvania, and Washington, D.C. Other Marylanders, anxious to join the fray, did not wait for the state to begin recruiting but enlisted in military organizations from northern states, especially those of Massachusetts, New York, and Pennsylvania, that passed through Maryland on their way to Washington.

The Maryland Brigade is representative of the units raised by the state for the Union during the war. In early September, 1862, during the Confederate invasion of Maryland, newly promoted Brig. Gen. Kenly commanded the newly formed 1st, 4th, 6th, 7th, and 8th Maryland infantry regiments and one battery of artillery. With the exception of the 1st Maryland Infantry (U.S.), the units of the new Maryland Brigade had recently formed under President Lincoln's July 2 call for three hundred thousand volunteers for three years' service and his August 15 draft proclamation for another three hundred thousand militiamen for nine months' service. The brigade remained intact until the end of the war although the 6th Maryland Infantry (U.S.) and Alexander's Baltimore Battery left for other duties in March, 1863. A total of 219 men served as captains and lieutenants in the companies of the four regiments that constituted the bulk of the Maryland Brigade.

The 1st, 4th, 7th, and 8th Maryland drew their officer personnel from Baltimore city and surrounding counties as well as from western Maryland. Although individual officers came from southern Maryland or the Eastern Shore, these areas did not contribute any entire companies to the Maryland Brigade (see Table 6). The year of birth has been determined for 206 officers in the Maryland Brigade, 94 percent of the company-grade infantry officers who held that position during the war. The average officer

20. *Ibid.*, 427.

Table 6. Geographic Origins of the Maryland Brigade

1st Maryland Inf. Regt.

Co. A	Baltimore city	Co. F	Baltimore County
Co. B	Baltimore city	Co. G	Baltimore County
Co. C	Baltimore city	Co. H	Frederick County
Co. D	Baltimore city	Co. I	Baltimore city
Co. E	Baltimore city	Co. K	Baltimore city/Washington County

4th Maryland Inf. Regt.

Formed with personnel from Baltimore city with the exception of Co. E from Carroll County. Regt. had no Co. K.

7th Maryland Inf. Regt.

Co. A	Washington County	Co. F	Carroll County
Co. B	Frederick County	Co. G	Frederick County
Co. C	Baltimore/Harford counties	Co. H	Baltimore city
Co. D	Baltimore city	Co. I	Washington County
Co. E	Frederick County		

Co. K formed in April, 1864, from elements of 10th Maryland Inf. (U.S.).

8th Maryland Inf. Regt.

Co. A	Baltimore city	Co. F	Baltimore city
Co. B	Baltimore city	Co. G	Baltimore city
Co. C	Baltimore city	Co. H	Baltimore city
Co. D	Baltimore city	Co. I	Baltimore city
Co. E	Frederick County		

Cos. H and I formed with draftees in 1862 and mustered out in 1863. These two companies replaced by two companies of Purnell Legion Cav. (U.S.) in 1864. Regt. had no Co. K.

Source: Wilmer, Jarrett, and Vernon, *History and Roster of Maryland Volunteers, War of 1861–65.*

was born in 1834 and would have been twenty-seven years old in 1861. The largest group of officers was born in 1840, followed by the years 1838, 1837, 1834, and 1836 (see Table 7).

First Lieut. William H. Allen was the oldest officer to serve in the Maryland Brigade. Born in 1810, Allen was a shoemaker and policeman in Baltimore's fifteenth ward when he joined the Baltimore Light Infantry in early 1862 and later served as an officer in the 4th Maryland Infantry (U.S.). The youngest officer in the brigade, Lawrence Tower, was born in New York on October 16, 1845, and enlisted in the 7th Maryland Infantry (U.S.) at Hagerstown three days after the battle of Antietam in 1862. After serving as a company first sergeant, Tower was appointed first lieutenant in 1863 just before his eighteenth birthday. Six months later, in early 1864, young Tower was promoted to captain of Company G.

The officers of the Maryland Brigade were predominantly natives of the state, although a substantial number hailed from neighboring states and even foreign countries. The birthplaces of 144 officers have been identified and show that 104 of these captains and lieutenants, or nearly 73 percent, were born in Maryland. Twenty-five of the remaining officers hailed from other states in the Union, mostly from Pennsylvania. Two of these officers claimed Virginia (later West Virginia) as their home when they joined the Union army. Only one officer, Levi T. Heath of the 1st Maryland Infantry (U.S.), came from the Deep South. Heath was born in South Carolina in 1835 and lived in Baltimore, where he taught orphans at the House of Refuge. Fifteen officers were born outside of the United States; 10 of these men came from the various German states, 3 were Irish, and 2 were from Great Britain. Military service and pension records as well as the 1860 census do not reveal the place of birth for 75 officers of the Maryland Brigade. It is likely that the nativity of these men would be similar to that of their comrades whose birthplace has been established (see Table 8).

The occupations of 150 officers at the time of their appointment or enlistment are known. The five largest occupational groups were those of clerks, farmers, carpenters, merchants, shoemakers, and printers (the last two occupations tied for fifth place). Maryland Union officers were overwhelmingly from two segments of the state's workforce. A sizable proportion (see Table 9) were proprietors, clerks, businessmen, or merchants while an even greater number were skilled workers before the war. Maryland's Union captains and lieutenants worked in a wide variety of skilled

Table 7. Years of Birth of Union Officers from Maryland

Year of Birth	Number	Year of Birth	Number
1810	1	1830	5
1811	1	1831	1
1816	1	1832	11
1818	3	1833	10
1819	1	1834	14
1820	5	1835	7
1821	2	1836	13
1822	3	1837	14
1823	2	1838	15
1824	6	1839	11
1825	5	1840	20
1826	4	1841	11
1827	5	1842	7
1828	7	1843	9
1829	5	1844	5
Unknown	13	1845	2

Sources: Compiled Service Records; 1860 Census; Pension Applications; Genealogical Sources.

occupations, including ship carpenters, cigar makers, and marble cutters. Relatively few men in the Maryland Brigade's junior officer corps could be considered professionals by nineteenth-century standards. More brigade officers were hotel or tavern keepers than lawyers.

The officers' economic standing closely matched their prewar occupational status. The vast majority of officers told census enumerators in 1860 that they had no personal or real estate wealth. In fact, the average personal estate value for all Union officers in the Maryland Brigade was $63 while their average real estate value was $31. Very few Maryland officers had any great holdings of their own at the outbreak of the war. John G. Johannes, who served variously as a field-grade and company-grade officer in several Maryland units, was one of the richest men in the Maryland Brigade. Johannes reported that as a jeweler at his shop at Wine Alley between Charles and Light streets in Baltimore, his real estate value

Table 8. Places of Birth of Union Officers from Maryland

	Number		Number
Maryland	104	Pennsylvania	13
New York	4	Ohio	2
New Jersey	1	Delaware	1
Virginia	1	West Virginia	1
South Carolina	1	District of Columbia	1
Germany	10		
Ireland	3		
Great Britain	2		
Unknown	75		

Sources: Same as for Table 7.

was $1,200 (he had a separate residence on West Fayette Street) and his personal estate value was $6,000 in 1860. Johannes employed a mulatto servant in his household.

Another officer in the Maryland Brigade also came from a prosperous background. James R. Hosmer, a lawyer, was born in New York City in 1834 and lived in Baltimore with his wife and child in 1860. Hosmer was appointed second lieutenant and shortly afterward assistant quartermaster for the 8th Maryland Infantry (U.S.) in 1862. Although he did not report his own wealth in the 1860 census, Hosmer and his family resided at his father-in-law's house in the eleventh ward. Augustus J. Albert, a city merchant and the father of Hosmer's wife, was one of the richest men in Baltimore with a combined personal and real estate value of over half a million dollars in 1860.[21]

The majority of Union officers in the Maryland Brigade lacked the wealth or family connections of Johannes or Hosmer. These officers received a common school education and then began their trade or occupation. Only a handful of officers received any higher education before the war. The relative dearth of educated officers in the four Maryland

21. Ironically, Hosmer's brother-in-law Augustus James Albert, Jr., served as a private in the 1st Maryland Battery (C.S.).

Table 9. Occupations of Union Officers from Maryland

	Number		Number
Ambrotypist	1	Marble cutter	2
Architect	1	Mariner	1
Artist	1	Mechanic	1
Barkeeper	4	Mechanic/tavern keeper	1
Blacksmith	3	Mechanic clerk	1
Bookkeeper	1	Merchant	7
Brass finisher	1	Miller	1
Bricklayer	2	Molder	3
Butcher	1	Painter	3
Cabinetmaker	4	Paper carrier	1
Carpenter	10	Plumber	2
Carriage maker/sheriff	1	Printer	5
Chandler	1	Property agent	1
Cheese/fish dealer	1	Railroad employee	2
Cigar maker	4	Ship carpenter	1
City magistrate	1	Shipping clerk	1
Clerk	19	Shipwright	1
Cooper	1	Shoemaker	5
Customs officer	1	Shoemaker/carpenter	1
Farmer	12	Shoemaker/policeman	1
Farmer/carpenter	1	Stock/bill broker	1
Furniture maker	1	Stonecutter (apprentice)	1
Gas fitter	1	Stonemason	1
General intelligence agent	1	Student	3
Grocer	1	Tailor	2
Hotelkeeper	1	Teacher	4
Ironworker	2	Tobacconist	1
Jeweler	1	U.S. marshal	1
Laborer	3	Veterinarian	1
Law student	2	Watchmaker	1
Lawyer	4	Wagonmaker (apprentice)	1
Lumber dealer	1	Wheelwright	2
Machinist	1		
Unknown	69		

Sources: Same as for Table 7.

regiments can be seen in the fact that there were only three men who listed themselves as students when they entered Union military service and another two men who claimed to be law students. One of these officers, Bowie F. Johnson, studied at Georgetown College and was scheduled to graduate in 1863. Johnson was appointed second lieutenant in the 8th Maryland Infantry (U.S.) in 1862 and never completed his college degree. Only two men are known to have graduated from college before the war. James R. Hosmer, a Baltimore lawyer, received his degree from Columbia University, and William B. Norman was an alumnus of Princeton College. Norman, a stock and bill broker in his father's firm, served as a lieutenant in the 8th Maryland Infantry (U.S.).[22]

No officers in the Maryland Brigade were listed in surviving records as illiterate. Several men, however, could not cope with their official duties because of their poor education. Francis G. F. Waltemeyer, a forty-one-year-old tavern keeper in Little Gunpowder, Baltimore County, and a captain in the 1st Maryland Infantry (U.S.), was placed under arrest for disobeying orders in December, 1861. Waltemeyer wrote his congressman for assistance. Waltemeyer's letter is evidence of his rudimentary education: "My Der Ser i have Ritten to you ——— ——— ——— and shall Rite this one to see if you Will tak the troble to See if the Sect of War and inform him of my Bing in a Rest for fifty Days and cant gett a trial i have aske to be tried But cant get No anser Nor ——— of aney one and if you will Due this for me you will oblige me."[23]

Another officer also found himself greatly hindered by his lack of education. William E. Andrews, a first lieutenant in the 8th Maryland Infantry (U.S.), took command of Company C in late 1863. Andrews attempted to resign on the grounds of incompetency. A board consisting of three officers convened in early 1864 to examine Andrews. When asked

22. The number of college graduates or attendees may have been slightly higher in the Maryland Brigade although these three men were the only officers identified by obituaries (GUAAR, or Ruby, *Blue and Gray*) as having attended higher education before the war.

23. F. G. F. Waltemeyer to Edward H. Webster, February 8, 1862, in CSR, Francis G. F. Waltemeyer, 1st Maryland Infantry (U.S.). Ironically, Waltemeyer served as a sutler for the regiment until replaced in September, 1863; see RG 393, Records of United States Army Continental Commands, 1821–1920, Part II, Progression 239 (Maryland Brigade) Entry 3786, Letters and Endorsements Sent and Orders Received, June, 1863–March, 1864, NA (hereafter identified by entry number, title, and record group).

about his name, rank, position, length of service, rank at resignation, and evidence proving incompetency or physical disability, Andrews claimed that he could not write well enough to perform his duties. The board asked if any noncommissioned officers or enlisted men could handle the clerical duties, to which Andrews replied that they could. Andrews, however, expressed concern that if they were killed or wounded, he would be "overboard" in running the company. Even though he submitted a sample of his poor handwriting, the board of examiners refused to permit Andrews to resign and he remained in the army until the end of the war.[24]

The Union regiments from Maryland had several officers with previous military experience. Maurice Albaugh, a Frederick shoe and boot merchant and a lieutenant in the 1st Maryland Infantry (U.S.), fought in the Mexican War as a private in the battles of Vera Cruz and Cerro Gordo. Another officer of the 1st Maryland Infantry (U.S.), Capt. Bladen T. F. Dulaney of Company A, spent fifteen years as an enlisted man in the Regular Army before the war. The captain of Company K, Thomas S. J. Johnson, was a lieutenant in the 8th U.S. Infantry from 1838 to 1845. Edward E. Nicholson was born in New Jersey in 1833, the son of Quaker parents. After the early death of his mother and father, Nicholson made his living as a farm laborer and a butcher before enlisting in the army as a private at Philadelphia in 1857. Nicholson served in the Utah Territory for the next five years with the 10th U.S. Infantry Regiment until his discharge in 1862. Returning east, Nicholson received an appointment as a second lieutenant in the 4th Maryland Infantry (U.S.) in 1863.[25]

John G. Johannes applied for a commission in the Regular Army on April 3, 1861, citing his eighteen years of service with volunteer companies in Maryland. A native of Baltimore, Johannes served as a major in the 53rd Maryland Regiment and commanded Company E of the 1st Regiment Light Artillery when the war began. This company, part of the Baltimore City Guard Battalion, remained overwhelmingly loyalist during those tumultuous spring days. Johannes promised that "should I be for-

24. Board of Examination, January 9, 1864, in CSR, William E. Andrews, 8th Maryland Infantry (U.S.).

25. Camper and Kirkley, *Historical Record*, 236–37, 254; CSR, Bladen T. F. Dulaney, 1st Maryland Infantry (U.S.); CSR and Pension Records, Thomas S. J. Johnson, 1st Maryland Infantry (U.S.); Francis B. Heitman, *Historical Register of the United States Army from Its Organization September 29, 1789, to September 29, 1889* (Washington, D.C., 1890), 577; CSR and Pension Records, Edward E. Nicholson, 4th Maryland Infantry (U.S.).

tunate enough to meet favor at the hands of the Administration I judge myself to stand by my country and use every effort in my power to sustain its dignity and glory against any foe who may assail its flag." His application was supported by numerous letters of recommendation from leading Maryland militia officers and politicians, including Henry Winter Davis. A fellow company commander described Johannes as "one of among the best in the Volunteers." Although he did not receive an appointment in the Regulars, Johannes soon accepted a field-grade commission in the Purnell Legion Infantry.[26]

Many of Maryland's German-speaking immigrants were veterans of military service in Europe or had gained some familiarity with war as combatants during the 1848 uprisings. Wilhelm Heine, appointed captain of Company I of the 1st Maryland Infantry (U.S.) by the secretary of war in the fall of 1861, was an engineer and scientist with the Prussian government in Asia and landed in Japan with Comm. Matthew C. Perry. When news of the outbreak of war in America reached the Far East, Heine set sail for San Francisco, where he applied for a position in the army.[27] Ernest F. M. Faehtz, born in Linz in 1823, studied law at the University of Vienna and fled his homeland after the suppression of the 1848 revolution in Austria. Traveling to Switzerland, France, England, and finally to the United States, Faehtz became a teacher in Pennsylvania. He raised Company I of the 5th Maryland Infantry (U.S.) and served as its captain for about a year when he resigned. In late 1862, Faehtz was commissioned as major of the 8th Maryland Infantry (U.S.) and ended the war as its lieutenant colonel. Another officer of the 5th Maryland Infantry (U.S.), Leopold Blumenburg, came to Baltimore from Prussia in 1854 and was a well-respected Jewish merchant in the city. Blumenburg's house had to be guarded against prosouthern rioters when he organized Company C and later served as major of the 5th Maryland Infantry (U.S.). Following a serious wound at Antietam, Blumenburg established a Unionist club for Germans in Baltimore in 1863, the Unionsverein.[28]

26. RG 107, Applications for Appointment, Maryland.

27. CSR and Pension Records, Peter Bernard Wilhelm Heine, 1st Maryland Infantry (U.S.). For further details on Heine in Japan, see Peter Booth Wiley, *Yankees in the Land of the Gods: Commodore Perry and the Opening of Japan* (New York, 1990).

28. Ernest F. M. Faehtz Papers, Harrisburg Civil War Round Table Collection, USAMHI; Cunz, "Maryland Germans," 413.

Maryland's Union officers not only came from diverse social and economic backgrounds but also had a wide variety of experiences before the war. Grayson M. Eichelberger resided near Creagerstown in northern Frederick County. His father and sister both died in 1854, followed by his mother three years later. He witnessed the execution of John Brown in 1859 with a cousin who lived in Virginia and later served in the Confederate army. In early 1861, Eichelberger moved to Ohio, where he took a job in a flour mill and worked there until the following summer. Offered a commission in an Ohio regiment, Eichelberger refused and returned to Maryland, where he enlisted in the 6th Maryland Infantry (U.S.).[29]

John H. Suter was the son of a prominent Baltimore furniture manufacturer and philanthropist who founded the Maryland Institute for the Promotion of the Mechanic Arts. Young Suter, born in 1832, left Maryland at the age of sixteen to seek his fortune in California. After eleven months in the West, Suter joined as a ship's carpenter on the *Governor Davis* for a return voyage to the eastern seaboard but was stranded in Peru for seven months. By the time he arrived in Baltimore, both of his parents had died. He took up his father's business and married Mary Jane Kidd, a native of Middlesex County, Virginia, in 1854. Like so many men of his generation, Suter became swept up in the turmoil of the 1850s. He joined the Vigilant Fire Department (volunteer fire companies often served as quasi-social and political clubs in prewar Baltimore) and was a member of the Bell and Everett Association of Minute Men in 1860. Following an attack by secessionists during the Baltimore riots in 1861, Suter served as a volunteer city policeman until he enlisted as a sergeant in Company A, 4th Maryland Infantry (U.S.), in the late summer of 1862. He received his appointment as second lieutenant in 1863.[30]

Gregory Barrett, Jr., also of the 4th Maryland Infantry (U.S.), was one of the most notorious officers in the Maryland Brigade. Employed as an officer in the state penitentiary and as a brass finisher in Baltimore's nineteenth ward, Barrett earned a reputation for his fierceness during the tumultuous gang wars of the decade preceding the Civil War. Years later, in 1898, an old Baltimorean recalled Barrett's exploits:

There was not a more reckless and absolutely fearless fellow in the city. I remember him first as connected with the Western Hose Company . . . one

29. Grayson M. Eichelberger Memoirs, Civil War Miscellaneous Collection, USAMHI.

30. *Biographical Cyclopedia*, I, 198–99.

of the unpaid volunteer companies that fought fires more for excitement than anything else. . . . Fierce jealousies existed between the different companies, and the bitterest kind of feuds grew up between them. Each had a large following of friends and supporters, and there was hardly a fire or an occasion for a run without a big fight between two or more companies, the numerous followers of each joining in the fray, until it assumed the size of a riot. Bricks and missiles of every kind were thrown, clubs and fire axes and hooks used with terrible effect, and often men would be seriously injured and sometimes killed outright.

Barrett was active in the Rip Raps, one of Baltimore's numerous gangs affiliated with the Know-Nothings. "One of the chief amusements of the 'Know-Nothing' clubs at that time, and principally were the 'Rip Raps' given to this, was to watch for the omnibuses which ran along Pennsylvania avenue to Green Street, rush out in a body, yelling and firing pistols, pull the driver down, give him a blow on the head, oust out all the passengers and take possession of the 'bus. They would then drive right into Lexington market, pillage the stalls, take whatever they wanted, fill up the 'bus and go across to MacPherson's, on the Anne Arundel side of the Patapsco, and hold a picnic." Barrett found his street-fighting experience of great benefit when he joined the 4th Maryland in 1862, and by the end of the war he was a brevet colonel.[31]

Officers of Barrett's caliber tended to be the exception rather than the rule in the Union Maryland regiments. Bowie F. Johnson had a well-connected background. His father, Reverdy Johnson, served as Maryland's senator in the 1840s as well as U.S. attorney general in Zachary Taylor's administration. Johnson, who had belonged to every party in Maryland's turbulent political arena, remained loyal to the Union despite his reluctance to support the Republican party. The younger Johnson was attending Georgetown College when the war began and served as an officer in the 8th Maryland Infantry (U.S.). Captain Daniel Rinehart of Carroll County's Company F, 7th Maryland Infantry (U.S.), was the brother of the noted nineteenth-century sculptor William H. Rinehart.[32]

Relatively few Union Maryland officers hailed from the first families

31. Baltimore *Sun*, August 7, 1898. Barrett remained in the army after the war and died of "brain fever" in Cuba during the Spanish-American War (*ibid.*; CSR, Gregory Barrett, 4th Maryland Infantry [U.S.]; and Heitman, *Historical Register*, 194).

32. GUAAR; Joseph G. E. Hopkins, ed., *Concise Dictionary of American Biography* (New York, 1964), 503, 866; Baltimore *Sun*, October 2, 1893. Klein, *Just South of Gettysburg*, 230.

of Maryland. Most officers in the Maryland Brigade were descended from recent settlers in the state's western portion or in the city of Baltimore. The paucity of Union officers from southern Maryland meant that only a handful of men from the state's original families were represented among the federal junior officer ranks. Bowie F. Johnson and his cousin Wallace A. Bowie (also an officer in the 8th Maryland Infantry [U.S.]) were exceptions, both from old Prince Georges County families, yet they served in the Union army. Edward Y. Goldsborough of Frederick was the son of Dr. Edward Y. Goldsborough, a medical graduate of the University of Maryland, whose family traced its roots to the early settlement of Kent Island in the Chesapeake Bay. The younger Goldsborough finished his formal education at the Frederick Academy in 1859 and worked as an apprentice in a law firm until admitted to the bar in 1861. Goldsborough later received a commission in the 8th Maryland Infantry (U.S.) when that regiment formed in 1862.[33]

Henry Wilhelm, born in 1836, the son of Peter B. and Elizabeth Kone Wilhelm, was typical of the officers in the Maryland Brigade. Henry Wilhelm's great-grandfather came to America at the time of the American Revolution. Settling in Baltimore County, the Wilhelms owned a respectable farm which they handed down through the generations. Henry Wilhelm received a basic education in the county's Sixth District and was employed as a carpenter when the war broke out. He enlisted in the 4th Maryland Infantry (U.S.) in 1862 and received a promotion to lieutenant in 1863.[34]

Just as few Union Maryland officers had extensive family connections in the state, only a handful of these men had claims to Maryland's patriotic past. Their lineages did not antedate Maryland's revolutionary experience, nor did they form the elite of Maryland's colonial society. Harrison Adreon, a young Baltimorean, was among the few Union Maryland officers who could take pride in his grandfather's exploits as a Maryland captain during the War of 1812. The vast majority of Union officers were not even affiliated with Maryland's militia or volunteer companies before the war.[35]

33. Bowie, *Across the Years*, 741, 746; T. C. J. Williams and Folger McKinsey, *History of Frederick County, Maryland* (2 vols.; 1910; rpr. Baltimore, 1967), II, 1241–42.

34. *Genealogy and Biography*, 191–92.

35. Scharf, *History of Baltimore City and County*, 495–96. Only five officers are known to have been involved in the state's prewar militia or volunteer units. They are John G.

For the most part, Maryland's Union officers represented a new and different element in Maryland society, one that had little connection to the educated, landowning, slaveholding, tobacco-growing society of old Maryland. In contrast to the captains and lieutenants in the Confederate Maryland Line, Union officers represented the vanguard of the state's growing white working class, which drew its economic base from the industrial and commercial development of Baltimore. This class, which had existed since the end of the eighteenth century, blossomed during the first decades of the nineteenth century. The Union officers in the Maryland Brigade symbolized the state's social and economic transformation to a northern- as opposed to a southern-oriented community. These men heralded the rise of a new order, setting itself apart from the rural and urban gentry who composed the bulk of the Confederate officer corps from Maryland.[36]

Johannes, James R. Hosmer, Josiah B. Coloney, John W. Wilson, and Martin Suter. Other future Union officers from the Maryland Brigade may have served in state military organizations before the war, but they are not listed in surviving records of these units.

36. For a full discussion of this new order, see Browne, *Baltimore in the Nation*; for a comparison with cities in the North experiencing similar developments, see Bruce Laurie, *Working People of Philadelphia, 1800–1850* (Philadelphia, 1980), and Richard B. Stott, *Workers in the Metropolis: Class, Ethnicity, and Youth in Antebellum New York City* (Ithaca, 1990).

·4·

Running the Blockade

If the decision to support the Confederacy was difficult for many Marylanders, the physical act of joining the southern army posed even greater challenges. Most Confederate Marylanders sought refuge in Virginia or in other friendly territories in order to enlist. The bulk of Maryland's Confederate lieutenants and captains served in a handful of state units that organized in Virginia, although men from Maryland fought under the banners of virtually every state in the Confederacy.

Maryland's junior officers encountered problems joining the Confederate army if they did not come to Virginia at the outset of the war in May and June of 1861. After that, "running the blockade" between the two states required careful planning to avoid unfriendly civilians and enemy patrols. The Potomac River marked not only the boundary between Maryland and Virginia but also the dividing line between the North and the South. Crossing the river was not easy. The stretch of river above Washington, D.C., though fordable, generally ran through territory hostile to the southern cause. The Potomac River, as it wends its way from Washington to Point Lookout at the Chesapeake Bay, widens considerably, making the voyage across the river even more difficult for recruits from southern Maryland. Natives of this region generally espoused the southern cause, forcing the Union to maintain a heavy military and naval presence throughout the war. Entering Virginia through Washington, D.C., became virtually impossible after the summer of 1861.[1]

1. For other accounts of Marylanders crossing the Potomac River to join the Confederate army, see Howard, *Recollections*, 16–21; Frederic B. M. Hollyday, ed., "Running the Blockade: Henry Hollyday Joins the Confederacy," *Maryland Historical Magazine*, XLI (1946), 1–10; Henry C. Mettam, "Civil War Memoirs of the First Maryland Cavalry,

G. Blanchard Philpot, a Marylander living in Jacksonville, Illinois, in 1861 could not bring himself to support the Union cause. He was, however, "not wise enough to keep a silent tongue in my head, but must express myself on all occasions." Philpot's northern neighbors did not appreciate his secessionist views, and he "soon found that it would not be healthy for me, either physically or financially, to remain" in Illinois. Philpot made his way back to Maryland, determined to join the Confederate army. Before crossing the Potomac, Philpot met a group of young men who shared the same objective. They found an unguarded ford on the upper Potomac and crossed with their horses. Arriving safely on the Virginia side, the group rested until dawn, when they set off to join Turner Ashby. Within a few weeks, Philpot's comrades elected him lieutenant of Company G, 7th Virginia Cavalry Regiment.[2]

George M. Emack, a teenager in Prince Georges County, acted as a messenger for the Confederacy when he was arrested by federal troops at Pleasant Springs, the home of Andrew J. Gwynn, in 1861. While under escort to Washington, Emack fatally stabbed a guard and escaped across the Potomac River. He received a commission as a cavalry lieutenant in October but was placed in command of Union prisoners at Libby Prison in Richmond. While performing this duty, Emack earned a reputation as a "Yankee killer." Emack was surprised to learn of his reputation among the enemy. Writing to his mother in 1862 from the Confederate capital, Emack stated, "I was not aware, until very lately, that I was such a desperate and fiendish character. I have neither bucked or gagged a prisoner, since they have been under my charge, nor had it done, but several have suffered that punishment, and very deservedly." Tiring of prison duty, Emack proposed to raise a company of "partisan rangers" in the spring of 1862 and later received a commission as a captain in the 1st Maryland Cavalry (C.S.).[3]

C.S.A.," ed. Samuel H. Miller, *Maryland Historical Magazine*, LVIII (1963), 139–45; and Ammen, "Maryland Troops in the Confederate Army," 82–85, 90–94.

2. G. B. Philpot, "A Maryland Boy in the Confederate Army," *Confederate Veteran*, XXIV (1916), 312–15, 361–63.

3. William A. Tidwell, James O. Hall, and David Winfred Gaddy, *Come Retribution: The Confederate Secret Service and the Assassination of Lincoln* (Jackson, 1988), 72–73, 118–99; George M. Emack to mother, date uncertain (Typescript copy in George M. Emack Papers, William A. Tidwell Collection); George M. Emack to George W. Randolph, May 19, May 12, and August 30, 1862, letters respectively filed as 80-E-1862, 86-E-1862, 165-E-

William I. Rasin took even greater risks to join the Confederate army. The war brought Rasin back to Kent County from Kansas, where Union detectives arrested him as a spy in February, 1862. Placed in confinement at the Old Capitol Prison in Washington, D.C., Rasin joined a Maryland Confederate officer, Henry A. Steuart, in a cell. Steuart had been captured in Maryland while procuring supplies for his troops.

Rasin, Steuart, and a third man plotted an escape from their wretched prison cell. The group sawed through one of the wooden bars with a sharpened table knife. Despite occasional checks by Union guards, the three men cut the bar until it could be removed by hand. Waiting until the time was right, the group selected Rasin to leave first. Rasin removed a rope, woven from an "old manila door mat," from its hiding place in a mattress, tied the rope to one of the firm bars, withdrew the cut bar, and climbed out the window.

It was a cold and rainy night, and the Union guards had little reason to suspect that a prisoner could escape from the cells several stories above street level. As Rasin began his descent, the rope snapped and he fell to the ground. His companions were certain that he had either fallen to his death or was seriously injured and had been apprehended by the sentries. They quickly pulled up the remaining rope and reinserted the wooden bar. Just before dawn, the wind knocked out the bar and it fell below, attracting the attention of the guards. The prison commander ordered an investigation and traced the wooden bar to Rasin's cell. Discovering that a prisoner was missing, the guards searched the neighborhood without success.

As it turned out, Rasin landed intact and unobserved because two guards were "engaged in a quiet flirtation with a girl." The Marylander passed these same two soldiers, who mistook Rasin for an officer and saluted him. The escaped prisoner hid in Washington for a couple of days before making his way across the Potomac and eventually arrived safely in Richmond.[4]

On May 8, 1861, Bradley T. Johnson led the first group of Marylanders to Virginia from Frederick, where they established a camp of rendezvous

---

1862, RG 109, Letters Received by the Confederate Secretary of War, 1861–65, M437, NA (hereafter referred to as LSOW and letter number).

4. Richard D. Steuart, "Henry A. Steuart—Rebel Spy," *Confederate Veteran*, XVI (1908), 332–34; Johnson, *Maryland*, 382–85. Henry A. Steuart was a lieutenant in the 3rd Maryland Battery (C.S.) at the time of his imprisonment.

for other exiled Marylanders to join the Confederate service. Johnson, formerly the chairman of Maryland's Breckinridge Democratic faction, intended that his volunteer company of western Marylanders rally "around it such Maryland men as could be collected together, to form a body which should try to represent the ancestral honor of that old Line, which before them, in another Revolution, had illustrated the fame of the State." Other companies soon followed, and by May 18, Johnson had eight Maryland companies at Point of Rocks and Harpers Ferry.[5]

Meanwhile, other Maryland companies gathered in Richmond as a skeletal battalion formed from prewar Baltimore militia and volunteer companies. The units in Richmond and in northern Virginia provided the foundation for the 1st Maryland Infantry (C.S.). The organization of these companies, however, was by no means complete, and Capt. Johnson faced enormous difficulties in clothing, feeding, and equipping the Marylanders at Harpers Ferry. Only two of the companies, for example, had proper uniforms; the remainder of the men wore the clothes they brought from home. McHenry Howard, one of the fortunate soldiers to be fully uniformed, described his appearance when he sent a photograph to his New York friend: "I send you something to aid you in keeping me in remembrance. It is half fatigue and half full uniform. The jacket is heavily trimmed with orange, the shirt blue with trimmings also orange. There should be added loose turkish pantaloons with a broad red sash."[6]

Jane Claudia Johnson, Capt. Johnson's wife, undertook a mission to North Carolina to appeal for uniforms, weapons, shoes, and other accoutrements to equip the destitute Marylanders. Unlike other southern states, which paid for military expenses, Maryland gave no support to the Confederates, who therefore relied on the efforts of private individuals or the central government. Mrs. Johnson, a native of North Carolina, went

5. Johnson, "Memoir of First Maryland Regiment," 348. For general histories of the 1st Maryland Infantry Regiment (C.S.), see Goldsborough, *Maryland Line*, 9–81; Johnson, *Maryland*, 37–88; Scharf, *History of Maryland*, III, 445–50, 473–80; Lamar Hollyday, "Maryland Troops in the Confederate Service," *SHSP*, III (1877), 130–39; Bradley T. Johnson, "The Maryland Line in the Confederate Army," *SHSP*, XI (1883), 21–26; and William M. Rommel, "A History of the First Maryland Confederate Infantry Regiment, 1861–1862" (M.A. thesis, University of Maryland, 1979).

6. McHenry Howard to "Dear Frank," May 18, 1861, in Howard Papers. A discussion of Maryland uniforms at the beginning of the war is found in Ross M. Kimmel, "Enlisted Uniforms of the Maryland Confederate Infantry: A Case Study, Part I," *Military Collector and Historian*, XLI (1989), 98–108.

there accompanied by Capt. Nicholas and Second Lieut. George M. E. Shearer and succeeded in raising enormous contributions from the Tarheel State as well as from Governor John Letcher of Virginia.

Mrs. Johnson brought back to Harpers Ferry several hundred .54 caliber Mississippi rifles, ten thousand cartridges, and thirty-five hundred percussion caps, as well as tents, blankets, shoes, and regulation gray uniforms. She accomplished her mission within two weeks after leaving camp, and the state of North Carolina recognized her for her sacrifice: "If great events produce great men, so, in the scene before us, we have proof that great events produce great women. . . . One of our own daughters, raised in the lap of luxury, blessed with the enjoyment of all elements of elegance and ease, had quit her peaceful home, followed her husband to the camp, and, leaving him in that camp, had come to the home of her childhood to seek aid for him and his comrades, not because he is her husband, but because he is fighting the battles of his country against a tyrant."[7] The support offered to the Confederate Marylanders in Virginia by many of the home folk, in the face of hardship and risk, contributed immensely throughout the war.

The organization of a Civil War company reflected nineteenth-century democratic beliefs with a tinge of anarchy.[8] Upon mustering for service, the men of each company elected their own commissioned and noncommissioned officers from captain to corporal. The volunteers believed that this process best expressed their faith in democratic principles in a military environment, although it did have drawbacks. The criteria for election seldom had anything to do with merit or competency to hold the position; rather, company elections often boiled down to popularity contests, rewards for those who organized the unit, or competition between rival factions. Elections tended to be divisive and resulted in hurt feelings among the sensitive volunteers.

Robert Lemmon, an enlisted man in a Maryland company in Richmond, wrote to his mother following his defeat for the position of sergeant and the failure of his company to elect William H. Murray as company commander: "I was a prominent candidate. Defeated, of course, owing &

7. Goldsborough, *Maryland Line*, 19–20; Johnson, *Maryland*, 37–41. The regiment's affection for Mrs. Johnson was expressed at her death in 1889 ("Memoir of Jane Claudia Johnson," *SHSP*, XXIX [1901], 33–45).

8. David Donald, "The Confederate as a Fighting Man," *Journal of Southern History*, XXV (1959), 178–93.

properly, too, to the fact that I am a recruit—I am hardly disappointed, tho I would have been much gratified at receiving the office. I was backed by all the commd. officers. The men are very fair. We did our best to keep the office of captn. for Murray [William H. Murray, later elected captain of another company], who would, most indubitably have been elected if here."[9]

After the election of company officers, the Maryland units mustered into service. Lieut. Col. George Deas swore the men of Companies A and B of what soon became the 1st Maryland Infantry Regiment (C.S.) into the service of the Confederate States for the period of one year at Point of Rocks on May 21. The following day at Harpers Ferry, Deas mustered the remaining companies into Confederate States service for the duration of the war. That Deas mustered the various companies into service for different terms later proved controversial in the 1st Maryland Infantry (C.S.). Many of the soldiers at Harpers Ferry were under the impression that they, too, would serve for only one year even though they signed their names beside the statement "for the war" on various muster rolls and enlistment papers.

The confusion over enlistment terms increased when several companies at Harpers Ferry were disbanded and consolidated and new companies were drafted from Richmond. Companies C, F, and H, commanded by Capts. Frank S. Price, Thomas H. Holbrook, and Henry Wellmore, respectively, disbanded in mid-June because they were of insufficient strength. The remaining companies at Harpers Ferry absorbed the soldiers from these units. Most of the company officers resigned and did not serve with any formal Maryland organization.[10]

New companies formed to replace the units that had disbanded. Second Lieut. J. Louis Smith of Company G was promoted to captain of the new Company F while Captain Holbrook of the original Company F became a first lieutenant in the successor company. Two new lieutenants, Joseph Stewart and William J. Broadfoot, were elected directly from the ranks to serve as subalterns of this company. The election of Lieut. Smith as Company F's new commander was based on merit rather than popularity because Smith played an important role during the evacuation of

9. Robert Lemmon to mother, May 23, 1861, in Lemmon Papers, MS 1352, Manuscripts Division, MHS.

10. Goldsborough, *Maryland Line*, 10.

Harpers Ferry on June 15. This operation resulted in the recovery of valuable equipment from the U.S. arsenal before its destruction by Confederate troops. General Joseph E. Johnston, the commanding officer at Harpers Ferry, noted the performance of the Maryland troops during this operation and commended the unit in special orders a week later.[11]

Three fresh companies from Richmond joined the Maryland troops in the lower Shenandoah Valley during the summer of 1861. Capts. Edward R. Dorsey and William H. Murray brought their companies to Winchester on June 25 and became second Companies C and H. In mid-August, after a frustrating wait for uniforms and equipment and then serving as guard details for Union soldiers captured at Manassas, Capt. Michael S. Robertson and his men joined as Company I. This gave the Maryland unit, designated as the 1st Maryland Infantry Regiment (C.S.) on June 16, its maximum strength of nine companies—one less than the regulation strength prescribed for a Confederate regiment. The tenth company, Capt. J. Lyle Clarke's Maryland Guard, never joined the Maryland regiment and ended up as Company B of the 21st Virginia Infantry Regiment.[12] Causing even more confusion in the new regiment, the two companies from Richmond had also enlisted for one year in Virginia service.

To command the various Maryland companies, Governor John Letcher of Virginia initially appointed a Marylander, Francis J. Thomas, as colonel and adjutant general of the Maryland volunteers then gathering in the state. Thomas had served in the Old Army and seemed a likely candidate for the position of colonel of the Maryland troops when he assumed nomi-

---

11. *Ibid.*, 11.

12. The assignment of this company to a Virginia regiment is often cited as a bureaucratic error on the part of the Confederate War Department. It appears, however, that Captain Clarke specifically requested his company's assignment to the 21st Virginia Infantry Regiment (Goldsborough, *Maryland Line*, 160; Captain Clarke to General Robert E. Lee, July 4, 1861, RG 109, Records of Virginia Forces, 1861, M998, NA). Clarke's, Dorsey's, and Robertson's companies in Richmond were part of a rough battalion under the command of Maj. J. Alden Weston. Before this battalion was disbanded and the three Maryland companies transferred, Capt. Edward R. Dorsey and fifty-three members of Company A, Weston Guard, as well as members of Capt. William H. Murray's company petitioned to stay with Weston (Petitions Received at the Confederate War Department on June 20 and 22, 1861, in RG 109, War Department Collection of Confederate Records, Muster and Pay Rolls for Maryland Units).

nal command on May 17. Thomas, with his commission in the Provisional Army of Virginia, wanted to organize three Maryland infantry regiments with other supporting units to be formed at a later date. Many of
the officers at Harpers Ferry, however, opposed Col. Thomas and preferred
to elect their own candidates for the regiment's chain of command. They
also wanted to raise Maryland troops under the state banner and not fall
under Virginia control. The Marylanders petitioned that the field-grade
positions be filled with familiar faces rather than strangers. They requested
the appointment of Charles S. Winder as colonel of the 1st Maryland
Infantry (C.S.) with Bradley T. Johnson and Edward R. Dorsey as lieutenant colonel and major. Winder, a native of Talbot County and an 1850
graduate of the United States Military Academy, had years of military
experience on the frontier. Both Johnson and Dorsey were already company commanders in Virginia and well-known among the Maryland companies.[13]

The Maryland opposition to Thomas was not personal, although that
officer had earned a poor reputation when he took two Maryland companies stationed at Richmond on an expedition to southeastern Virginia
in early June. Searching for Union troops reported in the area, Thomas'
scouts mistakenly identified fireflies as enemy pickets and opened fire. The
raw Maryland volunteers, fearing an ambush, hastily took battle positions
before the "enemy" was properly discovered. One enlisted man wrote
home claiming that Col. Thomas was inebriated during the entire expedition and returned to Richmond under arrest.[14]

Whether Thomas' conduct at Suffolk affected his command of the
Maryland troops is uncertain. His authority over the Maryland volunteers
proved short-lived in any case, and he was relieved of this duty on June
8. The Commonwealth of Virginia transferred control of her state troops
to the Confederate government and relinquished responsibility for Maryland forces in the state. President Jefferson Davis assigned two other Marylanders, both trained at West Point and possessing considerable military
knowledge, to command the 1st Maryland Infantry (C.S.). Arnold Elzey
took charge as colonel on June 16 with George H. Steuart as lieutenant

13. Johnson, *Maryland*, 42–43; Goldsborough, *Maryland Line*, 11–14.

14. Goldsborough, *Maryland Line*, 13; Robert Lemmon to mother, June 5, 1861, in
Lemmon Papers.

colonel. The central government awarded Capt. Johnson for his diligence in organizing the scattered Maryland companies by appointing him as major. In his stead as Company A's commander, the soldiers elected his cousin William W. Goldsborough as captain. Goldsborough, twenty-nine years old in the summer of 1861, had been a private in Capt. Dorsey's company and transferred to Company A as its new captain.[15]

Throughout the summer months, other Marylanders organized state units in Virginia. Capt. Gaither took his company, the Howard County Dragoons, from Baltimore and crossed the Potomac River at Point of Rocks. The company organized for one year's service at Leesburg as an independent unit, designated simply as the Maryland Cavalry. Gaither, the founder of the company and a Baltimore merchant, took formal command as captain on May 14 with George Howard and Samuel Worthington Dorsey as lieutenants. The company did not formally muster into Confederate service until August, when it joined the 1st Virginia Cavalry Regiment.

Marylanders also organized artillery units in 1861. The state eventually provided four regular batteries of light artillery to the Confederate cause, three of which served in the eastern theater. The first of these units, the Maryland Flying Artillery (better known as the Maryland Artillery), formed in the summer of 1861 under the command of a thirty-year-old Baltimore architect, R. Snowden Andrews. In addition to designing numerous public buildings, including the Governor's Mansion in Annapolis and the Baltimore Customs House, Andrews had an avid interest in artillery. In early 1861, Andrews went to the federal arsenal in Pikesville, where he made drawings of a twelve-pound Napoleon fieldpiece. Andrews intended to use these plans to design models of the cannon for production in a Baltimore foundry.

Andrews approached the state legislature in Frederick in the spring of 1861 to request funds to raise an artillery battery, complete with guns, limber, caissons, horses, and personnel. While discussing the overall issue of defense, Andrews realized that the legislature had no intention of securing the state against federal action. Andrews stood up and announced to the body, "Gentlemen, you are endeavoring to make a legal revolution. I do not believe a legal revolution to be possible. . . . I shall at once

15. E. Philip Schreier III, "Marylanders in the Civil War: William Worthington Goldsborough," *Maryland Line*, X (1990), 2–4.

proceed to Baltimore and break up my models, take my drawings and go to Virginia, to fight there for Maryland."[16]

Andrews journeyed to Harpers Ferry and then to Richmond, where he discussed his ideas for a Maryland artillery organization with Virginia officials. While at Richmond, Andrews gave his requirements for an artillery battery to Governor Letcher, who, in turn, passed them to the chief of ordnance for requisition. Andrews returned briefly to Baltimore to help his cousin Nicholas N. Snowden recruit for James R. Herbert's company, which had left the city for Harpers Ferry.

Avoiding Union patrols, Andrews returned safely to Virginia and went to Fredericksburg, where he actively recruited his own unit. A group of Marylanders, members of the Charles County Volunteer Cavalry, gathered in town to wait for their commander. When Andrews arrived, the Marylanders took up his offer to form a battery with the understanding that William F. Dement of Charles County would receive a commission as first lieutenant in the new battery. In mid-July, the Maryland artillerists went into camp near the Richmond Reservoir with Andrews as captain and Dement as first lieutenant. The new battery elected another cousin of Andrews', Charles S. Contee, as second lieutenant and Frederick Y. Dabney of Mississippi as third lieutenant.[17]

As the number of Marylanders serving in Virginia increased, the exiled soldiers felt the need for representation. The plan to raise several Maryland regiments failed, with the exception of the 1st Maryland Infantry (C.S.), and many Maryland volunteers were absorbed into Virginia units. With so many men in non-Maryland units, the exiled Marylanders had little ability to influence military affairs. Several members of Capt. Gaither's Maryland Cavalry met at Leesburg to form an association of Marylanders in Virginia on June 6. The purpose of this association, the Independent Maryland Line of 1861, was never clearly specified, and after drafting a constitution, it quickly disappeared.[18]

The idea of a separate Maryland brigade, or "line," never died, and proposals to form such a unit were made throughout the war. Bradley T. Johnson held this as his goal when he marched his company from Frederick to Point of Rocks in early May. After the riots, McHenry Howard

---

16. Tunstall Smith, ed., *Richard Snowden Andrews: A Memoir* (Baltimore, 1910), 35.
17. *Ibid.*, 29–40; Johnson, *Maryland*, 257–60.
18. Horace E. Hayden, "The Maryland Line," *SHSP*, IX (1881), 254–57.

in Baltimore exclaimed, "At present we can do nothing—save go to Virginia. Between one and two hundred men of my regiment have done so, and taken their uniform with them, intending to organize a Maryland line, to fight under the Maryland flag in the service of Virginia."[19] For the moment, however, Maryland officers had enough work organizing their companies.

The duties of the company-grade officer, whether captain or lieutenant, tended to be similar in both Union and Confederate armies. A company commander, the captain or his acting representative, was accountable for everything that happened, or did not happen, in the unit. His responsibilities included the health and welfare of his soldiers; the status and accountability of personnel, arms, ammunition, and equipment; the care and maintenance of animals, generally horses and mules, belonging to the unit; the training of all personnel in the company; and the performance of his unit in camp, on the march, and in battle.[20]

The commander's job depended on the number of men in the unit and the company's branch of service. Artillery battery commanders (field or light artillery companies were normally referred to as batteries) had the most work because these units had the most equipment and animals. In addition to these great demands, artillery officers had to be the most tactically proficient on the battlefield. The responsibilities of cavalry and infantry company commanders were almost equal. Unlike the infantry commander, the cavalry commander had to procure and care for mounts, but he also enjoyed a less structured command environment and often operated semiautonomously. Infantry officers did not have the opportunity for independent service and went into battle with their regiment or battalion. The chance for infantry commanders to shine in battle may have been somewhat less than in artillery or cavalry, but there was less likelihood that the captain of infantry would single-handedly botch an operation. Outweighing all of these factors, foot soldiers and their officers suffered far greater casualties than did their counterparts in the more mobile branches.

Each company commander had his own chain of command to assist

19. McHenry Howard to "Dear Frank," May 18, 1861, in Howard Papers. The original Maryland Line was one of the finest units in the Continental Army during the American Revolution and fought throughout the war exacting a heavy toll on the British enemy (Brugger, *Maryland*, 127–31).

20. Bell Irvin Wiley, *They Who Fought Here* (New York, 1959), 35–38.

him in the smooth operation and training of the unit. The Confederate infantry company had one captain as commander and three lieutenants as subalterns. The highest-ranking lieutenant, a first lieutenant, generally oversaw the day-to-day operations of the unit, freeing the captain to handle matters required by regimental headquarters. Two second lieutenants (the less senior officer was known as a junior second lieutenant or third lieutenant) commanded platoons within the company and ensured that the men were properly drilled, clothed, and armed. The highest-ranking noncommissioned officer, the orderly or first sergeant, acted as the commander's adviser on matters pertaining to the welfare of the company's enlisted men. The first sergeant also assisted the captain in keeping records such as the descriptive book (a register of company personnel), an order book (a record of orders received by the company from the regimental adjutant), and a morning report book that listed the company's strength on a daily basis and the whereabouts of personnel.[21]

In addition to the first sergeant, the War Department called for each Confederate infantry company to have an authorized strength of 4 sergeants, 4 corporals, and 65 to 125 privates. The sergeants commanded the company's four squads, and the corporals served as assistant squad leaders. According to *Regulations for the Army of the Confederate States,* published in 1863, the sergeants and corporals in the squads "will be held more immediately responsible that their men observe . . . that they wash their hands and faces daily; that they brush or comb their heads, that those who are to go on duty put their arms, accoutrements, dress, &c., in the best order and that such as have permission to pass the chain of sentinels, are in the dress that may be ordered." The number of officers, commissioned and noncommissioned, and enlisted men present for duty in the Maryland companies fluctuated as casualties, sickness, and details whittled away at unit strength.[22]

Training for combat was the most important duty of company-grade officers, whether artillery, cavalry, or infantry. At the beginning of the war, drilling the new volunteers required full-time commitments because most officers were as inexperienced as their soldiers. Officers, with the assistance of sergeants and corporals, commanded the company on the

21. *Official Records,* Ser. IV, Vol. I, 127–31; C.S. War Department, *Regulations for the Army of the Confederate States* (1863; rpr. Harrisburg, 1980), 12.

22. C.S. War Department, *Regulations,* 10.

parade ground and in battle. Cavalry and infantry officers were required to handle their own companies on the field and fight in conjunction with the battalion and regiment. Artillery officers had the even greater responsibility of coordinating their fire with other artillery batteries as well as supporting cavalry or infantry elements.

Officers drilled their companies daily to master the complicated maneuvers of nineteenth-century warfare. Once learned, drill had to be constantly rehearsed to maintain acceptable standards. This was very important during the winter months, when active campaigning ceased and officers and men tended to become lethargic. Innovative officers could make winter training as realistic as actual combat. The officers and men of the 2nd Maryland Infantry (C.S.) engaged the 1st Maryland Cavalry (C.S.) while in winter quarters at Hanover Junction, Virginia, on March 23, 1864. Using snowballs as weapons, the Maryland infantry assaulted the cavalry at their camp and fought a fierce battle throughout the morning. The units maneuvered as they did in actual combat under the command of their officers. That afternoon, soldiers from the 2nd Maryland Battery joined the cavalry in attacking the infantry. After two hours of snowball fights, the infantry "made a desperate charge, putting the cavalry and artillery completely to flight." Losses among the Marylanders were restricted to "black eyes and bloody noses," but the training experience was invaluable.[23]

Normally, units followed a strict training schedule when not involved in actual campaigning. Robert Lemmon in Richmond reported that his company had reveille at 5:30 A.M. and reported for parade half an hour later. Following inspection, breakfast, and washing, the company drilled from 9:00 to 11:00. The summer heat prevented much activity after lunch until 4:00, when the company drilled again, followed by a full parade two hours later.[24] Randolph H. McKim provided a similar account of the daily regime of the 1st Maryland Infantry (C.S.) in the summer of 1861 in a letter to his mother in Baltimore.[25]

Such training instilled confidence in both the officers and men of the

23. Ammen, "Maryland Troops in the Confederate Army," 125.

24. Robert Lemmon to mother, June 4, 1861, in Lemmon Papers.

25. McKim, *Soldier's Recollections*, 46–47. The benefits of the discipline instilled by close order drill were seen in the battle of Gaines' Mill on June 27, 1862, when the 1st Maryland Infantry (C.S.) withstood heavy fire and assaulted the enemy's line (Johnson, *Maryland*, 84–87).

company that they could perform as a unit in battle. The training that some officers and men had received in militia or volunteer companies before the war proved very useful during the drilling of the Confederate Maryland companies in Richmond and Harpers Ferry. When a drillmaster from the Virginia Military Institute tried to put Company C, 1st Maryland Infantry (C.S.), through the School of the Soldier in 1861, Capt. Dorsey told the cadet, "Let me give you a sample drill of my company." Dorsey began to issue commands to the company, many of whom had been members of various Baltimore volunteer units. The young drillmaster was so impressed with Dorsey's men on the parade field that he reported to the camp's commandant: "I cannot teach those Baltimore boys anything."[26]

In addition to the continual duties of preparing for battle, company officers had to handle numerous and never-ending administrative details. The commander was responsible for seeing that the company's morning report was prepared daily and forwarded to regimental headquarters. Likewise, the commander (who most often delegated these responsibilities to his lieutenants or orderly sergeant) completed the bimonthly muster roll to pay his company. The captain also prepared papers to discharge soldiers and descriptive lists that allowed his men to be paid at other duty stations or in hospitals. Furthermore, the company commander signed for all supplies and ammunition before issuing them to unit personnel. Captains and lieutenants (when acting in the commander's place) also prepared fuel and forage requisitions for the company; wrote recommendations for promotions of men under their command; conducted inspections of the soldiers and equipment assigned to the unit; administered the company's funds; and inventoried the personal effects of deceased soldiers.[27]

Officers were often detailed elsewhere in the regiment, or even brigade, while still nominally assigned to a line company. Commanders, at both regimental and brigade levels, frequently assigned company-grade officers to serve as adjutants, quartermasters, commissariats, provost marshals, ordnance, pioneer, and ambulance officers, or inspectors within the regiment or brigade.

Such appointments away from the companies had both advantages and disadvantages, as First Lieut. George W. Booth explained upon his selec-

26. Ammen, "Maryland Troops in the Confederate Army," 59.
27. For an example of the latter, see inventory of Pvt. Michael Logue's effects by Captain J. Louis Smith of the 1st Maryland Infantry (C.S.) in CSR.

tion as an adjutant of the 1st Maryland Infantry (C.S.) in 1861: "This service as Adjutant with Colonel Steuart was of immense advantage to me in the way of education for the duties of an officer, but the labors were very exacting, and I never felt altogether satisfied to be away from my company. . . . The men frequently would ask me to come back, and as I had enlisted many of them in Baltimore, I felt somewhat under obligation to stand by them." The regimental commander approved his request to return to his company, although he may have done so because Booth had gained so much weight during his recovery from illness in the Confederate capital.[28]

Assignment to the field and staff at regimental or brigade headquarters often constituted a promotion for the junior officer. The new duties challenged the lieutenant or captain as a manager of materiel, money, or administrative responsibilities. The assignment removed the officer from the grind of everyday duties with his company and reduced his exposure to combat. Officers reassigned from their companies were generally promoted and given extra pay and emoluments.[29] Not all officers received official appointments to these duties. Some were simply placed in an "acting" status, which forced regimental commanders to insist that appointment orders be made assigning the junior officer to the field and staff. After performing the duty of acting assistant quartermaster for the 1st Maryland Infantry (C.S.) for several months, First Lieut. Septimus H. Stewart of Company C still lacked an official appointment from the War Department. Twenty-three officers of the regiment petitioned the secretary of war in February, 1862, resulting in the appointment of Stewart, a former Baltimore bookkeeper, as captain and assistant quartermaster in April.[30]

In other cases, company officers were simply detailed to duties outside of the company and required to return when that duty was finished. Examples of duties of this nature included sitting on court-martial boards or commissions as a member or judge advocate and serving as recruiting officer or investigating officer for reports of survey, as provost marshal,

28. Booth, *Personal Reminiscences*, 21.

29. Lieutenants, for example, detailed as adjutants received an extra $10 to their monthly pay (*Official Records*, Ser. IV, Vol. I, 129).

30. Septimus H. Stewart to Judah P. Benjamin, February 22, 1862, Letter 448-S-1862, RG 109, Letters Received by the Confederate Adjutant and Inspector General, 1861–65, M474, NA (hereafter referred to by LAIG and letter number).

and on examination boards for promotion or competency. These extra responsibilities were usually assigned during the winter months when the army's active campaigning had ended.

Notifying the next of kin of the death of a member of the company was by far the most unpleasant command responsibility. In a war that grew increasingly bloody, summing up words of condolence was difficult for men numb from the horror of war. Faith in God and belief in the afterlife strengthened the will of many officers, as Capt. William H. Murray of the 1st Maryland Infantry (C.S.) recounted in a letter to the mother of Pvt. Edward L. West:

> My pen falters in the discharge of a most painful duty. Your noble son is dead. He died at Culpeper C.H. Nov. 20 of Pneumonia. I was with him. He was buried with military honors and his grave marked. As his commanding officer and friend I am proud to say that not one act or word of his ever caused the smallest complaint. As a Christian he lived as such he died his company bow with grief—to the will of God and to you broken hearted Mother I desire to present my heartfelt sympathy for the loss of a truly noble son. Grieve not he has gone to his God.[31]

The duties of both Union and Confederate company officers, both stated and unstated, were numerous and never-ending. The offices of captain and lieutenant demanded competent men, conscious of their responsibilities to their commanders and to their subordinates. Bell Irvin Wiley noted that the Civil War company "was very much like a large family. The captain was the father who supervised the daily routine" and molded the company in his image. "A good captain usually meant a good company," with the overall result that "as the company lived, marched, and fought together the members became so closely knit that they sometimes seemed to think and act as a single entity."[32] Unit cohesion resulted from the selection of suitable men to fill the junior officer positions and their demonstrated prowess and bravery on the battlefield.

31. William H. Murray to Mrs. E. L. West, n.d., in William H. Murray Letters, MS 1590, Manuscripts Division, MHS.
32. Wiley, *They Who Fought Here*, 35–38.

·5·

MARYLAND'S HIGH TIDE

The 1st Maryland Infantry (C.S.) experienced its baptism of fire at the Battle of First Manassas on July 21, 1861. The first unit from the state to see combat in the Civil War, it played a crucial role in supporting the Confederate line on Henry House Hill and driving in the Union right flank, collapsing the northern attack. Moving from the Shenandoah Valley to Manassas as a part of Joseph E. Johnston's army, the 1st Maryland Infantry marched from Winchester to Piedmont, a station on the Manassas Gap Railroad, in two days. Upon their arrival at Piedmont, "the men dropped on the ground where they halted with their guns in their hands." Capt. Murray tried to keep the men of his company on their feet, but "for my life I could not rouse them. They were to the eye dead. I gave it up as a bad job at the same time I knew if they had nothing to eat and no coffee to drink in the morning they would be broken down—so after a long time judging it was no use to wait I set myself to work to make coffee." When he roused his men the next morning, July 20, Murray said, "it repaid me to see them enjoy" the coffee.[1]

The 1st Maryland Infantry formed a part of a mixed brigade under Col. Elzey's command. After interminable delays while waiting for rail transport, the Marylanders joined the fray on the afternoon of the twenty-first. Up to this point, the battle had not gone well for the Confederacy and the division commander received orders to "go where the fire is hottest." Using the password *Sumter*, he led his men from Manassas Junction to the field, where they came across hordes of wounded men and stragglers who cheered them. The Marylanders joined the battle just as the division commander received several wounds, forcing him to relinquish command to Elzey. Elzey, in turn, placed the brigade near the Chinn House to wait for the enemy's advance.

1. William H. Murray to unknown, July, 1861, in Murray Letters.

Elzey soon discovered that his brigade overstretched the opposite Union line. The Maryland officer then ordered his troops to open fire on the unsuspecting Yankees, which devastated them. After several volleys, Elzey advanced the Confederate troops, sweeping the Union right flank off the field and rolling up the enemy. Panic soon enveloped the Union troops on Henry House Hill and forced their withdrawal and eventual rout toward Washington. In one of the forgotten moments of the war (as compared to Thomas J. Jackson's famous epitaph at Manassas), President Davis hailed Elzey as the "Blucher of the day" in the presence of Gens. Pierre G. T. Beauregard and Joseph E. Johnston.[2]

Manassas had been a hard-fought battle for the Marylanders. Among the officers who made their mark during the fighting was Capt. Charles C. Edelin of Company B, who captured a federal flag. Col. Elzey, who had boasted to Maj. Johnson that he would survive the battle with "a yellow sash or six feet of ground," earned an immediate promotion to brigadier general. Capt. Murray claimed that "the brave fellows of the North the pride of Old Abe—gave us but three shots and then we charged bayonets and they were not there. We sought them but they were no where to be found." Union prisoners captured after the battle told their captors that when they learned who opposed them, the word spread through the ranks, "Here come those d——d Baltimore men! It's time for us to git up and git!"[3]

In contrast to the performance of the enemy, Capt. Murray was extremely pleased with his brother's conduct as an enlisted man in Company H: "'Mr.' Clapham behaved beautifully I was by his side all day—and watched with intense anxiety of every bomb and flash of every gun." The captain poignantly admitted that "if he had fallen I did not wish to live." The aftermath of the battle was a new experience for the Maryland officers. Murray wrote that "the pen cannot describe the tongue cannot utter the horrors of war. It is left for the eye alone to convey to the mind an idea of a field of battle." Randolph H. McKim recoiled at the sufferings of the horses, victims of man's inhumanity.[4]

The Maryland regiment, now commanded by Col. Steuart, used the lengthy interlude of quiet after Manassas to perfect its drill and ceremony.

2. Winfield Peters, "First Battle of Manassas," *SHSP*, XXXIV (1906), 170–78; Johnson, "Memoir of First Maryland Regiment," 481–83; Goldsborough, *Maryland Line*, 21–27; Johnson, *Maryland*, 54–56.

3. Murray to unknown, July, 1861, in Murray Letters; McKim, *Soldier's Recollections*, 36.

4. Murray to unknown, July, 1861, in Murray Letters; McKim, *Soldier's Recollections*, 37.

Steuart, a Regular Army officer, whipped the unit into shape as a military formation and implemented as much of the old army discipline as possible. Junior officers became more confident under Steuart's tutelage, and the unit developed its identity during the final months of 1861. Somerville Sollers, an enlisted man in Company H, wrote from Fairfax Court House in August about life in the regiment:

> We are in fine spirits, & look upon the recognition of the Confederacy & the redemption of Md. as a Sure thing. . . . We have nothing to complain of, but our rations, which are miserable, driving us very often to the Hotel to eat by which our funds are nearly all gone. This is evidently something wrong in the Commissary Department of our Reg. . . . We received our uniforms a few days ago, grey pants & jackets & we look as gay as you please. Our's (Capt. Murray's Company) is the best in the Reg. numbering now 90—all gentlemen.[5]

Capt. Murray of the 1st Maryland Infantry reflected on his role as commander of Company H and his obligation to his men in a letter to a friend in early March, 1862:

> Just think it is nearly ten months since I left home "not banished but set free"—Not till now have I realized the responsibilities resting on one's shoulders. The force of example. The strict impartial rules—by which to govern—present their responsibilities fearfully plain to mind. . . . In other companies many officers laugh at moral corruption which is to me a source of anxiety and pain. How many anxious mothers . . . look to me as far as in me lies, to, shield and protect their sons from harm—This is but one care that is never absent.[6]

Murray cited a critical shortcoming among the junior officers of the 1st Maryland Infantry (C.S.) which originated with the election of officers. Many officers, particularly at the beginning of the war, rose to command for nonmilitary reasons. They often lacked the intellectual, physical, or moral stamina needed to set a proper example for soldiers. The removal of these incompetent or unqualified officers from the service disrupted unit efficiency. Incompetency, a broad term, covered failure of the officer to perform his administrative duties, to handle the company on the drill field, or to regulate the men in camp. Failure on the battlefield

5. Somerville Sollers to Meme, August 4, 1861, in Lucy Leigh Bowie Collection, MS 1755, Manuscripts Division, MHS.
6. William H. Murray to "My dear friend," March 2, 1862, in Murray Letters.

came to be seen in much harsher light, and the officer who did not pass the test of combat could easily be branded a coward.

Some of Maryland's junior officers resigned because they failed to meet the approval of the soldiers under their command. The Confederate soldier was a model of individualism; the nineteenth-century sense of egalitarianism gave enlisted men leeway in their treatment by their officers, whom they had elected as commanders. "The result," according to Gerald F. Linderman, "was a strong bent to resist the orders of any officer whose superior qualities were not immediately apparent to the privates."[7]

To achieve these "superior qualities," an officer had to establish a rapport with his soldiers based on the officer's own personal courage and inner strength. He had to understand his men's specific needs and motivate them in times of despair, reward them for their good deeds, and punish them justly when necessary. Leadership legitimacy was not derived simply from the rank on a man's collar. It had to be earned daily by the officer in front of his soldiers, as John H. Stone, a former enlisted man in the 1st Maryland Infantry, elected as first lieutenant in the 2nd Maryland Infantry (C.S.) in 1862, recognized when he wrote his sister from Camp Maryland in Richmond: "My time has been fully occupied in providing Quarter Master & Commissary stores for the men. If an officer wishes to gain the respect & confidence of his men, he must provide for their creature comforts, this I shall endeavor to do regardless of my own comfort."[8]

George Howard, a wholesale dry goods dealer from Baltimore and first lieutenant in Company M, 1st Virginia Cavalry (C.S.), apparently incurred the wrath of the enlisted men in his unit. Upon the company's formal muster into Confederate States service in August, 1861, Howard "found there was some dissatisfaction in the troop and I resigned." Soon after his resignation, Howard (while serving as a private in the company) was captured and held as a prisoner of war until paroled in late November. Howard went to Richmond to appeal to the adjutant general for rein-

---

7. Linderman, *Embattled Courage*, 37.

8. For a discussion of the qualities of an officer and leadership legitimacy, see Sam C. Sarkesian, ed., *Combat Effectiveness: Cohesion, Stress, and the Volunteer Army* (Beverly Hills, 1980), 263–65. Thomas G. Clemens, ed., "The 'Diary' of John H. Stone First Lieutenant, Company B, 2d Maryland Infantry, C.S.A.," *Maryland Historical Magazine*, LXXXV (1990), 115; this manuscript is in the Civil War Miscellaneous Collection, USAMHI.

statement and remained there until mid-1862. He continued to draw commutation for rations from the army during the entire period he waited for the War Department to act on his case.[9]

Perhaps more than most Civil War regiments, the commanders of Maryland's Confederate soldiers needed to restrain the ambitions of junior officers and enlisted men alike. The root of this dilemma lay in the high caliber of the unit's soldiers and their perceptions of their status in southern society. As Robert Lemmon wrote at the beginning of the war: "As a company in *social* standing we rank with the Palmettoes [South Carolinians] and in six weeks, I trust we will rival them in skill. Governor Letcher has spoken most highly of us and indeed we are the top of the ladder in popularity."[10]

One mess in Company H of the 1st Maryland Infantry (C.S.) provides a glimpse of the social standing of the regiment's enlisted personnel. Randolph H. McKim, a private, University of Virginia graduate, and candidate for the ministry in the Episcopal Church, shared duties with several other enlisted men with similar backgrounds: McHenry Howard, a Princeton graduate; Wilson Carr, a Baltimore lawyer; John Bolling, a graduate of the master's program at the University of Virginia; William Duncan McKim, a Harvard graduate; and George Williamson, a gentleman educated in Europe. All of these men joined the Confederate army because they initially believed they wanted to serve as private soldiers.[11]

After such men spent countless nights on picket duty around Washington and performed numerous tedious camp duties, the allure of enlisted life grew thin. They soon agitated for promotions, transfers to other companies where they thought duties were better, or discharges from the army.[12]

W. Jefferson Buchanan, a twenty-eight-year-old Baltimore lawyer serving as a private in the 1st Maryland Battery, received a discharge for atrophy of the heart in 1862. He immediately applied for several higher

9. George Howard to Gen. Samuel S. Cooper, December 12, 1861, in CSR, George Howard, 1st Virginia Cavalry Regiment. For further information, see his file in the 1st Maryland Cavalry (C.S.).

10. Robert Lemmon to mother, May 23, 1861, in Lemmon Papers.

11. McKim, *Soldier's Recollections*, 51; McHenry Howard discusses the same mess in *Recollections*, 64–65.

12. The propensity of men from the upper classes to serve in the Confederate enlisted ranks was a feature of the early part of the war; see Linderman, *Embattled Courage*, 38–39.

positions such as a commission in the artillery or Quartermaster Department or as a clerk in the Treasury Department. In a blunt letter to Jefferson Davis, Buchanan listed his qualifications for a lieutenancy in the Signal Corps. Like many of his Maryland comrades, he spared no effort in embellishing his story:

It is due to my family and to myself that I should freely and frankly state to you, Sir, who so kindly endorsed my application something of the surroundings of my position here. The first gun had not been fired in defence of the South & the Right ere I left the allurements and advantages of European life and Society to assist in our great and Just Cause. On the second day of my arrival in Virginia; fifteen months ago I enlisted as a private in the ranks of the Southern Army. I sought no position, I wished non[e]. My object was accomplished when I made myself a soldier of the South. I have four Brothers here, all in the ranks, one of them barely seventeen years of age, who left Europe for the Confederacy, with the blessing and approbation of both father & mother. I have an Uncle in Fort Warren, another in Fort McHenry. It was my relative John Merryman who struck the first blow for the Revolution in Maryland, and in whose case the writ of habeas corpus was for the first time suspended in this land. Another blow also has since been struck by another relative of mine, distasteful doubtless to our enemies. I mean by Admiral Buchanan late of the "Merrimac" whose letter to me I enclose. My first Cousin, a son of the late Col. John Rowan of Kentucky, a gentleman probably well known to you, fell at Shiloh; his brother died of Typhoid fever contracted in camp. But one male member of Col. Rowan's family line lives and he is in the ranks. Not a drop of my blood flows in the veins of any Northern man or woman. My father's dwelling house, in the City of Baltimore has been converted into a Federal Hospital. From the dome of his Country residence, near to the same City flies a Federal flag, marking the quarters of his foes. His entire property has been confiscated to the uses of his own and his Country's enemies. He is an exile now, in a foreign land and is growing old. As the eldest scion of his house he looked to me. And the duty of the worthy son of this honored father was clear and plain to me, and I am sure will so appear to me, when I made application for the comparatively humble position of 1st Lieut. in the Signal Corps.[13]

13. W. Jefferson Buchanan to Jefferson Davis, October 19, 1862, in CSR, W. Jefferson Buchanan, 1st Maryland Battery. Buchanan later wrote an eloquent appeal regarding Maryland's loyalty to the Confederate cause; see Buchanan, *Maryland's Hope: Her Trials and Interests in Connexion with the War* (Richmond, 1864). Another example of a request

To compound the frustration of the volunteers, the term of service for several of the companies of the 1st Maryland Infantry (C.S.) was due to expire in the spring of 1862. The Confederate government desperately sought to preserve the army in order to face the enemy in the upcoming campaign. Hastily passing the Bounty and Furlough Act in December, 1861, the Confederate Congress called for the reenlistment of Confederate troops to serve for three years (one year of which had already passed) in exchange for a bonus of $50 and sixty days' furlough. Additionally, the act permitted soldiers to organize new companies in the branch of their choice and to elect new officers. The Bounty and Furlough Act, rather than preserving the army, encouraged rivalry and disorder in the ranks.[14]

The act generated controversy among the Maryland Confederates and prompted Frank S. Price to write the secretary of war in March, 1862. Price had been the captain of the regiment's original Company C until it disbanded in the early summer of 1861. He remained in the regiment as an enlisted man while still drawing pay as an officer until August, 1861. The Maryland soldier (who had been absent from the regiment since October as either sick or on detached duty) inquired about the reenlistment options of Marylanders in Confederate service. Price signed his letter as captain when he asked: "If any one among those who were mustered in at Harper's Ferry, as members of the 1st Maryland Regiment, has the right to re-enlist and become entitled to the $50 bounty, has not every one, who enlisted on the same conditions, the same right?"[15]

Lieut. Col. Johnson (who had been promoted after Col. Elzey moved to brigade command) raised the issue of the period of enlistments for Companies A and B with officials in Richmond. In a January, 1862, letter Johnson reminded Lieut. Col. Deas at the Adjutant and Inspector General's Office (who had sworn the companies into Confederate service at

---

for a commission is found in John P. Marshall to Secretary of War, April 17, 1862, in Marshall file, GUAAR.

14. Freeman, *Lee's Lieutenants*, I, 171. See also Kevin Conley Ruffner, "Before the Seven Days: The Reorganization of the Confederate Army in the Spring of 1862," in *The Peninsula Campaign of 1862: Yorktown to the Seven Days*, ed. William J. Miller (Campbell, 1993), I, 46–69.

15. CSR, Frank S. Price, 1st Maryland Infantry (C.S.); Price to Benjamin, March 3, 1862, Letter 57-P-1862, LSOW. As late as December, 1863, Price sought restoration of rank as an officer and back pay; see Price to Capt. Kane, December 15, 1863, Letter 399-P-1863, LSOW.

Harpers Ferry and Point of Rocks) that Companies A and B had agreed to only one year's service. When the War Department received the company muster rolls, it had inadvertently changed the terms of enlistment to three years. The 1st Maryland's commander requested that the Confederate government correct this mistake, which, he believed, would uplift the spirits of the soldiers.[16]

The two Maryland companies most affected by the reenlistment offer, Companies A and B of the 1st Maryland Infantry (C.S.), accepted the terms of the Bounty and Furlough Act, as did a handful of men from other companies.[17] Company B's reenlistees went on furlough while Capt. Charles C. Edelin, their commander, proceeded to Richmond for additional recruits in early February. Edelin had still not returned to the regiment two months later and, instead, took his men to North Carolina to serve as a heavy artillery company. He claimed to have received permission from the War Department for this action but did not submit the transfer request through his chain of command.

Johnson protested Edelin's action to the adjutant general in April, 1862. He wrote that he "understood that Capt Edelin does not desire to return to this Regt. and intends also to keep the men who are with him." Johnson realized the dangers that the Bounty and Furlough Act posed to plans for a Maryland Line. He added: "Besides the service will lose the men who are in Richmond—having re-enlisted & recd the Bounty[.] This Regt is the only nucleus for a Maryland force in the army. All the men [who] belong to it are doubly precious for we have no resources to recruit from—Thus to scatter it, must destroy it. I beg therefore most earnestly to request that Capt Edelin be ordered forthwith to report to this Regt with all his men—Having him here I shall then be able to collect his scattered men & reorganize his Company." Edelin's company did not return until June, his absence weakened the 1st Maryland Infantry (C.S.) during the 1862 spring campaign in the Shenandoah Valley.[18]

16. Bradley T. Johnson to George Deas, January 21, 1862, Letter 60-J-1862, LAIG; Johnson to Deas, February 4, 1862, Letter 107-J-1862, LAIG.

17. See "List of Men in the 1st Md Regt who have Re-enlisted," February 8, 1862, in RG 109, War Department Collection of Confederate Records, Muster and Pay Rolls for Maryland Units, NA.

18. Bradley T. Johnson to Gen. Samuel Cooper, April 10, 1862, Letter 292-J-1862, LAIG; George H. Steuart to Gen. Samuel Cooper, March 30, 1862, Letter 292-J-1862, LAIG; Johnson, "Memoir of First Maryland Regiment," 488. After the war, Goldsborough

The Confederate Congress, responding to the demands of Steuart, Johnson, and other Marylanders, passed the "Act to Authorize and Provide for the Organization of the Maryland Line" on February 15, 1862. The act called for the voluntary enrollment of all Marylanders in the army now scattered throughout the Confederacy "into one or more brigades." The Confederate War Department, in turn, issued General Order 8 on February 26, which stipulated the transfer of Marylanders to the 1st Maryland Infantry (C.S.) and promoted Colonel Steuart to brigadier general in command of the Maryland Line, which was expected to grow to a complete brigade-sized element. At this point, the 1st Maryland Infantry and Andrews' 1st Maryland Battery were the only elements of the Maryland Line.[19]

---

described Edelin: "Captain Edelin alias Lum Cooper, who had by some means been elected to the command of a fine company, composed principally of young men from Baltimore. Without even the rudiments of a common school education, holding the truth in utter contempt, and a low swaggerer, he had nothing to recommend him but his having lighted the lamps in the streets of Washington for years, and beat a drum in the war with Mexico. His conduct everywhere in the army was disgraceful in the extreme, and reflected discredit, not only upon the regiment to which he belonged, but upon the State, of which he was neither a native nor a resident. Finally, despised and avoided by all who, without knowing the man, had associated with him in the regiment, he ran the blockade, took the Oath of Allegiance to the Federal Government and turned informer upon the Government of which he had been a sworn servant" (Goldsborough, *Maryland Line*, 32). Goldsborough's 1869 volume lacks the roster included in his 1900 work, but this portrayal of Edelin was not included in the later work. Edelin's name was mentioned in the 1861 congressional testimony about treasonous activity in Washington, D.C. He apparently worked at the U.S. Capitol as a lamplighter and took his alias from his stepfather. When Edelin was accused of flying a palmetto flag over his house, the commissioner of public buildings and grounds defended him by saying that he "is a man that has a great deal to say, and very little judgment, and often utters things without any foundation, I should think. He is very extravagant in his talk, though he is a little man; but he is a big bragger" (U.S. Congress, House, *Reports of the Select Committee of Five on Alleged Hostile Organization Against the Government Within the District of Columbia*, H.R. 79, 36th Cong., 2nd Sess., 1861, 19–20). Edelin's record at the National Archives is unclear after he left the 1st Maryland Infantry (C.S.). He was in a Confederate military prison in Richmond in 1864 and was captured by the enemy at Martinsburg in the summer of 1864. He was released from Old Capitol Prison when he took the oath of allegiance in 1865.

19. For a copy of General Orders 8, Adjutant and Inspector General's Office, 1862, see *Official Records*, Ser. IV, Vol. I, 953–54; for an order authorizing Marylanders to transfer to the Maryland Line, see *ibid.*, 1120–21; for the problems encountered with recruiting

Two months later, Gen. Steuart reported to the War Department that the Maryland Line had met with "very little success." Unit commanders were reluctant to permit their soldiers to transfer to the Maryland Line; consequently, Steuart's recruiting goals for the Line had not been achieved. Despite this gloomy picture, Steuart expressed confidence that "within a few weeks all can be assembled and ready to take the field. The First Maryland Regiment," he wrote, "being the largest body of Marylanders, could serve as a nucleus, and all the rest be ordered to report there immediately." Steuart believed the Maryland Line held great significance for the southern cause: "As Maryland is not represented in Congress nor an acknowledged State of the Confederacy, one great object which will be attained in forming the Maryland Line will be its representing the State. It will serve as a rallying point for all Marylanders, and will be constantly increased by men coming over from Maryland. It will serve also to keep up the spirits of our friends in Maryland by letting them know the State is represented by an organized and constantly increasing military body in the Confederacy."[20]

As the terms of enlistment for the companies of the 1st Maryland Infantry drew to a close, tension mounted within the regiment. The Confederate government, frustrated with the Bounty and Furlough Act, authorized conscription of southern men in April. The First Conscription Act called for the registration of all white males between the ages of eighteen and thirty-five. It forced all men of draft age to remain in the army, whether or not they had reenlisted. It did, however, permit the use of substitutes and later expanded the number of exemption categories. The government did not require nonresidents of the Confederate States to perform military duty, allowing Marylanders in the South to avoid compulsory military service because Maryland had not joined the Confederacy. This clause also permitted the discharge of those Marylanders already serving in the army as nonresidents.[21]

for the Maryland Line, see Gen. Steuart's correspondence with the War Department, *ibid.*, 946–47, 1102–1103; Johnson, "Maryland Line," 23–24.

20. *Official Records*, Ser. IV, Vol. I, 1102–1103.

21. Freeman, *Lee's Lieutenants*, I, 171–72. For a full discussion of the Confederate draft, see Albert B. Moore, *Conscription and Conflict in the Confederacy* (New York, 1963). For details on the Maryland companies that disbanded in 1861–62 upon the expiration of terms of service, and other unit changes, see Lee A. Wallace, Jr., *A Guide to Virginia Military Organizations, 1861–1865* (2nd ed.; Lynchburg, 1986).

In accordance with orders from brigade headquarters, Bradley T. Johnson, now colonel of the 1st Maryland Infantry after the promotion of George H. Steuart to brigadier general, formed the regiment for reelection of officers in Companies A, C, H, and I in late April. These companies had enlisted for one year and needed to reorganize to remain in service. Company A, which had already reenlisted in February, promptly reelected Capt. Goldsborough and First Lieut. George K. Shellman. The troops voted against Lieuts. Charles W. Blair and George M. E. Shearer and, instead, selected two enlisted men as officers. Orderly Sgt. John F. Groshon was elected second lieutenant and Sgt. William H. B. Dorsey took the position of third lieutenant. The defeat of Lieutenant Shearer jolted Col. Johnson, who immediately recommended the defeated officer, now without a position in the regiment, for appointment as a lieutenant in the Provisional Army of the Confederate States. Johnson noted that the "result [of the election] was surprising to his brother officers & myself who know his merits; had I suspected it, [it] could easily have been prevented."[22]

Johnson was shocked to learn that Companies C, H, and I refused to reorganize. Capt. R. Carter Smith of Company C reported that his company would not elect new officers, a situation repeated in Captain Murray's Company H and Captain Robertson's Company I. Johnson contended that these companies had legally organized as twelve-month companies from the Commonwealth of Virginia and were required to reorganize under the Conscription Act. Johnson warned his superiors that "there are now I think, ten thousand Marylanders in service, certainly from six to eight thousand. If any are exempt, all are, & they will everywhere claim their discharge, & thus the Government lose valuable soldiers at the crisis of the war, disorganizing many companies & Regts whose soldiers will fail to perceive the justice of exempting Marylanders from military service, when *they* are held. Maryland men who certainly have as much to fight for & I think more than any soldiers in the Confederate States."[23]

The refusal of these companies to reorganize threw the entire regiment into disorder. In May, 1862, the men of Company E petitioned the sec-

22. Bradley T. Johnson to George W. Randolph, May 2, 1862, Letter 345-J-1862, LAIG.

23. Bradley T. Johnson to Capt. T. O. Chestney, April 29, 1862, Letter 370-J-1862, LAIG.

retary of war for their release because they claimed also to have enlisted for one year. The soldiers cited illegal actions taken by the regimental commander the previous summer and claimed that "many of our officers now hold positions which they are utterly incompetent to fill."[24]

In addition to the confusion created by the various Confederate enactments, the rapid promotions of Elzey and Steuart to general officer ranks meant that replacements had to be found for the field-grade positions within the regiment. Under the system of seniority, Bradley T. Johnson and Edward R. Dorsey received promotions as colonel and lieutenant colonel, which still left the majority of the regiment vacant. Normally, the senior captain of the regiment would occupy this slot; however, the absence of Capt. Edelin prevented this from taking place. Gen. Steuart bitterly said that Edelin "has managed to get himself detached from the regt., is now in North Carolina, and I have been informed has stated that he is to be a Lt. Col. or Col. there, also that he stated publicly he would never come back to the regiment again."[25]

In Edelin's absence, Gen. Steuart proposed that Capt. Herbert of Company D be promoted to major. The War Department, however, failed to respond to Steuart's recommendation or to Gen. Elzey's suggestion a month later. Elzey initially wanted Capt. Murray to move up to major, and Murray himself had written the secretary of war on April 25 for an explanation of the Conscription Act and the election of field-grade officers. The government's response proved less than satisfactory, and Murray refused to be a candidate for the position. In his stead, Elzey selected Capt. Nicholas of Company G. Capt. J. Louis Smith of Company F also took it upon himself to write to the secretary of war on May 3 to recommend Capt. Nicholas for major.[26] The Confederate bureaucracy, despite numerous appeals, took no action concerning the vacant position of major in the 1st Maryland Infantry (C.S.).

24. Soldiers of Company E, 1st Maryland Infantry Regiment (C.S.) to Secretary of War George W. Randolph, May 8, 1862, in RG 109, War Department Collection of Confederate Records, Muster and Pay Rolls for Maryland Units.

25. George H. Steuart to Gen. Samuel Cooper, April 8, 1862, Letter 694-S-1862, LAIG.

26. William H. Murray to Secretary of War, April 25, 1862, Letter 443-M-1862, LSOW; Arnold Elzey to Gen. Samuel Cooper, May 2, 1862, Letter 141-E-1862, LAIG; J. Louis Smith to Secretary of War, May 3, 1862, in CSR, Wilson C. Nicholas, 1st Maryland Infantry (C.S.).

Despite Col. Johnson's warnings about releasing Marylanders from military service, the War Department ordered the discharge of members of Company C upon the expiration of its term of service in mid-May. Unhappy over the affairs in his regiment, Johnson stood in front of the regimental formation on May 17 and emphatically pointed the direction to the enemy as Company C disbanded. A member of the company, Pvt. George H. Weston, recorded the scene in his diary:

> Our muskets are stacked. Our knapsacks, cartridge boxes etc. etc. etc. all lying on the ground in order, ready to be delivered up when called for. Groups of our former companions in arms are around us, bidding a last adieu. Here & there can be seen men going to & fro with cooking utensils & blankets that we have thrown away. We are about to be mustered out in an hour when we will take the turnpike for Gordonsville. Happy are we, of our release, for as a company we have seen as hard, yes even harder service than any co. in the 1st Md. Regt.
>
> ½ past 9 The regt ordered into line to move off but before doing so, Col. Johnston [sic] read our Muster roll & discharged us from the service. Never did I feel so glad as when I stacked my gun on the parade ground of the 1st Md. Regt. for the last time. Not because of my hatred for the corps, nor the men (for I intend going into service again), but from the hatred & dislike I have for our field & staff officers.[27]

Four days later, Johnson discharged a number of soldiers from Companies A and B who had not reenlisted with their companies earlier in the year. At the same time, the remaining enlisted personnel of Companies D, E, F, and G clamored for discharge because they had enlisted for only twelve months at Harpers Ferry, not for the duration of the war. Johnson appealed to these soldiers to stay in the ranks while he tried to clarify the issue with the War Department. Notwithstanding the colonel's appeal, some Marylanders deserted or had to be placed under arrest because they refused to return to duty. Apparently, many soldiers disliked and distrusted Col. Johnson. Pvt. Weston complained that the commutation money for his clothing "had been stopped by our mean Col Bradley T. Johnson & Lt. Col. E. R. Dorsey."[28]

27. George H. Weston Diary, May 17, 1862, William R. Perkins Library, Duke University, Durham, N.C.
28. Johnson, "Memoir of First Maryland Regiment," 52; Booth, *Personal Reminiscences*, 31; McKim, *Soldier's Recollections*, 86; Weston Diary, May 13, 1862.

At the opening of the spring, 1862, campaign, the 1st Maryland Infantry was, in the words of its commander, "sullen and unhappy." After months of organizing and training for war, two Maryland regiments, one Union and the other Confederate, met on the field of battle. On May 23, the 1st Maryland Infantry (C.S.) moved toward Front Royal as a part of Stonewall Jackson's diversionary force in the Shenandoah Valley. During a break in the march, Col. Johnson received an urgent message from Gen. Jackson to advance his regiment forward "with all dispatch." Johnson shouted to his men that they were needed at the front but that he refused to lead dissatisfied soldiers into battle and would return the order to Jackson. He then beckoned his men to return to Maryland: "Boast of it when you meet your fathers and mothers, brothers, sisters, and sweethearts. Tell them it was you who, when brought face to face with the enemy, proved yourselves . . . to be cowards."[29]

Johnson's troops, both officers and enlisted men, heartily cheered the colonel and pleaded to be thrown into the fight. Indeed, one Maryland soldier wrote, "Col. Johnson made us a very inspiring speech, in which he reminded us of our friends confined in the dungeons of Fort Warren. When he had finished a shout rent the air and off we went under the impression that Baltimore was our destination."[30] With anxiety behind them, the Confederate Marylanders moved up and were greatly cheered by the news that the 1st Maryland Infantry (U.S.) held Front Royal. Jackson realized that the capture of the town and its bridges over the two forks of the Shenandoah River threatened the main Union army in the Shenandoah Valley proper.

The 1st Maryland Infantry (C.S.) formed the center of the Confederate line when they surprised the Union picket line on the outskirts of town. Sweeping into Front Royal, Col. Johnson's men encountered sporadic resistance in the drive to seize the first bridge over the South Fork. The Union commander, realizing that the town was lost, pulled his troops back to their main encampment on the heights near the North Fork bridge of the Shenandoah and prepared for a lengthy engagement. He

29. Johnson, "Memoir of First Maryland Regiment," 53; Robert G. Tanner, *Stonewall in the Valley: Thomas J. "Stonewall" Jackson's Shenandoah Valley Campaign, Spring 1862* (New York, 1976), 211.

30. Rosamond Randall Beirne, ed., "Three War Letters," *Maryland Historical Magazine*, XC (1945), 291; Booth, *Personal Reminiscences*, 31–32.

also sent a messenger to Strasburg to warn Gen. Nathaniel P. Banks of the Confederate advance and to arrange for the protection of the Union rear at Winchester.

The fighting raged for a short time as Jackson attempted to bring up his artillery to drive the Union Marylanders from the bluff. The battle for the North Fork bridge was crucial to Jackson because he needed to cross the river to continue his drive down the valley. Despite the attempts of Union soldiers to burn the bridge, the rebels managed to cross and charge the federals' camp. The failure to hold the bridge forced the Union withdrawal from Front Royal along the main road to Winchester. The Union Marylanders evacuated their position, under fire, in an "orderly military manner." The Union colonel planned to form a new defensive perimeter closer to Winchester, but Confederate cavalry struck the procession at Cedarville late in the afternoon of May 23.

After hitting both flanks, the southern cavalry chopped up the Yankee troops and scattered them. Struggling gallantly against the swiftly moving troopers, the commander of the 1st Maryland Infantry (U.S.) fell wounded, and shortly thereafter, Union troops threw down their weapons. Virtually all of the 1st Maryland Infantry (U.S.) was "gobbled up" by the jubilant Confederate Marylanders.[31]

The capture of so many northern Marylanders gave their southern counterparts ample opportunity to tease them, and Johnson's men quickly took up the chant that "the real First Maryland had whipped the bogus." As the Confederate Marylanders rounded up stray Union Marylanders, "recognitions among old acquaintances were highly amusing, although the conversations which generally passed between them were not of a polite or complimentary character." Capt. Murray came across one old acquaintance from Baltimore, William E. George, who had been captured while serving as the quartermaster of the 1st Maryland Infantry (U.S.). The two officers shook hands, and Murray said, "I am no longer a friend

---

31. For a discussion of the Battle of Front Royal, see Tanner, *Stonewall in the Valley*, 211–17; Goldsborough, *Maryland Line*, 40–44; Johnson, *Maryland*, 69–73; Scharf, *History of Maryland*, III, 473–75; Johnson, "Memoir of First Maryland Regiment," 53–56; Michael P. Musick, *6th Virginia Cavalry* (Lynchburg, 1990), 12–14. There was some controversy between the 6th Virginia Cavalry and Johnson's Marylanders as to who properly earned the battle honors at Front Royal; see "Cedar Creek. Between Winchester and Front Royal," in Daniel A. Grimsley, *Battles in Culpeper County, Virginia, 1861–1865* (1900; rpr. Orange, n.d.), 45–46.

of yours Lt George—but shall do all in my power to make you and all of you comfortable."[32]

Following the resounding victory at Front Royal, the 1st Maryland Infantry (C.S.) helped in the liberation of Winchester on May 25. The rewards of the capture of the town from the Yankees were immense. Lieuts. Booth and William Key Howard seized a fully equipped hospital and a supply depot while Lieut. Ward, of April 19 fame, captured a half dozen Union officers who had lost their units. The reception by the Virginia townspeople was, as Johnson recounted, "such an excited scene . . . never seen before or since—a whole people demented with joy and exhibiting all the ecstacy of delirium."[33]

One future Maryland officer, John Eager Howard Post, claimed that "our regiment was the first in town, and such wild demonstrations of joy and delight was depicted on the faces of every one, especially the ladies is inconceivable." A private in Company H, Post exclaimed, "I really thought they were going to hug us." Post's thoughts then turned to home, and he added, "If you had only known, my dear Ma, what a splendid opportunity this would have been for you to come up to see me, been there when we arrived and left when we did."[34]

After the glorious entry into Winchester, Jackson took most of his command to Harpers Ferry, where the 1st Maryland Infantry (C.S.) gazed across the Potomac River to the shores of Maryland. At Bolivar Heights, the commander of Company H poignantly wrote his mother of his sentiments from the town where the 1st Maryland Infantry (C.S.) had organized only a year before:

> I cannot tell you my feelings as I stood on the height which overlooks Harpers Ferry. I saw for the first time for more than twelve months—My native soil. I shed tears from a heart hardened by wrong. I thought Oh could I but stand once more upon her soil and say Thy Will be done I could be happy. At this moment a shell from the hills of My native land came hissing through the air. It seemed to say "Forbidden ground." I turned and looked not again at the land of my birth.[35]

32. Johnson, "Memoir of First Maryland Regiment," 55; William H. Murray to unknown, n.d., in Murray Letters.

33. Johnson, "Memoir of First Maryland Regiment," 99–100; Booth, *Personal Reminiscences,* 35.

34. Beirne, ed. "Three War Letters," 292.

35. William H. Murray to mother, June 28, 1862, in Murray Letters.

Pulling back from the jaws of a potential Union trap in the lower Shenandoah Valley, the 1st Maryland Infantry (C.S.) was heavily involved during the remainder of the Shenandoah Valley campaign. The pace of the fighting allowed the regiment's officers little time to contemplate their Maryland homes. Two officers of the 1st Maryland Infantry (C.S.) fell at the vicious fight near Harrisonburg on June 6, the same engagement in which the "Gallant" Turner Ashby lost his life. Leading the men in a charge, Capt. Robertson of Company I was struck by an enemy shell; despite his fatal wounds, the company commander rallied his troops, saying, "Go on, my men; don't mind me!" Second Lieut. Nicholas Snowden, the cousin of the artillerist, also died that day. Robertson and Snowden were the first officers of the 1st Maryland Infantry (C.S.) to die.[36]

The Marylanders turned the tide of the battle when they drove off an elite Union outfit, the Pennsylvania Bucktails, which had infiltrated Confederate lines. Capt. Nicholas of Company G captured the commander of the sharpshooter battalion, Lieut. Col. Thomas L. Kane, who cursed his men for leaving him wounded on the field. The division commander of the 1st Maryland Infantry (C.S.), Maj. Gen. Richard S. Ewell, ordered that the symbol of the Pennsylvania unit, a bucktail, be attached to the Marylanders' battle flag in recognition of their valor at Harrisonburg.[37]

Two days later, the regiment participated in another bloody engagement at Cross Keys, which Col. Johnson claimed as a "Maryland fight" because "it was the best fight that we have made" and because all the southern generals on the field were Marylanders or affiliated with the state. Johnson's Maryland infantry was supported by the Baltimore Light Artillery, and together they withstood the onslaught of three Union regiments during the day's action. Though low on ammunition, the regiment wanted to continue fighting but was pulled back at dusk. The spirit evinced by the Marylanders was reflected in the wounding of Second Lieut. Hezekiah H. Bean, the acting commander of Company I, who was struck in the foot. Pulling back from the line, Bean lifted his foot to show Col. Johnson, "See, I've got it, Colonel." The commander later wrote

36. Goldsborough, *Maryland Line*, 53; Johnson, "Memoir of First Maryland Regiment," 105.

37. Goldsborough, *Maryland Line*, 53; Johnson, "Memoir of First Maryland Regiment," 106–107.

about this incident: "The term of his [Bean's] company was to expire on the 15th—just a week off—and he was delighted at having so honorable a testimonial."[38]

The Valley campaign ended the next day at Port Republic with the 1st Maryland Infantry (C.S.) sitting in reserve during the entire battle.[39] The regiment did participate in the bloody engagements around Richmond later that month and in early July; however, the summer of 1862 was an uncertain time for Confederate Marylanders. In mid-June, Companies H and I of the 1st Maryland Infantry (C.S.) completed their twelve-month commitment, and the soldiers were discharged by Col. Johnson.[40]

There was a glimmer of hope that the regiment could still be maintained with fresh recruits. Capt. Edelin and the men of Company B returned to duty after their long sojourn in North Carolina. At the same time, a new company recruited from exiled Marylanders joined the regiment as the third Company C. The secretary of war gave Edmund Barry permission to raise a company of infantry in early March, 1862. He eventually formed enough men into a company with himself as captain, John P. Marshall (a Georgetown College graduate and former member of the 1st Virginia Infantry Regiment) as first lieutenant, and William H. H. Edelin (no relation to Capt. Edelin) and Thomas Washington Smith as second lieutenants. At the opening of the Seven Days' Battles, Johnson counted seven companies still in service with the 1st Maryland Infantry (C.S.) with the prospect that Capt. Murray would recruit yet another company.[41]

38. Johnson, "Memoir of First Maryland Regiment," 108–109. The importance of wounds as an outward symbol of courage is discussed in Linderman, *Embattled Courage*, 31–32. For Johnson's report on the regiment's participation in the Valley campaign from May 29 to June 9, 1862, see *Official Records*, Ser. I, Vol. XII, Pt. 1, pp. 817–18.

39. For an interesting account of the regiment's service in the Valley, see Robert H. Cushing to mother, June 13, 1862, in Folder 3, Robert H. Cushing Collection, Special Collections 931, MSA.

40. Johnson, "Memoir of First Maryland Regiment," 147–49.

41. *Ibid.*; Edmund Barry to Judah P. Benjamin, March 3, 1862, Letter 77-B-1862, LSOW; Marshall's letter to the secretary of war for a commission is in his file, GUAAR. The Maryland Line also opened a recruiting station in Richmond to facilitate the arrival of new recruits for the 1st Maryland Infantry (C.S.). See Maj. George H. Kyle, Recruiting Officer, Maryland Line, "Bounty List for Maryland Line Recruits," May–July, 1862, in RG

Col. Johnson's optimism evaporated after the Yankee threat to Richmond diminished. When active campaigning ended, the old complaints of the enlisted men of the regiment came to a head. Col. Johnson moved the regiment to Charlottesville in July to reorganize the companies, search for new volunteers, and get the regiment back in shape. Johnson had a secondary goal of formally organizing the Maryland Line while in camp in central Virginia. The soldiers of the four "war" companies, however, were in no mood to remain as a part of the 1st Maryland Infantry (C.S.). Twelve men of Companies D, E, F, and G petitioned the secretary of war on July 18 for their discharges in a lengthy letter:

> We as representatives of those Companies beg leave to make the following statement. . . . When we enlisted at Harpers Ferry in May 1861 it was understood by all of Companies E F & G, and by many of Company D, that the term of enlistment was for one year. During that year we served the Confederate States faithfully at the Battles of Manassas Front Royal Winchester and that near Port Republic against Genl Freemont [Frémont] will attest, but at the expiration of the year we claimed and still claim our discharges. We remained in after the year as we were promised by Col Bradley T. Johnson that everything should be satisfactorily arranged. We left the Regiment not considering ourselves bound to remain longer not for the purpose of leaving the service but because we wished to have our rights, as men fighting for these rights. When some of us requested discharge from the Colonel he said that he had no power to give them but advised us to leave in a quiet way. When this advice is given to some can the leaving of any of us be called desertion? Having set forth the above facts we as representatives request that Companies D E F & G of the First Maryland Regiment be discharged and that all the members of said Companies who have left and those who now remain (and in some companies that numbered eighty there are now but six or eight with the Regiment) be discharged and paid off so that they can enlist in any branch of the service they desire.[42]

Col. Johnson wrote to the secretary of war on August 3 from Charlottesville stating firmly that his regiment had enlisted for the period of the war at Harpers Ferry and that the men at that time "were satisfied & even gratified at their honorable position—soldiers for the war instead

---

109, War Department Collection of Confederate Records, Muster and Pay Rolls for Maryland Units.

42. Petition to George W. Randolph, July 18, 1862, Letter 429-L-1862, LSOW.

of 12 months as the State forces were." Johnson also submitted testimonials from Capt. Herbert of Company D and First Lieut. Edward C. Deppish of Company G that the men of their companies were fully aware of the lengthy enlistment term when they joined the army.[43]

The commander of the beleaguered regiment railed against the intrigues of Maryland refugees in Richmond and the Confederate government's overall unsupportive stance toward Maryland forces. Johnson specifically labeled J. Alden Weston as one of main conspirators in the capital city against the 1st Maryland Infantry (C.S.). Weston had formed a battalion of Maryland infantry in Richmond in the summer of 1861 which broke up to provide additional companies to the 1st Maryland (C.S.). Johnson felt that since that time Weston had harbored a grudge against him. "There a small discontent was sedulously nurtured by parties in Richmond, of whom a man named Weston who kept a store in Pearl St. actually sent up a Muster Roll to prevent re-enlistments in the Regt. & to secure men after their present term." The Confederate War Department had, in fact, authorized Weston in April, 1862, to raise his own cavalry battalion.[44] Johnson believed Weston gained recruits for this unit at the expense of the 1st Maryland Infantry (C.S.).

While Johnson faced criticism from members of his regiment and from Marylanders in Richmond, other soldiers appealed to the Confederate government for discharge on the basis of poor health or hardship. Pvt. John O'Neill of Company D wrote to the adjutant general from Charlottesville on August 4 about his predicament:

> I have four sisters & one female cousin all of whom are orphans. I am the only one to whom they can look for aid or support, which it is impossible for me to give in my present situation & position. The property left by my parents will soon be taken away from us, unless I can immediately do something toward paying the mortgage upon it, the interest of which has been accumulating ever since the death of my father in 1855. . . . If I can gain my discharge, I could obtain a situation & relieve the wants of my relatives.[45]

43. Bradley T. Johnson to George W. Randolph, August 3, 1862, Letter 295-J-1862, LSOW.

44. *Ibid.*; J. Alden Weston to George W. Randolph, April 11, 1862, Letter 204-W-1862, LSOW.

45. John O'Neill to Gen. Samuel S. Cooper, August 4, 1862, Letter 85-O-1862, LSOW.

As the litany of complaints and requests to leave the 1st Maryland Infantry (C.S.) mounted, the Confederate government's enthusiasm for a Maryland Line dwindled. On August 11, Secretary of War George Randolph ordered the disbandment of the regiment, including the newly reenlisted companies and those organized for the war. The War Department announced that "whereas doubts have arisen with reference to the terms of service of the men of the First Maryland Regiment," the unit will "be disbanded, and members thereof, with all natives and adopted citizens of Maryland desirous of enlisting into the service of the Confederate States, are invited to enroll and organize themselves in companies, squadrons, battalions, and regiments, the officers of which are to be elected. The organization will hereby be known as the Maryland Line."[46]

The haste with which the Confederate government abandoned the regiment disheartened many Marylanders. Corp. Washington Hands of Company D stated that the order caught the regiment by surprise and asked, "Could anything be more humiliating?" Second Lieut. Thomas W. Smith, on recruiting duty in Richmond with Capt. Barry's Company C, asked for commutation money from the government on August 8. Ten days later, he received a curt reply from the War Department: "Tell him that the 1st Md. Regt. has been disbanded."[47]

At least one Richmond newspaper expressed shock at the fate of the 1st Maryland Infantry (C.S.). "The Regiment is disbanded," wrote a columnist in the *Daily Enquirer* in late August. "The work of twelve months, of 'our Friends at Richmond,' has succeeded! The only organized, recognized body in the Southern Confederacy is wiped out; and now Maryland stands—unrepresented."[48]

It was a bitter blow to Johnson and his officers as the prospects for the Maryland Line faded from sight. The regiment (except Capt. Goldsborough and his company on prisoner of war duty in Richmond) held a last formation at Gordonsville, where Johnson discharged the soldiers and

46. *Official Records*, Ser. IV, Vol. II, 42; Johnson responded to the disbandment order in a letter to George W. Randolph, August 17, 1862, Letter 332-J-1862, LSOW.

47. Washington Hands Notebook (#10361), 77, Special Collections, Alderman Library, University of Virginia, Charlottesville; Tom Wash Smith to George W. Randolph, August 8, 1862, Letter 759-S-1862, LSOW.

48. The unsigned article by "W" describes the history of the 1st Maryland Infantry (C.S.) and its efforts on many battlefields. See "The First Maryland Regiment," Richmond *Daily Enquirer*, August 25, 1862.

settled their final payments. As a last act, the 1st Maryland Infantry (C.S.) folded its colors and appointed the color guard under Edwin Selvage (who had, ironically, signed the July petition to the secretary) to escort the flag to Charlottesville to present it to Mrs. Johnson as a token of appreciation.[49]

The dissolution of the 1st Maryland Infantry (C.S.) left its officers, from lieutenant to colonel, without any duties. Some of the officers, including Johnson, Goldsborough, and Booth, joined the main army and served as volunteers during the Second Manassas and Sharpsburg campaigns. Capt. J. Louis Smith of Company F acted as an army provost marshal in Winchester in October, 1862. Other officers sought military duties in the South. Capt. Septimus H. Stewart, the regiment's quartermaster, for example, formed Company N, 2nd Regiment, Virginia State Reserves, in Richmond in 1864 and enlisted two of his old 1st Maryland Infantry (C.S.) comrades, Alexander Cross and John Cushing, Jr.[50]

Some officers, however, wanted a complete change of branch of service or location of duty from what they had seen with the 1st Maryland Infantry (C.S.) in Virginia. William Dickenson Hough, originally a private in Company H and later lieutenant in Company F, resigned on account of ill health shortly after the battle of Port Republic, perhaps because of the unsettled conditions in his company. Hough later received an appointment as midshipman and captain's clerk on the CSS *Florida*. He fell into enemy hands and became a prisoner of war off the coast of Brazil in late 1864. John F. Groshon, who had received his commission as a lieutenant in Company A at its reorganization in April, 1862, applied for the rank of captain in the Provisional Army in the spring of 1863. Groshon had been employed as a quartermaster agent in Texas since the fall of 1862.[51]

49. George W. Booth, a first lieutenant and acting adjutant, acknowledged that the "thirst for position on the part of certain prominent Marylanders who were in Richmond," combined with overall dissatisfaction within the regiment, contributed to its demise (*Personal Reminiscences*, 57–58); Johnson, "Memoir of First Maryland Regiment," 219–20; Goldsborough, *Maryland Line*, 65–66; Johnson, *Maryland*, 87–88.

50. Goldsborough, *Maryland Line*, 66; CSR, J. Louis Smith, 1st Maryland Infantry (C.S.), and CGSO; CSR, Alexander Cross, John Cushing, Jr., and Septimus H. Stewart, 1st Maryland Infantry (C.S.) and 2nd Regiment, Virginia State Reserves.

51. CSR, William D. Hough, 1st Maryland Infantry (C.S.); CSR, John F. Groshon, 1st Maryland Infantry (C.S.) and CGSO.

Several officers of the 1st Maryland Infantry (C.S.) were fortunate to have connections with high-ranking officials in Richmond. The provost marshal of Richmond, Brig. Gen. John H. Winder, was a Marylander, and he employed several Marylanders on his staff (which had a reputation among city residents as being a gang of "plug uglies"). Winder added several of the unemployed officers of the 1st Maryland Infantry to his staff. Capt. Henry McCoy of Company E received an appointment as an assistant quartermaster in late 1861 with the Quartermaster Department. He was assigned to command the Confederate military prison in Salisbury, North Carolina, in early 1862 and spent the remainder of his military career in charge of prisons. First Lieut. John Lutts, Jr., also a member of Company E, was assigned to duties with the provost marshal's office in Richmond after 1862. Capt. Barry of the newly raised Company C tried to remain as a recruiting officer for the defunct Maryland Line but eventually ended up as the chief of detectives on the Rappahannock River, where he oversaw smuggling operations between Union and Confederate lines. Later in the war Barry was assigned to Camp Sumter for prisoners of war in Andersonville, Georgia, but served there only a few months, losing his post when the number of officers was reduced in 1865.[52]

Not all the officers of the 1st Maryland Infantry (C.S.) found suitable duty after the regiment disbanded. Second Lieut. William Key Howard enlisted as a private in the 4th Virginia Cavalry Regiment in early 1863. Several months later, Howard wrote to the secretary of war requesting reinstatement as an officer. He protested that his company had enlisted for the war but had been improperly disbanded. As a private, Howard received no pay (so he claimed), and he lacked a horse (each Confederate cavalryman had to provide his own mount). To press the matter before the secretary, Howard had his wife, Clara Randolph Howard, write to the secretary from Richmond, and his mother, née Key, also requested a commission for her son in a letter smuggled from Baltimore in 1863. These tactics failed and Howard remained a private for the rest of the war.[53]

52. John B. Jones, *A Rebel War Clerk's Diary at the Confederate States Capital* (2 vols.; Philadelphia, 1866), I, 144–45; CSR, Henry McCoy, 1st Maryland Infantry (C.S.), and CSGO; Kirby and Parker, *Roll Call*, 70; CSR, John J. Lutts, 1st Maryland Infantry (C.S.); CSR, Edmund Barry, 1st Maryland Infantry (C.S.), and CGSO.

53. Clara R. Howard to unknown, August 18, 1862; Howard to President Jefferson Davis, April 17, 1863; and William Key Howard to James A. Seddon, June 1, 1863, in CSR, William K. Howard, 1st Maryland Infantry Regiment (C.S.).

Second Lieut. Edward C. Deppish rejoined the army as a substitute for J. W. Marshall at Martinsburg on September 20, 1862. Deppish apparently served as a private without complaint in the 1st Virginia Cavalry Regiment and was imprisoned as such after his capture in the fall of 1864. Joseph H. Stewart, a lieutenant in Company F and later a sergeant in the 2nd Maryland Infantry (C.S.), became distinctly unhappy with his situation. He applied for a commission in the Provisional Army in the fall of 1862 without success. After a stint as an enlisted man, the frustrated soldier (who had previously attended the United States Military Academy but was dismissed for deficient conduct and knowledge of mathematics) wrote the secretary of war in January, 1864, that "all of my resigned West Point *classmates* have received their appointments, but, for the want of influential friends in the South, my case has been *forgotten* or *discarded.*" In February, Stewart received a commission as second lieutenant but remained unassigned in Richmond. A month later, he was forced to apply for a clerkship in the Treasury Department because "with my present pay of Eighty dollars per month, I cannot *live* in the City. It may be *months* until I receive my orders, and through *necessity*, I seek this position until ordered."[54]

At least one other officer of the 1st Maryland Infantry (C.S.) took civilian employment while waiting for orders to return to duty. Francis X. Ward applied as a clerk in the Second Auditor's Office of the Confederate Treasury Department in Richmond in 1864 until the War Department approved his appointment as aide-de-camp for a divisional commander.[55]

As the Confederate government received a mounting number of applications from former officers of the disbanded Maryland regiment, the War Department realized that deactivation of the regiment had created an enormous hardship for these men. In an attempt to correct the situa-

54. CSR, Edward C. Deppish, 1st Maryland Infantry (C.S.) and 1st Virginia Cavalry Regiment; Joseph H. Stewart to President Jefferson Davis, December 1863, Letter 2817-S-1863, LAIG; to George W. Randolph, September 11, 1862, to James A. Seddon, November 23, 1862; George H. Steuart to James A. Seddon, January 28, 1864; Joseph H. Stewart to James A. Seddon, January 28, 1864; and to C. C. Memminger, March 3, 1864, all in CSR, Joseph H. Stewart, 1st Maryland Infantry (C.S.); Dorothy Rapp, U.S. Military Academy Archives, to author, August 17, 1990, concerning Stewart's cadetship at West Point.
55. CSR, Francis X. Ward, 1st Maryland Infantry (C.S.), and CGSO.

tion, the adjutant general issued a special order in March, 1863, stating that the regiment had, indeed, been improperly disbanded and directed that the "officers of the same will remain in commission and reassemble and recruit their company without delay and report to Brig. Genl. Geo. H. Stewart [Steuart] commanding Maryland forces." The order, in reality, had little meaning, and one of the officers reinstated in 1863, Lieut. Alexander Cross, left the service again in September, 1864, after "having failed to accomplish the purpose of the Order and not having been assigned to other duty."[56]

The newly unemployed officers of the 1st Maryland Infantry (C.S.) were not the only members of the regiment to experience trouble. Two former officers of the original companies of the 1st Maryland Infantry encountered significant difficulties after leaving the regiment. Capt. Henry Wellmore raised Company H at Harpers Ferry on May 22, 1861; the unit failed to gain enough recruits, and the men it did have were distributed to the other companies in the regiment on June 30. This left Wellmore and his two lieutenants, Alexander McK. Pittman and Edward H. Walter, without any command. Wellmore was captured by Union troops at Charles Town, Virginia (now West Virginia) on July 23 and sent to Fort McHenry.[57]

Maj. Gen. John A. Dix, the Union commander at Baltimore, released Wellmore on a parole of honor after a short imprisonment. The captain's arrival at his house on 160 Mulberry Street led prosecessionists in town to believe that Wellmore was a Union spy. The rumors of Wellmore's suspected traitorous activity spread to Richmond, and the former 1st Maryland officer's name was besmirched in the newspapers there. A year later, Wellmore wrote Gen. Dix asking for an exchange so that he could go south and clear his name. It is uncertain whether Wellmore was vindicated in the Confederacy, and the last entry in his service records reveals that he took the oath of allegiance in Alexandria in November, 1864, because he was tired of living in the Confederacy.[58]

56. John Cushing, Jr., and John J. Lutts to James A. Seddon, April 22, 1863, Letter 201-L-1863, LSOW; Alexander Cross to Gen. Samuel Cooper, September 22, 1864, in CSR, Alexander Cross, 1st Maryland Infantry (C.S.).

57. As late as December, 1863, Johnson tried to get the Confederate government to pay Lieut. Walter for his short service with the 1st Maryland Infantry (C.S.). See Bradley T. Johnson to James A. Seddon, December 20, 1863, Letter 8-W-1864, LSOW.

58. CSR, Henry Wellmore, 1st Maryland Infantry (C.S.).

Frank A. Tormey, a clerk in his father's law firm, served as a second lieutenant in the original Company F of the 1st Maryland Infantry (C.S.). He submitted his resignation during the summer of 1861, but the War Department did not accept it immediately. Tormey again tried to resign in January, 1862, and the assistant adjutant general noted that "this officer is doing nothing, nor has been since some time in October." Col. R. H. Chilton contacted the regiment in late December, 1861, seeking information on Tormey's case. Col. Steuart responded in early January, acknowledging that Tormey had served in the regiment until he resigned when his company was disbanded. "Had he not he would have been dismissed by a Court Martial for being a confirmed liar and utterly unfit for the position of an officer; he was of no account whatever, unable to exercise command or authority, a butt of the private soldiers and for the good of the public service and the regt. it was not deemed expedient to force him to remain in camp." The commander of the 1st Maryland Infantry believed that Tormey had been arrested in Richmond for impersonating an officer and drawing government pay. Steuart wrote the War Department that "in the name of the whole of my regt I would most earnestly and respectfully request that such steps may be taken as will free us with any pretended connection with such an individual."[59]

The disbandment of the 1st Maryland Infantry (C.S.) shattered the dream of the Maryland Line. The lack of a strong organization to which Confederate Marylanders could rally became apparent in September, 1862, when Robert E. Lee and the Army of Northern Virginia crossed the Potomac River into Maryland. Col. Johnson, appointed provost marshal of his hometown of Frederick, issued a dramatic proclamation to his fellow Marylanders on September 8:

After sixteen months of oppression more galling than the Austrian tyranny, the victorious army of the South brings freedom to your doors. Its standard now waves from the Potomac to Mason and Dixon's Line. The men of Maryland, who during the last long months have been crushed under the heel of this terrible despotism, now have the opportunity for working out their own redemption, for which they have so long waited, and suffered and hoped. . . . You must now do your part. We have arms here for you. I

59. George H. Steuart to Col. R. H. Chilton, January 8, 1862, Letter 60-S-1862, LAIG; CSR, Frank A. Tormey, 1st Maryland Infantry (C.S.), and Unfiled CSR. For an account of Tormey at Fort Delaware, see George Baylor, *Bull Run to Bull Run; or Four Years in the Army of Northern Virginia* (1900; rpr. Washington, D.C., 1983), 106.

am authorized immediately to muster in for the war companies and regiments, the companies of one hundred men each, the regiments of ten companies. Come all who wish to strike for their liberties and homes. Let each man provide himself with a stout pair of shoes, a good blanket and a tin cup—Jackson's men have no baggage. Officers are in Frederick to receive recruits, and all companies formed will be armed as soon as mustered in. Rise at once!

Johnson concluded his call to arms: "Remember the cells of Fort McHenry! Remember the dungeons of Fort Lafayette and Fort Warren; the insults to your wives and daughters, the arrests, the midnight searches of your houses! Remember these, your wrongs, and rise at once in arms and strike for liberty and right!"[60]

Soon after Johnson's proclamation, Gen. Lee issued one of his own to Marylanders, stating that "our army has come among you, and is prepared to assist you with the power of its arms in regaining the rights of which you have been despoiled." Both Johnson and Lee hoped that Marylanders would respond by supplying fresh recruits for the Confederacy. One southern correspondent claimed at Frederick in early September that "recruiting here goes on rapidly. Within two days five companies have been formed, and it is stated that from the surrounding country over seven hundred entered our ranks while *en route*." Incredibly, the journalist even reported that dozens of Pennsylvania men had joined the Confederate army.[61]

Southern liberation of Maryland proved bitterly disappointing. Lee accomplished few of his original goals in his movement northward. One of those goals, "to afford her [Maryland] an opportunity of throwing off the oppression to which she is now subject," failed dismally.[62] Recruits were few, and the state gave only a lukewarm reception to the Confederate liberators. Of the 146 junior officers of the Maryland Line, only one man, Otis Johnson, joined the army as a result of the 1862 Maryland campaign. Two other men enlisted as private soldiers in late August at Manassas just before the Confederate offensive.

60. Johnson, *Maryland*, 90–91; Richmond *Daily Examiner*, September 18, 1862.

61. Johnson, *Maryland*, 89–90; Scharf, *History of Maryland*, III, 497.

62. James V. Murfin, *The Gleam of Bayonets: The Battle of Antietam and the Maryland Campaign of 1862* (Cranbury, N.J., 1965), 63–70, 378–79; Gary W. Gallagher, ed., *Antietam: Essays on the 1862 Maryland Campaign* (Kent, 1989), 5, 37–38. For a discussion of the 1862 Maryland campaign, see Richard R. Duncan, "Marylanders and the Invasion of 1862," *Civil War History*, X (1964), 141–48.

John W. Heard of Frederick, the former editor of the Frederick *Herald,* was among the few to answer Johnson's call for Maryland volunteers in September. Col. Johnson authorized Heard to recruit a company for Confederate service although illness prevented him from carrying out this task. Heard was captured in bed at the home of George Griffith near Winchester in December and paroled to recuperate in Frederick. Several months later, Union officials arrested Heard and charged him with recruiting within federal lines. A military commission at Fort McHenry found the Confederate officer innocent of the charge in September, 1863, but the Union army held Heard as a prisoner of war at Johnson's Island until early 1865.[63]

Johnson believed that "had the First Maryland regiment been with Jackson in Frederick during the three days he was there it would have filled up to two thousand men." Johnson linked the Confederate defeat in Maryland to the disbandment of his regiment. According to this officer, "Thousands wished to enlist. Every one asked 'Where is the First Maryland?' The disappointment and chagrin at finding it disbanded was extreme." Ultimately, the loss of the 1st Maryland Infantry (C.S.), which Johnson placed at the hands of Maryland schemers in Richmond, "inflicted a more deadly blow on the interests and future chances of the State than Hicks, Winter Davis and Bradford combined."[64]

The first year of the war had not been kind to pro-Confederate forces in Maryland. They were unsuccessful in getting the state to leave the Union and join the new Confederacy, and the enemy's forces placed a firm grip on Maryland and suppressed prosouthern agitation. Thousands of Marylanders fled to the South, where they joined Confederate units in Virginia and elsewhere. Attempts to raise the Maryland Line appeared doomed after the disbandment of the 1st Maryland Infantry (C.S.) in the summer of 1862. While officers and enlisted men debated over the rights of Marylanders in the Confederate service, the central government effectively settled the question to Maryland's ultimate disadvantage. The narrow vision of many Confederate Marylanders during the first year of the war proved detrimental to the overall war effort and threatened to have severe repercussions throughout the course of the struggle.

63. CSR, John W. Heard, 2nd Maryland Infantry (C.S.); Hartzler, *Marylanders in the Confederacy,* 31.

64. Johnson, "Memoir of First Maryland Regiment," 221–22.

·6·

The Shattered Vision

The breakup of the 1st Maryland Infantry (C.S.) and the lack of Maryland volunteers during the Sharpsburg campaign embittered many southerners who had regarded Marylanders as oppressed brothers in arms during the first months of the war. A Richmond newspaper, for example, welcomed volunteers from Maryland in 1861, exclaiming that "the gallant champions of Southern rights hailing from that section will be the nest-egg from which will be hatched a brood of avengers of Maryland's insulted honor, hard to understand—terrible to encounter."[1]

Somerville Sollers of the 1st Maryland Infantry joyfully recounted his reenlistment furlough in Alabama in mid-1862 in a letter to his mother: "I cannot express to you in words the kindness & hospitality with which we were recd, not only by our relatives, but strangers, being Marylanders, was a sufficient passport, & we were feasted by the old people, & so smiled upon by fair ladies, that the expiration of our furlough was most unwelcome tidings."[2]

By the end of 1862, sentiment in the South turned against the Marylanders. John P. Marshall, a future officer in the 1st Maryland Infantry, expressed the feeling to a Confederate doctor when he applied for a position at Chimborazo Hospital in Richmond in late 1861: "As a Marylander you know the difficulties I have to encounter, and I fear some are deep set prejudices. We are looked upon as persons willing to play upon the sympathies of the public. It is with confidence then since you are a Marylander—of not being misunderstood that I apply to you for employment." Many southerners began to regard Marylanders as opportunistic freeloaders who escaped the Union draft and then enjoyed a carefree life

---

1. Richmond *Daily Dispatch*, June 1, 1861.
2. Somerville Sollers to mother, July 30, 1862, in Bowie Collection.

in Richmond. Once in the South, the exiled Marylanders had no fear of Confederate conscription or other harsh wartime acts. Marylander John H. Winder, Richmond's provost marshal, and his officers contributed to this poor impression.[3]

John B. Jones, a native of Baltimore and employee of the War Department in Richmond, expressed disgust at the fact that many of Winder's agents were policemen from his hometown or other cities in the North. "Merely petty larceny detectives, dwelling in bar-rooms, ten-pin alleys, and such places," Jones lamented. "They are illiterate men, of low instincts and desperate characters." Jones predicted that most of Winder's detectives would soon be "on the pay-rolls of Lincoln," and he thereafter vented his frustration about the Richmond provost marshal's office in the pages of his diary. A Virginia soldier also complained that the officers in his unit were all Marylanders, none of whom had been elected by the troops. The anonymous correspondent wrote in the spring of 1863: "We would be much better satisfied with our situation here if we could have Virginia officers to take command of us instead of Maryland."[4]

Even Maryland officers in Confederate service grew frustrated with the inaction of fellow Marylanders. Gilbert G. Guillette, a second lieutenant in the 2nd Maryland Infantry (C.S.), resented the reaction of Marylanders during the 1863 Gettysburg campaign. Writing to his mother that summer, Guillette asked, "What is the matter with all the young men of Maryland. Do they expect to sit quietly down and wait for our little band to come and rescue our beloved state out of the yoke that the enemy has put upon her, and they lay idle and do nothing. *Tell them shame on them*; for they are not as brave as women. Tell them that I say that every ball that is fired does not hit and every one that hits does not kill, so that they can take their chances." Guillette commented that after the war, "I

3. CSR and CSGO, John P. Marshall; Mary Elizabeth Massey, *Refugee Life in the Confederacy* (Baton Rouge, 1964), 43–45, wrote that "many of the influential people about Richmond had a certain degree of contempt for the Marylander. . . . It was explained that the Marylander fled from his state to avoid the Federal Draft, and sought shelter in Virginia and became a corrupt and troublesome element." Marylanders were blamed for numerous bad deeds in Richmond and received little praise from city newspapers. See John William Ford Hatton Memoir, 675–76, LC. For a discussion of much lambasted General Winder, see Arch Frederic Blakely, *General John H. Winder C.S.A.* (Gainesville, 1990).

4. Jones, *Rebel War Clerk's Diary*, I, 71; Richmond *Daily Examiner*, April 30, 1863.

shall not know how to meet my old associates and those that I esteemed as brothers."[5]

The southern resentment against Maryland was so prevalent that Phoebe Yates Pember found it difficult to establish a ward for Maryland troops in Richmond's Chimborazo Hospital. "It was impossible to give them their due share of attention, so great was the feeling of jealousy existing. If an invalid required special attention, and he proved to be a Marylander, though perhaps ignorant myself of the fact, many eyes watched me, and complaints were made to the nurses, and from them to the surgeons, till a report of partiality to them on my part made to the surgeon-in-chief, called forth a remonstrance on his part, and a request that all patients should be treated alike." Pember "studiously" learned not to inquire about the homes of wounded or sick patients. Faced with such hostility, Marylanders reacted by publishing letters and poems in Virginia newspapers designed to raise their flagging spirits and publicize the state's sacrifices for southern independence.[6]

Even as the 1st Maryland Infantry disintegrated, new Maryland Confederate units formed to take its place. Two new artillery units for the Army of Northern Virginia joined Andrews' 1st Maryland Battery. The 2nd Maryland Battery, or the Baltimore Light Artillery, organized in August, 1861, in Richmond under the command of a Virginia lawyer, John B. Brockenbrough. Brockenbrough joined the Rockbridge Artillery at the beginning of the war and was wounded in the face at Manassas. After his recovery, he accepted the post of captain of the Baltimore Light Artillery in September, 1861. He initially had two lieutenants as subordinates: William Hunter Griffin, a Virginia-born salesman in Baltimore as first lieutenant and William Bennett Bean as second lieutenant.

By mid-September, 1861, the battery had three officers and fifty-five enlisted men at Camp Dimmock, and two months later, the battery's orderly sergeant, James T. Wilhelm, became third lieutenant. As a part of the Maryland Line in the 1862 Valley campaign, the battery showed

5. G. G. Guillette to mother, July 17, 1863, Erick Davis Collection (Transcript copy of letter provided by Thomas G. Clemens).

6. Phoebe Yates Pember, *A Southern Woman's Story: Life in Confederate Richmond*, ed. Bell I. Wiley (St. Simons Island, 1959), 44. An article examining Maryland's role in the Confederacy appeared in the Richmond *Daily Examiner*, November 10, 1862; two poems, "The March of the Maryland Line" and "Rise Maryland," appeared in the same paper on August 23 and November 25, 1862, respectively; for other poems about Maryland during the war, see Newman, *Maryland and the Confederacy*, 153–73.

its prowess at Winchester, Harrisonburg, and Cross Keys. One Confederate general commended Brockenbrough's men for their excellent work and awarded the unit with two captured Union guns. "I want you to have them," Gen. Richard Taylor proclaimed, "for what I saw of you yesterday, I know they will be in good hands."[7]

In early 1862, Joseph Forrest of St. Marys County organized Marylanders who had crossed the Potomac River to the Northern Neck of Virginia into an artillery battery known as the Chesapeake Artillery. It was formed as a Virginia organization in February, 1862, and Forrest served as captain with William D. Brown and John E. Plater as first and second lieutenants respectively. Forrest and Plater had both attended Georgetown College, the captain in the 1830s, his subaltern an 1857 graduate. Upon transferring to Camp Lee in Richmond for training in June, the battery reorganized and the men elected Lieut. Brown as captain, removing Forrest from command. Plater became first lieutenant, and John Grason, a private, was elevated to second lieutenant. A critical shortage of cannon and other artillery implements prevented the battery from entering active service until the summer of 1862.[8]

A third organization made its debut in 1862 when Col. Johnson disbanded his regiment. A group of Marylanders, members of Gaither's 2nd Company K, 1st Virginia Cavalry Regiment, refused to reenlist under Virginia's flag. Instead they gathered in Richmond in May to organize their own Maryland cavalry company. From a nucleus of just eighteen volunteers, the company grew rapidly as Marylanders throughout Virginia learned about the new unit. The volunteers elected officers, most of whom had been officers of the old Company K. Ridgely Brown, a twenty-eight-year old Montgomery County farm manager, was chosen as captain from his previous rank as first lieutenant. The unit selected Frank A. Bond as first lieutenant from his former rank of second lieutenant with Company K. Thomas Griffith, a former third lieutenant, became second lieutenant, while Sergeant James A. V. Pue was voted third lieutenant. The company participated in the fighting in the Shenandoah Valley, scouting for Jackson's army while Lieutenant Bond served as acting adjutant general for Gen. Steuart.[9]

7. Goldsborough, *Maryland Line*, 277.

8. *Ibid.*, 319; Ammen, "Maryland Troops in the Confederate Army," 178; Plater and Forrest files, GUAAR; Margaret K. Fresco interview, November 9, 1990.

9. Goldsborough, *Maryland Line*, 165–66; Horace Edwin Hayden, "The First Maryland Cavalry, C.S.A.," *SHSP*, V (1878), 251–53; John Gill, *Reminiscences of Four Years as a*

Despite the discontent felt throughout the South in 1862 over Maryland's wartime role, two new organizations formed that fall. The Maryland Cavalry, under Capt. Ridgely Brown, expanded into a battalion with the addition of five new companies. Mustered into service on November 25, 1862, the battalion under now–Lieut. Col. Brown later served as the 1st Maryland Cavalry Battalion (C.S.). At the same time, a new infantry battalion took the place of the old 1st Maryland Infantry with seven (later eight) companies in late 1862 and early 1863. The 2nd Maryland Infantry Battalion (C.S.) (originally designated as the 1st Maryland Infantry Battalion) had as its commander a former company commander in the original Maryland regiment, James R. Herbert. Both of the new battalions contained veterans from the 1st Maryland Infantry and other Confederate organizations as well as fresh recruits from Maryland.[10]

Even with these new units, the war lost much of its glamour for Confederate officers during 1862. The disappointment of Marylanders over the conduct of the war and the increasing violence exhibited toward civilians embittered many of them. Some officers developed a sense of fatalism about their chances of surviving the war. Robert Lemmon, still an enlisted man at the Battle of Kernstown in March, wrote home of his observations during the fight: "I amazed myself watching the countenances of those about me, some had their brows elevated & their pupils dilated showing a greater or lesser degree of fear. Others were only grave or their stern set features only showed resolution[,] of the latter class was Robt. C. Noonan of Frederick, Md., who was acting as our 2d Lieutenant. He remarked to me as a man told him to dodge the shells 'Lemon, I have come to the conclusion that if I am to die by a shell, why I'll die that's all.'" Before the battle was over, Noonan received a fatal wound. Lemmon commented, "Poor fellow, his hour was rapidly approaching." Contemplating his own life, Lemmon stated, "I think I am much changed since this war [began] in many respects tho' not in all."[11]

A year after the Battle of Harrisonburg, Lieut. Stone of the 2nd Maryland Infantry (C.S.) recalled the death of his former company com-

Private Soldier in the Confederate Army, 1861–1865 (Baltimore, 1904); Edward R. Rich, *Comrades Four* (New York, 1907); Joseph R. Stonebraker, *A Rebel of '61* (New York, 1899); Mettam, "Civil War Memoirs"; and Charles Ketterwell Letters, 1st Maryland Cavalry (C.S.), in Mrs. John H. Hopkins Collection, Letters and Other Memorabilia of the United Daughters of the Confederacy, Howard County, MSA.

10. Goldsborough, *Maryland Line*, 85–89.

11. Robert Lemmon to unknown, April 3, 1862, in Lemmon Papers.

mander, Capt. Michael S. Robertson: "Captain Robertson was detailing to me the future pleasure he would have after we should be mustered out of service. This was just one hour before the fatal bullet pierced his body killing him almost instantly." Stone remembered that "one hour before his death I warned him of the uncertainty of the future but to improve the present as that alone was his."[12]

Death or injury on the battlefield paid little regard to personalities, as Lemmon discovered at Kernstown. In a series of letters to his mother, Lemmon related the story of two Confederate officers at the battle. Capt. J. Pembroke Thom, a Virginia-born resident of Baltimore who commanded Company C of the 1st Virginia Infantry Battalion, received a wound in the wrist at Kernstown, and another bullet grazed his thigh. A third round struck Thom in the chest but hit a Bible in Thom's breast pocket. Thom's first lieutenant survived the battle unscathed, with a pack of cards in his pocket. Thus, Lemmon wrote, "both God & the devil looked after their own."[13]

Just after the disbandment of the 1st Maryland Infantry (C.S.), Capt. Murray became inflamed by the savagery of the Union army in northern Virginia. He wrote his sister in August, 1862: "If you ever get our papers you will see what the vandals—of Pope's army are doing to our people. Our government has at last said it shall be stopped cost what it may History stands appalled at their fiendish outrages. They dare not meet in the field the sons and brothers of those whom they cowardly insult because they are helpless." Murray demanded that "the law of retaliation is to be the law of our land & with a desperate people maddened to a degree beyond endurance it will be enforced to the letter."[14]

Murray found that he had changed during the war, as he wrote in 1863: "The happiest [day] I have ever spent in the South was I think the eight of June at Cross Keys I with rifle in hand had 15 others 20 most beautiful shots at a regiment of Yanks bearing their flag three different times did it fall in the dust under our fire. My heart danced for joy as the cheers of our dear little regiment made the echoes sing." Pondering the situation, Murray noted, "How strange for a people living in happiness together for so many years to delight and rejoice at the shot that hurls their now most bitter enemy to eternity."[15]

12. Clemens, ed., "'Diary' of John H. Stone," 130.
13. Robert Lemmon to mother, April 3, 12, 1862, in Lemmon Papers.
14. William H. Murray to sister, August 15, 1862, in Murray Letters.
15. William H. Murray to unknown, 1863 (exact date unknown), in Murray Letters.

The principles of honorable engagement slowly gave way as the war grew increasingly more violent. Capt. George W. Booth (who was promoted in 1863 for valor and skill) allowed one of his men to rob a Union prisoner of a silver watch. Booth reasoned that if the watch was not taken on the field, the Yankee would surely lose it when he was sent to the rear, and the man who captured the enemy soldier was more justified in taking enemy property than someone in the rear echelon. Booth did offer to pay the Union private three dollars for his extra pair of trousers, a bargain the northerner felt it wise to accept.[16]

During a sharp engagement at Greenland Gap in April, 1863, stubborn Union resistance infuriated the men of the 1st Maryland Cavalry (C.S.). When the Confederates finally subdued the Union holdouts in a church, the officers had to restrain their men from slaughtering the federal captives. After refusing repeated requests by the Confederates to surrender, the federal troops bitterly contested passage through the mountains and inflicted severe casualties among the Confederate brigade. The Marylanders lost a total of eleven men, including five of the unit's seven officers wounded.[17]

Lieut. Stone of the 2nd Maryland Infantry (C.S.) expressed horror at the lack of Christian sensibility shown by some of his fellow officers. Stationed in the Shenandoah Valley, Stone, a devout Catholic, wrote, "To-day a Priest visited our Camp. It is needless for me to say he is a welcome visitor. Tomorrow he will hear confessions & say Mass. This will give the Catholics of our Regiment [battalion] an opportunity of attending their religious duties, which they have not had an opportunity of doing during the past 2 months." In April, 1863, Stone had the sad duty of burying a member of the battalion who died of a "congestive chill." Unable to locate a priest, the Marylanders buried their comrade near camp. Just two hours after the funeral, "a race was made between two horses owned by Lt Blackstone [Henry C. Blackiston] the other by Lt Dorsey [William H. B. Dorsey] of the Cavalry [1st Maryland Cavalry (C.S.)]." Stone wrote that "the race was run over a portion of the same ground over which the funeral had just passed. This was too bad for men professing christianity. In vindication of our holy riligion, neither of them

16. Booth, *Personal Reminiscences*, 112–13.

17. Fritz Haselberger and Mark Haselberger, "The Battle of Greenland Gap," *West Virginia History*, XXVIII (1967), 285–304.

are Catholic." To make matters worse, the lieutenant added, "and this on Easter Sunday."[18]

Maryland's Confederate soldiers became weary of the increasingly heavy toll the war exacted. In the fall of 1863, Lieut. Samuel T. Mc-Cullough of the 2nd Maryland Infantry (C.S.) recorded in his diary that members of his battalion had deserted to the enemy and even committed self-mutilation to avoid duty. McCullough, however, commented that these men were "not Marylanders." On September 5, First Lieut. James S. Franklin commanded a squad from the 2nd Maryland Infantry that executed ten North Carolinians found guilty by a court-martial of desertion and murder. "Though I have seen death in its most horrid forms," McCullough wrote, "I never felt more gloomy and solemn than on this occasion."[19]

By the summer of 1864, Confederate forces were using counterterror measures against the enemy. The movement of Jubal A. Early's troops into Maryland in July, 1864, was accompanied by the ransoming of Frederick and drunkenness, looting, and burning by Confederates. The 1st and 2nd Maryland Cavalry Battalions (C.S.) participated in the abortive raid to free Confederate prisoners at Point Lookout prison camp in southern Maryland under now–Brig. Gen. Johnson. The raiders managed to sever communications around Baltimore and Washington as well as generally frighten Unionists but had little effect on the campaign itself. The destruction of the Maryland governor's country estate by a detachment of Maryland cavalry under the command of Second Lieut. Henry C. Blackiston was just one of the controversial actions of the campaign. The burning marked a change in Confederate policy and was done as revenge for destruction of the Virginia governor's house in Lexington, Virginia, by Union troopers.[20] Even the noted "Yankee killer" of the 1st Maryland

18. Clemens, ed., " 'Diary' of John H. Stone," 118–19, 127.

19. Diary entry for September 5, 1863, in McCullough Diaries and Letters, Hotchkiss Papers.

20. B. F. Cooling, *Jubal Early's Raid on Washington, 1864* (Baltimore, 1989), 27–29, 157–76; Bradley T. Johnson, "My Ride Around Baltimore in Eighteen Hundred and Sixty-Four," *SHSP,* XXX (1902), 215–25; Geoffrey W. Fielding, ed., "Gilmor's Field Report of His Raid in Baltimore County," *Maryland Historical Magazine,* XLVII (1952), 234–39; Booth, *Personal Reminiscences,* 123–28; Gilmor, *Four Years in the Saddle,* 191–203. The increasing bitterness of the war can also be seen in the death of First Lieut. Walter Bowie of Company F, 43rd Battalion, Virginia Partisan Rangers. Bowie, a Marylander and a

Cavalry (C.S.), Capt. George M. Emack, wrote after Early's raid, "I know the people of Maryland will never want to see us again. So many of our troops acted badly, and no discrimination between Southern and Northern."[21]

Shortly after Early's assault on Washington, D.C., Confederate cavalry reentered northern territory on a raid into Pennsylvania. Arriving at Chambersburg in the early morning hours of July 30, Brig. Gen. John McCausland with his brigade and Gen. Bradley T. Johnson's brigade demanded payment from the town elders. The councilmen refused to submit to rebel threats, and McCausland, obeying Early's orders, burned the town. The destruction of Chambersburg, with damage ranging up to $1.5 million, was readily denounced by Unionists and opposed by many of Early's own soldiers. McCausland passed the command to destroy Chambersburg to Maj. Harry Gilmor, in charge of the Maryland cavalry battalions, who at once set fire to the town's buildings and homes. Reports of looting marred the operation, but Gilmor followed orders in destroying virtually every structure in Chambersburg. He did, however, spare the house of a woman whose husband, a Union officer, had been generous to southerners in the Shenandoah Valley. Gilmor later wrote, "The burning of Chambersburg was an awful sight, nor could I look on without deep sorrow, although I had been hardened by such scenes in Virginia. . . . Who, then, taking a dispassionate view, will condemn our government for this act of righteous retribution."[22]

At least two officers in the Maryland Line submitted their resignations in protest of the conduct of Confederate troops during the Chambersburg raid. Second Lieut. William B. Bean of the 2nd Maryland Battery, which accompanied the cavalry on the raid, wrote angrily on August 9:

> My sense of honor and rights as a man, and my duty as a christian to my fellow beings, in view of the damning outrages perpetrated by our troops in the recent invasion of Maryland and Pennsylvania, will not permit me

member of John S. Mosby's command, led an abortive mission to kidnap Governor Bradford in October, 1864. They failed to do so, and Bowie was killed after his band of guerrillas robbed a store in Montgomery County (James O. Hall, "Marylanders in the Civil War: The Death of Walter Bowie," *Maryland Line*, X [1989], 2–3).

21. George M. Emack to Dora, July 27, 1864, in Emack Papers; Richard R. Duncan, "Maryland's Reaction to Early's Raid in 1864: A Summer of Bitterness," *Maryland Historical Magazine*, LXIV (1969), 248–79.

22. Freeman, *Lee's Lieutenants*, III, 571–72; Gilmor, *Four Years in the Saddle*, 209–12.

longer to fill the post I now occupy, to take place immediately, and do not hesitate to say, after waiting a reasonable time for the acceptance of this resignation I will not serve another day in this army, feeling as I do, that the disgrace of being cashiered would not be so great a dishonor, as indirectly lending my aid to the robbery of villages and burning of the houses of defenseless women and children.[23]

General Early immediately placed Bean under arrest and sent him to the army stockade in Staunton. The general could not understand his resignation "after all the outrages committed by the enemy in the Confederate States, & also in the native state of this officer." Early claimed that he was unaware of any outrages by southern troops in Maryland. Bean eventually reconsidered his action and wrote the adjutant general in Richmond on August 22: "My letter was written under a misapprehension with regard to the burning of Chambersburg and under the influence of excitement and indignation at outrages committed in my native State, Maryland, and I acknowledge not such as my calmer moments would have dictated and I respectfully ask that it be overlooked." The secretary of war subsequently dropped the charges of "mutinous insubordinate conduct" against Bean and ordered him to his unit. Even so, Bean remained uncertain whether his explanation had arrived in Richmond, and he submitted another copy of his August letter in March, 1865.[24]

Twenty-six-year-old John W. Goodman, also a second lieutenant in the 2nd Maryland Battery, was indignant at the conduct of Confederate forces and tendered his resignation in early September. "Not wishing to be longer connected with the army after the many individual acts of robbery and pillaging committed during the late invasion of Maryland & Pennsylvania and being conscientiously opposed to burning the houses of defenseless women and children in retaliation," Goodman immediately requested his release from the army. Gen. Early took offense at the junior officer's claim and demanded that Goodman be demoted to the ranks. Goodman's battalion commander thought that the "action of Lieut. Goodman is unmilitary & objectionable." As Goodman's letter of resignation made its way through the army's bureaucracy, Gen. Lee recom-

23. William B. Bean to Capt. J. Louis Smith, August 25, 1864, enclosing William B. Bean to Gen. Samuel Cooper, August 9, 1864, Letter 2353-B-1864, LAIG.

24. Endorsement, Jubal Early, August 30, 1864, to William B. Bean to Gen. Samuel Cooper, August 24, 1864, Letter 2458-B-1864, LAIG; Bean to Cooper, March 11, 1865, Letter 443-B-1865, LAIG.

mended Goodman's discharge and "that this officer be sent beyond the lines." The Confederate government dropped him from the service in early March, 1865, although Union troops paroled him as a Confederate officer in Winchester several weeks later.[25]

The war's increasing severity failed to dim the chivalric nature of the Maryland junior officers. A group of Union prisoners captured in the spring of 1863 "feelingly thanked" Lieut. Stone, who escorted them from the Shenandoah Valley to prison camp in Richmond. "They assured me, should the fate of war ever place me in their keeping I would receive none but the kindest treatment." Later that year, Lieut. Col. Herbert placed a notice in the New York *Herald* describing the last minutes on earth of Capt. David Brown. An officer in a New York regiment, Brown died of wounds received at the First Battle of Manassas. Col. Herbert (then a captain) "did all I could do to alleviate his suffering and stayed with him until his death." Herbert saved some letters from Brown's wife and his gold watch, which he returned to the widow after his own capture at Gettysburg.[26]

The plight of innocent civilians did not go unnoticed by Maryland's Confederate officers. Thomas H. Tolson, a young second lieutenant in the 2nd Maryland Infantry (C.S.), recorded in his diary a scene near Cold Harbor in June, 1864: "This morning we passed two families thus driven from their homes. They were compelled to leave without so much as a change of clothing. With the rest was a party of children nearly starved, and when one of the boys gave them a piece of bacon (we had no bread to give them) they eagerly devoured it raw. We sent them part of our rations when they came." Tolson added, "These scenes of suffering sicken men, and would to God this unnatural strife were ended."[27]

The war certainly did not dampen the interest of the Maryland officers in matters of the heart. Whenever the opportunity presented itself, officers and men paid visits to women in the neighborhood and spent many hours enjoying their company. One officer, Capt. George Thomas of the 2nd Maryland Infantry (C.S.), met his future wife, Ellen O. Beall, in a Richmond hospital while he was recuperating from severe wounds re-

25. John W. Goodman to Gen. Samuel Cooper, September 4, 1864, in CSR, John W. Goodman, 2nd Maryland Battery (C.S.).

26. Clemens, ed., "'Diary' of John H. Stone," 129; New York *Herald*, August 19, 1863, in Herbert's petition for presidential pardon, Amnesty Papers.

27. Ammen, "Maryland Troops in the Confederate Army," 149.

ceived at Gettysburg and Pegram's Farm. Maryland officers attracted attention from southern women for their gallantry in battle and their bravery in escaping from Yankee clutches.[28] Mary Louisa Kealhofer of Hagerstown recorded her anguish after the Battle of Gettysburg: "My heart sickens at the thought of these noble men—wounded & suffering & no friendly hand near. Maryland has suffered deeply—dreadfully. Last night I felt as if my brain was on fire—the constant anxiety is fearful to one deeply interested." Worried not only about her future husband, William F. Giles, Jr., "Lutie" expressed great concern about other Maryland officers: "I've just heard that our dear gallant Henry Douglas has been mortally wounded. I cannot, will not believe it. His last words—how they sing in my ears—'If I am wounded I will be carried straight here & you & your Ma must nurse me.'"[29]

A woman living in Shepherdstown wrote about the arrival of Maryland troops in the summer of 1864. "George [Emack of the 1st Maryland Cavalry (C.S.)] was almost the first one I saw. He rode up to the door looking so *brave* and *handsome*, I almost felt like kissing him, but I knew he would have been *shocked* by such an outburst of enthusiasm, so I restrained myself. I was so delighted to see him, and could hardly talk fast enough." She was so impressed with the Marylanders that she thought that "the Yanks are beginning to see that the Rebels are not so 'insignificant' as they thought them, but can accomplish everything they want to. I saw a *great many* of my friends, and made numerous acquaintances, as we do every time they come."[30]

Harry Gilmor of Baltimore represented the beau ideal of the Confederate Maryland officer corps. Dashing and brave, Gilmor was twenty-three years old at the outbreak of the war when he enlisted in Turner Ashby's cavalry in the Shenandoah Valley. Commissioned in the 12th Virginia

28. Pogue, *Yesterday in Old St. Mary's County*, 165. A granddaughter of John C. Calhoun of South Carolina, living in Maryland in 1864, exclaimed when she met some Maryland officers, "They were *so* handsome. So noble looking, Oh!" (Charles M. McGee, Jr., and Ernest M. Lander, Jr., *A Rebel Came Home: The Diary and Letters of Floride Clemson, 1863–1866* [rev. ed.; Columbia, 1989], 37).

29. Fletcher M. Green, "A People at War: Hagerstown, Maryland, June 15–August 31, 1863," *Maryland Historical Magazine*, XL (1945), 258. For a Maryland woman's concern about officers from her state in the Charlottesville hospital, see Kevin Conley Ruffner, "A Maryland Refugee in Virginia, 1863," *Maryland Historical Magazine*, LXXXIX (1994), 447–52.

30. Nannie to Dora, August 17, 1864, in Emack Papers.

Cavalry Regiment in 1862, Gilmor went on to form his own battalion of partisan rangers in 1863. His exploits on the field attracted much attention, including this unusual, and forward, letter from Eva Lee, a teenaged girl in Staunton in the spring of 1864:

> The pleasure I have experienced in your society the few times I have been so happy makes me feel anxious to solicit another, or rather, *many more* such opportunities. I am so perfectly pleased with what I have seen of you that I *entreat* your permission to cultivate a more intimate acquaintance. It may surprise you when I tell you I have long *loved* you with the utmost fondness but till this moment could never resolve to make a disclosure of my possessions. Say then my dear Sir will you permit me to make you an offer of my hand and heart? Will you suffer me to indulge the pleasing expectation of receiving from you a return of mutual love? I can safely say you will never regret the slip for my friends have always told me I was gentle, lovely, and amiable and the greatest of inducements I have a nice little fortune of my own. . . . By understanding to accept my proposal and by uniting your destiny with mine you will as I have said make me the happiest among women. Then shall my life be devoted to the constant promotion of your happiness.[31]

Few soldiers received offers of this nature from southern women. For many Maryland officers, life was often lonely away from family and home. Communications with their family members in Maryland were infrequent. The mother of the Gilmor brothers (Harry had two brothers serving as officers in his battalion) wrote in 1863 that "we are obliged to be very careful about holding any correspondence with the 'Confederacy' or we will have the 'skunk' after us." In fact, Sarah Hutchins of Baltimore was sentenced by a Union court-martial to five years' imprisonment in 1864 for corresponding with Harry Gilmor and giving him a sword.[32]

Federal authorities often intruded into the personal affairs of the families of Maryland's Confederate officers. The conduct of Union soldiers disgusted the mourners of Capt. William D. Brown of the 4th Maryland Battery. After he was killed at Gettysburg, his family held a funeral service at Greenmount Cemetery in Baltimore on July 31, 1863. W. Jefferson Buchanan, a former enlisted man in the 1st Maryland Battery and later

31. Eva Lee to Maj. Harry Gilmor, April 9, 1864, in Harry Gilmor Papers, MS 1288, Manuscripts Division, MHS.

32. Mary Gilmor to Richard Gilmor, October 2, 1863, *ibid.*; Baltimore *American*, November 26, 1864.

a staff officer, wrote, "Not only is there in Maryland on the part of her oppressors no regard for the Southerner dying, but insult is heaped on him when dead." As Brown's coffin was about to be placed in the ground, Union soldiers arrested the male members of the funeral party. "The coffin was then broken open and *a new Confederate uniform* in which his friends had lain him stripped from the frigid limbs of the resistless soldier."[33] Death provided no shelter from the war and its bitterness.

For other officers, the lack of news from home created hardships. Second Lieut. Gilbert G. Guillette of the 2nd Maryland Infantry (C.S.) asked his mother, "Why have you or Sis not written for so long a time for you could have done so if you had wished to for all the boys from that neighborhood received letters as late as the 1st of July [1863]. If you knew what pleasure it gave me to receive a letter from home you would write oftener for I have not received but one letter from you and one from Hellen in two years."[34]

Occasionally Maryland officers expressed their homesickness and loneliness. Robert G. H. Carroll, brother of a former governor of Maryland and aide-de-camp to Gen. Ewell, wrote his new wife from Orange Court House in 1863: "I am in the worst possible spirits, as my only real wish is to go back & see you. Oh my darling why can I not catch you in my arms & kiss you a thousand times. This is not the proper style for a soldier but I am entirely unwarlike now. I want to be free of this place."[35]

Other officers were dismayed at the conduct of women during the war. Capt. Emack, for example, expressed concern when he learned that a Maryland girl had married a Unionist. "It seems all the girls in Maryland are taking advantage of our absence and getting married to the first handsome face who proposes, laying aside politics. None of us can have any regard for any lady who would lower herself to be wedded to a Yankee."

---

33. Buchanan, *Maryland's Hope*, 22; Newman, *Maryland and the Confederacy*, 181.

34. G. G. Guillette to mother, July 17, 1863, in Davis Collection. The capture of correspondence between the Confederacy and Maryland may account for the lack of communication with Maryland's officers in Virginia. For examples of such "intercepted" letters, see RG 109, War Department Collection of Confederate Records, Entry 189, Intercepted Letters, Baltimore, Maryland, and Entry 199, Records of Confederates in Union Prisons, Station Rolls, "Maryland Duplicates," NA.

35. "Harper" Carroll to wife, September 20, 1863, in Robert Goodloe Harper Carroll Papers, MS 1683, Manuscripts Division, MHS.

Lieut. Stone had an unusual encounter with a young woman in Richmond. Sitting on a bench near the Confederate capitol, Stone was approached by a girl who claimed to be a refugee from Texas. After talking about her life in Richmond and the lack of clothing, the fourteen-year-old asked Stone for some tobacco. She claimed, "I do not chew because I like tobacco, but merely as a past time." Not wishing to learn more about this strange girl, the Maryland officer deemed that "it was time to leave." Whether Stone's "adventure" could have gone further, he did not say. Medical records of Maryland Confederate officers suggest that some of Maryland's junior officers indulged in the pleasures of Richmond's numerous bawdyhouses. At least four officers received medical treatment for syphilis or gonorrhea in hospitals during the war.[36]

Visiting prostitutes went unpunished in the Confederate army, although the army took disciplinary action against several Maryland junior officers for official misconduct. Eugene Digges, a native of Charles County and an 1857 Georgetown College graduate, faced trial before a general court-martial at Swift Run Gap in the spring of 1862 for allowing a prisoner to escape. Col. Johnson accused Digges, a second lieutenant in the 1st Maryland Infantry (C.S.), of violating the 81st Article of War (concerning the proper release of military prisoners) and neglect of duty. While serving as officer of the guard on May 11, Digges allowed a deserter from the regiment to go to the woods to relieve himself. The unescorted prisoner absconded. Claiming that regimental orders did not forbid prisoners from moving about camp without guard, Digges maintained his innocence. The court-martial, however, found Digges guilty of the charges and specifications and ordered his arrest for ten days.[37]

As the war continued, military infractions committed by Maryland's captains and lieutenants increased in severity. Lieut. George Howard of the 1st Maryland Cavalry (C.S.) was found guilty of absence without leave in 1863 and sentenced to forfeit one month's pay. The court also ordered that the battalion commander publish Howard's sentence before a formation of the entire unit. The army dropped Second Lieut. Benjamin

36. George M. Emack to sister, April 5, 1863, in Emack Papers; Clemens, ed., "'Diary' of John H. Stone," 115; CSR, John W. Goodman, Thomas P. Lecompte, William I. Rasin, John B. Wells, various units.

37. "Proceedings of a General Court Martial which convened near Swift Run Gap, Va. by Virtue of General Orders No. 12, HdQr 3rd Divn. May 9th 1862," transcript in CSR, Eugene Digges, 1st Maryland Infantry Regiment (C.S.).

F. Divinney of Company G, 2nd Maryland Infantry (C.S.), for absence without leave as it did another officer in that company because he had never served a day in the unit.[38]

John E. Plater, an officer in the Chesapeake Artillery, was tried and convicted in September, 1863, of misbehavior before the enemy at Gettysburg and conduct unbecoming an officer and a gentleman. During the fighting in July, Plater abandoned a caisson without orders and then tried to blame the loss on his commanding officers. When recommending a successor to command the 4th Maryland Battery after Capt. Brown's death at Gettysburg, Maj. Snowden Andrews (formerly commander of the 1st Maryland Battery) advocated the promotion of First Lieut. Charles S. Contee of the 1st Maryland Battery. Contee's "uniform Soldierly conduct generally, and in particular for gallantry in the battle of Jordan Spring (near Winchester)," Andrews wrote, "attracted the attention of the Division by the manner in which he repulsed some four or five charges of Infantry, and holding a bridge for one hour and a half against the enemys Sharpshooters."[39]

In contrast, Andrews found "no officer with the Chesapeake Artillery [who] is competent or suitable to be made Capt." The court-martial sentenced Lieut. Plater to be dismissed from the army although President Davis later commuted this sentence to a suspension from duty for four months. Plater returned to duty in February, 1864, only to be dropped four months later.[40]

Although Maryland units suffered from desertion throughout the war, only a handful of officers abandoned their posts. Those who did desert were, for the most part, men who had lost their positions in the army. Capt. Henry Wellmore of the original Company H, 1st Maryland Infantry (C.S.), surrendered to Union officials in 1864. Charles C. Edelin, the notorious "Lum Cooper," fell into enemy hands under questionable cir-

38. General Orders Number 100, November 20, 1863, in RG 109, War Department Collection of Confederate Records, Orders and Circulars Issued by the Army of the Potomac and the Army and Department of Northern Virginia, C.S.A., 1861–65, M921, NA; Bradley T. Johnson to Gen. Samuel Cooper, January 13, 1864, Letter 14-J-1864, LAIG.

39. R. Snowden Andrews to Lieut. Col. A. S. Pendleton, August 6, 1863, in CSR, Charles J. Raine, Lee Battery (Virginia).

40. Bradley T. Johnson to Gen. Samuel Cooper, April 26, 1864, Letter 689-P-1864, LAIG.

cumstances. Alexander McK. Pittman, the one-armed filibuster veteran in Wellmore's company, briefly rejoined a Confederate outfit in 1862 and worked as a superintendent in a saltworks in Alabama. He gave himself up to a Union detective at Lancaster Wharf on the Potomac River in early 1865 and sought to take the oath of allegiance. Instead, Union officials in Washington placed Pittman in prison at Fort Delaware. Second Lieut. Joseph P. Quinn of the 2nd Maryland Infantry (C.S.) was captured "through his own indiscretion" at Winchester in 1863. Quinn, who claimed to be a British subject, ended up at a Union prisoner of war camp in Ohio.[41]

A former enlisted man in the 1st Maryland Infantry (C.S.), James A. Davis, was elected lieutenant in the 2nd Maryland Infantry (C.S.) in 1862. After he was wounded in the back at Gettysburg, a board of examiners ruled on his competency as an officer in December, 1863. Davis, a resident of Dorchester County, tendered his resignation in January, 1864, citing physical disability. Davis remained in Virginia until October, when he and an enlisted man from the 1st Maryland Battery left Richmond for Northumberland County. After crossing the Potomac River in a small boat, Davis went to Salisbury, where he reported to the Union provost marshal. Davis gave his captors a simple reason for his leaving the Confederacy: "I left because I got tired of the war & wanted to come home."[42]

One of the most notorious officers in a Confederate Maryland unit staunchly supported the southern cause in 1861. Christopher C. Callan, an Irish-born resident of Georgetown, District of Columbia, enlisted in Company H, 7th Virginia Infantry Regiment, at the beginning of the war. Callan attended Georgetown College and worked as a lawyer before the war. After being discharged from the Virginia regiment in late 1861, Callan wrote the secretary of war outlining his interest in obtaining employment with the Confederate government: "Having rendered myself obnoxious to the Abolitionist dynasty at Washington, I was compelled to abandon my practice, leave my property (which was very valuable, and I learn is now in the hands of the Enemy) desert my wife and children, and escape to the safer and more hospitable shores of Virginia." Callan added,

41. Pittman statement, in Turner-Baker Files; CSR, Joseph P. Quinn, 2nd Maryland Infantry (C.S.); Goldsborough, *Maryland Line*, 95.

42. CSR, James A. Davis, 2nd Maryland Infantry (C.S.).

"I sacrifice all my feelings of military pride and ambition for rank in the one better and purer feeling of a desire to serve the Cause of Southern independence in any capacity."[43]

Frustrated in his attempts to make a living in Richmond as a lawyer, Callan tried to organize an "Irish Regiment" or "Brigade" in early 1862. He instead settled for a captaincy in Maj. John Scott's 24th Battalion, Virginia Partisan Rangers, "a rowdy and useless unit."[44] Callan found that "in the meantime the scales fell from my eyes. Secession deprived of its novelty, lost all its glittering charms, and I discovered that instead of battling for liberty and independence, I was struggling to build up a despicable tyranny." Callan remained an officer in the partisan battalion although the Confederate army imprisoned him at Castle Thunder in Richmond because of the numerous desertions from his command. Claiming to have paid $800 to the "Chief of Detective Police" in Richmond, Callan managed to gain his release from prison.[45]

Evading army officials until February, 1863, Callan was once again thrown in prison until the summer, when, "at the suggestion of one of Gen. Winder's officers the Captaincy was offered" to Callan, who formed a new company. Callan raised the Winder Rangers for cavalry service, but it ended up in the 2nd Maryland Infantry (C.S.) in August, 1863. A month later, Callan was court-martialed for signing false returns and embezzling unit funds. Through a technicality, the court acquitted Callan, although Gen. Lee refused to approve the court's findings. Callan's dissatisfaction with the Confederacy grew after this point, and he encouraged his men to desert. Taking advantage of President Lincoln's amnesty proclamation of December 8, 1863, Callan left the Confederate army in January, 1864, near Gordonsville, Virginia, and gave himself up to Union cavalry pickets near Warrenton. Thrown into Old Capitol Prison in

43. For a full description of Callan's life in his own words, see Kevin Conley Ruffner, "Civil War Letters of a Washington Rebel," *Washington History: Magazine of the Historical Society of Washington, D.C.*, IV (1992–93), 56–71; Callan file, GUAAR; Christopher C. Callan to Judah P. Benjamin, November 27, 1861, Letter 7925-1861, LSOW.

44. Christopher C. Callan to Judah P. Benjamin, February 24, 1862, Letter 25-C-1862, LSOW; CSR, Christopher C. Callan, 24th Battalion, Virginia Partisan Rangers; Robert K. Krick, *Lee's Colonels: A Biographical Register of the Field Officers of the Army of Northern Virginia* (2nd rev. ed.; Dayton, 1984), 288.

45. Christopher C. Callan to President Lincoln, February 22, 1864, in Turner-Baker Files.

Washington, Callan appealed to President Lincoln for aid and departed upon taking the oath of allegiance on March 15.[46]

Although the war brought out a mixture of emotions and personalities (Callan certainly was one of the more unusual in the Maryland Line), the hardships of camp life and the battlefield brought men together. As the officers learned their duties, feelings of mutual respect grew between the ranks. The enlisted men of Company B, 1st Maryland Cavalry (C.S.), for example, presented an exquisite sword to Lieut. Mason E. McKnew in 1862 as "a mark of their regard and admiration for his character and his services in the cause of Southern independence."[47]

Capt. William D. Brown of the 4th Maryland Battery told acquaintances in Virginia about his unit's activities since their departure in the spring of 1862. "We have seen much hard service since leaving the Northern Neck. Our stay there," Brown admitted, "is the one bright spot in our career as a company. We did not know then what a soldier's life was. It may please you to know that our battery has made its mark in all the battles fought from 'Cedar Mountain' to Fredericksburg. I am proud of my command & would not relinquish it for a regiment."[48]

Officers protected their soldiers in a variety of ways, including sparing their lives when they were arrested for military crimes. Capt. Wilson C. Nicholas appealed to Jefferson Davis to pardon a deserter from his old company. In his letter to the president, Nicholas praised Patrick Rattie as "among the first who left their homes in defense of the South. If anything can be done towards having him reprieved, by doing so you will greatly oblige a large numbers of his friends and relatives."[49]

46. *Ibid.*; General Orders Number 90, September 25, 1863; see also Gen. John H. Winder to Gen. Samuel Cooper, November 4, 1863, Letter 2078-W-1863, LAIG; CSR, Christopher C. Callan, 2nd Maryland Infantry (C.S.); Philip Van Doren Stern, ed., *The Life and Writings of Abraham Lincoln* (New York, 1940), 789–93. Ironically, Callan had twin sons born in August, 1864, whom he named Beauregard and Lee (David Callan to Kevin Conley Ruffner, August 24, 1990). For Callan's postwar activities, see Ruffner, "Letters of a Washington Rebel."

47. Richmond *Daily Enquirer*, October 11, 1862.

48. Brown to unstated recipient, May 9, 1863, Letter 910, Book 5, in Ward Family Papers, LC. This extensive collection of nineteenth-century letters of a Virginia family also contains some correspondence from John G. Hooff, an enlisted man in the 4th Maryland Battery (C.S.).

49. Wilson C. Nicholas to President Jefferson Davis, October 27, 1862, Letter 1121-H-1862, LSOW.

The fortitude of the Maryland soldiers in 1863 during an expedition in western Virginia inspired Capt. William H. Murray of the 2nd Maryland Infantry (C.S.). In horrendous winter weather, Murray's company made its way across swollen creeks and treacherous mountains. Setting up camp, the "men worn out from fatigue and depressed by hunger, wrapped themselves in their blankets, and stretched upon the cold ground." The battalion was soon roused by the beat of the drum: "The poor fellows came, their feet one mass of inflamed blisters and asked 'Captain how far are we to go,' I answered the order is to march until further orders, it is to meet the enemy. I told them, all those without shoes and unable to keep up must remain with the wagons; to a man they said, 'We will follow you' how proud I felt of my *brave* boys, to see them stand shoulder to shoulder when there was danger, though it was against the will of Nature."[50]

The death of beloved officers took a heavy toll on unit *esprit de corps*. Seventeen junior officers, or nearly 12 percent of those men in the Maryland Line, lost their lives during the war. This figure includes those who were killed in action, died of their wounds, and died of disease. Surprisingly, there were only three men in the last category, and just one officer in the entire group who died in a Union prison. Eight of the combat deaths occurred among Maryland infantry officers, four among cavalry, and two in the artillery branch. The death of Capt. Murray at Gettysburg and that of Lieut. Col. Ridgely Brown (a former lieutenant and captain), in particular, deeply affected the exiled Marylanders.

To express their loss, unit comrades customarily published a tribute to the deceased officer in local newspapers and forwarded it, if possible, to the next of kin. Col. Brown's death at South Anna River on June 1, 1864, brought more than usual remorse. Col. Bradley T. Johnson issued the following order after the death of this popular officer:

> He died, as a soldier prefers to die, leading his men in a victorious charge. As an officer, kind and careful; as a soldier, brave and true; as a gentleman, chivalrous; as a Christian, gentle and modest; no one in the Confederate Army surpassed him in the hold he had on the hearts of his men, and the place in the esteem of his superiors. Of the rich blood that Maryland has lavished on every battle-field, none is more precious than his. . . . His command lost a friend most steadfast, but his commanding officer is deprived

50. William H. Murray to sister, January 10, 1863, in Murray Letters.

of an invaluable assistant. To the first he was ever as careful as a father; to the latter as true as a brother.[51]

Officers grew accustomed to the event of death, whether at the hands of the enemy or from natural causes. Yet they often exhibited emotion over the deaths of fellow officers and friends. First Lieut. Charles W. Hodges, an officer in the 2nd Maryland Infantry (C.S.), was killed instantly at Hatcher's Run in early 1865 when a bullet smashed into his forehead as he peered from behind a tree. His friends, not wanting to leave his body on the field, volunteered to return to the woods later that evening and retrieve it. Enemy gunfire prevented them from reaching the spot, and they reluctantly withdrew. Two weeks later, his remains were recovered from the federals during a truce, "in a good state of preservation and looks very natural." Lieut. Tolson escorted Hodges' remains to Richmond's Hollywood Cemetery for interment. Tolson commented in his diary, "It was the saddest duty I ever performed. Charley Hodges, my best friend, hid away in the cold earth! May he rest in peace!"[52]

As sad as the loss of these men was to their comrades in the army, it was a heartrending blow on the home front. Edward Beatty, a twenty-four-year-old lieutenant in the 1st Maryland Cavalry (C.S.), was captured in 1863 and imprisoned at Johnson's Island, Ohio. Suffering from chronic diarrhea, Beatty weakened and eventually died on March 24, 1864, despite attempts by friends and doctors to save him. Beatty's father had died in battle in 1862, and now another member of the family was lost in Confederate service. Beatty's mother expressed her feelings in a letter to a friend in June:

> My hopes and aspirations were directed to a bright earthly future of my darling my idolized son but *now* I look forward to joining him in a far brighter immortality where "sorrow and sighing shall forever flee away." This last stroke has made the iron enter more deeply into my soul than ever, and I feel at times ready to exclaim, "Oh could not this sorrow have been averted? Could not I have been spared this heavy blow?" but we are told that "afflictions are mercies in disguise, and I pray God to enable me to look upon this as such, and enable me to say 'tho he slay me, yet will I

51. Goldsborough, *Maryland Line*, 200–201; this tribute also appears in the Richmond *Daily Dispatch*, June 7, 1864. Another example of a published tribute to a Maryland officer can be found in the Richmond *Daily Dispatch*, May 29, 1863, upon the death of Noah Dixon Walker at Chancellorsville.

52. Ammen, "Maryland Troops in the Confederate Army," 169–70.

trust in Him." It may seem a dark and mysterious dispensation, and that I thank God that he has given me strength to endure my many sorrows, but I do not doubt that time will manifest to us how much mercy has been bound up in this severe trial.[53]

Maryland's Confederate junior officers suffered greater losses from wounds and capture than from disease during the four years of war. The short existence of the 1st Maryland Infantry (C.S.) helped minimize officer casualties. The three artillery batteries and three battalions of cavalry and infantry, however, were plagued by injuries and loss to the enemy. Thirty-nine men who served as junior officers in the Maryland Line were wounded at some point during the fighting. These men were struck by enemy fire a total of fifty-five times. Capt. Andrew J. Gwynn of the 2nd Maryland Infantry (C.S.) and Second Lieut. Edward H. D. Pue of the 1st Maryland Cavalry (C.S.) each sustained three injuries on various fields of battle. The wounds often proved debilitating, forcing the officers to undergo extensive hospitalization and long periods of recuperation before returning to field duty. Some officers never rejoined their units because their injuries were so severe. First Lieut. Charles S. Contee earned a recommendation from the corps commander for promotion to captain during the fighting near Winchester in 1863. Contee, however, suffered grievous wounds in his knee and never returned to the 1st Maryland Battery. He spent the rest of the war in hospitals or as an enrolling officer with the Conscript Bureau in southwestern Virginia.

Maj. Andrews (formerly captain of the 1st Maryland Battery) had a close call with death following his wounding at Cedar Mountain in 1862. While he was directing the fire of Jackson's artillery on horseback, a shell took out the right side of his stomach and cut across his thigh and hip. The wound appeared fatal to all onlookers and medical personnel, and they thought it merely a matter of time before he died. Yet the Maryland officer hung on to his life and cursed the doctors around him. With his abdomen wide open, Andrews said, "If you damned doctors would do something for me I'd get well. I once had a hound dog that ran a mile with its guts out and caught a fox." He added, "I know I am as good as any damned dog that ever lived, and can stand as much." He was taken off the battlefield, and surgeons tried desperately to clean his wounds of

53. Mrs. Beatty to Mary, June 1, 1864, in Bowie Collection; Washington Bowie Memoirs, P 939, in Minnesota Historical Society.

shell fragments and dirt. Amazingly, they succeeded and Andrews recovered without any disabling effects or infection. Cases such as Andrews' were rare during the war.[54]

The chances of being taken prisoner by the enemy were even greater than those of dying in battle or sustaining injuries. Fifty-two officers were captured at some point during the war (not including those officers who surrendered at the end of the war). Two great disasters each resulted in the capture of seven Maryland junior officers. Union cavalry nearly destroyed the 1st and 2nd Maryland Cavalry (C.S.) in August, 1864, at the Battle of Moorefield. The brigades of McCausland and Johnson had camped on two sides of the south branch of the Potomac River in West Virginia after the Chambersburg raid. The camp's layout split the small Confederate cavalry force into several sections, none of which could easily support the others.[55]

During the early morning hours of August 7, Union soldiers dressed as Confederates infiltrated Johnson's camp, followed by regular troopers. The Confederate pickets, under the command of Second Lieut. Samuel G. Bonn of the 1st Maryland Cavalry (C.S.), fell asleep at their posts and were easily nabbed by the federals. The enemy charged into Johnson's camp, shouting, "Surrender, you house-burning scoundrels!" and "Kill every damned one of them!" Within minutes, the Union soldiers rounded up the Maryland Confederates or put them to flight. Second Lieut. Fielder C. Slingluff of the 1st Maryland Cavalry (C.S.) was rudely disturbed by a kick, which he thought came from a horse. Raising his head from under his blanket, Slingluff saw a pair of pistols pointed at him and several gruff Yankee cavalrymen standing over him. "Get up, you ——— Chambersburg burning ———!," they exclaimed. The officer was then stripped of his possessions, including fine new boots and a hat.[56]

Capt. Booth of Gen. Johnson's staff was one of the fortunate survivors of the Moorefield disaster. He was sleeping on the porch of a nearby house when the Union cavalry charged into camp. Booth tried to get the 2nd Maryland Battery into action. The enemy's horsemen prevented Booth from reaching the artillery camp, and he took cover in a "small clump of elder bushes." He lay there for hours while Union soldiers gathered cap-

54. Robert K. Krick, *Stonewall Jackson at Cedar Mountain* (Chapel Hill, 1990), 379–83.

55. Freeman, *Lee's Lieutenants*, III, 572–74.

56. Fielder C. Slingluff, "The Burning of Chambersburg," *SHSP*, XXXVII (1909), 160–63; Gilmor, *Four Years in the Saddle*, 223.

tured equipment off the battlefield. Finally, Booth and another staff officer who had also sought shelter in the bushes made their break and charged across an open plain into a nearby patch of tall corn. The two men were safe from the enemy but had to find their way back to the Confederate lines. After days of wandering through the countryside, Booth met a gang of Confederate bushwhackers who directed him to Johnson's new camp in the Shenandoah Valley, and he rejoined the main army.[57]

An acrimonious struggle over the cause of the Moorefield disaster ensued among Confederate commanders. Gen. Johnson requested a court of inquiry to clear his name and castigated Gen. McCausland for the terrible performance of his troops in Maryland and Pennsylvania. Johnson believed that "had there been less plunder [during the campaign] there would have been more fighting at Moorefield." The Confederate army, however, took no action, and the southern cavalry in the Shenandoah Valley experienced a marked drop in morale and fighting prowess after Moorefield.[58]

The other significant capture of Maryland's junior officers occurred in the final days of the war at Hatcher's Run. Six lieutenants and one captain of the 2nd Maryland Infantry (C.S.) and numerous men of the battalion were cut off from the main Confederate force and compelled to surrender on April 2. The battalion held the far right of the Confederate line, and when the Union army launched its final assault on Petersburg, the 2nd Maryland Infantry (C.S.) had only 250 soldiers to defend its overextended positions. Fighting desperately, the Maryland rebels were pushed back through their winter encampment and finally withdrew from the field. Two companies detached as pickets did not partake in this portion of the battle; instead, they maintained a skirmish front until surrounded by federal troops. The seesaw fighting and the confusion that ensued led to the scattering of the battalion and the capture of many personnel. Lieut. Tolson of Company C noted that he was well treated by his captors and provided with ample rations.[59]

At least two officers were captured when they traveled to Maryland to

57. Booth, *Personal Reminiscences*, 134–39. Another account of the disaster at Moorefield and the Chambersburg raid is found in Malcolm Fleming to mother, August 10, 1864, Malcolm Fleming Letter, University of Virginia, Charlottesville.

58. Booth, *Personal Reminiscences*, 140–42; *Official Records*, Ser. I, Vol. XLIII, Pt. 1, pp. 4–8.

59. Ammen, "Maryland Troops in the Confederate Army," 175–78.

visit relatives. Second Lieut. Mason E. McKnew, an officer with the 1st Maryland Cavalry (C.S.), received a forty-two-day furlough and had already spent some time in Loudoun and Westmoreland counties in Virginia. McKnew crossed the Potomac to St. Marys County. Unfortunately, he became sick and was forced to seek bedrest. Union patrols captured McKnew on June 2, 1863. He was sent to various prisons until exchanged in 1864.[60] First Lieut. Somerset B. Burroughs, also a member of the 1st Maryland Cavalry (C.S.), fell into Union hands while returning to Maryland in December, 1863. He remained a prisoner of war until June, 1865.

Running the blockade between Virginia and Maryland entailed risks, although the rewards were great for those who succeeded. Travel to Maryland allowed officers an opportunity to visit home and loved ones as well as to enlist fresh recruits and obtain scarce items. In March, 1864, Col. Johnson expressed his intention to reorganize the 2nd Maryland Infantry (C.S.) into a mounted battalion for cavalry service. Doing so, of course, required the permission of the Confederate War Department (it was denied) and a large amount of cash to fund the refitting of the unit.

Second Lieut. William P. Zollinger and another member of the battalion left Confederate territory and made their way to Baltimore to raise money for this venture. The two men succeeded in getting money from wealthy benefactors in Maryland and began their journey back to the army. Zollinger crossed the Potomac River above Washington, D.C., and rejoined the battalion on June 22. A soldier in the unit wrote about his arrival in Virginia: "He brought me some very welcome articles—shoes, paper, soap, &c.—sent me by homefolks." His partner was not as fortunate and was arrested by Union troops in southern Maryland with the money.[61]

The Union army imprisoned Maryland Confederate officers in camps scattered throughout the North. For the most part, they received treatment similar to that accorded other southern soldiers, although they were looked upon with more hostility.[62] On occasion, Maryland soldiers suf-

60. CSR, Mason E. McKnew, 1st Maryland Cavalry (C.S.); for a letter from McKnew to his wife on the steamer *New York* at Baltimore en route to his exchange, see McKnew to wife, April 25, 1864, in Civil War Collection, MS 1860, Manuscripts Division, MHS.

61. Bradley T. Johnson to Gen. Samuel Cooper, March 16, 1864, Letter 274-J-1864, LAIG; Johnson to Cooper, March 20, 1864, Letter 294-J-1864; LAIG; and Ammen, "Maryland Troops in the Confederate Army," 150.

62. Union troops captured Capt. Warner G. Welsh of the 1st Maryland Cavalry (C.S.) on the outskirts of Winchester in 1863 and held him as a bushwacker. Federal authorities

fered from Union atrocities as patience wore thin on both sides. For example, Pvts. Churchill Crittenden and John Hartigan, members of the 1st Maryland's Company C, were surprised and captured by Union cavalry while on a foraging expedition in October, 1864. The Union commander immediately ordered the summary execution of both soldiers although Crittenden had been wounded. Union troopers shot both men and left their bodies exposed to the elements as a warning to residents and Confederate soldiers alike.[63]

Although the Union army committed no such crimes against Confederate officers in the Maryland Line, other violations of common decency occurred. The northern army, for example, imprisoned five officers of the Maryland Line at Morris Island, South Carolina, in 1864 and held them as hostages while under fire from friendly artillery in nearby Charleston. Capt. Eugene Digges of the 2nd Maryland Cavalry (C.S.), Maj. William W. Goldsborough of the 2nd Maryland Infantry (C.S.), Capt. William H. Griffin of the 2nd Maryland Battery, and Capt. George Howard and Second Lieut. James A. V. Pue of the 1st Maryland Cavalry (C.S.) were among the "Immortal Six Hundred" held in inhumane conditions during the summer and fall of 1864.[64]

Herman F. Keidel's experience as a prisoner of war is typical of those in the Maryland Line. Keidel enlisted in Gilmor's cavalry company, which joined the 12th Virginia Cavalry Regiment in the spring of 1862. Gilmor appointed the thirty-year-old native of Germany and Baltimore County store clerk as adjutant of the 2nd Maryland Cavalry Battalion (C.S.). Keidel, who had yet to receive his official assignment as adjutant from Richmond, was captured during a raid on the Baltimore and Ohio Railroad in October, 1863.[65]

Keidel wrote to his brother from Fort McHenry in Baltimore in late October, asking him to send clothing, a blanket, writing materials, and food. Prison life soon grew dull without any recreation, and Keidel hoped to spend his time usefully: "We read here any thing that we can lay hands

---

refused to parole Warner, forcing him to escape from Fort McHenry in Baltimore and make his way to friendly territory (CSR, Warner G. Welsh, 1st Maryland Cavalry [C.S.]).

63. Goldsborough, *Maryland Line*, 215; Crittenden's wartime letters are in Churchill Crittenden Letters, 1863–64, Crittenden Family Papers, University of Washington, Seattle.

64. J. Ogden Murray, *The Immortal Six Hundred: A Story of Cruelty to Confederate Prisoners of War* (Roanoke, 1911).

65. Keidel Family Papers, LC.

on I dont wish to surround myself with books, that will be lost, or be an incumbrance. Anything [dealing] with my profession, with the occurrences of the present day—pamphlets, &c.—but no Yankee periodicals, if you please." He likened his experience to Napoleon's exile.[66]

Keidel's morale fluctuated in prison as he heard news from the front and learned about activities at home. He saw his circle of civilian friends dwindling because of his own standing as a Confederate prisoner. "Mc's excuse must stand as a good one and answer for many other friends. I am getting used to it, & learn that acquaintances and friendships of the past, formed & consecrated in the career & walks of life & in the clubs & drawing room can't survive in these times. It has," Keidel acknowledged, "caused some regrets, this experience—I become reconciled to it though by degrees." After the fighting at the Wilderness and Spotsylvania, other Confederate officers joined Keidel at Point Lookout prisoner of war camp in St. Marys County, where he had been sent from Fort McHenry in January, 1864. "One hundred officers of late captures were left at this point last night, & came to our camp. . . . I found among the number the Adjutant of my old Regt, 12th Va, & you can easily imagine how much this fact heightened my interest, how great my pleasure to listen to his accounts, & to news from dear friends & comrades. The esprit de corps is still powerful drawing me to the old 12th & I feel if I had still a claim to share this glory; it is in Rosser's Brigade."[67]

Keidel spent time at three major Union prisons during the war: Fort McHenry, Point Lookout, and Fort Delaware. He saw little of the outside world except while in transit from one camp to another. The feeling of freedom from confinement was sensational, as Keidel described when shipped from Baltimore to southern Maryland. "The trip down the Bay was exhilarating. The sea boundless as our hopes, before me." Keidel's hopes for exchange were continually dashed, and he remained in prison until the end of the war. One of his last letters from Fort Delaware in May, 1865, reflects the despair of Confederate officers at that prison at the collapse of the Confederacy:

> The hand of God is hard & heavy upon me, upon us. It would be perhaps worse than useless to attempt to give you an idea of what struggles & trials our souls endure. Two thousand men that have met death rampant in the field of battle unflinchingly, who have obeyed the voice of honor & duty

66. Herman F. Keidel to Louis, October 25, 1863, March 8, May 29, 1864, *ibid.*
67. Herman F. Keidel to Louis, March 8, May 15, 1864, *ibid.*

as a child follows the beck of his father, are thrown into a deep distressing state of doubt & uncertainty & trouble. How faintly is our state described in those words, I give up. I have seen men weep around me, & we pray that God would enlighten us.

Keidel and his prison comrades faced a difficult decision in taking the oath of allegiance in 1865. "I have weight the matter in all is length, breadth & depth. My conscience my honor are left to me as yet free & pure, such shall they remain to me to the end. I cannot contract a new allegiance so long as I owe allegiance to the C.S. I cannot change my present status as C.S. officer, Prisoner of War so long as my coleurs are upheld by an army in legitimate warfare. I cannot do the former w. committing perjury before God & my conscience, the latter without disgrace and dishonor."[68]

Lieut. Samuel T. McCullough of the 2nd Maryland Infantry (C.S.), a prisoner at Johnson's Island in Ohio, received a letter from his friend Lieut. James S. Franklin, also a captured Maryland officer, at Fort Delaware. McCullough, whose father had just died in Annapolis, read Franklin's words with great interest in early May, 1865:

My principal object in writing you now is that I thought you would like to know the action of the officers here, especially the Md. Offrs. upon the question of taking the Oath of Allegiance. Maj. Goldsborough, Maj. Davis & Shearer, Capts. Griffin & Digges & Lieuts. Guillette & myself have determined to take it. I have not heard Lt. Murray's ultimate determination. We considered that we had done all that could be required; that there was no longer an armed & organized force E. of the Mississippi; that the Confederacy is surely virtually at an end its chief Magistrate a fugitive & its armies dispersed, & that in particular Gen Lee himself, to whom we all looked for example, had evidently given up the struggle as a hopeless one. Under the circumstances, we considered that other duties—to ourselves & our families required that we should no longer for the sake of an empty purpose, self-subject ourselves to the further continuance of troubles & hardship, but adapt our course as readily as possible to the necessities of the Situation.[69]

Confederate officers from Maryland faced numerous situations that tested their devotion to the cause. In combat officers were expected to

68. Herman F. Keidel to Louis, January 25, 1864, May 1, 1865, *ibid.*
69. James S. Franklin to Samuel T. McCullough, April 30, 1865, in McCullough Diaries and Letters, Hotchkiss Papers.

exhibit boundless bravery under fire. Prison and hospital life challenged their stamina in a different way, as they experienced deprivation and pain. Even daily camp life grew wearisome. The rewards of army life seemed very distant at times. Inflation ravaged junior officers' buying power and frequently left officers in debt. An infantry captain earned $130 per month while lieutenants drew $80–$90. This salary, generous in 1861, could not keep pace with the jump in prices for all southern goods. Lieut. Stone reported that clothing was "out of sight" in the Shenandoah Valley in 1863, while in Richmond a suit cost $600.[70]

The high cost of uniforms forced several Maryland Confederate officers to wear issue uniforms for enlisted men at the war's end. Lieut. Tolson in the 2nd Maryland Infantry (C.S.), for example, wore a Richmond Depot blue-gray wool shell jacket with nine Maryland state buttons. The only visible sign of rank was a single gold strip on his collar denoting that he was a second lieutenant. Tolson, however, did spend his own money to have his uniform lined. A study of uniforms worn by the soldiers of the Maryland infantry units reveals that men from the state generally wore uniforms of the proper style and condition throughout the war. There were shortages of uniform items and footwear at times, but these were made up by clothing drawn from the Confederate government and from private sources throughout the South and in Maryland.[71]

The Confederate Maryland officer, like the men he commanded, was always hungry. The amount and quality of rations fluctuated, depending on the season, whether in camp or actively campaigning, and on transportation conditions. Junior officers usually supplemented their rations by purchasing local items, especially vegetables. Lieut. Tolson, like other officers, took advantage of a lull in the action to dine in civilian establishments. On November 23, 1864, he "went to Petersburg and came back to camp this evening—distance walked about ten miles—for the sake of a good square meal."[72]

At the beginning of the war, some Maryland officers brought servants or slaves with them to camp. Capt. Robertson of Company I, 1st Maryland Infantry (C.S.), completed a requisition for wood on July 12, 1861, at

70. *Official Records*, Ser. IV, Vol. I, 129; Clemens, ed., "'Diary' of John H. Stone," 126; Ammen, "Maryland Troops in the Confederate Army," 124.

71. Ross M. Kimmel, "Enlisted Uniforms of the Maryland Confederate Infantry: A Case Study, Part II," *Military Collector and Historian*, XLI (1989), 184, 187–88.

72. Ammen, "Maryland Troops in the Confederate Army," 164.

Richmond for three officers, sixty-seven enlisted men, and three laun-dresses or servants. As late as June, 1864, the 2nd Maryland Infantry (C.S.) employed four Negroes as cooks for the battalion, and one soldier reported that his mess gave their black cook a furlough in November of that year.[73] The number of officers with personal servants declined after the beginning of the war, and later several officers encountered former slaves on the battlefield as soldiers wearing Union blue. Maryland officers identified the black soldiers when Confederate troops brought them into southern lines as prisoners during the fighting around Richmond in July, 1864.[74]

Food always aroused great interest among junior officers, and enlisted men sometimes played tricks to obtain rations. Capt. Joseph L. McAleer of Company D, 2nd Maryland Infantry (C.S.), procured a ham during the winter of 1863. Thoughts of such a delicacy played havoc with the ap-petites of his troops. Planning to savor the meal the next day, McAleer carefully strung the ham on a tree limb, under which the captain made his camp. During the night, McAleer's men scaled the tree and cut the ham from it. When the officer woke up the next morning, he found only the bones of his prized dinner dangling overhead.[75]

Foraging was a popular, if unauthorized, pastime for both officers and men. Lieut. McCullough found "the greatest profusion of black and den-berries" near Sperryville in the summer of 1863. He "considered them a luxury, contrasted with our scant rations." This same officer was not above indulging in the illicit activities of the men in his company. The day before Christmas, 1862, McCullough stated that "several members of my company went out on a foraging expedition for whiskey, and much to my gratification & surprise succeeded in getting some, out of which, we man-aged, by a little ingenuity, to manufacture a nifty pot full of tolerably fair egg-nogg." A private in the 1st Maryland Cavalry recalled after the war

73. CSR, Michael S. Robertson and James P. Crane, 1st Maryland Infantry (C.S.) and 59th Virginia Infantry Regiment, respectively; Ammen, "Maryland Troops in the Con-federate Army," 165.

74. Capt. Dement had a black servant named Jack throughout the war (Hatton Mem-oir, 688); Ammen, "Maryland Troops in the Confederate Army," 151, 156. For a descrip-tion of a Negro soldier guarding a Maryland Confederate officer, see George M. Anderson, ed., "A Captured Confederate Officer: Nine Letters from Captain James Anderson to His Family," *Maryland Historical Magazine*, LXXVI (1981), 65.

75. Ammen, "Maryland Troops in the Confederate Army," 96.

that he raided a watermelon patch in the summer of 1863 and returned to his camp with a pumpkin. His company officer, First Lieut. Nathaniel Chapman, very much enjoyed the pumpkin the next morning.[76]

As the war wound on, and especially as casualties mounted, the role of the junior officer grew in importance. Company commanders often found themselves acting as battalion commanders, and lieutenants frequently substituted for captains in charge of companies. These men provided the sinew for their units in the face of adversity and despair. In an overwhelmingly volunteer army with little professional assistance, Confederate junior officers were a vital presence in camp and on the battlefield. The success or failure of Maryland's units depended, in many cases, on the strength and spirit of their captains and lieutenants.

76. Diary entries for July 27, 1863, and December 24, 1862, in McCullough Diaries and Letters, Hotchkiss Papers; Rich, *Comrades Four,* 66–69.

Members of the Maryland Guard Battalion, 53rd Maryland Regiment, as they appeared prior to the war. Many officers and men in this volunteer unit from Baltimore later served with the Maryland Line.

(Courtesy of the U.S. Army Military History Institute)

Bradley T. Johnson organized Maryland's volunteers at Point of Rocks and Harpers Ferry in the spring of 1861. He commanded the 1st Maryland Infantry Regiment (C.S.) and oversaw its disbandment in August, 1862. Johnson re-formed the Maryland Line in 1863 and commanded a Confederate cavalry brigade in 1864. He took a deep interest in recording Maryland's role in the Confederacy after the war.

(Courtesy of the Library of Congress)

Arnold Elzey, the first colonel of the 1st Maryland (C.S.), earned his laurels as the "Blucher of the day" at First Manassas. Promoted to brigadier general, Elzey was wounded during the fighting around Richmond in 1862. He was promoted to major general and briefly commanded the camp of the Maryland Line in Staunton in 1864.

(Courtesy of the Eleanor S. Brockenbrough Library, Museum of the Confederacy, Richmond, Va.)

Following Elzey's promotion to brigadier general in the summer of 1861, George H. Steuart, a West Point graduate, rose to the command of the 1st Maryland Infantry (C.S.). With Johnson, Steuart actively promoted the idea of the Maryland Line in 1862, which earned him promotion to brigadier general. He commanded an infantry brigade with the Army of Northern Virginia that included the 2nd Maryland Infantry Battalion (C.S.) at Gettysburg.

(Courtesy of the Eleanor S. Brockenbrough Library, Museum of the Confederacy, Richmond, Va.)

Edward R. Dorsey commanded Company C of the 1st Maryland Infantry (C.S.). He became the unit's major and later lieutenant colonel, which he remained until the 1st Maryland disbanded in the summer of 1862.

(Ambrotype reproduced courtesy of the Maryland Historical Society, Baltimore)

Wilson C. Nicholas, son of a U.S. naval officer and the grandson of a Virginia governor, commanded Company G of the 1st Maryland Infantry (C.S.). Like many officers of that regiment, Nicholas had no position in the army after the unit's disbandment. He later obtained a staff assignment with Colonel Johnson's Maryland Line until his capture in 1864.

(Courtesy of the Eleanor S. Brockenbrough Library, Museum of the Confederacy, Richmond, Va.)

William I. Rasin faced difficulties in joining the Confederate army, although he managed to escape from Old Capitol Prison in Washington, D.C. He later commanded a company in the 1st Maryland Cavalry (C.S.) and participated in the unit's final charge at Appomattox.

(Courtesy of the Eleanor S. Brockenbrough Library, Museum of the Confederacy, Richmond, Va.)

Like Captain Rasin, Capt. George E. Emack escaped Union capture, and he earned notoriety as a "Yankee killer" for stabbing a Union soldier and fleeing Maryland. Emack raised Company E, 1st Maryland Cavalry (C.S.), and served with that unit throughout the war. His battalion, however, demonstrated little enthusiasm for Emack's promotion and assumption of command.

(Courtesy of William A. Tidwell)

One of the best known and loved officers of the 1st and 2nd Maryland Infantries (C.S.), Capt. William H. Murray fell leading his troops at Gettysburg. His men remembered him fondly years after the war.

(Courtesy of the Maryland Historical Society, Baltimore)

Capt. Joseph Forrest of St. Marys County raised the Chesapeake Artillery (later the 4th Maryland Battery) in early 1862. The richest officer in the Maryland Line, Forrest served only briefly in the Confederate army. He spent most of the war in Texas with his wife, Henrietta Cecilia Forrest.

(Courtesy of Margaret K. Fresco)

Henrietta Cecilia Forrest, wife of Capt. Joseph Forrest.
(*Courtesy of Margaret K. Fresco*)

A cousin of Bradley T. Johnson, William W. Goldsborough joined the Confederate army as a private in the spring of 1861. He was elected captain of Company A, 1st Maryland Infantry (C.S.), upon the promotion of Johnson to major. Goldsborough continued to serve as a company commander and later as major in the 2nd Maryland Infantry (C.S.). He was wounded and captured at Gettysburg and imprisoned as one of the "Immortal 600."

(Courtesy of the Eleanor S. Brockenbrough Library, Museum of the Confederacy, Richmond, Va.)

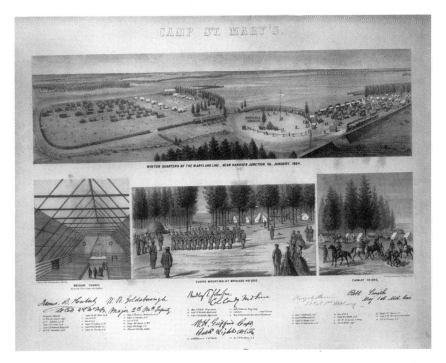

Camp St. Mary's of the Maryland Line near Hanover Junction, Virginia, during the winter of 1863–64. For the only time in the brief history of the Confederate Maryland Line, almost all of the Maryland units encamped at one location under the command of Col. Bradley T. Johnson. The bottom of the illustration reproduces the signatures of the senior officers of the Maryland Line.

(Courtesy of the Maryland Historical Society, Baltimore)

Capt. Christopher C. Callan of Company H, 2nd Maryland Infantry (C.S.), had a shaky record of service with the Confederate army. Released from prison to form his unit for the Maryland Line, Callan deserted to the enemy in early 1864. He later took the oath of allegiance and was released from Old Capitol Prison. Ironically, he named his twin sons after prominent Confederate generals.
(Courtesy of the Historical Society of Washington, D.C.)

Harry Gilmor earned a fierce reputation as a Confederate cavalryman, but his command of the 2nd Maryland Cavalry (C.S.) left much to be desired. Although his unit wreaked havoc on the enemy, it was troublesome to Confederate commanders.

(Tinted photograph by D'Almaine, 1862, reproduced courtesy of the Maryland Historical Society, Baltimore)

Brig. Gen. John D. Imboden, commander of Confederate forces in the Valley District, often had to respond to charges leveled against Gilmor's cavalry battalion and other partisan forces.

(Courtesy of the Library of Congress)

James L. Clark initially served with the 1st Maryland Infantry (C.S.) as a staff officer and later as a company commander with the 12th Virginia Cavalry Regiment. His company transferred to Gilmor's 2nd Maryland Cavalry in the summer of 1864. Captain Clark remained with Gilmor for only a brief period as he was captured at Moorefield in August, 1864.

(Courtesy of the Eleanor S. Brockenbrough Library, Museum of the Confederacy, Richmond, Va.)

John R. Kenly, a hero of the Mexican War, rallied pro-Unionist Marylanders during the dark days of 1861. Colonel Kenly commanded the 1st Maryland Infantry Regiment (U.S.) and was taken prisoner with his command at Front Royal. Following his exchange, Kenly raised the Maryland Brigade and served as its first commander.

(Courtesy of the Massachusetts Commandery, Military Order of the Loyal Legion, and the U.S. Army Military History Institute)

Capt. Thomas S. J. Johnson, Company K, 1st Maryland Infantry (U.S.), had previously served in the Regular Army nearly twenty years before the war. Johnson's conflict with one of his subordinate officers, First Lieut. William E. George, resulted in appeals to the regiment's commander at Harpers Ferry in early 1863. Johnson was taken prisoner at Cold Harbor a year later and died of disease in a Confederate prison.

(Courtesy of the Roger D. Hunt Collection, U.S. Army Military History Institute)

A Frederick boot and shoe merchant, Maurice Albaugh had fought as an enlisted man during the Mexican War. He joined the 1st Maryland Infantry (U.S.) as a second lieutenant and rose to command a company. Following his wounding at Petersburg, Albaugh was discharged from the army.

(Courtesy of the Carol L. Porter Collection, U.S. Army Military History Institute)

A German immigrant, Peter Bernard Wilhelm Heine never served with the 1st Maryland Infantry (U.S.), although he had a commission as captain of Company I. A topographical engineer, Captain Heine was assigned as a staff officer but encountered problems with the army's bureaucracy. He also fell into Confederate hands and later resigned his commission in December, 1862. He rejoined the Union army, however, as colonel of a New York regiment and ended the war as a brevet brigadier general.

(Courtesy of the Massachusetts Commandery, Military Order of the Loyal Legion, and the U.S. Army Military History Institute)

John W. Wilson, formerly captain of Company G, 1st Maryland Infantry (U.S.), and later major, lieutenant colonel, and colonel, fell at Dabney's Mill in early 1865. Wilson's brother Robert, a second lieutenant in Company G, died of wounds received at the same battle.

(Courtesy of the Roger D. Hunt Collection, U.S. Army Military History Institute)

A good example of the Union army's meritocracy, David L. Stanton rose from private in 1861 to colonel of the 1st Maryland Infantry (U.S.) in 1865. He commanded the Maryland Brigade during the last campaign of the war and earned a brevet promotion to brigadier general.

(Courtesy of the Roger D. Hunt Collection, U.S. Army Military History Institute)

Isaiah Lightner enlisted as a sergeant in the 7th Maryland Infantry (U.S.) in 1862. As captain of Company F, Lightner was wounded at Five Forks.
(Courtesy of the Tom Gordon Collection, U.S. Army Military History Institute)

A carriage maker and the sheriff of Washington County, Edward M. Mobley raised Company A, 7th Maryland Infantry (U.S.), and served as captain. He received a promotion to major and later brevet promotions to lieutenant colonel and colonel. Mobley was wounded at Bethesda Church in May, 1864, and mustered out a year later.

(Courtesy of S. Roger Keller and Charles L. Mobley, Jr.)

Edward Y. Goldsborough, a Frederick lawyer, served as a first lieutenant with the 8th Maryland Infantry (U.S.). He resigned in order to take office as the Frederick County's state's attorney in late 1863.

(Courtesy of the Massachusetts Commandery, Military Order of the Loyal Legion, and the U.S. Army Military History Institute)

George W. Shriver of Westminster initially enlisted in a District of Columbia unit and then joined Company K (Nine Months Drafted Men and Substitutes) of the 8th Maryland Infantry (U.S.) in late 1862. He became captain of that company in March, 1863, and served until his discharge a year later. Shriver then served as an enlisted man and officer in the 12th Maryland Infantry (100 Days) (U.S.).

(Courtesy of the Maryland Historical Society, Baltimore)

James R. Hosmer (on ground, second from right), a lawyer and the son-in-law of one of Baltimore's richest citizens, was appointed a second lieutenant in the 8th Maryland Infantry (U.S.) in September, 1862. After briefly serving with his company, Hosmer became the regiment's AQM. He resigned his commission in order to accept the position of captain and AQM of U.S. Volunteers. In this role, he served with Gen. Philip Sheridan (seated at center). After the war, Hosmer entered the diplomatic service. He rejoined the army during the Spanish-American War.

(Courtesy of the Massachusetts Commandery, Military Order of the Loyal Legion, and the U.S. Army Military History Institute)

·7·

DEATH THROES OF THE MARYLAND LINE

The success or failure of a Civil War unit depended on several tangible factors: its size, training of personnel, weapons and equipment, and logistical support. Three other factors, less definable but certainly critical, affected the unit—the quality of its leadership, discipline, and cohesion in the companies and the regiment. Positive marks in all of these areas contributed to the unit's ability to fight and win on the battlefield as well as to overcome other adversities. Casualties and other losses easily altered this delicate balance.

In a long conflict such as the American Civil War, regimental and company officers struggled to keep their units in top fighting form. An examination of the Maryland Line reveals the challenges that commanders faced in the last months of the war. The wartime experiences of two Maryland units, the 2nd Cavalry Battalion and the 2nd Infantry Battalion, underscore the role that junior officers played in honing an effective command. Although the two units had different missions, the quality of leadership proved the fundamental difference between a successful unit and an unsuccessful one in both cases.

Unlike professional armies, in which noncommissioned officers are generally considered the backbone of company-sized units, junior officers (especially company commanders) played an influential role in shaping the Maryland commands. Officers set the tone for their companies and determined whether they marched and fought as a cohesive body or whether they remained a mob of armed men. Officers, by virtue of their location in front of the troops on the battlefield, set the example for their men as well as for other observers.

The 2nd Maryland Infantry Battalion (C.S.), formed in the wake of the disbandment of the 1st Maryland Infantry Regiment in the summer of 1862, initially did not offer much promise. The companies of Capts.

William H. Murray and J. Parran Crane mustered into service at Richmond on the same day, August 27, 1862. Disagreement between the two officers had already become rancorous when the battalion organized with five companies a month later. Murray and Crane each claimed that his company deserved the designation as the senior company, or Company A, of the new battalion. Murray stated that his company had been organized and ready for mustering before Crane's although the mustering officer swore the latter officer's men into Confederate service first. Officials in Richmond finally decided the question of seniority in favor of Murray's company.

Crane, in turn, complained to Gen. Steuart in Charlottesville, who also ruled for Murray. Crane, a native of St. Marys County and a former commander of a volunteer company of students from the University of Virginia, still insisted that his company deserved the senior designation. Finally, the district commander in the Shenandoah Valley ordered that a simple drawing be held in camp to determine the seniority of the 2nd Maryland Infantry (C.S.). Murray, a veteran of the 1st Maryland Infantry (C.S.), won once again, and the "vexed question" was settled.[1]

In addition to the seniority crisis, unit elections threatened to divide the new battalion. The five companies elected Capt. Herbert of Company C as major on October 2, 1862. The addition of Capt. Gwynn's Company F on October 28 entitled the battalion to have a lieutenant colonel and a major. Gen. Steuart, the former colonel of the 1st Maryland Infantry (C.S.), ordered new elections to determine the commander of the 2nd Maryland Battalion (C.S.). Maj. Herbert protested because he thought this was unnecessary, and he appealed for assistance from the War Department. When he had not heard from Richmond, Herbert conducted the election on January 8, 1863, and the men chose Col. Bradley T. Johnson as the battalion's new lieutenant colonel.

Two hours after the election, Herbert received a dispatch from the Confederate capital. The War Department officially recognized Herbert as the lieutenant colonel of the battalion with his date of rank matching the date of the addition of the sixth company—October 28, 1862. Col. Johnson graciously declined the post of commander, thus avoiding an embarrassing situation, and Herbert moved up to the rank of lieutenant

---

1. Goldsborough, *Maryland Line*, 85–86.

colonel.[2] To fill the vacancy caused by Herbert's promotion, the War Department appointed (rather than permit unit elections) Capt. Goldsborough of Company G as major of the 2nd Maryland Infantry (C.S.). After that point, empty officer slots in the battalion were filled by promoting company officers on the basis of seniority. The election of junior second lieutenants from the enlisted ranks proved to be the only exception, a practice that continued throughout the war despite opposition from the army's hierarchy.

Despite these initial problems, the 2nd Maryland Infantry quickly developed a reputation as an effective unit. After service in the Shenandoah Valley during the first half of 1863, the 2nd Maryland Infantry joined Brig. Gen. George H. Steuart's brigade in the Second Corps of the Army of Northern Virginia. When the brigade arrived at Gettysburg on the afternoon of July 1, it moved to the Confederate left flank, where, in the evening of July 2 and the early morning hours of July 3, the battalion engaged the enemy. After a series of fruitless attacks on the strongly fortified federal forces, the Maryland battalion was spent. Dozens of men were strewn on the hillside, dead or dying, while many more suffered from wounds. Among the losses, Capt. William A. Murray of Company A fell at the front of his troops. Gettysburg marked Maryland's ultimate sacrifice for the Confederate cause, and that one engagement wiped clean the slate of embarrassments the state had suffered in Confederate service over the past year. The unit's performance at Culp's Hill during the second day's fighting at Gettysburg marked one of the finest moments in the annals of Confederate Maryland history.

The fighting at Gettysburg, however, unleashed a chain of events that eventually destroyed the battalion's officer corps. A survey of the 2nd Maryland Infantry shows that the battalion's officer promotion system broke down under the strain of combat. There were never enough officers in the unit, and this problem compounded after the battalion entered the fray in the summer of 1864. The eight companies had a total of thirty-five men who served as company officers from 1862 until the battalion's surrender in 1865. Nineteen of these men had previous military experi-

2. CSR, James R. Herbert, 2nd Maryland Infantry (C.S.); J. Parran Crane to the Secretary of War, November 25, 1862, Letter 2364-C-1862, LAIG; James R. Herbert to Capt. Martin, December 2, 1862, Letter 2379-H-1862, LAIG; Goldsborough, *Maryland Line*, 87–88.

ence in the Confederate army before their election as officers in the 2nd Maryland Infantry. Eight of these veterans had been officers while the remainder were enlisted men. This meant that sixteen men had no previous military experience during the war until they joined the battalion.

The war caused heavy attrition among the junior officer corps of the 2nd Maryland Infantry. Six men died in combat while another ten men had to be assigned to light duties because of disabling wounds. Twelve officers were captured by the enemy, and never returned to the unit. Three officers resigned for various reasons during the war, two deserted, and the army dropped one for absence without leave. Only one company officer, Capt. John W. Torsch, remained when the battalion surrendered at Appomattox on April 9, 1865.

The battalion did not suffer its heaviest losses until the final months of the war, but even before that point, casualties were not replaced with fresh officers. Company E's first lieutenant was killed at Gettysburg a month after the Union army captured its junior second lieutenant at Winchester. The surviving second lieutenant received an automatic promotion to first lieutenant. Thus two second lieutenant slots were left unfilled until the end of the war. Company H, commanded by Capt. Callan, had no officers after the entire company's chain of command either deserted, resigned, or was dropped by order of the War Department. The company elected Second Lieut. James T. Bussey of Company D as the new captain of Company H in February, 1864. No other men became company-grade officers of that company; Bussey had his hands full running the company by himself.

Officers absent from the command because of hospitalization, imprisonment, or detached duties posed the biggest hindrance to officer promotions. These men, no matter how long they were absent, were still assigned to the 2nd Maryland Infantry (C.S.), so their positions remained open until the missing officer died, resigned, or was dropped for unexcused absence. Consequently, the battalion held slots for missing officers who, in all likelihood, would never return to duty. This archaic promotion system, derived from peacetime personnel constraints, crippled the battalion's command structure.

The inability to replace officers affected every rank from junior second lieutenant to lieutenant colonel. For example, both Lieut. Col. Herbert and Maj. Goldsborough were taken prisoner at Gettysburg, leaving battalion command to a shifting gallery of captains. The army, believing that

Maj. Goldsborough had died of wounds, promoted Capt. Crane to major because he was the senior officer in the battalion in June, 1864. Crane returned the commission several months later, stating, "I hasten to disclaim all right to it upon that ground: as I have the gratification to state, that I have very recently received a letter from Major Goldsborough from Flag of Truce, and that he is not only alive, but perfectly recovered from the wounds which he has suffered so long: and is now a prisoner at Fort Delaware."[3]

Although Crane's sentiment was gentlemanly, it did not help the battalion, which needed officers. Holding slots for absent officers (Maj. Goldsborough was not released from prison until June, 1865) meant that the burdens of command fell on a diminishing number of officers. Administrative and logistical capabilities declined, and not all of the company commanders who served as temporary battalion commander were suited to lead the battalion into combat. The heavy workload fell unequally upon those officers remaining in the 2nd Maryland Infantry, which may account for Captain McAleer's resignation in early 1865. McAleer was in command of the battalion in January but submitted his letter of resignation on February 15: "Feeling conscious of the rectitude of my own conduct, I must say that my usefulness in the battalion has in a great measure at least, been destroyed by petty contentions and jealousies, and my resignation may restore more harmony in the command while it will enable me to serve the Confederacy more usefully in some other position."[4]

As combat losses further eroded the structure of Maryland's Confederate junior officer corps, Col. Bradley T. Johnson achieved his long-desired goal of the formation of the Maryland Line. Following the disbandment of the 1st Maryland Infantry (C.S.), the concept of the Maryland Line lay dormant. Neither Gen. Steuart nor Col. Johnson was in a position to advocate its regeneration as long as they held no commands and only a handful of Maryland companies existed in Confederate service. After persuading the secretary of war of the merits of a Maryland organization, Johnson received permission to organize a regiment from

---

3. J. Parran Crane to Lieut. Colonel E. R. Palfrey, March 18, 1865, Letter 2752-C-1864, LAIG. Crane also returned his October, 1864, major's commission to the adjutant general in this communication.

4. Joseph L. McAleer to Gen. Samuel Cooper, February 15, 1865, in CSR, Joseph L. McAleer, 2nd Maryland Infantry (C.S.).

the various Maryland battalions. The timing could not have been worse when Johnson reported for this duty with the Army of Northern Virginia at the Battle of Gettysburg. In the simple language of Gen. Ewell, "This is no time to be swapping horses." Consequently, Johnson took temporary command of a Virginia brigade as the army retreated from Pennsylvania.[5]

In the fall of 1863, the seed that Johnson had planted in the Confederate War Department germinated. The Confederate army formally reconstituted the Maryland Line on October 31, 1863, with three subordinate elements: the Maryland infantry and cavalry battalions and the 2nd Maryland Battery. To avoid confusion, the army designated the Maryland infantry battalion as the 2nd Maryland Infantry (C.S.) and Brown's cavalry battalion as the 1st Maryland Cavalry (C.S.) on January 19, 1864. Johnson took his new command to Hanover Junction to recruit and train as a single entity while in winter quarters near the Confederate capital. The Maryland Line commander organized his staff on the same basis as that of a regular brigade, even though the Line had elements of all three combat branches.[6]

The months spent at Hanover Junction were the most enjoyable of the entire war. The officers of the various Maryland units organized a ball for the women of the neighborhood; the 2nd Maryland Infantry had a glee club that performed frequently; rations were good; and both officers and men received furloughs to visit nearby Richmond or other areas of the state. The Marylanders neatly constructed their camp, and the men even built a chapel for visiting priests and ministers from Richmond.[7]

The Confederate hierarchy continued to express interest in the Maryland Line during the spring of 1864. On March 23, the Confederate adjutant general authorized the transfer of all Marylanders in the service to the Maryland Line. This act allowed Marylanders, regardless of command or location, to enlist in either the artillery, cavalry, or infantry

5. Johnson, *Maryland*, 114–15; Johnson, "Maryland Line," 24–25.

6. Special Orders No. 269, October 31, 1863; Johnson, "Maryland Line," 25; Special Orders No. 15, January 19, 1864; Goldsborough, *Maryland Line*, 122–23; Johnson, *Maryland*, 115–16.

7. Ammen, "Maryland Troops in the Confederate Army," 124–25; Rich, *Comrades Four*, 69–72. One member of the 1st Maryland Cavalry (C.S.) even had time to send a poem about picket duty near the Maryland Line encampment. See Spencer C. Jones to Miss Mary V. Ward, April 25, 1864, enclosing "All Quiet Along the Pamunkey," in Soldier Songs, Box 4, Ward Family Papers.

components of the Maryland Line. Col. Johnson's units remained in Hanover Junction at Camp Howard while Gen. Elzey took overall command of the Maryland Line at Camp Maryland in Staunton. First Lieut. Charles S. Contee, still recuperating from the wounds he had received the previous summer, established an office in Richmond in late April to direct new recruits to the Maryland commands. The order also called for the drafting of all Marylanders not in military service into the Maryland Line, no doubt to rectify the oversight of the conscription acts. George P. Kane, the former police marshal of Baltimore and a great friend of Maryland Confederates, hailed the new Maryland Line: "This would secure the three great elements which a Maryland organization has always lacked so far—viz.: concentration, harmony, and an *esprit de corps* of purpose and principle."[8]

The Maryland Line ultimately lacked two of the three elements Kane listed. Col. Johnson battled higher headquarters to pull Maryland units from their assigned commands. Naturally, few commanders wanted to let good troops leave, although recruiting initially proceeded well for Johnson at Camp Howard as Marylanders in units throughout the Army of Northern Virginia applied for transfers to the Maryland Line. Gen. Elzey, however, had little luck in attracting men in the Shenandoah Valley for the Maryland Line. Marshal Kane and Capt. Torsch of the 2nd Maryland Infantry returned empty-handed from an attempt to lure Marylanders from units stationed in South Carolina. Col. Johnson detailed Capt. Thomas R. Stewart of the 2nd Maryland Infantry, severely wounded at Gettysburg, to serve as a recruiting officer for the new Maryland Line in Richmond. A letter published in the Richmond *Daily Examiner* revealed that Stewart had yet to receive his additional pay as a recruiting officer. "Every one is aware that a captain's salary will not pay his board in Richmond, and that Captain Stewart, during his stay in Richmond, must have drawn extensively upon his private means, to obtain even the necessaries of life." Bureaucratic snags hindered recruitment in more ways than one.[9]

Likewise, the officers and men of the 1st Maryland Battery protested

8. General Orders No. 38, Adjutant and Inspector General's Office, reforming the Maryland Line, is found in Letter 716-G-1864, LAIG; Johnson, "Maryland Line," 26; *Official Records*, Ser. IV, Vol. III, 507; Richmond *Daily Examiner*, March 16, 24, 1864.

9. Goldsborough, *Maryland Line*, 243–44; *Official Records*, Ser. IV, Vol. III, 510–12; Ammen, "Maryland Troops in the Confederate Army," 125; CSR, Thomas R. Stewart, 2nd Maryland Infantry (C.S.); Richmond *Daily Examiner*, March 28, 1864.

that their unit had not been assigned to the Maryland Line at Hanover Junction. Writing to Gen. Elzey on April 2, Capt. Dement stated, "It is somewhat singular that the very object of Genl Order No 38 [dealing with transfers to the Maryland Line] should be so completely ignored by Genl Lee, and that our attempts to take the position assigned to us, should be denied." The 4th Maryland Battery joined the Maryland Line on April 14, and Dement's 1st Maryland Battery followed five days later.[10]

The concentration of the Maryland units in Virginia with the Maryland Line at Hanover Junction proved short-lived. The opening of the spring campaign in Virginia split the Maryland Line because infantry was needed at one battlefield and cavalry at another. The artillery batteries returned to their earlier assignments with the army's regular artillery battalions in the field. Finding it tactically impossible to command a "combined arms" team in the Civil War, Col. Johnson remained with the Maryland cavalry. The Maryland Line continued to be an elusive dream.

The harmonious relations between Marylanders in Confederate service was always of questionable duration. The Maryland artillery batteries never experienced the same discord that destroyed the 1st Maryland Infantry (C.S.) in 1861–1862. The peaceful relationship between officers and men in the 1st Maryland Battery, however, took a dramatic turn for the worse in the summer of 1864. In July of that year, the three-year term of service for the enlisted men expired, and they sought release from military service. Capt. Dement appealed to the Confederate president for assistance in obtaining the discharges of the Maryland artillerists on July 20.[11]

The War Department denied Dement's initial request. Fearing that the 1st Maryland Battery would be destroyed if its members were separated, the army took the view that all soldiers, regardless of residence or nativity, were liable for military service under the 1864 Conscription Act. This act held soldiers already in the army for the indefinite term of the war. Dement had no choice but to hold his men in the service, and they responded by suing him in a Richmond court for writ of habeas corpus. In a long, drawn-out trial, conducted on an individual basis, the court

10. William F. Dement to Brig. Gen. Arnold Elzey, April 2, 1864, enclosing petition of officers and soldiers of the 1st Maryland Battery, Letter 764-M-1864, LAIG; Ammen, "Maryland Troops in the Confederate Army," 125; Hatton Memoir, 553–55.

11. Bradley T. Johnson to Gen. Samuel Cooper, April 20, 1864, Letter 458-J-1864, LAIG; *Official Records*, Ser. IV, Vol. III, 545.

declared that Dement had illegally detained his soldiers and ordered him to discharge all soldiers whose enlistments expired in 1864. The Richmond judge also prohibited the Confederate government from conscripting these same men because of their prewar domicile.[12]

Discharges and desertions drained the 1st Maryland Battery of its personnel. Pvt. Albert Tolson of Prince Georges County returned home to see his mother because he was "tired." Although he still supported the Confederacy, Tolson a twenty-year-old student, reported to Union officials in Washington, D.C., who arrested him and placed him in the Old Capitol Prison. Despite his mother's efforts to get him released, Tolson did not return home again until the summer of 1865, when he took the oath of allegiance at Fort Warren prison in Boston Harbor.[13]

Losses such as these compelled Capt. Dement to ask permission to recruit fresh men from Maryland. Gen. Ewell denied the request, saying, "I have the highest opinion of this Battery but do not think that the benefit to be derived from sending recruiting agents in Md. would be commensurate with the risk incurred."[14] By March, 1865, the artillery commander of the Army of Northern Virginia recommended the consolidation of the three Maryland batteries (1st, 2nd, and 4th) into a single unit because their ranks were so diminished.[15]

The officers and men of the 1st Maryland Cavalry (C.S.) expressed great dissatisfaction at Gen. Lunsford L. Lomax's plan to consolidate

12. *Official Records*, Ser. IV, Vol. III, 546–47, 550–51; For a discussion of the suit against Capt. Dement by a soldier in the battery, see Hatton Memoir, 675–79, 688; Richmond *Daily Examiner*, September 28, 1864; Richmond *Daily Dispatch*, September 14, 15, 20, 22, October 4, 1864; Jones, *Rebel War Clerk's Diary*, II, 233. See also J. H. Gilmer to President Jefferson Davis, October 12, 1864, in RG 109, War Department Collection of Confederate Records, Uninventoried Records, "C.S.A. Printed and Written Reports Secretary of War Court of Inquiry—Fall of New Orleans," NA.

13. Mary H. Tolson to Assistant Secretary of War, August 29, 1864, in CSR, Albert Tolson, 1st Maryland Battery.

14. Dement to Gen. Ewell, January 6, 1865, and to James A. Seddon, January 6, 1865, Letter 40-D-1865, LAIG; Because of the lack of men in the battery Dement had to give his horses to the 4th Maryland Battery on October 23, 1864 (Hatton Memoir, 674). The condition of Dement's horses raised questions within the Confederate command structure; see E. P. Dandridge to Gen. William N. Pendleton, November 7, 1864, in CSR, William F. Dement, 1st Maryland Battery. The subsequent report of a survey and Dement's response are in his compiled service record.

15. *Official Records*, Ser. I, Vol. XLVI, Pt. 2, pp. 1319–20.

that battalion with Gilmor's partisans in the fall of 1864. Earlier that summer, the question of command of the 1st Maryland Cavalry generated a heated letter to the president of the Confederacy opposing the promotion of the "Yankee killer," Capt. George M. Emack, upon the death of Lieut. Col. Brown and the incapacity of Maj. R. Carter Smith to serve in the field. Twelve officers signed the petition on June 6 stating that "Capt Emack is in point of *age* the *youngest officer* in the command . . . has *experienced less* of *service* than any officer *in the command*, that on all occasions when he has had command of the Battalion his conduct has been of such a *rash* & *reckless* nature, marked with a lack of judgement as to call for the censure of both officers & men." The officers, claiming to represent those men absent from command, wanted to elect their own major or have Capt. Frank A. Bond of Company A appointed as the unit's commander.[16]

Emack, realizing the sentiment against him, apparently did not press his promotion as the senior officer in the battalion. In September Lomax raised Emack's name for promotion to major when he proposed to merge the two Maryland cavalry units. The four company-grade officers still serving with the 1st Maryland Cavalry vigorously protested once again to President Davis: "We do hereby enter our most solemn protest against a Consolidation of the said commands or the appointment of the above officers over us. We are *volunteers*, and having earned a reputation under the *leadership* of the lamented 'Col Ridgely Brown which we are all proud of, we do not wish' that fair name at this late date, to be sullied by the command which it is the intention of uniting us with."[17]

Gen. Lomax, rebutted in his initial recommendation, used a new act of Congress that allowed division commanders to promote officers for "distinguished skill and valor." Lomax selected Capt. Gustavus W. Dorsey of Company K as the battalion's commander. As the newest company in the 1st Maryland Cavalry, Dorsey and his men transferred to the battalion

16. Maj. Gen. L. L. Lomax to Lieut. Col. A. S. Pendleton, September 14, 1864, Letter 1244-L-1864, LAIG; Petition of the officers of the 1st Maryland Cavalry (C.S.) to President Jefferson Davis, June 6, 1864, Letter 1562-M-1864, LAIG. This file also contains a separate petition on June 4, 1864, from the battalion's enlisted men who submitted Frank Bond's name as major.

17. Booth, *Personal Reminiscences*, 122; Capt. William I. Rasin and officers of the 1st Maryland Cavalry (C.S.) to President Jefferson Davis, September 15, 1864, Letter 2130-W-1864, LAIG.

in August, 1864. A resident of Montgomery County, Dorsey rose through the ranks with the Maryland company of the 1st Virginia Cavalry Regiment. Lomax felt that he deserved promotion for his bravery throughout the fighting in the Valley. This time, the officers and men of the battalion did not protest Lomax's action.[18]

The opposition of the 1st Maryland Cavalry (C.S.) to merging with their comrades in the 2nd Battalion is understandable when one examines the history of that command. In an effort to boost military strength, the Confederate Congress adopted the "Act to Organize Bands of Partisan Rangers" in April, 1862, authorizing President Jefferson Davis to form partisan units to conduct operations against enemy forces. The law stipulated that partisans would receive the same pay, rations, and quarters as members of the regular army, as well as extra pay for seized enemy arms and ammunition.[19]

The Partisan Ranger Act capitalized on southern interest in guerrilla warfare. Throughout the spring and summer of 1862, the government authorized the formation of partisan units. Army commanders, however, expressed displeasure at these new units because they tended to be poorly trained and equipped.[20]

Within months, the army refused to transfer soldiers from the regular army to partisan units and officers who recruited among the main forces faced court-martial charges. Further orders specifically required officers to recruit only nonconscripts, or men ineligible for drafting into the army, for partisan commands. Recruitment of partisans was prohibited in certain military districts, such as the Department of Henrico.[21]

18. CSR, Gustavus W. Dorsey, 1st Maryland Cavalry (C.S.) and 1st Virginia Cavalry Regiment; *Official Records,* Ser. IV, Vol. III, 190.

19. For a discussion of the manpower situation in the Confederacy in 1862, see Moore, *Conscription and Conflict.* The role of partisan rangers in the southern war effort is discussed in Jeffrey D. Wert, *Mosby's Rangers* (New York, 1990), 69–71. The Confederate Partisan Ranger Act, as announced in General Orders Number 30, April 28, 1862, is in *Official Records,* Ser. IV, Vol. I, 1094–95. Further discussion of Gilmor's role is found in Kevin Conley Ruffner, "'More Trouble Than a Brigade': Harry Gilmor's 2d Maryland Cavalry in the Shenandoah Valley," *Maryland Historical Magazine,* LXXXIX (1994), 388–411.

20. For one Confederate officer's complaints against the use of state partisan rangers even before the act's passage by the Confederate Congress, see Brig. Gen. Henry Heth's letter to the governor of Virginia, *Official Records,* Ser. I, Vol. LVI, Pt. 2, p. 526. Heth also heard a similar complaint from a citizen of western Virginia; *ibid.,* 531–32.

21. *Official Records,* Ser. IV, Vol. I, 1151–52, Ser. IV, Vol. II, 26.

In early 1863, James A. Seddon, the Confederate secretary of war, reported to the president that the "policy of organizing corps of partisan rangers has not been approved by experience. The permanency of their engagements and their consequent inability to disband and reassemble at call precludes their usefulness as mere guerrillas," Seddon noted, "while the comparative independence of their military relations, and the peculiar rewards allowed for captures induce much license and many irregularities."[22]

At Seddon's urging, the War Department refused to authorize new partisan units and merged existing units with regular battalions and regiments. Samuel Cooper, the Confederate adjutant and inspector general, introduced new regulations for the partisan ranger units to "promote their efficiency and the interest of the service" in June, 1863. By this time, many units raised in 1862 had already disbanded.[23]

Even though the Confederate government lost much of its enthusiasm for partisan warfare by 1863, there were notable exceptions. John S. Mosby, perhaps the most famous partisan leader of the Civil War, led a daring raid in March of that year, capturing a Union general. Mosby's successes behind Union lines in northern Virginia earned the "Gray Ghost" promotions and eventual command of a partisan ranger regiment. By the end of the war, some nineteen hundred officers and men had served with Mosby, striking terror into the hearts of Union soldiers and civilians around the northern capital.[24]

Mosby raised his first company of partisan rangers in June, 1863; at the same time, Capt. Harry Gilmor received permission from the secretary of war to organize an independent battalion of Maryland cavalry for service behind Union lines. Gilmor earned his laurels as a dashing cavalryman under Turner Ashby in the Shenandoah Valley in 1861. He formed his own company in the early spring of 1862; it was soon assigned to the 12th Virginia Cavalry Regiment. Following service in the Valley, Gilmor moved into Maryland with the main army in September. On a lark, he visited his home in Baltimore County, where Union soldiers took him prisoner. Gilmor was held as a spy at Fort McHenry in Baltimore until

22. *Ibid.*, Ser. IV, Vol. II, 289.
23. *Ibid.*, 585.
24. Among the many books that discuss Mosby's military career and the history of his unit, see Wert, *Mosby's Rangers*, 47, 74.

his father gained his parole to wait for his formal exchange in February, 1863.[25]

Gilmor, who was twenty-five years old when he returned to Confederate soil, hailed from one of Maryland's wealthiest families. His father, Robert Gilmor III, owned a Baltimore shipping firm, and the family staunchly supported the South despite the state's occupation by Union troops. Three of the Gilmor sons served in the Confederate army, as did numerous other relatives. Gilmor's prowess on the battlefield was enhanced at Kelly's Ford in March, and Maj. Gen. J. E. B. Stuart, cavalry commander of the Army of Northern Virginia, commended him for bravery.[26]

Gilmor encountered little difficulty in gaining army approval to form his own partisan ranger unit. On May 7, he addressed a short note to the secretary of war in Richmond stating that "having become satisfied that a battalion of Maryland Cavalry can be raised in the Valley of Virginia I respectfully ask that authority may be granted me to raise such a Battalion." Gilmor failed to indicate what prompted this request, nor did he say why he thought his unit could enlist Marylanders who had not already joined the Confederate army. Gilmor also asked that "in case the authority is granted me that I may be allowed to operate outside our lines until my Battalion is mounted and equipped, and that it may be considered *an independent command* until its organization is complete."[27]

That the War Department granted Gilmor's request to raise a battalion for independent service is unusual in light of the numerous problems that other partisan commands had experienced in procuring suitable recruits, officers, mounts, equipment, and weapons. Nevertheless, Seddon endorsed Gilmor's proposal and told the adjutant general that

25. Gilmor's *Four Years in the Saddle* is an autobiography of his Civil War service. It was one of the first books by a Confederate officer after the war. One modern Civil War historian has questioned the book's authorship and authenticity. See James I. Robertson, Jr., "The War in Words," *Civil War Times Illustrated*, XVI (1977); 48. This criticism is dismissed by Daniel Carroll Toomey in his introduction to the Butternut and Blue Press edition of Gilmor's book.

26. Harry Gilmor's brothers, Meredith and Richard T. Gilmor, were also officers in the 2nd Maryland Cavalry Battalion. For the commendation, see Goldsborough, *Maryland Line*, 243.

27. Harry Gilmor to James A. Seddon, May 7, 1863, in CSR, Harry Gilmor, 12th Virginia Cavalry Regiment.

same day to "allow the authority to Capt Gilmor (with the approval of Genl Stuart with who he is now serving) to raise within or near the enemys lines a Battalion of Marylanders for the Prov. Army." The secretary added that Stuart could post Gilmor "with any companies he may raise to service of an independent or partisan character until his full Command be raised."[28]

To the army's later detriment, Seddon failed to specify any date by which Gilmor's "full command be raised." Consequently, the Confederate chain of command exercised little control over Gilmor's organization and leadership of his new unit—an oversight that created enormous problems.

Capt. Gilmor resigned his commission in the 12th Virginia Cavalry on May 23 at Camp Ashby near Harrisonburg to raise his new battalion as its major. Gen. Robert E. Lee accepted Gilmor's letter of resignation reluctantly, commenting that "I know nothing of the probability of success of raising this Battn. It takes a man from the cavy of this Army."[29]

Raising his new unit proved more difficult than Gilmor initially expected. In early June, he wrote the Confederate adjutant general for permission to join Brig. Gen. Albert G. Jenkins' cavalry brigade. E. A. Palfrey, assistant adjutant general in Richmond, told Gilmor on June 11 that the War Department would assign the new Maryland unit to a specific brigade only when the battalion had been duly organized and the muster rolls had been forwarded to the Confederate capital.[30]

The movement of the Confederate army into the Valley and across the Potomac River delayed Gilmor's organizational efforts. He temporarily abandoned recruiting and scouted for the army as it moved northward into Pennsylvania. Gilmor commanded Lieut. Col. Ridgely Brown's regular Maryland cavalry battalion and entered Gettysburg shortly after the Union withdrawal. He then served as the town's provost marshal, gathering captured Union prisoners, supplies, and equipment and assisting in the care of the wounded. He relinquished this duty on July 2, and, as he later recalled, "I amused myself by riding from point to point to watch

28. *Ibid.*

29. Endorsement, Harry Gilmor to Gen. Samuel Cooper, May 23, 1863, in CSR, Harry Gilmor, 12th Virginia Cavalry Regiment.

30. E. A. Palfrey to Harry Gilmor, June 11, 1863, RG 109, War Department Collection of Confederate Records, Letters and Telegrams Sent by the Confederate Adjutant and Inspector General, 1861–65, Roll 4, M627, NA.

the fight." Gilmor took part in the fighting the following day and during the retreat to Virginia.[31]

As the southern army made its precarious way back to the Old Dominion, Gilmor's first company joined him at Williamsport, Maryland. This company, commanded by Capt. Nicholas Burke, formed while Gilmor was with the Army of Northern Virginia. Gilmor designated Burke's unit as Company B. To serve as Company A in the new battalion, Gilmor planned to use his own Company F from the 12th Virginia Cavalry. By early August, the 12th's commander demanded the return of Company F to his regiment, forcing Burke's company to become Company A of Gilmor's battalion by default.[32]

Major Gilmor spent the remainder of the summer of 1863 raising new companies for his battalion. In early August from his camp near Fishers Hill Gilmor told Gen. Cooper that he had authorized six men to form new companies: Nicholas Burke, T. Sturgis Davis, Charles A. Bragonier, George E. Shearer, W. Y. Glenn, and J. Redmond Burke. He still could not fully organize the battalion and even complained that Confederate conscript officers had disbanded a company under Captain Frank Ingle when it was "fully equipd and ready to take the field." Gilmor requested permission from Cooper to continue recruiting for his battalion without harassment from regular army recruiters.[33]

As it turned out, only two of the six men that Gilmor appointed actually went on to command companies in the battalion. Nicholas Burke took command of Company A while J. Redmond Burke (no known relation) raised Company D. The other men either failed to raise companies or, after raising a company, refused to join Gilmor's battalion.[34] Indeed, Gilmor commissioned a mixed group of men; in some cases, they proved to be rugged fighters, whereas one, Shearer, was a bushwacker.

Twenty-five-year-old J. Redmond Burke proved to be one of the more

31. Gilmor, *Four Years in the Saddle*, 98.

32. *Ibid.*, 77. For a discussion of the circumstances of the return of Gilmor's old company to the 12th Virginia Cavalry Regiment, see Harry Gilmor to Walter H. Taylor, March 2, 1864, in CSR, Harry Gilmor, 2nd Maryland Cavalry Battalion (C.S.).

33. Harry Gilmor to Gen. Samuel Cooper, August 5, 1863, Letter 746-J-1863, LAIG. No record has been found concerning Ingle's company.

34. T. Sturgis Davis refused to join Gilmor's battalion; George E. Shearer was captured by Union troops; and the record is uncertain as to the status of Bragonier's and Glenn's companies.

successful officers in Gilmor's unit. A resident of Berkeley County, Burke joined a Virginia infantry unit in 1861 and then transferred to the 1st Virginia Cavalry Regiment. He fought with his father, Redmond Burke, who earned the sobriquet of the "Potomac Scout" for his exploits with J. E. B. Stuart. Following his father's death at enemy hands in 1862, Burke continued the struggle and was captured twice by the Union army.[35]

Gilmor demonstrated less selectivity when he appointed George E. Shearer as a recruiting officer for the battalion. A native of Winchester, Shearer had no prior military service in the Confederate army; in fact, he preyed on helpless citizens in the area.[36] In early 1863, Shearer threatened to burn a house with its inhabitants still inside. Following his apprehension by Union forces in February, the provost marshal recorded that "the loyal citizens of this vicinity had learned to fear him for his many deeds of cruelty and villainy." Despite these charges, the federals exchanged Shearer only two months later.[37] Maj. Gilmor's association with Shearer gravely damaged the reputation of the new Maryland unit and had numerous ramifications within the Confederate chain of command.

Finding untapped reservoirs of volunteers within the war-torn Shenandoah Valley proved to be one of Gilmor's greatest headaches. In May, he assumed that he could easily raise a battalion of Marylanders. Three months later, he had learned that there were very few men from that border state who desired to join the Confederate army and had not already done so. In his letter to the Confederate adjutant general in August, Gilmor asked to be allowed to recruit Virginians for his battalion. He followed this letter by paying a visit to Richmond to make a verbal appeal

35. J. Redmond Burke to James A. Seddon, May 9, 1863, in CSR, J. Redmond Burke, 2nd Maryland Cavalry (C.S.) and 1st Virginia Cavalry; Robert J. Driver, Jr., *1st Virginia Cavalry* (Lynchburg, 1991), 156. There is some confusion in the records between Redmond Burke and his son J. Redmond Burke. The latter served as a company commander in Gilmor's unit.

36. Confusion also exists in the records between George M. E. Shearer, who served as an officer in the 1st Maryland Infantry Regiment (C.S.) and later as a staff officer, and George E. Shearer of the 2nd Maryland Cavalry (C.S.). The former was taken prisoner twice in 1862 and 1864 and held until the end of the war. Capt. George E. Shearer of Gilmor's battalion was a resident of Frederick County, Virginia, but never served as a lieutenant in either the 51st Virginia Militia (from Frederick County) or the 51st Virginia Infantry Regiment.

37. Capt. W. D. Alexander, Provost Marshal at Winchester, to Provost Marshal at Martinsburg, February 12, 1863, in George E. Shearer, Unfiled CSR.

for permission to recruit Virginians. Brig. Gen. John D. Imboden, a former partisan officer and now commanding the Valley District, supported Gilmor in a letter to the secretary of war on August 27.[38]

These letters and Gilmor's visit displeased Secretary Seddon, who replied: "No Virginians liable to Conscription are allowed to be recruited. Only non Conscripts. It is evident that the power granted [to raise the battalion] has been exceeded. . . . I am greatly tempted to revoke it." In a letter to Gen. Imboden in September, the War Department prohibited Gilmor's recruitment of men who were liable to conscription.[39]

Gilmor had few sources from which to draw recruits. The partisan service's long reputation as a haven for deserters from the main army proved no exception in Gilmor's battalion. The root of the problem was the failure of officers to uphold tough recruiting standards. In several cases, men received commissions as officers in the Maryland battalion while still absent without leave from their original commands.[40]

Soon Gilmor's battalion sheltered men who had left the main army under less than desirable conditions. These soldiers created similar disciplinary problems in their new unit. Capt. Nicholas Burke charged two of his men, Pvts. John Birchell and George Wagoner, with desertion in July while at Harrisonburg. Birchell, already a deserter from the Union army, soon escaped and returned to federal lines, where, ironically, he took the oath of allegiance and was released. Wagoner, a deserter from a Louisiana regiment, begged Capt. Burke for mercy: "Will you be kind enough to reliese me from the guard House and take me to the Company again and I will go to my duty and doe it like a man. Capt doe not send me to Richmond for god sake for they will shoot me and capt I doe not think you want my blood on your hands, doe try me once more and you will not have any caus to regret it I will doe all you require of me and will be a Dutifull an Obediant Soldier."[41]

38. Harry Gilmor to Gen. Samuel Cooper, August 5, 1863, Letter 746-J-1863, LAIG; John D. Imboden to James A. Seddon, August 27, 1863, Letter 746-J-1863, LAIG.

39. Seddon's endorsement to Gilmor's letter, August 5, 1863, Letter 746-J-1863, LAIG; E. A. Palfrey to John D. Imboden, September 15, 1863, Letters and Telegrams, Roll 4.

40. Capt. J. Redmond Burke was among the officers absent without leave. Officer absenteeism drew the attention of Gen. Lee and the secretary of war; see *Official Records*, Ser. I, Vol. XXXIII, Pt. 2, pp. 1120–21.

41. CSR, John Birchell, 2nd Maryland Cavalry (C.S.); George Wagoner to Capt. Burk[e], July 26, 1863, RG 109, War Department Collection of Confederate Records, Entry 143, Departmental Records (carded), Department of Henrico, NA.

Whether Burke released the penitent private is uncertain although he continued to rely on deserters to fill his company's ranks. In October, Burke dispatched one of his lieutenants to Richmond to recruit ten "Yankee deserters" for Company A. The War Department permitted Burke to recruit these deserters from Richmond prisons.[42]

Maj. Gilmor overlooked numerous disciplinary infractions in his new organization. By early August, Gilmor's men brought attention to themselves in the Shenandoah Valley—attention that was not particularly distinguished. Seventeen residents of Winchester protested to the Confederate government about the conduct of Gilmor's troops:

> We have been, and now are, very much harassed and annoyed by small roving bands of Confederate Cavalry or who profess to belong to our army. They say that they belong to Maj. Gilmers cavalry and to Capt. Shearers' company of cavalry. They are riding about the country in small parties very frequently intoxicated, many of them stealing horses, or whatever else they may want, sometimes arresting citizens, and in fact doing as much, if not more injury to us, than the Yankees. There seems to be an utter want of discipline, and the most of the men, in a state of demoralization. Between them and the Yankees, very few horses are left in the country, and it is with great difficulty that we can be furnished with wood even in the warm weather. If this seizing and carrying off horses is to be continued, we do not see what is to become of us in the winter.[43]

The Winchester petition marked the beginning of an almost endless stream of complaints by civilians and military officials alike against Gilmor's men. Gilmor responded to the charges of his men's misconduct on October 6. He acknowledged that he had authorized Capt. Shearer to raise a company for his battalion but told the War Department that Shearer had been taken prisoner only days before the citizens drew up their petition. Gilmor asserted that his entire battalion was under his

42. J. H. Carrington to Capt. W. S. Winder, October 16, 1863, Letter 831-C-1863, LSOW. For an example of men recruited for Gilmor's battalion and other units in Richmond, see C.S. War Department, Conscription Bureau Enrolling Book, 1863–64, Virginia Historical Society. Recruitment notices for the battalion appeared in Richmond *Daily Dispatch*, January 27 and February 1, 1864.

43. Citizens of Winchester to James A. Seddon, August 11, 1863, Letter 1489-W-1863, LAIG; another complaint by a citizen about Gilmor's men is found in R. E. Byrd affidavit, October 2, 1863, Byrd Family Papers, Virginia Historical Society.

personal command and "is & always has been subject to the strictest discipline & I conduct an inspection of it at any time."[44]

Gilmor further stated that his command was on outpost duty between Fishers Hill and New Market, with additional scouts deployed in Frederick, Clarke, Berkeley, and Jefferson counties. According to Gilmor, "I meet with favors of unflinging [unflinching] attachment to our country & assurances that the presence of my command is encouraging & benefiting to them." The thievery described by the civilians, he claimed, resulted from a "dangerous class of outlaws, Union refugees, deserters, conscripts," and not from his soldiers.[45]

Gen. Lee received the petition from the War Department and told Gen. Imboden on September 10 that "prominent citizens of the valley have made serious complaints of the conduct of Captain Shearer's company, of Gilmor's battalion. I wish you would see to it. If they cannot be brought under proper discipline, and continue to harass our own citizens by their bad conduct, they had much better be disbanded."[46]

Although Imboden's response to Lee's communique has not been located, it apparently eased the mounting criticism against Gilmor and his unit. Maj. Charles Marshall, Lee's aide-de-camp, told Imboden on September 21 that Lee was "gratified to learn that injustice has been done to Major Gilmor and his command. He says that he considers it necessary that every means should be used to capture or destroy the lawless men who have brought discredit upon the army. The interests of the cause and the character of our troops, particularly that of Major Gilmor's command,

---

44. Gilmor's response to the Winchester petition, October 6, 1863, Letter 1489-W-1863, LAIG. Capt. Shearer was captured by Union troops in Winchester on August 8, 1863. He was tried by a Union military commission on the charge of "being a guerrilla" and was found guilty and sentenced to fifteen years' hard labor in the spring of 1864. Shearer escaped from Fort McHenry in Baltimore on May 15, 1864, and was later reported in the Winchester area. For more details on this renegade officer, see CSR, George E. Shearer, 2nd Maryland Cavalry (C.S.); Unfiled CSR, George E. Shearer; George E. Shearer, RG 109, War Department Collection of Confederate Records, Union Provost Marshal's File of Papers Relating to Individual Civilians, M345, NA; George E. Shearer, RG 109, Union Provost Marshal's File of Papers Relating to Two or More Civilians, M416, NA; and Baltimore *American*, August 18, 1863, and May 17, 1864; *Official Records*, Ser. I, Vol. XXIX, Pt. 1, p. 74; and RG 153, Records of the Judge Advocate General, Proceedings of a Military Commission US v. George E. Shearer, NN107, NA.

45. Gilmor's response, Letter 1489-W-1863, LAIG.

46. *Official Records*, Ser. I, Vol. XXIX, Pt. 2, p. 709.

require that these deserters be arrested or destroyed, and a stop put to their marauding." Lee ordered Imboden to "instruct your officers and men to take them whenever they can, dead or alive. They must be exterminated, and every one who comes across them must take or shoot them."[47]

While still undergoing organization, Gilmor's battalion met mixed success on the field of battle. A party of Union cavalry nearly captured Gilmor in Jefferson County as he was returning from an unsuccessful raid into Maryland to seize horses. Gilmor and his men evaded the enemy after killing the federal commander. In the middle of October, Gilmor launched a raid on the Baltimore and Ohio Railroad. He allowed John C. Blackford, a former cavalry partisan commander whose company had disbanded, to lead the column.[48] While Gilmor lingered (according to one Union account to "see a rebel maiden"), the remainder of his men pressed on across North Mountain.[49]

Meanwhile, Gilmor's movement alerted Union forces at Martinsburg. Detachments from the 1st New York and 12th Pennsylvania Cavalry rode hard into the night of October 15 and, with infantry support, attacked the southern camp. The federals utterly routed the sleeping partisans and seized thirty-seven men, including Blackford, Capt. Eugene Digges of Company B, First Lieut. William Reed of Company D, and Gilmor's acting adjutant, Herman F. Keidel.[50] The loss of these men at Hedgesville, West Virginia, severely reduced Gilmor's effective strength of personnel

47. *Ibid.*, 739.

48. Gilmor, *Four Years in the Saddle*, 107–12. Gilmor's account is vague as to which Capt. Blackford commanded the raiding party. It was not Capt. William Willis Blackford, who served in the 1st Virginia Cavalry Regiment and later on Stuart's staff. According to his memoirs, *War Years with Jeb Stuart* (New York, 1945), Blackford was with the Army of Northern Virginia at the time of the raid. For confirmation that John C. Blackford led Gilmor's men, see F. K. Shawham to Provost Marshal, Baltimore, October 16, 1863, in Unfiled CSR, John C. Blackford. For further details on Capt. John C. Blackford's military career, see CSR, John C. Blackford, 2nd Maryland Cavalry (C.S.), and Wallace, *Guide*, 54.

49. An article by "Grapeshot" labeled Gilmor's men "the knights of the order of the rum punch." (Baltimore *American*, October 21, 1863). This article was reprinted in Frank Moore, ed., *The Rebellion Record: A Diary of American Events with Documents, Narratives, Illustrative Incidents, Poetry, Etc.* (12 vols.; 1864; rpr. New York, 1977), VII, 565–66.

50. For descriptions of the engagement, see *ibid.*; *Official Records*, Ser. I, Vol. XXIX, Pt. 1, p. 483; Baltimore *American*, October 19, 23, 1863. Keidel's subsequent experiences as a prisoner of war are described in Chapter 6.

equipped with proper mounts—always an important consideration for Confederate cavalrymen, who had to furnish their own horses.[51]

Only days after the loss of Blackford's party, Gilmor's battalion participated in the capture of Charles Town, West Virginia. In a daring assault on the morning of October 18, Gen. Imboden's command gained the small county seat and forced the 9th Maryland Infantry Regiment (U.S.) to evacuate. The northerners fled in the direction of Harpers Ferry, where they encountered Confederate cavalrymen, including Gilmor's small battalion (only ninety-five mounted and dismounted troopers). After slight resistance, the nine-month soldiers from Baltimore threw down their arms and surrendered to the southern raiders. The victory at Charles Town, which netted 15 officers and 345 enlisted men, partially offset Gilmor's disaster at Hedgesville.[52]

For the remaining months of 1863 and into early 1864, Gilmor and his men patrolled the Shenandoah Valley. Their presence continued to raise questions about the status of the battalion as well as that of other independent Confederate units in western Virginia. Days after his victory at Charles Town, Gen. Imboden responded to a complaint presented by a member of the Virginia House of Delegates that Gilmor had stolen horses from a farmer in 1862. Imboden admitted that deserters ran rampant throughout the Valley. Imboden felt that there was "but one mode of remedying these evils & that is to consolidate & organize the small companies now in this Dist: deprieve them of their partizan character, and thus have a homogenous force in the Valley, & then begin a war of extermination on the Deserters & the vagabonds from Balt: who have come here for plunder & not to serve in the army." The general complained that "there are a great many Marylanders in this Dist. who are not in the army, & who do much of the mischief complained of, which is laid to the door of the soldiers."[53]

In late October Imboden requested that Gilmor's battalion be placed under his direct command and converted from partisan status to that of

51. Gilmor, *Four Years in the Saddle*, 112.

52. *Ibid.*, 113–17. For a review of the defeat at Charles Town from the Union perspective, see Paul E. Barr, Jr., and Michael P. Musick, eds., "'They Are Coming': Testimony at the Court of Inquiry on Imboden's Capture of Charles Town," *Magazine of the Jefferson County Historical Society*, LIV (December, 1988), 15–53.

53. John D. Imboden to James A. Seddon, October 26, 1863, Letter 1086-L-1863, LAIG.

regular troops. Imboden noted that the various partisan units in the Valley, "are all good troops, but for want of organization they are necessarily less efficient than they might be made and having no staff they are more trouble to subsist and manage than a Brigade." He added, "Their partizan character is also very objectionable—it is giving rise to discontent & dissatisfaction amongst the other troops." Imboden told the adjutant general of the difficulties he experienced in the Valley District: "The great extent of territory—a line extending from Harper's Ferry to Beverly over 200 miles under my command—renders it impossible to enforce good discipline & prevent wrongs to private property." The assistant secretary of war admitted on November 5 that the "partisan corps when left to themselves are little better than highwaymen."[54]

In the face of these difficulties, Maj. Gilmor failed to attract new soldiers. Upon the formation of his battalion in May, Gilmor expected to bring his old company in the 12th Virginia Cavalry with him. When the regimental commander revoked this transfer, Gilmor did not give up hope. In November, he obtained the support of A. R. Boteler, the Confederate congressman from the Shenandoah Valley. Boteler asked the secretary of war to transfer Gilmor's old company from the 12th Virginia to his new battalion. In its place, Boteler proposed that a new cavalry company under Capt. Fielding Helms Calmes be assigned to that regiment. Gilmor delivered Boteler's letter to Richmond, but it met with no success.[55]

Gen. Imboden questioned the presence of yet another Maryland cavalry unit in the lower Valley, one commanded by Capt. T. Sturgis Davis. This company, originally recruited by Davis for Gilmor's battalion, refused to join that unit. Gilmor told the War Department in October that Davis

---

54. John D. Imboden to Gen. Samuel Cooper, October 26, 1863, Letter 947-J-1863, LAIG. For an example of Imboden's inability to maintain law and order, see John D. Imboden to Winchester Town Council, November 27, 1863, in John D. Imboden Papers, LC.

55. A. R. Boteler to James A. Seddon, November 4, 1863, Letter 803-B-1863, LSOW. Calmes's company was later assigned to the 23rd Virginia Cavalry Regiment although Maj. Calmes (he was promoted in the process) was captured by Union troops. A northerner described Calmes as one of "the most notorious horse-thieves and bushwhackers in the country" (Wallace, *Guide*, 62–63; *Official Records*, Ser. I, Vol. XXXVII, Pt. 1, pp. 386–87).

had even established a separate camp. Davis, who had served with Gilmor in the same company at the beginning of the war, claimed that he planned to join Lieut. Col. Brown's battalion of Maryland cavalry with the main army. When this assignment did not take place, Davis organized his own cavalry battalion in the Valley.[56]

The presence of so many Confederate cavalry units raised havoc in the Valley, where they all foraged for limited food, horse fodder, and shelter. These units also became involved in petty disturbances with civilians throughout the region. In mid-January, 1864, a band of southern troopers rode into Winchester and seized William Dooley while he was at church. According to Union sources, the Confederates belonged to Gilmor's battalion under the charge of a Lieut. Gilmor.[57]

Col. R. S. Rodgers, the Union commander at Martinsburg, wrote on January 21 that "the arrest of a private citizen for holding loyal sentiments to the Government of the United States will certainly be punished by retaliation." In fact, northern soldiers had already taken two prominent residents of Winchester on January 18 as hostages until Dooley's safe return. Ironically, one of the prosouthern civilian detainees, Robert Y. Conrad, had signed the August, 1863, petition of residents protesting Gilmor's actions around Winchester.[58]

By this time, the lower Shenandoah Valley had a notorious reputation in both North and South. The Washington *Evening Star* commented on February 3 that bands of robbers along the Shenandoah River in Jefferson and Clarke counties were "more dreaded than the Yankees." The disappointing performance of partisan troops during a raid in West Virginia prompted Brig. Gen. Thomas L. Rosser, commanding a brigade of regular Confederate cavalrymen in the Valley, to protest the presence of so many "irregular bodies of troops which occupy this country."[59]

---

56. Harry Gilmor to James A. Seddon, October 6, 1863, Letter 1489-W-1863, LAIG. Davis later expanded his company into yet another battalion, which eventually became part of the 23rd Virginia Cavalry (Wallace, *Guide*, 63).

57. *Official Records*, Ser. I, Vol. XXXIII, 393; Roger U. Delauter, Jr., *Winchester in the Civil War* (Lynchburg, 1992), 63–64; and Washington *Evening Star*, January 22, 1864. The Lieut. Gilmor mentioned appears to have been Richard T. Gilmor.

58. *Official Records*, Ser. I, Vol. XXXIII, 400–401.

59. Washington *Evening Star*, February 3, 1864; *Official Records*, Ser. I, Vol. XXXIII, 1081–82.

Maj. Gen. Jubal Early, detailed to duty in the Shenandoah Valley in late 1863, was also disgusted with the cavalry that he found when he reported to his new post. He criticized Imboden's command, prompting that officer to ask Gen. Lee for a formal court of inquiry to investigate the "good order, discipline, courage, and soldierly qualifications" of the Northwestern Brigade. The request caused a minor stir at army head-quarters, but Lee thought such an examination to be disadvantageous to the service and let the matter rest.[60]

A new chorus of outrage against Maj. Gilmor's battalion resounded in early 1864. On the morning of February 12, Gilmor and twenty-eight of his men cut the Baltimore and Ohio Railroad between Martinsburg and Harpers Ferry at a whistle stop named Brown's Shop. The raiders placed obstacles across the track to halt the express train from Baltimore. Meeting only slight resistance, the southerners tried to open the train's safe. When they failed, the Confederate commander ordered his soldiers to burn the train except for the carriage carrying female passengers. While he was preoccupied with the safe, Gilmor learned that his men were robbing passengers of their valuables.

Eyewitness accounts vary as to what actually transpired on the train. One witness wrote in the New York *Times* that the raiders were "lavish of profane, vulgar and threatening language, but perpetrated no bodily injury, took nothing from the ladies, with a single exception, performed the whole affair with the clumsiness of novitiates in robbery, and retired in haste from the 'sleeping car' on the accidental discharge of a pistol, before completing their work there leaving quite a number of persons undisturbed, except by a very great fright."[61]

Another paper stated that the southern raiders robbed the train "most thoroughly, with all the grace and sang froid of experienced highway-men." According to this account, "those who did the robbing were ac-companied by pistol holders, who thrust the muzzles under the noses of

---

60. *Ibid.*, 1166–68; Freeman, *Lee's Lieutenants*, III, 326–28. Early's first impression of Confederate cavalry in the Valley was not favorable, and this had later ramifications when he commanded the Valley District in 1864. See Robert K. Krick, "'The Cause of All My Disasters': Jubal A. Early and the Undisciplined Valley Cavalry," in *Struggle for the Shenandoah: Essays on the 1864 Valley Campaign*, ed. Gary W. Gallagher, (Kent, 1991), 77–106.

61. Gilmor, *Four Years in the Saddle*, 143–46; Virgil Carrington Jones, *Gray Ghosts and Rebel Raiders* (New York, 1956), 215–17; New York *Times*, February 15, 1864; *Official Records*, Ser. I, Vol. XXXIII, 151.

their victims whilst they were being plundered."[62] The arrival of an east-bound train with federal troops scattered Gilmor's men.

A Baltimore paper reported that "the parties who committed this robbery are sons of some of the chivalry and Rebel sympathizing Baltimoreans. They constitute a portion of Gilmor's band. Beside Baltimore born robbers, there were engaged some of the sons of the wealthy and heretofore respectable residents of Jefferson and Berkeley counties, Virginia. It is said that there were in the party the sons of Marylanders and distinguished gentlemen living in and in the neighborhood of Cumberland."[63]

Reports that Gilmor's men had robbed a Jewish merchant in the Valley near Strasburg immediately followed the news of his controversial action on the Baltimore and Ohio train. A resident of Winchester complained to Gen. Early on February 15 that seven Confederate cavalrymen robbed a merchant who was transporting goods along the Valley Turnpike. The merchant, named Hyman, lost about $6,000 in gold pieces and personal items. One of the members of the caravan, a young teenager named Ezekiel, lost a woman's watch to the renegade Confederates. When the group arrived in Richmond, Ezekiel's father reported the crime to the city's provost marshal, who dispatched two detectives to the lower Valley to investigate and arrest the culprits. The two policemen returned to Richmond without success although a Confederate officer in Harrisonburg claimed that the investigators had been bribed not to make any arrests. This officer, Maj. E. W. Cross, told the Richmond authorities that the identity of the guilty party was known throughout the region. Cross specifically blamed Maj. Gilmor and said that Gilmor had "boasted that he had arranged the whole affair" and that he could "manage the whole detective force of the Government."[64]

62. Jones, *Gray Ghosts and Rebel Raiders*, 216–17.

63. Baltimore *American*, February 16, 1864; see also account of Charles Eichler, Baltimore *American*, February 17, 1864. The reference to wealthy residents of Cumberland, Maryland, may pertain to William W. McKaig, Jr., the son of a leading Cumberland family. McKaig was a cadet at the Virginia Military Institute in 1861 and later served as an officer in Company A of Gilmor's battalion. He was captured a month after the train raid. For a description of his wartime activities and his postwar career, see Helene L. Baldwin, Michael Allen Mudge, and Keith W. Schlegel, eds., *The McKaig Family Journal: A Confederate Family of Cumberland* (Baltimore, 1984). Details about McKaig's murder in Cumberland and other records are found in his alumni file at the Virginia Military Institute.

64. *Official Records*, Ser. I, Vol. XXXIII, 152–53; and Jones, *Gray Ghosts and Rebel*

The news from the Valley disturbed Gen. Lee, who told the secretary of war on March 6 that "I have heard that a party of Gilmor's battalion, after arresting the progress of a train of cars on the Baltimore and Ohio Railroad, took from the passengers their purses and watches." While protesting the action of Union raiders under Gen. Hugh Judson Kilpatrick and Col. Ulric Dahlgren around Richmond, Lee observed of Gilmor's raid that "as far as I know no military object was accomplished after gaining possession of the cars, and the act appears to have been one of plunder. Such conduct is unauthorized and discreditable. Should any of the battalion be captured the enemy might claim to treat them as highway robbers."[65]

Lee ordered an investigation of the train incident, and Imboden once again wrote to Confederate headquarters on February 29 requesting clarification of the status of Gilmor's battalion. He found that the unit had been the source of many complaints and wanted the Marylanders transferred to Stuart's cavalry in eastern Virginia. "Otherwise," Imboden declared, "I see no means of repressing the lawlessness in the lower Valley where every Cut throat & vagabond, who is not in the army, passes through the country on the claim of being 'one of Gilmor's men.' Remove Gilmor's command and the mode of escape will be cut off from these fellows."[66]

The entire Confederate chain of command concurred with Imboden's recommendation. J. E. B. Stuart wrote on March 7 that "Gilmor's command be disbanded except such companies as may elect to join some regt. in the organization of April 16, 1862." Lee likewise supported the conversion of Gilmor's partisan battalion to a regular organization. Maj. Samuel W. Melton of the Adjutant and Inspector General's Office stated later in March that Gilmor's unit should be offered the opportunity to report to Camp Maryland at Staunton to join the newly revived Maryland Line under Maj. Gen. Arnold Elzey or face disbandment.[67]

In the meantime, the Confederate War Department ordered Gen. Imboden to investigate the circumstances surrounding the train incident

---

Raiders, 217. A search through the Compiled Service Records fails to provide any clues as to the identity of Maj. E. W. Cross in Staunton.

65. *Official Records*, Ser. I, Vol. XXXIII, 222–23.

66. John D. Imboden to Col. R. H. Chilton, February 29, 1864, Letter 234-J-1864, LAIG.

67. *Ibid.*; *Official Records*, Ser. I, Vol. XXXIII, 1312.

and the robbery complaints in the Valley. The results of this investigation are briefly summarized in the *Official Records* and point to Gilmor's culpability in not controlling his men. According to testimony provided by Capt. David M. Ross of Company C, Major Gilmor "arranged the affair of robbing the Jew; had put the men concerned all right, and had stood off and seen the thing well done."[68]

Gilmor concedes in his postwar memoir that a military court-martial convened in Staunton to try him on unspecified charges in early April. The major's comments (one paragraph in his book) are the only known account of this trial. The charges and specifications do not survive, nor are there any transcripts of the court-martial. Likewise, if the results of the court-martial were published, the general orders have not been located. Interestingly, Gilmor does not mention the robbery in the Valley in his book, and he contends that his court-martial dealt only with the train robbery. He admits that the proceedings lasted one week but states that the court, presided over by Col. Richard H. Dulany of the 7th Virginia Cavalry Regiment, took only five minutes to acquit him.[69]

While Gilmor was facing court-martial charges, other commanders in the Valley vented their spleen against him. Capt. T. Sturgis Davis reported to Gen. Imboden on April 8 that "Gilmor's battalion has now only thirty-five horses fit for duty, and his transportation is entirely useless, more of an encumbrance than anything else." Davis, who had refused to join Gilmor the previous summer, now commanded an independent battalion in the Valley. He claimed that "it is a shame that no better care has been bestowed upon it. The neglectful manner in which the affairs of that battalion have been administered is certainly culpable in the extreme. I found scarce any one connected with it devoted to the service."[70]

68. *Official Records*, Ser. I, Vol. XXXIII, 152–54. Other Confederate soldiers also admitted that Gilmor's men lived on captured plunder. Pvt. William Delisle of Company A told a federal interrogator in 1863 that "all the plunder we capture it is divided among those engaged in the fight. Every private in Harry Gillmore Independent Battalion makes about two thousand dollars a month besides there pay from the government" (Statement of William Delisle to Michael Graham, October 15, 1863, RG 393, Records of U.S. Army Continental Army Commands, Part II, Entry 3980, Box 9, Miscellaneous Letters, Reports, and Lists Received, 1861–65, NA).

69. Gilmor, *Four Years in the Saddle*, 146. Ironically, the general orders recording the charges, specifications, and verdicts of a court-martial for enlisted men in Imboden's brigade at Staunton for the same period survive at the University of Virginia.

70. *Official Records*, Ser. I, Vol. LI, Pt. 2, p. 853.

By mid-April, complaints against Gilmor and the few remaining partisan ranger units still in Virginia reached a crescendo, forcing the War Department to act. On April 21, the secretary of war approved Gen. Lee's recommendation that Gilmor's battalion be mustered into Confederate service and issued orders to that effect on May 5. Gilmor received instructions to report to Camp Maryland at Staunton, where Gen. Elzey would enlist the Marylanders into regular service as the 2nd Maryland Cavalry Battalion. Members of the battalion who were not Marylanders had permission to transfer to other commands.[71]

As it turned out, the exigencies of war prevented Gilmor from reporting to Elzey. Pressure from Union forces in the Shenandoah Valley in May, 1864, coupled with the movement of enemy troops toward Richmond, forced Confederate commanders to call upon all troops to defend the state. Gen. Ezley furnished Maj. Gilmor with a handful of fresh troops, but he never formally reorganized Gilmor's battalion. By mid-June, Elzey admitted the futility of recruiting for the Maryland Line at Staunton. He subsequently requested that the War Department close Camp Maryland and that he be assigned to new duties.[72]

Maj. Gilmor and his command served with Confederate forces in the Shenandoah Valley, around Lynchburg, and on the drive to Washington throughout the spring and summer of 1864. Gilmor is perhaps best remembered for his raid around Baltimore County during Early's movement on Washington in July. This daring raid behind the enemy's lines resulted in the capture of a Union general. Gilmor's men once again demonstrated their carelessness because this officer, Maj. Gen. William B. Franklin, escaped from his captors while they slept.[73]

Gilmor commanded his battalion throughout the summer and played a prominent role in the destruction of Chambersburg, Pennsylvania. This raid was marked by numerous acts of depredation by ill-disciplined southern horsemen. Upon the return of Early's cavalry, under Brig. Gens. John McCausland and Bradley T. Johnson to West Virginia, Union forces

---

71. *Ibid.*, Vol. XXXIII, 1252–53.

72. *Ibid.*, Vol. XL, Pt. 2, p. 650. Gilmor's battalion received new recruits transferred from South Carolina; see Richard P. Weinert, Jr., *The Confederate Regular Army* (Shippensburg, 1991), 92–95.

73. Gilmor, *Four Years in the Saddle*, 148–208; Fielding, ed., "Gilmor's Field Report of His Raid in Baltimore County," 234–39. For a discussion of Gilmor's role in the Maryland campaign, see Cooling, *Jubal Early's Raid*, 157–76.

launched a surprise attack at Moorefield during the early morning hours of August 7. The bulk of the 2nd Maryland Cavalry (C.S.) fell prisoner, including Capt. James L. Clark, whose Company F had finally transferred to Gilmor's command from the 12th Virginia Cavalry. It was a devastating blow that crippled the small Maryland unit, which lost six officers and forty-five men.[74]

Following the debacle at Moorefield, Confederate commanders attempted to correct some of the problems of the mounted branch in the Shenandoah Valley. Two weeks after Moorefield, Gen. Robert Ransom recommended that the two battalions of Maryland cavalry, the 1st and 2nd, be consolidated. Maj. Gen. Lomax made the same suggestion to Gen. Early on September 14 and stated that the two battalions should form a regiment. Lomax observed that "the command is now very indifferently organized and is insufficient from its perfect want of discipline."[75]

The 1st Maryland Cavalry counted 598 officers and men present and absent (with nearly 300 of that number absent in prison, detached, or wounded), but the 2nd Maryland Cavalry had fewer than 100 men present for duty. Capt. Gustavus W. Dorsey, who had recently transferred with his company from the 1st Virginia Cavalry Regiment, commented on the 2nd Maryland's morning report that "it is impossible to obtain a correct report from Co's B, C, and E. Their Company officers are all captured, & the rolls lost."[76]

To command this new regiment, Lomax recommended that Maj. Gilmor be promoted to colonel and Capt. Dorsey assume the rank of lieutenant colonel. Lomax felt that Capt. George M. Emack, a company commander in the 1st Maryland Cavalry, should assume the majority as these officers "have [proven] themselves to be gallant and efficient soldiers, and competent for the position."[77] Lomax's proposed consolidation

74. Gilmor, *Four Years in the Saddle*, 221–25; *Official Records*, Ser. I, Vol. XLIII, Pt. 1, pp. 4–8. For further details on the transfer of Capt. Clark and his men from the 12th Virginia Cavalry, see Petition of Officers and Men to Gen. Arnold Elzey, April 2, 1864, Letter 244-V-1864, LAIG; and James L. Clark to Gen. Samuel Cooper, March 6, 1865, Letter 443-C-1865, LAIG.

75. *Official Records*, Ser. I, Vol. XLIII, Pt. 1, pp. 1003–1004. Maj. Gen. L. L. Lomax to Lieut. Col. Alexander S. Pendleton, September 14, 1864, Letter 1244-L-1864, LAIG; for General Early's approval of this proposal, see *Official Records*, Ser. I, Vol. XLIII, Pt. 2, p. 874.

76. Lomax to Pendleton, September 14, 1864, Letter 1244-L-1864, LAIG.

77. *Ibid.*

plan failed, in part because of resistance from members of the 1st Maryland Cavalry and inaction on the part of the Confederate government.

The Maryland cavalry consolidation also failed to win official recognition because Maj. Gilmor suffered a wound in his upper neck and shoulder blades at Bunker Hill on September 3. From that point on, Gilmor's command "dwindled away" and he never really tried to reform it after the multiple disasters at Third Winchester, Fishers Hill, and Cedar Creek. In December, Gilmor took leave and traveled throughout the South. When he returned to the Shenandoah Valley, Gen. Early ordered him to proceed to Hardy County, West Virginia. Early wanted Gilmor to refit his own battalion and strengthen it by taking command of two independent partisan companies, Jesse C. McNeill's and Charles H. Woodson's Missouri rangers. Not surprisingly, both companies refused to join Gilmor, and Early appealed to Gen. Lee on January 31 to abolish the partisan ranger status of McNeill's unit.[78]

In addition to these troubles, Gilmor failed to reorganize his own command. He told the adjutant general's office on January 22 that he could not provide a roster of officers because "when I returned to duty a short time ago I found only two officers with the remnant of my battalion & but 15, or 20 men. The balance are scattered all over the lower Valley, but are principally with Mosby."[79]

Within days after authorities in Richmond received Gilmor's communique, he fell into Union hands. Gilmor's capture on February 3, under less than heroic circumstances, ended the threat that his presence posed to Union forces in the Shenandoah Valley.[80] Major General Philip Sheridan stated in his official report in 1866 that the loss of Gilmor severed "the last link between Maryland and the Confederacy."[81] He ended the war in a Union prison cell in Boston Harbor and was not released until the summer of 1865.

The last months of the Confederacy were the most trying in the short history of that nation. Confronted with diminishing resources in the face of mounting pressure from the enemy, some units, such as Gilmor's 2nd

78. Gilmor, *Four Years in the Saddle*, 257, 276–77; *Official Records*, Ser. I, Vol. LI, Pt. 2, pp. 1060–61; and Roger U. Delauter, Jr., *McNeil's Rangers* (Lynchburg, 1986), 92–93.

79. Harry Gilmor to Jon W. Riley, January 22, 1865, Letter 85-G-1865, LAIG.

80. For a description of Gilmor's capture, see John Bakeless, "Catching Harry Gilmor," *Civil War Times Illustrated*, X (1971), 34–40; and Gilmor, *Four Years in the Saddle*, 277–91.

81. *Official Records*, Ser. I, Vol. XLIII, Pt. 1, p. 56.

Maryland Cavalry, essentially dissolved because of internal problems as well as losses in combat. Other units, however, like the 2nd Maryland Infantry, remained viable until the end.

The key difference lay in the quality of unit leadership. Gilmor's battalion lacked discipline from its inception, and though a brave soldier, Gilmor never exercised strict control over his command. His company commanders likewise failed to perform their duties, which resulted in many lapses and earned the battalion notoriety that Gilmor perhaps did not initially intend it to have. When confronted with major losses on the battlefield, the 2nd Maryland Cavalry fell apart. In contrast, faced with the loss of its commanding officers, the junior officers of the 2nd Maryland Infantry (C.S.) readily assumed responsibility for the battalion. The unit maintained tight coherence because its captains and lieutenants proved to be able officers.

The 2nd Maryland Infantry, in fact, gained a reputation as the most steadfast command in its brigade (an amalgamation of two separate brigades with troops from Alabama, Maryland, Tennessee, and Virginia) during the last months of the war. Second Lieut. Tolson recorded in his diary the "sad fact that desertions from our division are becoming very numerous. Last night over eighteen men left the picket line, and went over to the enemy. . . . Our Cause is in great danger; for if this continues but a little while, we shall have nothing to oppose to the enemy." Indeed, Tolson glumly saw a near mutiny in a neighboring unit when the soldiers refused to obey the orders of their officers. The Maryland troops squelched what could have been a potentially dangerous situation along the Confederate front line.[82]

From Cold Harbor in June, 1864, until the surrender, the 2nd Maryland Infantry (C.S.) served in the thick of fighting with the Army of Northern Virginia. Somerville Sollers, an enlisted man in Company A, described the battalion's activities during the summer of 1864:

> Since you heard from me last, we have had fighting to our hearts content; there has not been a day since our fight at Cool Harbour [sic] that we have not been under fire more or less. Around Petersburg, we lived entirely in the trenches, & I assure you it is a mean life to lead! . . . Our lines & the enemies are from 75 to 200 yds apart. . . . Our pickets & theirs were only some 50 yards apart. Fortunately for us, we found that an agreement had

82. Ammen, "Maryland Troops in the Confederate Army," 170–71.

been entered by the pickets not to fire unless it was really necessary, & when we entered the trenches the same agreement prevailed. But still, we were continually exposed to danger, for the firing on our left was kept up 'Morning noon & night' & the stray balls were always hissing over us & among us, so that seldom a day passed but what some were killed & wounded, & then the Yanks would take it into their heads that we were all asleep I suppose & wanted rousing, & open about a dozen guns, & the way Sheel & Solid Shot would whiz over us was a caution, & then our batteries would answer, & altogether there would be the most infernal din for an hour or more, keeping us poor fellows squeezed in the smallest possible space behind the 'works' & in Boom [sic] proofs, afraid to show our heads.[83]

The end came quickly after Union troops assailed the Petersburg fortifications in early April, 1865. Maryland Confederate troops held the line gallantly at Hatcher's Run and Fort Gregg, stemming the Union avalanche.[84] After suffering heavy losses, Capt. Torsch was the only company officer present with the 2nd Maryland Infantry when the battalion stacked its arms at Appomattox Court House. Dorsey's 1st Maryland Cavalry refused to surrender, broke through the Yankee encirclement, and made its way westward. Riding hard into southwest Virginia to rally with other Confederate forces, the Marylanders planned to continue the struggle. Near Salem, Virginia, the battalion held its last formation. Lieut. C. Irving Ditty of the 1st Maryland Cavalry posted the last order of Brig. Gen. Thomas T. Munford, disbanding the battalion: "You, who struck the first blow in Baltimore and the last in Virginia, have done all that could be asked of you. Had the rest of our officers and men adhered to our cause with the same devotion, to-day we would have been free from the Yankees. May the God of battles bless you!"[85]

The Confederate Marylanders, despite their internal squabbling, proved to be determined patriots of southern independence. The success

---

83. Sollers to Meme, September 12, 1864, in Bowie Collection.

84. Goldsborough, *Maryland Line*, 151; E. C. Cottrell, "The Fight at Fort Gregg," *Confederate Veteran*, VII (1899), 308.

85. John R. Stonebraker, "Munford's Marylanders Never Surrendered to Foe," *SHSP*, XXXVII (1910), 309–12; Frank Dorsey, "Last Days of the First Maryland Cavalry," *Confederate Veteran*, XXVII (1919), 254–55; Raphael Semmes, "Vignettes of Maryland History from the Society's Collections of Broadsides," *Maryland Historical Magazine*, XL (1945), 53.

of the Maryland Line on battlefields as varied as First Manassas, Cross Keys, Gaines Mill, Second Winchester, Gettysburg, and Cold Harbor, and during the fierce fighting around Petersburg, is a tribute to the bravery and professionalism of the captains and lieutenants who served in its units.

·8·

Uncertain Yankees

One of the first items of business for all Civil War units upon mustering for service was the presentation of the battle flag. The 1st Maryland Infantry (U.S.) assembled on June 18, 1861, and "a bevy of young ladies, thirty-four in number, each representing a state, and dressed in white, wearing a beautiful floral wreath upon their heads, and preceded by several gentlemen having the flag in charge" went to the front of the regiment. Emma Lawrenson presented the banner to Col. John R. Kenly while a civic-minded city lawyer spoke to the troops: "Our country, torn by dissensions, and trembling in the throes of an attempted revolution, has appealed to its loyal hearts and strong arms for support. . . . You, brothers and soldiers, have sought and found service in your country's cause. Mothers, sisters, wives and children will look upon you with a tearful anxiety as you take up the march for the battlefield, upon the triumphs of which hang the destinies of your country." Kenly accepted the flag for the regiment and promised that the 1st Maryland Infantry would "fight valorously for the Government their fathers had given to their keeping." The women then sang "The Star-Spangled Banner," which had special meaning for Marylanders, as the regiment returned to camp. Such flag presentations helped indoctrinate soldiers to the cause for which they had taken up arms and bound the regiment to the home community.[1]

Organizing Union regiments from Maryland proved to be a difficult

1. Camper and Kirkley, *Historical Record*, 8–12; Wiley, *Life of Billy Yank*, 28–30. The importance of the flag presentation was evident when a Union volunteer company attempted to form in Queen Annes County on the Eastern Shore in 1861. A local newspaper wrote dramatically, "This fine organization will carry no other banner than the Stars and Stripes. Have we not patriotic ladies enough to see that they shall soon have a standard to carry which shall once more gladden our eyes?" (Emory, *Queen Anne's County*, 497–98).

task. Recruitment was hindered by uncertainties about the responsibilities of the state and federal governments for appointing officers and providing supplies for the new Maryland regiments. In April, 1861, the War Department issued "Instructions for Making Muster-rolls and Mustering into Service of Volunteer and Militia" to aid officers in organizing their troops. The instructions specified that each Union infantry company have one captain, one first lieutenant, two second lieutenants, four sergeants, four corporals, a drummer, and a fifer as well as no fewer than eighty privates before it could be mustered into service. The company commander and a surgeon conducted an in-ranks physical examination of all enlisted personnel in approximately thirty minutes. Following this rudimentary check, the company commander and the mustering officer (usually a Regular Army officer or a civil magistrate) mustered the company into federal service.

Each member of the company, including officers, took off his cap and raised his right hand as the mustering officer administered the oath. "All and each of you do solemnly swear (or affirm as the case may be) that you will bear true allegiance to the United States of America, and that you will serve them honestly and faithfully against all their enemies or opposers whatsoever, and observe and obey the orders of the President of the United States and the orders of the officers appointed over you according to the Rules and Articles for the government of the armies of the United States; so help you God." To remind the soldiers of their responsibilities, the Articles of War were to be read by the company commander twice yearly while the troops were in formation.[2]

Maryland's Union units enlisted for periods of three years, one year, nine months, six months, or one hundred days, but there was confusion about the authority to appoint officers and the system for filling under-strength units. James Cooper, a Maryland-born Pennsylvania politician, wrote the secretary of war in late April, 1861, protesting the appointment of volunteer officers by the state of Maryland. Claiming that the "executive authority [was] being controlled by an organization unfriendly to the object of the President of the United States," Cooper asked if the federal government could directly commission officers for Maryland units. The federal government declined to adopt any system of direct appointments of junior officers for Maryland volunteer units and left this matter

2. *Official Records*, Ser. III, Vol. I, 961–64.

in the governor's hands. President Lincoln, however, directly commissioned Cooper as a brigadier general of Maryland volunteers.[3]

Maryland's new governor, Augustus Bradford, still felt uncertain about appointing officers when he wrote the secretary of war in mid-March, 1862. Referring to the removal of Col. John C. McConnell of the 3rd Maryland Infantry (U.S.) by the War Department, Bradford asked that "your Department should definitely determine whether it or the Executive of Maryland will exercise the power of appointing the regimental and company officers of the volunteers which have been raised and organized in that State." The federal government replied that Bradford indeed had the authority to appoint officers for Maryland organizations.[4]

In permitting the organization of Maryland regiments for home defense and the Purnell Legion in 1861, the War Department reserved the right to "revoke the commissions of officers who may be found incompetent for the proper discharge of their duties." Responding to the governor's letter, the War Department once again stated that incompetent officers must appear before an army board in Baltimore.[5] After this point, the general rule was that the Maryland governor appointed officers and the federal government removed them. The War Department initially permitted the election of officers but quickly abandoned this means of officer selection in the Union army. Occasionally, the federal government appointed junior officers in the Maryland regiments who later did not serve with these units.[6]

The seemingly interminable delay in sending Maryland's units to the front frustrated many Union officers. The state organized its first unit in the spring of 1861, but it did not see combat until a year later. Brig. Gen. James Cooper, appointed to command a brigade of Marylanders in 1861, was still without a command in March, 1862. He appealed to Montgomery Blair, Lincoln's postmaster general and a Maryland politician, for aid in consolidating the scattered state units under Cooper's command at Annapolis and then dispatching them to the army.

3. *Ibid.*, Ser. I, Vol. I, 138, 210; Clark, "Recruitment of Union Troops," 154–55.

4. *Official Records*, Ser. I, Vol. I, 930–31, 951.

5. *Ibid.*, 427, 482, 951. The authority of the northern state governors to appoint officers was initially stated in War Department General Orders Number 45 on July 19, 1861 (*ibid.*, 339).

6. For a discussion of Union officers, see Francis A. Lord, *They Fought for the Union* (Harrisburg, 1960), 190–97.

Cooper wrote emotionally that "the wish of the men to see active service in the field is increased by the taunts of the disloyal amongst us, who are always ready to whisper mischief into any ears open to receive it. These people tell the troops that the Government distrusts either their loyalty or courage or both, and will not, therefore, confide to them any duty they could betray." The general noted that this was "galling to their pride and patriotism alike, and they feel a sense of injury and degradation in remaining idle while others are fighting and dying in a cause that they love as devotedly as the best of those who have shed their blood for it. . . . Both officers and men have besought me, and on more than one occasion with tears, that I should exert myself to have them sent into the field, where they could vindicate their hereditary claim to loyalty and manhood."[7]

The low strength of several Maryland units compounded the problem of deploying the state's troops. Maryland had a quota of 15,578 men to fill its regiments under the president's proclamation of May 3, 1861. The actual number of volunteers from Maryland, however, never reached this level, and the state provided only 9,355 men under the three-year proclamation.[8] With the exception of the 1st Maryland Infantry (U.S.), most of the state's regiments formed during the winter of 1861–1862. Kenly's regiment, meanwhile, picketed the upper Potomac River and occasionally skirmished with the enemy.

James J. Gillette, a civil engineer before the war, fought with the 71st New York Volunteers at First Manassas, where he was captured and later imprisoned in Richmond. Upon his exchange, Gillette obtained a post in the German Rifles, then recruiting in Baltimore. In a letter to his father on February 18, 1862, Gillette discussed the organization of his new unit. "The Regt. is not yet full and will be stationed near Balto. for some time." The young New Yorker was encouraged by Union victories in North Carolina and Tennessee and the upcoming movement of the Army of the Potomac. Gillette mustered in as first lieutenant of the German Rifles on March 1, and the unit was designated as the 4th Maryland Infantry Regiment (U.S.). He wrote his mother in late March from Baltimore:

The secesh never had any expectation of retaining Virginia—they were merely using her as a tool. Living off of her and they now, having eaten

7. *Official Records*, Ser. III, Vol. I, 931–33.
8. Clark, "Recruitment of Union Troops," 153–54.

her up, abandoning her for new country in which to find subsistence. You will see them eventually narrowed down to the gulf states where they will make a desperate stand & there will be *a battle* we have not had yet but the exception of Bull Run, Pea-Ridge and perhaps Donelson. We have not had anything more than skirmishes—In a European war they would be laughed at if called battles.[9]

A month later, Gillette's enthusiasm ebbed, not from military defeat but because "matters are culminating which I think will result disastrously for our Maryland troops. There are a set of men here who are endeavoring to destroy the Maryland regiments by a process known as consolidating—that is putting two or three small regiments together and forming one large one." The lieutenant described the consolidation of the German Rifles and the 3rd Maryland Infantry (U.S.): "It is a wise plan when properly managed; but when regiments are crushed together without some regard paid to the feelings of the men or some settled plan by which the most deserving officers—(those commanding the largest companies) are selected for the positions in the new organization—then ruin and demoralization results the regiments loose the 'esprit de Corps' and desertion and insubordination is the result."[10]

Upon the consolidation of the German Rifles (the original 4th Maryland Infantry [U.S.]) and the Baltimore (or Dix's) Light Infantry with the 3rd Maryland Infantry (U.S.), Gillette was chosen as adjutant for the new 3rd Maryland Infantry (U.S.) from a pool with three other candidates. He attributed his appointment as an "honor not through favoritism but rather as a discrimination of merit" on the part of Gen. Cooper.[11] The merging of Union regiments from Maryland soon became a familiar means of uniting understrength units. The 4th Regiment, Potomac Home Brigade Infantry, consolidated with the 3rd Potomac Home Brigade a few months after Gillette wrote about the problems of the new 3rd Maryland Infantry (U.S.). Other Maryland units consolidated during the war although the army never fully resolved the problem of excess officers.

Within the first months of military service, the Union Maryland regi-

9. James J. Gillette to father, February 18, 1862, and to mother, March 31, 1862, in James J. Gillette Papers, LC. A partial typescript of the Gillette Papers is in the *Civil War Times Illustrated* Collection, USAMHI.

10. Gillette to mother, May 2, 1862, in Gillette Papers. The proposal to consolidate Maryland's units is found in *Official Records*, Ser. I, Vol. I, 799.

11. Gillette to father, May 9, 1862, in Gillette Papers.

ments underwent a shakedown in personnel as the army removed incompetent or unfit officers from the service or these men tendered their resignations. The removal of these officers initially disrupted unit harmony but eventually improved efficiency. Col. Kenly of the 1st Maryland Infantry (U.S.) spent much of his time in 1861 getting rid of officers from the regiment whom he deemed ineffective. Thirteen officers resigned their commissions in the 1st Maryland Infantry during the last half of 1861 as the war lost its allure. Second Lieut. Charles E. Colegate of Company C, for example, resigned because of poor health, claiming "chills and Rheumatism." In his letter of resignation Colegate appealed to Col. Kenly that "as soon as possible with your permission I will return Home feeling so very 'sick.'" Kenly accepted Colegate's resignation only because he believed that officer to be incompetent.[12]

In a letter regarding the resignations of three officers from the 1st Maryland Infantry (U.S.), Gen. Cooper wrote the adjutant general that "the commander of the Regt., Colonel Jno. R. Kenly, strongly urges the acceptance of all the above resignations. I unite with him in doing so. . . . So far from regarding the resignation of the above named officers a matter of regret, it was a subject for congratulation with the officers of the Regiment generally."[13]

The commanders of the various Maryland units were occasionally demonstrative in endorsing the resignations of their subordinates. David C. Huxford, a thirty-nine-year-old painter from Baltimore and lieutenant in the 1st Maryland Infantry (U.S.), submitted his resignation on August 22, 1861, without stating any cause. Kenly requested approval of the resignation in early October "by reason of his utter incompetency and no hope of improvement." Another thirty-nine-year-old officer in the 1st Maryland Infantry, Second Lieut. Julius Veidt of Company K, requested a discharge to join Col. McConnell's 3rd Maryland Infantry (U.S.). Kenly refused to transfer Veidt and demanded his dismissal "by reason of his utter incompetency . . . I cannot recognize Mr. Veidt as an officer of my Regt. and disapprove of his request to be assigned to the 3rd Maryland Regiment."[14]

12. Charles E. Colegate to Col. John R. Kenly, October 22, 1861, in CSR, Charles E. Colegate, 1st Maryland Infantry (U.S.).

13. Brig. Gen. James Cooper to Brig. Gen. Lorenzo Thomas, September 29, 1861, in CSR, William T. Hilleary, 1st Maryland Infantry (U.S.).

14. Col. John R. Kenly to Lieut. Col. S. Williams, October 11, 1861, in CSR, David

In the case of another officer in the 1st Maryland Infantry (U.S.), Joseph Bailey Orem, Gen. Cooper wrote that "in transmitting you the request of this officer [to transfer to another command] I refrain from any recommendation. His excuse for resigning is certainly not a valid one; but his services in the Regiment, as an officer, are not of account enough to induce any one to wish to retain him in it." Despite this lackluster report, Orem later served as a captain in the 4th Maryland Infantry (U.S.) although his military career was marked with disciplinary infractions before he was wounded and discharged in 1864.[15]

Henry C. Hack submitted his resignation as second lieutenant of the 1st Regiment's Company I on October 8, 1861, to attend "important Business which demands my early attention." Col. Kenly immediately urged the acceptance of Hack's resignation "by reason of a generally insubordinate conduct," and the army released Hack on October 22. Three days later, Hack received an appointment as second lieutenant in the 1st Maryland Cavalry Regiment (U.S.) at Baltimore. He once again submitted his resignation from the army in the fall of 1862 because "important private interests are suffering for want of attention." His commander, however, endorsed the resignation on the grounds that Hack's "character is such as to render him very obnoxious to all the Officers in the Regiment—he has at various times of *danger* absented himself from the Regt without leave—and has shown himself utterly incompetent to command the respect of either Officers or men."[16]

Every Union Maryland regiment experienced turmoil in the officer ranks. Illnesses, disabling wounds, incompetence, cowardice, commitments to loved ones at home, and business matters all prompted officers to resign. Capt. Henry R. Gillingham of Company I, 1st Maryland Infantry (U.S.), a Baltimore machinist, entered the service in the spring of 1861 but was forced to resign in early 1863 because of "excessive corpulency." The regiment's surgeon testified that Gillingham was so fat that

C. Huxford, 1st Maryland Infantry (U.S.); and Kenly to Capt. R. Morris Copeland, October 24, 1861, in CSR, Julius Veidt, 1st Maryland Infantry (U.S.).

15. Brig. Gen. James Cooper to Brig. Gen. Lorenzo Thomas, December 11, 1861, in CSR, J. Bailey Orem, 1st Maryland Infantry (U.S.). See also CSR, J. Bailey Orem, 4th Maryland Infantry (U.S.).

16. Henry C. Hack to Col. John R. Kenly, October 8, 1861; Kenly to Lieut. Col. S. Williams, October 11, 1861, and Henry C. Hack to Maj. George Thistleton, December 1, 1862, in CSR, Henry C. Hack, 1st Maryland Cavalry (U.S.).

he had had to ride in an ambulance for the past three months. Charles Davis Irelan, a captain in the 8th Maryland Infantry (U.S.), was also unfit for army life because of his weight. Joshua T. Dayhoff, a Frederick saloon owner and a second lieutenant in the 7th Maryland Infantry (U.S.), resigned in 1864 because his poor eyesight prevented him from reading a newspaper in the daytime without spectacles.[17]

First Lieut. William H. Allen, the oldest officer in the Maryland Brigade, resigned because of old age and chronic rheumatism in early 1863. The surgeon of the 4th Maryland Infantry (U.S.) wrote that "Lieut Allen is past 53 years of age, and has been for some years laboring under *Chronic Rheumatism*, at times suffering severely. . . . He can scarcely get about, and is hardly ever free from pain in the limbs, back, and chest. I am satisfied his condition is such as to disqualify him from further military duty, nor is he able to withstand the exposure incident to the life of a soldier."[18]

Wounds and other injuries often prevented officers from returning to duty. Capt. William D. Morrison of the 7th Maryland Infantry (U.S.) resigned in early 1865 after his right knee was smashed in a train accident. He gave up his position as a company commander in the regiment because "I wish those who are doing the duty to hold the position." Edward E. Nicholson, a lieutenant in Company C, 4th Maryland Infantry (U.S.), was obliged to resign for disability following a concussion to his back at the Wilderness in 1864. George L. Tyler, the first lieutenant of Company F, 7th Maryland Infantry (U.S.), and the regiment's adjutant, likewise resigned following his wounding at the same battle.[19]

Arthur J. Weise, a twenty-four-year-old lieutenant from Hagerstown,

17. Report of E. R. Baer, Assistant Surgeon, January 18, 1863, enclosed in Henry R. Gillingham to Lieut. Col. W. D. Whipple, January 18, 1863, in CSR, Henry R. Gillingham, 1st Maryland Infantry (U.S.); C. Davis Irelan to Lieut. Col. W. W. Cheseborough, April 22, 1863, in CSR, Charles Davis Irelan, 8th Maryland Infantry (U.S.); Joshua T. Dayhoff to Lieut. Col. C. Kingsbury, Jr., February 26, 1864, with surgeon's certificate by J. H. Jarrett, February 26, 1864, in CSR, Joshua T. Dayhoff, 7th Maryland Infantry (U.S.).

18. William H. Allen to Lieut. Col. William D. Whipple, March 3, 1863, enclosing Surgeon William W. Volk to Lieut. Colonel William D. Whipple, March 5, 1863, in CSR, William H. Allen, 4th Maryland Infantry (U.S.).

19. William D. Morrison to Maj. A. C. Storker, January 15, 1865, in CSR, William D. Morrison, 7th Maryland Infantry (U.S.); Special Orders Number 215, Adjutant General's Office, June 21, 1864, in CSR, Edward E. Nicholson, 4th Maryland Infantry (U.S.); George L. Tyler to Brig. Gen. Lorenzo Thomas, October 25, 1864, in CSR, George L. Tyler, 7th Maryland Infantry (U.S.).

tendered his resignation from the 7th Maryland Infantry in late 1864 upon the death of his father. Weise returned home to care for his widowed mother and three sisters. Officers often disliked quitting the army in its hour of need. The captain of Company C, 8th Maryland Infantry (U.S.), William F. Larrabee, resigned in early 1863 because "circumstances have occurred in his domestic relations which imperatively demand his presence at home." Larrabee concluded, "It is perhaps, not improper here to state that he greatly regrets the necessity of this step and that he will hereafter as a private Citizen earnestly sustain the government in its efforts to put down this rebellion."[20]

William W. Roderick resigned in early 1864 as a second lieutenant in the 8th Maryland Infantry when his wife became gravely ill. He wrote his letter of resignation while on recruiting duty in Washington, D.C., in January 1864. "As reasons of this my respectful request allow me to state that no dissatisfaction with the service or my superiors, or fellow officers—no disappointment in promotion or ambition for a better position in or out of the service—no softly succumbing to the hardships or cowardly fear of the dangers of my position—but solely the rapidly declining health of my wife (who lays prostrated by an incurable disease) and the hence emanating utter derangement of my domestic affairs, could induce me to leave the service of my country and the Regiment, in which I have served for the past 17 months with credit to myself & to the satisfaction of my superiors." Roderick's wife was so desperate for her husband's return that she wrote President Lincoln on February 17, 1864, citing her husband's response to the call for volunteers in 1862 when he brought with him thirty recruits during the invasion of Maryland. Roderick was discharged from the army in March. His wife lived until 1902.[21]

Other officers did not share Roderick's reluctance to leave military service. First Lieut. John K. Smith of the 7th Maryland Infantry (U.S.) tendered his resignation in late 1862 after three months' service because he considered himself "incompetent to discharge the duties of my position as a military man." William T. Hilleary, who resigned as a second lieu-

20. A. James Weise to Brig. Gen. Lorenzo Thomas, October 6, 1864, in CSR, Arthur J. Weise, 7th Maryland Infantry (U.S.); William F. Larrabee to Col. A. W. Denison, January 5, 1863, in CSR, William F. Larrabee, 8th Maryland Infantry (U.S.).

21. William W. Roderick to the Adjutant General, January 1, 1864, and Amanda E. Roderick to Abraham Lincoln, February 17, 1864, in CSR, William W. Roderick, 8th Maryland Infantry (U.S.).

tenant in the 1st Maryland Infantry (U.S.) in October, 1861, received a commission as captain in the 3rd Maryland Infantry (U.S.) in February, 1863. A little over a month later, Hilleary resigned because he believed himself incompetent.[22]

Resignations were often prompted by officials higher in the chain of command. The commander of Company C, 1st Maryland Infantry (U.S.), Capt. George Smith, resigned at Camp Murray in Baltimore on September 11, 1861, "because I consider myself wronged by my Colonel for not complying with Army Regulation Article IV." The commander of the regiment thought Smith incompetent and did not provide further details. Richard R. Brouner, the adjutant of the 7th Maryland Infantry (U.S.) and later a company commander, initially enlisted as a corporal in the 5th New York Volunteers in early 1861. By the summer of that year, Brouner was a lieutenant in the regiment and later its adjutant. Brouner abruptly offered his resignation on June 12, 1862, while the regiment was on the outskirts of Richmond. He cited the need to return home to New York to take care of his widowed mother and family. The regimental commander and acting brigade commander, Col. Gouverneur K. Warren (of later Gettysburg fame), gave a different version of Brouner's sudden resignation: "Lt. Brouner was promoted to this place on my recommendation while in Baltimore, but I have not been altogether satisfied with his qualifications for the post in the field, and yesterday I, in a moment of vexation, for an irregularity committed by him, which led to the discharge of my Drum Major without my approval, advised him to resign."[23]

Some officers resigned because of dissatisfaction among subordinates in their companies. Alphreod C. Bragonier, the twenty-year-old commander of Company G, 7th Maryland Infantry (U.S.), wrote his letter of resignation on March 28, 1863. "My command," Bragonier noted, "was enlisted in August last and before it was regularly mustered in as a company we were ordered into the field and the men are still doing duty without the regular company organization. This together with the fact that promises were made to the men which I have not been able to fulfill

22. John K. Smith to R. R. Brouner, December 23, 1862, in CSR, John K. Smith, 7th Maryland Infantry (U.S.); William T. Hilleary to Lieut. Col. Rogers, March 25, 1863, in CSR, William T. Hilleary, 3rd Maryland Infantry (U.S.).

23. George Smith to Col. N. T. Dushane, September 2, 1862, in CSR, George Smith, 1st Maryland Infantry (U.S.); Endorsement of Col. G. K. Warren, June 12, 1862, in CSR, Richard R. Brouner, 5th New York Volunteers.

and the lack of necessary officers to assist me, have tended to demoralize the Co. and I deem it for the good of the regt and the service that I be discharged therefrom."[24]

Companies H, I, and K of the 8th Maryland Infantry (U.S.) consisted of men drafted for nine months of service under the president's proclamation of August 1, 1862, asking for three hundred thousand recruits. The companies formed at Camp Bradford in Baltimore although the governor did not appoint the officers until 1863. By the spring and summer of that year, the officers of the drafted companies agitated for release from the service. Nineteen-year-old McKendree C. Furlong, drafted on October 28, 1862, was promoted to be Company K's second lieutenant on March 19, 1863. He submitted his resignation on August 8, stating, "After having served five months as a private, I was commissioned by the Governor of Maryland as 2nd Lieut of Co 'K' 8th Reg't Md. Vols, & accepted the commission under the impression that I would not be held longer than the nine months for which I was drafted, otherwise I would have respectfully declined the commission & with cheerfulness have served out my time as a private." Furlong gained his release from the army on September 26, 1863.[25]

Bernard N. Graeser, a native of Erfurt, Germany, and a merchant in Baltimore, was drafted on October 15, 1862. Appointed first lieutenant of Company H, 8th Maryland Infantry (U.S.), on January 3, 1863, Graeser tendered his resignation eight months later to obtain his discharge from the army, which he received on November 1.[26]

To replace the three drafted companies in the 8th Maryland Infantry that disbanded in 1863, two companies of the Purnell Legion Cavalry transferred to the regiment in November, 1864. Companies B and C of the Purnell Legion Cavalry became new Companies H and I of the 8th Maryland Infantry. The transfer, however, did not meet the approval of two officers who resented being assigned to the infantry without their consent. Capt. Theodore Clayton and Second Lieut. Joseph J. Janney

24. Alphreod C. Bragonier to Lieut. Col. William H. Chesebrough, March 28, 1863, in CSR, Alphreod C. Bragonier, 7th Maryland Infantry (U.S.).

25. McKendree C. Furlong to Lieut. Col. William H. Chesebrough, August 8, 1863, in CSR, McKendree C. Furlong, 8th Maryland Infantry (U.S.).

26. Bernard N. Graeser to Brig. Gen. Lorenzo Thomas, September 8 and 10, 1863, in CSR, Bernard N. Graeser, 8th Maryland Infantry (U.S.).

both submitted their resignations in protest of the transfer and were discharged from the army on December 17, 1864.[27]

The growing number of resignations forced the army to establish formal procedures to regulate officers' conduct. The War Department issued General Order 51 in August, 1861, which dictated that all resignations had to be processed through the officer's chain of command before he actually left the service.[28] Permitting officers to resign did not, however, solve the problem of those who were incapable of performing their duties or who refused to behave like officers. Established court-martial procedures were often lengthy and unsuitable for units in the midst of campaigning, so other measures were instituted to discipline the Union officer corps.

The "Act to Authorize the Employment of Volunteers of 1861" contained a section enabling army and department commanders to convene military boards to examine the "capacity, qualifications, propriety of conduct, and efficiency" of volunteer officers. Although imperfect, the examination board system "meant that the army could by-pass regular court-martial proceedings in ridding itself of unqualified volunteer officers through the rank of colonel."[29] Similarly, the secretary of war issued General Order 91 in 1862, giving the president the power to dismiss officers without a court-martial or formal hearing. This order enabled the government to get rid of officers who had been absent without leave from their commands.[30]

The Maryland regiments, like all Union volunteer regiments, formed hastily at the beginning of the war and contained only a few men with any practical military experience. The regulations issued by the government, combined with the test of combat, shaped a professional officer corps in the Maryland Brigade from its decidedly nonmilitary cadre. The process was not easy, as attested by the service records of numerous officers. Drunkenness was the largest single reason for the breakdown of

27. Special Orders Number 439, Adjutant General's Office, December 10, 1864, in CSR, Theodore Clayton and Joseph J. Janney, 8th Maryland Infantry (U.S.).

28. *Official Records*, Ser. I, Vol. I, 384.

29. Stanley L. Swart, "The Military Examination Board in the Civil War: A Case Study," *Civil War History*, XVI (1970), 227–45. For an example of the questions of one officer's examination, see John W. Powell, "How to Pick Out Bad Officers," *Civil War Times Illustrated*, XXX (1991), 46–49.

30. Lord, *They Fought for the Union*, 197.

discipline among Maryland's Union officers. Alcohol abuse became rampant in both enlisted and officer ranks of Maryland's Union troops and created numerous difficulties.[31] Capt. James S. Baer of Company G, 1st Maryland Infantry (U.S.), born in Baltimore in 1834, joined the army as a clerk in 1861. Baer was cited on several occasions for his intemperance. Lieut. Col. John W. Wilson, commanding the 1st Maryland Infantry, charged Baer with failing to appear at the afternoon regimental inspection near Mountain River in Virginia on September 18, 1863. Wilson found that Baer was so drunk as to be unfit to command his company during the inspection. A month later, Baer was charged with drunkenness on duty while in charge of a picket detail near Bristoe Station. Baer soon faced new charges of disobedience of orders when he went to the quarters of the commanding officer and sought permission to visit his men in the guardhouse. Wilson refused permission and ordered Baer to his own quarters until in "a fit condition to leave them." Instead, Baer went to the guardhouse. The last straw for Wilson came in August, 1864, when Baer "was so intoxicated as to be unable for any duty whatever" near Reams Station. A general court-martial finally dismissed Baer from the service in September with the forfeiture of all pay and allowances.[32]

Other officers of 1st Maryland Infantry ran into problems as a result of heavy drinking. John J. Knoppel, the first lieutenant of Company E, allowed his men to straggle into camp after picket duty. For this oversight, the army charged him with neglect of duty in early 1864. He was later cited as drunk on duty while on the skirmish line on August 25, 1864. Knoppel remained in the service until October 10, when a federal court-martial dismissed him for drunkenness.[33] Thomas Saville, a middle-aged Baltimore policeman and shoemaker, commanded Company B when the army dropped him in 1863. As early as December, 1861, Saville had been absent from the regiment without leave. In the fall of 1862, the regimen-

31. Wiley cites the prevalence of alcohol abuse in the Union army in *The Life of Billy Yank*, 252–54. For studies of drunkenness in nineteenth-century America and the temperance movement, see Ian R. Tyrrell, *Sobering Up: From Temperance to Prohibition in Antebellum America, 1800–1860* (Westport, 1979), and W. J. Rorabaugh, *The Alcoholic Republic: An American Tradition* (New York, 1979).

32. The various charges and specifications preferred against Baer by Wilson are found in CSR, James S. Baer, 1st Maryland Infantry (U.S.).

33. The various charges and specifications preferred against Knoppel by Wilson are found in CSR, John J. Knoppel, 1st Maryland Infantry (U.S.).

tal commander placed Saville under arrest, but he escaped from the guard in February of the following year. Saville had been convicted of drunkenness and disorderly conduct. In a note to the provost marshal of Baltimore, Col. Nathan T. Dushane wrote that Saville "lives on the North side of Ross St. about 4 doors west of Preston . . . very likely he has left of his uniform, and dresses in citizens clothing. He is well known to the Police." Six days later, Union officials in Baltimore placed the delinquent officer in confinement and dismissed him shortly afterward.[34] Henry Haugh, an officer in Company D of the 1st Maryland Infantry, was so drunk that he could not perform his duties at brigade drill at Mountain River in September, 1863. Unlike Baer, this officer corrected his behavior (or at least did not overindulge when it interfered with duty); he was promoted to captain in 1864 and mustered out with the regiment at the end of the war.[35]

A Baltimore tobacconist, Albert S. Husband, joined the 4th Maryland Infantry (U.S.) as the first lieutenant of Company H in 1862. On January 28, 1863, while in camp on Maryland Heights, overlooking Harpers Ferry, Husband was "grossly intoxicated in the presence of officers and soldiers of the Regiment." While in this condition, Husband attempted to assault the sutler's clerk in front of his troops, and when arrested, Husband used profane language to intimidate the guards and said, "never mind, it will be my turn to be on guard soon." Charged with conduct prejudicial to good order and military discipline and leaving his quarters while under arrest, Husband was found guilty and cashiered from the army.[36]

Capt. J. Bailey Orem, formerly with the 1st Maryland Infantry (U.S.) and later assigned to the 4th Maryland Infantry (U.S.), was detailed to recruiting duty at his home on the Eastern Shore in late 1862. Instead, Orem went to Baltimore. The new commander of his regiment ordered his arrest and return to camp at Maryland Heights. Orem protested this action in a letter in which he stated that the resignation of Col. William

34. Henry R. Gillingham to Lieut. William H. Taylor, October 14, 1862; Col. N. T. Dushane to Brig. Gen. John R. Kenly, February 7, 1863; Dushane to Provost Marshal, February 18, 1863, in CSR, Thomas Saville, 1st Maryland Infantry (U.S.).

35. "Charges and Specifications preferred against 2d Lieut. Henry Haugh 1st Regt. Maryland Infantry," by Lieut. Col. John W. Wilson, September 29, 1863, in CSR, Henry Haugh, 1st Maryland Infantry (U.S.).

36. General Orders Number 71, Middle Military Department, 8th Army Corps, December 31, 1863, in CSR, Albert S. Husband, 4th Maryland Infantry (U.S.).

J. L. Nicodemus on November 27, 1862, had made his position in the regiment "very disagreeable." Orem claimed, "I do not wish to leave the good cause that I am fighting for but to stand up against a fire in front and rear it is rather more than any one man can stand." A Dr. Ward endorsed Orem's cryptic message in a note to the Maryland governor saying that he had heard that the new commander of the 4th Maryland Infantry, Lieut. Col. Richard N. Bowerman, and his officers played cards and drank with enlisted men.[37]

The presence of liquor in camp and the fact that many officers drank to excess made its prohibition very difficult. Charles A. Moulton, an enlisted man in a Massachusetts regiment, witnessed drunkenness in many Maryland units while he was detailed as a provost marshal clerk at Harpers Ferry. Moulton realized that "an officer holding a commission may go off on a spree and get as drunk as a beast and it is all right, but should a private follow the example he would be thrown into the guard house to await a court martial, and then have $10 or $20 taken from his pay." Pvt. David K. Wantz of Company A, 7th Maryland Infantry (U.S.), provided an account similar to Moulton's when he wrote his sister on March 4, 1863, about an incident in camp:

> When I was home me and bill harris [another private in Company A] promise to treat the boys we box up 4 bottles of whiskey a piece and sent them to camp not be open until we got Back and they where not open befor we got Back when we got to camp we open the box the boys where singing a little loud because we had come back. In this time one of the Boys slip out and invited two officers Down to take a drink. The boys got two singing Louder when the captain [Edward M. Mobley] came and grab the Bottle of the Lieutenant hand and that made us mad then a dispute the captain said he whould report bill Harris for fetching Whiskey in camp I then told him to report me at the same time as I had as much to do with it as he had Listen there has been nothing said About it since we where not reported good that He [Capt. Mobley] diden for he whould have been sorry for it He knowed that he had good reasons for not Reporting us if he whould there whould have Been an other one reported he knowed that There are as good feeling between us and the Captain.[38]

37. J. Orem Bailey to Dr. Ward, March 15, 1863, and Dr. Ward to Gov. Bradford, March 19, 1863, Executive Papers, 1863–65, MSA.

38. Lee C. Drickamer and Karen D. Drickamer, eds., *Fort Lyon to Harpers Ferry: On the Border of North and South with "Rambling Jour": The Civil War Letters and Newspaper*

Officers committed other infractions not related to the bottle. Maryland's Union officers did not easily take to military bureaucracy and often failed to follow proper procedures when on furlough or sick leave. Capt. Frank M. Collier of the 1st Maryland Infantry (U.S.) was dismissed in early 1863 because he tried to resign when "leave of absence for 48 hours was refused him, he having at the time but recently returned from a five months' absence from his command."[39]

Second Lieut. Oscar A. Mace of the 4th Maryland Infantry (U.S.) left camp during the afternoon of October 12, 1862, and did not return until early the next morning. Lieut. Col. Bowermen charged the Baltimore cigar maker with disobedience of orders, and he resigned on October 14 rather than face a court-martial.[40]

In many cases, the army took disciplinary action against officers when they were absent from their commands while in hospitals or at home recovering from wounds or illnesses. Thomas McNulty, a lieutenant in the 1st Maryland Infantry (U.S.), was discharged for disability and absence without leave in 1864. McNulty had been first injured in 1862 when he was run over by Confederate cavalry at Front Royal. He subsequently lost the use of his voice during fighting in the Wilderness and suffered pains in his side and chest which caused him to spit blood. The army released him because McNulty "failed to file in this Office [Adjutant General's Office] the necessary Surgeon's Certificates of Disability as required by the regulations of the War Department."[41]

The army also often took disciplinary action against officers who were absent for reasons beyond their control. Capt. Eugene J. Rizer of Company D, 8th Maryland Infantry (U.S.), was dismissed for unauthorized absence in the fall of 1863. A later investigation determined that Rizer had been

---

Dispatches of Charles H. Moulton (34th Mass. Vol. Inf.) (Shippensburg, 1987), 91; David K. Wantz to sister, March 4, 1863, in Lewis Leigh Collection, Book 42, no. 17, USAMHI. For an example of one enlisted man (later officer) in the 5th Maryland Infantry (U.S.) who repented for his abuse of alcohol, see John D. Babb, Jr., to father, August 16, 1862, in John D. Babb Family Papers, Emory University.

39. General Orders Number 83, Adjutant General's Office, February 19, 1863, in CSR, Frank M. Collier, 1st Maryland Infantry (U.S.).

40. "Charges and Specifications preferred against 2d Lieut Oscar A. Mace 4th Regt Maryland Infantry" by Lieut. Col. Richard N. Bowerman, October 13, 1862, in CSR, Oscar A. Mace, 4th Maryland Infantry (U.S.).

41. Special Orders Number 274, Adjutant General's Office, August 18, 1864, in CSR, Thomas McNulty, 1st Maryland Infantry (U.S.).

sick with typhoid fever in Baltimore with proper medical authorization when he was dropped. The army subsequently restored Rizer to command in March, 1864, but there were no vacancies for him in the regiment at that time. Robert B. Meade, a first lieutenant in the 4th Maryland Infantry (U.S.) and a Baltimore shipwright, left the army on a surgeon's certificate in late 1863. A few months later, the army placed him under arrest for failing to report as a witness in a court-martial. By the spring of 1864, Meade was reappointed as an officer directly from civilian status "to fill a vacancy caused by his own resignation. The cause for such resignation having been revoked."[42]

The army cashiered First Lieut. Joseph O. Broadfoot of the 8th Maryland Infantry (U.S.) on March 21, 1865, for being absent in late 1864. A military commission composed of three officers from the Maryland Brigade determined in January, 1865, that Broadfoot should be tried before a court-martial for disobedience of orders and absence without leave because he failed to return to Petersburg by the "regularly established U.S. Mail Route via Washington D.C." Instead, the officer went by boat to Norfolk, and weather and transportation problems delayed his return to the unit. The court-martial found Broadfoot, a Baltimore molder, guilty of being absent without official leave, and he was placed "out of service" before the opening of the war's final campaign. An investigation in 1900, however, ruled that Broadfoot had not been absent without leave because he had been properly admitted to the Annapolis general hospital in December, 1864, with an injury to the spine and then returned to duty. At that late date the War Department revoked Broadfoot's dismissal because the charge was erroneous.[43]

The absence rate of regimental officers caused severe embarrassments for unit commanders. Col. Edwin H. Webster of the 7th Maryland Infantry (U.S.) provided a formal account of the circumstances surrounding the absence without leave of Capt. Richard R. Brouner. An officer in

---

42. Special Orders Number 110, Adjutant General's Office, March 8, 1864, in CSR, Eugene J. Rizer, 8th Maryland Infantry (U.S.). Rizer later served as an enlisted man and officer in the 11th Maryland Infantry (U.S.). Capt. George V. Massey to Lieut. Col. William H. Chesebrough, January 27, 1864, in CSR, Robert B. Meade, 4th Maryland Infantry (U.S.).

43. "Proceedings of a Military Commission Convened at camp of 4th Md. Vol. Inf. near Weldon RR Va.," January 27, 1865, in CSR, Joseph O. Broadfoot, 8th Maryland Infantry (U.S.).

the 7th's Company G, Brouner incurred the wrath of yet another commanding officer during the summer of 1863. On August 23, Col. Webster endorsed Brouner's summary dismissal because of the latter officer's impatience with army bureaucracy. Webster stated that Capt. Brouner's "conduct . . . has been so unbecoming that his further association with the Regiment, would in my judgment, be injurious to it and the service."[44]

Many of the disciplinary problems among Maryland's officer corps resulted from personality conflicts that led to acts of insubordinate behavior. The commander of Company I, 4th Maryland Infantry (U.S.), absented himself without permission from dress parade while in camp near the Rappahannock River in 1863. When Maj. Henry P. Brooks approached Capt. Louis A. Carl about his whereabouts, Carl replied in a "rude & disrespectful manner that 'he had no reason & he didn't want any excuse.'" The next morning, while under arrest, Carl proclaimed at the regimental headquarters in the presence of officers and enlisted men that "Brooks is the greatest rum head I ever saw." For similar disrespect, First Lieut. William J. Crawford, also of the 4th Maryland Infantry (U.S.), was dismissed in 1864.[45]

Disagreements occasionally flared into complicated legal problems. Capt. Thomas S. J. Johnson of Company K, 1st Maryland Infantry (U.S.), arrested his first lieutenant, William E. George, on January 23, 1863, for absence without leave, disobedience of orders, conduct subversive to good order and military discipline, and conduct unbecoming an officer and a gentleman while the company was stationed at the Outer Battery on Maryland Heights. When ordered by his commander to state in writing the reason for his absence, George responded, "I respectfully report that being in the Camp of the 1st Md Regt, I did not consider myself absent, at the same time I was there with your knowledge." Johnson immediately responded: "There is no question as to your absence with leave on the 19th Inst. and in regard to your absence without leave during the night of the 19th and the day following your letter of this date is in no regard

44. Col. Edwin H. Webster to [unstated], August 23, 1863, in RG 393, Records of U.S. Army Continental Commands, Entry 3786, Letters and Endorsements Sent and Orders Received, June, 1863–March, 1864.

45. "Charges and Specifications against Captain Louis A. Carl Co. I 4th Md. Regiment Vol. Infty," by Maj. H. P. Brooks, September 19, 1863, in CSR, Louis A. Carl, 4th Maryland Infantry (U.S.); General Orders Number 90, Army of the Potomac, December 6, 1864, in CSR, William J. Crawford, 4th Maryland Infantry (U.S.).

satisfactory." Johnson added, "It is hoped that you will be able to make a more admissible explanation, and to assign a sufficient reason for not complying with my first order on this subject." The two officers continued to wrangle, and the matter came to the attention of the regiment's commander, Col. Dushane. On January 22, George appealed to Dushane for release from confinement. "My relation with the Commander of Co K 1st Md Regt being disagreeable and utterly devoid of any amicable feeling; I respectfully ask to be transferred to some other position." Johnson forwarded his charges to Dushane on January 27: "This officer though not devoid of sense, is, seemingly in utter want of both personal and official sensibility and admonition appears to be entirely thrown away upon him. The preliminary steps I have taken for a legal investigation of his conduct seem to be the only remedy left to impress him with the absolute necessity of obedience and discipline." Johnson emphasized that "I am firmly convinced that nothing short of his present trial and punishment will have a salutary effect that without it he may become worse than useless to the public service." Dushane was not convinced of the need to try George, and he soon released the lieutenant and even promoted him to the command of Company I two months later.[46]

Some personality conflicts were not easily resolved. First Lieut. John W. Isaacs of Company H, 4th Maryland Infantry (U.S.), was detailed as aide-de-camp for the brigade commander. First Lieut. Robert M. Gorsuch reported to duty as the officer in charge of the picket at brigade headquarters on April 2, 1864. Without provocation, Isaacs struck Gorsuch in front of several witnesses. Gorsuch pressed charges although they were dropped when he died of wounds received at the Wilderness in May.[47]

Such disrespectful behavior occurred not only between men of equal rank or as insubordination on the part of lower-ranking officers. First Lieut. Levi T. Heath charged Lieut. Col. John W. Wilson, commander of the 1st Maryland Infantry (U.S.) and a former company commander, with conduct unbecoming an officer and a gentleman and prejudicial to good

---

46. William E. George to Col. N. T. Dushane, January 22, 26, 1863; Thomas S. J. Johnson to Dushane, January 27, 1863; "Charges and Specifications preferred against First Lieutenant William E. George of Company K 1st Maryland Regiment," by Thomas S. J. Johnson, January 27, 1863, in CSR, William E. George, 1st Maryland Infantry (U.S.).

47. "Charges and Specifications preferred against Jno. W. Isaacs 1st Lieut Co H 4th Regt Md Vol and A.D.C. to Commanding Officer 3rd Brigade 2nd Division 5th Corps," by R. M. Gorsuch, April 10, 1864, in CSR, John W. Isaacs, 4th Maryland Infantry (U.S.).

order and military discipline in 1863. Heath, a member of the 1st Maryland Infantry (U.S.) and the Maryland Brigade's acting assistant adjutant general, requested entrenching tools from Wilson for use by the brigade commander. Wilson, in turn, berated Heath in public for carrying out his official duties, and Heath then pressed charges.

The court-martial convicted Wilson of prejudicial conduct and sentenced him to a public reprimand. Brig. Gen. Kenly issued the reprimand on September 15, 1863: "The language used by Lieut Col Wilson and which was the basis of the charges against him, directed to an officer of his Regiment, inferior in rank, and without the favor of reply was so outrageous and so violent in its character, that the only presumption which can arise, is that Lt Col Wilson was at the time, so completely under the control of passion that he was bereft of reason and ignorant of the enormity of which he was found guilty."[48]

First Lieut. William H. Leonard, acting adjutant of the 8th Maryland Infantry (U.S.), witnessed the violent treatment of one enlisted man in his regiment by a field-grade officer in 1864. Lieut. Col. John G. Johannes, a Baltimore jeweler, seized Pvt. Adam Hudson by the throat in the camp of the 8th Maryland Infantry (U.S.) on June 30 and then struck him several times with a stick or club. Leonard testified in a court-martial that Hudson was under escort to the regimental guardhouse when Johannes attacked him. The court found Johannes guilty of striking a soldier and subjected him to a public reprimand. "Lieut Col Johannes," the tribunal noted, "can felicitate himself, upon the wonderful forbearance of the Court."[49]

Bladen T. F. Dulaney resigned his commission in the 1st Maryland Infantry (U.S.) in late 1861 to organize his own company but was unsuccessful and later received an appointment as a first lieutenant in the 2nd Maryland Cavalry Regiment (U.S.), a six-month regiment. The Maryland cavalrymen were placed on guard duty around the many Union camps

48. General Orders Number 2, 1st Army Corps, February 5, 1864; L. T. Heath to Lieut. Col. C. Kingsbury, Jr., January 24, 1864, in CSR, John W. Wilson, 1st Maryland Infantry (U.S.); Special Orders Number 88, 1st Army Corps and reprimand, in RG 94, Regimental Order Books and Papers, 4th Maryland Infantry (U.S.).

49. "Charges and Specifications against Lieut. Colonel John G. Johannes, 8th Maryland Vol. Infantry," by Lieut. George L. Choisey, June 30, 1864, and General Orders Number 6, 2nd Division, 5th Army Corps, August 15, 1864, in CSR, John G. Johannes, 8th Maryland Infantry (U.S.).

and hospitals in Annapolis. About 6:00 on the evening of November 17, 1863, Dulaney went to the house of Pvt. Henry M. Billheimer in Annapolis. Billheimer, a member of Company A, had previously accused the lieutenant of stealing his dog. Dulaney, who "appeared to be in liquor," began to castigate Billheimer's wife, saying that she "is a poxy arsed whore, and gave me the clapp once, and I had to procure Doctor Bowen of Annapolis to cure her and I also had to pay the Doctor's bill." Naturally, Billheimer objected to the officer's behavior and ordered him out of his house. Dulaney continued to make abusive remarks in front of several enlisted men, and the two men nearly came to blows. Billheimer's wife, the former Amelia F. Arnold, stepped in and demanded that Dulaney leave. The army subsequently arrested Dulaney and held him for court-martial. At the trial, Dr. William Bowen testified that he had never treated Mrs. Billheimer for any "secret diseases," only intermittent fever. Dulaney's conduct besmirched the officers of the regiment although the court never reached a verdict and Dulaney mustered out with his unit in early 1864.[50]

Officers also encountered problems with the army through no fault of their own. Wilhelm Heine became tangled in an unrelenting army bureaucracy. Heine, a Prussian scientist and artist, came to the United States from the Far East when he heard about the outbreak of war in America. He offered his services to the North, and the secretary of war commissioned him as captain of Company I, 1st Maryland Infantry (U.S.), on December 9, 1861. Heine, however, never served with the unit; instead, he served as a topographer with the Army of the Potomac. During the Virginia Peninsula campaign, Heine was placed under arrest and on May 4, 1862, was confined in Fort Wool. The army gave no reason for his apprehension, and Heine vainly sought redress from Gens. Philip Kearny and George B. McClellan, as well as from President Lincoln. Heine protested his imprisonment to Gen. Seth Williams, the adjutant general of the Army of the Potomac: "Still I am kept in confinement without even charges preferred against me, beyond a vague intimidation that I am suspected of disloyalty. Is this lawful?"[51]

On June 10, 1862, the provost marshal general of the Army of the

50. Charges and affidavits against Dulaney are in CSR, Bladen T. F. Dulaney, 2nd Maryland Cavalry (U.S.).

51. Heine's voluminous correspondence with Union officials is in CSR, Wilhelm Heine, 1st Maryland Infantry (U.S.).

Potomac revealed that Heine had been arrested for making a map of Union positions at Yorktown, which was subsequently published in *Harper's Weekly*. Heine vigorously denied the charge and claimed that a sergeant in the 20th New York Volunteers was actually responsible for the breach in security. Williams ordered Heine's release in mid-June and restored him to duty. Heine nevertheless requested a formal court of inquiry on June 14. Sixteen days later, while conducting a reconnaissance near Bottoms Bridge, Heine fell into enemy hands and was imprisoned at Libby Prison in Richmond. He managed to get exchanged (after appealing to Gen. Dix in Baltimore for help) in August and furloughed to go to New York to recover his health. Returning to the army, Heine was arrested again and thrown into a cell at Fort Monroe in Hampton Roads. He once again requested a court of inquiry and told Williams that "I have never and in any manner direct or indirect allowed any maps showing fortifications and positions of camps or troops of our army permitted to go into other hands than those of persons designated by the different generals to whom I reported." Heine protested his arrest as "an undeserved cruelty to an innocent loyal and zealous officer."[52]

Apparently, Heine's troubles ceased after his resignation in December, 1862. He signed on as colonel of the 103rd New York Volunteers in the spring of 1863. Following service in South Carolina and Virginia, Heine was honorably discharged near the close of the war and received a brevet promotion to brigadier general in 1868 for "faithful and meritorious service."[53]

The turmoil the junior officer corps experienced from resignations and disciplinary action was just one facet of the war for these men. By 1865, the Union army had an efficient system to handle the personnel actions of its officers, and Maryland's regiments could concentrate on fighting the war. The Union regiments from Maryland had their fair share of troublesome officers and men not suited for the responsibilities of their positions; most of these officers had departed by the time the Maryland Brigade saw its fiercest battles.

52. *Ibid.*
53. CSR, Wilhelm Heine, 103rd New York Volunteers.

·9·

THE MARYLAND BRIGADE'S DESPAIR

The Maryland Brigade, the state's largest contribution to the Union war effort, fought in some of the fiercest battles of the Civil War. Combat claimed fourteen captains and lieutenants in the brigade either killed in action or dead of wounds. Another three junior officers died of disease at home, in Union hospitals, or in enemy prison camps. Altogether, nearly 8 percent of the men who served as junior officers in the Maryland Brigade became casualties of the war. Although this was not a large percentage, the loss of comrades was devastating, particularly after the opening of the spring campaign in Virginia in 1864.

Harrison Adreon of Baltimore joined the 4th Maryland Infantry (U.S.) as a first lieutenant in 1862. Two years later, he had received several promotions and was known as the "fighting major." After mustering the unit for pay in the trenches before Petersburg in the summer of 1864, Adreon wrote to his mother:

> It was a sad thing to read some names over, of those who were not here to answer. In some companies especially this was the case—for instance "E" comp'y—one of the best in the regiment—all quiet, obedient and brave men—as we called over their names commencing with the Captain a prisoner Lt Mills wounded Orderly Sergt killed two sergts killed & wounded then the corporals several of whom are killed and wounded then the names of privates killed, wounded, until looking around upon those noble fellows who are left we only count eighteen sergeants Corporals and privates and this . . . was the finest Co. and only numbered one or two less, than the largest then in the Regiment. In the same way the companies have had their losses more or less and as the names were called the faces of all were sad as they answered he was killed, he was wounded.[1]

1. Harrison Adreon to mother, n.d., in Civil War Collection, MHS.

Virtually every Maryland regiment at the front during 1864 suffered the same casualty rates as the 4th Maryland Infantry. Lieut. Col. Wilson of the 1st Maryland Infantry (U.S.), for example, told the state adjutant general in October, 1864, that his regiment had lost 16 officers and 263 soldiers killed or wounded in action over a five-month-period.[2]

Maryland's officers often inspired their troops in moments of great trial. An Irish cheese and fish dealer in Baltimore, James H. Bride, rallied the troops of the Maryland Brigade during the fierce fighting at Laurel Hill, near Spotsylvania Court House, on May 8, 1864. Seizing his regiment's flag, Capt. Bride shouted: "Come on, my brave boys! Follow me, Marylanders!" As the 8th Maryland Infantry (U.S.) surged forward, Bride was struck by a Confederate shell and died holding the flag.[3] First Lieut. Alfred D. Reynolds of the 1st Maryland Infantry (U.S.), a brother of another officer in the regiment, fell in action at the Battle of Weldon Railroad on August 18, 1864. As he lay dying, Reynolds told his men, "I die content; my peace is made with my Maker, and I have fallen in a glorious cause; it shall not be said that I died a coward's death."[4]

Three officers of the Maryland Brigade earned the newly authorized Medal of Honor for their gallantry during the war. Capt. William Taylor of the 1st Maryland Infantry was cited for two acts when he was awarded the medal in 1897. As a sergeant in 1862, Taylor was trying to burn a bridge at Front Royal when he received a painful wound. Two years later, at Weldon Railroad, Taylor, now a second lieutenant, volunteered for a dangerous reconnaissance mission behind enemy lines and was captured.[5]

Brevet Capt. Francis M. Smith received the Medal of Honor decades after the war. Smith, an apprentice stonecutter in Frederick County, was

2. John W. Wilson to Adjutant General, October 16, 1864, Adjutant General's Papers, 1864, MSA.

3. CSR and Pension Records, James Bride, 8th Maryland Infantry (U.S.). Bride's father applied for a pension after the war and submitted tributes to his dead son that appeared in the Baltimore *American*, May 18, 1864, and a resolution of the 8th Maryland Infantry (U.S.) issued on December 1, 1864.

4. Camper and Kirkley, *Historical Record*, 255. "The dying were most concerned to fix their courage, but families were equally anxious for reassurance of the soldier's purity. They cherished worthy last words as a special remembrance, as a moral summation of life about to be lost and as a declaration of religious faith" (Linderman, *Embattled Courage*, 87).

5. CSR, William Taylor, 1st Maryland Infantry (U.S.); U.S. Army Public Information Division, *The Medal of Honor of the United States* (Washington, D.C., 1948), 110–11.

born in 1842 and enlisted as a private in the 1st Maryland Infantry (U.S.) in 1861. After serving as an enlisted man, he received promotions to second lieutenant in 1864 and then to first lieutenant and adjutant later that year. Wounded three times during the last year of war, Smith remained with the dead body of his colonel and brought the remains off the field after the Battle of Dabney's Mills (or Hatcher's Run) in 1865.[6]

The army awarded the Medal of Honor to First Lieut. Jacob Koogle of the 7th Maryland Infantry (U.S.) for capturing an enemy battle flag at Five Forks. The twenty-three-year-old farmer from western Maryland wrote on May 21, 1865: "I have the honor to acknowledge the receipt of the 'Medal of Honor' granted me by the 'Secretary of War' for services though rendered for the good of 'our cause' I am happy to find have attracted his favorable notice."[7]

The loss of Maryland's Union officers was particularly tragic for the comrades who survived as well as the next of kin and friends at home. Three Wilson brothers served as officers in the 1st Maryland Infantry (U.S.). John W. Wilson, a staunch Unionist during the tense days of April, 1861, was killed at Dabney's Mills on February, 6, 1865. His brother Robert, a lieutenant in Company G, was wounded in the shoulder at the same battle, and the ball lodged in his lungs. He died of his injuries at home on February 14. Isaac, the third brother and a lieutenant in Company E, was left to bury his brothers in the family plot at the Presbyterian church cemetery in Chestnut Grove, Baltimore County. A fourth brother had already fallen as an officer in the 2nd Maryland Infantry (U.S.) at the Battle of Antietam in 1862.[8]

The officers and men of the various Maryland regiments often published their respects to their dead comrades in the form of resolutions. The expression of grief over the death of Capt. Josiah B. Coloney of the 1st Maryland Infantry (U.S.) from wounds received at Weldon Railroad in 1864 was heartrending:

> Where as Our Grief over the previous losses of beloved and respected officers & comrades in this command is painfully intensified by the death

6. CSR and Pension Records, Francis M. Smith, 1st Maryland Infantry (U.S.); U.S. Army, *Medal of Honor,* 185.

7. Jacob Koogle to George D. Ruggles, May 21, 1865, in CSR, Jacob Koogle, 7th Maryland Infantry (U.S.); U.S. Army, *Medal of Honor,* 190.

8. Camper and Kirkley, *Historical Record,* 253; James I. Robertson, Jr., ed., "A Federal Surgeon at Sharpsburg," *Civil War History,* IV (1960), 137, 139.

of J. B. Coloney who had been wounded whilst in the noble discharge of his duties as Adjutant and although on account of his Merits & Bravery was commissioned as Major of this Regiment was by the will of a Superior power was not allowed to join us in that capacity.

Resolved   That Whilst we are glad that the appreciation of his value as an officer expressed in his promotion must have cheered the last moments of his useful life and comforted him in the agony upon his death bed, We doubly lament his loss at the time when this increased vacant of his Efficiency as an Officer entitled us to expect still more glorious manifestations of his patriotism and military abilities. Resolved That we express our deep Sympathy with his Bereaved Widow & mourning orphans and send to them from the battlefield the assurance of our sincere confidence and lasting friendship.

Resolved   That whilst our hearts are aching over the repeated blows, a wicked Rebellion strikes in our ranks the same hearts are swelling for anger to revenge the noble victims of Patriotism and to imitate their heroic conduct.

Resolved   That a copy of these resolutions be sent to the family of the deceased & copies to the Balt American & Balt Clipper for publication.[9]

The knowledge of an officer's death, though painful to his family, was perhaps preferable to the uncertainty that plagued families whose loved ones were missing in action or taken prisoner. Deborah O'Neill asked for information regarding her husband: "I have heard that Capt. Charles Z. O'Neill was a prisoner, and wounded in Richmond, if you know anything of his whereabouts, or condition, will you be so kind as to let me know through flag of truce. . . . By doing so you will confer a great favor to his *distressed* wife." Mrs. O'Neill later learned that her husband fell in battle at Laurel Hill with his regiment, the 4th Maryland Infantry (U.S.), and was buried by Confederate soldiers in an unmarked grave.[10]

Margaret A. Johnson received a letter from her husband, Capt. Thomas S. J. Johnson, from a prison camp in Charleston, South Carolina, in September, 1864. He had been captured that spring while serving as the

9. CSR, Josiah B. Coloney, 1st Maryland Infantry (U.S.); Camper and Kirkley, *Historical Record*, 253–54.

10. Mrs. Charles Z. O'Neill to William Burns, August 16, 1864, in CSR, Charles Z. O'Neill, 4th Maryland Infantry (U.S.).

Maryland Brigade's inspector. Johnson told his wife on September 8 that "my health is good—thanks only to a good constitution and to god; whom I pray to guard and bless you and our baby." Mrs. Johnson did not hear from her husband again, and she wrote the government for assistance in December. She learned in the summer of 1865 that Capt. Johnson of the 1st Maryland Infantry (U.S.) died of chronic diarrhea on November 20, 1864, while a prisoner of war in South Carolina. A fellow prisoner reported that while in a southern hospital, Johnson ate mostly cornmeal and sorghum molasses, which aggravated a stomach ailment.[11]

Tidbits of information provided some consolation to surviving family members. A clerk in the Fredericksburg hospital told Mrs. Gorsuch that her son Robert M. Gorsuch of the 4th Maryland Infantry (U.S.) had died of wounds on May 16, 1864. "He was brought here on the 9th inst and remained here until his death . . . he had the best possible care under the circumstances. It was his last wish that his love be sent to his Mother, Grandmother, Brothers and Sisters." The orderly added, "He was buried near the Hospital and the grave plainly marked and could be easily found at any future time."[12]

Officers frequently transmitted bad news about troops under their command to their families. Second Lieut. Thomas Ocker of Company F, 6th Maryland Infantry (U.S.), tried to explain the circumstances surrounding the disappearance of Pvt. Richard I. Gist at the Wilderness. In a letter to Gist's sister, Ocker stated that "Richard was wounded & supposed seriously from the fact he otherwise would have went to the Rear." During the battle, the regiment had to fall "Back 3 or 4 hundred yards from the Enemys fire it was impossible to Recover all the Wounded. Richard was among the unfortunate & Left on the ground. After which I & some of the Rest of the officers consented for some from each company to go back & try to get the Wounded Back." The men of the 6th Maryland Infantry were unable to evacuate their wounded and dead comrades, which grieved Ocker. "I would just say here you may think hard of friends leaving a field & not careing for there wounded comrades. Could you But Witness the Sight you would not be at a Loss to account for it. It is one of the most

11. Margaret A. Johnson to Brig. Gen. Henry W. Wessells, December 18, 1864, in CSR, Thomas S. J. Johnson, 1st Maryland Infantry (U.S.).

12. James Whitman to Mrs. Gorsuch, May 18, 1864, in Pension File, Robert M. Gorsuch, 4th Maryland Infantry (U.S.).

Humiliating things to a Regt. to loose their woun[d]ed in Battle, but such is the fate of many." Coming off the field at Cold Harbor, Ocker added, "Should I be spared & so fortunate as to get any further information Reliable, it will afford me pleasure to transmit it immediately to you."[13]

Sixty-five officers of the Maryland Brigade were wounded during the course of the war, nearly 30 percent of the junior officer corps. This figure excludes men who died of their wounds. These sixty-five men suffered a total of eighty-two separate woundings. Some officers, such as Medal of Honor recipient Francis M. Smith, suffered more than one wound. With the exception of eleven officers of the 1st Maryland Infantry (U.S.) injured at Front Royal in 1862, the vast majority of lieutenants and captains were wounded in the last eleven months of fighting. The brigade lost heavily at such contests as the Wilderness and the fighting near Spotsylvania in the opening days of the Overland Campaign. The brigade suffered its single greatest loss, fifteen officers wounded, at the Weldon Railroad near Petersburg in August, 1864. The number of injured officers did not diminish as the war drew to a close; three men were hit by enemy gunfire at Dabney's Mills in February, 1865, and another eight at Five Forks two months later.

Unlike many Union regiments that suffered heavy losses throughout the four years of fighting, the four regiments of the Maryland Brigade did not see continuous action until the end of the war. This period, however, was as bloody as Antietam, Chancellorsville, or Gettysburg. The fighting in May–June, 1864, and the numerous engagements around Petersburg tore deep holes in the ranks of Maryland's Union officers.[14]

Laurel Hill near Spotsylvania typifies the horror that the officers of the Maryland Brigade faced in 1864. The brigade, with the 1st, 4th, 7th, and 8th regiments, formed the lead element of the Union V Corps in the race to seize the vital crossroads at Spotsylvania Court House on May 8. Marching through the night of May 7 on dust-choked roads and burning underbrush in the Wilderness, the Maryland Brigade moved down Brock Road when they were urged forward by the corps commander, Gouverneur K. Warren. He reportedly shouted to the exhausted Marylanders: "Never

---

13. Thomas Ocker to Mary S. Gist, June 5, 1864, in Gist Family Collection, LC; copies of these letters are in Gist Family Papers, MS 2007.1, Manuscripts Division, MHS.

14. For a discussion of Maryland units in the fighting around Petersburg, see Richard J. Sommers, *Richmond Redeemed: The Siege at Petersburg* (New York, 1981).

mind cannon! Never mind bullets! Press on and clear this road. It's the only way to get your rations."[15]

The 4th Maryland Infantry (U.S.), detached as skirmishers with another brigade, had already engaged the enemy early in the morning. The remainder of the brigade formed columns along the road and went into the attack with a "hearty cheer." Heavy Confederate fire halted the Marylanders, creating a jam as Union Marylanders in the rear kept pushing forward. For a brief time, the northerners engaged the rebels in a fierce duel, but the Confederates were protected by hastily built entrenchments while the troops of the Maryland Brigade were exposed. The brigade commander went down with a serious wound, as did his successor. Capt. Bride of the 8th Maryland Infantry (U.S.) lost his life as he tried to keep his regiment intact in the face of ferocious Confederate shot and shell. A round also struck Col. Charles E. Phelps of the 7th Maryland Infantry (U.S.), the brigade's acting commander, as he rode his horse across the field. When the horse fell, it crushed Phelps. Despite the best efforts of Capt. Ephraim F. Anderson to rescue his commander, both men fell into enemy hands. At the same time, Confederate bullets struck Anderson, a Hagerstown lawyer, three times, and he eventually lost the index finger of his right hand. The survivors of the brigade fell back to the comparative safety of Union lines after having lost a total of 192 officers and men in a matter of minutes.[16]

One of the soldiers wounded at Laurel Hill passed the flag to Capt. Bride of the 8th Maryland Infantry (U.S.) just before that gallant officer fell. This soldier, Pvt. John H. McCracken, belonged to Capt. Louis R. Cassard's Company A of the 8th Maryland Infantry and later described his plight that May morning:

> I tried my best to crawl off, but I could not move. I did make out to get
> up on my foot, but my wounded leg pained me so, I was glad to lay down
> again. I now commenced to suffer for water; it was so hot and dusty, my
> throat and tongue was dry as a chip. I begged the Rebs to bring me some
> water, but they would not. Night came at last; it became cooler, which

15. Wilmer, Jarrett, and Vernon, *History and Roster*, 271.

16. William D. Matter, *If It Takes All Summer: The Battle of Spotsylvania* (Chapel Hill, 1988), 60–62; Wilmer, Jarrett, and Vernon, *History and Roster*, 271–73; CSR, Ephraim F. Anderson, 7th Maryland Infantry (U.S.). For an interesting story of the acting commander of the Maryland Brigade, see H. H. Walker Lewis, "The Schizophrenic Diary of Colonel Phelps," *Maryland Historical Magazine*, LXXVI (1981), 383–85.

relieved me greatly. I soon went to sleep and slept soundly till wakened by the roar of artillery and small arms. The morning now became foggy and the firing ceased for a while. The Rebs came out to where I was laying. I begged one of them for some water, but he had none. I now asked him to cut a canteen off a dead man and bring it to me, but he did not seem inclined to do it. I had a gold pen and a pencil, so I offered him that. He did not like to come out; he was afraid our men would shoot him, but I begged him so hard, at last he got it for me. It was full. I drank nearly the whole of it without stopping.

McCracken's agony was not over. Renewed shelling drove the Confederates back to their trenches, and the Union wounded were subjected to friendly fire. The private wrote: "I hugged mother earth as close as I could. The bullets were so thick over me that the sing of them was like a swarm of bumble bees. They tore up the ground all around me and some of them grazed my clothes. . . . At last one hit me. I thought I was killed this time." McCracken survived this second wound and after a torturous second night lying on the battlefield, he could see Confederate soldiers moving closer. "I begged them to bring me some water, but I might as well have asked a bird flying over." Finally, southern troops evacuated the wounded Marylanders from Laurel Hill and McCracken was able to quench his thirst and have his wounds treated.[17] McCracken's suffering was similar to that of countless Union Maryland officers and enlisted men who fell on numerous battlefields during the war.

The hideous scene of the battlefield when fighting had ceased impressed Maryland's officers with the horror of man's inhumanity. Graham Dukehart, a Maryland soldier in a New York regiment, recorded after the ferocious battle of Antietam that "the enemy sent in on that day [September 18, 1862] a flag of truce asking permission to bury his dead, as the number was very large, it was granted & he took advantage of the truce to skedaddle leaving the dead to rot where they lay we yesterday passed over the field in our advance, & saw not less than 500 dead rebels, & a large number of our own men, whom they were engaged in burying, the sight was a horrid one, & God grant I may never see, or participate in an other battle, the ground over which on the 17th we engaged, was literally strewed with dead." First Lieut. James H. Rigsby, a thirty-year-old officer in Battery A, 1st Maryland Light Artillery (for-

17. Huntsberry and Huntsberry, *Maryland in the Civil War*, Vol. II: *The North*, 47–49.

merly part of the Purnell Legion), also described the scene at Antietam: "It was awful in the extreme; the stench was awful, the field still being full of dead Rebels, who, their comrades, in their haste to get away, left unburied."[18]

Injury in battle was indiscriminate. One officer in the 8th Maryland Infantry (U.S.) told his father of his close calls at the Battle of Weldon Railroad: "I made two very narrow escapes of being shot on Saturday attack a ball pass through my hat so close to my head that it suffed [snuffed] my hair and on Sunday fight a ball struck me on the four [fore] part of my right arm but did not enter the flesh although it pained my arm very much."[19]

Officers tried to reduce the risks of battle injuries, as First Lieut. James J. Gillette of the 3rd Maryland Infantry (U.S.) wrote his mother: "I promise to make myself as little as possible in the target line when the day of battle finds me again. We do not wear much uniform in the field. Blouses are worn on almost all occasions by the officers as well as the men." The Unionist promised, "I would no sooner uselessly seek danger than I would dishonorably fly from it." In an optimistic spirit in 1862, he concluded that "the war may end without my being again under fire, stranger things occur. . . . In this war especially the soldiers' risks are not so great as the outside public imagine."[20]

Maryland's Union officers had more to be wary of than the battlefield. Several men received serious injuries while not actually engaged with the enemy. Pvt. Isaac Reed shot Skipworth C. Gorrell, a farmer from Harford County and a lieutenant in the 7th Maryland Infantry (U.S.), in the left arm in the early morning hours of May 22, 1863. Reed mistakenly fired on Gorrell, who was in charge of a detail of Union pickets on Loudoun Heights near Harpers Ferry. The wound forced Gorrell to resign at the age of forty-three in late 1863. William H. Moffett, Jr., a young private from Baltimore and the brother of an officer, served in a Maryland battery and witnessed a terrible accident. A new breechloading cannon exploded while being tested, killing the battery's drummer and injuring five other soldiers. Moffett wrote, "I was standing behind the gun & along side of

18. Graham Dukehart to sister, September 20, 1862, in Graham Dukehart Papers, MS 1862, Manuscripts Division, MHS; "Three Civil War Letters of James H. Rigby, a Maryland Federal Artillery Officer," *Maryland Historical Magazine*, LVII (1962), 158.

19. Edwin W. Moffett to father, August 24, 1864, in Moffett Papers.

20. James J. Gillette to mother, August 4, 1862, in Gillette Papers.

him [the drummer]; it was a miracle that so few were hurt as nearly the whole battery were standing there at the time."[21]

Several members of the Maryland Brigade were injured in the withdrawal of Union troops from Harpers Ferry during the Confederate invasion in 1863. Lieut. Col. Johannes of the 8th Maryland Infantry (U.S.) experienced temporary loss of vision from the flash of the regiment's exploding ammunition magazine on Maryland Heights on July 1. Second Lieut. George W. McCulloh of the 8th's Company C burned his hands and face as the regiment pulled back from its defensive positions overlooking the junction of the Potomac and Shenandoah rivers.[22]

Other officers suffered disabilities while riding horses, marching, or drilling on the parade field. Eighteen-year-old George W. Shealey, a cavalryman in the Purnell Legion Cavalry and a future officer in the 8th Maryland Infantry (U.S.), ruptured his abdomen in a horse accident in Wilmington, Delaware, in 1863. Alexander Murray, also of the 8th Maryland Infantry, damaged his left knee when he was thrown from a horse that same year. First Lieut. William B. Norman claimed that his sides were ruptured when he fell from a horse. Another first lieutenant, John K. Green of the 7th Maryland Infantry (U.S.), sprained his ankle in late 1864 while on an expedition near Petersburg. Capt. Edward J. Hyde of the 4th Maryland Infantry (U.S.) was discharged in the summer of 1863 for an "inguinal hernia" that occurred while he was drilling troops at the Lafayette Square Barracks in Baltimore the preceding year. Even moving through woods could be dangerous for Union officers, as Capt. William H. Colklessor of the 7th Maryland Infantry discovered. Losing his direction during the fierce Wilderness fighting, Colklessor stepped over a fallen tree, and "one of the branches struck him in the crotch, injuring his privates."[23]

21. Skipworth C. Gorrell to Maj. Gen. Robert C. Schenck, June 26, 1863, in CSR, Skipworth C. Gorrell, 7th Maryland Infantry (U.S.); William H. Moffett to father, December 1, 1862, in Moffett Papers.

22. Statement of Surgeon A. A. White, April 16, 1864, in CSR, John G. Johannes, 8th Maryland Infantry (U.S.), and Statement of Acting Assistant Surgeon M. M. Townshend, August 15, 1863, in CSR, George W. McCulloh, 8th Maryland Infantry (U.S.).

23. Pension Files, George W. Shealey, Alexander Murray, and William B. Norman, 8th Maryland Infantry (U.S.), and John K. Green, 7th Maryland Infantry (U.S.); Edward J. Hyde to Capt. L. C. Baird, August 1, 1863, in CSR, Edward J. Hyde, 4th Maryland Infantry (U.S.); Pension Files, William H. Colklesser, 7th Maryland Infantry (U.S.).

Accidents occurred when soldiers became careless and indifferent to danger. Graham Dukehart had just been relieved from picket duty when Confederate shells landed in camp. The first round "startled us all, & well it might, for the ball came directly toward us, & buried itself in the side of the hill." It was "followed by several others, the balls coming rather nearer every time" until a Union battery silenced the enemy's fire. "While all the firing was going on our supper bell, which is by the way (a cowbell) rang, & then you should have seen the scampering regardless of the enemy or their shots we sat down & ate like veterans careing nothing for them." The Union soldier admitted that there is "a great deal of truth in the old proverb, that familiarity breads contempt." He promised his father that "I never expose myself more than is necessary."[24]

Officers became victims of the war in other ways. First Lieut. John H. Millender of the 4th Maryland Infantry (U.S.) was discharged in the spring of 1864 for "nervous disability and inability to travel." A doctor noted that Millender "seems to be melancholy his skin is pale, a general feeling of nervousness and lassitude, no appetite, his tongue is clean." Another officer in the regiment, John A. Tucker, the commander of Company H, had to be discharged in 1865 for injuries to his right shoulder and arm when he fell into the campfire near Weldon Railroad on February 14 during an epileptic attack. Tucker suffered extensive burns and was unable to perform any further military service.[25] Such injuries underscored the general feeling of despair that seeped into the Army of the Potomac as its officer ranks were decimated during the last year of the war.[26]

The Confederates captured many Union Maryland officers during the course of the war. The Maryland Brigade, for instance, lost 41 junior officers as prisoners during the war. With the exception of a handful of men taken during the fighting in 1864–1865, almost all of these officers came from the 1st Maryland Infantry, which fell into rebel hands at Front Royal on May 23, 1862. In a short fight against Stonewall Jackson's army,

24. Graham Dukehart to sister, October 8, 1861, to father, August 22, 1861, in Dukehart Papers.

25. General Orders No. 173, Adjutant General's Office, May 10, 1864, in CSR, John H. Millender, 4th Maryland Infantry (U.S.); Statement of Surgeon Charles W. Cadden, February 14, 1865, in CSR, John A. Tucker, 4th Maryland Infantry (U.S.).

26. This aspect of the "simmering down" process of Civil War armies is discussed in Linderman, *Embattled Courage*, 245–48.

Col. Kenly's 1st Maryland Infantry attempted to hold the town against advancing Confederates. Kenly's men were outnumbered and lacked sufficient warning either to hold the town or to evacuate. As a result, 21 officers and 514 enlisted men of the 1st Maryland Infantry surrendered.[27]

The news of Kenly's capitulation struck terror in the hearts of many northerners. Five officers of the regiment, Lieuts. Charles Camper, John McF. Lyeth, Thomas Saville, and George W. Thompson and Capt. George Smith, escaped the trap at Front Royal. Far from the scene of the battle, these officers reported from Hagerstown: "The rebel infantry forded the North Branch stream [of the Shenandoah River] and flanked us on the left. We were again ordered to move, left in front, up the road toward Winchester. We had marched about two miles when a wild shout was heard, and rebel cavalry came dashing into our lines, cutting from right to left, showing no quarter, displaying a black flag. . . . A severe fight was kept up until our whole force was cut to pieces."[28]

This incident incited Unionist crowds in Baltimore, Frederick, and Hagerstown to attack the homes of known southern sympathizers. A mob stormed the office of the Hagerstown *Mail*, destroying the building and the paper's presses. Other Unionist rioters attacked Baltimore's German newspaper, *Der Deutsche Correspondent*, for failing to fly the national flag after the Front Royal disaster. Despite rumors to the contrary, the Confederate troops from Maryland treated their Union counterparts well. Col. Kenly thanked Capt. William H. Murray of the 1st Maryland Infantry (C.S.) for his kindness to him and his men. Murray responded by touching his cap and saying, "Col.—I have done only my duty."[29]

The capture of the 1st Maryland Infantry (U.S.) at Front Royal essentially eliminated that unit from the federal order of battle. The Confederates took the Maryland soldiers to Winchester after the battle and then, as the fighting spread up the Valley, removed them to territory securely in their own grip. Col. Kenly wrote in his official report that "our treat-

27. Camper and Kirkley, *Historical Record*, 31–38; for Kenly's report of the battle, see *Official Records*, Ser. I, Vol. XII, Pt. 1, pp. 555–58.

28. Goldsborough, *Maryland Line*, 43; *Official Records*, Ser. I, Vol. XII, Pt. 1, pp. 558–59.

29. Scharf, *History of Maryland*, III, 474; Cunz, "Maryland Germans," 414–15; William H. Murray to sister, August 15, 1862, in Murray Letters; Goldsborough, *Maryland Line*, 44.

ment has been kind and considerate, except that but a scanty allowance of food has been given us, which I ascribe to its scarcity among them than to any disposition on their part to deprive us of it."[30]

The rebels left some of the seriously wounded, including twenty-four-year-old Frederick C. Tarr, a first lieutenant in Company D and the regiment's adjutant, at Front Royal, where they were soon liberated by Union troops. Col. Kenly and another wounded officer, Capt. Charles W. Wright of Company D, were released on parole in Winchester because of the severity of their wounds. Wright lingered for nearly two weeks at the Union Hotel hospital before dying from his injuries on June 12; he was the first officer in the Maryland Brigade to die.[31]

The remaining officers of the regiment accompanied the prisoners in the march up the Valley until they reached Harrisonburg. The Confederates then separated the officers from the enlisted men and paroled the officers to report on their own accord to Staunton. They regrouped there and were finally sent to Salisbury, North Carolina, where they waited to be exchanged in early August. The enlisted men were sent to Lynchburg and Richmond, where they suffered heavily from the lack of food and proper medical attention until exchanged in September. The Union army reconstituted the regiment with returning prisoners and men who escaped from Front Royal during the summer and fall of 1862. The 1st Maryland Infantry (U.S.) served as the foundation of the Maryland Brigade when it organized in September.[32]

Two other Maryland Union regiments suffered the rigors of imprisonment that year. The 1st and 3rd Regiments, Potomac Home Brigade Infantry, were captured intact when Harpers Ferry fell to Stonewall Jackson on September 15, 1862. These two regiments, with 56 officers and 1,257 enlisted men, formed a substantial portion of the total Union loss of 435 officers and 12,085 soldiers. Losses by death or wounds were minimal.[33]

30. Goldsborough, *Maryland Line*, 44.

31. Camper and Kirkley, *Historical Record*, 49, 254; CSR and Pension Files, Charles W. Wright, 1st Maryland Infantry (U.S.).

32. Camper and Kirkley, *Historical Record*, 47–80, 82–84; Special Orders Number 66, Department of the Shenandoah, June 3, 1862, reforming the 1st Maryland Infantry (U.S.), in Civil War Papers, 1862, MSA.

33. *Official Records*, Ser. I, Vol. XIX, Pt. 1, p. 549; testimony of the commander and a company-grade officer of the 1st Potomac Home Brigade at the inquiry into the Harpers Ferry capitulation, *ibid.*, 556–58, 713–14.

The daring escape of Union cavalry under Col. Benjamin F. Davis was the only bright aspect of the entire Union debacle at Harpers Ferry. Guided by Hanson T. C. Green, a second lieutenant in Cole's Maryland Cavalry, the Union cavalry force crossed the Potomac River into Maryland and evaded the Confederate army. Maj. Cole led his battalion of four companies in advance of the Union foray while two companies of the 1st Maryland Cavalry (U.S.) brought up the rear and even managed to capture a Confederate supply train.[34]

Maryland Unionists met disaster again in 1863 at the hands of the enemy. During the fighting at Stephenson's Depot near Winchester in June, the 5th Maryland Infantry (U.S.) lost heavily, mainly through capture, and the 6th Maryland Infantry (U.S.) barely escaped the Confederate trap.[35] The capture of the entire 9th Maryland Infantry (U.S.) on October 18, 1863, at Charles Town was a major defeat and humiliation for Union Marylanders.

The 9th Maryland Infantry, a six-month regiment, occupied Charles Town and guarded the approach to Harpers Ferry. The regimental commander, Col. Benjamin L. Simpson, had vague orders to hold the town unless pressed by enemy troops, in which case he was to fall back to the main post at Harpers Ferry. Union plans called for reinforcements to assist Simpson and his unbloodied troops. On the morning of October 18, Simpson discovered that Confederate cavalry under Brig. Gen. John D. Imboden had surrounded Charles Town. The regiment's colonel prepared to fight the enemy and refused rebel offers to surrender. As Confederate artillery shells landed in the town's center, the regiment's adjutant, Lieut. Charles H. Richardson, was struck in the right leg by a shell fragment. Simpson quickly lost control of his men, who became panic-stricken. The escape routes out of Charles Town had been cut by the Confederates, and only Col. Simpson and a handful of officers and men managed to evade capture. Imboden's raiders rounded up 15 other officers and 345 soldiers and sent them off to Confederate prisons.[36]

34. Murfin, *Gleam of Bayonets*, 149–54.

35. William Sturtevant Nye, *Here Come the Rebels!* (Baton Rouge, 1965), 108–23. For an account of a private soldier's escape from Winchester, see J. Polk Racine, *Recollections of a Veteran; or, Four Years in Dixie* (Elkton, 1894), 61–72. Letters of one officer of the 5th Maryland Infantry (U.S.) captured at Winchester and imprisoned at Libby Prison in Richmond are located in Babb Family Papers.

36. Barr and Musick, eds., "'They Are Coming!'"

A soldier in the 34th Massachusetts Infantry Regiment in nearby Harpers Ferry recorded his disgust at the performance of the Union Marylanders: "Much blame is attached to the 9th Md., in surrendering as it did, without firing a single gun. Instead of making any effort at all toward defending themselves until reinforcements arrived they began to break their guns to pieces, with which the road was filled when our regiment arrived on the spot. . . . All the field and staff officers looked out for their own precious bodies, and left the regiment to take care of itself." A court of inquiry relieved Simpson of responsibility for the loss of his regiment at Charles Town although he never again resumed military duties.[37]

Conditions for Union prisoners of war deteriorated after the first year of the war. Most officers captured in 1861 and 1862 were speedily paroled and then exchanged, a system that alleviated the strains of housing and feeding thousands of captured men. After 1863, the cartel system broke down, forcing Confederates to establish massive camps throughout the South to house growing numbers of Union prisoners. Overcrowding, lack of food and medicine, and poor sanitation afflicted Marylanders who surrendered to Confederate forces. Twenty-nine officers from Maryland, held in Richmond's Libby Prison, petitioned the governor of Maryland on September 23, 1863, for assistance in obtaining their exchange. The officers, mainly from the 5th Maryland Infantry (U.S.), noted that "our imprisonment has become almost intolerable. Deprived of *pure air*, the sweet sunshine, and an accustomed diet, we continue to sink gradually under the debilitating influence."[38]

As the situation of Union prisoners of war grew more desperate, escape seemed the only hope. First Lieut. Christopher R. Gillingham, one of three brothers who served as officers in the 1st Maryland Infantry (U.S.), was captured at Front Royal. He attempted to escape on June 3, 1862, but was recaptured four days later. The commander of Company G, Robert S. Smith, escaped on June 6 while in Staunton and made his way back to the Union army. Unlike the other paroled officers in the regiment, Smith broke his word of honor when he escaped and he subsequently found it impossible to get exchanged. He resigned at the end of 1862

37. Drickamer, and Drickamer, eds., *Fort Lyon to Harpers Ferry*, 144; Barr and Musick, eds., "'They Are Coming!,'" 16–17.

38. *Historical Times Illustrated Encyclopedia of the Civil War* (New York, 1986), s.v. "Prisons," by Peggy Robins; Petition of Maryland Officers to Governor Bradford, September 23, 1863, Executive Papers, 1863–65, MSA.

because "I have not been able to obtain information of my exchange necessary to justify in engaging in active service."[39]

Such niceties of the early war period were quickly forgotten as Maryland's officers began to suffer the horrors of lengthy imprisonment. John Sachs was born in Germany in 1826, moved to the United States in 1850, and took up dairy farming near Gettysburg, Pennsylvania. In 1861 he joined his family in Canton, a neighborhood in Baltimore, and received an appointment as a lieutenant in the 5th Maryland Infantry (U.S.). Taken prisoner with his regiment at Winchester in June, 1863, Sachs was among the many officers of the regiment held at Libby Prison in Richmond. When more Union prisoners arrived in the spring of 1864, Sachs was transferred to Confederate prisons in Danville, Macon, and Charleston. After a miserable train trip from Charleston to Columbia, he witnessed the murder of a fellow officer who was bayoneted by a guard for reaching out of the train for food offered by a friendly citizen.

This cold-blooded act infuriated Sachs, who, along with three other men, escaped from the prison at Columbia on September 29, 1864, and headed for the South Carolina backwoods. Aided by friendly Negroes, the Union officers joined other escaped prisoners of war and began the long journey northward. When they encountered white southerners, Sachs passed himself off as a member of the 32nd Georgia Infantry Regiment, the unit that guarded the Columbia prison camp. Their luck did not hold, however, and the escapees were surprised by two Confederates with hound dogs. One of the Maryland officers was recaptured. Despite this mishap, Sachs and his band made their way northward until they met Union sympathizers who aided them in reaching a Union army outpost at Cleveland, Tennessee. Sachs and three fellow officers from the 5th Maryland Infantry (U.S.) finally returned home to Baltimore on January 3, 1865.[40]

William Taylor, the officer in the 1st Maryland Infantry (U.S.) who earned the Medal of Honor for his exploits at Front Royal and at Weldon Railroad, was taken prisoner in late 1864. He jumped off a train carrying

39. Camper and Kirkley, *Historical Record*, 52; Robert S. Smith to Col. N. T. Dushane, December 11, 1862, in CSR, Robert S. Smith, 1st Maryland Infantry (U.S.).

40. "Experiences of Lieut. John Sachs as a Prisoner of War, 1863–1865," Civil War Miscellaneous Collection, USAMHI. For a description of the Columbia prison, see George C. Fraser, ed., *A Petition Regarding the Conditions in the C.S.M. Prison at Columbia, S.C.* (Lawrence, 1962).

Union prisoners from Salisbury to Danville on October 2. Crossing the Smoky Mountains in North Carolina, Taylor arrived at Knoxville, Tennessee, on January 12, 1865. He reported to Union troops "entirely devoid of outer garments, and shoeless."[41]

Other Maryland Brigade officers did not have the opportunity to escape and waited for exchange. Capt. Ephraim Anderson, who received three wounds at Laurel Hill while rescuing Col. Phelps, was held at Libby Prison but was among the fortunate officers to be paroled in September, 1864, and then exchanged because of the seriousness of his injuries. Peter A. Hagan, a twenty-year-old officer in the 7th Maryland Infantry (U.S.), fell into enemy hands during the 1863 Bristoe Station campaign and remained a prisoner until March, 1865, when he was paroled in North Carolina. Capt. William H. Davis of the 4th Maryland Infantry (U.S.) was captured at the Wilderness and also paroled. Joseph T. Addison, another officer in the 4th, fell into enemy hands at Weldon Railroad in September, 1864, and was paroled on the James River early in the new year after being held at Libby Prison and Salisbury.[42]

Following the parole of these officers, Union vessels transported them to Camp Parole in Annapolis to await their formal exchange, generally within a few weeks after their arrival in Maryland. They then received furloughs to visit home before returning to duty. Lieut. Hagan was paroled in North Carolina on March 1, 1865. He arrived at the Maryland capital four days later and was given thirty days' leave on March 11. He returned to duty on April 13 and was sent to his regiment on May 2. He had been absent from the 7th Maryland Infantry (U.S.) for over eighteen months.[43]

The detailing of officers to duties outside of the company hindered unit efficiency. Lieutenants and captains from the Maryland regiments served on court-martial boards or commissions as members or judge advocates, as recruiting officers or investigating officers for reports of survey, and on examination boards for promotion or competency. In July, 1863, at least seven officers from the Maryland Brigade reported to Baltimore, Annapolis, or Washington to take charge of draftees. Later that year, and again

41. CSR, William Taylor, 1st Maryland Infantry (U.S.); Camper and Kirkley, *Historical Record*, 240.

42. CSR, Ephraim F. Anderson, 7th Maryland Infantry (U.S.); CSR, Peter A. Hagan, 7th Maryland Infantry (U.S.); CSR, William H. Davis, 4th Maryland Infantry (U.S.); CSR, Joseph T. Addison, 4th Maryland Infantry (U.S.).

43. CSR, Peter A. Hagan, 7th Maryland Infantry (U.S.).

in 1864, more officers and enlisted men were detailed to duties away from the Maryland regiments and did not return to their companies until late April, only days before the opening of the spring, 1864, campaign. They had little time to familiarize themselves with field living or prepare for the upcoming battles.[44]

In another example of the problems caused by detailing officers, Col. John W. Wilson of the 1st Maryland Infantry (U.S.) wrote the secretary of war in late 1864 requesting that First Lieut. Robert N. Wharry rejoin his company. Twenty-six years old in 1864, Wharry, a carpenter from Baltimore, had been assigned to a military commission in his native city since mid-August. Wilson desperately needed Wharry to take command of Company C. The commanding general in Baltimore, however, refused to release Wharry until a replacement could be found. As a result, Wharry did not rejoin the 1st Maryland Infantry until February, 1865, despite the secretary's orders that he leave Baltimore two months earlier.[45]

In September, 1864, the V Corps commander determined that far too many officers and enlisted men were not serving on the front lines with their regiments, and he ordered a reduction in the number of special- or extra-duty billets. At that time, the four regiments and one infantry battalion assigned to the Maryland Brigade had 19 officers and 283 enlisted men detailed to other duties while another 144 soldiers were listed as absent without leave.[46]

This continual attrition of Union officers in the Maryland Brigade through resignations, dismissals, battle casualties, and detachments generally caused only temporary dislocation. After the heavy fighting in the summer of 1864, Lieut. Col. Barrett of the 4th Maryland took command of the 7th Maryland. That unit's commander, Maj. Edward M. Mobley, had been temporarily incapacitated from wounds. The appointment or-

44. Brig. Gen. John R. Kenly to Gov. Augustus W. Bradford, August 11, 1863, Executive Papers, 1863–65, MSA. Kenly protested the loss of these officers and asked for more troops for the Maryland Brigade. Col. Dushane also protested to Gen. Kenly that the detailed officers and men on duty for the draft in Baltimore were "doing nothing" and he requested their return (Dushane to Kenly, August 25, 1863, in RG 393, Entry 3786, Letters and Endorsements Sent and Orders Received, June, 1863–March, 1864).

45. Col. John W. Wilson to Edwin M. Stanton, November 26, 1864, in CSR, Robert N. Wharry, 1st Maryland Infantry (U.S.).

46. General Orders No. 12, 2nd Brigade, 2nd Division, 5th Army Corps, September 14, 1864, in RG 393, Records of U.S. Army Continental Commands, Entry 3792, Special Orders, June, 1863–June, 1865.

ders commended Barrett for his "well-known firmness and discretion." The brigade commander, however, criticized the 7th Maryland, which had become "sadly demoralized because of the inefficiency and want of attention on the part of some of the line officers." Barrett had the full authority to "bring the regiment back to its former efficiency, and to this end he will report to these headquarters all officers who do not freely and fully do their duty."[47]

The Union army devised an efficient officer-replacement system in the Army of the Potomac, which supplied the Maryland regiments with the full quota of company- and field-grade officers. The heavy fighting in 1864 and 1865 sorely tested this system, but it proved reliable as experienced noncommissioned officers rose to the junior officer ranks. The replacement system maintained unit cohesion and fostered an "aristocracy of merit" within the Union Maryland regiments rather than bringing inexperienced and unknown appointees into the officer corps.[48]

The Union regiments practiced promotion by seniority throughout the war, and as replacements were needed, regimental officers identified capable enlisted men and nominated them to the state governor for appointment.[49] Later in the war, all of the enlisted men nominated for lieutenancies had served in the ranks for months, if not years, and had endured the trials of the battlefield. They were capable men (most had already risen from private to first sergeant), and they knew the duties of both commissioned and noncommissioned officers.

The case of David L. Stanton of Baltimore is a good example of the promotional opportunities available to capable enlisted men in the Maryland regiments. Stanton, a pattern maker, was born in 1840 and enlisted as a private in the 1st Maryland Infantry (U.S.) at the beginning of the war. He soon became Company A's first sergeant and was promoted to second lieutenant in November, 1861. He rose to first lieutenant in December, 1862, and then moved to Company I as its captain in March, 1864. At the end of the year, Stanton earned his gold oak leaves and in February, 1865, became lieutenant colonel. A month later, he assumed command of the regiment as its colonel. In addition to commanding the

47. *Official Records*, Ser. I, Vol. XLII, Pt. 1, pp. 345–46.

48. Linderman, *Embattled Courage*, 233.

49. For an example of a letter of recommendation for promotion of an enlisted man to officer, see J. H. Stonebraker to Col. Frederick T. Locke, December 3, 1864, in CSR, James T. Armacost, 1st Maryland Infantry.

1st Maryland Infantry, Stanton commanded the Maryland Brigade during the final campaign of the war. His gallantry at Five Forks brought Stanton a promotion to brevet brigadier general in 1867, his date of rank coinciding with the battle. During the course of the war, Stanton was captured at Front Royal and wounded at Harris Farm and at Weldon Railroad.[50]

Most officers in the Maryland Brigade did not experience as meteoric a rise as Stanton, although the Union army generally handled its officer promotion and replacement system in an orderly fashion. There appears to have been little dissatisfaction among Maryland's officers regarding their chances for advancement in the army because vacancies always existed.[51]

Assignment to the field and staff or to duties completely outside of the regiment often resulted in promotions for junior officers. The new duties were challenging, requiring management of materiel or funds, and removed the officer from the grind of daily duties in the company as well as reducing exposure to combat. First Lieut. James J. Gillette of the 3rd Maryland Infantry (U.S.) wrote his mother about his detachment from the regiment to "act as Commissary of Subsistence for the brigade" in the summer of 1862: "This being a position on the staff and one of more importance than my adjutancy I am anxious to hold it. The officer whom I have succeeded in the charge of the Deptmt was ordered back to his regt by Gen. Sigel for *incompetency*. I am strenuous in my exertions to suit the stomachs of the soldiers in order that a similar Fate may not be mine." Gillette admitted: "I am somewhat startled when selected for the responsible duty of providing subsistence for four thousand hungry soldiers, but like all other responsibilities it seemed most terrifying at a distance. A nearer view," he stated, "with a few days experience has taught me that with good supplies within a days distance an active commissary has no excuse for permitting his store house to get empty—provided his means of transportation are good."[52]

---

50. CSR and Pension Files, David L. Stanton, 1st Maryland Infantry (U.S.); Camper and Kirkley, *Historical Record*, 230–31.

51. The brevet system of promotion was not generally employed in the Maryland Brigade until the end of the war. Most brevet promotions, in fact, were given after 1865 in recognition of gallant and meritorious service performed by Maryland officers throughout the war and at specific battles. This system of promotion is discussed in C. F. Eckhardt, "A Problem of Rank," *Civil War Times Illustrated*, XXIX (January–February, 1991), 52–54.

52. James J. Gillette to mother, June 28, 1862, in Gillette Papers. Gillette later advised

The effectiveness of the officer replacement system is evident in the experiences of the forty-three men who served as captains and lieutenants in the 4th Maryland Infantry (U.S.) from 1862 to 1865. Of the regiment's nine original captains in 1862 (the 4th Maryland Infantry had only nine companies), one officer was eventually promoted to brevet colonel; one was killed in action; six were discharged for wounds or disabilities; and one remained as a captain until mustered out in 1865. Of the remaining nineteen original officers, all first and second lieutenants, one first lieutenant became major and eventually earned a brevet lieutenant colonelcy at the end of the war; one became a brevet captain and mustered out of service; one resigned to accept a captaincy in the United States Volunteers; five resigned their commissions without promotion beyond their original rank; four were promoted to captain and ended the war with the regiment; two died of wounds after promotion from second to first lieutenant; two were discharged without promotion; one was promoted to captain and subsequently discharged; one was dismissed without promotion; and one second lieutenant was promoted to the next higher grade and mustered out in 1865.

To fill the gaps in the company-grade leadership structure caused by losses, fifteen enlisted men were appointed officers in the 4th Maryland Infantry (U.S.). Ten of these soldiers held the top noncommissioned officer position of first sergeant in their respective companies before being promoted to the officer corps. Two of the remaining five held the regiment's senior post of sergeant major when they became lieutenants. Two men were still sergeants, and one served as the regiment's quartermaster sergeant. Half of the newly minted officers were commissioned in the critical year of 1864, two were commissioned in 1862, three in 1863, and three in 1865. Ten of the soldiers received direct commissions as first lieutenants and five as "shavetails," second lieutenants in Union army jargon.[53]

his brother against seeking a staff position because "so many leave the service after a short trial and so many fail to come up to the mark that, in the line, advancement is certain. It is difficult in the staff and Dan [his brother] would do well to refuse any detail which may be offered him. A Lieutenant once detailed is always a Lieutenant. He closes the avenue of promotion in his regiment, and the chances are against his confirmation in the Department to which he is detailed" (James J. Gillette to father, April 9, 1863, *ibid.*).

53. John M. Priest, "Lieutenants and Captains in the Army of the Potomac: The

Only two of the fifteen men made it to the rank of captain because of their late appointment to the officer corps. Ten of the men promoted from the ranks mustered out with the regiment in 1865. Two were dismissed and another two discharged for disability. One of the new lieutenants died of wounds.

The situation was similar in the other regiments of the Maryland Brigade as new officers replaced those who received promotions, resigned, left the service for other reasons, or died. The Maryland regiments continued to face the same problems they first encountered in 1862. As casualties increased and sources for fresh volunteers dried up, several Maryland units consolidated so as to maintain a viable strength at the end of the war. The Purnell Legion Cavalry consolidated with the 8th Maryland Infantry (U.S.) while its infantry counterpart merged with the 1st Maryland Infantry (U.S.). The same pattern could be seen among other Maryland regiments as the 2nd Regiment Eastern Shore Infantry consolidated with its sister unit, the 1st, which in turn amalgamated with the 11th Maryland Infantry (U.S.), itself a one-year hybrid of an earlier one-hundred-day regiment raised in 1864.

Many Union Maryland officers opposed these consolidations because they reduced the number of available command positions. The officers of the 3rd Maryland Infantry (U.S.) protested the idea of consolidation or disbandment of their regiment in a letter to the governor in 1863.[54] Despite the recommendations of the officers that recruitment be done at home, the army downgraded the regiment to a battalion. Replenishing the diminished ranks of Maryland's regiments was difficult because many men in Maryland were reluctant to join the army.[55]

Competition for volunteers was intense and resulted in a rancorous letter-writing battle between the 1st Maryland Infantry (U.S.) and the 5th Maryland Infantry (U.S.) in early 1864. The latter regiment, while

---

Creation of a Professional Army," paper presented at the 1990 conference of the Civil War Society, Crystal City, Arlington, Va., August 23, 1990.

54. Petition of Officers of 3rd Maryland Infantry (U.S.) to Gov. Augustus W. Bradford, June 6, 1863, Executive Papers, 1863–65, MSA. The proposal to consolidate regiments in the Maryland Brigade evoked some protest; see Edwin W. Moffett to father, January 20, 1863, in Moffett Papers.

55. The problems of getting Marylanders to join the Union army are discussed in Clark, "Recruitment of Union Troops," 159.

in Baltimore on reenlistment furlough, attempted to sway fresh recruits and transfers from other units by billing itself as the "1st Maryland Volunteer Infantry." Col. Nathan Dushane of the original 1st Maryland Infantry strongly opposed this effort on the part of Col. William Louis Schley: "We are now where we have ever been, since we left Baltimore in 1861—facing the enemies of our country, and not in some safe and comfortable place in the rear." In another newspaper notice, Lieut. Col. Wilson also criticized the commander of the 5th Maryland Infantry, which led Schley to prefer charges against Wilson.[56]

The reason behind the intense recruiting efforts was obvious to Union officers. The quality of new soldiers brought in under the federal and state draft calls was deplorable and affected the morale of the Maryland veterans in the field. Col. Joseph M. Sudsberg of the 3rd Maryland Infantry (U.S.) summed up his feeling about the substitutes in his regiment:

> Devoid of patriotic sentiment, religious faith, or manliness, these scroundels entered the service only to make money; they made it and deserted. The example is demoralizing in the extreme. For our soldiers who enlisted eighteen months since (for three years) no bounty was required to stimulate their participation. They have not only been doing battle with the enemy in the Field, but have suffered privations patiently on the march, and endured sickness in the Camp. The Government neglecting to pay them for seven months, the brave fellows had to suffer in mind as well as in body, when they heard from Home and of their wives and children often destitute even of bread. But like good Soldiers they bore up well against these complicated evils, until the nine months Substitutes came to us, full of money. The contrast was too great, their patience was overburdened and exhausted, to see men, and worthless ones too, paid in advance for expected service only, whilst they who had fought the battles of the Country were coldly neglected.[57]

56. Baltimore *American*, January 8, February 23, 1864. The charges were dropped by the brigade commander on March 8, 1864 (RG 393, Records of U.S. Army Continental Commands, Entry 3786, Letters and Endorsements Sent and Orders Received, June, 1863–March, 1864).

57. Col. Joseph M. Sudsberg to Gov. Augustus W. Bradford, February 10, 1863, Executive Papers, 1863–65, MSA. Lieut. Gillette noted after the Battle of Antietam that "another battle will annihilate my regiment and the Government will muster us out of service, those that are left. . . . The 3rd Md. number now only 150 men. We were 900 when we left Baltimore; 300 killed, wounded, and prisoners in three engagements. The rest deserters and sick. One million men may be recruited, but if not prevented from

The litany of complaints against these men grew as their motives became evident. One of the most notorious bounty jumpers, Samuel W. Downing, initially enlisted in a Maryland regiment in the fall of 1862 and deserted in 1863. He amassed a fortune of $7,750 over the period of ten months from substitute payments and enlistment bounties. The army finally tracked Downing (which may not be his actual name) and executed him in September, 1864. Executions of Maryland soldiers were not infrequent, and military courts sentenced at least nine enlisted men to death for various crimes.[58]

Unfortunately, corruption also tainted Maryland's Union officer corps. William E. George, the officer who had so much trouble with his company commander in the 1st Maryland Infantry (U.S.) in 1863, was charged with conduct prejudicial to good order and military discipline in 1864. By this time, George had resigned from the 1st Maryland Infantry on account of ill health. He later received an appointment as major in the 11th Maryland Infantry (U.S.), a one-hundred-day regiment that served during the summer and fall of 1864. Following his muster out in October, the army discovered that George had siphoned money from substitute brokers instead of paying the actual substitutes. Because he was now a civilian, the army could not take any action against George for his illegal activities.[59]

Capt. Edward E. Gillingham left the 1st Maryland Infantry (U.S.) and was later appointed as a company commander in the 13th New York Cavalry Regiment. Gillingham did not exercise much care in recruiting men for his unit. The regimental commander of the 2nd New York Artillery identified one of Gillingham's new soldiers as a deserter from his regiment at Fort Whipple in Virginia on September 23, 1863. Gillingham, however, failed to return the deserter to his original unit, and charges

---

deserting and straggling will not fill up the army" (James J. Gillette to mother, September 23, 1862, in Gillette Papers).

58. Robert I. Alotta, *Civil War Justice: Union Army Executions Under Lincoln* (Shippensburg, 1989), 129–30. For a review of conscription in Maryland, see Report of Brevet Brig. Gen. William H. Browne, September 4, 1865, in RG 110, Records of the Provost Marshal General's Bureau (Civil War), Historical Reports of State Acting Assistant Provost Marshals General and District Provost Marshals, 1865, M1163, NA.

59. "Charges and Specifications against William E. George 2 Lieut. of the 11th Regt. Maryland Vol. Infty," [undated]; Col. William H. Browne to Lieut. Col. Samuel G. Laurence, November 21, 1864, in CSR, William E. George, 11th Maryland Infantry (U.S.) (100 Days).

258 • Maryland's Blue and Gray

were later placed against him. Rather than face a court-martial, Gillingham resigned in the spring of 1864, citing disease to his liver.[60]

As a result of the lack of volunteers for lengthy military service, Maryland raised a number of short-term units. Some of these units, such as the 11th Maryland Infantry (U.S.), served for a little over three months and were ad hoc formations hastily assembled to deal with Confederate forays across the Potomac River. Other units, such as the 3rd Maryland Cavalry Regiment (U.S.), were so hard-pressed that they recruited Confederate prisoners of war at Union prison camps.[61] As a result, the state of Maryland continually formed new units from untrained personnel and repeated the devastating cycle that had plagued the state's original units in 1861–1862.

The deficiencies of the officers in the new units are evident in several letters to the state's governor regarding Battery D, 1st Maryland Light Artillery, in the Washington defenses in 1865. The battery, raised in late 1864, had five officers during its six months of existence, three of whom had been dismissed. The commander of Fort Whipple told Governor Bradford that "the Battery needs a rigorous and steady hand to break it into thorough discipline and make it efficient. Its whole existence seems to have been so loose and unsoldierly and its training so vicious that very little advantage can be expected from promoting from its ranks." Because there was no strong battery commander, "each day's delay now is a dead loss to the Government and an injury to the organization."[62]

First Lieut. Richard M. Ray, the battery's sole remaining officer, also pleaded with the governor for leadership: "My duties at present are more than one officer can properly attend to, as in my position as Lieut., I am obliged in my regular turn to perform all that is required of an officer of that grade, such as officer of the day, and Officer of the Pickets, which in connection with the entire duty of the Battery (as Comd'g Officer) resting upon me, does not really afford me sufficient time to devote to the interests of the men of my own Battery, which I should wish to give. The want of a Captain is seriously felt in the Battery in many respects."[63]

60. CSR, Edward E. Gillingham, 13th New York Cavalry.

61. *Official Records*, Ser. III, Vol. IV, 1203.

62. Capt. Robert J. Nevin to Gov. Augustus W. Bradford, March 13, 1865, Civil War Papers, 1864–65, MSA.

63. Richard M. Ray to Gov. Augustus W. Bradford, April 3, 1865, *ibid*. A postwar report on Ray by his superior officers noted that he was "not competent in any respect to

Maryland's junior officers played a key role in commanding their units. Whether in garrison or in the field, the captains and lieutenants wielded far greater influence than they would have in a peacetime, professional military. These officers molded Maryland's companies and batteries, thereby shaping the effectiveness of their regiments and brigades. These men little realized the full extent of their authority and responsibilities at the outbreak of the war.

---

fill the office he now holds" ("Report of Board of Officers Convened by Virtue of General Orders 86 War Department A.G.O. May 9th 1865 in Case of Officers of Batty 'D' 1st Md. Light Artillery," in RG 94, 1865 Officers Reports of Various Divisions [uninventoried records]). The only other report of a Maryland unit is of the 2nd Maryland Infantry (U.S.). For a copy of General Orders Number 86, see *Official Records*, Ser. III, Vol. V, 15.

·10·

MARYLAND REDEEMED

Maryland's officers relied on their families at home for material support to supplement army rations and supplies. The women of Frederick, under the direction of Mrs. Schley, knitted one hundred havelocks for her husband's company in the 1st Maryland Infantry (U.S.) during the summer of 1861. The soldiers graciously accepted the havelocks, a popular but useless uniform item, and most ended up as rags to clean muskets. The women of Hagerstown presented this same company with a silk flag for their "soldierly bearing and good conduct." Food quickly became the most sought-after gift from home. Company F of the 1st Maryland Infantry (U.S.) placed a note in the Baltimore *American* in November, 1864, thanking the Union ladies of Ellicott's Mills with the "highest regard" for providing turkey dinners on Thanksgiving.[1]

Civic groups warmly welcomed Union regiments from Baltimore and Frederick when these troops returned home on their reenlistment furloughs in 1864. Despite these open expressions of support, Union Marylanders suspected their state of harboring strong Confederate sentiment. Robert H. Hergesheimer, an eighteen-year-old first sergeant in Company E, 7th Maryland Infantry (U.S.), and a future second lieutenant, complained to his father in early 1863: "It is really astonishing that the people of Frederick allow such men as Heard, Markel, and men of that kidney to remain in Frederick, preaching the terrible heresy of secession, and awaiting with anxiety a favorable opportunity to put their doctrines into practicable operation at the expense perhaps of thousands of valuable lives." Hergesheimer, who fell in battle in 1864, wrote: "We are fighting against the rebels in the field, it seems to me strange, that those, who

---

1. Camper and Kirkley, *Historical Record*, 19, 21–22; Baltimore *American*, November 24, 1864.

profess to be loyal, have not even the *courage* to drive from their homes those black hearted traitors, that infest their firesides. They ought to be repudiated, and cast out scorn and contempt."[2]

A soldier in the 6th Maryland Infantry (U.S.) expressed the same opinion to his brother about the residents of Carroll County in 1862: "The neighbors are very much tainted with that hellish rebellion which has cause many a widow and orphan and friend to cry out for vengeance at the hand of God. It seems that the rebels are determined to ruin and make desolate our once happy and peaceful State how many traitors have we in the midst of us who have done all that lays in their power to free as they say the state of Maryland."[3]

Many Unionists also had their doubts about Maryland's loyalty. Baltimore's prewar reputation as a town of roughs tarred soldiers from the city. James H. Herring, a sergeant in 1864, a member of the Purnell Legion Cavalry, and a future officer in the 8th Maryland Infantry (U.S.), was arrested near Baltimore with three members of his company while on a scout. The provost marshal confined Herring in the Central Guardhouse in Washington, D.C., for lacking written orders authorizing his absence from his unit. Asked by a prison captain about his unit, Herring replied and was answered in a "volley of invective calling us 'God damned Baltimore Plug Uglies,' Scape Gallows, and escaped convicts from the State Prison." Even as late as 1864, the army did not allow Maryland units to perform all duties. The secretary of war received a recommendation that the 5th Maryland Infantry (U.S.) be replaced by another unit as guards at Fort Delaware because "it has too many sympathizers in it to be intrusted with the charge of prisoners of war." A short-term Ohio regiment, formed with one-hundred-day men, replaced the Maryland unit.[4]

Union soldiers who spent any time in the state often found it securely Unionist, which helped to allay previous concerns. One man wrote to a Baltimore family in late 1862 about the city's aid to the army after the Battle of Fredericksburg: "I was very glad to hear that your city did so nobly by the sick and wounded soldiers it will help to prove to some

2. Baltimore *American*, February 19, 29, March 3, April 9, May 7, 1864; Robert H. Hergesheimer to father, February 6, 1863, in Pension Files, Robert H. Hergesheimer, 7th Maryland Infantry (U.S.).

3. Richard J. Gist to brother, October 12, 1862, in Gist Family Collection.

4. James H. Herring to Capt. Thomas B. Watkins, April 22, 1864, in CSR, James H. Herring, Purnell Legion Cavalry; *Official Records*, Ser. II, Vol. VII, 187, 193.

people that the *good* citizens of Baltimore are not the bloodthirsty people that they were popularly supposed to be."[5]

Lieut. Gillette told his father in 1862 that he "attended a tremendous party last eve & met all the celebrated officers of the department." In Gillette's opinion, "It is a libel on Balto. that it is said that all the ladies are secession. There were present twenty or thirty of the most refined and heavily pursed ladies of the city *all Union*." The city was heavily festooned with national flags, and Gillette concluded, "I don't see how it can be said that it is secession in feeling."[6]

Maryland's Union officers played a key role in keeping the state in the Union. They participated in state and national elections and maintained a federal presence to enforce draft laws and to subdue local secessionists. As early as October, 1861, Gen. Dix recognized the importance of Maryland's Union troops in border state politics. He told Gen. McClellan, "I think it very important for our future quietude that the Union ticket should not merely be carried, but that it should have an overwhelming majority." Estimating the number of Maryland's voters in the military at six thousand, Dix emphasized "that the Government will make all practicable arrangements to enable the voters in the Maryland corps to attend the polls in the districts in which they reside."[7]

A Massachusetts soldier reported in 1863 that "the Maryland troops all start for home tomorrow to vote at the coming state election. Soldier's votes tell the story now-a-days at elections and their side generally carries the day with overwhelming success." Officers in the Maryland Brigade received leave to return to their residences to vote, and Frederick County voters elected First Lieut. Edward Y. Goldsborough of the 8th Maryland Infantry (U.S.) as state's attorney in 1863.[8]

Maryland's Union troops overwhelmingly supported the government's policies throughout the war in their actions on the home front and at

5. John McGeehan to William H. Moffett, December 28, 1862, in Moffett Papers.
6. James J. Gillette to father, February 18, 1862, in Gillette Papers.
7. *Official Records*, Ser. I, Vol. I, 628–29. The role of soldier voting in Maryland is discussed in Charles L. Wagandt, "Election by Sword and Ballot: The Emancipationist Victory of 1863," *Maryland Historical Magazine*, LIX (1964), 143–64.
8. Drickamer and Drickamer, eds., *Fort Lyon to Harpers Ferry*, 145; Charles S. Knodle to Lieut. Col. George Sangster, October 27, 1863, in CSR, Charles S. Knodle, 7th Maryland Infantry (U.S.); Edward Y. Goldsborough to Lieut. Col. Charles Kingsbury, Jr., December 17, 1863, in CSR, Edward Y. Goldsborough, 8th Maryland Infantry (U.S.).

the ballot box. Union officers initially served as police fillers in Baltimore when the regular constabulary disbanded. Officers of the 1st Maryland Infantry (U.S.) helped to establish Union control in the city and participated in the arrests of suspected Confederate sympathizers. Capt. Gregory Barrett took his company from the 4th Maryland Infantry (U.S.) to Westminster in Carroll County, where he conducted a large-scale sweep of the town in late August, 1862. His men apprehended sixteen citizens on trumped-up charges and forcibly took them back to Baltimore. Barrett's reputation as a Baltimore thug grew with his action in Westminster although the army later dropped the charges and released the Marylanders.[9]

During the war years, Maryland held a gubernatorial election and a constitutional referendum to abolish slavery in addition to the 1864 presidential election.[10] The soldier vote in these elections and others was critical to the victory of the Unionist ticket. Although Maryland's white Union troops had little regard for blacks, be they slave or free, and little investment in slavery, the Maryland Brigade voted overwhelmingly in favor of ending slavery in the state.[11] In the presidential race between Abraham Lincoln and George McClellan in 1864, Maryland's troops threw their support behind their war leader. It is impossible to determine who actually voted for each candidate, but the total results highlighted the army's willingness to follow the Republican party. In the words of one correspondent from a Maryland artillery battery, "We yesterday opened a poll, and not being engaged *in front*, we determined to '*fire to the rear*'; accordingly we gave our *whole* vote—present—for the *right* men, and against the *home* enemies of our government."[12]

The returns for several Union Maryland units are as follows:[13]

9. Klein, ed., *Just South of Gettysburg*, 10–14. A discussion of the Union army in Maryland is found in Charles B. Clark, "Suppression and Control of Maryland, 1861–1865: A Study of Federal-State Relations During Civil Conflict," *Maryland Historical Magazine*, LIV (1959), 241–71.

10. For a full discussion of the various elections, see Baker, *Politics of Continuity;* Wagandt, *Mighty Revolution;* Fields, *Slavery and Freedom;* Clark, *Politics in Maryland;* and Josiah Henry Benton, *Voting in the Field: A Forgotten Chapter of the Civil War* (Boston, 1915), 223–49.

11. The Maryland Brigade voted 780 to 91 in favor of the new state constitution that abolished slavery (Camper and Kirkley, *Historical Record,* 780).

12. Baltimore *American*, November 11, 1864.

13. *Ibid.* For results within the Maryland Brigade, see Gen. Warren's note to the acting

	Lincoln	McClellan
1st Maryland Infantry	475	2
4th Maryland Infantry	272	0
7th Maryland Infantry	304	30
8th Maryland Infantry	227	12
12th Maryland Infantry	175	31
Cole's Cavalry	376	48
Alexander's Battery	95	0
Rigby's Battery	98	0

Richard King, an assistant to the state governor, arrived at City Point from Baltimore on November 2, 1864, to oversee election activities in the Maryland units. At the camp of the 1st Maryland Cavalry (U.S.) he distributed ballots for the upcoming election on the eighth. He found the soldiers expressing "much interest in the coming Election also to know they were not forgotten at home." King then went to the 5th Maryland Infantry (U.S.), which had just suffered heavy casualties at Fort Harrison, outside of Richmond. He found the regiment in good spirits but with few officers. King told the governor that the regiment should be assigned to the Maryland Brigade, whose camp he visited on November 6. Officers from the 2nd and 3rd regiments came to the brigade's camp to pick up ballots for their units. Election day was a festive occasion in the camp of the Maryland regiments because all nonessential duties were suspended. "We think it will be a long remembered day by every man in the Brigade," King added. Following the elections, King visited Marylanders in army hospitals and also went to the isolated Maryland regiments, the 2nd and 3rd. All the Maryland troops, he declared, appreciated the packages, tobacco, stationery, and sewing material that he had brought from home, and they all wanted to know when the governor would visit. King returned to Maryland with several hundred dollars to deposit in Baltimore banks and to give to families at home.[14]

Maryland officers who served on the home front often encountered hostility from their neighbors, sometimes social ostracism but also open violence. The Baltimore *American* reported in January, 1862, that First

---

adjutant general of the Army of the Potomac in *Official Records*, Ser. I, Vol. XLII, Pt. 2, p. 576.

14. Richard King to Gov. Augustus W. Bradford, November 11, 1864, Adjutant General's Papers, 1864, MSA.

Lieut. Isaac L. Boyd of the Baltimore Light Infantry (later the 4th Maryland Infantry [U.S.]) was "brutally assaulted and beaten" "while in a shaving saloon in South Baltimore, by the notorious Joseph Edwards—He was assaulted in a chair undergoing a tonsorial operation, when Edwards, who had frequently been arraigned by the Lieutenant, then acting as Magistrate of the Southern Police Station, and by him committed to jail for his ill deeds, approached and made some offensive remarks. Before Boyd could arise from his chair Edwards struck him repeatedly about the face and beat him severely."[15]

Capt. Jesse D. Childs of the 1st Maryland Infantry (U.S.) suffered a concussion in 1865 when an unknown assailant attacked him in the city. Childs had had a rifle butt smashed into his eye at Cold Harbor only a few months previously. Second Lieut. Samuel N. Whittle of the 7th Maryland Infantry (U.S.) received knife wounds to his left shoulder while on guard duty at the polls in Baltimore County in the spring of 1864.[16]

Capt. Thomas H. Watkins had just returned to his home in Anne Arundel County after his army discharge when a local horse thief killed him. Watkins had raised Company B of the Purnell Legion Cavalry in 1861 and spent most of the war on provost marshal duty at Annapolis until his company was ordered to the front in 1864. After receiving a bullet wound to his head near Petersburg, Watkins recuperated in Maryland and decided to go riding to regain his strength. His horse, however, had been stolen, and Watkins and his brother tracked the culprit and arrested him. The thief, John H. Boyle, did not surrender without a fight and struck Watkins, aggravating his already serious head injury. After Watkins' return to civilian life, Boyle surprised the convalescent captain in his own house and murdered him. Another officer, Capt. John McF. Lyeth of the 1st Maryland Infantry (U.S.), lost his house and all his possessions when Confederate troops burned it after the Battle of Monocacy in 1864.[17]

The morale of the Union officers from Maryland sometimes lagged

15. Baltimore *American*, January 6, 1862.

16. Jesse D. Childs to Brig. Gen. Lorenzo Thomas, March 15, 1865, enclosing medical certificate of Surgeon Alexander B. Hasson, March 14, 1865, in CSR, Jesse D. Childs, 1st Maryland Infantry (U.S.); CSR, Samuel N. Whittle, 7th Maryland Infantry (U.S.).

17. Daniel Carroll Toomey, "Murdered—A Yankee Marylander, Captain Thomas H. Watkins," *Maryland Line*, X (December, 1989), 2–3; Pension Files, John McF. Lyeth, 1st Maryland Infantry (U.S.).

when they faced enemies both at home and at the front. At times, Union victory appeared elusive and these men despaired of ever defeating the Confederates and going home. One Maryland soldier in the 6th Maryland Infantry (U.S.) recorded his frustration with the war effort in the fall of 1862: "There seems to be a dark shadow impeding our national affairs the [Emancipation] Proclamation of the President has a great dissatisfaction in the army the defeat and utter failure of Burnside to capture and drive the rebels from their fortifications at Fredericksburg has tended to prolong the war perhaps another long summer and impeded the progress of the army in its campaign towards the Confederate Capital."[18]

James J. Gillette, commissioned a captain and commissariat in the fall of 1862, grew increasingly frustrated with the conduct of the war. Writing from Harpers Ferry after the Battle of Antietam, Gillette "could not help remembering today, as I saw the enemy from Maryland Heights, that five months ago we occupied the same relative position as now. Five months lost by practical intermeddling with General McClellan. How surely does wickedness recoil in the evil doers. General Banks and McClellan stand today on a prouder station in the eyes of their fellow countrymen, than ever they did before." Gillette seemed unconcerned about his own fate: "I don't care much what they do with me. This life gives one a heathenish and careless way of living that is appalling when one reflects. Our men live worse than brutes. The rebels are like starved jackals. Winter will break down the rebellion or inaugurate a disgraceful peace."[19]

Gillette strongly supported McClellan after the general's removal from command of the Army of the Potomac. In late January, 1863, Gillette protested that "the government is a stupid association of grandmothers that are bound to ruin us while they have the power. Our best Generals are all gon[e]—McClellan, Burnside, Porter, Sumner, Shields and Franklin." The new commander of the Army of the Potomac, Joseph Hooker, is "a broken down teamster from California." A few weeks later, Gillette exclaimed: "I am waiting anxiously for McClellan to take charge of us. So does every soldier wait. 'No one but McClellan' is the watchword and will be until he and the army he created are again joined."[20]

As late as the summer of 1863, Gillette still supported "Little Mac"

18. Richard J. Gist to aunt, January 7, 1863, in Gist Family Collection.
19. James J. Gillette to mother, September 23, 1862, in Gillette Papers.
20. James J. Gillette to mother, January 29, 1863, to parents, February 5, 1863, *ibid.*

and was bitterly disappointed when George G. Meade was placed in command. When the Union army marched into Frederick in pursuit of the Confederate force, Gillette was shocked at the undiscipline of the troops, a "sad contrast" to their appearance during the 1862 Maryland campaign. "People may scoff at McClellan and it may be that he is not a great General, but we know the fact that without him all seems chaos and disorder. Nor can the combined efforts of a thousand presses and ten thousand newspaper scribblers in the pay of the other faction, convince us to the contrary although the people may be and are blinded."[21]

Officers from Maryland rarely encountered problems in obtaining leave because they could easily travel home from the army's camps in Virginia. Officers from the Maryland Brigade received furloughs to get married as well as to take care of other personal or business matters. Christopher R. Gillingham of the 1st Maryland Infantry (U.S.) requested leave "for as long a time as can be consistently granted to go to Cincinnati Ohio to fulfill a matrimonial engagement" on April 15, 1863, while the unit was posted at Camp Pleasant near Harpers Ferry. Ferdinand Chenoweth, a nineteen-year-old first lieutenant in the 4th Maryland Infantry (U.S.), returned to Baltimore in 1865 to discuss his property arrangements with his guardian. New officers obtained leave to obtain their uniforms and equipment in Baltimore because officers, unlike enlisted men, were not authorized to draw government issue items.[22]

During the last winter of the war, the number of Maryland officers

21. James J. Gillette to parents, July 2, 1863, *ibid.* Soldiers of the Army of the Potomac long supported McClellan as a general but failed to support his bid for the presidency in 1864. In the words of Bruce Catton, "McClellan had always been a great symbol. He was the trumpets these soldiers had heard and the flags they had carried and the faraway, echoing cheers they had raised: the leader of an unreal army which had come marching out of the horn gates with golden light on its banners, an impossible sunrise staining the sky above its path, and now it had gone into the land of remembered dreams" (*Army of the Potomac*, III, 323).

22. Christopher R. Gillingham to Lieut. Col. William H. Chesebrough, April 15, 1863, in CSR, Christopher R. Gillingham, 1st Maryland Infantry (U.S.); Ferdinand Chenoweth to Brig. Gen. S. Williams, January 18, 1865, in CSR, Ferdinand Chenoweth, 4th Maryland Infantry (U.S.); William D. Ratliff to Lieut. Col. William H. Chesebrough, March 27, 1863, in CSR, William D. Ratliff, 7th Maryland Infantry (U.S.); William H. Leonard to Col. Frederick T. Locke, April 19, 1864, in CSR, William H. Leonard, 8th Maryland Infantry (U.S.); and Thomas J. Sterling to Col. Frederick T. Locke, April 19, 1864, in CSR, Thomas J. Sterling, 8th Maryland Infantry (U.S.).

applying for furloughs jumped dramatically. Regimental adjutants read countless letters each day from loved ones in Maryland and other states in the North imploring the release of their menfolk in the army. These officers were usually allowed to go home to reassure their families during the quiet interlude on the front. Several letters attest to the precarious balance that officers had to maintain between their responsibilities at home and their official duties. John Reese, a German who had changed his name from Johann Riess, had just risen to officer rank in the 1st Maryland Infantry (U.S.) when he submitted his furlough application in March, 1865: "I have a letter from a friend informing me of the dangerous illness of my wife; she being too ill to write herself. She is very anxious for me to come home, believing herself on her death bed [so] that I may make some arrangement for the care and protection of my five children who would be left in a most destitute condition in the event of her death."[23]

Capt. Joseph A. Harkins of the 7th Maryland Infantry (U.S.) received this letter from his sister in Harford County in late 1864: "I am sorry to have to write you such a letter as duty impels me to write you now. Mother is quite ill and is so very anxious to see you that I do hope you will try to come home at once for a few days if you can possibly get off. I fear she will not last long and she talks so much about you and Nathan [Harkins' brother, a private in the same company]. Oh! Brother do try to get home."[24]

Letters from home stressed the necessity for the officers to come home to visit sick or dying family members. Capt. James B. Cochran's sister urged him to leave the 7th Maryland Infantry in late 1864: "Please do not write as you have done before that you cannot come, let us hear from you soon." Such letters taxed the officers' ties to kin and their duties with the regiment. First Lieut. John Ball, in the same regiment and a native of England, received a pitiless letter from his sister in New York: "I have no encouraging news from you poor Anna is much worse. Dr Buchanan says there is no hope and that she cannot last much longer. John I can

23. John Reese to Lieut. Col. Frederick T. Locke, December 16, 1864, in CSR, John Reese, 1st Maryland Infantry (U.S.).

24. Ann C. Johnson to Joseph A. Harkins, November 28, 1864; Joseph A. Harkins to Brig. Gen. S. Williams, December 2, 1864, in CSR, Joseph A. Harkins, 7th Maryland Infantry (U.S.).

carry her in my arms she has fallen away so, poor Mamma is sick too she sends her love to you John if you want to see Sis. in this world you must come home at once."[25] Despite the constant need for regimental officers, the army furloughed as many lieutenants and captains as possible during the hard winter of 1864–1865.

Sometimes it appeared that officers had all the benefits while enlisted men suffered at the hands of petty tyrants. That officers had greater pay, allowances, and furlough opportunities and could resign when they wished alienated many enlisted men. A Massachusetts private whose regiment was in the vicinity of Maryland units at Harpers Ferry commented about officers: "It is the private, we all know, who enlists with a patriotic intent, and not the officers. The latter enlist for money, and get large salaries, while the private does all the work. It would be no more than an act of justice to decrease their pay and add it to the privates."[26]

A Baltimorean, Edwin W. Moffett, was serving as first sergeant in the 8th Maryland Infantry (U.S.) when he wrote a bitter letter complaining about the state of affairs in his regiment at Harpers Ferry in 1863. Commissioned a year later, Moffett witnessed firsthand the poor treatment of enlisted men. Moffett's regiment was "situated at the base of a mountain and all the water drain from the mountain and settle in our Camp which keeps the ground under our feet continually damp." The men suffered from the effects of the weather and poor sanitation, leading Moffett to declare emphatically, "It is nothing but neglect that cause the death instead of sending them to the General Hospital where they can be tended to properly but put up in a cold tent with no fire and laid on the damp ground to die from Neglect and want of attendance." Moffett held his officers accountable for this disaster: "The Surgeon & Asst Surgeon loaf about drinking Liquor almost ready to bust but that is a mear [mere] sample of what is done in the Brigade for the Head Officers are spreeing from morning until night and the poor Enlisted Man is entirely for goten & neglected."[27]

25. Mary Emma to James C. Cochran, November 29, 1864, in CSR, James B. Cochran, 7th Maryland Infantry (U.S.); Mary Ball to John Ball, November 28, 1864; John Ball to Brig. Gen. S. Williams, December 3, 1864, in CSR, John Ball, 7th Maryland Infantry (U.S.).

26. Drickamer and Drickamer, eds., *Fort Lyon to Harpers Ferry*, 68.

27. Edwin W. Moffett to father, January 20, 1863, in Moffett Papers. The situation

The familiarity of Maryland's soldiers with war led to an unfortunate rise in wanton violence against civilians. Graham Dukehart told his father in Baltimore in 1861 that "so far as burning & distroying houses. . . . We (that is our Regt) have never had any hand in it at all & most of the soldiers with whom I have talked deprecate all such proceedings." Dukehart believed that "it is done by a few evil disposed ones who thereby bring discredit on the whole army."[28]

First Lieut. James J. Gillette, detached from his duties with the 3rd Maryland Infantry (U.S.) and acting as a brigade commissary officer in Maj. Gen. John Pope's Army of Virginia, wrote about the military's poor discipline in August, 1862: "It is become sadly demoralized, from pilfering secessionists they have come to indiscriminate marauding and from that to stealing from each other, so that it is not safe to leave anything out of sight five minutes. An officer stole one of my horses two days since and today he is reported to me as riding the stolen animal on the march, having cut off its mane and tail to prevent recognition. The act will cost him dearly. Indiscriminate thieving seems the order of the day."[29]

Occasionally, enlisted men committed acts of violence against their officers. Poor treatment, however, does not appear to have been the cause of the criminal actions. Pvt. George Smith assaulted Second Lieut. George Gamble of the 8th Maryland Infantry (U.S.) and ruptured Gamble's left testicle in 1862. While taking the train from Baltimore to Harrisburg, Gamble ordered his soldiers to stop firing at cattle in passing fields. Smith refused to obey and hit Gamble in the crotch. He then threatened to kill

---

had not improved in the 1st Maryland Infantry (U.S.) a year later when the medical director of the First Army Corps commented in his inspection report on March 18, 1864: "The Camp of this Regiment [1st Maryland Infantry (U.S.)] is extremely irregular, the huts are exceedingly close, are overcrowded, and built in the most imperfect manner. The most inexcusable feature of all, is the police of Quarters, which is Odious. In fact this is the worst Camp in the Corps, and I strongly recommend that another Camp be at once constructed upon new grounds. The health of the men demands this change, even if the new quarters are not occupied longer than a week." Realizing that this was the direct responsibility of the regiment's officers, the corps commander ordered that a new camp be established for the 1st Maryland Infantry (U.S.) and that no leaves of absence or furloughs be given until the regiment occupied its new quarters (Report by J. Thomas Heard, Medical Director, First Army Corps, March 18, 1864, in RG 393, Entry 3786, Letters and Endorsements Sent and Orders Received, June, 1863–March, 1864).

28. Graham Dukehart to father, October 8, 1861, in Dukehart Papers.

29. James J. Gillette to father, August 7, 1862, in Gillette Papers.

Gamble in the first battle. After less than sixty days in the service, Gamble left the army because of his injuries.[30]

Pvt. William Kuhnes of the 2nd Maryland Infantry (U.S.) shot Second Lieut. David Whitson to death at Camp Carroll on December 10, 1861. Kuhnes killed the officer with no apparent provocation while the unit formed for parade. For this crime, the army hanged Kuhnes at Fort Mc-Henry in March, 1862, in the presence of the fort's garrison and volunteer troops.[31]

Enlisted men also perpetrated acts of violence against one another. Lieuts. Coloney and Thompson of the 1st Maryland Infantry (U.S.) witnessed the murder of Pvt. George W. Young in the regiment's camp on Maryland Heights on the evening of June 13, 1863. Young was trying to stop a fight between three other soldiers when Pvt. John Grady pulled a knife and screamed, "Look out you sons of Bitches: I will stab some of you." The other soldiers ran away after hitting Grady. The drunk private then turned and attacked Young, stabbing him in the stomach, chest, and back of the neck. He died the following day. Coloney and Thompson arrested Grady and testified at his court-martial.[32]

Junior officers also vented their frustrations against their commanders by refusing to obey orders or deliberately sabotaging their authority. John G. Johannes received an appointment as lieutenant colonel of the Purnell Legion Infantry in September, 1861. The next spring, Johannes tendered his resignation because "I cannot remain in the Regiment under present circumstances—subalterns in the staff are incessantly undermining and subverting all my efforts to establish proper discipline and my feeling as an officer and a man will not allow me to remain in the army." Col. Thomas B. Allard of the 2nd Maryland Infantry (U.S.) expressed the same view when he resigned in early 1864. Allard noted in his diary on January 7 that he did not want to stay in the regiment when "I was so objecnable [objectionable] to the officers."[33]

30. Certificate of Disability by Surgeon A. A. White, September 26, 1862, in CSR, George Gamble, 8th Maryland Infantry (U.S.). Such violence was not restricted to officers on active duty. For an account of the murder of a former officer of the 5th Maryland Infantry (U.S.), see Racine, *Recollections*, 193.

31. Alotta, *Civil War Justice*, 54; Baltimore *American*, March 6, 7, 8, 1862.

32. Deposition of Adjutant J. B. Coloney, June 14, 1863, in CSR, George W. Young, 1st Maryland Infantry (U.S.).

33. John G. Johannes, Jr., to Col. William J. Leonard, April 15, 1862, in CSR, John

Relations between junior officers and their commanders and subordinates usually improved once they began to work as a team on the battlefield. Similarly, men of diverse social and economic backgrounds accommodated themselves to the army's rank structure, which demanded complete obedience. Officers who were unable to submit to the army's way of life usually did not remain long. As officers and men began to know one other, they developed a long-lasting mutual respect. The soldiers of Company F, 1st Maryland Cavalry (U.S.), presented First Lieut. Charles H. Bankard, a former enlisted man in the company, with a saber, sash, and belt as a "token of their personal esteem and a mark of their regard for him as a bold, competent and efficient officer."[34]

Officers who expressed genuine concern for the welfare of their troops and demonstrated personal courage on the battlefield won the undying gratitude of the men. Pvt. Henry Devallin of Company H, 4th Maryland Infantry (U.S.), told his wife about his lieutenant in early 1864:

> I was taken sick after coming off of picket, and had a very hard time of it. I was taken with the Rheumatism in the back and shoulders, and could scarcely move, and might have died had it not been for our Lieutenant, the Regt. moved off and left me with the understanding from my officers that an ambulance would be there to take me to the hospital. I waited and waited, but no ambulance came and might have lain there all night, but my Lieutenant discovered me, and had me conveyed to the hospital.[35]

The best testimony to the faith that officers and men in the 1st Maryland Infantry (U.S.) had in one another was their willingness to reenlist when their term of service expired in early 1864. Soldiers who reenlisted received thirty days' leave in Maryland and were feted by the citizens at home. Soldiers who did not accept the reenlistment offer were discharged and returned to civilian life. The 1st Maryland Infantry was one of several

---

G. Johannes, Purnell Legion Infantry; Allard Diary, October, 1862–January, 1864, entry for January 7, 1864, in Thomas B. Allard Papers, MS 1953, Manuscripts Division, MHS. Allard had been examined by a military commission as to his competency as a field-grade officer in 1862. He was found proficient in company leadership tasks but not for battalion-level command or higher (Gov. Bradford to Gen. Burnside, July 18, 1862, Civil War Papers, 1862, MSA).

34. Baltimore *American*, April 6, 1864.

35. Henry Devallin to wife, January 14, 1864, in CSR, Henry Devallin, 4th Maryland Infantry (U.S.).

Maryland units whose three-year enlistment expired in 1864; the remaining regiments in the Maryland Brigade had another year or more to serve. Twenty-seven officers and 306 enlisted men in the regiment accepted the army's offer to continue the struggle as veteran volunteers and reenlisted in the spring of 1864. Only six officers declined to continue to serve in the 1st Maryland Infantry (U.S.). Previous war injuries and disabilities were the major reasons that prevented these men from staying in the regiment.[36]

In 1864, Maryland's Union officers wanted to finish the task they had started three years earlier and avenge the deaths of their comrades.[37] Major Adreon of the 4th Maryland Infantry (U.S.) put it bluntly when he said, "Let the traitors in front quail, for each and every one of the boys now with us, when the time comes, will strike harder and make them feel the vengeance in store for Rebels." The Maryland Brigade keenly shared this sentiment in late 1864 near Petersburg when "numbers of our soldiers were found all along the road murdered. It was done by citizens," a soldier in the 1st Maryland Infantry (U.S.) reported. "As we went down safeguards were put on their property and that is how we were repaid. As soon as the men were found orders were issued to burn everything for five miles on each side of the road. It was done with a vengeance. It was a track of fire day and night and was a sublime but awful sight. In one cellar three of the 2nd Corps were found murdered and buried. The owner of the house was hung without judge or jury. . . . The whole country was left a barren waste. It was an awful sight to see those who the guerrillas had killed. I have walked over battlefields where dead and wounded lay in piles but I never saw anything that harrowed my feelings so before."[38]

The quest for vengeance also drew a number of Union officers from Maryland to serve along the Virginia–Maryland–West Virginia borders on antipartisan raids with Cole's Cavalry or other units that sought to eradicate Confederate guerrillas in the lower Shenandoah Valley. Cole's western Maryland troopers engaged in sharp skirmishes with Mosby's and

36. Camper and Kirkley, *Historical Record*, 124.

37. Catton, *Army of the Potomac*, III, 33–35; Linderman, *Embattled Courage*, 261–62; Lord, *They Fought for the Union*, 12–14.

38. Harrison Adreon to mother, n.d., in Civil War Collection, MHS; Lord, *They Fought for the Union*, 274.

Gilmor's men as well as with renegades who ravaged the no-man's-land along the Blue Ridge Mountains. In such fights, quarter was neither offered nor expected.[39]

Even when Union Maryland officers left their original regiments, they often sought other military duties. Many joined newer organizations from Maryland, enlisted in other northern regiments, or served in the Veteran Reserve Corps. These men brought their combat experience and a knowledge of military tactics to their new units. Edward Y. Goldsborough, who resigned in 1863 to take up his elected post as state's attorney for Frederick County, served as a volunteer officer during the fighting around his hometown in 1864.[40] Capt. Virgil T. Mercer of the 1st Maryland Infantry (U.S.) was wounded in the left forearm at Harris Farm and was discharged because of disability. He wrote the colonel of the regiment asking for a recommendation for appointment in the Veteran Reserve Corps: "I have an honorable discharge from the service of the United States on account of physical disability, from wounds received in action." Mercer added: "Such discharge is no fault of my own, and I wish it could have been otherwise. My wound continues to annoy me very much, and I have no use of my arm, or hand." Mercer closed his letter by saying: "I suppose you have heard of Sheridans late victory in the Valey. it was most thorough and complete. three cheers for Sheridan and three *rousing* cheers for uncle Abe and Andy Johnson." One officer, Bowie F. Johnson, enlisted as a substitute in a New Jersey regiment in 1865 so he could return to combat duty.[41]

Despite the hardships and horrors that company officers faced during the war, military life had its benefits. Graham Dukehart, an enlisted man and later an officer in a New York regiment, wrote his father in Baltimore, "On the whole pa soldiering is not so laborious a life as represented the only thing we have to complain is a sameness of food every day viz crack-

---

39. For a description of one such fight, see Newcomer, *Cole's Cavalry*, 93–107. The latest description of the dueling between Cole and Mosby in northern Virginia is in Wert, *Mosby's Rangers*, 131–37, 143–45.

40. CSR and Pension Files, Edward Y. Goldsborough, 8th Maryland Infantry (U.S.); Edward Y. Goldsborough, *The Appeal of Frederick City to the Congress of the United States* (Frederick, 1989); and Cooling, *Jubal Early's Raid*, 45.

41. Virgil T. Mercer to Lieut. Col. John W. Wilson, September 28, 1864, in CSR, Virgil T. Mercer, 1st Maryland Infantry (U.S.); CSR and Pension Files, Bowie F. Johnson, 4th New Jersey Infantry Regiment.

ers Bread Pork & Beans, Bacon Beef & Coffee." Maj. Adreon, formerly a lieutenant in the 4th Maryland Infantry (U.S.), remarked to his father about his meal in the trenches near Petersburg: "Coffee, 'slap-jacks' fresh peaches (canned) and ginger cakes what do you say to this out here? style, ain't it!" The brother of a Maryland officer, serving as a private in a Maryland battery on a transport ship in 1862, stated that "we have every thing very nice aboard have plenty of Chickens, Eggs & in fact everything heart could wish. . . . I take a bath every morn & night equal to Cape May. . . . I am in excellent health never felt better in my life. I think I am getting fat."[42]

Even when food was poor, Civil War officers detected an improvement in their physical condition as soldiers. Dukehart noted that "there is a great change come over me since I saw you last, you will scarcely believe what your delicate son can now stand, I am almost as tough as a young bull I think nothing of standing all night in a rain storm, the night as dark as pitch." Robert H. Hergesheimer of the 7th Maryland Infantry (U.S.), who died in battle in 1864, recounted his opinion of army life:

I have now been six months a soldier, and I cannot say that I am tired of the life, or anxious to be rid from of any of the responsibilities it imposes upon me. On the contrary I am rather pleased than otherwise with the lot in which I have been cast. For what is more democratic and independent than the freedom of a soldier. We eat when we have got anything to eat, and we do with out when the wherewith is not on hand. We lie upon the ground or roost in a tree just as necessity requires it. We burn a man's fence rails, or kill his chickens or pigs just as it pleases us. None is better satisfied with our humble fare than a soldier, and none knows better how to dispose of rich dainties than he. He is contented to take things just as they come and no mishap ever befells him but what he turns it to good.[43]

In the midst of combat, Maj. Adreon found something spectacular to tell the folks at home: "Last night there was a novel sight (to me) and a very beautiful one too. The mortars opened and the ball of fire could be traced

42. Graham Dukehart to father, July 28, 1861, in Dukehart Papers; Harrison Adreon to father, June 28, 1864, in Civil War Collection, MHS; William H. Moffett to father, August 5, 1862, in Moffett Papers.

43. Graham Dukehart to father, August 22, 1861, in Dukehart Papers; Robert H. Hergesheimer to father, February 6, 1863, in Pension Files, Robert H. Hergesheimer, 7th Maryland Infantry (U.S.).

in its course, as it gracefully curved towards the rebel works, and with a loud report and brilliant light burst inside their lines."[44]

The long hours in camp afforded junior officers ample time to enjoy nature, read, write, play cards, and talk with friends. William H. Daneker, a second lieutenant in the 9th Maryland Infantry (U.S.), wrote from his camp in Harpers Ferry in 1863: "I never felt better in my life, & another feature under the supervision of some of the men I'm making good progress at swimming, this evening after *tea*, I took twelve down to bathe in the waters of the Potomac, which by the by have swollen 7 feet today." Daneker, a twenty-two-year-old carpenter from Baltimore, added, "Heuh! while I write Capt. & dickie (all Lieuts are termed Dickies) are snoozing away for dear life, I am immediately on the Capt's right & writing on a first rate home-made table (of course I made it) made of chest nut legs, cracker-box ledger & crossties & top of the same material, in our large wall tent all the other officers of the Regt. having these A tents but I tell you ours is sumptious."[45]

Robert Hergesheimer spent his time well while encamped near Harpers Ferry in the spring of 1863: "I went a fishing the other night and caught some of the nicest fall fish and eels I ever saw. The country surrounding us is the most beautiful and enchanting. The scenery along the Rail Road is truly grand. . . . There is a natural curiosity not far from our camp called Browns Cave after old John Brown. Several of us explored it and found its dimensions most astonishing. In it there is a most beautiful spring of the purest water."[46]

James J. Gillette wrote about his situation in camp near Baltimore in early 1862: "I have a tent on the right of the Col. and am getting used to sleeping in it—though the flapping canvass disturbs me. . . . We mess in what is called the Officers Mess and the living is very good." This lieutenant's first days in a Maryland unit were not difficult at all. "I never knew it could be so comfortable in camp life. My boy does everything for me that would be unpleasant for me to perform and leaves me nothing to think of save my military & social duties."[47]

44. Harrison Adreon to father, June 28, 1864, in Civil War Collection, MHS.

45. William H. Daneker to family, July 31, 1863, in William H. Daneker Correspondence, MS 1252, Manuscripts Division, MHS.

46. Robert H. Hergesheimer to father, April 17, 1863, in Pension Files, Robert H. Hergesheimer, 7th Maryland Infantry (U.S.).

47. James J. Gillette to mother, March 3, 1862, in Gillette Papers.

Camp life, however, did have some drawbacks, including inspections by higher headquarters. Col. Bowerman of the 4th Maryland Infantry (U.S.) ordered an inspection of his regiment at 8:00 on the morning of September 16, 1863, at Rappahannock Station in preparation for the brigade inspection by Col. Dushane to follow at 9:00. Bowerman told his company commanders that the troops must appear in full uniform, carrying knapsacks, ponchos, canteens, and haversacks with three days' rations. The colonel also informed his officers that the morning reports of each company must be ready for the brigade inspector and that all shortages of equipment or uniform apparel should be duly noted before the actual inspection. Bowerman required all weapons to be clean and in good order, cartridge boxes full with forty rounds, all brass polished, and shoes and leather items neatly blackened. The colonel emphasized to his officers that "as this inspection is to be a most thorough one, it is hoped the Company officers will join with the Commandant in getting it up in the best possible manner."[48]

These inspections almost always proved a nuisance to both company officers and men. Graham Dukehart reported that his regiment underwent extreme deprivation during an inspection held in the summer of 1861: "We started about 8 ½ oclock to the plains below the Arlington house about by the road 4 miles over a dusty road & stood about 4 hours on the ground to be inspected by General McClenan [McClellan] Pres Lincoln & Sec Seward afterwards passing in review before them we marched back to quarters arriving there at 5 o'clock looking and feeling like veterans choked with dust nothing to eat or drink since leaving camp & as dirty as any man at the mill with the dust."[49]

Inspections were long and tedious, yet they boosted the morale of both observers and participants. Edwin W. Moffett of the 4th Maryland Infantry (U.S.), still Company F's first sergeant, expressed his pride in a letter to his father in late 1862. "We had a Brigade Inspection yesterday morning and it was a grand sight I can tell you it was composed of all the Infantry cavalry & Artillery in the Brigade. Our Company received the praise of the best looking & cleaness Set of men in the Brigade in the Infantry Service."[50]

48. Special Orders Number 76, September 15, 1863, in Regimental Order Books and Papers, 4th Maryland Infantry (U.S.).

49. Graham Dukehart to Mr. Starr, August 31, 1861, in Dukehart Papers.

50. Edwin W. Moffett to father, December 4, 1862, in Moffett Papers.

278 • Maryland's Blue and Gray

After years of frustration, Maryland's soldiers eagerly awaited the opening of the spring campaign in 1865. Maj. Adreon expressed the feeling in his regiment: "There is the utmost confidence in the ability and skill of our Generals and the troops are in the most jubilant spirits anticipating victory whenever the command 'forward' is given by Genl Grant." The officers and men of the Maryland Brigade participated in the war's final battles when they broke the Confederate defenses at Five Forks and forced the southern army to evacuate Richmond and Petersburg. The identity of the first Union troops to enter the Confederate capital has been a subject of contention, but one source claims that First Lieut. David S. Keener of the 5th Maryland Infantry (U.S.) was the first northern officer in Richmond. Col. William W. Bamberger of the 5th Maryland Infantry reportedly raised the first Stars and Stripes over the burning city.[51]

The Maryland Brigade pursued the enemy from Petersburg to Appomattox Court House. A corporal in the 8th Maryland Infantry (U.S.) recounted the last minutes of the war in Virginia:

Yesterday [April 9, 1865] we were advancing in line of battle and were about to *finish* Lee's army when a flag of truce was seen coming into our lines, and in a few moments the firing had almost ceased. We had fixed our bayonets for a grand charge upon the enemy, and we waited in suspense to hear the news. In a short time Genl. Ayers [Romeyn B. Ayres] and Staff came towards us waving their hats. We knew then it was all right. You should have heard the cheering then and seen the flags waving, and hats flying in the air. A short time afterward when the men were quiet, Genl. Ayers rode in front of the Division and announced that arrangements were being made for the terms of surrender of Lee's army. This of course renewed the cheering. . . . I felt like singing the good old doxology: "Praise God from whom all blessings flow."[52]

For the junior officers of the Maryland Brigade the long road to victory ended at Appomattox. The regiments then returned to Washington, where they took part in the massive parade of the Army of the Potomac. Later, they received a warm welcome in Baltimore by the governor and

51. Harrison Adreon to parents, March 28, 1865, in Civil War Collection, MHS; Baltimore *American*, April 15, 1865.

52. David J. Scott to Maud, April 10, 1865, in *Civil War Times Illustrated* Collection, USAMHI. For another account of the end of the war, see Edward Schilling, "My Three Years in the Volunteer Army of the United States of America," *Journal of the Alleghenies*, XX (1984), 9–11.

the Union citizens of the city. A handful of Maryland officers, including Gregory Barrett, remained in the Regular Army after the war, although most tried to put army life behind them. In 1871, Gen. Warren wrote about the Marylanders who fought so valiantly in his old corps during the last year of the Civil War: "It should hereafter be enough glory for any man to say, 'I bore an honorable reputation in the Maryland Brigade.'"[53] The junior officers of the brigade bore this pride to their graves.

53. *Official Records*, Ser. I, Vol. XLVI, Pt. 1, pp. 1186–87; Camper and Kirkley, *Historical Record*, 221.

CONCLUSION

Thirty years before Capt. Torsch surrendered the 2nd Maryland Infantry (C.S.) to the four regiments of the Union Maryland Brigade, Alexis de Tocqueville envisioned the impact of war on the officer corps of a democratic society:

> A long war produces upon a democratic army the same effects that a revolution produces upon a people; it breaks through regulations, and allows extraordinary men to rise above the common level. Those officers whose bodies and minds have grown old in peace, are removed, or superannuated, or they die. In their stead a host of young men are pressing on, whose frames are already hardened, whose desires are extended and inflamed by active service. . . . The principle of equality opens the door of ambition to all, and death provides chances for ambition. Death is constantly thinning the ranks, making vacancies, closing and opening the career of arms.[1]

Such was the case with the officers of the Confederate Maryland Line and the Union Maryland Brigade. Losses from combat, resignations, illness, and capture wore down the once-mighty regiments that so eagerly rallied around the flags in 1861 and 1862. Although casualties among Maryland's junior officer corps were not unusual by the standards of the day, the chances of a man starting the war as an officer with a Maryland Confederate or Union regiment and finishing the war with that same unit were not great.[2]

1. Tocqueville, *Democracy in America*, II, 533–34.
2. The 2nd Maryland Infantry (C.S.) had only one company officer present for duty at Appomattox and the 2nd Maryland Cavalry (C.S.) had few, if any, still remaining with that battalion at war's end. Union units were in similar shape. William F. Fox, the noted compiler of casualty lists of Union regiments, ranked the 1st Maryland Infantry (U.S.) among the fighting Union organizations. The regiment had 8 officers (including several in the field and staff) and 110 enlisted men killed in action or died of wounds while 1

Confederate Marylanders suffered greater losses in combat than their northern counterparts and were less likely to return to duty with their units. This resulted, in great part, from their longer time in service on the whole and because the Confederate Maryland units engaged in heavy action earlier in the war than the regiments of the Maryland Brigade. Confederate officers taken prisoner after 1863 rarely rejoined their commands. Northern officer casualties were concentrated during the last year of the war, and few men were captured in this period. The officers of the 1st Maryland Infantry (U.S.) who surrendered at Front Royal in 1862, for example, were paroled within months and reentered the fight shortly thereafter.

Surprisingly, deaths of Union and Confederate Maryland officers in battle far outweighed mortalities from disease or imprisonment. Maryland's officers, while exposed to all the rigors of army life, appear to have been inured to the "deadliest foe" which cut swaths through the ranks of both armies. The commonly accepted figure that three men died of disease for every man killed in battle was not true for the captains and lieutenants from Maryland. No single explanation accounts for this except that officers, particularly Union, had better opportunities for furloughs home to seek medical care or to be admitted into army hospitals.[3]

This, however, did not mean that Maryland's officers maintained good health throughout the war. Hospital records and furlough applications reveal that these men were constantly sick or suffering from wounds or other disabilities. But the greatest losses came from resignations, discharges, dismissals, and the disbandment of units; such losses plagued regiments from Maryland on both sides throughout the war. Union regiments experienced many resignations for disabilities as well as for disci-

---

officer and 133 soldiers died from diseases, accidents, or in prison from a total strength of 1,885. This corresponds to a casualty rate of 13 percent and does not include losses from wounds or capture. In a single engagement at the Weldon Railroad on August 19, 1864, the 1st Maryland Infantry (U.S.), for example, suffered 10 killed, 64 wounded, and 6 missing in action. The 6th Maryland Infantry (U.S.), briefly in the Maryland Brigade, had the second highest casualty losses of any Maryland units in Union service. See William F. Fox, *Regimental Losses in the American Civil War, 1861–1865* (Albany, 1889), 308–309, 455, 489–90.

3. Wiley, *Life of Johnny Reb*, 244–69. The comparison of officer casualties with those of enlisted men and some explanations are found in Fox, *Regimental Losses*, 38–40; for a modern-day comparison, see Trevor D. Dupuy, *Attrition: Forecasting Battle Casualties and Equipment Losses in Modern War* (Fairfax, 1990), 61–63.

plinary problems. Drunkenness among officers affected Maryland's Union regiments to a greater degree than the Confederate. More Confederate officers, however, were admitted to hospitals for treatment of venereal diseases than Union Maryland officers. Maryland's Confederate officers tended to grow dissatisfied with their lot more quickly than their Union counterparts. The officers' dissatisfaction, in turn, created dissension within the ranks. No Union officers in the Maryland Brigade deserted to the enemy, whereas there were relatively infrequent desertions among the officers of the Maryland Line.[4]

Confederate Maryland units also experienced greater turmoil as a result of the "democratic" process of electing officers. Although the Union system of appointment of regimental and company officers by the governor was imperfect, it avoided much of the trouble that affected the various Maryland Confederate units throughout the war. The ambition of many officers and enlisted men in the Confederate units from Maryland could not be restrained, leading to tremendous agitation in 1861–1862 and again in 1864. The uproar destroyed two fine units, the 1st Maryland Infantry (C.S.) and the 1st Maryland Battery (C.S.)—the equivalent of the destruction of those units in battle. Indeed, Bradley T. Johnson contends that the disbandment of Maryland's only Confederate regiment altered the outcome of the 1862 Maryland campaign.

Union regiments were not impervious to change in the form of con-

---

4. Some Union Maryland officers did desert to the Confederacy. Ralph Abercrombie, a first lieutenant in the 13th U.S. Infantry and an officer at the Alton, Illinois, prison, resigned in 1862 and then attempted to cross into Confederate lines to join Gilmor's battalion in 1863. He later served briefly in a Virginia unit and was placed under arrest in late 1863. In 1865, Abercrombie was captured in Baltimore and thrown into prison by Union officials. Another Union officer, John C. Henry, a captain in the 1st Regiment, Eastern Shore Infantry, also resigned in 1862 and later served as an enlisted man in the 2nd Maryland Infantry (C.S.). The Eastern Shore regiments in the Union army experienced considerable turmoil over military obligations, which resulted in the piecemeal disintegration of the 1st Regiment, Eastern Shore Infantry, by 1864. See CSR, Ralph Abercrombie, 1st Virginia Infantry Battalion; Baltimore *American*, April 19, 1865; CSR, John C. Henry, 2nd Maryland Infantry (C.S.); "Union Soldier Slave Owners," 408. A detailed examination of the disciplinary problems in the 1st Eastern Shore Infantry is found in K-893 (VS)-1864, RG 94, Records of the Volunteer Service Branch. For an account detailing the refusal of that regiment's Company K to leave the Eastern Shore to participate in the Gettysburg campaign, see the petition of Capt. Littleton Long, Jr., to the secretary of war, July 31, 1863, *ibid*

solidation or other bureaucratic measures taken to improve overall military strength. These actions, made at levels far removed from the units, deeply affected officer morale because they limited opportunities for promotion and changed the identity and integrity of units. Consolidation of Maryland's Union regiments (done mainly in early 1862 and again at the end of the war) had little effect on the four regiments of the Maryland Brigade. The brigade increased its strength through the consolidation of the infantry and cavalry portions of the Purnell Legion in late 1864 with no loss of identity to either the 1st or 8th Maryland Infantry (U.S.). Maryland's Union regiments instead suffered to a greater extent from the lack of dedicated recruits when the draft was implemented after 1862.

The travail of camp life and the battlefield weeded out men who were incompetent or unable to serve as officers in both armies. Tocqueville noted that "the interest and the tastes of the members of a democratic community divert them from war" in peacetime. He found the opposite to be true of Americans in time of war. "Their habits of mind fit them for carrying on war well: they soon make good soldiers, when they are roused from their business and their enjoyments."[5]

This was indeed the case for many officers in the Maryland units during the Civil War. Only a minority had any practical military experience in the antebellum period, yet many readily took up military life. By 1865, the Army of the Potomac and the Army of Northern Virginia contained a professional officer corps. The Maryland Confederate units enjoyed overall better leadership at the company level through 1863 but proved unable to sustain their officer ranks when casualties depleted them. The Union army, on the other hand, replenished its losses by promoting experienced noncommissioned officers. A key to the success of the Union army lay in its ability to develop natural talent within the officer and enlisted ranks and promote men worthy of command.

The overall administration of the Union Maryland regiments was more efficient than that of the Confederate units. Although Maryland units on both sides never shared the complete confidence of the central governments, the state's Union regiments were less susceptible to the acrimonious divisions that often hindered the exiled Marylanders in the Confederacy. The vision of a Maryland Line proved elusive to Confederate Marylanders. Attempts by Bradley T. Johnson and George H. Steuart to

5. Tocqueville, *Democracy in America*, II, 334.

form the Line from Marylanders scattered throughout the South were admirable but impractical. The exemption of Marylanders from conscription until the end of the war detracted from efforts to unify pro-Confederate Marylanders into a single military body.

In any case, the formation of the Maryland Line in late 1863 and early 1864 was tactically unsound, and the Line had a limited life span. Marylanders supporting the southern cause were rarely satisfied with their role as soldiers in the Confederacy. Tired of infantry service in 1862 and demanding their right to choose their own course of action after a year of military service, the 1st Maryland Infantry (C.S.) disbanded without any practical plan to reorganize. The companies that formed in late 1862 and early 1863 had little overall guidance, and the new 2nd Maryland Infantry (C.S.) soon encountered many of the same problems as its predecessor. Of the two existing Maryland mounted units, only the 1st Maryland Cavalry (C.S.) served as a regular unit. The 2nd Maryland Cavalry (C.S.), fighting as partisans, generally created more trouble than it was worth. The three artillery batteries with the Army of Northern Virginia were the most stable Maryland organizations throughout the war and, even then, the 1st Maryland Battery nearly disbanded after a controversial fight over the terms of enlistment. Altogether, the Maryland Confederates never enjoyed the success that their compatriots from Kentucky found with the Orphan Brigade.[6]

Despite the enormous difficulties that Maryland's officers faced in the war, many men made good soldiers on the battlefield and in camp. William H. Murray was perhaps the best-loved Confederate junior officer from Maryland. He earned the respect of his subordinates and his commanding officers for his valor on the field, his trustworthiness, and the concern he showed for his men. His death at Gettysburg was greatly mourned by Confederate Marylanders. Survivors of his two companies revered his memory and dedicated a monument in his name at the Loudoun Park Cemetery twelve years after the bloody fighting at Culp's Hill that took his life. His former soldiers later organized the Murray Confederate Association, which had fifty members in 1893.[7]

6. Davis, *Orphan Brigade*, 270. The dissatisfaction that Marylanders felt during the war may have led one former Maryland soldier to recall years after the war that "there has never yet been given to the Maryland Boys the credit due them" (W. Kennedy Jenkins to Miss King, n.d., in Special Collections, MSA).

7. *Addresses Delivered at the Dedication of the Monument Erected in Loudoun Park Ceme-*

Union officers also made their mark on the battlefield. The "fighting major" of the 4th Maryland Infantry (U.S.), Harrison Adreon, rose through the ranks even though he was only twenty-four when he ended the war as a brevet lieutenant colonel for bravery at Five Forks. The "principle of equality," fostered by losses within the army, was true in Adreon's case as he described the fighting at Weldon Railroad in the summer of 1864 in a letter to his father:

> The Rebel skirmishers advanced driving in (as we intended they should) our pickets it was the most beautiful sight I ever witnessed. Three lines of battle advanced with their battleflags streaming in the wind our cavalry fell back in good order retiring slowly and without excitement. On came the Rebel lines steadily until they got within about charging distance when our batteries and infantry sent such a deadly fire into their ranks as to completely break every line away went flags the men seemed to melt away before the deadly fire we gave we captured just on the right of our brigade a whole Rebel Brigade. About a dozen Rebel officers and 150 men came in on my front. We annihilated them they never came up again. They have been as quiet as mice ever since. Two battle flags captured on our front.

The cost of this victory was heavy; the commander of the Maryland Brigade fell in battle, as did his immediate replacement. Maj. Adreon took charge of the 4th Maryland Infantry (U.S.), "just what I wanted." The new commander placed his regiment on the picket line of the brigade when the enemy renewed the attack. An officer next to Adreon was struck by a shell, and the major found himself in the thick of the fight. "The Rebs were trying for me, as they could see me pushing forward the men a Battery horse was shot right by me, and like to fell on me it was

---

tery to Captain Wm. H. Murray and His Soldiers who Fell in the Confederate War (Baltimore, 1875); *The Murray Confederate Association, Confederate Relief Bazaar Association* (N.p., 1885); "History of Confederates in Maryland," *Confederate Veteran*, X (1902), 166; "Confederate Association in Maryland," *Confederate Veteran*, I (1893), 71. There were nine different Confederate veterans' groups in Maryland in 1893, including the Murray Association. The largest, the Society of the Army and Navy of the Confederate States in Maryland, had eleven hundred members, while the Association of the Maryland Line had six hundred and the Beneficial Association of the Maryland Line had three hundred. There were four company- or battery-size veterans' groups, the Murray Association, the Baltimore Light Artillery Association, and reunion groups for Companies A and C of the 1st Maryland Cavalry (C.S.); several posts of the Union Grand Army of the Republic were active in Maryland. For a history of this organization, see Mary R. Dearing, *Veterans in Politics: The Story of the G.A.R.* (Baton Rouge, 1952).

very hot." As the action grew fiercer, Adreon noted that "the sharp-shooters tryed their best but, thank God, I was saved the fire was so severe that some of the men hesitated, Capt. Crouch also. I had therefore to push them up be a little more conspicuous than I would have been had they gone promptly." Adreon's quick reaction on the field kept his regiment in line and held the enemy.[8]

Murray and Adreon as well as dozens of other men formed the bedrock of the junior officer corps of Maryland's Civil War regiments. They shared a pride of service that was reflected in a wartime article concerning the promotion of one Union officer in 1864:

> Lieutenant Robert Watson, of Company A, 4th Maryland Volunteers, has recently been promoted to the Captaincy of that Company, and as such has received a commission from Gov. Bradford. . . . Immediately on the breaking out of the rebellion he enlisted in one of the regiments of the State, and on the organization of the 4th accepted the First Lieutenancy of the above Company, in discharging the duties of which he has ever shown himself competent and prompt. Though two years have elapsed since the command has been on duty, he has never applied for leave of absence, but continued with his regiment, which under the command of Col. Bowerman, has greatly distinguished itself.[9]

Thrust into an increasingly savage war, these men, in their own ways, made military life a little more bearable for their soldiers. The officers showed good leadership qualities, and their examples motivated their troops in some of the war's bloodiest battles. No more could have been asked of Maryland's Union and Confederate lieutenants and captains.[10]

The Union and Confederate Maryland junior officers shared similar experiences with their counterparts from other states in either the Army

8. Harrison Adreon to father, August 22, 1864, in Civil War Collection, MHS.
9. Baltimore *American*, March 9, 1864.
10. The principles of leadership are, as defined by the modern U.S. Army, to know yourself and seek self-improvement; be technically and tactically proficient; seek responsibility and take responsibility; make sound and timely decisions; set the example; know your soldiers and look out for their well-being; keep your soldiers informed; develop a sense of responsibility in your subordinates; ensure that the task is understood, supervised, and accomplished; train your soldiers as a team, and employ your unit in accordance with its capabilities. Military leadership, according to the army, "is a process in which a soldier influences others to accomplish the mission." (U.S. Department of the Army, FM 22-100, *Military Leadership* [Washington, D.C., 1983], 41-44).

of the Potomac or the Army of Northern Virginia. The shock of combat and the bonding among these men over the years was repeated among the officer corps of numerous regiments on both sides. Yet few northern or southern states had such a difficult time establishing a military, or even political, identity as Maryland did as either a loyal member of the United States or a potential ally of the Confederate States of America. The pre-war uncertainty that afflicted Maryland continued to overshadow the state during the Civil War. Wooed by both sides, Maryland was trusted by neither. This ambivalence, unique only to the border states (primarily Maryland and Kentucky), affected the status of Maryland's soldiery.

The civil war that divided Maryland was fought between two elements of that state's antebellum society. The officers of Maryland's Confederate units, on the whole, represented the state's landed gentry who traced their roots to the early days of the Chesapeake Bay settlements. As a group, these men were well educated and formed the state's highest stratum. The number of men who earned a living as professionals or semiprofessionals was more than double the number who were farmers or planters before the war. Workers, skilled or unskilled, were rare among the Confederate Maryland junior officer corps. Officers hailed from all four regions of Maryland with Baltimore and southern Maryland predominating, al-though western Maryland, particularly Frederick County, claimed a fair share of the state's Confederate leadership. Politically, Confederate offi-cers from Maryland supported the Democratic party before the war and appear to have had only minor personal ties to slavery. Their decision to support the Confederate cause may have derived from their belief in the "fundamental principle of honor, family, and race supremacy, one and indivisible."[11]

The vast majority of the Confederate officers were natives of Maryland with extensive family connections throughout the state and other parts of the South. A large number of junior officers in the Maryland Line were communicants in the Roman Catholic Church, befitting that denomi-nation's role in the founding of Maryland as a religious refuge. They left Maryland of their free will to take up the cause of southern independence and to free their home from the perceived tyranny of the "Black Repub-licans." Altogether, the captains and lieutenants in Maryland's Confed-

---

11. Bertram Wyatt-Brown, *Yankee Saints and Southern Sinners* (Baton Rouge, 1985), 212.

erate companies or batteries represented a distinctive section of the state's total white population. Bradley T. Johnson and his contemporaries were certainly justified in exulting the distinguished background of Maryland's Confederates.

The Union officers in the Maryland Brigade represented an entirely different stratum of society. Coming almost exclusively from western Maryland and Baltimore, these men made their living with their hands, either as farmers or as workers. They possessed little higher education by the standards of the day. Although many were natives of Maryland, their ties to the state were looser than those of their Confederate counter-parts. Many Union officers, in fact, were born in neighboring northern states or in other countries. Ironically, Maryland's Union regiments at-tracted both foreigners and nativists who supported the tenets of Know-Nothingism. These men went to war in support of the Union with little regard for blacks, slave or free. Union Maryland officers were at the fore-front of a new order that drew its base from the industrial development of Baltimore and surrounding areas. Of working- or lower-middle-class origins, they had little in common with the aristocratic neighbors against whom they took up arms in 1861.[12]

Maryland's junior officers do not fit neatly into Marcus Cunliffe's cate-gories of the Quaker, Rifleman, and Chevalier, nor do they precisely re-flect Grady McWhiney and Perry Jamieson's Celtic or Anglo-Saxon tribes or William R. Taylor's Cavalier and Yankee.[13] Very few Marylanders, northern or southern, held the pacifist notions of the Quaker model. Men who opposed the war or the use of violence avoided service in either army. Many Marylanders of military age did not touch a weapon during the four years of war despite Union efforts to force them into the army or Confederate hopes that they would rally around the southern banner.

Maryland, and Baltimore in particular, had a reputation for electoral violence and political gangs. "Mobtown" seethed with martial spirit, as shown by the number of men who served in militia units. This training

12. A fictional account of Marylanders during the war is George Alfred Townshend, *Katy of Catoctin or the Chain-Breakers*, introduction by Harold R. Manakee (Cambridge, Md., 1959).

13. Grady McWhiney and Perry D. Jamieson, *Attack and Die: Civil War Military Tactics and the Southern Heritage* (University, Ala., 1982), 170–91; William R. Taylor, *Cavalier and Yankee: The Old South and American National Character* (New York, 1961).

proved of benefit when these men went to war. Even so, martialism took on different dimensions among men who became officers in the Maryland Line as opposed to those in the Maryland Brigade. In this regard, Cunliffe provides some insight into the makeup of these soldiers. Union officers had several features in common with the Rifleman model: diligence and ruggedness coupled with ferocity in battle. Although the Union Maryland officer grew tired of military life and often resorted to drinking when bored and committing acts of violence or disobedience, he proved a steady character and saw the war to its finish. Cunliffe describes the Rifleman as usually serving as an enlisted man, a rank initially held by many Union junior officers.

His Confederate counterpart at first glance appears as a fine example of the Chevalier. A romantic hero, the Confederate officer as Chevalier is as much a postwar conception as it was an actual wartime figure. Maryland's southern lieutenants and captains saw themselves as the embodiment of a Sir Walter Scott tale (indeed, the first and middle names of one Confederate officer were Walter and Scott). War was an adventure to be enjoyed, especially for the benefit of young female admirers.

The reality of the war bitterly disappointed these Chevaliers for whom glory proved transitory. When neither glory nor victory appeared imminent, these men resorted to the model of the Rifleman and quickly demanded changes in their status. Confederate Marylanders were as intelligent a set of men as could have served in the Confederate army but proved better suited as staff officers than infantry company commanders. The drudgery of foot service had little appeal to these cavaliers, who longed for excitement. The Confederate army's need for pawns and not knights greatly disappointed Marylanders. The Maryland Line harkened to the hallowed days of the first War of American Independence and fit nicely with the psychological pattern of the Chevalier. After the war, the term "Maryland Line" assumed almost mythic proportions.[14]

In essence, the men who served as junior officers in the Maryland

14. Much of the interest in the Maryland Line after the war was generated by Bradley T. Johnson, who funded a variety of activities, such as the paintings of various Confederate Maryland units in action. The art of Allen C. Redwood (a veteran of the Line) and William Ludwell Sheppard spurred the public's awareness in the Maryland Line, as did the numerous postwar veterans' groups. See Mark E. Neely, Jr., Harold Holzer, and Gabor S. Boritt, *The Confederate Image: Prints of the Lost Cause* (Chapel Hill, 1987), 214–16.

Line and the Maryland Brigade came from two societies within one state. Despite the vast differences among them, both as types and as individuals, both groups of officers "embodied the faith and pride" of their Maryland.[15]

15. Quote from Johnson, *Maryland*, 98.

Appendix:
Roster of Union and
Confederate Junior Officers

This roster contains the service records and brief genealogical data for 365 captains and lieutenants who served in the Union Maryland Brigade and the Confederate Maryland Line. The roster forms the basis for the statistical sample of Maryland's junior officers and is derived from many sources. It is organized alphabetically for all Confederate officers because these men often served in more than one unit. The Union officers are also listed in alphabetical order among the four regiments of the Maryland Brigade.

My main sources of information were the Compiled Service Records of Confederate Soldiers Who Served in Organizations from the State of Maryland and the Compiled Service Records of Volunteer Union Soldiers Who Served in Organizations from the State of Maryland. These records are a postwar compilation of muster rolls, pay, clothing, and medical records, and other documents as well as prisoner of war records. Microfilm editions of the Compiled Service Records are available at the National Archives, Washington, D.C.

In addition to the Compiled Service Records of Union and Confederate Marylanders, I checked service records of Marylanders who served in military organizations from other states—in particular, Marylanders who served in Virginia units (often, material is intermingled in the different compiled service records). For Confederate officers who also served in staff or nonregimental positions, I found items of interest in the Compiled Service Records of Confederate General and Staff Officers and Non-Regimental Enlisted Men. I also located various documents pertaining to Marylanders in Unfiled Papers and Slips Belonging to Confederate Compiled Service Records, and Case Files of Applications from Former Confederates for Presidential Pardons, 1865–1867.

For the many Union Marylanders serving in regiments from other northern states, I also examined the military records to provide further information for the roster. Of particular assistance in this regard is the Organization Index to Pension Files of Veterans Who Served Between 1861 and 1900. This microfilmed index is broken down by regiment and company and provides the pension numbers needed to obtain individual pension applications. For Union soldiers, the pension records provide the bulk of the genealogical background used in this roster. Such information as birth date, postwar occupation, marriage and residence date, and death date and place is often unavailable without extensive research through municipal or church records.

Although the pension records proved to be the most valuable source on Union officers after the Compiled Service Records, several other sources were also helpful. Francis B. Heitman's *Historical Register of the United States Army from Its Organization September 29, 1789, to September 29, 1889* is a handy reference for officers from Maryland who also served in the Regular Army. The War Department's *Official Army Register of the Volunteer Force of the United States Army for the Years 1861, '62, '63, '64, '65, Part III*, contains rosters of officers in Maryland's volunteer regiments. Similar information is also found in Camper and Kirkley's *Historical Record of the First Maryland Infantry* and Wilmer, Jarrett, and Vernon, *History and Roster of Maryland Volunteers, War of 1861–65*.

The Compiled Service Records for Confederate officers from Maryland tend to be of uneven quality. Those records of officers who served in the 1st Maryland Cavalry, the 2nd Maryland Infantry, and the Maryland artillery batteries are generally good. The records of the 1st Maryland Infantry and the 2nd Maryland Cavalry are piecemeal and less reliable. For the latter unit, Gilmor's battalion, only a handful of records pertain to its officers while the 1st Maryland Infantry lacks many records after late 1861 despite the regiment's short existence. To overcome the lack of official documentation, I employed the standard Confederate references for Marylanders, as outlined in the Introduction. These were helpful in piecing together the careers of officers who served in more than one Confederate unit.

Additionally, the names of Union and Confederate officers have been cross-referenced with Ronald Vern Jackson's *Maryland 1860 Census Index Except the City of Baltimore* as well as with the Reamy's *1860 Census of Baltimore City*, the 1859 Frederick City directory, the 1860 Baltimore City directory, and the 1860 directory for Washington, D.C., and Georgetown. Though useful for individuals with uncommon names or known residences, the 1860 census and other contemporary sources have pitfalls. The fact that many officers were underage in 1860 and are therefore not listed in the 1860 census indexes complicates the search.

Personal data given in the 1860 census must be viewed with caution. For example, some men were actually older or younger than stated in the census. This seems to be more of a problem with Maryland's Confederate officers for whom I found several discrepancies between known birth dates and ages as provided at the time of the census enumeration in 1860. Likewise, the wealth of a man at the time of the census (or that of his father) may not be represented accurately. In most cases, the census does not provide any information as to a man's real estate or personal estate value (this is shown in the roster as $———/$———). This lack unfortunately clouds modern-day understanding of the economic standing of nineteenth-century Americans.

To overcome some of these problems, I consulted a number of self-published books from Maryland and Baltimore for postwar biographical sketches of Maryland Civil War officers. These are a fruitful source, as are local histories and church and cemetery records. *Maryland Mortuaries from the Baltimore Sun Almanac* is replete with references to the thinning ranks of blue and gray Marylanders. One useful guide, Margaret K. Fresco's *Marriages and Deaths: St. Mary's County, Maryland, 1634–1900*, saves the researcher many hours of searching for records on Confederates from southern Maryland. College and university alumni records are also a potential source of information but again of uneven quality. The Delman-Hayward biographical card files at the Maryland Historical Society contain much valuable information (mostly obituary clippings) on Civil War soldiers from Maryland. Finally, interviews with descendants provide a wealth of information that can never be matched in libraries or archives.

Using a variety of sources, I was able to form a thumbnail sketch of each man who served as a lieutenant or captain in the Maryland Brigade and the Maryland Line. This information is intended as a handy reference for the reader perusing the pages of this work.

Abbreviations

corp.	corporal	sgm.	sergeant major
sgt.	sergeant	1lt.	first lieutenant
1sg.	first sergeant	2lt.	second lieutenant

3lt.	third lieutenant	1860 cen.	1860 census
cpt.	captain	em.	enlisted men
maj.	major	enl.	enlisted
ltc.	lieutenant colonel	ETS	expiration of term of
col.	colonel		service
gen.	general	exch.	exchanged
		F&S	field and staff
AAG	assistant adjutant general	furl.	furloughed
ADC	aide-de-camp	inf.	infantry
AADC	acting aide-de-camp	GAR	Grand Army of the
abs.	absent		Republic
AACS	acting assistant	GCM	general court-martial
	commissariat	GH	general hospital
ACS	assistant commissariat	grad.	graduated or graduate
adj.	adjutant	HA	heavy artillery
adm.	admitted	KIA	killed in action
AGO	Adjutant General's	MDO	medical director's office
	Office	MIA	missing in action
AIG	assistant inspector	MO	mustered out
	general	MR	muster roll
appt.	appointed or	MWIA	mortally wounded in
	appointment		action
AQM	assistant quartermaster	NFR	no further record
ass.	assigned	OCP	Old Capitol Prison
asst.	assistant	OOA	oath of allegiance
att.	attached	ord.	ordnance
AWOL	absent without official	PACS	Provisional Army of the
	leave		Confederate States
bn.	battalion	PM	provost marshal
btry.	battery	PMO	Provost Marshal's
bde.	brigade		Office
bvt.	brevet	POW	prisoner of war
c.	circa	pres.	present
cav.	cavalry	prom.	promoted
CH	courthouse	qm.	quartermaster
Chimb.	Chimborazzo Hospital	RA	Regular Army
Co.	Company or County	RE	real estate
dir.	directory	recd.	received
disch.	discharged	reenl.	reenlisted
DOD	died of disease	regt.	regiment
DOR	date of rank	rel.	released
DOW	died of wounds	res.	residence

RQM	regimental quartermaster	surg.	surgeon
RTD	returned to duty	trans.	transfer or transferred
SOW	secretary of war	VRC	Veterans Reserve Corps

Confederate Maryland Junior Officers

ANDREWS, RICHARD SNOWDEN. Born Washington, D.C., 10/29/1830. Son of Col. T. P. Andrews of Ireland, a prominent U.S.A. officer who was promoted to brevet brigadier general in Mexican War and later served as Union paymaster general. Educated in Washington and Georgetown and served as apprentice carpenter. Moved to Baltimore in 1849, where he worked with firm Niernsee & Nelson architects. Designed such buildings as hospital for insane in Weston, W.Va., south wing of Treasury Department, and the U.S. Custom House in Baltimore. Member of Emmanuel Church at Cathedral and Read streets. 1860 city dir. shows architect at 7&8 Carroll Hall; res. 48 Mt. Vernon Place. 1860 cen.: res. 11th Ward. $16,000/———; wife Marcy C. Lee and three children; lived with father; had two white and four black servants. Appt. cpt. 5/29/61 of Maryland Artillery (1st Md. Btry.). Accepted appt. as maj. of cavalry 6/14/61 but resigned to accept appt. as cpt. artillery 7/31/61. Fuel requisition of btry. shows 1 cpt., 3 lts., 97 em's, and 2 servants or laundresses. Pres. 9–10/61 through 1–2/62. Prom. maj. 7/15/62. WIA at Mechanicsville 6/26/62. Severely WIA Cedar Mt. 8/9/62. Ass. Ord. Bureau 10/15/62. Prom. ltc. 11/4/63. Ordered to Europe for ord. duty 1/11/64. After war worked on railroad in Mexico until he returned to Baltimore in 1867. Appointed militia general of artillery by Md. governor. Died Baltimore 1/6/1903.

BARBER, JOSEPH W. Born in Md. 11/8/1837. 1860 cen.: res. Annapolis, Anne Arundel Co.; age 16; student; son of J. B. and Mary Barber; for father no occupation listed; $9,000/$1,000; three other children. Enl. as pvt. in Co. C, 2d Md. Inf. at Richmond 9/11/62. Elected 2lt. 10/2/62. DOW: fractured thigh 7/20/63 from Gettysburg. Obituary in Baltimore *Daily Gazette* 8/11/63.

BARRY, EDMUND. 1860 Washington, D.C., city dir. shows res. at 584 New Jersey Ave., N.W. Requested permission to raise infantry company as cpt. in letter to SOW from Richmond 3/3/62. This company later became 3rd Co. C, 1st Md. Inf. Regt., with Barry as cpt. Barry ordered to recruiting duty for Md. Line 12/22/62. Ordered to duty with Gen. Lee 5/22/63 but later revoked and ordered to Gen. Elzey 6/1/63. Ordered to take command of detectives along Rappahannock River to oversee transportation of prisoners and goods across lines 9/24/63. Relieved of this duty 8/9/64 and ass. to duty with Gen. Winder at Andersonville

9/10/64. Relieved of this duty because of a reduction of officers 3/22/65. Paroled at Washington, D.C., 7/31/65.

BAYLEY, JAMES P. Signed forage requisition 8/21/64 as cpt. of Co. B, 2nd Md. Cav. NFR.

BEAN, HEZEKIAH HENRY. Born 1820. Recd. M.D. from the Univ. of Baltimore in Baltimore 1847. Res. Charlotte Hall, St. Marys Co. Appt. 2lt. of Co. I, 1st Md. Inf. Regt., 6/15/61. Pres. 9–10/61 as commanding company. Pres. 11–12/61. WIA foot Cross Keys 6/8/62. Military record after this point is uncertain. Married Mary A. Miltmore 10/30/49. Postwar doctor in Charles and St. Marys Counties. Adm. Confederate Soldiers' Home 8/17/88. Died there 3/18/1903. Buried at Loudoun Park Cemetery in Baltimore.

BEAN, WILLIAM BENNETT. Born in Md. 1860 cen.: age 19; merchant in St. Iningoes and Ridge P.O., St. Marys Co.; RE value $1,000. Appt. 2lt. 2nd Md. Btry. 8/15/61 at Richmond. Pres. 9–10/61. Abs. sick at Front Royal 11–12/61. Commanded btry. during summer of 1864. Wrote letter of resignation to protest conduct of CSA troops during march to Chambersburg 8/9/64. Placed under arrest by Gen. Early 8/22/64. Ordered released by SOW and RTD 9/1/64. Bean was still trying to explain his actions as late as March, 1865. Postwar farmer in St. Marys Co. Wife, Willie C. Bean, and five children in 1880.

BEATTY, EDWARD. Born in Md. 1860 cen.: res. Baltimore, 10th Ward. (1860 city dir. shows res. at Lanvale Lane opposite Greenmount Cemetery); age 19; son of Edward and Maria Beatty, both born in Md. Father was Baltimore customs officer who fired first shot during April 19, 1861, riot in Baltimore. Later member of 1st Md. Inf. Regt. and KIA at Harrisonburg 6/6/62. Three other children. Family had six mulatto servants. The younger Beatty was appt. 3lt. in Co. A, 1st Md. Cav. 11/12/62. Previously corp. of above company. WIA shoulder at Greenland Gap 4/25/63. POW Brandy Station 10/11/63. Sent to Johnson's Island from OCP 11/14/63. DOD chronic diarrhea 3/24/64. Buried there but remains later removed to Rockville.

BLACKISTON, HENRY CURTIS. Born in Md. 6/9/38. Son of William H. Blackiston. 1860 cen.: res. Sassafras, Kent Co., age 22; farmer; $2,200/$900; single; one black laborer. Elected 2lt. in Co. B, 1st Md. Cav. 9/10/62. Pres. 11–12/62 and 7–12/63. Adm. GH Charlottesville 10/10/63. RTD 11/3/63. Furl. 24 days 1/23/64. Adm. GH 4, Richmond, 3/8/64. RTD 4/17/64. KIA Bunker Hill 8/13/64. Buried at Episcopal Church Cemetery in Bunker Hill.

BLAIR, CHARLES W. 1860 cen.: res. 9th Ward, Baltimore; age 23; clerk; born in Md.; lived in boardinghouse with James Blair, bookkeeper. Appt. 2lt., Co. A, 1st Md. Inf. Regt. at Harpers Ferry 5/21/61. Pres. 9–12/61. Reenl. 2/8/62. Appears as 2lt. and general recruiting officer in spring and summer of 1862. Also served as 2lt. 2d Co. C, 19th Va. Heavy Artillery Bn. (Deas Artillery) 9–10/62. Resigned 11/5/62. NFR.

BOND, FRANCIS A. Born 2/6/38 at Bel Air, Harford Co., Md. Son of Maj. William B. and Charlotte (Richardson) Bond. Father was lawyer and state's attorney for Harford Co. Educated at Bel Air Academy and finished in 1856. Farmer in Anne Arundel Co. before war. Married in 1859. Enl. as pvt. 2nd Co. K, 1st Va. Cav. Regt. at Leesburg by Capt. Gaither 5/14/61. Elected 2lt. 8/1/61 from corp. Pres. 9/61 through 4/62. Dropped 4/23/62. Served as lt. and AAG to Gen. Steuart 5/29–6/9/62. Appt. cpt., Co. A, 1st Md. Cav. 11/12/62. Company formed from nucleus of Bond's old co. in the spring of 1862. Served in Maryland in fall of 1862 until bn. organized in 11/62. WIA leg and POW Hagerstown 7/8/63. Exch. 4/27/64 from Pt. Lookout for cousin of Bradley T. Johnson. Adm. GH 4, Richmond, 5/1/64. Furl. 5/5/64. Examined as permanently disabled at Richmond 7/27/64. Applied for retirement 10/25/64. Paroled Greensboro, N.C., 5/1/65 as Maj., 1st Md. Cav. but no formal record of promotion found. Appt. as Maryland adjutant general in 1874 by state governor. Elected chairman of the Maryland Democratic party 6/1907. Superintendent of the House of Corrections. First wife died in 1875 and he remarried two years later. Died of pleurisy in Philadelphia 11/12/1923. Buried at Loudoun Park Cemetery, Baltimore.

BONN, SAMUEL G. 1860 cen.: res. 15th Ward, Baltimore; age 23; clerk; born in Md.; son of Anthony and Elizabeth Bonn; father was city merchant; ————/$30,000; eleven other children; one Irish servant. POW records show Samuel Bonn was born c. 1838. Merchant, light complexion, brown hair, gray eyes, res. 172 W. Pratt St., Baltimore. Enl. as pvt. in 2nd Co. K, 1st Va. Cav. Regt. at Richmond by Cpt. Gaither 4/10/62. Pres. 3–4/62. Appears to later have enl. 5/1/62 at Yorktown under Cpt. Brown. Served as pvt. in Co. A, 1st Md. Cav. Regt. until trans. to Co. F when elected 2Lt. 7/16/63. Pres. 7–12/63. Adm. Charlottesville with dysentery 9/25/63. Trans. GH 4, Richmond, 10/16/63. Applied for 15 days furl. 2/26/64 at Hanover Junction. Abs. as acting ord. officer on furl. 4/1/64. POW Moorefield 8/7/64. Sent to Camp Chase from Harpers Ferry and Wheeling 8/12/64. Trans. to City Point for exch. 3/2/65. Paroled in Richmond by 20th N.Y. Cav. 4/22/65.

BOOTH, GEORGE WILSON. Born 7/29/44. Served as a member of 53rd Md. Militia Regt. Appt. 1lt. in Co. D, 1st Md. Inf. Regt. at Harpers Ferry by Ltc.

Deas 5/22/61. Pres. 9–12/61. Acting adj. of regt. at Mechanicsville 6/26/62. Volunteer aide to Col. Johnson at 2nd Manassas where Booth was wounded. Appt. 1lt./adj. for 1st Md. Cav. 1/20/63. WIA thigh Greenland Gap 4/25/63. Accompanied Cpt. Bond into Pennsylvania in 1863 despite severe wound. Served as AAG for Md. Line upon its organization in the fall of 1863. Prom. cpt. for valor and skill 9/25/63. Furl. 30 days from Hanover Junction 2/19/64. Served with Gen. Johnson during summer campaign in Maryland and later with him at Salisbury, N.C., prison. Resigned 3/25/65. Paroled at Richmond by 20th N.Y. Cav. 4/22/65. Returned to Baltimore in 1879 where he worked as clerk and comptroller for Baltimore and Ohio Railroad. President of the Society of the Army and Navy of the Confederate States in the state of Maryland. Died 1/6/1914.

BREWER, HENRY WILMOT. Born 1834 in Georgetown. Civil engineer. Served in U.S. Navy as master's mate on U.S. coast survey 1858–61. Also listed as clerk with Treasury Department in 1860 Washington, D.C., city dir. Res. 149 West Street, Georgetown. 5'1", brown hair, gray eyes, fair complexion. Enl. as 2lt., Co. H (Washington Volunteers), 7th Va. Inf. Regt. 4/22/61. Abs. sick 10–12/61. Pres. 1–3/62. Prom. 1lt. 4/26/62. Company disbanded 5/16/62. Brewer appears as asst. engineer with Richmond defenses and in Mississippi in 1862–63. Ass. to recruiting duty with Maryland Line summer 1863 through early 1864. Later appears as 1lt. and cpt. of Co. E, 2nd Md. Cav. POW Moorefield 8/7/64. Sent to Harpers Ferry, to Wheeling, and to Camp Chase 8/11/64. Trans. to City Point for exch. 3/2/65. Paroled at Lynchburg 5/23/65. Postwar civil engineer in Georgetown. Buried July, 1900, in Oak Hill Cemetery, Washington, D.C.

BRIGHTHAUPT, GEORGE A. Born in Washington, D.C., c. 1839. Butcher. 1860 res. in Washington on M Street near North Capitol Street. Enl. as pvt., Co. E, 1st Va. Inf. Regt. at Richmond 5/2/61. Trans. Co. H, 7th Va. Inf. and disch. 5/23/62. Enl. as pvt., Co. C, 19th Bn. Va. H.A. 5/3/62. Trans. as pvt. to Co. G, 2nd Md. Inf. 12/17/62. Elected 2lt. 1/26/64. Pres. 2–3/64 as commanding co. WIA both legs at Pegram's Farm 9/30/64. Adm. GH 4, Richmond, 10/2/64. Left leg amputated. DOW 10/15/64. Buried at Hollywood Cemetery, Richmond.

BROADFOOT, WILLIAM J. 1860 cen.: res. 13th Ward, Baltimore; age 22; clerk; born in Md.; single. Possibly the son of Joseph O. Broadfoot, a molder, at 44 North Liberty. Appt. 2lt., Co. F, 1st Md. Inf. Regt. at Richmond 6/18/61. Abs. 9–10/61 sick in Centreville. Not stated 11–12/61 "in arrest." Appt. 1lt. Co. E, 2nd Md. Inf. 9/13/62. Pres. 11/62. WIA Gettysburg 7/2–3/63. DOW 8/4/63.

BROCKENBROUGH, JOHN BOWYER. Born 4/6/36 in Lexington, Va. Att. Washington College 1855–56, grad. University of Virginia 1857, grad. Washington College LL.D. 1859. Lawyer in Lexington. Appt. 1lt. in Rockbridge Artillery (Va.) 4/29/61. WIA in face 1st Manassas 7/21/61. Resigned 8/26/61. Appt. cpt. Baltimore Light Artillery (2nd Md. Btry.) 8/15/61 and accepted position 9/17/61. Pres. 9–10/61. Abs. sick at home 11–12/61. WIA Fredericksburg 12/13/62 while acting chief of artillery for 1st Division, Jackson's Corps. Prom. maj. and chief of artillery 3/2/63. Also served as second in command of artillery bn. Retired for disability 3/24/64. Married in 1864. Postwar lawyer in Lynchburg 1864–86, when appt. special agent for Department of Interior by President Cleveland. Moved to Baltimore 1900. Died Evanston, Wyoming, 11/15/1901. Buried at Loudoun Park Cemetery, Baltimore.

BROWN, GEORGE W. Elected 1lt. in Co. H, 2nd Md. Inf. 7/23/63. Dropped 1/18/64. Adm. MDO with chest wound 4/19/64. Fit for duty. NFR.

BROWN, RIDGELY. Born in Montgomery Co. 11/12/33. 1860 cen.: res. at "Elton" near Unity, Montgomery Co.; age 26; farm manager; born in Md. Brown was the son of Amos Brown (died 1845) and Sarah Ridgely Griffith; mother was listed as farmer in 1860; $9,000/$6,100. Ridgely Brown was a first cousin of Frank and Thomas Griffith II. Enl. as pvt. in 2nd Co. K, 1st Va. Cav. Regt. at Leesburg 5/14/61. Elected 1lt. 8/1/61; previously 3sgt. Pres. 9–12/61. Abs. recruiting service in Richmond 2/27/62. Pres. 3–4/62. Dropped 4/23/62. Appears as cpt., Co. A, 1st Md. Cav. in 1862. Prom. maj. 11/12/62 and ltc. 8/20/63. WIA leg Greenland Gap 4/25/63. KIA South Anna River 6/1/64. Reburied at "Elton" in Montgomery Co. in 1866. Memorial plaque dedicated to Brown at St. John's Church in Olney, Md.

BROWN, WILLIAM DAWSON. Served in Baltimore City Guards before the war. Appt. 1lt. Chesapeake Artillery (4th Md. Btry). Pres. 1–2/62. Paid as cpt. 6/62. Served as acting chief of artillery Ewell's Division 12/62. WIA and POW Gettysburg. Both legs fractured and one amputated. DOW 7/11/63. Obituary in Baltimore *Sun* 7/14/63.

BURKE, FRANCIS W. "Polk." Born c. 1846. Res. Harpers Ferry. 5'7", fair complexion, gray eyes, black hair. Occupation student. Pvt., Co. F, 1st Va. Cav. Regt. POW Clarke Co., Va. 12/26/62. Sent from Cumberland, Md., to Wheeling, W.Va., 12/31/62. Trans. Camp Chase sometime after and then to City Point 3/28/63 for exch. 4/1/63. POW near Berryville 4/21/63. Sent to Martinsburg 4/25/63 and at Ft. McHenry 4/28/63. Trans. to Ft. Monroe for exch. 4/30/63. Burke later served as 2lt., Co. D, 2nd Md. Cav., in 1863 and 1864. Paroled Harrisonburg 5/8/65.

BURKE, JOHN REDMOND. Born c. 1838. Res. Berkely Co., W.Va. 5'7", dark complexion, black hair, hazel eyes. Occupation stonecutter. Enl. as corp., Co. K, 2nd Va. Inf. Regt., at Harpers Ferry 4/20/61. Trans. to Co. B, 1st Va. Cav. Regt., 8/8/61. Pres. 9–10/62. Detached to Gen. Stuart's headquarters for scouting duty and earned fame as the "Potomac Scout." Recommended for promotion by Stuart on 3/19/62 and by S. Bassett French on 3/24/62. Apparently no action taken. POW Shepherdstown 11/62 and sent to Ft. McHenry. Exch. at City Point 12/4/62. POW again at Berryville 4/4/63. At Ft. McHenry 4/11/63 and sent to Ft. Monroe for exch. 4/19/63. Paid as exch. prisoner in Richmond 5/6/64. Burke is noted as AWOL on 1st Va. Cav. Regt. muster rolls through late 1863 and early 1864. Adm. Staunton hospital 2–3/64. Appears as cpt., Co. D, 2nd Md. Cav. 8/31/64. Adm. Stuart Hospital, Richmond, with scabies 2/3/65. Trans. to private quarters 2/26/65. Paroled at Staunton 5/1/65.

BURKE, NICHOLAS. 1860 Baltimore city dir. shows a man by this name living at 41 Greenmount Ave. and as city bailiff. Light complexion, dark hair, blue eyes, 5'8". Obituary lists a Nicholas Burke, age 69, who died in Baltimore Co. on 1/10/1881. Had previously served as deputy warden, city jail detective, and rent collector in Baltimore. Burke served in the Mexican War. His father commanded a Maryland regt. in the War of 1812. Appears as cpt., Co. A, 2nd Md. Cav. No service record except offering resignation 1/27/64. Appears AWOL on 10/25/64 for 65 days and no steps taken to have him dropped. Burke was later dropped from command 1/3/65. He died in 1874. A Nicholas Burke is shown paroled at Baltimore Co. 7/26/65.

BURROUGHS, SOMERSET B. Born c. 1839. Res. Prince Georges Co. 5'9", dark complexion, black hair, brown eyes. Occupation farmer. Enl. 12/16/62 at Richmond as pvt. in Winder Cavalry Co. under Cpt. R. B. Winder, later organized as Co. E, 1st Md. Cav. Regt. Prom. 2lt. 1/20/63 and 1lt. 2/1/63. Adm. Charlottesville with remittent fever 8/15/63. RTD 9/10/63. Adm. Charlottesville with hepatitis 10/26/63. RTD 12/5/63. Furl. 30 days 12/19/63. POW on Potomac River 12/29/63. At Ft. McHenry from PMO, Washington, D.C., 1/13/64. Trans. Pt. Lookout 1/23/64. Trans. Ft. Delaware 6/23/64. Took OOA and rel. 6/8/65.

BUSSEY, JAMES THOMAS. 1860 cen.: res. 5th Ward, Baltimore; age 18, born in Md.; son of Bennet T. and Maria Bussey, both born in Md.; father is listed as physician ———/$200; four other children. CSA discharge records show James T. Bussey as born in Cecil Co. c. 1838. 5'7", fair complexion, blue eyes, brown hair. His occupation is listed as dentist. 1860 Baltimore City dir. shows Bussey's res. as southwest corner Hillen and Exeter. Served as 2lt. in the Winans Guards, 5th Md. Militia Regt. Enl. as pvt. in Co. C, 1st Md. Inf. Regt., at Fairfax CH

8/17/61. Pres. 9–12/61. Disch. 5/22/62 as nonresident. Appt. 2lt. in Co. D, 2nd Md. Inf., at Richmond 9/11/62. Abs. detached service in Richmond on unit business since 6/10/63. RTD 3/15/64. Elected cpt., Co. H, 2nd Md. Inf. 1/27/64. Pres. 2–3/64. WIA left hip Weldon Railroad 8/19/64. Adm. GH 4, Richmond, 8/20/64. Abs. sick since 12/8/64. Imprisoned at Libby Prison 4/9/65 and paroled in Richmond 4/19/65. Postwar member of Confederate Veterans camp in New York City. Died sometime between 5/1922 and 5/1923.

BYUS, WILLIAM R. Born in Baltimore c. 1840. Res. in Easton. 5'11", fair complexion, dark hair, blue eyes. Enl. as pvt., 2nd Co. H, 47th Va. Inf. Regt. 6/15/61. Pres. 3–6/62. Elected 2lt. Co. E, 2nd Md. Inf. 9/13/62. Pres. in arrest under charges by Cpt. Murray at New Market 12/62. Prom. 1lt. 8/4/63. Pres. 2–3/64 as commanding company. WIA left arm 8/19/64 at Weldon Railroad. Adm. GH 4, Richmond, 8/20/64. Furl. 40 days to Hanover Junction 8/27/64. Adm. GH 4, Richmond, 10/4/64. RTD 10/29/64. Adm. private quarters 1/6/65. RTD 1/20/65. POW Hatcher's Run 4/2/65. Sent OCP 4/5/65. Trans. Johnson's Island 4/11/65. Took OOA and rel. 6/18/65. Died in Baltimore 7/26/1910. Buried in Confederate lot at Loudoun Park Cemetery, Baltimore.

CALLAN, CHRISTOPHER CHARLES. Born in Ireland 1/3/37. Att. Georgetown College 1853–54. Married in Washington in 1858. 1860 Washington, D.C., city dir. shows Callan as lawyer. Res. 623 7th West Street in Georgetown. 5'6", light complexion, dark hair, gray eyes. Formed Co. C of the National Volunteers Bn. in Washington, D.C., before the war. Enl. as pvt. in Co. H, 7th Va. Inf. Regt., at Alexandria 4/22/61. Disch. 11/10/61 for myopia. Commissioned cpt., Co. A, 24th Bn. Va. Partisan Rangers 5/23/62. Company mustered as dismounted cavalry at Gordonsville 5/17/62. Resigned for physical and other reasons 8/12/62 but paid until 1/29/63 when company disbanded. Adm. GH 13, Richmond, with fever 4/1/63. Became cpt. of Winder Rangers, which mustered into service at Camp Maryland in Richmond by Cpt. Winder 7/27/63. This co. was attached to 2nd Md. Inf. as Co. H on 8/26/63. Callan court-martialed for conduct unbecoming an officer and gentleman for signing false returns and embezzlement. He was found not guilty and acquitted although findings were disapproved because neither judge advocate nor court was duly sworn 9/25/63. Resigned 1/20/64 and soon thereafter deserted to 1st Massachusetts Cav. at Warrenton. Committed to OCP 1/21/64. Rel. on OOA and sent to Philadelphia 3/15/64. Postwar lawyer in Washington until 1873. Moved to Texas and was lawyer in Fredericksburg. Also served as commander of Gillespie Co. Texas Rangers. Died 4/9/86.

CHAPMAN, NATHANIEL. Born in Charles Co. 8/26/42. 1860 cen.: res. Pomonkey, Charles Co.; age 18; student; son of Person and Mary Chapman; father was planter $40,000/$15,000. 5'6", light complexion, dark hair, blue eyes. Studied at Charlotte Hall and Jefferson College. Served as a pvt. with Hampton Legion. Wrote letter on 8/26/62 at Richmond for a government job, claiming poor health after one year of military service. Enl. as pvt., Co. E, 1st Md. Cav., at Richmond 11/12/62. Prom. 3lt. 1/20/63 and 1lt. 3/20/63. Pres. 7–12/63. Adm. GH 4, Richmond, with mobicutis 11/10/63. RTD 12/2/63. Pres. 7–8/64 and 11–12/64. Appears on 78 days' detached service 10/25/64. Claims paroled at Fredericksburg. Lived in Va. immediately after the war. Grad. University of Maryland Medical College in 1872. Later M.D. in Charles Co. and Washington, D.C. Died in Washington, D.C., 8/16/98.

CHEW, WALTER SCOTT. Born c. 1841. 1860 res. 114 Prospect St., Georgetown. 5'6", fair complexion, light hair, blue eyes. Student at Georgetown College and member of class of 1862. Father was superintendent of Chesapeake and Ohio Canal. Enl. as 1sg., Chesapeake Artillery (4th Md. Btry.) at Machodoc 1/1/62. Pres. 1–2/62 through 1–2/65. Prom. 1lt. 5/1/63 and cpt. 6/6/64. POW Petersburg 4/2/65. Sent to OCP 4/5/65 and then to Johnson's Island 4/9/65. Took OOA and rel. 6/2/65.

CLARK, JAMES LOUIS. Born c. 1841. Res. Baltimore. 5'9", light complexion, light hair, blue eyes. Son of Maj. Michael M. Clark, U.S. Army. Appt. cpt./AQM for 1st Md. Inf. Regt. 11/20/61. Dropped from duty 2/24/62. Applied for lieutenancy in C.S. Regular Army 9/29/62. Served on Gen. J. E. B. Stuart's staff in 1863 and appt. as cpt., Co. F, 12th Va. Cav. Regt., 6/17/63. Pres. 7–8/63. Adm. Culpeper hospital 10/18/63. Trans. to GH 4, Richmond, 11/3/63. RTD 2/2/64. Pres. 3/31/64. Applied for transfer to Maryland Line 4/2/64. Transfer approved 4/29/64. Placed under arrest 4/30/64, reason not stated. Had horses killed under him at Todd's Tavern 5/6/64 and Ashland 6/1/64. Appears as cpt., Co. F, 2nd Md. Cav., 7/27/64. POW Moorefield 8/7/64. Sent to Harpers Ferry 8/8/64, then to Wheeling 8/10/64. At Camp Chase 8/12/64. Trans. Pt. Lookout for exch. 2/12/65. Paroled at Appomattox 4/10/65.

CONTEE, CHARLES SNOWDEN. Born at Pleasant Prospect, Prince Georges Co. 10/31/30. Son of Lt. John and Anne L. Contee. Father was an officer in U.S. Navy. 1860 res. Annapolis, Anne Arundel Co.; age 24, farmer. $21,600/$21,200. Appt. 1lt., Md. Artillery (1st Md. Btry.) 7/14/61. Pres. 9–10/61 through 1–2/62. WIA left knee Stephenson's Depot 6/15/63. Recommended by Gen. Ewell and other officers for promotion to cpt. for gallantry at this action. Adm. Charlottesville hospital 8/25/63. Trans. Richmond 9/19/63. Adm. Farmville hospital 10/3/63 and sent to private quarters 1/18/64. Declared unfit for field duty and ordered to report to Conscript Bureau 6/23/64. Assigned as enrolling officer for

Wythe Co., Va. 6/25/64. Military record after this point is uncertain. Married Elizabeth Bowling 6/15/60. Eight children. Wife died in 1885.

COOKE, ADOLPHUS. Born c. 1841 near Beltsville, Prince Georges Co. Son of Dr. S. J. Cooke. Occupation farmer. 5'11", light complexion, light hair, blue eyes. Enl. as pvt., 2nd Co. K, 1st Va. Cav. Regt., at Manassas 7/21/61. Pres. 7/61 through 5/62. Prom. corp. 4/2/62. Disch. 5/19/62. Appt. 2lt., Co. B, 1st Md. Cav., 9/10/62. Pres. 9/62. POW Williamsport 7/14/63. At Cotton Factory hospital in Harrisburg, Pa., 8/63. Sent to West's Building hospital, Baltimore, from Harrisburg 9/4/63. Trans. Johnson's Island from Ft. McHenry 9/29/63. Took OOA and rel. 6/11/65. Died in Baltimore Co. 7/30/1905. Left widow and six children. Buried at Druid Hill Cemetery, Baltimore.

COSTELLO, THOMAS. Res. Baltimore. Appt. 2lt., Co. B, 1st Md. Inf. Regt., at Harpers Ferry by Ltc. Deas 5/21/61. Pres. 9–12/61. Detailed to unknown duty 4/28/62. He appears later at various Richmond hospitals in 1863–64. Paroled in Richmond and Lynchburg 4/65. NFR.

CRANE, JAMES PARRAN. Born in St. Marys Co. 8/6/1838. Son of James E. Crane and Sarah A. Spencer. Educated at Charlotte Hall Academy. 1860 census: res. Great Mills, St. Marys Co.; age 21; student at the University of Virginia; farmer; $3,000/$10,000. Formed a company of students at University of Virginia and mustered in as the University Volunteers 7/20/61. Co. assigned as 2nd Co. G, 59th Va. Inf. Regt., 8/13/61. Crane served as cpt. until co. disbanded by order of War Department at Salem 1/13/62. Later served as a staff officer for Brig. Gen. Wise. Applied for appointment as drillmaster at Richmond 5/5/62. Appt. cpt., Co. B, 2nd Md. Inf., at Richmond 8/27/62. Abs. sick in Winchester and Richmond 10/27/62. Requested to report for court-martial duty at Harrisonburg because of chronic diarrhea 4/6/63. Ordered before board of examiners 12/17/63. Pres. 3/64 as acting commander of unit since 7/4/63. WIA contusion from blow of musket at Weldon Railroad 8/19/64, which caused partial paralysis to left arm and left leg. Adm. GH 4, Richmond, 8/22/64. Furl. to Charleston, S.C., 11/14/64 and leave extended 12/1/64. Ordered to report to Gen. Ewell for court-martial duty in Richmond 12/24/64. Crane was promoted to maj. 9/27/64 with a DOR of 6/3/64 but this was subsequently canceled at Crane's request because Maj. Goldsborough was still alive as a Union POW. Paroled Salisbury, N.C., 5/1/65. Postwar lawyer, state's attorney, and judge in St. Marys Co. Married Laura Ann Hammett at St. Andrews Protestant Episcopal Church, St. Marys Co. 5/31/71. Wife died 8/10/85. Crane married Mollie Dent in Baltimore 6/16/87. Six children. Crane died at Jarboesville, St. Marys Co., 1/5/1916. Buried at St. Andrews P.E. Church. Obituary in Baltimore *Sun* 1/19/1916.

CROSS, ALEXANDER. Res. 113 N. Exeter St., Baltimore. Served as 2Lt. in Co. A, 5th Md. Militia Regt. Appt. 1lt., Co. G, 1st Md. Inf. Regt., 5/23/61. Abs. sick near Centreville and Richmond 10/28/61. Recruiting officer 1862. Resigned his position in Maryland unit 9/24/64 although he already had enlisted as pvt. Co. N, 2nd Va. State Reserves, on 4/15/64. Paroled in Richmond 4/18/65.

CUSHING, JOHN, JR. 1860 cen.: res. 14th Ward, Baltimore; age 23; merchant; born in Md.; son of John and Frances Cushing; father was merchant born in New Hampshire; mother born in Md.; four other children and one Irish servant; $10,000/$5,000. 1860 Baltimore city dir. shows res. at southwest corner of Lombard and Paca Sts. 5'9", fair complexion, light hair, light eyes. Enl. as sgm. in Co. E, 1st Md. Inf. Regt., at Harpers Ferry 5/22/61. Prom. 2lt. 8/18/61. Pres. 9–12/61. Paid as clerk with provost marshal's office in Winchester 9/24–11/1/62. Cushing requested to be reinstated in the new 2nd Md. Inf. while at Richmond 4/22/63. He had the approval of Col. Johnson, Gen. Steuart, and Senator Louis Wigfall. Not known what action was taken on Cushing's appeal. Cushing served as 1lt., Co. N, 2nd Va. State Reserves, in the summer of 1864. Paroled Charlottesville 5/17/65 and again at Gordonsville 6/23/65.

DABNEY, FREDERICK Y. Res. Dry Grove, Hinds Co., Miss. Occupation civil engineer with Southern Railroad. Son of Judge A. L. Dabney of Hinds Co. Appt. 2lt., Md. Artillery (1st Md. Btry.) on unknown date. Pres. 9–10/61 through 1–2/62. Resigned to accept appt. as 1lt. of Engineers 5/23/62. POW Port Hudson 7/9/63. Exch. after stay at Ft. Columbus, N.Y., and Johnson's Island 9/25/64. Suffered from chronic diarrhea throughout winter of 1864–65. Paroled Jackson, Miss. 5/18/65.

DAVIS, JAMES A. Born c. 1824 in Dorchester Co. 6'2", dark complexion, dark hair, dark eyes. Enl. as pvt., Co. H, 1st Md. Inf. Regt., at Fairfax CH 7/27/61. Abs. sick throughout 1861–62 until disch. 6/8/62. Appt. 2lt., Co. G, 2nd Md. Inf., 12/24/62. Prom. 1lt. 1/26/63. WIA back at Gettysburg 7/2–3/63. Adm. GH 4, Richmond, 7/26/63. Furl. 30 days to Forsyth, Ga. 8/6/63. Adm. GH 4, Richmond, for rheumatism 11/17/63 and furl. 11/30/63. Ordered before board of examiners 12/12/63, but Davis wrote letter of resignation 12/30/63. Gen. Johnson requested immediate acceptance of Davis' resignation on 1/18/64, which was done two days later. A James A. Davis crossed the Potomac River from Virginia in 10/64 to desert to Union troops. Davis stated that he "left because I got tired of the war & wanted to come home." Desired to take OOA.

DEMENT, WILLIAM FENDLEY. Born in Charles Co. 1826. Black hair, dark eyes, dark complexion. 1860 cen.: res. Duffield, Charles Co.; age 32; planter; wife

Eliza and two children; $2,000/$3,000. Att. Georgetown College 1841. Appt. 1lt. Md. Artillery (1st Md. Btry.) 7/13/61. Pres. 9–10/61 through 11–12/64. Prom. cpt. 7/4/62. Abs. sick at Charles Town 9/22/62. Given 30 days' leave 1/10/63. Appt. to court-martial duty 2/20/64. Noted as AWOL 1–2/65. Paroled Appomattox 4/9/65. Applied for presidential pardon 9/8/65. Postwar employee in U.S. Treasury Department. Died at Pomfret, Charles Co., 5/31/1907.

DEPPISH, EDWARD CHRISTIAN. 1860 cen.: res. 7th Ward, Baltimore; age 29; tinner; born in Md.; wife Sarah and three children; ———/$200. 1860 Baltimore city dir. shows res. at 112 North Gay. Served as sgt. in Co. E, 5th Md. Militia Regt. Appt. 2lt. in Co. G, 1st Md. Inf. Regt., at Harpers Ferry by Cpt. Nicholson 5/23/61. Pres. 9–12/61. Noted as commanding co. since 10/28/61. Resigned 7/15/62. Enl. as pvt. and substitute for J. W. Marshall in Co. G, 1st Va. Cav. Regt. at Martinsburg 9/20/62. Pres. 9–10/62 through 7–8/64. Without horse 3/15–4/30/63. Adm. Chimb. hospital with fever 5/18–24/64. POW Strasburg 10/9/64. Sent to Harpers Ferry 10/20/64. Trans. Pt. Lookout. Took OOA and rel. 5/13/65.

DEVINNEY, BENJAMIN F. Elected 2lt. in Co. G, 2nd Md. Inf. 7/27/63. Dropped for AWOL 1/18/64. NFR.

DIGGES, EUGENE. Born 10/27/38. Res. Allen's Fresh, Pt. Tobacco, Charles Co. Grad. 1857 from Georgetown College. 5'10", fair complexion, brown hair, blue eyes. Studied law in New York before war. Descendant of first Va. governor. Roman Catholic. Appt. 2lt. in Co. I, 1st Md. Inf. Regt., 7/19/61. Pres. 9–12/61. Digges later claimed service in Topographical Engineers and left to join Md. Line. In Richmond on unassigned duty 8/63. Appears as cpt. in Co. B, 2nd Md. Cav. POW Martinsburg 10/15/63. Sent to Ft. McHenry 10/18/63. Applied to SOW from Staunton for leave from Ft. McHenry to visit mother in Charles Co. and help her arrange household 11/1/63. Trans. Pt. Lookout 1/23/64. Sent to Ft. Delaware 6/25/64. Trans. Hilton Head 8/20/64. One of the Immortal Six Hundred. At Ft. Pulaski 10/22/64. RTD Hilton Head 11/64. RTD Ft. Delaware 3/12/65. Took OOA and rel. 6/1/65. Postwar lawyer and state's attorney in Charles Co. Moved to San Antonio, Texas, 12/79. Served as state attorney for Texas and state librarian. Member of John B. Hood Confederate Veterans Camp. Died at Austin 6/29/99.

DITTY, CYRUS IRVING. Born 9/26/36 at Dryad Hill, Anne Arundel Co. Att. West River Classical Institute. Grad. Dickinson College, Pa., 1857. Entered law practice in Baltimore and admitted to bar in 1859. Enl. as pvt. in 2d Co. K, 1st

Va. Cav. Regt., at Leesburg 5/14/61. Pres. 9–12/61. Prom. corp. 8/31/61. Abs. sick since 2/25/62. Apparently enl. as sgt. sometime in 1862 in Co. A, 1st Md. Cav. Trans. to Co. F upon promotion to 1lt. 7/16/63. Pres. 9–10/63. Abs. furl. 11–12/63. WIA thigh Old Church 3/2/64. Listed as AWOL for 52 days 10/25/64. Paroled Beaver Dam 5/11/65. Returned to Baltimore to resume law practice. Married sister of Cpt. Schwartze in 1868. Five children. Postwar Republican and witnessed 1876 presidential election in Louisiana. Assailed in Cross Street market hall riot in Baltimore. Collector of internal revenue under President Arthur for six months until paralyzed. Died in Baltimore 10/3/87. Buried at Loudoun Park Cemetery, Baltimore.

DORSEY, EDWARD RUTLAND. 1860 Baltimore city dir. shows Dorsey as a clerk with Baltimore and Ohio Railroad. Res. 116 South Sharp in Baltimore. Served as adj. of Baltimore City Guard. Appt. cpt. in 2nd Co. C, 1st Md. Inf., 5/17/61. Prom. maj. 9/10/61 and ltc. 3/18/62. WIA shoulder at Winchester 5/25/62.

DORSEY, GUSTAVUS WARFIELD. 1860 cen.: res. Damascus and Unity, Montgomery Co.; age 21; farmhand; born in Md.; son of Samuel and Mary Dorsey, farmer, $3,400/$35,000. Obituary shows Dorsey born c. 1839 at Brookville, Montgomery Co. Enl. as pvt. in 2d Co. K, 1st Va. Cav. Regt., at Leesburg 5/14/61. Pres. 9–10/61 through 1–2/64. Prom. 1sg. 8/31/61. Prom. 1lt. 4/23/62. Prom. cpt. 10/1/63. Company transferred to 1st Md. Cav. 8/64. Prom. Ltc. for valor and skill 9/16/64. WIA Fredericksburg and Fisher's Hill 9/22/64. Reported to have assisted J. E. B. Stuart when MWIA at Yellow Tavern 5/11/64. Died Brookville 9/6/1911 and buried in Owens Family Cemetery.

DORSEY, WILLIAM H. B. Res. Carroll Co. 6', fair complexion, brown hair, blue eyes. Enl. as pvt. in Co. A, 1st Md. Inf., at Harpers Ferry 5/21/61. Pres. 9–12/61. Prom. sgt. 9/1/61. Prom. 2lt. 4/29/62. Dorsey appears later as 1lt. in Co. D, 1st Md. Cav., at Winchester 9/20/62. Pres. 11–12/62 and 9–12/63. Pres. 4–12/64. Paroled at Frederick 9/18/65. Applied for presidential pardon from Mt. Airy, Carroll Co., 9/28/65.

DUVALL, FERDINAND C. 1860 cen.: res. Millersville, Anne Arundel Co.; age 25; farmer; born in Md.; $20,000/$8,000; lived with mother and brother and black farmhand. 5'7", dark complexion, dark hair, blue eyes. Enl. as pvt. in Co. C, 2nd Md. Inf. at Richmond 8/30/62. Prom. 1lt. 9/11/62 and cpt. 10/2/62. Pres. 10–12/62. WIA right knee at Winchester 6/14/63. Adm. GH 4, Richmond, 7/22/63. Furl. 40 days to Bainbridge, Ga. 7/27/63. Furl. 30 days 10/31/63. Pres.

2–3/64. WIA right thigh at Peebles Farm as commander of bn. 9/30/64. Adm. GH 4, Richmond, 10/1/64. Furl. 40 days to Bainbridge, Ga. 10/24/64. Adm. Stuart Hospital 12/3/64. Furl. 30 days 12/7/64. Adm. Stuart Hospital 12/29/64. Trans. private quarters 1/10/65. POW Hatcher's Run 4/2/65. Sent OCP 4/5/65. Trans. Johnson's Island 4/9/65. Took OOA and rel. 6/18/65. Applied for presidential pardon from Anne Arundel Co. 9/4/65. Died after the war and buried in Crofton Cemetery, Anne Arundel Co.

EDELIN, CHARLES COLUMBUS. Res. Baltimore. Appt. cpt. in Co. B, 1st Md. Inf. at Harpers Ferry 5/21/61. Abs. sick at Centreville 10/29/61. Pres. 11–12/61 through 3–4/62. Edelin later appears in N.C. in 1862. He then appears at Howard's Grove GH 1/13/63. RTD 1/27/63. Edelin also seems to have been a member of Winder Legion from Eastern Military District and released for service in front of Richmond 8/3/64. He simultaneously appears as POW Martinsburg 8/3/64. Sent to OCP and rel. on oath 2/22/65. Apparently rearrested and committed at OCP 2/22/65. U.S. SOW ordered release of Ltc. Edelin upon taking OOA at OCP 4/11/65. Edelin was not held in high regard by his fellow officers.

EDELIN, WILLIAM H. H. 1860 cen.: res. Piscataway, Prince Georges Co.; age 20; planter; born in Md.; $10,000/$5,000; lived with mother and other people. Enl. as pvt. in 2nd Co. C, 1st Md. Inf. Regt. at Richmond 3/26/62. Prom. 2lt. 7/1/62. Ordered to recruiting duty with Md. Line 12/22/62. In command of Camp Maryland 6/30/63. Ordered to take newly enlisted men to Col. Johnson 6/26/63. Appt. 2lt./acting ord. officer of Maryland Line 7/15/63. Abs. furl. 20 days 3/27/64. NFR.

EMACK, GEORGE M. 1860 cen.: res. Beltsville, Prince Georges Co.; age 17; student; born in Md.; son of A. G. and Margaret Emack, farmer; $12,000/$5,000. George Emack escaped to Virginia by stabbing a Union guard and was appointed as a lieutenant in the Richmond prison system for Union soldiers. Requested permission to raise company of sharpshooters from Richmond 5/62 and 8/62. Appt. as 2lt. in cavalry 10/8/61 but cashiered 9/15/62. Elected cpt. of Co. B, 1st Md. Cav., 9/10/62. Pres. 11–12/62 through 11–12/64. Adm. Charlottesville hospital 8/4/63. RTD without regular discharge 9/24/63. Ordered to report to Maj. Gen. Jones for court-martial 11/7/63. WIA during raid on Richmond 3/64 and again in right hand summer 1864. Adm. Charlottesville hospital with diphtheria 3/1/65. Trans. Stuart hospital 3/9/65. RTD 4/2/65. Postwar resident of New Orleans and Kentucky. Married after the war. Died in Versailles, Ky., 5/86.

FINIGAN, JAMES. (Name also appears as Finnegan although he signs his name as Finigan). Elected as 2lt. in Co. H, 2nd Md. Inf. Wrote letter of resignation at

Hanover Junction claiming physical disability 1/1/64. Resignation accepted 1/11/64. NFR.

FORNEY, GEORGE W. Forney appears as 2lt. in Co. C, 2nd Md. Cav., when he submitted resignation 11/28/63. Gen. Imboden approved his resignation stating, "I have no doubt a much [better] officer can be secured in place of Lieut. Forney, & the *morale* of the service be benefitted." A man by this name was a pvt. in Co. A, 11th Va. Cav. Regt. Difficult to ascertain if it was the same Forney.

FORREST, DAVID CRAWFORD. Enl. as pvt. in Co. F, 2nd Md. Inf., at Richmond 8/30/62. Elected 2lt. 10/28/62. Pres. 10/62 through 1–2/65. Served as PM at Hanover Junction 1/15/64. Relieved of command of Companies A and G; took command of Co. F 1/28/65. Adm. Stuart Hospital with "old wound" 3/28/65. RTD 4/2/65. Appears among "refugees and deserters" at Washington 5/30/65.

FORREST, JOSEPH. Born at Forrest Hall, St. Marys Co. 9/5/21. Son of Gen. James Forrest and Ann Edwards. Roman Catholic. 1860 cen.: res. Oakville, St. Marys Co.; age 38; farmer and planter; wife and 4 children; $51,650/$63,000. Att. Georgetown College 1833–36. Reentered 1838 but left that same year. Formed Chesapeake Artillery (later 4th Md. Btry.) as cpt. at Heathville, Va. Apparently defeated for election when battery reorganized. Forrest moved his family and slaves to Texas at the beginning of the war and suffered severe property losses when he returned to Md. after 1865. Took OOA at Galveston, Texas, 7/17/65. Received presidential pardon 10/9/65. Postwar farmer in St. Marys Co. Married Henrietta Cecilia Plowden at Bushwood Manor, St. Marys Co., 7/26/48. Twelve children; only a few survived to adulthood. Forrest died at Cole's Farm, St. Marys Co., 3/8/89. Buried at St. Francis Xavier Roman Catholic Church, Newtown. Wife died 10/27/98.

FRANKLIN, JAMES SHAW. Born 12/9/37. 1860 cen.: res. Annapolis, Anne Arundel Co.; age 32, lawyer; born in Md.; ———/$1,700. A 14-year-old mulatto boy lived with Franklin. 5′9″, light complexion, light hair, blue eyes. Elected 1lt. in Co. D, 2nd Md. Inf., 9/12/62. Pres. 5–6/63 through 1–2/64. Adm. Charlottesville hospital with chronic diarrhea 8/7/63. RTD 8/29/63. Readmitted Charlottesville hospital 9/18/63. Trans. Richmond 10/7/63. Commanded co. at Cold Harbor. POW Weldon Railroad 8/19/64. At OCP 8/22/64. Sent to Ft. Delaware 8/27/64. Took OOA and rel. 6/17/65. Applied for presidential pardon 7/19/65. Postwar attorney, clerk of the court of appeals, and state's attorney in Annapolis. Died 3/7/81.

GALE, JOHN. 1860 cen.: res. Potato Neck, Somerset Co.; age 34; merchant; born in Md.; ———/$4,000. Enl. as sgt. in Md. Artillery (1st Md. Btry.) at Richmond 7/16/61. Pres. 9–10/61 through 1–2/65. WIA 6/25/62. Appt. 1lt. 8/20/62. WIA Second Manassas 8/29/62. Adm. GH 8, Richmond, with typhoid fever 9/1/62. Furl. 60 days 9/11/62. WIA right leg at Fredericksburg 5/3/63. Adm. GH 4, Richmond, 9/4/63. Furl. 90 days to Buckingham Co., Va., 10/2/63. Gen. J. H. Winder wrote note to Col. Gorgas requesting Gale's assignment until fit for field duty 10/15/63. Gale requested his return to field duty from Richmond 5/6/64. Paroled Appomattox as btry. commander.

GILMOR, MEREDITH. Born c. 1844. Res. Baltimore Co. Youngest son of Robert Gilmor and brother of Maj. Harry Gilmor and Cpt. Richard T. Gilmor. 6'1/2", florid complexion, auburn hair, gray eyes. Farmer. Gilmor appears as 2lt. in Co. A, 2nd Md. Cav. POW Johnstown, Va., by 54th Pa. Cav. 7/22/63. Sent to Wheeling 7/29/63 and then to Camp Chase 7/30/63. Trans. to Johnson's Island 10/10/63. Gilmor was on list of POWs wanting to take OOA and not be sent south or exchanged. Gilmor took OOA and rel. 5/16/65. Gilmor enlisted as pvt. in Co. C, 10th U.S. Inf. Regt., 2/2/80 through 2/1/85. He reenlisted at Ft. Marcy, N.M., as pvt. in Co. C, 22nd U.S. Inf. Regt., 3/1/1885. Gilmor was injured by a blow to his stomach when he tripped getting out of a cart and fell on a shovel handle. He was disch. at Ft. Lyon, Colo., for aneurism of the abdominal aorta 7/8/85. Inmate at the U.S. Soldier's Home in Washington, D.C., 1886. Gilmor was found dead at the Govanstown Hotel in Baltimore Co. 9/21/1900. Officials believed that he died from an overdose of morphine as he was known to have been an addict. Gilmor never married. Buried at the family vault at the Westminster Cemetery, Baltimore.

GILMOR, RICHARD TILGHMAN. Born at Glen Ellen, Baltimore Co., c. 1840. Son of Robert Gilmor and brother of Maj. Harry Gilmor and 2Lt. Meredith Gilmor. Arrested during the April 19, 1861, riot in Baltimore and held for $13,000 bail. Released and ordered to go south but stopped at Ft. Monroe and confined on board the USS *Cumberland*. Released and ordered to Baltimore. Gilmor instead went to Richmond. Appt. 2lt. in 2nd Co. H, 1st Md. Inf. Regt., at Richmond 6/18/61. Pres. 9–12/61. He later appears to have enl. as pvt. in Co. F, 12th Va. Cav. Regt., at Bartonsville 2/15/62. Abs. sick at GH 1, Lynchburg, 7–8/63. Noted as AWOL in Madison Co. since 9/18/63 although he is listed as abs. furl. from GH 9, Richmond, 10/8/63. Gilmor signed various requisition forms as 1lt. and cpt. of Co. C, 2nd Md. Cav., from 10/12/63 until 6/12/64. Paroled at Campbell CH 5/27/65. Gilmor returned to Baltimore 8/65 and later served as bailiff in Baltimore Criminal Court. He died at the Confederate Soldiers Home in Pikesville 8/23/1908. Buried in family lot at Loudoun Park Cemetery, Baltimore.

GOLDSBOROUGH, WILLIAM WORTHINGTON. Born 10/6/31 in Frederick Co. Son of Dr. and Mrs. Leander Goldsborough. 1860 res. 20 Jackson St., Baltimore. 5'11", fair complexion, light hair, brown eyes. Cousin of Bradley T. Johnson. Member of Baltimore City Guard in 1861. Enl. as pvt. in Co. C, 1st Md. Inf. Regt., at Richmond 5/17/61. Trans. to Co. A and elected cpt. upon promotion of Bradley T. Johnson to maj. 6/25/61. Pres. 7–12/61. Following disbandment of 1st Md., Goldsborough placed in command of company of 48th Va. at Second Manassas. WIA left side at Second Manassas. Elected cpt. of Co. G, 2nd Md. Inf., 12/14/62. Prom. maj. 1/26/63. WIA left side and back and POW at Gettysburg 7/2/63. Adm. Letterman hospital 8/10/63. Sent to GH 10/14/63. Received at West's Building hospital from Ft. McHenry 4/23/64. Sent to Ft. Delaware 6/16/64. Forwarded to Hilton Head, S.C., 8/20/64. One of the Immortal Six Hundred. At Ft. Pulaski 10/20/64. Returned to Ft. Delaware 3/12/65. Took OOA and rel. 6/12/65. Postwar newspaper shop foreman in Philadelphia. Run over by bicycle in 1896 and forced to use crutches. Died in Philadelphia 12/25/1901. Buried at Loudoun Park Cemetery, Baltimore.

GOODMAN, JOHN W. Born c. 1838. Res. 241 South Paca St., Baltimore. 5'10", fair complexion, dark hair, blue eyes. Occupation clerk. Enl. as pvt. in Baltimore Light Artillery (2nd Md. Btry.) at Richmond 8/15/61. Pres. 9–10/61 through 9–10/64. Adm. GH 21, Richmond, with diarrhea 4/19/62. RTD 5/13/62. Goodman appears as disch. for disability 1/2/63, but this does not seem to have been official. Prom. 2lt. 7/8/63. Adm. GH 4, Richmond, with syphilis 9/29/63. RTD 11/1/63. Commanded btry. after fall of 1864. Goodman wrote a scathing letter about conduct of southern troops during 1864 summer campaign in Maryland and Pennsylvania and requested to be released from the army 9/4/64. He was apparently dropped 3/2/65. Paroled at Winchester 4/21/65 and sent to Baltimore.

GRASON, JOHN. 1860 cen.: res. Queenstown, Queen Anne Co.; age 34; no occupation listed; born in Md.; son of William and Susan Grason, farmer; $20,000/$20,000; both parents born in Md.; six other children. Enl. as pvt. in Chesapeake Artillery (4th Md. Btry.) at Heathville 2/10/62. Apparently prom. to 2lt. as he is paid as such 5/24–7/1/62. KIA Fredericksburg 12/13/62. Obituary in Baltimore *Daily Gazette* 1/6/63.

GREEN, THOMAS J. No record of enlistment in Co. C, 1st Md. Cav. Appears as prom. 2lt. 6/1/63. Pres. 7–12/63 and 4/1/64. Member of board to investigate factors connected with dismounted men in camp at Hanover Junction 11/14/63. Furl. 20 days to Essex Co. 1/27/64. WIA right shoulder at Rockville 7/14/64. Nearly taken POW but released by Confederate forces. Given furl. to Essex Co. because of disability for three months. Adm. Stuart Hospital, Richmond, 11/22/64 but deserted 2/22/65. Appears at Paroled and Exchanged Camp 3/22/65. NFR.

GRIFFIN, JOSEPH. Born c. 1836. Res. Baltimore. Appt. 2lt. in Co. B, 1st Md. Inf. Regt., at Harpers Ferry by Ltc. Deas 5/21/61. Pres. 9–12/61. Pres. in arrest for reasons unknown 11–12/61. Tendered letter of resignation at Camp Chesapeake 1/2/62 as "there are changes prefered against me for which reason I prefer to resign my commission." Appt. 2lt. in Co. B, 24th Bn., Va. Partisan Rangers 5/20/62. Prom. cpt. 7/6/62. Placed under arrest by bn. commander at time bn. disbanded 1/5/63. Appealed to Confederate government for reinstatement 5/26/63, 8/31/63, 1/18/65. Griffin later appears on staff of Gen. Fitzhugh Lee. WIA in thigh and POW at Hamilton 3/21/65. At Island hospital at Harpers Ferry 3/22/65. Trans. Ft. McHenry 3/25/65. Ordered not to be exchanged during war as "his pretended rank is hardly credited it being strongly suspected that he is a member of Mosby's Guerillas." Took OOA and rel. 6/10/65.

GRIFFIN, WILLIAM HUNTER. Born in Southampton Co., Va. 1860 res. Fountain Hotel in Baltimore. 5'10", ruddy complexion, dark hair, hazel eyes. Appt. 1lt. in Baltimore Light Artillery (2nd Md. Btry.) at Richmond 8/15/61. Pres. 9–12/61. Fuel requisition shows 1 cpt, 2 lts, and 55 em's at Camp Dimmock 9/21/61. Submitted resignation 2/19/63 but apparently not accepted. Prom. cpt. 3/22/63. POW Yellow Tavern 5/11/64. Sent to Ft. Monroe and Pt. Lookout. Trans. to Ft. Delaware 6/25/64. Forwarded to Hilton Head 8/20/64. One of the Immortal Six Hundred. At Ft. Pulaski 10/20/64. Returned to Ft. Delaware 3/12/65. Took OOA and rel. 6/16/65. Postwar resident of Galveston, Texas. Married twice. Died in Galveston 11/23/96 and buried in Galveston City Cemetery.

GRIFFITH, FRANK or FRANCES M. 1860 cen.: res. Clarksburg, Montgomery Co.; age 29; farmer; born in Md.; wife Elizabeth and one son; $3,000/$2,100. Grew up at Edgehill. Son of Thomas Griffith I. Brother of Thomas Griffith II and first cousin of Ridgely Brown. Enl. as corp. in 2nd Co. K, 1st Va. Cav. Regt., at Leesburg 5/14/61. Pres. 7–8/61 through 1–4/62. Appears to have enl. as sgt. in Co. A, 1st Md. Cav., at Camp Jackson 2/10/62. Pres. 7–12/63 through 4/1/64. Abs. furl. 9/1–25/63. Signed as 2lt. commanding co. 11–12/64. Fuel requisition for co. shows 1 lt. and 42 em's 12/1/64. NFR. Postwar farmer at Edgehill, fifteen miles north of Olney, Md. Died there in 1892.

GRIFFITH, THOMAS II. Born in Md. 1831. Res. Olney, Montgomery Co. 5'11", fair complexion, dark hair, blue eyes. Occupation farmer. Grew up at Edgehill. Son of Thomas Griffith I. Brother of Frank Griffith and first cousin of Ridgely Brown. Enl. as corp. in 2nd Co. K, 1st Va. Cav. Regt., at Leesburg 5/14/61. Prom. 2lt. 8/1/61. Pres. 7–8/61 through 1–4/62. Dropped 4/23/62. Appt. 1lt. in Co. A, 1st Md. Cav., 11/12/62. Served as 1lt/AQM 11–12/62. Applied for 20-day furl. to visit Montgomery Co. 1/3/63. Pres. 9–12/63 and 4/1/64. Company fuel requisition shows 2 lts. and 87 em's at Hanover Junction 1/64. POW Moorefield 8/7/64. Sent to Camp Chase from Harpers Ferry, then Wheeling 8/12/64. Trans. to City Point for exch. 3/2/65. Paroled Mechanicsville 4/25/65. Postwar farmer in Montgomery Co.

GROSHON, JOHN F. Born c. 1838 in Frederick Co. 1860 Frederick city dir. shows res. at southwest corner Patrick and Carroll Sts. Clerk. Enl. as 1sg. in Co. A, 1st Md. Inf. Regt., at Harpers Ferry 5/21/61. Pres. 9–12/61. Reenl. as 1sg. 2/8/62. Elected 2lt. 4/29/62. Employed as quartermaster agent in Texas since the fall of 1862. Requested appt. as cpt. in PACS while at San Antonio, Texas, 5/1/63. Had letters of recommendation from former governor of Md., Gen. Ezley, and Col. Johnson. NFR.

GUILLETTE, GILBERT G. Born c. 1835 in Somerset Co. Teacher. 5'8", dark complexion, dark hair, dark eyes. Enl. as pvt. in Co. B, 19th Va. H.A. Bn. at Norfolk 2/21/62. Prom. sgt. during 1862. Pres. until trans. to Md. Line 12/15/62. Elected 2lt. in Co. G, 2nd Md. Inf., 5/13/63. Prom. 1lt. in place of James A. Davis 1/20/64. Passed board of examiners. Abs. furl. 3/26/64. POW Weldon Railroad 8/19/64. At OCP 8/22/64. Sent to Ft. Delaware 8/27/64. Took OOA and rel. 6/14/65.

GWYNN, ANDREW JACKSON. Born 11/24/36 at Pleasant Springs, Piscataway, Prince Georges Co. Son of John Hilleary Gwynn and Ann Eliza Dyer. 1860 cen.: res. Piscataway, Prince Georges Co., age 25; farmer; lived with two other families; $8,000/$19,000; Roman Catholic. Enl. as pvt. in Md. Line at Richmond 5/19/62. Reenl. as pvt. in Co. F, 2nd Md. Inf., at Richmond 8/26/62. Elected cpt. 10/28/62. Pres. 10–12/62 and 2–3/64. WIA slightly at Gettysburg 7/3/63, at Cold Harbor 6/3/64, and at Peebles Farm 9/28/64. Gwynn was absent from the command in various hospitals after this wounding. Paroled Greensboro, N.C., 5/1/65. Postwar traveling salesman for New York firm. Married Marie Louise Keen 1/8/68. Six children. Moved to Spartanburg, S.C., in 1875. Prominent resident and served on city council. Gwynn died 8/4/1908. United Daughters of the Confederacy chapter named for Gwynn in Prince Georges Co. His wife died in 1913.

HARRISON, JOHN SPENCER. Born c. 1838. Res. Church Hill, Queen Anne Co. 5'5", fair complexion, light hair, blue eyes. Paid as sgt. in Co. B, 2nd Md. Cav., in Richmond 7–8/63. Appears as 1lt., commanding co. 9/19/64. POW Piedmont 6/15/64. Sent to Camp Morton, then Johnson's Island 6/22/64. Took OOA and rel. 5/13/65.

HERBERT, JAMES R. Born 8/18/33 at Woodstock, Howard Co. Son of Dr. Thomas Snowden Herbert and Camilla A. Hammond. Att. school in Howard Co. and at Hallowell College in Alexandria, Va. Went to sea at age 13 and survived cholera epidemic. Entered father's store business at age 16 until father's death in 1852. Formed tobacco, grain, and produce commerce business with brother after that. 1860 Baltimore city dir. shows res. 89 North Paca. Served as 2lt. in Independent Greys. Appt. cpt. of Co. D, 1st Md. Inf. Regt., at Harpers Ferry by Ltc. Deas 5/22/61. Pres. 9–12/61. Elected cpt. of Co. C, 2nd Md. Inf., 9/11/62. Prom. maj. 10/2/62 and ltc. 1/26/63. WIA and POW Gettysburg 7/3/63. Sent to Johnson's Island from Baltimore 9/29/63. Sent to Ft. Monroe for exch. 10/8/64. At Richmond hospital 1/24/65. Furl. 30 days to Charlottesville. Adm. Richmond MDO 3/13/65. Paroled Greensboro, N.C., 5/1/65. Applied for presidential pardon 6/26/65. Pardoned 7/26/65. Returned to Baltimore and reopened business. Elected col., 5th Regt. Md. National Guard, 1867 and appt. brig. gen. by governor in 1871. Served as Baltimore city police commissioner 1877–83 and reappt. for another six-year term. Commanded troops during 1877 labor riots. Member of Masons, Democratic party, and Episcopal church. Married to Elizabeth Coleman Alexander and had six children. Died at Woodstock, Howard Co., 8/5/84. Buried at Loudoun Park Cemetery, Baltimore.

HILL, WILLIAM ISAAC. Born at Baltimore Manor 12/28/41. 1860 cen.: res. Upper Marlboro, Prince Georges Co.; age 21; son of William and Catherine Hill; planter; no wealth listed; four other children; Father born in Md. and mother in D.C. Enl. as corp. in Md. Artillery (1st Md. Btry.) at Fredericksburg 6/27/61. Pres. 9–12/61. Abs. on recruiting duty 1–2/62. Pres. 7–8/64. Abs. sick 9–10/64. Pres. 11–12/64 through 1–2/65. Elected 2lt. 7/25/62. Paroled Appomattox 4/9/65 and again in Washington, D.C., 4/22/65. Applied for presidential pardon 6/5/65. Pardoned 7/6/65. Postwar lawyer in Prince Georges Co. Married Henrietta S. Sasscer 10/11/66. Seven children. Hill died at Upper Marlboro 7/17/98. His wife died 10/14/1912.

HOBBS, NATHAN CHEW. Born c. 1837. Res. Howard Co. 6'2", dark complexion, brown hair, gray eyes. Enl. as sgt. in 2nd Co. K, 1st Va. Cav. Regt., at Leesburg 5/14/61. Pres. 7–12/61. Abs. furl. 2/8/62. Pres. 3–4/62. Elected 2lt. 4/26/62. POW Catlett Station 8/22/62. Paroled 9/1/62 and exch. 9/21/62. Pres.

11–12/62. WIA right thigh and POW at Hagerstown 7/12/63. Sent to Harrisburg, then Pt. Lookout 1/22/64. Exch. 3/3/64. Meanwhile, prom. 1lt. 10/1/63. Pres. 3–8/64. Trans. to Co. K, 1st Md. Cav., 8/64. WIA at Winchester 9/19/64. Adm. GH 4, Richmond, 9/25/64. Furl. 10/15/64. Adm. Charlottesville hospital 10/21/64. Trans. to Richmond 10/25/64. NFR until paroled at New Market 4/19/65.

HODGES, CHARLES W. 1860 cen.: res. 10th Ward, Baltimore; age 22; clerk; born in Md.; lived in boardinghouse. 1860 Baltimore city dir. shows res. at 171 West Lombard. Enl. as pvt. in Co. C, 2nd Md. Inf., at Richmond 8/30/62. Elected 2lt. 9/11/62. Prom. 1lt. 10/2/62. Detailed as ord. officer for unit 12/30/62. Commanded co. at Gettysburg. Ordered before board of examiners 12/17/63. Pres. 2–3/64 and 9–10/64. Detailed as acting adj. 9/1/64 and also served as commander for Companies G and H. Struck in head and KIA at Hatcher's Run 2/5/65.

HOLBROOK, THOMAS H. 1860 cen.: res. Tyaskin, Somerset Co.; age 33; farmer; born in Md.; wife and one child; two black servants; $2,500/$500. Appt. 1lt. in 1st Co. F, 1st Md. Inf. Regt., at Harpers Ferry by Ltc. Deas 5/22/61. Resigned 9/16/61. He later appears to have formed an artillery btry. but it was never officially organized.

HOUGH, WILLIAM DICKINSON. 1860 cen.: res. 11th Ward, Baltimore; age 25; merchant; born in Md.; ———/$1,000; son of Robert and Mary Hough; father is merchant, ———/$60,000; both parents born in Md.; two other children and two servants (one white, one black). 1860 Baltimore city dir. shows res. at 228 North Charles. Served as 1lt. of Co. A, 39th Md. Militia Regt., 1857. Enl. as pvt. in 2nd Co. H, 1st Md. Inf. Regt., at Fairfax CH 6/18/61. Trans. to Md. Artillery (1st Md. Btry.) 6/25/61. Returned to 1st Md. Inf. Regt. 8/15/61. Elected 1lt. and trans. to 2nd Co. F 10/8/61. Abs. sick in Richmond 1–2/62. Resigned because of ill health 6/12/62. Resignation accepted 7/1/62. Later Hough appears as midshipman and captain's clerk on the CSS *Florida*. POW at Bahia, Brazil, by USS *Wachusett* on 10/7/64. Arrived at Pt. Lookout 11/15/64. Trans. to Washington, D.C., then back to Pt. Lookout 11/18/64. Recd. at Ft. Warren 11/28/64. Rel. and ordered to leave the United States in ten days and to commit no hostile actions 2/1/65.

HOWARD, GEORGE. Appt. 1lt. in 2nd Co. K, 1st Va. Cav. Regt., at Leesburg 5/14/61. Resigned 8/1/61 and took rank as pvt. POW at Lewinsville 9/10/61. Paroled at Washington, D.C., 11/6/61 and sent to Ft. Monroe for exch. Appears at Richmond 12/12/61 when he wrote the adjutant general to apply for a commission. He was paid for commutation of rations at Richmond while a paroled prisoner 12/1/61 through 6/18/62. Elected 1lt. of Co. C, 1st Md. Cav., 8/4/62. Pres. 11/62. Abs. court-martial duty 12/62. Abs. 7–8/63. Prom. cpt. 8/25/63. Pres. 9–12/63. Howard was court-martialed as a lieutenant for absence without leave and found guilty. He was sentenced to forfeit one month's pay and be publicly reprimanded by the unit commander in dress parade. Order was published 11/20/63. Company fuel requisition shows 1 cpt., 2 lts., and 72 em's in 12/63. The next month's requisition shows an additional six em's. Adm. GH 4, Richmond, 3/2/64. RTD 4/12/64. POW at Pollard's Farm 5/27/64. Arrived at Pt. Lookout from White House Landing 6/8/64. Trans. Ft. Delaware 6/23/64. Sent to Hilton Head 8/20/64. One of the Immortal Six Hundred. At Ft. Pulaski 10/20/64. Delivered for exch. 12/13/64. In Richmond 1/23/65. Paroled at Winchester 4/30/65. Resident of Baltimore in 1891.

HOWARD, WILLIAM KEY. Member of 53rd Md. Militia Regt. Appt. 2lt. in Co. D, 1st Md. Inf. Regt., at Harpers Ferry by Cpt. Herbert 6/1/61. Abs. furl. 9–10/61. Pres. in arrest 11–12/61. Howard later appears to have enl. as pvt. in Co. E, 4th Va. Cav. Regt., at Culpeper 3/19/62. Pres. until POW at Front Royal 8/16/64. Sent to OCP, then to Elmira 8/16/64. Exch. 2/25/65. Paroled in Richmond 4/21/65. While a member of this command, Howard wrote the SOW from Richmond requesting reinstatement in a Maryland unit 6/1/63. Howard's wife and mother also bombarded CSA officials with similar appeals.

HYLAND, JOHN G. Born c. 1840 in Somerset Co. Lawyer. 5'11", light complexion, brown hair, hazel eyes. Enl. as pvt. in Co. C, 1st Md. Inf. Regt., at Richmond 5/17/61. Abs. sick at hospital 10/8/61. Disch. as nonresident 6/9/62. Elected 2lt. in Co. F, 2nd Md. Inf., at Richmond 9/10/62. Pres. 10/62. WIA left side at Gettysburg 7/3/63. Adm. GH 4, Richmond, 7/23/63, and furloughed the same day. Pres. 2–3/64. Abs. sick in Richmond 4/11/64. Paroled at Greensboro 5/1/65.

JOHNSON, OTIS. Born c. 1842 in Frederick Co. Farmer. 5'8", dark complexion, dark hair, gray eyes. Enl. as pvt. in Co. A, 1st Md. Cav., at Urbanna 9/12/62. Pres. 7–8/63 and 4/64. Elected 2lt. 6/18/64. POW Moorefield 8/7/64. Sent to Camp Chase from Wheeling 8/12/64. Trans. to City Point for exch. 3/2/65. Paroled Charlotte 5/16/65. Pardoned 9/20/65. Died at Cumberland 2/17/81.

KEMP, WILLIAM H. Enl. as pvt. in Co. F, 12th Va. Cav. Regt., at Harrisonburg 4/9/62. POW at Berryville 11/29/62. At OCP 12/3/62. Trans. to City Point for exch. 3/29/63. Paid in Richmond as paroled POW 3/31/63. Paid 7/1/62 through

10/1/62 as 2sgt. and 10/1/62 through 2/28/63 as 1sg. Pres. 7–8/63. Appears as AWOL since 9/21/63. Kemp is then shown as paid as 2lt. in Co. C, 2nd Md. Cav., 1/12–3/12/64. KIA at Moorefield 8/7/64. Obituary in Baltimore *Sun* 9/2/64.

LAWRENCE, STEPHEN DEMETT. Elected as 2lt. in Co. D, 1st Md. Cav., at Winchester 9/20/62. Pres. 11–12/62 and 7–10/63. Abs. furl. 11–12/63. Resigned because of poor health at Hanover Junction 1/29/64.

LECOMPTE, THOMAS P. Born 5/6/41. 1860 Baltimore city dir. shows a man by this name living at 32 Williamson St. and making a living as engineer. Enl. as sgt. in Chesapeake Artillery (4th Md. Btry.) at Machodoc 1/1/62. Pres. 1–2/62 Adm. GH 21, Richmond, with syphilis 5/1/62. RTD 6/27/62. Pres. 5–10/63 as Sgm. Prom. 1lt. for valor and skill 4/29/64. Pres. 9–10/64 through 1–2/65. NFR. Died 3/21/73.

LUTTS, JOHN J. 1860 cen.: res. Frederick City; age 17; apprentice tailor; born in Md.; son of Michael and Mary Lutts; father born in Bavaria; tailor, $600/$100; one other child. Appt. 2lt. in Co. E, 1st Md. Inf. Regt., at Harpers Ferry by Ltc. Deas 5/22/61. Pres. 9–12/61. Prom. 1lt. after the resignation of Cpt. McCoy. Detailed to service with Gen. Winder in Richmond 2/62. Requested reinstatement in Md. Line in letter to SOW from Richmond 4/22/63. Claim supported by Col. Johnson, Gen. Steuart, and Senator Louis Wigfall. NFR.

McALEER, JOSEPH L. Res. Emmitsburg. Elected cpt. of Co. D, 2nd Md. Inf., 9/12/62. Pres. 10–12/62. Pres. 5–6/63 and 2–3/64. Adm. GH 4, Richmond, with dysentery 1/16/64. Furl. 1/25/65. Adm. GH 4 with colitis 8/16/64. Furl. 8/28/64. Readm. GH 4 with hemmorhoids 9/23/64. Furl. 10/9/64. Submitted letter of resignation stating that "my usefulness in the battalion has in a great measure at least, been destroyed by petty contentions and jealousies." Requested to be placed in some other position 2/15/65. Resignation accepted 2/22/65. NFR.

McCARROLL, WILLIAM J. Appears as 1lt. of Co. D, 2nd Md. Cav. Paid as such as patient in hospital on 12/15/64 for 3/1–4/30/64 and again on 1/17/65 for 5/1–30/64. Listed as AWOL 12/31/63 through 8/31/64. Dropped from rolls 1/3/65. NFR.

McCOY, HENRY. 1860 cen.: res. 11th Ward, Baltimore; age 27; salesman; born in Md. 1860 Baltimore city dir. lists res. as 205 Saratoga. Served briefly as cpt. of Co. E, 1st Md. Inf. Regt. Paid for service 5/21–8/18/61. Appt. cpt./AQM and ordered to report to quartermaster general 11/7/61. Spent majority of the war on prison duty in Salisbury, Danville, and in northern Alabama settling quarter-master claims. Paroled at Salisbury as cpt./ADC to Gen. Johnson 4/26/65. Post-war commission merchant with Cpt. Rasin in Baltimore. Died 12/28/66.

McCULLOUGH, SAMUEL THOMAS. Born 1842. Res. Annapolis, Anne Arundel Co. Lawyer. 5'8", fair complexion, dark hair, blue eyes. Elected 2lt. of Co. D, 2nd Md. Inf., 9/12/62. Pres. 10–12/62. Pres. 5–6/63 and 2–3/64. Severely WIA upper right thigh at Cold Harbor 6/3/64. Adm. Chimb. hospital 6/7/64. Furl. 8/3/64. Adm. Chimb. 9/12/64. Furl. 20 days 9/13/64. Pres. 1–2/65 as commanding Companies D, G, and H. POW Hatcher's Run 4/2/65. Sent to OCP 4/5/65. Trans. to Johnson's Island 4/9/65. Took OOA and rel. 6/19/65. Postwar attorney and city council member in Annapolis. Married twice, the second marriage to the daughter of Jedediah Hotchkiss. Died 4/20/97.

McKAIG, WILLIAM WALLACE, Jr. Born in Cumberland, Md., 5/5/42. 1860 cen.: res. Cumberland, Allegheny Co.; age 18; VMI cadet; son of William W. McKaig and Priscilla E. Beall; father was Cumberland lawyer, industrialist, member of Md. legislature, and first mayor of Cumberland; father born in Ohio and mother in Md.; four other children; $8,000/$3,700. 5'11", fair complexion, light hair, gray eyes. Entered VMI in 1859. Member of class of 1864. Drilled new recruits in Richmond after outbreak of war. Claims to have participated in the Battle of First Manassas as unassigned to any unit 7/21/61. Appt. 2lt. of Co. I, 1st Va. Inf. Regt., at Fairfax CH 9/14/61. Resigned 4/26/62. Reportedly served in 12th Va. Cav. Regt. Shown as 1lt. and cpt. of Co. A, 2nd Md. Cav. POW in Hampshire Co., W.Va., 3/23/64. Sent to Wheeling and then Camp Chase 3/28/64. Trans. to City Point for exch. 2/25/65. Paroled at Winchester 4/24/65. Married Laura Hughes of Rippon, W.Va. 10/25/65. One child. Postwar iron manufacturer, member of Cumberland city council, and colonel in the Md. National Guard. McKaig apparently "guilty of a grave charge against a sister of Mr. Harry W. Black." Black met McKaig on a Cumberland street and shot the latter in the back and killed McKaig 10/17/70. Black was defended by Daniel W. Vorhees, a congressman from Indiana, and released. Black later earned a fortune in coal and lived in Baltimore.

MCKNEW, MASON E. Enl. as pvt. in Co. D, 1st Md. Inf. Regt., at Harpers Ferry 6/1/61. Pres. 9–10/61. Prom. sgt. 9/1/61. Abs. furl. 11–12/61. Adm. GH 21, Richmond, 4/21/62. Elected 2lt. of Co. B, 1st Md. Cav., 9/10/62. Abs. on detailed duty to purchase horses 11/62. Pres. 12/62. POW along Potomac River 6/2/63. Had been in St. Marys Co. for a visit of six days during furl. of 42 days in which time he also visited Loudoun and Westmoreland Cos. in Va. Became sick in St. Marys Co. and did not get to see wife. Sent OCP 6/8/63 and then to Johnson's

Island 8/12/63. Trans. Pt. Lookout for exch. 4/22/64. Adm. GH 4, Richmond, with diarrhea 5/1/64. RTD 5/5/64. Adm. Charlottesville hospital 6/8/64. RTD 6/13/64. Company fuel requisition shows 1 cpt., 2 lts., and 46 em's 8–9/64. Appears WIA left side in fall 1864. Adm. Charlottesville hospital 9/27/64. RTD 10/17/64. Abs. furl. 12/23/64. NFR.

MCNULTY, JOHN R. Born in Ellicott City, Md., c. 1836. Appt. 2lt. of Baltimore Light Artillery (2nd Md. Btry.) 7/8/63. POW at Culpeper CH 9/13/63. At OCP 9/14/63. Trans. to Ft. McHenry 9/24/63. Sent to Johnson's Island 9/28/63. "Sent away surreptiously in place of Wm. M. Brown" 2/9/64. Abs. detailed as acting adjutant on Gen. B. T. Johnson's staff 2–8/64. Pres. as 1lt. commanding btry. 9–10/64. Paid 2/8/65. Military service after this point is uncertain. Postwar coffee merchant and founder of New York Coffee Exchange. Founder of Harlem and Sangamore Democratic Clubs. Died at home in Blauvelt, Rockland Co., N.Y. 1/11/1912. Three sons survived.

MARRIOTT, JOSEPH G. W. Res. Frederick, Md. Appt. cpt. of Co. A, 39th Regt. Md. Militia, by Md. governor 10/30/57. Appt. 2lt. in Co. E, 1st Md. Inf. Regt., at Harpers Ferry by Ltc. Deas 5/22/61. Pres. 9–12/61. Appears to have been prom. 1lt. following resignation of Cpt. O'Brien 7/23/62. Appealed for reinstatement in Md. Line as officer in letter to SOW from Strasburg 12/3/62. Marriott was at that time with Maj. Ridgely Brown of the Md. Cav. NFR.

MARSHALL, JOHN PREVOST. Res. Washington, D.C. Grad. of Georgetown College 1859. Enl. as pvt. in Co. F, 1st Va. Inf. Regt., at Manassas 6/19/61. Trans. to Co. C, 1st Va. Art. Regt., sometime later. Abs. sick in Charlottesville 11/61. Disch. 11/13/61. Enl. as pvt. in 3rd Co. C, 1st Md. Inf. Regt., 3/25/62. Prom. 1lt. 7/1/62. Ordered to recruiting duty with the Md. Line 12/23/62. Marshall requested promotion to cpt. Ordered to duty with Gen. Lee 5/19/63. Served as acting ord. officer for Md. Line 5–8/63. Gen. Steuart requested Marshall's transfer to the South because of poor health 8/10/63. Marshall then ordered to S.C. 9/5/63. Relieved of duty at his own request 2/8/64 and assigned to light duty with Invalid Corps in Va. 3/9/65. Reportedly died shortly after the war from the effects of poor health.

MITCHELL, HUGH. Born in Charles Co. 8/9/38. Son of Gen. Walter Mitchell. Att. Charlotte Hall Academy and Princeton College. Appt. 1lt. in Co. I, 1st Md. Inf. Regt., 6/15/61. WIA at Upton's Hill 8/27/61. Pres. 11–12/61. Mitchell claimed later service with C.S. Signal Service at Pope's Creek to send messages across Potomac River between Md. and Va. Postwar farmer in Charles Co. Married Mary Risteau Jennifer at Good Hope, Baltimore Co., 11/15/71. Three children. Mitchell was a Democrat but changed allegiance to the Populist party and served as first Md. State president of that party. Offered colonelcy in Md. National Gd. by governor but refused. Died of Bright's disease at Linden in LaPlata 9/27/99.

MULLAN, JAMES. Served as 1lt. of Co. D, 39th Md. Militia Regt. Appt. 1lt. in Co. B, 1st Md. Inf. Regt., at Harpers Ferry by Ltc. Deas 5/21/61. Pres. 9–12/61. Listed in arrest 11–12/61 but no reason given. NFR.

MURRAY, CLAPHAM. Born 1838 at Woodstock in West River, Anne Arundel Co. Son of Alexander John Murray and Mary Clapham Murray. Brother of Cpt. William H. Murray. Went to Baltimore in 1855 to work. 1860 cen.: res. 11th Ward, Baltimore; age 19; clerk. 1860 Baltimore city dir. shows res. at 37 McCullough. 6'0", fair complexion, dark hair, dark eyes. Member of the Maryland Guard. Enl. as corp. at Richmond in 2nd Co. H, 1st Md. Inf. Regt., 6/18/61. Pres. 9–12/61. Prom. to sgt. 4/62. Disch. ETS 6/18/62. Enl. as pvt. in Co. A, 2nd Md. Inf., at Richmond 8/20/62. Elected 2lt. 8/27/62. Pres. 10–12/62. Prom. 1lt. 7/3/63. Furl. 30 days 10/31/63. Pres. 2–3/64. POW Weldon Railroad 8/19/64. At OCP 8/22/64. Sent to Ft. Delaware 8/27/64. Took OOA and rel. 5/31/65. Postwar Baltimore banker and tax official. Married Mary C. Gibson and had three children. Died at Woodstock 6/5/1925 and buried at Christ Church, West River.

MURRAY, WILLIAM H. Born at Woodstock in West River, Anne Arundel Co. 4/30/39. Prewar businessman in Baltimore and cpt., Co. D (Maryland Guard), 53rd Md. Militia, 1859–61. Appt. cpt. of 2nd Co. H, 1st Md. Inf. Regt., at Richmond 6/18/61. Abs. sick 9–10/61. Pres. 11–12/61. Considered for prom. to maj. in spring 1862 but refused. Elected cpt. in Co. A, 2nd Md. Inf., at Richmond 8/27/62. Pres. 10/62. Served as provost marshal at New Market 12/23/62. KIA at Gettysburg 7/3/63. Buried on the field and body later returned to West River. Monument dedicated to Murray at Confederate Lot, Loudoun Park Cemetery, Baltimore, 10/22/74.

NICHOLAS, WILSON CAREY. Born at Brooklyn Navy Yard, N.Y., 9/3/36. Son of Cpt. John S. Nicholas of the U.S. Navy and Esther Stevenson. Descended from early settlers in Va. and Md. Paternal grandfather commanded Washington's Life Guard during the American Revolution and later served as member of Va. House of Delegates, U.S. Congress, and governor of Va. Grandfather was friend of Thomas Jefferson and is buried at Monticello. Wilson C. Nicholas moved to Baltimore as a baby and was raised by aunt there. Educated in Baltimore and at

Oxford College, Md. Worked with B&O Railroad before the war. 1860 cen.: res. Reistertown, Baltimore Co. Appt. cpt. of Co. G, 1st Md. Inf. Regt., at Harpers Ferry by Ltc. Deas 5/22/61. Abs. sick at Charlottesville 10/1/61. Pres. 11–12/61. Recommended for promotion to maj. 5/3/62 but not appt. Appt. 1lt./drillmaster on Col. B. T. Johnson's staff 9/1/62. Resigned 10/4/62. Later recommended by Col. Johnson for appt. as cpt./AAG but denied 2/19/63. Ordered to duty with Col. Johnson 3/25/63 and appears as cpt/AIG with Col. Johnson 6/63. Nicholas then served as cpt/AIG of Md. Line 6/18/64. POW at Rockville 7/12/64. At OCP 7/13/64 and sent to Ft. Delaware 7/22/64. On list of POWs to be sent to Hilton Head, S.C., 8/20/64 but did not go. Exch. 10/31/64. Nicholas claims prom. to maj. and paroled at Charlottesville 5/10/65. Postwar farmer at Atamsco in the Caves Valley area of Baltimore Co. Married Augusta Moale 10/66 and had ten children, eight living. Nicholas was a Democrat, Mason, and did not belong to any church.

O'BRIEN, EDMUND. 1860 cen.: res. Carroll Co.; age 30; lived in hotel; born in Md. Appt. 1lt. of Co. E, 1st Md. Inf. Regt., at Harpers Ferry 5/22/61. Prom. to cpt. 8/18/61. Pres. 9–12/61. Adm. GH 21, Richmond, with fracture 3/20/62. RTD 5/5/62. Wrote letter of resignation at Pt. Republic for broken ankle and unfitness 6/13/62. Resignation accepted 7/23/62. Requested to be assigned to duty from Charlottesville 11/28/62. NFR.

PITTMAN, ALEXANDER McK. Born c. 1835. Bookkeeper. 1860 Baltimore city dir. shows res. at 28 N. Greene St. Son of Edward Pittman, stockbroker. 5'10", dark complexion, black hair, black eyes. Pittman served in Nicaragua with filibuster Walker 1855. Lost his arm there 4/11/55. Appt. 1lt. in 1st Co. H, 1st Md. Inf. Regt., at Harpers Ferry 5/21/61. All the officers of this co. resigned. Appt. 2lt. of Co. B, 24th Bn. Va. Partisan Rangers, 5/20/62. Tendered resignation at Charlottesville because of ill health 9/1/62. POW 10/1/62. At OCP and sent to Ft. Monroe 10/31/62. Exch. at Aiken's Landing 11/2/62. Applied for position as drillmaster or enrolling officer in Richmond 5/1/63. Pittman later worked as superintendent of saltworks in Alabama. Pittman left Richmond 12/64 and surrendered to Union officials at Lancaster Wharf on the Potomac River 1/16/65. Held at Pt. Lookout and forwarded to Washington. Desired to take OOA. Judged to be dangerous and ordered to be held at Ft. Delaware. Sent from Washington to Ft. Delaware 2/3/65. Took OOA and rel. 5/10/65.

PLATER, JOHN EDWARD. Res. Nottingham, Baltimore Co. Son of Dr. William Plater. Att. Georgetown College 1849–55. 1860 Baltimore city dir. shows res. at southeast corner of Franklin and Park sts. Bookkeeper. Appears as 2lt. of Chesapeake Artillery (4th Md. Btry.). Pres. 1–2/63 and 5–6/63. According to sentence of court-martial held at Ewell's Corps 9/5/63, Plater was tried and convicted of misbehavior before the enemy and ordered to be dismissed. Pres. Davis later commuted the sentence to suspension of pay and rank for four months to date from 9/23/63. Plater was restored to duty 2/20/64. Dropped from the service 6/6/64. NFR. A John R. Plater, a native of Talbot Co. and 73 years old, is noted in an obituary in the Baltimore *Sun* as dying of heart disease in a boardinghouse in Baltimore 11/8/96. The paper describes Plater as a C.S. veteran (unit not specified) who married a woman from Lynchburg, Va., during the war. The couple separated and Plater returned to Talbot Co. In the summer of 1871, the wife visited Plater in Md. but returned to Va. shortly afterward. She then came back in Dec. 1871 and was shortly found dead in a field with a bottle of chloroform and an envelope of strychnine. She was initially thought to have committed suicide, but later her husband was arrested and convicted of manslaughter. Plater was sented to the state penitentiary for five years (2/8/73–4/2/78) but pardoned by the governor before the completion of sentence. It is not clear if John E. and John R. Plater are the same.

POLK, JOHN W. 1860 cen.: res. Princess Anne, Somerset Co.; age 26; clerk; born in Md.; son of William T. G. Polk, merchant; $18,500/$18,000. 5'9", dark complexion, dark hair, hazel eyes. Enl. as pvt. in Co. F, 2nd Md. Inf., at Richmond 9/10/62. Elected 1lt. 10/28/62. Pres. 10–12/62. Pres. 9–10/64 and 1–2/65. Commanded co. at Weldon Railroad 8/64 and listed as commander through early 1865. Abs. furl. 30 days 1/28/65. POW Hatcher's Run 4/2/65. At OCP 4/5/65. Sent to Johnson's Island 4/9/65. Took OOA and rel. 6/19/65.

PRICE, FRANK S. Served as cpt. of 1st Co. C, 1st Md. Inf. Paid as such 7/1/61 through 8/24/61 although co. disbanded before that time. Appears to have enl. as corp. in 2nd Co. C, 1st Md. Inf., at Richmond 5/21/61. Abs. sick since 10/9/61. Wrote letter to SOW 3/3/62 and again in 1863. NFR.

PUE, EDWARD H. D. 1860 cen.: res. Bel Air, Harford Co.; age 20; born in Md.; son of Michael E. and Elizabeth Pue; farmer; $20,000/$5,000. 6'1", light complexion, light hair, light eyes. Occupation farmer. Enl. as pvt. in 2nd Co. K, 1st Va. Cav. Regt., at Leesburg 5/14/61. Pres. 8/61 through 12/64. Adm. Chimb. hospital 11/29/61. RTD 12/13/61. Appears as disch. for ETS 5/14/62 but Pue must have reenl. Elected 2lt. 10/1/63. Later served as 2lt. in Co. K, 1st Md. Cav. Claimed to have been WIA at Gettysburg, Spotsylvania, Reams Station, and three times during the Shenandoah Valley campaign. NFR. Postwar farmer in Harford Co. Married Cornelia Dunn and had four children. Pue died of Bright's disease at Woodview near Bel Air 12/23/1905. Buried at St. Mary's Episcopal Church in Emmorton.

PUE, JAMES A. VENTRESS (or VENTRIS). Born 7/20/41. Res. Howard Co. 6'1", light complexion, light hair, blue eyes. Enl. as sgt. in 2nd Co. K, 1st Va. Cav. Regt., at Leesburg 5/14/61. Pres. 7–8/61. Adm. Chimb. hospital with icterus 10/22/61. RTD 11/20/61. Pres. 11–12/61 through 3–4/62. Appt. 2lt. in Co. A, 1st Md. Cav., 11/12/62. Pres. 11–12/62. WIA shoulder Greenland Gap 4/25/63. Pres. 9–10/63 through 4/64. WIA thigh at Beaver Dam 5/9/64. Pue and Cpt. Schwartze were taken to nearby house of Mr. Redd and later made POW 5/24/64. Both men taken by Union troops to Fredericksburg and placed on U.S. hospital steamer *Connecticut* 5/25/64. At OCP 7/4/64 and later at Lincoln Hospital, Washington, D.C., 7/11/64. Sent to Ft. Delaware 7/22/64. Sent to Hilton Head 8/10/64. One of the Immortal Six Hundred. At Ft. Pulaski 10/20/64 and 12/26/64. Returned to Ft. Delaware 3/12/65. Took OOA and rel. 6/16/65. Postwar judge in Texas.

PURNELL, GEORGE WASHINGTON. Born 1841. Res. Snow Hill, Worchester Co. Son of William V. and Eleanor H. (Robins) Purnell. Descendant of early Md. settlers. Att. Snow Hill Academy. Entered University of Virginia in 1858 but forced to leave because of poor health. Att. Princeton College 1859 but forced to leave at outbreak of the war. 5'8", dark complexion, dark hair, hazel eyes. Enl. as pvt. in Co. M, 23rd Va. Cav. Regt. (Sturgis Davis' former co.), at Richmond 6/20/63. Prom. 2lt. in Co. B, 2nd Md. Cav., 9/63. POW Piedmont 6/5/64. Sent to Johnson's Island 6/25/64. Took OOA and rel. 6/15/65. Applied for presidential pardon from Snow Hill 8/21/65. Returned to Worchester Co. after war and tried to establish business. Grad. University of Virginia law school 1868 and adm. to Md. Bar at Snow Hill. Opened own practice and married Margaret D. Bowen in 1870. Three children. Successful lawyer and large landowner in Worchester Co. Served as presidential elector on Democratic party ticket in 1896. Died of Bright's disease at Snow Hill 5/8/99.

QUINN, JOSEPH P. Claimed to be a British subject. Elected. 2lt. in Co. E, 2nd Md. Inf., 9/13/62. Pres. 10–12/62. Under arrest with charges preferred by Cpt. Murray at New Market 12/62. POW "through his own indiscretion" at Winchester 6/13/63. Sent to Ft. McHenry from Harpers Ferry 6/26/63. Sent to Johnson's Island 7/20/63. Trans. to Pt. Lookout 3/14/65. Exch. 3/22/65. NFR.

RASIN, WILLIAM INDEPENDENCE. Born 7/4/42 in Kent Co. Son of Macall Medford Rasin. Moved to St. Louis in 1848 to live with uncle there after father's death. Went to Leavenworth, Kan., to establish own business in 1858. Served in Missouri with Sterling Price. Returned to Md. at outbreak of the war. Appt. cpt. of Co. E, 1st Md. Cav., at Richmond 1/20/63. WIA saber cut to head at Middletown 6/12/63. Pres. 7–8/63. Adm. Charlottesville hospital with fever

9/23/63. RTD 10/13/63. Company fuel requisition shows 1 cpt., 3 lts, and 40 em's present 11/63. Two months later there was one less lt. and two more em's. Adm. GH 4, Richmond, 3/8/64. RTD 4/17/64. Pres. 7–8/64. Adm. Charlottesville hospital for wound on left side of head 10/6/64. RTD 10/18/64. Readm. Charlottesville hospital with gonorrhea 11/10/64. RTD without regular disch. 2/28/65. Listed as pres. in arrest (cause unknown) 11–12/64. Rasin participated in last C.S. charge at Appomattox 4/9/65. Unit disbanded without parole. Postwar commission merchant in Baltimore with Henry McCoy and later city revenue collector. Later worked in Newport News, Va., with English shipping company. Married in 1867 to Mary A. Garnett. He died at Newport News 6/18/1916.

RICHARDSON, WILLIAM H. Born c. 1838. Res. Harford Co. 5'11", fair complexion, light hair, blue eyes. Enl. as pvt. in Co. F, 12th Va. Cav. Regt., at Staunton 5/26/62. Pres. 7–8/63 and 3–4/64. Trans. to Co. F, 2nd Md. Cav., 4/29/64. Appears as 1lt. of Co. F. POW Moorefield 8/7/64. Sent to Wheeling from Harpers Ferry 8/10/64. Then sent to Camp Chase 8/12/64. Trans. to City Point for exch. 3/2/65. Paroled at Staunton 5/27/65. Listed as living in Austin, Texas, 1918.

ROBERTS, BENJAMIN G. 1860 cen.: res. Sudereville, Queen Anne Co.; age 27; farmer; born in Md.; $2,500/$1,000; lived with another farmer who had four black field hands. Elected 2lt. in Chesapeake Artillery (4th Md. Btry.) after the death of John Grason at Fredericksburg 12/13/62. Pres. 5–6/63 and 9–10/63. Possibly WIA at Gettysburg 7/2/63. Adm. Charlottesville hospital 11/18/63. Died of typhoid fever at Charlottesville 12/1/63.

ROBERTS, JOSEPH KENT, JR. Born 3/13/40 at Rosemount in Bladensburg, Prince Georges Co. Son of Joseph K. Roberts and Amelia Williams. Att. Georgetown College 1854. Also att. St. John's College. Lawyer. 5'5, light complexion, light hair, blue eyes. Enl. as pvt. in Co. E, 1st Md. Cav., at Richmond 10/31/62. Prom. 2lt. 2/1/63. Pres. 7–12/63. Adm. Charlottesville hospital with acute diarrhea 9/30/63. RTD 10/27/63. Appt. judge advocate for court-martial duty with Fitz Lee's Cavalry Division 10/6/63. Pres. 4/1/64 and 7–12/64. WIA right hip at Winchester 9/19/64. Adm. Charlottesville hospital with acute diarrhea 9/30/64. RTD 10/27/64. NFR. Att. University of Virginia after the war. Postwar planter and lawyer in Prince Georges Co. Member Md. legislature 1880. Appt. U.S. collector of internal revenue 1886. Married Edith P. Bowie 6/7/66. Died at Upper Marlboro, Prince Georges Co., 10/1/88. Buried at Holy Trinity Church, Bowie. Gen. Johnson and Cpt. Torsch attended funeral and presented resolutions of the Confederate Society of the Army and Navy. Cpt. Rasin served as committee member to raise funds for monument to Roberts.

ROBERTSON, MICHAEL STONE. 1860 cen.: res. Tompkinsville, Charles Co.; age 22; farmer; born in Md.; ———/$8,500. Appt. cpt. of Co. I, 1st Md. Inf. Regt., 6/15/61. Co. fuel requisition shows 1 cpt., 2 lts., 67 em's, and 2 laundresses or servants 7/12/61. Abs. sick at Centreville 10/29/61. Pres. 11–12/61. KIA at Harrisonburg 6/6/62. Eugene Digges served as administrator of will.

ROSS, DAVID M. Born c. 1835. Res. Kent Co. 6'0", fair complexion, black hair, blue eyes. Ross appears as a pvt. in Co. K, 12th Va. Cav. Regt. AWOL 9–10/62. He is then listed as cpt. of Co. C, 2nd Md. Cav. No date of appt. given. Signed for ord. stores 10/18/63. Abs. detached service for 115 days to gather grain for Gen. Early's army 10/25/64. Paroled at Staunton 5/24/65.

ROUSSELOT, C. A. Resigned as 2lt. of Co. D, 2nd Md. Cav., 2/23/64. Cpt. Redmond Burke of Co. D declared Rousselot "incompetent to fulfill the duties of an officer." NFR.

SCHWARTZE, AUGUSTUS F. Born c. 1839 in Baltimore. Enl. as pvt. in Co. A, 1st Md. Cav., at Manassas 8/31/62. Trans. to Co. F upon prom. to cpt. 7/16/63. Pres. 9–12/63. Co. fuel requisition shows 1 cpt., 3 lts., and 38 em's at Hanover Junction 11/63. Two months later the number of em's decreased by 11. WIA at Beaver Dam 5/27/64. Removed to house of Mr. Redd until taken by Union troops as POW. DOW at Lincoln GH, Washington, D.C., 6/12/64. Buried at National Cemetery.

SHEARER, GEORGE M. E. Born c. 1841. Res. Nevada Co., Calif. 6'2", fair complexion, light hair, blue eyes. Appt. 2lt. in Co. A, 1st Md. Inf. Regt., at Harpers Ferry by Ltc. Deas 5/21/61. Pres. 9–12/61. Defeated for reelection 4/29/62. POW near Hancock, Md., by 1st Vermont Cav. 7/25/62. Sent to Ft. McHenry 7/29/62. Trans. to Ft. Delaware 8/12/62. Returned to Ft. McHenry 10/10/62. Exch. at Aikens Landing 11/10/62. Appt. 1lt./drillmaster to 1st Md. Cav. 12/5/63. Listed in Baltimore *American* on 1/6/64 as political prisoner at Ft. Delaware for burning bridges on the B&O Railroad 7/25/62 and making maps of roads in Washington and Frederick Co.s for use by C.S.A. POW at Hagerstown 7/5/64. Sent to Ft. Delaware from Harrisburg 7/9/64. Sent to Ft. McHenry 8/14/64 and then to Washington, D.C., as witness in spy case of Hammond Claude. Returned to Ft. Delaware from OCP 10/23/64. Took OOA and rel. 6/17/65.

SHELLMAN, GEORGE KREBS. 1860 cen.: res. Frederick, Md.; age 40; born in Md.; lived in hotel. Noted as lawyer in obituary. Appt. 1lt. in Co. A, 1st Md. Inf. Regt., at Harpers Ferry by Ltc. Deas 5/21/61. Pres. 9–12/61. Acting qm. since

9/22/61. Appt. Cpt./ACS for 1st Md. but declined 4/15/62. Exch. at Aikens Landing 10/6/62. Not known where POW. Paid in Richmond 6/63 while awaiting orders 1–4/63. Ordered to report to Gordonsville for PM duty 8/25/63. Paroled at Appomattox 4/9/65. Remained in Va. until 1876, when he returned to Frederick. His health deteriorated and Shellman entered the Confederate Soldiers Home at Pikesville, where he died 5/25/91.

SLINGLUFF, FIELDER CROSS. Born 6/16/42 in Baltimore Co. Son of Jesse Slingluff and Frances E. Cross. Father was descended from a German Dunker family that moved to Baltimore after the American Revolution. By time of the war, Jesse Slingluff was city banker and merchant. 6'0", light complexion, brown hair, gray eyes. Occupation student. Grad. Yale College. Enl. as pvt. in Co. A, 1st Md. Cav., at Manassas 8/31/62. Trans. to Co. F upon prom. to 2lt. 7/16/63. Pres. 9–12/63. Adm. GH 4, Richmond, with gonnorhea 2/25/64. POW at Moorefield 8/7/64. Sent from Harpers Ferry to Wheeling 8/10/64. Sent to Camp Chase 8/11/64. Trans. to City Point for exch. 3/2/65. Paroled at Mechanicsville 4/29/65. Postwar lawyer in Baltimore. Died of heart disease in Baltimore 5/20/1918. Buried in Greenmount Cemetery, Baltimore.

SMITH, JOHN LOUIS. Res. Baltimore. Appt. 2lt. in Co. G, 1st Md. Inf. Regt., at Harpers Ferry by Ltc. Deas 5/22/61. Trans. to Co. G upon prom. to cpt. 7/1/61. Pres. 9–12/61. Served as PM of Winchester 10/62. Appt. cpt./AAG 1/8/63 with DOR 12/2/62. Served as cpt./AAG at Richmond 4/17/63 through 3/23/64. Ordered to Danville and Petersburg to inspect staffs 8/4/63 and 10/26/63. Recommended for promotion to maj. by Gen. Elzey 12/21/63. This does not appear to have taken place. Relieved of duty with Department of Richmond and ordered to Md. Line 4/30/64. Took command of Camp Maryland 8/5–9/21/64. Ordered to Gen. Gardner at Richmond 10/4/64. Served as inspector of various C.S. units till end of war. NFR.

SMITH, ROBERT CARTER. Born 1828 in Baltimore. Grandson of Baltimore War of 1812 gen. Samuel Smith, who also served as congressman and mayor of Baltimore. 1860 Baltimore city dir. shows res. at 23 Hamilton St. Clerk. Member of Co. C, Md. Guard, 1860. Signed petition as 2lt. in Co. A, Weston's Bn., in Richmond 1861. Appt. 2lt. in 2nd Co. C, 1st Md. Inf. Regt., at Richmond 5/17/61. Prom. cpt. 10/9/61. Abs. sick at Charlottesville 10/29/61. Pres. 11–12/61. Elected cpt. of Co. C, 1st Md. Cav., 8/4/62. WIA at Greenland Gap 4/25/63. Abs. from command through summer 1863. Pres. 9–12/63. Co. fuel requisition shows 3 lts. and 72 em's at Hanover Junction 11/63. Prom. maj. 8/20/63 and ltc. 6/1/64. Unable to accept latter promotion because of disabling wounds. Retired to Invalid Corps 12/2/64. Briefly detailed as commandant of

Danville military prison 10/64. Paroled at Salisbury, N.C., 5/1/65. Unmarried. Died at Catonsville 2/13/1900. Buried at Loudoun Park Cemetery, Baltimore.

SMITH, THOMAS JEFFERSON. Born c. 1824. Res. Baltimore. Farmer. 5'9", dark complexion, dark hair, gray eyes. Smith was paid as 2lt. in Co. G, 7th Va. Cav. Regt., 10–11/61 and 1–2/62. Elected 2lt. in Co. C, 1st Md. Cav., 8/4/62. Abs. with broken leg from Sharpsburg at Charlottesville 11–12/62. Pres. 7–8/63. Prom. 1lt. 8/25/63. Abs. 15 days furl. to Albermarle Co. to visit relatives 1/3/64. Pres. 4/1/64. POW at Moorefield 8/7/64. Sent to Wheeling from Harpers Ferry 8/10/64. Sent to Camp Chase 8/12/64. Trans. for exch. 3/2/65. NFR.

SMITH, THOMAS WASHINGTON. Res. Cecil Co. Enl. as pvt. in Cpt. Davidson's Btry., Va. Light Artillery (Letcher Artillery) in Richmond 2/17/62. Trans. to 3rd Co. C, 1st Md. Inf. Regt., 3/26/62. Prom. 2lt. 7/1/62. Resigned at Richmond 10/23/62. NFR.

SMYTH, WILLIAM. 1860 cen.: res. 15th Ward, Baltimore; age 29; clerk; born in Ireland; lived in National Hotel. Signed petition as sgt. in Co. A, Weston's Bn., at Richmond 1861. Enl. as pvt. in 2nd Co. C, 1st Md. Inf. Regt., at Richmond 5/17/61. Pres. 9–12/61. Prom. 1sg. 9/1/61. Prom. to 2lt. sometime after 12/61. NFR.

SNOWDEN, NICHOLAS N. 1860 cen.: res. Avondale near Laurel Factory, Prince Georges Co.; age 32; farmer; born in Md; wife and four children; $10,000/ $40,000. Att. Georgetown College 1843–46. Married Henrietta Stabler in 1850. Appt. 2lt. in Co. D, 1st Md. Inf. Regt., at Harpers Ferry by Ltc. Deas 6/1/61. Pres. 9–12/61. KIA at Harrisonburg 6/6/62. Recd. posthumous prom. to maj. His widow returned to her home in Montgomery Co. and lived at Ingleside until her death 5/1907.

STEWART, JOSEPH H. Born 5/10/41 in Cambridge, Dorchester Co. Son of John T. and Henretta Stewart. Farmer. Eleven other children. 5'11", fair complexion, brown hair, hazel eyes. Appt. as cadet to U.S. Military Academy from First Congressional District in Md. 7/1/60. Dismissed from West Point as deficient in mathematics and conduct 3/17/61. Enl. as sgt. in 2nd Co. H, 1st Md. Inf. Regt., at Richmond 6/18/61. Trans. to Co. F when elected 2lt. sometime in summer–fall 1861. Pres. 9–10/61. Pres. in arrest (reason not stated) 11–12/61. Applied for commission in RA 9/11/62. Stewart later served as sgt. in Co. A, 2nd Md. Inf. Noted as AWOL 12/20/62. POW Centreville 4/5/63. At OCP

4/23/63. Trans. Pt. Lookout 9/26/63. Exch. 12/24/63. Adm. Chimb. hospital with debility 12/29/63. Deserted 1/4/64. Wrote letter to SOW from Richmond for commission 1/28/64. Supported by letters of Gen. Steuart and Gov. Letcher. Also applied for appt. in Treasury Department 3/3/64. He recd appt. as 2lt. 2/17/64. Paroled in Macon as 1lt. 5/4/65. Paroled again at Nashville 7/24/65 and arrived in Middle Military Department 8/2/65. Died at New York City 8/14/90.

STEWART, SEPTIMUS H. 1860 Baltimore city dir. shows res. at Howard House. Bookkeeper. Appt. 1lt. in 2nd Co. C, 1st Md. Inf. Regt., at Richmond 5/17/61. Abs. sick at Centreville 10/29/61. Pres. 11–12/61. Appt. cpt./AQM 4/16/62 with DOR of 3/15/62 but appears as POW at Manassas 3/9/62. Exch. at Aikens Landing from Ft. Delaware 8/5/62. Adm. Richmond MDO 8/26/62. Dropped as cpt./AQM 8/30/62. Stewart later served as cpt. of Co. N, 2nd Regt. Va. State Reserve Forces. Paroled at Appomattox 4/9/65. At PMO Washington, D.C., 4/22/65.

STEWART, THOMAS RICHARD. 1860 cen.: res. Cornersville, Dorchester Co.; age 28; farmer; born in Md. Married within the year to Hester. Enl. as pvt., Co. G, 2nd Md. Inf., at Richmond 10/31/62. Elected 1lt. 12/24/62 and then cpt. 1/26/63. WIA severely at Gettysburg 7/3/63. Unable to return to unit because of wounds and appt. recruiting officer for Md. Line 12/7/63. Assigned to duty at Andersonville prison 8/22/64. Relieved because of reduction in officers 3/22/65. Paroled at Augusta, Ga., 5/6/65. Died in Baltimore 11/26/1908.

STONE, JOHN H. Born 8/12/32 in Charles Co. Son of Joseph and Sara Stone. Father was county tax collector and planter. After father's death in 1846, family split and John Stone lived with uncle and, later, older brother. 1860 Cen.: res. Doncaster, Charles Co.; age 28; farmer; ———/$1,200; owned one slave; unmarried; Roman Catholic. Enl. as sgt. in Co. I, 1st Md. Inf. Regt., at Richmond 6/15/61. Pres. 9–12/61. Adm. GH 1, Danville, with diarrhea 1/21/62. Trans. to Charlottesville and Richmond. Disch. 6/30/62. Elected 1lt. of Co. B, 2nd Md. Inf., at Richmond 8/27/62. Pres. 10–12/62. Pres. 2–3/64. Commanded co. at Cold Harbor and WIA left leg 6/2/64. Adm. Chimb. hospital 6/6/64. Furl. 50 days 9/17/64. Adm. Chimb. hospital with chronic diarrhea 9/22/64. Furl. 50 days 9/28/64. Adm. GH 4, Richmond, 10/3/64. Furl. 50 days to Bainbridge, Ga., 11/1/64. Adm. Stuart hospital with debilitas 12/2/64. RTD 2/2/65. Requested assignment to light duty because of wounds 12/5/64. Ordered to Salisbury, N.C., in early 1865. NFR. Returned to Charles Co. briefly after war. Worked with sewing machine manufacturing company throughout the South. Died in Baltimore from effects of broken hip 1/6/1907 and buried at Cathedral Cemetery.

STONESTREET, JOSEPH HARRIS. 1860 cen.: res. Port Tobacco, Charles Co.; age 33; planter; born in Md.; $14,000/$20,000; single; son of Charles H. Stonestreet. Att. Georgetown College 1839–42. Enl. as sgt. in Md. Artillery (1st Md. Btry.) at Fredericksburg 6/27/61. Pres. 9–10/61 through 1–2/65. WIA in chest at Mechanicsville 6/25/62. Elected 2lt. 7/25/62. Adm. Charlottesville hospital 8/11/62. RTD 8/23/62. Apparently court-martialed 12/26/63. Offered to resign 8/1/64 but not accepted. Paroled at Appomattox 4/9/65 and again at Washington, D.C., 4/22/65.

SUDLER, JOHN EMORY. 1860 ccn.: res. Still Pond, Kent Co.; age 21; farmer; son of Emory and Elizabeth Sudler, farmer; $12,000/$5,500. Cpt. of Co. E, 2nd Md. Cav. Paroled at Mechanicsville 4/25/65.

THOMAS, GEORGE. Born at Mattaponi, St. Marys Co. 8/35. 1860 cen.: res. Great Mills, St. Marys Co.; age 25; farmer; son of Jan Thomas, farmer; $25,000/ $36,000. Appears as 1lt. of Co. D, Weston's Bn., 1861. Appt. 1lt. of 2nd Co. H, 1st Md. Inf. Regt., at Richmond 6/18/61. Pres. 9–10/61 as commanding co. Served as 1lt./adj. 9/61 through 3/62. Adm. Charlottesville hospital with debility 10/4/61. RTD 10/12/61. Elected 1lt. of Co. A, 2nd Md. Inf., at Richmond 8/23/62. Pres. as acting adj. 10–12/62. Severely WIA in left thigh at Gettysburg 7/2/63. Prom. cpt. 7/3/63. Ordered to appear before examination board 12/17/63. Abs. furl. 3/25/64. Severely WIA at Pegram's Farm 9/30/64. Appears on furl. after that date until ass. to Ord. Department duty in early 1865. Paroled by 6th Army Corps (place not stated) 5/25/65. Thomas gave the dedication speech of the unveiling of the Md. Monument at Gettysburg 11/19/86. President of Confederate Society of St. Marys Co. Married Ellen Beal of Norfolk after the war. She was a nurse in Richmond and helped Thomas. He died 5/14/1903.

THOMAS, WILLIAM P. Member of Co. A, Weston's Bn., 1861. Appt. 2lt. of Co. C, 1st Md. Inf. Regt., at Richmond 5/17/61. Pres. 9–10/61. Commanding co. 10/29/61. Abs. sick in Richmond 12/19/61. NFR.

TOLSON, THOMAS HILL. Born in Prince Georges Co. 2/9/40. Moved to Baltimore in 1849. 1860 Baltimore city dir. shows office at 209 Ross St. and res. at 13 George St. Occupation clerk. 5'8", fair complexion, light hair, blue eyes. Enl. as pvt. in Co. C, 2nd Md. Inf., at Richmond 9/1/62. Elected 2lt. 11/24/62. Pres. 12/62. Slightly WIA at Gettysburg 7/2–3/63. Pres. 2–3/64. Severely WIA in right knee/thigh at Cold Harbor 6/3/64. Adm. Chimb. hospital 6/6/64. Furl. 40 days 7/7/64. Remained on furl. or at different hospitals throughout the fall of 1864. RTD 11/26/64. Signed fuel requisition at Petersburg showing 1 lt. and 24 em's in co. 12/15/64. Reported at Richmond headquarters 2/19/65. POW at Hatcher's Run 4/2/65. Sent OCP and then to Johnson's Island 4/9/65. Took OOA and rel. 6/20/65. Postwar resident of Baltimore and member of Society of the Army and Navy of the Confederate States and Confederate Veterans camp.

TORMEY, FRANK A. Born in Frederick c. 1834. 1860 Baltimore city dir. shows Tormey as a clerk with res. at 160 N. Calvert St. He may be the son of Francis D. Tormey, a Baltimore attorney. 5'9", fair complexion, dark hair, hazel eyes. Roman Catholic. Served as 2lt. of Winans Guard, 5th Md. Militia Regt. Tormey initially served as 2lt. of Co. F, 1st Md. Inf. Regt., but was forced out by the small size of the co. He resigned in the summer of 1861 although this resignation was lost. Attempted to resign again at Centreville 1/11/62. Noted by AAG that "this officer is doing nothing, nor has been since some time in October." Tormey later appears in Baltimore, where he surrendered to the Union PMO 12/17/62. Claimed to be an acting lt. of an independent Md. btry. (Holbrook's Btry.) with prior service at First Manassas, Leesburg, Vienna, Shiloh, Farmington, Memphis, and Vicksburg. Came to Baltimore to visit sick mother. When he reported to PMO, Tormey was drunk. He was held as a spy at Ft. McHenry 12/18/62. Declared innocent of the charges 12/24/62 and sent to Ft. Delaware 1/26/63. Returned to Baltimore and sent to City Point 4/6/63. POW near Memphis, Tenn., as cpt. of the 42nd Tenn. Cav. (a nonexistent unit) 10/15/63. Adm. Memphis hospital with gunshot wound 12/15/63. RTD as prisoner 12/20/63. Sent to Johnson's Island 12/23/63. Took OOA and rel. 5/16/65. Postwar manager of National Fireproofing Co. Married twice and had one son. Died of heart failure in Baltimore 2/5/1905. Buried from St. Ignatius R.C. Church in Baltimore.

TORSCH, JOHN W. Born in Baltimore 1834. Son of Henry F. Torsch. Educated in city public schools. Went to New York City to work as wood engraver with *Frank Leslie's* and *Harper's*. Returned to Baltimore and founded Baltimore *Illustrated News* but paper failed in Panic of 1857. Member of Law Greys, 53rd Md. Inf. Regt. 1860 Baltimore city dir. shows Torsch living at 44 Hill and office at 117 W. Baltimore St. 1860 cen. shows res. in hotel in 10th Ward. Appt. as 2lt. in Zarvona Zouaves, 2nd Co. H, 47th Va. Inf. Regt., 6/15/61. Pres. 3–4/62. Abs. sick in Richmond 4/30–6/15/62. Torsch later petitioned SOW for permission to make sketches of Richmond battlefields as a civilian 7/23/62 and 8/19/62. Apparently denied permission on both occasions. Elected cpt. of Co. E, 2nd Md. Inf., 9/13/62. Pres. 10–12/62. Abs. on recruiting duty in Charleston, S.C., 3/4/64. WIA in neck at Cold Harbor 6/3/64. Adm. Chimb. hospital 6/9/64. RTD 8/27/64. Pres. 9–10/64 and 1–2/65 as commanding unit. Signed fuel requisition for co. showing 1 cpt. and 18 em's 12/31/64. Paroled at Appomattox 4/9/65. Postwar Baltimore studio owner, militia officer, and city councilman. Organized James R.

Herbert Confederate Veterans camp. Died in Baltimore from complication of diseases 10/1/98. Buried at Loudoun Park Cemetery, Baltimore.

TURNBULL, S. GRAEME (or GRAHAM). 1860 cen.: res. Lauraville, Balti-more Co.; age 21; clerk; born in Md.; son of Henry C. and Anna G. Turnbull, farmer; $46,000/$2,000. Father born in Pa. and mother in Md. Graham was designated to recruit in Md. and obtain weapons for Weston's proposed unit in early 1862. Elected 2lt. of Co. C, 1st Md. Cav., 8/4/62. Abs. to get clothing in Richmond 11/18/62. Pres. 12/62. Died of diphtheria at Lacey Springs, Rocking-ham Co., 3/30/63. Obituary in Baltimore *Sun* 4/23/63.

WALTER, EDWARD H. 1860 cen.: res. 14th Ward, Baltimore; age 19; clerk; born in Md. 5′8″, light complexion, brown hair, brown eyes. Served as 2lt. in Co. C, 39th Md. Militia Regt., 1857. Appt. 2lt. in 1st Co. H, 1st Md. Inf. Regt. Paid for service 5/22–6/28/61. Later served as a scout for Fitz Lee. Paroled at Winchester 4/23/65.

WALTERS, JAMES D. Born c. 1834. Res. Harford Co. 5′0″, light complexion, red hair, blue eyes. Enl. as pvt. in Co. C, 1st Md. Cav., at Richmond 9/7/62. Pres. 7–8/63 through 11–12/64. Prom. corp. 8/1/63. Elected 2lt. 6/18/64. Signed fuel requisition for co. showing 1 lt. and 73 em's 9/30/64. Adm. Stuart hospital with scabies 2/24/65. RTD 3/11/65. Paroled at Staunton 5/15/65.

WARD, FRANCIS XAVIER. Born in Baltimore 7/11/39. Son of William Ward. Grad. Georgetown College 1859. Appt. secretary to U.S. legation to Central America by Pres. Buchanan. Resigned after Walker filibuster scandal. Returned to Baltimore to study law. 1860 Baltimore city dir. shows res. at 118 E. Baltimore St. Ward served as 1sg. of Co. F, Md. Guard, 1860–61. Struck by bullet in right hip during Baltimore riots 4/19/61. 2lt. in Co. D, Weston's Bn., 1861. Appt. 2lt. of 2nd Co. H, 1st Md. Inf. Regt., at Richmond 6/18/61. Abs. sick throughout most of 1861. Appt. 1lt./adj. 5/1/62. Served on Gen. Elzey's staff after disband-ment of 1st Md. Applied for clerkship with C.S. Treasury Department. 7/6/64. Appt. cpt./ADC to Gen. Wilcox 3/17/65. Paroled at Appomattox 4/9/65 and again in Richmond 5/29/65. Returned to Georgetown College for M.A. degree 1867. Postwar lawyer in Baltimore and Philadelphia. Ward's first wife was Mary Patten Wolfe. They appear to have been married during the war. He married second wife, Ellen Topham Evans, in 1874. She was a descendant of the first Md. governor after the American Revolution. Three children. Ward was a Democrat. Died in Philadelphia 8/9/1914. Buried from St. Ignatius Church in Baltimore.

WELLMORE, HENRY. Claimed res. in both Baltimore and Washington, D.C. 5'8", ruddy complexion, brown eyes, brown hair. Served as cpt. of 1st Co. H, 1st Md. Inf. Regt. All the officers of this co. resigned in late June 1861. POW at Charles Town, W.Va., 7/23/61. Held as prisoner in Baltimore and released on parole 8/6/61. Wellmore was suspected of being a Union spy and wrote Gen. Dix for assistance in getting exchanged. Wellmore later appears at PMO, Alexandria, Va., 11/16/64. He left the South because he was tired of the Confederacy and claimed that he had not been in service since 4/63. NFR.

WELLS, JOHN B. Born c. 1841. Res. Baltimore. 5'9", dark complexion, brown hair, hazel eyes. Appears as 2lt. of Co. A, 2nd Md. Cav., 2/1–8/31/64. Adm. Stuart hospital with syphilis 12/19/64. RTD 2/24/65. Paroled at Staunton 5/1/65 and again at Winchester 6/19/65.

WELSH, MILTON. Born c. 1843. Res. Hancock. 5'11", fair complexion, gray hair, brown eyes. Elected 2lt. of Co. D, 1st Md. Cav., at Winchester 9/20/62. Pres. 7–8/63 through 4/1/64. Abs. detached service to collect horses and stragglers in Shenandoah Valley in fall 1864. Pres. as commanding co. 11–12/64. Fuel requisition for co. shows 1 lt. and 57 em's 8–9/64. Paroled at Winchester with four enlisted men 4/28/65.

WELSH, WARNER GRIFFITH. 1860 cen.: res. Hyattstown, Frederick Co.; age 38; merchant; born in Md; widowed with seven children; $2,000/$21,560. Represented Montgomery Co. at state convention at Baltimore to advocate secession 2/18/61. Welsh served in the 7th Va. Cav. Regt. at the beginning of the war. Appt. 1lt. of Co. F, 12th Va. Cav. Regt., 4/10/62. Elected cpt. of Co. D, 1st Md. Cav., at Winchester 9/20/62. Pres. 11–12/62. POW near Winchester 5/10/63. Held by Union forces as a bushwacker because he was absent from unit with orders to attack Union pickets. Forwarded to Martinsburg 5/19/63 and then to Ft. McHenry 5/22/63. Escaped 6/10 or 6/15/63. Pres. 7–12/63 and 4/1/64. Fuel requisition for co. shows 1 cpt., 3 lts., and 42 em's at Hanover Junction 11/63. Requested 20 days furl. to visit Shenandoah Valley 2/22/64. Noted as AWOL 10/25/64 although listed as abs. sick on MR 11–12/64. Paroled at Salisbury, N.C., 5/1/65.

WILHELM, JAMES T. Born in Leonardtown, St. Marys Co., 1839. 1860 Baltimore city dir. shows Wilhelm as a clerk living at 169 Hanover St. Enl. as 1sg. of Baltimore Light Artillery (2nd Md. Battery) at Richmond 8/15/61. Pres. 9–12/61. Elected 2lt. 11/30/61. Adm. GH 21, Richmond, with chronic catarrhus

2/13/62. RTD 3/22/62. Pres. 12/62. Resigned 2/10/63. POW at Heathville 6/2/63. At OCP 7/1/63. Sent to Johnson's Island 8/8/63. Sent to Ft. Monroe suffering from chronic diarrhea 10/8/64. Exch. 10/11/64. Furl. 30 days from Richmond MDO 10/17/64. NFR. Grad. from University of Maryland Medical College after the war. M.D. in Baltimore. Married daughter of Walter Dorsey of Howard Co. Wilhelm died in Baltimore 12/26/82.

WILSON, JAMES HEBB. Born in St. Marys Co. 9/18/38. Res. Great Mills, St. Marys Co. Grad. St. John's College 1858. Taught school in Leonardtown. Adm. to bar in 1860. Lawyer. Served as pvt. in Co. B, 21st Va. Inf. Regt. Elected 2lt. of Co. B, 2nd Md. Inf., at Richmond 8/27/62. Pres. 10–12/62. WIA right elbow at Gettysburg 7/3/63. POW at Martinsburg 7/20/63. At Ft. McHenry from West Building hospital 10/22/63. Sent to Pt. Lookout 1/23/64. Applied for permission to visit "very sick" father in St. Marys Co. from Pt. Lookout 4/14/64. Exch. 4/27/64. Applied for clerkship with Treasury Department 5/25/64. Ass. to duty at Macon, Ga., POW camp 7/16/64. Given per diem while in charge of transporting Union POWs from Camp Lawton, Ga., to Florence, S.C., 11/21–28/64. Listed among C.S. troops surrendered to Union troops in Richmond hospitals 4/3/65. Adm. to Jackson hospital 4/10/65. Paroled 4/25/65. Postwar lawyer in St. Marys Co. Never married. Died in City Hospital, Baltimore, of congestion of the lungs 6/24/83. Buried at Poplar Hill Cemetery, St. Marys Co.

WISE, CHARLES BENNETT. Born c. 1840. Res. Great Mills, St. Marys Co. Son of Susanna Abell and Charles L. Wise. Entered Georgetown College 1859. Member of class of 1863 but did not graduate. 5'10", florid complexion, sandy hair, blue eyes. Enl. as pvt. in 2nd Co. H, 1st Md. Inf. Regt., at Fairfax CH 8/6/61. Pres. 9–12/61. Disch. 6/18/62. Elected 2lt. in Co. B, 2nd Md. Inf., at Richmond 8/27/62. Pres. 10–12/62. Pres. 2–3/64 through 1–2/65. Commanded co. 9–10/64. Fuel requisition shows 1 lt. and 30 em's at Petersburg 12/31/64. Tendered resignation 2/19/65. POW at Hatcher's Run 4/2/65. Sent OCP 4/5/65 and then to Johnson's Island 4/9/65. Took OOA and rel. 6/20/65. Postwar magistrate in St. Marys Co. Married Catherine Greenwell 12/27/65. Seven children. She died in 1882. Wise married Emily E. Cecil 1/6/84.

WRIGHTSON, WILLIAM C. Res. Hicksburg, Dorchester Co. Elected 2lt. of Co. G, 2nd Md. Inf., 12/24/62. KIA at Gettysburg 7/3/63.

ZOLLINGER, WILLIAM P. Born c. 1841. Res. 269 Madison Ave., 12th Ward, Baltimore. Occupation clerk. Born in Md. 5'8", light complexion, light hair, blue eyes. Enl. as pvt. in 2nd Co. H, 1st Md. Inf. Regt., at Richmond 6/18/61. Abs.

sick in hospital 10/6/61. Pres. 11–12/61. Disch. 6/30/62. Enl. as pvt. in Co. A, 2nd Md. Inf., at Richmond 8/20/62. Elected 2lt. 8/27/62. Pres. 10–12/62. Pres. 2–3/64 through 1–2/65. Commanding co. 9–10/64 and 1–2/65. Fuel requisition shows 1lt. and 36 em's at Petersburg 12/31/64. POW at Hatcher's Run 4/2/65. Sent OCP 4/5/65 and then to Johnson's Island 4/9/65. Took OOA and rel. 6/20/65. Postwar merchant. Died 7/11/89.

Union Officers of the 1st Maryland Infantry Regiment

ALBAUGH, MAURICE. Born c. 1824. 1860 Frederick city dir. shows Albaugh as a boot and shoe merchant on the west side of Market St. between Church and 2nd Sts. Enl. as pvt. in Co. F, 1st Pa. Vols., 12/15/46. Fought at La Hoya, Vera Cruz, Pueblo, Perote, Huamantla, Cerro Gordo, and Atlixco. Disch. 7/28/48. Appt. 2lt. of Co. H, 1st Md. Inf. Regt., at Frederick 5/20/61. POW at Ft. Royal 5/23/62. Paroled at Aiken's Landing 8/17/62. At Camp Parole in Annapolis 9/15/62. Exch. and sent to regt. 11/3/62. Prom. 1lt. 9/1/62 and cpt. of Co. E 4/16/63. WIA left thigh at Petersburg 7/8/64. Disch. for ETS 10/4/64. Albaugh was postwar resident of Baltimore. Married Frances M. Crumm at Frederick 10/23/62. No children. Albaugh died in Baltimore 10/28/75. His wife remarried and died 1/28/1913.

ARMACOST, JAMES T. 1860 cen.: res. Towsontown, Baltimore Co.; age 22; stonemason; born in Md.; wife born in Md. ———/$100. 5′7″, dark complexion, dark hair, black eyes. Enl. as pvt. in Co. G, 1st Md. Inf. Regt., at Relay House 5/27/61. Prom. corp. 3–4/62. POW at Ft. Royal 5/23/62. Prom. sgt. 11/25/62. Served as color sgt. 5–6/63. WIA at Weldon Railroad 8/18/64. Appt. 1lt. of Co. C 12/15/64. WIA minié ball in left thigh and into right hip at Five Forks 4/1/65. Prom. bvt. cpt. for gallant and meritorious service at Five Forks 4/1/65. MO 7/2/65. Postwar resident of Baltimore. Married Mary A. Smith at Brooklynville, Baltimore Co., 12/21/58. One child. Armacost died of heart disease in Baltimore 9/3/84. Buried at Baltimore Cemetery. His wife died 3/24/1902.

ARMACOST, LEWIS. Born in Baltimore c. 1840. 5′9″, light complexion, brown hair, gray eyes. Enl. as pvt. in Co. E, 1st Md. Inf. Regt., at Muddy Branch 11/10/61. Noted as AWOL 1/24–2/10/62. Sentenced to forfeit one month's pay. Prom. sgt. 5/25/62. Prom. 1sg. 9/17/64. Appt. 2lt. of Co. A 12/1/64. KIA at Dabney's Mill 2/6/65. Body left behind in enemy lines. Married Mary A. LaCount at Methodist Episcopal Church in Baltimore 4/19/64. She gave birth to Lewis Wilson Armacost 9/9/65 after death of the father. Widow remarried 3/23/69.

BAER, JAMES S. Born in Baltimore 7/17/34. Clerk. 5'5", light complexion, dark hair, dark eyes. Appt. 2lt. of Co. A, 1st Md. Inf. Regt., at Baltimore 6/30/61. Prom. 1lt. 11/1/61. WIA at Ft. Royal and POW 5/23/62. Prom. cpt. of Co. G 12/16/62. Baer was charged by Ltc. Wilson with violation of the 44th Article of War and drunkenness 9/19/63. Charged again by Ltc. Wilson with disobedience of orders and drunkenness on duty 12/15/63. Once more Baer was charged by Ltc. Wilson with drunkenness near Reams Station: "Was so intoxicated as to be unable for any duty whatever." Sentenced by general court-martial to be dismissed and to lose all pay and allowances 9/28/64. Baer later had a special act of Congress introduced which honorably discharged him from the army 8/9/1912. Married Susan Kimble Gessler at Timber Grove, Baltimore Co., 11/23/65. Three children. Wife died 8/7/1914. Baer died at Tannery, Carroll Co., 3/4/1917.

BAKER, JOHN J. Appt. 2lt. of Co. E, 1st Md. Inf. Regt., at Williamsport 9/23/61. Prom. 1lt. of Co. F 9/22/62. Dismissed from the service 3/30/63 with an effective date of 3/30/63. Recommended for reinstatement. NFR.

BAZIN, CASIMER. Born c. 1828. Enl. as pvt. in Co. K, Purnell Legion Regt. Inf., at Pikesville 3/19/62. Prom. corp. and later sgt. 1–2/63. Prom. 1sg. 10/1/63. WIA at Weldon Railroad 8/18/64. Trans. to 1st Md. Inf. Regt. upon muster out of Purnell Legion 10/23/64. Appt. 2lt. 12/6/64. Furl. 20 days to visit sick son in Wilmington, Del., 1/1/65. Tendered resignation to take care of business 5/29/65. Resignation accepted 5/31/65. NFR.

BRADSHAW, JOHN J. Appt. 2lt. of Co. C, 1st Md. Inf. Regt., at Williamsport 9/5/61. He resigned 9/7/61 and was dropped from the rolls 10/31/61. A man by the same name appears to have enl. as a pvt. in Co. C, 1st Md. Cav. Regt., 10/15/61. Deserted 7/16/62. Likewise, a John J. Bradshaw was appt. cpt. of Co. I, 6th Md. Inf. Regt., 8/25/62, at age 25. Prom. maj. (but not mustered) 4/25/65. Prom. bvt. maj. for gallant and meritorious service at Petersburg 4/2/65. MO 6/20/65.

BRASHEARS, WILLIAM G. Born in Md. c. 1840. Enl. as pvt. in Co. D, 1st Md. Inf. Regt., at Baltimore 5/16/61. Prom. sgt. 1/62. POW at Ft. Royal 5/23/62. Prom. 1sg. 11/23/62 and sgm. 12/16/62. Appt. 2lt. of Co. H 5/1/63. Suffered injuries to the spine when run over by a horse at Laurel Hill 5/8/64. WIA right thigh at Weldon Railroad 8/18/64. Disch. for disability 11/2/64. Postwar dry goods salesman in Baltimore. Married Mary E. Pattison sometime after the war. One child. Wife died 2/24/83. Brashears was adm. to Southern Branch National Home for Disabled Volunteer Soldiers after death of wife for epileptic attacks caused by war injuries. He died in Baltimore while on furl. from home 3/18/94.

CAMPER, CHARLES. Born c. 1833. Student in 1861. 5'5", dark complexion, dark hair, gray eyes. Appt. 2lt. of Co. K, 1st Md. Inf. Regt., 9/22/61. Prom. 1lt. of Co. D 9/22/62 and cpt. 3/6/64. WIA left arm between wrist and elbow at Harris Farm 5/19/64. Disch. for ETS 10/13/64. Enl. as pvt. in General Service with AGO 5/25/67. Disch. for ETS 5/25/70. Reenl. 5/25/71. Prom. sgt. 7/1/71. Disch. 7/1/74. Served as clerk with AGO. Married Elizabeth Hayne at Roman Catholic Church in Baltimore 4/26/64. Camper wrote *Historical Record of the First Regiment Maryland Infantry* in 1871. Camper died 12/2/85.

CARROLL, CHARLES. Born in Harford Co. c. 1842. Cooper. 5'8", fair complexion, sandy hair, blue eyes. Enl. as corp. in Co. I, 1st Md. Inf. Regt., at Relay House 5/27/61. WIA and POW near Harpers Ferry 8/27/61. Confined in Richmond and New Orleans. Delivered to Washington, D.C., 6/2/63. In meantime, Carroll prom. sgt. 9/62 and sgm. 4/12/63. Appt. 1lt. of Co. B 12/6/64. Appt. acting adj. 4/1/65. Tendered resignation to resume business 6/8/65. Resignation accepted 6/10/65. NFR.

CHASE, JOHN H. Born in Baltimore c. 1843. Occupation cigar maker. 5'7", fair complexion, light hair, blue eyes. Enl. as pvt. in Co. C, 1st Md. Inf. Regt., at Relay House 6/2/61. Prom. sgt. 7/4/61. WIA and POW at Ft. Royal 5/23/62. Paroled at Aikens Landing 9/13/62. Charged with AWOL at Maryland Heights 1/29–2/11/63. Pleaded guilty and sentenced to forfeit $13 2/11/63. WIA at Weldon Railroad 8/18–20/64. Prom. 1sg. 3/10/65. Appt. 2lt. of Co. A 4/26/65. MO 7/2/65. NFR.

CHILDS, JESSE D. Born in Baltimore c. 1840. 5'9", light complexion, light hair, blue eyes. Enl. as pvt. in Co. E, 1st Md. Inf. Regt., at Relay House 5/20/61. Prom. corp. 11/1/61, sgt. 1/1/62, and 1sg. 11/22/63. Childs captured a C.S. soldier at Spotsylvania 5/19/64. Received injury to eye by butt of musket at Cold Harbor 6/4/64. Appt. 1lt. of Co. C 9/13/64. Furl. 10 days to visit "aged mother" in Baltimore 11/15/64. Prom. cpt. of Co. F 12/15/64. Childs suffered contusion of head when assaulted in Baltimore 3/13/65. Prom. bvt. maj. for gallant service at Dabney's Mill 2/6/65. Appt. division pioneer officer 4/29/65. MO 7/2/65. Enl. as pvt. in U.S. Army for General Mounted Service 7/11/66. Served as recruiting sgt. in New York City when he became blind in both eyes. Disch. at St. Louis Barracks, Mo., 6/7/77. Childs married Sarah A. Eckles at Fourth Street Bethel Church in Carlisle, Pa., 11/14/66. No children. Childs died of paralysis of pneumogastric nerve in Carlisle 9/14/78. His wife died 1/4/1901.

COLEGATE, CHARLES E. Born c. 1828. Appt. 2lt. of Co. C, 1st Md. Inf. Regt., at Baltimore 5/11/61. Tendered resignation at Poolesville, Md., for "chills

& rheumatism" 10/22/61. Col. Kenly requested approval of resignation because otherwise he would have cashiered Colegate 10/29/61. Resignation accepted 11/2/61. NFR.

COLLIER, FRANK M. Born in Howard Co. 3/26/36. 1860 res. in Ellicott's Mills. Mechanic and clerk. 5'10", light complexion, dark hair, blue eyes. Appt. 1lt. of Co. F, 1st Md. Inf. Regt., at Relay House 5/20/61. POW at Ft. Royal 5/23/62. Prom. cpt. of Co. C 9/22/62. Dismissed for conduct unbecoming an officer 2/19/63. The order noted that "in tendering his resignation when leave of ab-sence for 48 hours was refused him, he having at the time but recently returned from a five months' absence from his command." Married Drucilla Harding at the First Presbyterian Church in Ellicott City 11/13/64. Four children. Collier died of intemperate use of tobacco and organic disease of the heart in Baltimore 9/19/1915. Buried at Loudoun Park Cemetery. His wife died 11/9/1925.

COLONEY, JOSIAH B. Born in Akron, Ohio, 6/3/35. Had an "academical edu-cation." Moved to Baltimore in 1852. Printer. Member of Baltimore City Guards before the war. Appt. 1lt. of Co. I, 1st Md. Inf. Regt., at Baltimore 5/15/61. Served as acting PM at Williamsport 8/9–10/15/61. POW at Ft. Royal 5/23/62. Appt. 1lt./adj. 10/4/62. Detailed to obtain drafted men in Baltimore and Wash-ington, D.C., 7/21/63. Coloney imprisoned at Ft. McHenry 10/13/63 and OCP 10/31/63 (no cause given). RTD 4/25/64. WIA in back and right hip at Weldon Railroad 8/21/64. Prom. maj. (but not mustered) 9/6/64. DOW in Philadelphia 10/9/64. Married Myron Herndon at Eutaw Street Methodist Episcopal Church in Baltimore 9/9/57. One child born 12/26/63. Wife died 3/25/1928.

CULLIMORE, WILLIAM H. Born c. 1837. Blacksmith. Enl. as sgt. in Co. G, 1st Md. Inf. Regt., at Baltimore 5/27/61. Prom. 1sg. 2/1/62. POW at Ft. Royal 5/23/62. Appt. 2lt. of Co. A 12/13/62. Broke right leg while on detached service in Baltimore in 1863. Disch. for disability in right leg 6/27/64. Postwar fruit grower and farmer in Centralia, Marion Co., Ill. Married in Cleveland, Ohio, 9/14/57. No children. Cullimore died 9/30/1908.

DEITZ, CHARLES ALOYSIUS. 1860 cen.: res. 2nd Ward, Baltimore; age 28; cuttler (tailor); born in Saxony, Germany; wife and three children; ———/$100. 5'8", light complexion, light hair, gray eyes. Enl. as sgt. in Co. B, 1st Md. Inf. Regt., at Baltimore 5/11/61. WIA by saber to forehead, left eye, lower lip, and right middle finger at Ft. Royal 5/23/62. POW at same battle. Prom. 1sg. 5/22/64. Appt. 2lt. of Co. E 12/6/64. Furl. 10 days to visit family in Baltimore 1/8/65. WIA in left side of face, impairing vision in left eye, at Dabney's Mill 2/5/65.

MO 7/2/65. Postwar tailor in Baltimore. Married Anna Maria Etzel at St. Alphonsus Roman Catholic Church in Baltimore 1/18/52. Deitz died of cirrhosis of the liver and kidney in Baltimore 7/18/1900. Buried at Holy Redeemer Cemetery. His wife died 12/26/1908.

DUDROW, CHARLES EDWIN. Born in Frederick Co. 4/13 or 30/39. Son of G. W. and M. E. Dudrow. Cigar maker. 5'9", fair complexion, light hair, gray eyes. Enl. as sgt. in Co. F, 1st Md. Inf. Regt., at Relay House 5/20/61. Prom. sgm. 11/16/61. Lost in action at Ft. Royal one dress coat, one overcoat, and one blanket 5/23/62. Appt. 2lt. 5/24/62. Noted as commanding co. 7/22/62. Tendered resignation at Baltimore 1/31/63 citing ill health and spine disease "which cause my *Inefficient Service* to the government." Col. Dushane refused to accept resignation because Dudrow was AWOL. Dudrow was ordered to report for examination. Resignation accepted 2/13/62. Appt. 1lt. of Co. A, 2nd Md. Cav. Regt., at Baltimore 6/18/63. Appt. RQM 10/1/63. MO 1/26/64. Postwar resident in Baltimore until 1908. Married Kate V. Donohue at St. Vincent's Roman Catholic Church in Baltimore 9/29/70. No children. Dudrow entered National Soldiers' Home in Hampton, Va., in 1908 and died there 10/20/1909. Wife died 7/5/1921.

DULANEY, BLADEN T. F. Born c. 1818. 1860 Baltimore city dir. shows res. at 85 Washington St. Service record claims that Dulaney served in prewar U.S. Army. Appt. cpt. of Co. A, 1st Md. Inf. Regt., 6/11/61. Resigned 11/4/61 to raise a new unit. Apparently this was not accomplished. Dulaney was later appt. 1lt. in Co. B, 2nd Md. Cav. Regt., at Baltimore 7/8/63. Dulaney court-martialed for accusing wife of an enlisted man of giving him a venereal disease. Commander at Annapolis recommended Dulaney for dishonorable disch. for conduct unbecoming an officer and gentleman 11/19/63. Dulaney had earlier shot a saloon owner in Annapolis 8/63. MO 1/26/64. NFR.

DUTTON, NORRIS B. 1860 cen.: res. 19th Ward, Baltimore; age 38; restaurant keeper; born in Delaware Co., Pa.; married with six children; ———/$300. 1860 Baltimore city dir. shows Dutton as barkeeper at 427 Saratoga St. Enl. as pvt. in Co. B, 1st Md. Inf. Regt., at Baltimore 5/11/61. Prom. corp. 6/23/61, 1sg. 8/4/61. Appt. 2lt. of Co. C 12/13/61. POW at Ft. Royal 5/23/62. Prom. 1lt. 5/1/63. Resigned because of physical disability 6/11/64. Postwar laborer in Baltimore. Married Margaret Bear in Delaware Co., Pa., 4/10/42. Dutton died 7/3/79.

EVANS, THOMAS R. Born c. 1837. Ambrotypist in Baltimore. 5'11", light complexion, brown hair, blue eyes. Appt. cpt. of Co. E, 1st Md. Inf. Regt., at Relay House 5/20/61. Abs. sick since 8/1/61. Tendered resignation for ill health at Boteler's Ford 9/19/61. Resignation accepted 9/21/61. Col. Kenly approved Evans' resignation 9/29/61 because otherwise he would have cashiered the officer. Postwar photographer in Washington, D.C. Married twice. One child. Evans was admitted to Central Branch of the National Home for Disabled Volunteer Soldiers 4/27/85. Evans died of alcohol and morphine poisoning in Louisville, Ky., 8/28/99. His widow testified that "the soldier was in the habit of going on sprees. He used to have a spree from 2 to 3 weeks about twice a year usually when he got his pension money. No, he was not a regular habitual drinker."

GALLAHER, JOHN H. Enl. as pvt. in Co. C, 1st Md. Inf. Regt., at Baltimore 6/10/62. Prom. corp. 11–12/62, sgt. 2/5/63, and 1sg. 7/27/63. Appt. 1lt. of Co. A 3/9/65. Furl. 20 days to visit brother in Baltimore who was wounded 4/20/65. MO 7/2/65. NFR.

GEORGE, WILLIAM E. 1860 cen.: res. Lauraville, Baltimore Co.; age 28; clerk; born in Md.; lived in hotel. 5'10", light brown hair, blue eyes. Appt. 1lt. of Co. K, 1st Md. Inf. Regt., 1/31/62. Appt. RQM 2/1/62. POW at Ft. Royal 5/23/62. RTD 8/31/62. George was held in close confinement at Maryland Heights 1/23/63 and charged by Cpt. Thomas S. J. Johnson with AWOL, disobedience of orders, conduct subversive to good order and military discipline, and conduct unbecoming an officer and gentleman. Col. Dushane reported on 1/30/63 that "this officer has been in close confinement since the 23rd Inst. by order of Cpt. Johnson commanding the detachment at outer battery—and in my judgment the good of the service will not be enhanced by his trial or further punishment." Prom. cpt. of Co. I 3/28/63. Abs. sick since 8/9/63. Resigned for disability 11/19/63. George wrote letter to Gov. Bradford asking for appt. with 100-day volunteers 6/4/64. Appt. maj. of the 11th Md. Inf. Regt. (100 days) 6/13/64. Charged with conduct prejudicial to good order and military discipline for taking money that should have been paid to substitutes. MO 10/1/64. Postwar court clerk in Baltimore. Married 6/5/67. No children. George entered Maryland Hospital for the Insane at Towsontown 7/15/78. He alleged that his insanity resulted from his having diarrhea and rheumatism along the Rappahannock River in 1863, which caused "softening of the brain." He suffered from delusions of grandeur and convulsive attacks. No signs of syphilis detected. He died at the hospital of general paresis paralysis 3/3/82. Buried at Greenmount Cemetery.

GILLINGHAM, CHRISTOPHER R. Born in Cockeysville, Baltimore Co., 1/2/44. 1860 cen.: res. 16th Ward, Baltimore; age 17; clerk; son of Edward and Catharine Gillingham; Father a conductor with B&O Railroad; six other children and one black servant; ———/$150. Brother of Edward and Henry Gillingham. 1860 Baltimore city dir. shows res. at 139 South Paca St. 5'11", dark complexion, brown hair, black eyes. Appt. 2lt. of Co. D, 1st Md. Inf. Regt., at Baltimore 5/16/61. Prom. 1lt. 2/1/62. POW at Ft. Royal 5/23/62. Prom. cpt. 4/12/63. Requested leave "for as long a time as can be consistently granted to go to Cincinnati Ohio to fulfill a matrimonial engagement" from Camp Pleasant near Harpers Ferry 4/15/63. Abs. on detailed service in Baltimore 3–4/64. Listed as AWOL 5/3/64. MO for ETS 5/23/64 (official notice received 8/3/64). Postwar clerk and general agent for Merchants' and Miners' Transportation Co. in Baltimore. Married Eliza J. Ebaugh 6/14/70. She died 6/22/70. Married Deblona M. Covey at Cambridge 9/16/79. One child. Died of apoplexy in Baltimore 12/16/1911.

GILLINGHAM, EDWARD E. 1860 cen.: res. 16th Ward, Baltimore; age 21; conductor with B&O Railroad; born in Baltimore; son of Edward and Catharine Gillingham; Father also a conductor with B&O Railroad; six other children and one black servant; ———/$150. Brother of Christopher and Henry Gillingham. 1860 Baltimore city dir. shows res. at 139 South Paca St. Appt. 2lt. of Co. E, 1st Md. Inf. Regt., 5/27/61. Prom. cpt. 9/21/61. Tendered resignation (no reasons stated) at Maryland Heights 12/24/62. Resignation accepted 1/13/63. Appt. cpt. of Co. B, 13th N.Y. Cav. Regt., at Camp Sprague, N.Y., 5/25/63. Charged with violation of 22nd Article of War by harboring a deserter from another unit in his co. at Ft. Haggerty 9/23/63. Abs. with leave 10/31–11/12/63. Noted as AWOL after that date until 12/17/63 although he was abs. on surgeon's certificate. Tendered resignation for disability at Vienna 3/31/64. Resignation accepted 4/4/64.

GILLINGHAM, HENRY RABORG. Born in Baltimore 1837. 1860 cen.: res. 16th Ward, Baltimore; age 24; conductor with B&O Railroad; son of Edward and Catharine Gillingham; father also a conductor with B&O Railroad; six other children and one black servant; ———/$150. Brother of Christopher and Edward Gillingham. 1860 Baltimore city dir. shows res. at 139 South Paca St. and occupation machinist. Appt. 2lt. of Co. B, 1st Md. Inf. Regt., at Baltimore 5/11/61. Prom. 1lt. 11/1/61. Prom. cpt. of Co. I 12/13/62. Tendered resignation because of "excessive corpulency" 1/19/63. Asst. surg. reported Gillingham had to ride in ambulance for the last three months. Resignation accepted 1/25/63. Postwar civil engineer in Baltimore, Washington, D.C., and North Carolina. Gillingham married Lizzie Morrice. He divorced her in Washington, D.C., 1/4/82. Married Alberta Stith Jones in Lutheran Church in Ward Mine, Davidson Co., N.C., 4/5/1905. Gillingham died 4/15/1905. In a letter to a congressman, Gillingham's second wife wrote about his first marriage: "You will understand that after Capt. Gillingham, first left the service, he was in dreadful health, for a long time, and as I understand, there was some woman, who acted in the capacity, of nurse, and he told me, that one morning, when he awoke, she told him, that they were married, had been married the night before, and he not knowing a word of it. . . . He told her, that he would not live with her, but she could go and get a divorce, putting all of the blame on him." Gillingham's second wife died in Cid, N.C., 2/21/1933.

HACK, HENRY C. Born c. 1833. 1860 Frederick city dir. shows Hack as a general intelligence agent in Frederick at 8 North Frederick St., res. 142 Lexington St. Appt. 2lt. of Co. I, 1st Md. Inf. Regt., at Relay House 5/27/61. Tendered resignation to attend "important Business which demands my early attention" 10/8/61. Col. Kenly requested the acceptance of his resignation "by reason of a generally insubordinate conduct" 10/11/61. Resignation accepted 10/22/61. Hack was later appt. 2lt. of Co. F, 1st Md. Cav. Regt., at Baltimore 10/25/61. Tendered resignation at Centreville to attend to "important private matters" 10/3/62. His commander requested approval because Hack was ordered before the examining board. "His character is such as to render him very obnoxious to all the Officers in the Regiment—he has at various times of *danger* absented himself from the Regt without leave—and has shown himself utterly [sic] incompetent to command the respect of either Officers or men." Disch. 12/1/62.

HAGGERTY, JOHN B. Born in Baltimore Co. c. 1836. Farmer. 5'7", dark complexion, black hair, brown eyes. Enl. as pvt. in Co. G, 1st Md. Inf. Regt., at Relay House 5/27/61. Served as regt. wagonmaster 8/61 through 6/62 and bde. wagonmaster 9/62 through 6/63. POW at Ft. Royal 5/23/62. Reduced to ranks 11/25/62. Appt. QM sgt. 8/22/63. Appt. 2lt. of Co. B 3/16/64. WIA at Harris Farm 5/19/64. Disch. for disease of lungs and throat contracted at the Wilderness 1/21/65. Postwar commission dealer in Elmira, N.Y. Married Elizabeth A. Kelley 8/54. She died 6/17/64. One child. Married Hannah A. Lunn at Methodist Episcopal Church in Elmira, N.Y., 7/13/66. Haggerty died of chronic bronchitis and tuberculosis in Elmira 5/17/78.

HAUGH, HENRY. Enl. as pvt. in Co. B, 1st Md. Inf. Regt., at Harrisonburg, Va., 4/24/62. POW at Ft. Royal 5/30/62 but released the same day. Prom. sgm. 9/18/62. Appt. 2lt. of Co. E 10/1/62. Requested furl. to receive legacy left by deceased relative at Frederick 5/28/63. Charged with drunkenness and conduct prejudicial to good order and military discipline by Ltc. Wilson 9/29/63. Prom. 1lt. of Co. D 3/6/64. Prom. cpt. of Co. B 10/24/64. Furl. 15 days to visit sick wife in Philadelphia 3/19/65. MO 7/2/65. NFR.

HEATH, LEVI THEODORE. Born in S.C. c. 1835. Instructor at the House of Refuge in Baltimore. Enl. as corp. in Co. G, 1st Md. Inf. Regt., at Relay House

5/17/61. Prom. sgt. 2/1/62. Noted as co. commander 6/21/62. Appt. 2lt. of Co. H 10/1/62. Prom. 1lt. 4/16/63. Served as bde. inspector 6/11/63. Preferred charges against Ltc. Wilson 11–12/63. KIA at the Wilderness while acting as bde. inspector 5/5/64. Body fell into enemy hands. Married Fannie Windsor at the Church of the Intercessor in Philadelphia 5/5/60. One child. Widow remarried 8/21/73.

HEINE, PETER BERNARD WILHELM. Born in Dresden, Germany, 1/30/27. Served as artist with Commodore Perry in his voyage to Japan. Appt. as cpt. of Co. I, 1st Md. Inf. Regt., by the U.S. SOW 12/9/61. Heine never served with 1st Md. He was on topographical engineer staff of Maj. Gen. John A. Dix at Ft. Monore in the spring of 1862. Heine was arrested 5/4/62 because a map of the approaches to Yorktown appeared in *Harper's Weekly* although Heine claimed he did not make the map or give it to the paper. Heine appealed to Gens. Kearney, McClellan, and Dix and President Lincoln. He wrote to Gen. Williams from Ft. Wool 5/16/62: "Today is the twelfth day since my arrest and still I am kept in confinement without even charges preferred against me, beyond a vague intimation that I am suspected of disloyalty. Is this lawful?" Heine was released and ordered to his regt. 6/14/62. POW near Bottoms Bridge 6/30/62. Imprisoned at Libby Prison. Wrote to Gen. Dix for assistance from Richmond 7/14/62. Exch. at Aikens Landing 8/12/62. Requested furl. to go to New York to recover health and business 8/22/62. Heine was rearrested and held at Ft. Monroe 9/62. Requested court of inquiry 10/8/62. Resigned 12/7/62. Heine was later appt. col. of 103rd N.Y. Inf. Regt., the German Rifles, 5/13/63. Served in S.C. Prom. bvt. brig. gen. of U.S. Volunteers 3/13/65. MO in New York City 3/17/65. Postwar scientist, painter, and author in the United States and Germany. Received pension for dislocated right shoulder when he was ridden over by the enemy's cavalry upon his capture. Heine was admitted to the National Soldiers Home in Hampton, Va. Weighed 300 pounds and could barely walk in 1885. Heine died in Dresden 10/5/85 and is buried there.

HENRY, THOMAS. Born 1/19/38. Enl. as sgt. in Co. D, 1st Md. Inf. Regt., at Relay House 5/16/61. Appt. QM sgt. 2/1/62. Appt. 2lt. of Co. D 5/1/63. WIA left arm and leg at Laurel Hill 5/8/64. RTD 7/23/64. WIA at Weldon Railroad 8/18/64. Prom. 1lt. of Co. K 12/5/64. Furl. 15 days to visit sister in Baltimore who fell down stairs 1/31/65. Sentenced by court-martial to forfeit six months' pay for AWOL 2/65. Prom. cpt. of Co. H 4/10/65. MO 7/2/65. Henry died of heart disease in Baltimore 7/6/66. He never married.

HILLEARY, WILLIAM T. Born in Upper Marlboro, Prince Georges Co., 4/1/30. Son of William Hilleary and Mary A. Willet. House and sign painter. 5'7", dark complexion, black hair, hazel eyes. Appt. 2lt. of Co. E, 1st Md. Inf. Regt., at Relay House 5/20/61. Tendered letter of resignation 9/24/61. Resignation accepted 10/8/61. Served as cpt. of Co. I, 3rd Md. Inf. Regt., 2/1/63. Tendered resignation at Aquia Creek because he believed himself incompetent 3/25/63. Resignation accepted 3/31/63. Applied for post of detective in Baltimore 1/64. Enl. as sgt. in Battery D, 1st Md. Light Artillery, 2/28/64. MO 6/24/65. Postwar resident of Baltimore and Harford Co. Married Margaret Ann Ware 9/29/57. She died at Baltimore 1/24/63. One child. Married Margaret J. B. Kennard in Washington, D.C., 11/29/66. Two children. Hilleary died of cerebral hemorrhage 3/21/1911. Buried at Grove Cemetery in Aberdeen. Wife died 3/11/1919.

HUXFORD, DAVID C. Born c. 1822. 1860 Baltimore city dir. shows Huxford as a painter living at 25 Somerset St. Appt. 2lt. of Co. A, 1st Md. Inf. Regt., at Baltimore 5/10/61. Tendered resignation 8/22/61. Col. Kenly requested approval of Huxford's resignation at Williamsport 10/11/61 "by reason of his utter incompetency and no hope of improvement." Resignation accepted with effective date 8/22/61. Huxford enl. as QM sgt. in Battery A (2nd), Md. Light Artillery, "Junior Artillery," at Baltimore 6/23/63. MO 1/19/64. He reenl. as QM sgt. in Battery D, Md. Light Artillery, 2/28/64. MO 6/24/65. NFR.

JOHNSON, THOMAS SCOTT JESUP. Born c. 1820 in Pa. 5'11", light complexion, gray hair, light eyes. Appt. 2lt. in the 8th U.S. Inf. Regt. 7/7/38. Prom. 1lt. 12/31/42. Cashiered 5/30/45. Appt. cpt. of Co. K, 1st Md. Inf. Regt., at Relay House 5/28/61. Abs. sick in Frederick 7/19–8/18/62. Commanded regt. 9/18–10/16/62. Detailed bde. and division inspector 8/29/63. POW near Cold Harbor 5/31/64. Died of chronic diarrhea while a prisoner in Charleston, S.C., 11/20/64. Johnson had already been prom. to ltc. 10/30/64. Married Margaret A. Stuck in Frederick 11/3/60. Two children. Johnson's wife was not officially informed of his death until 6/6/65. She died in Washington, D.C., 1/19/1920.

KNOBELOCK, SIMON. 1860 cen.: res. 2nd Ward, Baltimore; age 34; teacher; born in Hesse, Germany; wife and three children; Wife born in Hanover, Germany; ———/$100. 1860 Baltimore city dir. shows res. at 257 Aliceanna St. Enl. as pvt. in Co. K, 1st Md. Inf. Regt., at Relay House 5/28/61. Prom. corp. 9/19/61, sgt. 9/20/61, and 1sg. 2/1/62. POW at Ft. Royal 5/23/62. Exch. at Aikens Landing 9/14/62. Appt. 2lt. 5/1/63. Prom. 1lt. 8/21/64. Furl. 15 days to visit wife 10/22/64. Prom. cpt. of Co. D 12/4/64. Furl. 20 days to visit wife 4/24/65. Charged with AWOL 6/20/65 when Knobelock overstayed 24-hour pass on 5/27/65 and did not return until 6/14/65. Dismissed from the service 7/11/65 with effective date of 6/19/65, but Knobelock had already mustered out 7/2/65. This dishonorable disch. was revoked 1/19/99. Knobelock had been married, although his wife died in 1855. Married Doris Mayer at First German United Evangelical Church in Baltimore 5/1/56. Three children. Knobeluck died of rheumatism in Baltimore 7/13/68. His widow died 1/24/1902.

KNOPPEL, JOHN JOSEPH. Born in Germany c. 1830. Son of John Joseph and Margaret Knoppel. Came to United States c. 1847. 1860 Baltimore city dir. shows Knoppel as a carpenter living at 348 Bond St. Enl. as sgt. in Co. I, 1st Md. Inf. Regt., at Relay House 5/27/61. Appt. 2lt. 10/12/61. POW at Ft. Royal 5/23/62. Prom. 1lt. 12/13/62. Charged with neglect of duty when he allowed pickets to straggle into camp "not in a military manner" 1/20/64. Later charged with drunkenness on duty while on picket and placed under arrest 8/25/64. Found guilty of charge by GCM and dismissed from the service 10/10/64. Postwar cabinetmaker in New York City. Married Catharine Schroder at the Zion Church in Baltimore 5/14/60. Two children. Knoppel died of pneumonia in a New York tenement 8/21/1903.

KUGLER, GEORGE W. Born c. 1839. Appt. 1lt. of Co. A, 1st Md. Inf. Regt., at Baltimore 5/10/61. Prom. cpt. 11/1/61. WIA and POW at Ft. Royal 5/23/62. Exch. at Aikens Landing 8/17/62. RTD 9/20/62. Disch. for ETS 5/23/64. NFR.

LEWIS, JOHN WESLEY. Born in Baltimore 7/16/41. Shoemaker. 5'9", light complexion, dark hair, blue eyes. Enl. as pvt. in Co. B, 1st Md. Inf. Regt., at Baltimore 5/11/61. Prom. sgt. 6/20/61. WIA and POW at Ft. Royal 5/23/62. Prom. commissary sgt. 10/1/64. Appt. 2lt. of Co. B 2/14/65. Prom. 1lt. but not mustered 6/23/65. MO 7/2/65. Postwar resident of Baltimore. Member of the GAR. Married Lavinia C. Taylor at the Franklin Street Methodist Episcopal Church in Baltimore 4/14/64. Five children. Lewis died of rheumatism 3/8/1913. Buried at Loudoun Park Cemetery. His wife died 3/28/1916.

LYETH, JOHN McF. Born c. 1821. Occupation marble cutter. Frances M. Smith apprenticed with Lyeth in Frederick 1858–61. 1860 Frederick city dir. shows res. at 3rd St. between Middle and Chapel Alleys. 5'8", light complexion, light hair, gray eyes. Appt. 1lt. of Co. H, 1st Md. Inf. Regt., at Frederick 5/20/61. Appt. RQM 5/1/62. Prom. cpt. of Co. H 8/22/62. Disch. for ETS 5/23/64. Spent most of the latter part of the war sick in Frederick. Lyeth's house at Monocacy Junction was ransacked by C.S. troops during the 1864 battle. Postwar resident of Baltimore. No record of marriage. Lyeth must have died after 1892.

LYON, LEMUEL Z. Born c. 1820. Veterinary surg. 5'10", light complexion, light brown hair, blue eyes. Appt. cpt. of Co. I, 1st Md. Inf. Regt., at Relay House

5/27/61. Tendered resignation to enter another branch as a "horseman" 10/20/61. Given leave to recruit cavalry co. in Baltimore 10/21/61. Resignation accepted 10/31/61. Lyon does not appear to have served in the military after this point. Postwar resident of Baltimore. Lyon's first wife died about 1858. Married Kate A. Edwards at Littletown, Pa., 9/18/60. Uncertain if there were any children. Died of senility in Baltimore 9/26/98. His wife died 1/28/1908.

McCONNELL, JOHN C. Born c. 1811. 1860 Baltimore city dir. shows Mc-Connell as a property agent with res. at 144 South Fremont St. Appt. cpt. of Co. A, 1st Md. Inf. Regt., at Baltimore 5/10/61. Resigned to accept promotion as col. of the 3rd Md. Inf. Regt. 8/5/61. Disch. 2/18/62. McConnell requested a court-martial to investigate why he was deprived of his command 3/6/62. Died in Baltimore 4/14/83.

McNULTY, JOSEPH. Born in Howard Co. c. 1839. Blacksmith. 5'8", light complexion, brown hair, brown eyes. Enl. as pvt. in Co. F, 1st Md. Inf. Regt., at Relay House 5/20/61. Prom. corp. 3–4/62. POW at Ft. Royal 5/23/62. Prom. sgt. 2/5/64, 1sg. 11/29/64. Appt. 2lt. of Co. H 2/11/65. Prom. bvt. 1lt. for gallant and meritorious service at White Oak Road 3/31/65. Charged with AWOL 6/25/65 for violating 24-hour pass at Arlington Heights 6/20/65. MO 7/2/65. Died in Baltimore 6/11/1920.

McNULTY, THOMAS. Born c. 1840. Res. Clarksville, Howard Co. Blacksmith. Enl. as corp. in Co. F, 1st Md. Inf. Regt., at Relay House 5/20/61. Prom. sgt. 11/21/61. Served as color sgt. 1–4/62. POW at Ft. Royal 5/23/62. Suffered injuries to breast when run over by enemy cavalry. Appt. 2lt. 3/31/63. Lost his voice at the Wilderness and began to spit blood. WIA in left arm at Spotsylvania 5/9/64. Disch. for disability and AWOL 8/8/64. "Having failed to file in this Office [AGO] the necessary Surgeon's Certificates of Disability, as required by the regulations of the War Department." Postwar worker with B&O Railroad and Cumberland and Savage Railroad. Married at Mt. Savage 1/27/68. Two children. McNulty died 5/22/90. His wife died 4/29/97.

MANSFIELD, JAMES T. Born c. 1836. Res. Eutaw and Henrietta Sts. in Baltimore. Bricklayer. Enl. as sgt. in Co. E, 1st Md. Inf. Regt., at Relay House 5/20/61. Prom. 1sg. 3–4/62. Appt. 2lt. of Co. I 12/16/62. Furl. to visit sick wife in Baltimore 1/28/64. Prom. 1lt. of Co. B 3/12/64 and cpt. of Co. H 8/21/64. Abs. to recuperate health in Baltimore 9/24/64. Resigned for disability 3/24/65. Postwar resident of Baltimore. Married 5/27/58. No children. Mansfield died of smallpox 4/5/72. Wife remarried 12/23/75 after repeatedly trying to get U.S. pension.

MERCER, VIRGIL T. 1860 cen.: res. Ellicotts Mill, Howard Co.; age 35; wheelwright; born in Md.; no value listed. Appt. 2lt. of Co. F, 1st Md. Inf. Regt., at Relay House 5/20/61. POW at Ft. Royal 5/23/62. Prom. 1lt. of Co. B 5/24/62 and cpt. 4/10/63. WIA left forearm at Harris Farm 5/19/64. Disch. for disability 8/17/64. Applied for commission in VRC 9/28/64. Postwar resident of Baltimore and Ellicott City. Married Mary MacKenzie 2/11/64. She served as a nurse at Harrison's Landing on a hospital ship and at hospitals in Washington, D.C. Not known if there were any children. Mercer died of senile degeneration at Ellicott City 4/25/1906.

MORRIS, ROBERT A. Born in Ireland c. 1830. Mariner. 5'5", light complexion, light hair, hazel eyes. Appt. 1lt. of Co. E, 1st Md. Inf. Regt., at Relay House 5/20/61. Served as acting rqm. Tendered resignation at Washington, D.C., to raise another unit 10/31/61. Col. Kenly approved of resignation citing his good service. Enl. as pvt. in Co. A, 2nd Md. Cav. Regt., at Baltimore 6/22/63. Appt. qm. sgt. 7/1/63. MO 1/26/64. Enl. as sgt. in Co. G, 1st Regt. Potomac Home Brigade Infantry, 2/21/65. Trans. to Co. G, 13th Md. Inf. Regt., 4/8/65. MO 5/29/65. Postwar janitor. Married Emma A. Orrell in Baltimore 12/24/58. Three children. Morris died of bronchitis in Washington, D.C., 2/20/1907. His wife died 4/2/1926.

NEELY, ROBERT. Born in Baltimore 3/17/38. Farmer in Cockeysville. 5'11", light complexion, brown hair, gray eyes. Enl. as 1sg. of Co. G, 1st Md. Inf. Regt., 5/27/61. Appt. 2lt. of Co. G 2/1/62. Served as adj. until 4/14/63. POW at Ft. Royal 5/23/62. Commanded Co. G 9/15–12/14/62. Prom. 1lt. 3/27/63. Abs. on detached service for recruiting 7/21/63 through 3/10/64. WIA at Weldon Railroad 8/18/64. Prom. cpt. of Co. C 8/20/64 and maj. 2/21/65. Commanded regt. since 4/1/65. MO 7/2/65. Appt. 2lt. of 41st U.S. Inf. Regt. 7/28/67. Prom. 1lt. 9/20/67. Trans. to 11th U.S. Inf. Regt. 11/11/69. Dropped for three months AWOL at Ft. Brown, Texas, 10/5/74. Postwar laborer in New Orleans, Baltimore, and Washington, D.C. Married Elizabeth Neely 3/15/64. Not known if there were any children. Neely was adm. to Mountain Branch, National Home for Disabled Volunteer Soldiers, in Johnson City, Tenn. Adm. to St. Elizabeth's Hospital in Washington, D.C., 2/3/1912. Died there of senile psychosis 11/3/1916. His wife died 11/7/1930.

OREM, JOSEPH BAILEY. Born in Cambridge, Dorchester Co., c. 1828. Carpenter. Appt. 1lt. of Co. C, 1st Md. Inf. Regt., at Baltimore 5/11/61. Tendered resignation to accept captaincy in another unit 12/1/61. Brig. Gen. Cooper wrote on 12/11/61: "In transmitting you the resignation of this Officer I refrain from any recommendation [*sic*]. His excuse for resigning is certainly not a valid one;

but his services in the Regiment, as an officer, are not of account enough to induce any one to wish to retrain him in it." Resignation accepted 1/2/62. Appt. cpt. of Co. C, 4th Md. Inf. Regt., at Baltimore 7/9/62. Abs. detailed recruiting service in Easton 11–12/62. Orem apparently did not recruit on the Eastern Shore; instead he went to Baltimore. Unit wrote for his arrest 2/10/63. Pres. in arrest 3/10/63. To forfeit one month's pay by court-martial 6/10/63. Noted as AWOL 7/13/63. WIA at Weldon Railroad 8/18/64. Noted as AWOL 10/15/64. Disch. 10/31/64. Postwar builder in Baltimore. Had private act introduced into Congress on 6/6/1906 to allow pension for sunstroke suffered in the summer of 1863. Married Caroline P. Skinner at Caroline Street Methodist Episcopal Church in Baltimore 7/31/51. One child. Orem died in Baltimore 7/16/1911. Buried in Greenmount Cemetery. Wife died 12/25/1911.

REED, SETH G. Born in Baltimore Co. c. 1840. Teacher. 5'7", fair complexion, brown hair, gray eyes. Enl. as pvt. in Co. A, 1st Md. Inf. Regt., at Baltimore 5/10/61. Prom. sgt. 8/18/61 and 1sg. 11/1/61. WIA in right leg at Ft. Royal 5/23/62. Appt. 2lt. of Co. K 9/22/62 and 1lt. 3/28/63. Served as 1lt./adj. 9/63 through 4/64. Commanded Co. K since 5/5/64. Prom. cpt. of Co. A 8/16/64. WIA right arm and shoulder at Weldon Railroad 8/20/64. Commission as cpt. revoked 11/17/64 because unfit for duty. Abs. 1–3/65 and resigned for disability 3/23/65. Disch. revoked 4/8/65 upon recovery although Reed could not be re-instated as cpt. 5/1/65. He was, however, prom. to ltc. 5/26/65. MO 7/2/65. Married Sarah J. McCurley at the First English Lutheran Church in Baltimore 7/13/65. One child. Reed died of disease of the brain and spinal cord 6/26/80. No symptoms of syphilis found. Suffered from convulsions and total blindness.

REESE, JOHN. [Name also appears as Johan Riess.] Born in Germany c. 1832. Tailor. 1860 Baltimore city dir. shows res. at 17 Somerset St. 5'8", light com-plexion, light hair, blue eyes. Enl. as 1sg. of Co. K, 1st Md. Inf. Regt., at Relay House 5/27/61. Noted as AWOL 9–10/61. WIA by saber blow to head and POW at Ft. Royal 5/23/62. Appt. 2lt. 12/6/64. WIA in left leg at Hatchers Run 10/27/64. Furl. 15 days to visit sick wife in Baltimore 3/25/65. Failed to return in time and charged with AWOL. Prom. 1lt. 6/23/65 but not mustered. MO 7/2/65. Postwar tailor in Baltimore. Married Catherine Maul at Zion Church in Baltimore 7/22/65. Six children. Reese died of aortic stenosis in Baltimore 4/22/1905. Buried in Baltimore Cemetery.

REYNOLDS, ALFRED D. 1860 cen.: res. Ellicotts Mills, Baltimore Co., age 22; carpenter; born in Md.; son of Hosea and Sarah Reynolds. Brother of Robert W. Reynolds. Received a "common-school education." 5'8", light complexion, dark hair, blue eyes. Enl. as pvt. in Co. F, 1st Md. Inf. Regt., at Relay House 5/27/61.

Prom. corp. 11/21/61 but reduced to the ranks 1–2/62. Prom. corp. 3/11/62 and sgt. 12/15/62. Abs. on detached service in Baltimore to recruit 7/63 through 4/64. Appt. 1lt. of Co. C 7/28/64. KIA at Weldon Railroad 8/18/64. As he died, Reynolds said, "I die content; my peace is made with my Maker, and I have fallen in a glorious cause; it shall not be said that I died a coward's death." Married Roxanna V. Aler at Union Square Station Methodist Episcopal Church in Baltimore 4/21/64. She later remarried but divorced on grounds of abandonment. She died 3/25/1924.

REYNOLDS, ROBERT W. Born c. 1833. Son of Hosea and Sarah Reynolds. Brother of Alfred D. Reynolds. Appt. cpt. of Co. F, 1st Md. Inf. Regt., at Relay House 5/20/61. Received a blow to the testicles and small of the back and POW at Ft. Royal 5/23/62. RTD 12/12/62. Abs. furl. 1/19–29/64 and 3/19–4/3/64. Disch. for ETS 5/23/64. Brig. Gen. Kenly requested that the governor appoint Reynolds in one of the 100-day units 6/24/64. This apparently did not take place. Postwar resident of Baltimore. Married Elizabeth Nichols at Ellicotts Mills 12/28/56. Not known if there were any children. Reynolds died of diabetes and bronchitis in Baltimore 5/19/92. Buried at St. Mary's Cemetery. Wife died about 1903.

RUHL, HENRY (signs as Rule). Born in Germany c. 1843. Cigar maker. 5'7", dark complexion, auburn hair, gray eyes. Enl. as corp. in Co. I, 1st Md. Inf. Regt., at Relay House 5/27/61. Prom. sgt. 9/1/61. POW at Ft. Royal 5/23/62. Prom. 1sg. 5/27/64. WIA in right foot at Weldon Railroad 8/20/64. Appt. 2lt. 1/1/65. WIA in head at Hatcher's Run 2/6/65. Disch. for disability 5/8/65. Postwar resident of Baltimore. Married Mary Weller at Zion Church in Baltimore 11/27/65. Ruhl died of chronic meningitis in Baltimore 7/11/94. Buried at Baltimore Cemetery.

SAVILLE, THOMAS. 1860 cen.: res. 19th Ward, Baltimore; age 32; shoemaker; born in Md.; wife and four children; wife born in Va.; ———/$100. Appt. 1lt. of Co. B, 1st Md. Inf. Regt., at Baltimore 5/11/61. Detached service with Co. D 9/16/61. Noted as AWOL 12/31/61. Prom. cpt. of Co. B 5/24/62. Pres. in arrest 9–10/62. Noted as AWOL while awaiting decision of court-martial 12/1–31/62. Name sent for dismissal. Saville again appears as AWOL 2/1/63. Col. Dushane wrote Brig. Gen. Kenly that Saville had escaped from the guards and had left for Baltimore. He was under arrest for drunkenness and disorderly conduct 2/7/63. Col. Dushane also wrote the PM that Saville was in Baltimore and "very likely he has left of his uniform, and dresses in citizens clothes. He is well known to the Police." Placed under arrest by PMO in Baltimore 2/24/63. He was dismissed 3/9/63 with an effective date of 2/22/63. Saville applied for a pension 5/24/98.

He wrote requesting information for his pension application 5/16/1905. The application was denied. NFR.

SCHLEY, BENJAMIN H. 1860 cen.: res. Frederick City; age 26; lawyer; born in Md.; son of Margaret Schley; ten other children; $32,000/$18,000. Appt. cpt. of Co. H, 1st Md. Inf. Regt., at Frederick 5/20/61. POW at Ft. Royal 5/23/62. Prom. maj. 8/22/64. Disch. for ETS 5/23/64. NFR.

SMITH, FRANCES M. Born in Frederick (or possibly Baltimore) 11/29/42. Son of D. F. and S. E. Smith. Marble cutter. 5'9", fair complexion, brown hair, black eyes. Apprentice with John McF. Lyeth. Enl. as pvt. in Co. H, 1st Md. Inf. Regt., at Relay House 5/17/61. Prom. corp. 5/27/61 and 1sg. 11/25/62. Appt. 2lt. of Co. E 3/12/64. WIA in groin at Cold Harbor 6/3/64. WIA in left hand and thigh at Petersburg 6/18/64. Appt. 1lt./adj. 9/9/64. Awarded the Medal of Honor for gallantry at Dabney's Mills (Hatcher's Run) 2/6/65. Smith remained with the dead body of Col. Wilson and brought it off the field under a heavy fire. Medal of Honor awarded 8/13/95. WIA left leg at Five Forks 4/1/65. Prom. bvt. cpt. for gallant and meritorious service at Five Forks 4/1/65. MO 7/2/65. Postwar post office worker in Baltimore. Member of the GAR. Married Mary E. Nicholson at Union Square Methodist Episcopal Church in Baltimore 10/4/65. No children survived him. Smith died of chronic bronchitis and angina pectoris in Baltimore 9/22/1917. Buried at Loudoun Park Cemetery. Wife died 7/22/1923.

SMITH, GEORGE. Born c. 1825. Appt. cpt. of Co. C, 1st Md. Inf. Regt., at Baltimore 5/11/61. Smith placed in command of remnants of the regt. after Ft. Royal in the spring of 1862. Tendered resignation at Camp Murray in Baltimore 9/11/62. "I consider myself wronged by my Colonel for not complying with the Army Regulation Article IV." Col. Dushane claimed that Smith was incompetent. Resignation accepted with an effective date 9/4/62. NFR.

SMITH, ROBERT S. Born c. 1821. Res. Warren, Baltimore Co. Appt. 1lt. of Co. G, 1st Md. Inf. Regt., at Baltimore 5/27/61. Acting commander of Co. H 7/16–8/3/61. Appt. rqm. 10/1/61. Prom. cpt. of Co. G 2/1/62. POW at Ft. Royal 5/23/62. Smith escaped while on parole at Staunton. Tendered resignation on account of disability and "that I have not been able to obtain information of my exchange necessary to justify in engaging in active service" 12/1/62. Resignation accepted with effective date 12/7/62. Later applied for pension but claim was rejected because Smith did not provide any evidence after the original filing date 9/12/79.

SMOOT, WILLIAM SIDNEY. Born in Va. 1860 Baltimore city dir. shows Smoot as a clerk with res. at 549 West Fayette St. Appt. 1lt. of Co. F, 1st Md. Inf. Regt., by the U.S. SOW 12/24/63. Smoot had previously served in the Ord. Department. Ordered before board of examiners for Ord. Department in Washington, D.C., 1/16/64. Appt. 2lt. of ord. in the U.S. Army 7/2/64. Prom. bvt. 1lt. for meritorious service in that department 3/13/65. Prom. 1lt. 3/7/67. Disch. at own request 12/31/70. Died 2/18/86.

STANTON, DAVID LEROY. Born in Baltimore 2/2/40. Father was born in Conn. and mother in Md. 5'10". Enl. as pvt. in Co. A, 1st Md. Inf. Regt., at Baltimore 5/10/61. Prom. 1sg. immediately after enlistment. Appt. 2lt. 11/1/61. POW at Ft. Royal 5/23/62. Prom. 1lt. 12/12/62. Prom. cpt. of Co. I 3/7/64. WIA in right foot at Harris Farm 5/19/64 and again at Weldon Railroad 8/18/64. Prom. maj. 12/2/64, ltc. 2/21/65, and col. 3/20/65. Commanded Md. Bde. at Five Forks and Appomattox. Prom. bvt. brig. gen. for gallant conduct at Five Forks 4/1/65 (date of bvt. 6/22/67). MO 7/2/65. Postwar lawyer in Baltimore. Represented many former Md. U.S. soldiers in pension cases. Member of the GAR. Married 2/9/65. Number of children unknown. Stanton died of acute nephritis in Baltimore 12/26/1919. Buried at the National Cemetery. His wife died 7/30/1921.

STARKWEATHER, NORRIS G. Born c. 1816. 1860 Baltimore city dir. shows Starkweather as an architect with office at 83 West Fayette St. and res. at 42 Lexington St. Appt. 1lt. of Co. K, 1st Md. Inf. Regt., at Relay House 5/27/61. Abs. with leave until 7/1/61. Noted as AWOL 9–10/61. Dishonorably disch. 1/31/62 to take effect 10/30/61. Starkweather served as 1lt. of Co. K, 6th Md. Inf. Regt., 8/27/62. Submitted letter of resignation for old age at Fredericksburg 5/15/64. Disch. for chronic nephritis 5/24/64.

STIFFLER, JOHN NELSON. Born in Baltimore Co. 12/18/41. Son of George and Elizabeth Stiffler. Occupation shoemaker or carpenter. 5'10", dark complexion, dark hair, dark eyes. Enl. as pvt. in Co. G, 1st Md. Inf. Regt., at Baltimore 5/17/61. POW at Ft. Royal 5/23/62. Prom. sgt. 11/25/62 and 1sg. 12/1/63. Suffered injuries to back when large tree fell on him while sleeping 9/12/64. WIA at Poplar Grove Church 10/1/64. Appt. 1lt. of Co. H 10/26/64. WIA at Five Forks 4/1/65. MO 7/2/65. Postwar Union Pacific Railroad worker. Married Mary E. Hanson in Baltimore 11/65. She died 2/7/67. No children. Married Mary E. Funk in Omaha, Neb., 9/7/68. Four children. Stiffler died in Pace, Fla., 1/14/1920. His wife died 5/15/1932.

STONEBRAKER, JOSEPH H. Born 8/2/41. Enl. as sgt. in Co. H, 1st Md. Inf. Regt., at Baltimore 5/17/61. POW at Ft. Royal 5/23/62. Appt. 2lt. of Co. G 5/1/63. Detailed ambulance officer 7–8/63 through 7–8/64. Prom. 1lt. of Co. H 6/25/64 and cpt. of Co. G 10/24/64. Furl. to visit family in Baltimore Co. "to make arrangements" 12/20/64. Furl. to visit sick father in Harford Co. 4/25/65.

MO 7/2/65. Postwar resident of Johnstown, Pa. Injured in Great Flood. Married at some point and had at least three children who escaped to Baltimore during the flood. Stonebraker died in Johnstown, Pa., 1/21/1915.

TARR, FREDERICK CREY. 1860 cen.: res. 10th Ward, Baltimore; age 21; clerk.; born in Md.; lived with dentist and family. Appt. 1lt. of Co. D, 1st Md. Inf. Regt., in Baltimore 5/16/61. Appt. 1lt./adj. 6/11/61. WIA by saber to nose, head, right elbow, and left thumb at Ft. Royal 5/23/62. Prom. cpt. 9/1/62. Appt. cpt./AAG of U.S. Volunteers 9/29/62 and ass. to Md. Bde. Appt. maj./paymaster of U.S. Volunteers 2/23/64. MO 11/1/65. Prominent Baltimore businessman after the war. Member of the GAR, Union Veterans Association, and Military Order of the Loyal Legion of the United States. Married Mary Shoop at Williamsport Presbyterian Church 3/14/63. Three children. Wife died 3/5/1903. Tarr died of heart complications in Baltimore 4/22/1911. Buried at Loudoun Park Cemetery, Baltimore.

TAYLOR, WILLIAM. Born in Washington, D.C., c. 1834. Enl. as sgt. in Co. H, 1st Md. Inf. Regt., at Relay House 5/27/61. WIA right hand at Ft. Royal 5/23/62. Detailed to duty with bde. ambulance corps 11/62 through 2/63. Appt. 2lt. of Co. C 4/12/63. Charged with AWOL when regt. commander wanted to inspect the trenches at Petersburg 8/12/64. POW at Weldon Railroad while establishing picket line 8/19/64. Sent to Salisbury, N.C., 10/2/64. Escaped by jumping from rail cars while traveling to Danville, Va., 10/19/64. Arrived at Knoxville, Tenn., 1/12/65. On detached service in Baltimore 1–4/65. Prom. cpt. of Co. E 6/7/65. MO 7/2/65. Taylor was later awarded the Medal of Honor for attempting to burn the bridge at Ft. Royal and for voluntarily taking the place of a wounded officer and leading a hazardous reconnaissance behind enemy lines at Weldon Railroad. Awarded medal 8/2/97. Postwar bricklayer in Baltimore. Married at some point before the war. Four children. Wife died 6/15/75. Married Mary R. Lawrence 5/3/98. They had previously been recognized as common-law husband and wife in Washington, D.C., 11/19/83. Taylor died of heart disease in Baltimore 4/6/1902. Buried at the National Cemetery. His wife died 10/24/1933.

TAYLOR, WILLIAM H. Born in Baltimore c. 1832. Appt. 2lt. of Co. I, 1st Md. Inf. Regt., 10/9/61. Trans. to Co. B 11/1/61. Detached for recruiting service in Baltimore 2/4/62. Served as acting adj. 8/22/62. Prom. 1lt. of Co. I 10/4/62. In charge of bde. bakery 3/63. Detached for light duty at Camp Tyler in Baltimore 5–10/63. Disch. 7/13/65. Postwar resident of Baltimore. Married Josephine K. Norris at Baltimore 8/17/53. She died 1/2/71. Two children. Married Martha E. Frederick at Baltimore 6/5/73. Two children. Taylor died of consumption in Baltimore 10/15/77. Buried at Loudoun Park Cemetery, Baltimore. His wife died 2/13/85.

THOMPSON, GEORGE W. Born in Baltimore 2/6/33. Bricklayer. 6'0", fair complexion, light hair, gray eyes. Enl. as sgt. in Co. H, 1st Md. Inf. Regt., at Baltimore 5/27/61. Appt. qm. sgt. 6/18/61. Appt. 2lt. of Co. D 2/1/62. Furl. 10 days "for the purpose of visiting home to fill an engagement or in other words to get *married* hoping the above may receive a favorable consideration." Prom. 1lt. of Co. B 4/8/63. Furl. to visit sick brother in Washington, D.C., 11/19/63. Disch. for chronic diarrhea 3/2/64. Appt. 1lt. of Co. I, 11th Md. Inf. Regt. (one year), at Baltimore 3/21/65. MO 6/15/65. Postwar resident of Baltimore. Married Emma D. Achenbach at the Seventh Baptist Church in Baltimore 3/21/63. One child. Thompson died of senility cystitis in Baltimore 2/16/1912. Buried at Loudoun Park Cemetery, Baltimore. His wife died 2/6/1913.

VEIDT, HENRY JACOB JULIUS. Born in Brunswick, Germany, c. 1822. Cabinetmaker. Appt. 2lt. of Co. K, 1st Md. Inf. Regt., at Relay House 5/28/61. Tendered resignation to transfer to 3rd Md. Inf. Regt. in early 9/61. Col. Kenly, however, denied permission for the transfer "by reason of his utter incompetency. . . . I cannot recognize Mr. Veidt as an officer of my regt. and disapprove of his request to be assigned to the 3rd Maryland Regiment" 10/24/61. Resignation accepted 10/31/61. Veidt does not appear in any other Md. unit although he claims he was drafted in 1864. Postwar cabinetmaker in Washington, D.C. Married Johanne Caroline Fredrike Dohring at the German Universal Christian Church in New York City 4/13/49. Four children. Veidt died in Washington, D.C., 1/8/93. Buried at Prospect Hill Cemetery. His wife died 3/31/1906.

VINK, JOHN E. Born in Anne Arundel Co. c. 1834. Bricklayer. 5'5", light complexion, light hair, blue eyes. Enl. as corp. in Co. F, 1st Md. Inf. Regt., at Relay House 5/20/61. POW at Ft. Royal 5/23/62. Prom. sgt. 12/15/62. Appt. qm. sgt. 9/1/64. Appt. 2lt. of Co. F 12/6/64. Furl. 15 days to visit sick wife and child in Howard Co. 2/28/65. Noted as AWOL 3/19/65. MO 7/2/65. Postwar bricklayer with B&O Railroad. Resident of Steubenville, Ohio, Howard Co., and Baltimore after the war. Married at some point before the war. Applied for pension claiming rheumatism and general poor health 1898. Pension examiner wrote about his investigation of members of the unit regarding Vink: "It appears rather remarkable that these men could remember that he had rheumatism in the service, when they can apparently remember little else about him," 3/5/90. Pension was denied.

WALKER, JOSEPH E. Born in Philadelphia 1/26/34. Painter. 5'11", dark complexion, dark hair, gray eyes. Enl. as pvt. in Co. D, 1st Md. Inf. Regt., at Baltimore 5/16/61. Prom. corp. 7/19/61 and sgt. 2/1/62. Charged $5 for AWOL at Hagerstown 11/12/62. Prom. 1sg. 1/13/63. WIA left side of the back at Harris Farm 5/19/64. Appt. 1lt. of Co. D 10/24/64. Furl. 10 days to visit sick mother 12/15/64.

WIA at Five Forks 4/1/65. Prom. bvt. cpt. for gallantry and meritorious service at White Oak Road and Five Forks 4/1/65. MO 7/2/65. Postwar resident of Baltimore. Married Elizabeth C. Waltgen at St. Paul's Lutheran Church in Baltimore 10/67. No children. She was the widow of Pvt. George H. F. Waltgen of Co. A, 2nd Md. Inf. Regt., who was KIA at Antietam 9/17/62. Wife died 4/93. Walker adm. to National Soldiers Home in Hampton, Va., 1912. Died there 3/14/1916.

WALTEMEYER, CHARLES. Born in Baltimore c. 1835. Molder. 1860 Baltimore city dir. shows res. at 730 West Baltimore St. 5'9", fair complexion, brown hair, blue eyes. Enl. as corp. in Co. H, 1st Md. Inf. Regt., at Relay House 5/27/61. POW at Ft. Royal 5/23/62. Prom. sgt. 2/1/63 and 1sg. 4/1/64. WIA in face at Harris Farm 5/19/64. Appt. 1lt. of Co. F 12/6/64. Furl. 15 days to visit brother in Annapolis who had just returned from POW camp 2/10/65. MO 7/2/65. Postwar molder in Baltimore and Washington, D.C. Married Sarah C. Easterly in Baltimore 5/31/70. She died 1/2/79. Married Estelle Gray at Chatsworth Church in Baltimore 3/22/81. One child. Waltemeyer died of chronic diarrhea in Baltimore 8/23/1902. His wife died 11/17/1932.

WALTEMEYER, FRANCIS G. F. 1860 cen.: Res. Little Gunpowder, Baltimore Co.; age 40; tavernkeeper; born in Md.; wife and four children; $600/$250. Appt. cpt. of Co. B, 1st Md. Inf. Regt., at Baltimore 5/11/61. Waltemeyer was placed under arrest for disobedience of orders 12/15/61. He wrote a barely literate letter to the U.S. SOW appealing for assistance 2/8/62. Remained in the service until 4/62. NFR.

WATSON, HUGH. Born in Tyrone, Ireland, c. 1825. Chandler. 1860 Baltimore city dir. shows res. at 116 East Monument St. 5'8", light complexion, light hair, blue eyes. Enl. as pvt. in Co. E, 1st Md. Inf. Regt., at Relay House 5/25/61. Prom. corp. 9/1/61 but reduced to ranks 10/31/61. Noted as AWOL for 14 days 7–8/62. Prom. corp. 10/1/62 and 1sg. 12/16/62. Appt. commissary sgt. 11/22/63. Appt. 1lt. of Co. B 8/30/64. WIA in right breast at Five Forks 4/1/65. MO 7/2/65. Postwar chandler and letter carrier in Baltimore. Married Eveline Hamington 11/22/49. Two children. Wife died 5/26/75. Watson died 12/14/83.

WHARRY, ROBERT N. Born in Baltimore c. 1838. Occupation carpenter. 5'8", dark complexion, dark hair, dark eyes. Enl. as sgt. in Co. F, 1st Md. Inf. Regt., at Relay House 5/20/61. Prom. 1sg. 11–12/61. POW at Ft. Royal 5/23/62. Appt. 2lt. of Co. B 12/16/62. Prom. 1lt. of Co. A 3/7/64. WIA in left arm at Harris Farm 5/19/64. Detached service on court-martial board in Baltimore 8/15/64. Col. Wilson requested Wharry's return 11/26/64 but he remained on board until

2/65. Prom. cpt. of Co. C 3/8/65. Furl. two days to visit sick child in Ellicotts Mill 6/1/65. MO 7/2/65. Postwar carpenter in Washington, D.C. Married Matilda J. Wilson at Catonsville 7/29/60. One child. Wharry died of bronchitis in Washington, D.C., 5/13/94. Buried at Arlington National Cemetery.

WILLIAMS, EDWARD. Born in Philadelphia 1/9/37. Watchmaker. 5'7", light complexion, light hair, gray eyes. Enl. as pvt. in Co. B, 1st Md. Inf. Regt., at Relay House 5/29/61. Prom. corp. 11/12/61. POW at Ft. Royal 5/23/62. Prom. 1sg. 12/16/62. Appt. 2lt. of Co. I 4/7/64. WIA thigh at Weldon Railroad 8/18/64. Furl. 20 days to visit relatives in Baltimore 9/2/64. Prom. 1lt. of Co. B 11/16/64 and cpt. of Co. I 12/3/64. Furl. 15 days to visit sick mother in New York City 3/8/65. MO 7/2/65. Postwar resident of Baltimore and various locations in Del. and Pa. Married Johanna Carroll at some point before the war. She died in Baltimore 11/7/59. Married Rosena Heales in New York City 3/19/65. Three children. She apparently died before Williams. He was adm. to National Soldiers Home in Hampton, Va., 12/9/1907 and died there 7/2/1914.

WILSON, ISAAC. Born in Lancaster Co., Pa., c. 1832. Farmer. Brother of John W. and Robert A. Wilson. 5'9", light complexion, brown hair, blue eyes. Appt. 2lt. of Co. G, 1st Md. Inf. Regt., at Relay House 5/17/61. Prom. 1lt. 2/1/62. POW at Ft. Royal 5/23/62. Escaped from enemy at Harrisonburg 6/4/62. Noted as AWOL 12/24–29/62 and 1/18–2/28/63. Dismissed from the service 2/22/63. Held in arrest in Baltimore 3/22/63. Wilson was recommended for a commission in the 12th Md. Inf. Regt. 8/5/64. He enl. as sgt. in Co. F, 1st Md. Inf. Regt., at Baltimore 9/17/64. Appt. 1lt. of Co. E 12/13/64. Applied for leave to carry remains of his two brothers who DOW from Dabney's Mill 2/6/65. Disch. for disability because of tonsillitis 4/25/65. Postwar butcher in Baltimore Co. Married Mary A. Olliver at some point before the war. Two children. She died in Baltimore in 1870. Married Teresa Clark in Baltimore 1891. Wilson died 10/5/1902.

WILSON, JOHN W. Born in Lancaster Co., Pa., 2/2/28. Farmer. Brother of Isaac and Robert A. Wilson. Received a "common school education." Served in the Mexican War. Appt. cpt. of Co. G, 1st Md. Inf. Regt., at Relay House 5/17/61. Prom. maj. 2/1/62. POW at Ft. Royal 5/23/62. Prom. ltc. 8/22/62. Abs. on detached service to recover deserters 12/22/62. Wilson was charged with disrespect and conduct prejudicial to good order and military discipline by 1lt. Levi T. Heath, bde. inspector, for not releasing entrenching tools 11–12/63. Held under guard 12/29/63. Court-martial found Wilson guilty of disrespect and sentenced him to reprimand in general orders by army corps commander 2/5/64. Prom. col. 10/30/64. Furl. 10 days to settle claim of a brother killed earlier in the war 11/1/64. KIA at Dabney's Mill 2/6/65. Buried at the Presbyterian Church Cemetery in Chestnut Grove, Baltimore Co. A monument is dedicated to Wilson in the cemetery. Wilson had married 3/27/53. Five children. His wife died 9/20/1902.

WILSON, ROBERT A. Born in Lancaster Co., Pa., 3/20/26. Farmer. Brother of Isaac and John W. Wilson. Received a "common school education." Appt. cpt. of Co. F, 1st Md. Cav. Regt., at Cockeysville 9/1/61. Resigned for ill health at Camp Carroll 5/9/62. Enl. as pvt. in Co. G, 1st Md. Inf. Regt., at Baltimore 8/25/62. Prom. corp. 11/26/62 and sgt. 4/3/63. Detailed to ambulance corps 7–8/64. Appt. 2lt. 12/6/64. WIA shoulder with bullet lodging in the lungs at Dabney's Mill 2/6/65. DOW at home in Baltimore Co. 2/14/65. Buried at Presbyterian Church Cemetery in Chestnut Grove, Baltimore Co.

WRIGHT, CHARLES WESLEY. Born c. 1828. Appt. cpt. of Co. D, 1st Md. Inf. Regt., at Baltimore 5/16/61. WIA right shoulder at Ft. Royal 5/23/62. Adm. to Union Hotel hospital in Winchester 5/29/62. DOW in Baltimore 6/12/62. Married Emma Wright in Philadelphia 10/18/57. One child.

Union Officers of the 4th Maryland Infantry Regiment

ADDISON, JOSEPH T. Born c. 1840. Plumber. Enl. as pvt. in Co. G, 4th Md. Inf. Regt., at Baltimore 8/20/62. Prom. sgt. 9–10/62 and 1sg. 11–12/62. Listed as AWOL 12/28/63. Appt. 1lt. of Co. G 7/16/64. POW at Weldon Railroad 9/16/64. Confined at Libby Prison 9/17/64. Sent to Salisbury, N.C., 10/2/64. Returned to Richmond 2/18/65. Exch. at James River 2/22/65. RTD 4/12/65. MO 5/31/65. Postwar clerk in Baltimore in 1869. NFR.

ADREON, HARRISON. Born in Baltimore 1/12/41. Son of William Adreon and grandson of Christian Adreon, who commanded a Md. company in War of 1812. Educated in Baltimore public schools and City College. 1860 cen.: res. 15th Ward, Baltimore; age 18, clerk; father was an auctioneer; ———/$5,000; six other children and two black servants. 5'6", light complexion, dark hair, blue eyes. Appt. 1lt. of Co. A, 4th Md. Inf. Regt., at Baltimore 6/28/62. Prom. cpt. of same co. 1/17/63 and maj. 1/5/64. Prom. bvt. ltc. for gallant and meritorious service at Five Forks 4/1/65. MO 5/31/65. Returned to Baltimore and studied law. Adm. to bar in 1866. Clerk of Baltimore City Court and secretary of the Republican State Central Committee. Later served as state pension agent and postmaster for Baltimore. Founder of GAR in Md. Married Jane Augusta Kelso at Baltimore 6/6/68. She died 11/17/84. They had one child, who was supported as a "lunatic" until death 10/11/1926. Adreon died in Baltimore of phthisis pulmonalis 5/25/91. Buried in Greenmount Cemetery.

ALLEN, WILLIAM H. Born c. 1810. Shoemaker and prewar Baltimore policeman. 1860 cen.: res. 15th Ward, Baltimore; born in Md.; wife, Mary, and one son. Appt. 1lt. of Co. C, Baltimore Light Infantry, 1/16/62. MO 5/27/62. Appt. 1lt. of Co. C, 4th Md. Inf. Regt., at Baltimore 7/9/62. Tendered resignation because of old age and chronic rheumatism 3/9/63. Resignation accepted 3/9/63. Allen's first wife must have died sometime in this period as he married Louvina D. Owins at Baltimore 2/28/74. She died 5/94. Allen died at Crisfield, Somerset Co., 3/8/94.

BANKERD, JOSIAH. 1860 cen.: res. 12th Ward, Baltimore; age 26; hotel keeper; born in Md.; wife and possibly two children; $1,000/$1,400. Appt. 1lt. of Co. I, 4th Md. Inf. Regt., at Baltimore 10/4/62. Detailed service as ord. officer with 3rd Division since 8/17/63. Appears as AAAG of 3rd Bde., 2nd Division, 5th Army Corps 4/1/64. WIA in left knee at Cold Harbor 6/4/64. Prom. cpt. of Co. C 11/19/64. Furl. 15 days to visit Baltimore for business 12/26/64. Appt. cpt./AAG of U.S. Volunteers 2/14/65. Disch. from 4th Md. to accept new rank 4/30/65. MO 8/10/65. Married Annie E. Waltz at Unionville, Frederick Co., 9/20/55. Died of nephritis at Baltimore 1/5/89. Buried in Baltimore Cemetery.

BARBER, JOHN G. 1860 cen.: res. 18th Ward, Baltimore; age 23; merchant; born in Md.; wife and two children; wife born in Md., ———/$400. 1860 Baltimore city dir. shows res. at 26 South Poppleton St. Appt. 2lt. of Co. E, 4th Md. Inf. Regt., at Baltimore 7/25/62. Resigned because of hernia 12/8/62. Married Margaret Johnson at Ellicott City 6/8/58. Three children. Barber died of consumption at Baltimore 12/29/76. Wife died 9/12/1913.

BARRETT, GREGORY, JR. 1860 cen.: res. 19th Ward, Baltimore; age 24; brass finisher; born in Md.; wife born in Ohio; ———/$200. 1860 Baltimore city dir. shows res. at 115 North Fremont St., and Barrett is listed as an officer at the penitentiary. Barrett was a noted firefighter and political thug in prewar Baltimore. Appt. cpt. of Co. F, 4th Md. Inf. Regt., at Baltimore 8/15/62. Abs. sick 8/30–10/29/63. Prom. ltc. 3/9/64. Abs. furl. to visit sick brother in Baltimore 4/6–11/64. Prom. bvt. col. 1/4/65. Abs. furl. to visit sick mother in Ohio 2/21/65 and 4/29/65. MO 5/31/65. Appt. 1lt. of 26th U.S. Inf. Regt. 7/28/66. Appt. RQM 3/1–5/19/69. Trans. to 10th U.S. Inf. Regt. 5/16/69. Ass. RQM 7/12/69 to 4/8/84. Prom. cpt. 4/8/89. Died of brain fever at Santiago 8/7/98.

BISHOP, JOHN L. Born c. 1832. Occupation U.S. deputy marshal. Served on U.S. police force in Baltimore as cpt. 1861–62. Appt. cpt. of Co. E, 4th Md. Inf. Regt., at Baltimore 8/14/62. Detailed court-martial at Harpers Ferry 3/15/63. Abs. sick since 9/17/63. Disch. for hemorrhoids 11/10/63. Postwar tinner and roofer in construction business in Baltimore. NFR.

BOYD, ISAAC L. Born c. 1818. 1860 Baltimore city dir. shows Boyd as city magistrate for 17th Ward with office at 213 Montgomery St. Res. 73 William St. Appt. 1lt. of Co. D, Baltimore Light Infantry, 1/6/62. Assaulted by Joseph Edwards while in a barber shop 1/4/62. MO 4/1/62. Appt. cpt. of Co. A, 4th Md. Inf. Regt., at Baltimore 6/28/62. Disch. for hernia 1/14/63. Postwar steamboat freight agent in Annapolis. Married in Anne Arundel Co. 7/9/39. Boyd died 9/6/82.

BROWN, JOHN W. Born c. 1841. Appt. 1lt. of Co. B, 4th Md. Inf. Regt., at Baltimore 6/28/62. Charged by Col. Dushane with being absent from duty as officer of the guard 9/4/63. Disch. for diarrhea and rheumatism 3/19/64. Postwar engineer. Married Laura V. Howard at Baltimore 1/26/66. One child. He died of chronic dysentery at Baltimore 1/31/71. Wife remarried 12/91.

CARL, LOUIS ADOLPH. Born c. 1832 in Pa. Son of Joseph Carl and Charlotte Hannan. 1860 Baltimore city dir. shows res. at 122 Franklin St. Shipping clerk at a tobacco warehouse. Appt. cpt. of Co. I, 4th Md. Inf. Regt., at Baltimore 10/4/62. Charged by court-martial with disrespectful conduct and sentenced to forfeit 5 weeks' pay 11–12/63. Furl. 10 days 2/12–22/64. Acting bde. AQM 1/26/65. MO 5/31/65. Married Louisa C. H. Pickett at in New York City 12/31/79. She had been married previously to a soldier who died at Andersonville during the war. Carl and Pickett lived together for five years in Newark, N.J., before marrying. Moved to Baltimore in 1881. No children. Carl died from an operation to relieve rupture on right side caused by being kicked by a horse at Petersburg 11/11/64. Death occurred at Newark, N.J., 5/19/85. Buried in Fairmount Cemetery. His widow remarried in 1914.

CHENOWETH, FERDINAND. Born 2/24/45 in Baltimore. 5'6", dark complexion, dark hair, dark eyes. Clerk. Enl. as sgt. in Co. H, 4th Md. Inf. Regt., at Baltimore 8/16/62. Prom. 1sg. 11–12/62. Abs. sick in Washington, D.C., hospital 10/10/63. Appt. 1lt. of Co. C 10/24/64. Furl. 15 days to discuss property matters with guardian in Baltimore 1/18/65. MO 5/31/65. After the war married Roseanna Davis, but they divorced. Married Sarah Olivia Walker at the Lutheran Church in Baltimore 1872. Three children. She died 7/4/93. Chenoweth lived in Baltimore and at various soldiers' homes in the United States. He apparently died after 1915.

CRAWFORD, WILLIAM J. Born c. 1840. Enl. as sgt. in Co. B, 4th Md. Inf. Regt., at Baltimore 5/30/62. Prom. 1sg. 10/11/62. Sentenced by regimental court-martial to forfeit $10 for conduct prejudicial to good order 9–10/63. Appt. 1lt. of Co. B 6/28/64. WIA at Petersburg 6/18/64. Found guilty by general court-martial of conduct prejudicial to good order and military discipline and disrespect to superior and commanding officer. Sentenced to be dismissed 12/6/64. He applied for a military pension from Gallup, N.M., 2/3/91, but it was disapproved on grounds of his dishonorable discharge.

CROUCH, DAVID. Born 10/14/28. Served as a civilian teamster with QM Department in Mexico. Enl. at Baltimore 10/2/47. Disch. at Vera Cruz 12/17/47. Appt. 2lt. of Co. F, 4th Md. Inf. Regt., at Baltimore 8/15/62. Prom. 1lt. 1/5/63. Detailed to procure drafted men 7/26/63 until the spring of 1864. Prom. cpt. 4/21/64. MO 5/31/65. Postwar laborer in Baltimore. Married Charlotte Clements 10/48. She died at Baltimore 2/6/81. Married Effie Gise at Baltimore 6/3/90. Crouch died of strangulations of the bowels 7/17/98. Wife gave birth to a daughter in Washington, D.C., 10/14/98. Wife died in Washington 9/18/1930.

DAVIS, THOMAS H. Born c. 1834. 1860 Baltimore city dir. shows Davis as a paper carrier living at 173 East Pratt St. Enl. as corp. in Co. F, 4th Md. Inf. Regt., at Baltimore 7/30/62. Prom. 1sg. 1/5/63. Appt. 1lt. of Co. F 9/24/64. Furl. 15 days to visit sick wife in Baltimore 2/16/65. Appears AWOL 3/15/65. In arrest awaiting results of military commission 5/31/65. MO 5/31/65. Received pension in Baltimore for blindness and rheumatism 1891. Died sometime in 1896.

DAVIS, WILLIAM H. Born 3/10/24. 5'11", light complexion, sandy hair, blue eyes. Painter. Appt. 1lt. of Co. D, 4th Md. Inf. Regt., at Baltimore 7/30/62. Prom. cpt. of Co. E 12/5/63. POW at the Wilderness 5/5/64. At prisons in Lynchburg, Macon, Charleston, Columbia, and Charlotte. Exch. at Northeast Ferry, N.C., 3/1/65. At Camp Parole, Annapolis, 3/5/65. RTD 5/2/65. MO 5/31/65. Married before the war. Four children. Wife died in 1894. Davis died in Baltimore 3/18/1915.

DEVENEY, JOHN. Born c. 1838. Appt. 1lt. of Co. E, 4th Md. Inf. Regt., at Baltimore 8/14/62. Tendered resignation for syphilis 10/7/62. Resignation accepted 10/19/62. NFR.

EASTON, WILLIAM THOMAS. 1860 cen.: res. Franklinville, Carroll Co.; age 24; wheelwright; born in Md., ———/$200; wife and one child. Enl. as sgt. in Co. E, 4th Md. Inf. Regt., at Carroll Co. 8/12/62. Prom. 1sg. 6/1/64. Appt. 1lt. 1/10/65. Commanded co. 1/14–5/7/65. Furl. 15 days to visit sick wife in Carroll Co. 4/25/65. MO 5/31/65. Postwar traveling photographer. Married in Winfield, Md., 4/11/55. Three children. Husband and wife did not get along well. Easton and his partner (Robert E. Richardson, also of the 4th Md.) were in Pa. when Easton stole money in 1869 and then went west. He was never heard from again. Wife applied for and received pension. Easton presumed dead after 1898. Wife died 12/19/1926.

ELLERS, JOHN T. Born in Baltimore 6/27/37. Enl. as corp. in Co. B, 4th Md. Inf. Regt., at Baltimore 5/30/62. Prom. sgt. 7/18/62. Deserted from Baltimore 12/6/62. RTD 1/23/62. Reduced to pvt. Prom. sgt. 3/1/63. Reduced to ranks again 7/30/63. Prom. 2sg. 8/1/64 and 1sg. 8/16/64. Appt. 1lt. of Co. B 1/17/65. MO 5/31/65. Married Annie Courtney at Eutaw Street Methodist Episcopal Church in Baltimore 10/31/60. Three children. Died in Baltimore 11/28/1920.

ELLIOTT, JOSEPH. Born c. 1829. Ship carpenter. 5'6", fair complexion. 1860 Baltimore city dir. shows res. at 13 South Spring St. Enl. as pvt. in Co. A, 4th Md. Inf. Regt., at Baltimore 6/1/62. Prom. sgt. 7/17/62 and QM sgt. 9–10/62. AWOL after 12/28/63. Pres. 1–2/64. Claimed WIA twice at Weldon Railroad 8/18/64. Appt. 1lt. of Co. D 2/4/65. Detailed to duty to QM Department from 2/4/65. Furl. 20 days to visit home in Baltimore 2/28/65. Listed as AWOL 3/25/65. MO 5/31/65. Married Catharine Clayton at Annapolis 12/26/50. Three children. He died of heart disease 2/16/73. Wife died 3/18/1907.

GORSUCH, ROBERT McINTIRE. Born c. 1843. Res. Baltimore. Son of Robert and Sophronia Gorsuch. Appt. 2lt. of Co. I, 4th Md. Inf. Regt., at Baltimore 8/6/62. Prom. 1lt. of Co. D 2/29/64. Assaulted by 1lt. Isaacs at brigade head-quarters while serving as officer of the pickets 4/2/64. Pressed charges against Isaacs 4/11/64. WIA in eye at the Wilderness 5/5/64. DOW at Fredericksburg 5/16/64.

HUSBAND, ALBERT S. 1860 Baltimore city dir. shows res. at 29 Courtland St. Tobacconist at 280 1/2 West Baltimore St. Appt. 1lt. of Co. H, 4th Md. Inf. Regt., at Baltimore 8/15/62. Charged by general court-martial at Harpers Ferry with conduct prejudicial to good order and military discipline and violation of the 77th Article of War 3/13/63. Husband was accused of being drunk on Mary-land Heights 1/28/63 and assaulting the sutler's clerk. He also left his quarters while under arrest without permission 1/28/63. Found guilty and sentenced to be cashiered. Sentence approved by Gen. Schenck 6/2/63. Husband was on detached service with ambulance corps 6/20/63. He was cashiered 12/31/63. NFR.

HYDE, EDWARD J. Born at Baltimore 7/10/39. Appt. cpt. of Co. B, 4th Md. Inf. Regt., at Baltimore 6/28/62. Tendered resignation for hernia when he ruptured his side at the Lafayette Square Barracks in Baltimore while on drill 8–9/62. Resignation accepted 8/7/63. Married Caroline R. Clemm at Baltimore 3/25/68. Four children. He died in Baltimore 4/3/1917.

ISAACS, JOHN W. Born c. 1838. Appt. 2lt. of Co. H, 4th Md. Inf. Regt., at Baltimore 7/18/62. Detached service as ADC to Col. Dushane 11/24/63 till end of the war. Prom. 1lt. of Co. H 2/4/64. Charged with conduct unbecoming an officer and conduct prejudicial to good order and military discipline for assaulting 1lt. Gorsuch at bde. headquarters 4/2/64. Ordered to be tried by divisional commander 4/11/64 (results not known, and Gorsuch died of wounds month later). Furl. 12 days to visit family in Baltimore 8/1/64. Prom. bvt. cpt. for gallant and meritorious service at White Oak Road and Five Forks 4/1/65. MO 5/31/65. Postwar restaurant owner. First wife died 6/2/95. No children. Married Mary B. Henchy at St. Peter's Church in Baltimore 6/10/95. Isaacs died of apoplexy in Baltimore 11/1/1910. Buried at U.S. National Cemetery. Wife died 6/30/1917.

KEMP, THOMAS EDWIN. Born c. 1840 in Baltimore. Enl. as pvt. in Co. F, 4th Md. Inf. Regt., at Baltimore 8/15/62. Prom. corp. 9/3/62 and sgm. 1/7/64. Appt. 1lt. of Co. D 9/24/64. Appt. 1lt./adj. 12/19/64. MO 5/31/65. Postwar draftsman and stonecutter in Baltimore. Married to Belinda Gorsuch Patterson. First child born in 1866 and three others before wife's death 6/23/83. Married Edwina B. Burnett at Ashland, Baltimore Co., 2/17/86. Kemp died in Baltimore of apoplexy 1/1/99. Buried in Baltimore Cemetery. Wife died 12/10/1923.

MACE, OSCAR A. 1860 cen.: res. 7th Ward, Baltimore; age 28; cigar maker; born in Md.; wife and three children; wife born in Md. 1860 Baltimore city dir. shows res. at 87 McElderry St. 5'8", dark complexion, dark hair, brown eyes. Appt. 2lt. of Co. C, 4th Md. Inf. Regt., at Baltimore 7/9/62. Charged by Ltc. Bowerman with disobedience of orders and leaving camp without permission at Williamsport 10/13/62. Mace tendered resignation 10/14/62, which was accepted 10/16/62. He enl. as pvt. in Co. A, 9th Md. Inf. Regt. (6 months), at Baltimore 6/18/63. Prom. 1sg. 7/1/63. Reduced to the ranks 1/24/64. MO 2/23/64. Reenl. as pvt. in Co. K, 13th Md. Inf. Regt., at Sandy Hook 1/21/65. MO 5/29/65. Postwar cigar maker in Baltimore. Married Virginia E. Wright in Baltimore

6/5/53. Mace lived in the Soldiers Home in Hampton, Va., and died of Bright's disease while on leave in Baltimore from the Soldiers Home 8/25/93. Buried at U.S. National Cemetery. Wife died in 1900.

MEADE, ROBERT B. Born c. 1829. Shipwright. 5'11", fair complexion, auburn hair, blue eyes. Appt. 2lt. of Co. D, 4th Md. Inf. Regt., at Baltimore 7/18/62. Prom. 1lt. of Co. C 3/16/63. Disch. from army on surgeon's certificate at Georgetown 10/9/63. Meade was ordered to be arrested for failure to appear as witness for court-martial of Cpt. William H. Weizel 1/27/64. Apparently the victim of army bureaucracy, Meade was restored to his rank at Culpeper 4/27/64 "to fill a vacancy caused by his own resignation. The cause for such resignation having been revoked." Meade claimed prom. to cpt. of Co. D 10/24 or 31/64. MO 5/31/65. Meade filed a pension claim for a ruptured left side that occurred while building breastworks at Funkstown in summer 1863. He must have died immediately after making the claim 5/82 because no other information is available after that date and no certificate was issued.

MILLENDER, JOHN HENRY. Born c. 1834. Lumber dealer. Appt. 1lt. of Co. G, 4th Md. Inf. Regt., at Baltimore 9/16/62. Listed as AWOL 4/7/64; the charge was revoked 5/81. Disch. for "nervous disability and unable to travel" 5/11/64. Surg. noted that Millender "seems to be melancholy his skin is pale, a general feeling of nervousness and lasitude, no appetite, his tongue is clean." Married Elizabeth Ann Sauble at Manchester Lutheran Church in Baltimore Co. 5/16/54. Millender died at Cerado, W.Va., of a stomach tumor 4/5/98. His wife died in Kenova, W.Va., 6/11/1917.

MILLS, THOMAS ALLEN. Born c. 1834. 1860 Baltimore city dir. shows Mills as a grocer and liquor dealer at Calverton Mills near the almshouse. Appt. 2lt. of Co. G, 4th Md. Inf. Regt., at Baltimore 7/22/62. Prom. 1lt. of Co. E 4/27/64. WIA left foot at Laurel Hill 5/8/64. WIA right leg at Weldon Railroad 8/21/64. Died while leg was being amputated at City Point 8/23/64. Married in Washington, D.C., 11/11/56. Three children. Wife died 3/28/1917.

NICHOLSON, EDWARD E. Born at Salem, N.J., 1/7/33. Parents were Quakers and died when Nicholson was young. He worked on a farm and then as a butcher. Enl. as pvt. in Co. K, 10th U.S. Inf. Regt., at Philadelphia 6/11/57. Joined co. from Ft. Columbus, N.Y., 7/3/57. Deserted at Camp Scott, Utah Territory, 5/17/58. Arrested and restored to duty without trial. Disch. at Ft. Kearney, Nev., upon ETS 7/24/62. Appt. 2lt. of Co. C, 4th Md. Inf. Regt., 12/23/62. Abs. on detailed service with Cpt. Daniels, Signal Corps, 6/23/63. RTD 6/30/63. Detailed to receive drafted men 7/25/63. RTD 4/27/64. WIA in back by shell concussion at the Wilderness 5/5/64. Resigned for disability 6/21/64. Married three times. First wife died 7/16/65. Second wife died 5/28/79. Married Kate E. Cazier at Wilmington, Del., 5/26/80. Nicholson lived in Soldiers Home, Vineland, N.J., at time of death from vabular disease of the heart 8/7/1909. Buried at Soldiers Home Cemetery. Wife died 2/26/1933.

O'NEILL, CHARLES Z. Born c. 1831. Appt. 1lt. in Co. G, 2nd Md. Inf. Regt., at Camp Carroll 8/9/61. Tendered resignation "regretting that circumstances are such that I am compelled to resign" 6/6/62. Resignation accepted 6/9/62. Appt. cpt. of Co. H, 4th Md. Inf. Regt., at Baltimore 8/21/62. Furl. 10 days to visit sick wife in Baltimore 3/18/64. MWIA at Laurel Hill 5/8/64. Body fell into C.S. hands and wife did not know O'Neill's fate as of 8/16/64. O'Neill appears on a list of POWs at Lynchburg, Va., 6/2/64 although it is not known if this was correct. Married at Baltimore 3/8/54. Three children.

OREM, JOSEPH BAILEY. See 1st Md. Inf. Regt. entry.

PLACIDE, PAUL D. Born in Baltimore c. 1833. 1860 Baltimore city dir. shows Placide as a clerk with res. at 255 West Madison St. Enl. as pvt. in Co. I, 4th Md. Inf. Regt., at Baltimore 8/22/62. Adm. to Steuart's Mansion hospital in Baltimore with chronic diarrhea 2/18/63. Deserted 5/16/63. Arrested in Washington, D.C., 9/18/63. Placed in Forrest Hall prison but escaped. Rearrested in Washington, D.C., 10/29/63. RTD 10/30/63. Charges dropped without conditions 12/17/63. Prom. sgt. and later sgm. 10/1/64. Appt. 1lt. of Co. I 11/22/64. Furl. 15 days to visit sick father in Baltimore 1/18/65. MO 5/31/65. Married in Baltimore 2/17/69. Four children, the first born six weeks after the wedding. Placide died of consumption in Baltimore 11/26/75. Buried at Cathedral Cemetery. Wife died 12/20/1927.

RECKERD, JOHN WILLIAM. Born in Howard Co. 9/11/35. Prewar farmer and carpenter in Woodbine, Carroll Co. 5'9", light hair, hazel eyes. Enl. as 1sg. of Co. E, 4th Md. Inf. Regt., at Baltimore 8/7/62. Appt. 2lt. of Co. E 12/22/62. Adm. to Georgetown officers' hospital 8/20/63. Listed as AWOL 12/24/63. The commander of the 4th Md. requested the assistance of PMO in Carroll Co. for information on Reckerd 12/5/63. Dismissed for AWOL 1/4/64. Postwar resident of Pittsburgh, Pa., Kansas City, Kan.; Dallas, and Denver; returned to Carroll Co. in 1901. Married Amanda Leatherwood 9/25/57. No children. Applied for pension claiming debility from typhoid fever and injury to left leg. Claim rejected in 1909 because of dishonorable discharge. At that time, Reckerd lived at Methodist Episcopal Home in Baltimore. NFR.

RIMBY, JACOB. Born c. 1827. Customs officer at tobacco warehouse. 6'0", dark complexion, black hair, dark gray eyes. Enl. as 1sg. of Co. F, 4th Md. Inf. Regt., at Baltimore 8/15/62. Appt. 2lt. of Co. D 4/5/63. Prom. 1lt. 5/20/64. WIA near Petersburg 6/19/64. Applied for sick leave to visit home in Baltimore because of chronic diarrhea. Died of dysentery in Baltimore 8/31/64. Married Annie E. Butler in Baltimore 2/25/51. One child. Wife remarried 12/13/65.

RUTHS, GEORGE. Born c. 1836. Appt. 2lt. of Co. B, 4th Md. Inf. Regt., at Baltimore 6/28/62. Prom. 1lt. of Co. E 10/11/62. Commanded co. since 3/15/63. Prom. cpt. of Co. B 5/18/64. WIA in left leg at Cold Harbor 6/3/64. Furl. 15 days to visit sick wife in Baltimore 1/15/65. MO 5/31/65. Postwar cigar maker in Baltimore. Married Margaret Nity at the Lutheran Church on Eastern Ave. near Broadway in 1862. Six children. Wife died 7/2/98. Ruths died of heart failure on a public highway 1/7/1910. Buried in Baltimore Cemetery.

SCHLEY, JOHN. Born in Frederick City 8/23/38. Occupation printer. 5'6", dark complexion, black hair, dark eyes. Enl. as pvt. in Co. A, 11th Indiana Inf. Regt., at Indianapolis 4/19/61. MO 8/4/61. Appt. 2lt. of Co. F, 4th Md. Inf. Regt., at Baltimore 7/18/62. Prom. 1lt. 8/15/62. Appt. 1lt./adj. 12/9/62. Furl. 10 days to visit Baltimore on personal business 4/1/64. WIA in left leg by spent cannonball at Laurel Hill 5/8/64. Prom. cpt. of Co. G 11/26/64. Furl. 15 days to visit Indianapolis, where he had purchased town lots before the war 12/14/64. MO 5/31/65. Married Emily Isabella Smith at Central Christian Church in Indianapolis 8/22/67. Four children. First son was lost at sea as a U.S. Naval Academy cadet in 1886. Schley entered the Protestant Deaconess Hospital in Indianapolis 11/1918. Died there 1/27/1924.

SUTER, JOHN H. Born in Baltimore 9/12/32. Son of Charles and Henrietta Suter. Father was prominent furniture manufacturer and founder of Maryland Institute for the Promotion of the Mechanic Arts. John H. Suter att. school in Baltimore and went to California in 1849 during the gold rush. Was stranded in South America for seven months while returning to the East. Became a furniture manufacturer and was a member of Vigilant Fire Department and "Bell & Everett Association of Minute Men." Attacked by rioters 4/19/61 and served as volunteer officer in Unionist police force till 1862. 1860 Baltimore city dir. gives res. at 188 East Monument St. Enl. as sgt. in Co. A, 4th Md. Inf. Regt., at Baltimore 8/29/62. Prom. 1sg. 9/1/62. Appt. 2lt. in Co. A 1/17/63. Appt. acting RQM 8/17/63 and later bde. QM. Prom. 1lt. of Co. A 2/9/64. Furl. 10 days to visit sick wife in Baltimore 4/9/64. Furl. 15 days to visit family in Baltimore 12/21/64 and 5 days to visit sick children in Baltimore 5/15/65. MO 5/31/65. Postwar Baltimore circuit court clerk and clerk to auditor of the customs house. Married Mary J.

Kidd at First Reformed Church in Baltimore 5/17/55. Four children. Member of Republican party, GAR, Masons, IOF, Knights of Pythias, and Red Men Mechanics. Suter died of hemorrhoids contracted during the war in Baltimore 2/27/94. Buried at Loudoun Park Cemetery. Wife died 6/23/1913.

SUTER, MARTIN. Born in Hagerstown 11/26/20. 1860 cen.: res. 1st District, Baltimore Co. Reistertown P.O.; age 39; butcher; born in Md.; wife and six children; wife born in Md. ———/$600. 1860 Baltimore city dir. shows res. on Garrison Lane near the almshouse. Served as cpt. of Taylor Light Dragoons as part of 1st Light Cav. Regt., Md. Militia 10/29/57. Appt. cpt. of Co. G, 4th Md. Inf. Regt., at Baltimore 8/20/62. Detached service to receive drafted men in Baltimore 7/25/63. Furl. 15 days to visit Baltimore to look after children upon the death of his wife 8/7/64. Disch. for rheumatism and disease of the throat 11/25/64. Suter was appt. cpt. of the 1st Reg. Eastern Shore Inf. at Baltimore 1/18/65. Trans. to Co. E, 11th Md. Inf. Regt. (one year) that month. Prom. maj. 2/18/65. MO 6/15/65. Married Ann Maria Vilen in Martinsburg 11/9/42. Eight children. Married Ann Virginia Inlose at Baltimore 12/29/64. She died in Chicago 9/15/77. Suter died in Ireton, Iowa, 1/11/1917.

TUCKER, JOHN A. Born c. 1841. Enl. as pvt. in Co. G, 4th Md. Inf. Regt., at Baltimore 8/13/62. Prom. sgt. 1/1/63. Appt. 1lt. in Co. E 9/15/64. Prom. cpt. of Co. H 1/14/65. Suffered from extensive burns received near Weldon Railroad 2/4/65 after "falling in the fire owing to a rush of blood to the head." Tucker burned his right shoulder and arm after fulling into the fire during an attack of epilepsy "which he has recently become subject." Disch. for epilepsy 5/18/65. Married Elizabeth J. Gardner at Methodist Episcopal Church in Baltimore 5/11/65. Two children. Tucker died of epilepsy at Cockeysville 7/25/73. Wife remarried 9/24/74. She died in Baltimore 4/28/1920.

VON HAGEN, SIGISMUND. Born c. 1818. Enl. as 1sg. of Co. B, 4th Md. Inf. Regt., at Baltimore 6/9/62. Appt. 2lt. of Co. B 10/11/62. Disch. for disability 2/23/64. Adm. Annapolis GH 3/4/64. Disch. 3/14/64.

WATSON, ROBERT. Born c. 1824. Appt. 2lt. of Co. A, 4th Md. Inf. Regt., at Baltimore 6/28/62. Prom. 1lt. 1/17/63 and cpt. 1/29/64. Disch. for chronic diarrhea 9/5/64, contracted at North Anna River 5/24/64. Married Mary J. Mooney in Baltimore 1847. Watson died in the spring of 1904.

WILHELM, HENRY. Born in Middletown, Baltimore Co., 5/17/36. Son of Peter B. Wilhelm and Elizabeth Kone, descended from a German family that settled in Baltimore Co. after the American Revolution. Carpenter. 5'10", dark complexion, black hair, black eyes. Enl. as pvt. in Co. F, 4th Md. Inf. Regt., at Baltimore 7/29/62. Prom. sgt. at unknown date. Appt. 2lt. of Co. F 1/5/63. Detailed to ambulance duty 3/15/64. Prom. 1lt. 4/21/64. WIA in skull at Laurel Hill 5/8/64. WIA in thigh at Cold Harbor 6/3/64. Appears as bde. AADC 8–9/64. Prom. cpt. of Co. A 3/15/65. MO 5/31/65. Postwar conductor with B&O Railroad and Baltimore Co. farmer. Appt. tax assessor of his district in 1896. Married Chloe Dorsey in Middletown 3/12/68. Two children. Member of GAR, reasons, Summit Grange, and Republican party. Wilhelm died of emphysema at Middletown 7/13/1911. Buried at Middletown Cemetery. Wife died 12/6/1924.

WILLIAMS, ANTHONY C. Born in Philadelphia 1/3/32. 1860 cen.: res. 3rd Ward, Baltimore; age 30; shoemaker; wife and two children; ———/$500. 5'8", dark complexion, dark hair, brown eyes. Appt. cpt. of Co. D, 4th Md. Inf. Regt., at Baltimore 7/30/62. Abs. sick leave in Baltimore 10/13/62. Williams left unit 11/15/63 and applied for pass in Washington, D.C., to rejoin unit 11/20/63. Apparently Williams was tried for his absence 12/9/63 and sentenced to forfeit one month and six days' pay. WIA in right arm above the wrist at Weldon Railroad 8/18/64. Disch. for disability 9/9/64. Prom. bvt. maj. for gallant and meritorious service during the war 3/13/65. Married Mary A. Rice in 1852. Seven children. Williams died in Philadelphia 6/29/1911. Buried in Holy Cross Cemetery.

Union Officers of the 7th Maryland Infantry Regiment

ANDERSON, EPHRAIM F. Born c. 1839. Lawyer. Enl. at Hagerstown 8/25/62. Appt. cpt. of Co. I 9/5/62. WIA in right hand, left hand and palm, and right thigh at Laurel Hill 5/8/64. POW at same battle. Index finger of right hand was amputated. At Libby Prison 5/22/64. Exch. at Varina 9/22/64. Furl. for 48 hours to visit Washington, D.C., 9/22/64. Resigned because of disability 11/30/64. Prom. bvt. maj. for gallantry at the Wilderness 3/13/65 and bvt. ltc. for conspicuous gallantry at Laurel Hill 3/13/65. Farmer in Hagerstown 1866 and in 1871 resided in Howard Co. with a business address in Baltimore. Date of death unknown.

BALL, JOHN K. Born c. 1840 in London, England. Occupation clerk. Enl. as pvt. in Co. K, 27th N.Y. Inf. Regt., at Elmira, N.Y., 5/21/61. Prom. corp. 3/1/62 and sgt. 12/1/62. MO 5/31/63. Enl. as pvt. in Co. C, 10th Md. Inf. Regt., at Baltimore 6/20/63. Prom. corp. 6/26/63 and sgt. 1/7/64. MO 1/29/64. Appt. 1lt.

of Co. G, 7th Md. Inf. Regt., at Baltimore 4/1/64. Prom. 1lt./adj. 11/18/64. Requested leave of absence to visit sick sister in western N.Y. 12/3/64. MO 5/31/65. Married Mary Jane Murphy in Albion, N.Y., 2/18/64. No children. Ball was a resident of Soldiers' Home in Dayton, Ohio, 1891. He died in Baltimore 12/27/1903. Buried in Loudoun Park Cemetery. Wife died 4/2/1923.

BEACHUM, F. STANLEY. Appt. 2lt. of Co. C, 7th Md. Inf. Regt., 9/9/62. Appears as abs. sick 4/19–5/3/63. Deserted from Baltimore hospital 8/15/63. Dismissed from the service 10/12/63. NFR.

BENNETT, DAVID T. Born c. 1829 in Md. 1860 Frederick city dir. shows Bennett as a carpenter residing on the south side of 3rd St. between Market and Public Sts. Appt. 2lt. of Co. E, 7th Md. Inf. Regt., 8/21/62. Prom. cpt. 8/28/62. Prom. ltc. 7/2/64. WIA upper jaw at the Wilderness 5/5/64. WIA in left leg below knee at Five Forks 4/1/65. Prom. bvt. col. for gallant and meritorious service at Five Forks 4/1/65. MO 5/31/65. Married Charity A. James at Evangelical Lutheran Church in Frederick 5/8/55. Six children. Postwar carpenter and builder in Baltimore. Member of the Odd Fellows. He died of tumor in Baltimore 10/2/89 after falling down stairs and breaking ribs. Buried in Loudoun Park Cemetery. Wife died 8/31/1911.

BOULDIN, RICHARD E. Born in Bel Air, Harford Co., 11/26/37. 1860 cen.: res. Bel Air, Harford Co., age 23; printer; son of Charles and Mary Bouldin; father was clerk; $2,000/$1,000. two other children; two black servants; all born in Md. 5'9", fair complexion, auburn hair, blue eyes. Appt. 2lt. of Co. C, 7th Md. Inf. Regt., 8/13/62. Prom. cpt. 9/4/62. WIA saber cut to right arm during Bristoe Station campaign in fall 1863. Tendered resignation at Baltimore for injuries 9/23/64. Disch. for disability 10/8/64. Married Martha Christabill Gough at Charles Street Methodist Episcopal Church in Baltimore 2/4/64. Five children. Postwar Harford Co. newspaper editor. Died 3/12/1920.

BRAGONIER, ALPHREOD C. Born near Hagerstown 5/6/42. 5'7", fair complexion, brown hair, brown eyes. Merchant. Appt. 2lt. of Co. G, 7th Md. Inf. Regt., 8/12/62. Prom. cpt. 9/12/62. Resigned "for the good of the service" 3/28/63. Resignation accepted 4/7/63. Postwar merchant in Baltimore. Married first wife 11/8/60. Eleven children. She died in Frederick 11/4/97. Married Victoria Royston in Baltimore 6/11/1902. Died 8/7/1911. Buried in Middletown.

BREWER, VALENTINE G. Born 5/14/40 in Hagerstown. Cabinetmaker. 1860 cen.: res. Clear Spring, Washington Co.; son of Henry and Elizabeth Brewer;

father farmer born in Pa., mother born in Md.; $3,000/$150; six other children. 5'6", fair complexion, brown hair, gray eyes. Enl. as sgt. in Co. A, 7th Md. Inf. Regt., at Hagerstown 8/8/62. Prom. 2lt. 1/21/64. Prom. 1lt. 11/10/64. Detailed as bde. pioneer officer 4/15/64 until MO 5/31/65. Requested 15 days leave of absence to visit sick mother in Clear Spring 3/15/65. Postwar cabinetmaker for lumber co. in Gunnison, Col. Married Bethena Beath in Gunnison 5/29/82. One child. He died there 4/7/1924. His wife died 1/8/1941.

BROUNER, RICHARD R. Born in Sing Sing, N.Y., c. 1826. Bookkeeper. 5'6", light complexion, dark hair, gray eyes. Enl. as pvt. in Co. A, 5th N.Y. Zouaves, at New York City 5/9/61. Prom. 1sg. 6/26/61. Appt. 1lt. 8/14/61. Appt. 1lt./adj. 1/15/62. Tendered resignation at camp near New Bridge to take care of widowed mother and family 6/12/62. Col. G. K. Warren recommended approval because "I have not been altogether satisfied with his qualifications for the post in the field." Resignation accepted 6/13/62. Appt. 1lt./adj. of 7th Md. Inf. Regt. 9/16/62. Prom. cpt. of Co. G 4/23/63. Requested leave of absence to visit sick mother in New York City in spring 1863. Noted as AWOL since 8/17/63. Dismissed from the service for "having failed to make satisfactory defence before the Military Commission" 11/3/63. Enl. as pvt. in Co. D, 165th N.Y. Inf. Regt., in New York City 2/10/64. Prom. sgt. 11/6/64 and sgm. 1/1/65. Reduced to ranks 3/5/65. Abs. on detached service in Winchester 4/7/65. Later served with QM Department in Washington, D.C. MO in Washington, D.C., 8/31/65. Married Annie R. Drayton in Washington, D.C., 10/1/66. Four children. Brouner was confined at St. Elizabeth's Hospital in 1902. He died 11/16/1903.

BURNHAM, WILLIAM H. Born in Kiskaton, Greene Co., N.Y. 5/19/44. 5'7", fair complexion, brown hair, hazel eyes. Machinist. Enl. as pvt. in Co. H, 5th N.Y. Inf. Regt., at Ft. Schuyler 5/9/61. Prom. corp. 7/20/61 and sgt. 8/19/61. Reduced to ranks 12/23/61. Disch. for hypertrophy and palpitations of the heart at Harrison's Landing 8/8/62. Enl. as pvt. of Co. B, 10th Md. Inf. Regt., at Baltimore 6/23/63. Appt. 2lt. and trans. to Co. E 7/10/63. MO 1/29/64. Appt. 2lt. of Co. K, 7th Md. Inf. Regt., 4/4/64. Suffered from contusion in fall 5/20/64. No duty performed after 7/20/64. MO 5/31/65. Married Isabella Hertell at Cedar Street Baptist Church in Buffalo, N.Y., 6/27/65. Four children. Burnham died of consumption in Buffalo 5/30/84. Buried in Forest Lawn Cemetery, Buffalo.

BURROWS, HILLARY T. Born c. 1844 in Montgomery Co., Md. 5'8", light complexion, brown hair, blue eyes. Enl. as pvt. in Co. C, 7th Md. Inf. Regt., at Baltimore 8/20/62. Prom. 1sg. 9/4/62. Appt. 1lt. 1/21/64. WIA left side and chest at the Wilderness 5/5/64. Unable to perform field duty and ass. to court-martial duty in Washington, D.C., 6/8/64 until end of the war. Requested to be relieved of this duty to be mustered out with regt. in Baltimore 6/10/65. Claimed reenl. in Co. G, 9th U.S. Veteran Volunteers, 8/5/65. Disch. 4/19/66 or 5/30/66. Lived in Washington, D.C., in 1897. Died 5/8/98.

COCHRAN, JAMES B. Born in New Castle, Del., 10/13/36. Res. Havre de Grace. Merchant. Appt. cpt. of Co. H, 7th Md. Inf. Regt., at Baltimore 9/4/62. Prom. bvt. maj. for gallant and meritorious service at White Oak Road and Five Forks 4/1/65. MO 5/31/65. Lived in Baltimore, New York City, and Philadelphia after the war. Married Clara Cochran after the war. Two children. She died 1/23/78 in Philadelphia. Married Hattie Yardley Buckman 2/20/90. Cochran died in Philadelphia 1/8/1913. Wife died 9/17/1926.

COLKLESSER, WILLIAM H. 1860 cen.: res. Hagerstown, Washington Co.; age 27; shoemaker; born in Md.; ———/$100. Appt. 1lt. of Co. A, 7th Md. Inf. Regt., at Hagerstown 8/8/62. Prom. cpt. 1/21/64. Abs. on detailed service with subsistence department after 11/11/64. MO 5/31/65. Married Amelia A. Oden at Boonsboro 2/17/55. Two children. In pension claim, Colklesser stated that he got lost between the lines during the fighting in the Wilderness, and "one of the branches struck him in the crotch, injuring his privates." He died of Bright's disease in Washington, D.C., 2/17/71. Buried at Hampstead, Carroll Co., Md. His wife died in Washington 2/2/1920.

CONNER, CHARLES A. Born in Havre de Grace c. 1836. Newspaper editor and journalist. Appt. 2lt. of Co. D, 7th Md. Inf. Regt., at Baltimore 8/13/62. Prom. 1lt. 8/26/62. WIA in hipbone at Weldon Railroad 8/18/64. Abs. on detailed service in Philadelphia after wounding. Prom. cpt. 5/6/65 but disch. for disability in Philadelphia 5/15/65. Postwar editor of the Baltimore County *Union* and Havre de Grace *Republican*. Member of the GAR. Married Cornelia R. Lee at Presbyterian Church in Gowanstown, Md., 2/22/65. Two children. She died about 1873. Connor died of bronchitis in Baltimore 12/25/1901.

CREAGER, NOBLE HARWOOD. 1860 cen.: res. Mt. Pleasant District, Frederick Co.; age 17, born in Md.; son of Ephraim and Mary Creager; farmer; $10,000/$2,000; both parents born in Md.; five other children; one black boy lived with family. Enl. as corp. in Co. E, 7th Md. Inf. Regt., at Frederick 8/15/62. Prom. 1sg. 10/63. WIA in right side and right arm at the Wilderness 5/5/64. Appt. 1lt. 1/25/65. MO 5/31/65. Lived in Frederick and Baltimore after the war.

Appt. maj./QM of U.S. Volunteers 5/20/98. MO 4/17/99. Appt. cpt./QM of U.S. Army 2/2/1901. Died in Orlando, Fl. 12/31/1914.

CROMWELL, WILLIAM H. Born in Frederick Co. 6/11/33. 1860 cen.: res. Woodboro District, Frederick Co.; age 27; carpenter; born in Md.; $800/$200; wife, Elizabeth, and two children. 5'10", black hair, black eyes. Appt. 2lt of Co. E at Frederick 8/28/62. Resigned because of poor health at Maryland Heights 10/9/62. Postwar building contractor; sheriff in Frederick in 1891. Democrat. Died of debility at Walkersville, Frederick Co., 1/12/1910. Buried at Mt. Olivet Cemetery, Frederick.

DAYHOFF, JOSHUA T. 1860 cen.: res. Frederick city; age 27; restaurant owner; born in Md.; ———/$100; wife, Ann, and two children. 1860 Frederick city dir. shows res. at south side of Patrick St., west of Bentz. Owner of saloon at Dayhoff and Rice on the east side of Market St. between Patrick and All Saints. Appt. 2lt. of Co. B, 7th Md. Inf. Regt., at Frederick 8/20/62. Tendered resignation for poor eyesight 2/26/64. Resignation accepted 4/19/64. NFR.

DEVILBLISS, ISAIAH. 1860 cen.: res. Frederick city; age 30; merchant; born in Md.; ———/$2,000; wife and one child. Appt. 1lt. of Co. E, 7th Md. Inf. Regt., at Frederick 8/21/62. Died of typhoid fever at Culpeper CH 9/24/63. Married at Methodist Episcopal Church in Frederick 4/4/50. Widow remarried 4/7/65 and died 3/22/1906.

DUNPHY, RICHARD G. 1860 cen.: res. Lauraville, Baltimore Co.; age 40; laborer; born in Md.; $800/$300; wife and six children. Enl. as pvt. in Co. D, 7th Md. Inf. Regt., at Baltimore 8/14/62. Appt. 2lt. 8/26/62. Served as asst. PM at Harpers Ferry 3–6/63. Requested 15 days leave of absence to visit dying sister in Baltimore Co. 3/15/65. MO 5/31/65. Married Elizabeth Ann Bowen in Baltimore 4/5/41. He died 3/19/91. Wife died in 1894.

GORRELL, SKIPWORTH C. 1860 cen.: res. Hopewell, Harford Co.; age 41; farmer; born in Md.; $2,000/$500; wife and one child. Appt. 1lt. of Co. H, 7th Md. Inf. Regt., at Baltimore 9/4/62. WIA left arm near shoulder while on picket duty to capture guerrillas on Loudoun Heights, Va. 5/23/63. Shot accidentally by Pvt. Isaac Reed at 2 A.M. Abs. in hospital in Baltimore after 6/11/63 and at home 7/7/63. Resigned because of disability 11/25/63. Married Priscilla Hopkins near Level, Md., 1/18/42. Gorrell died 1/11/92 and his wife died 5/13/92.

GREEN, JOHN KIRKWOOD. Born in Harford Co. 9/6/29. 5'10", florid complexion, light hair, blue eyes. Mechanic and tavern keeper. Enl. as sgt. in Co. H,

7th Md. Inf. Regt., at Baltimore 8/21/62. Listed as AWOL 1/28–2/6/63. Appt. 1lt. 1/26/64. Requested 15 days leave of absence to purchase property 1/13/65. MO 5/31/65. Married Alice A. Fulton at Presbyterian parsonage near Stewartstown, Pa., 10/12/54. Two children. He died of gastritis 3/7/1907. Buried at Stewartstown, Pa. Wife died in Philadelphia 10/2/1913.

HAGAN, PETER AUGUSTUS. Born 4/8/43 at Braddock Heights, Md. 1860 cen.: res. Jackson District, Frederick Co.; worked as laborer for Jonathan Keller, farmer; $7,000/$1,500. Hagan had attended school within the year. 5'6", light complexion, brown hair, blue eyes. Enl. as sgt. in Co. C, 7th Md. Inf. Regt., at Middletown 8/13/62. Appt. 2lt. 2/28/63. POW at Haymarket 10/19/63. Confined in Richmond 10/23/63. Sent to Macon, Ga., 5/7/64. Exch. at Northeast Ferry, N.C., 3/1/65. Furl. 30 days 3/11/65. RTD 4/13/65 and sent to regt. 5/2/65. He still was at Camp Parole, Md., 5/5/65. MO 5/15/65. Postwar messenger for the superintendent of the architect's office in the U.S. Treasury Department. Married Mary Emily Harrison in Baltimore 10/30/66. Four children. He died of pneumonia and heart failure 12/4/1913. Buried at Middletown. She died 6/17/1938 and was buried at Methodist Episcopal Church in Middletown.

HARKINS, JOSEPH A. Born c. 1840 in Md. Brother also enlisted in same unit. Enl. as sgt. in Co. C, 7th Md. Inf. Regt., at Baltimore 8/21/62. Appt. 2lt. 11/27/63 and cpt. 1/18/65. Requested 15 days leave to visit sick mother in Harford Co. 12/2/64 and again 4/24/65. MO 5/31/65. Married Lorena Slade at Chestnut Hill in Harford Co. 12/21/65. Six children. He died 8/17/1914 at Chestnut Hill. She died 11/26/1917.

HARN, THOMAS W. Born c. 1824. Farmer in Unionville, Frederick Co. Appt. 1lt. of Co. B, 7th Md. Inf. Regt., at Frederick 8/20/62. Furl. 15 days to visit sick mother in Frederick Co. 2/22/65. WIA right hip at Five Forks 4/1/65. MO 5/31/65. He died about 1/21/92. NFR.

HERGESHEIMER, ROBERT H. Born c. 1843 in Frederick Co. Son of James Hergesheimer. 5'8", light complexion, black hair, gray eyes. Student. Enl. as sgt. in Co. E, 7th Md. Inf. Regt., at Frederick 8/15/62. Prom. 1sg. 1/28/63. Appt. 2lt. 11/9/63. KIA at Weldon Railroad 8/21/64. Buried at Mt. Olivet Cemetery.

HORINE, WILLIAM HENRY HARRISON. Born in Md. 4/20/40. Mechanic. 1860 cen.: res. Hagerstown, Washington Co.; son of Henry and Elizabeth Harrison; farmer; $4,000/$1,000; both parents born in Md.; three other children. 5'7", fair complexion, gray hair, brown eyes. Enl. as corp. in Co. A, 7th Md. Inf.

Regt., at Hagerstown 8/8/62. Appt. 2lt. 11/10/64. Furl. 15 days to visit aged father in Hagerstown 3/20/65. MO 5/31/65. Postwar merchant. Lived in Md. and Ill. after the war. Married Annie Bell, widow of Simeon A. Sprague, at Carlinville, Ill., 7/16/74. Two children. Wife born in Cherokee Co., Ala. Horine died of uremia in St. Louis, Mo., 3/20/1916.

HOWARD, JOHN. 1860 cen.: res. Mechanicstown District, Frederick Co.; age 33; laborer; born in Berkley Co., W.Va.; wife, Sarah, and seven children; wife born in Md. 5'10", light complexion, light hair, blue eyes. Enl. as 1sg. of Co. E, 7th Md. Inf. Regt., at Frederick 8/19/62. Appt. 2lt. 1/2/63, 1lt. 11/9/63, and cpt. 12/5/64. Furl. 15 days to visit sick child in Frederick city 2/13/65. MO 5/31/65. Died in Cumberland Co., Pa., 7/30/1907.

KNODLE, CHARLES S. Born 8/9/37 in Hagerstown. 1860 cen.: res. Hagerstown, Washington Co.; son of John and Christiana Knodle. father shoemaker, born in Pa.; mother born in Md.; $2,000/$1,500; four other children. Appt. 2lt. of Co. I, 7th Md. Inf. Regt., at Hagerstown 8/18/62. Furl. 10 days to vote in Hagerstown and visit family 11/1/63. Detached service to receive drafted men at Annapolis 7/25/63. RTD 4/23/64. Detailed as bde. ambulance officer 11–12/64. Furl. 10 days to visit sick sister in Hagerstown 2/17/65. Requested to be relieved of this duty to return to regt. 5/31/65. MO 5/31/65. Postwar merchant and clerk in Baltimore. Married Caroline Josephine Bingham at Somerville, Mass., 11/24/68. Two children. He died of indigestion after eating fried oysters in Baltimore 1/31/1906. Buried at Hagerstown. His wife died 9/7/1923.

KOOGLE, JACOB. Born 12/5/41 at Wyersville, Md. 1860 cen.: res. Frederick Co.; son of Magdalena Koogle; $3,220/$350; four other children. 5'8", fair complexion, sandy hair, gray eyes. Farmer. Enl. as pvt. in Co. G, 7th Md. Inf. Regt., at Middletown 8/13/62. Prom. 2sg. 4/10/63 and 1sg. 10/7/63. Appt. 1lt. 11/18/64. Furl. 15 days to visit sick mother in Frederick Co. 1/19/65. Awarded the Medal of Honor for capturing an enemy battle flag at Five Forks 4/1/65. MO 5/31/65. Married Mary Manerva Poffenberger at Hagerstown 12/28/71. Five children. He died at Hagerstown 3/16/1915.

LIGHTNER, ISAIAH. Born 10/30/41 at Union Bridge, Md. Clerk. 5'10", sallow complexion, light hair, blue eyes. Enl. as sgt. in Co. F, 7th Md. Inf. Regt., at Baltimore 8/22/62. Appt. 2lt. 1/3/63; 1lt. 11/11/63; and cpt. 12/12/64. Furl. 15 days to visit sick mother and oversee property in Carroll Co. 1/13/65. WIA left hip at Five Forks 4/1/65. MO 5/31/65. Postwar resident of Union Bridge, Santee Agency, and Monroe, Neb. Married Fannie R. Haines at Union Bridge 12/3/67.

Six children. She died 4/14/1911. He married Catharine Pound DePeel at Neleigh, Neb., 10/26/1912. He died in Pasadena, Calif., 3/2/1923.

MAKECHNEY, JOHN. Born in Pottsville, Pa., 11/2/27. 1860 cen.: res. Frederick City; age 28; gas fitter; lived in hotel. Appt. 2lt. of Co. B, 7th Md. Inf. Regt., at Frederick 8/12/62. Appt. cpt. 8/20/62. Abs. furl. 12/12–22/63 and 4/23–28/64 to visit dying mother-in-law in Trenton, N.J. Commanding regt. 6/7/64. Detached duty at draft rendezvous in Elmira, N.Y., 12/13/64 until disch. 6/3/65. Postwar engineer in Trenton, N.J. Married Catharine Gantz in Pottsville, Pa., 1848. She died in 1856. Two children. Married Louisa Baumford in Philadelphia 9/13/70. She died in 1902. Makechney died 12/4/1905.

McALLISTER, JOHN A. Born c. 1837. Enl. as pvt. in Co. C, 4th Regt. Potomac Home Brigade, at Middletown 11/11/61. Deserted at Williamsport 5/3/62. Appt. 2lt. of Co. F, 7th Md. Inf. Regt., 8/14/62. Noted as "missing" 8/28/62 but appears to have been a deserter. POW at Harpers Ferry 9/15/62. Paroled 9/15/62 and sent to Alexandria, Va. NFR.

McMORRIS, JOHN. Born c. 1837. Carpenter. Enl. as sgt. in Co. H, 7th Md. Inf. Regt., at Baltimore 8/21/62. Appt. 2lt. of Co. C 1/31/65. MO 5/31/65. Married Bathsheba L. Stone at Marietta, Ohio, 12/20/66. One child. He died of heart disease (but also listed as syphilis) 8/17/70. Widow died 4/8/1923.

MOBLEY, EDWARD M. Born in Frederick City 1/20/25. Son of Eli and Sophia Mobley. Father was a drummer at Ft. McHenry in the War of 1812. Carriage maker and elected to sheriff of Washington Co. on Union ticket in 1859. 1860 cen. shows that Mobley had ———/$450. Appt. cpt. of Co. A, 7th Md. Inf. Regt., at Hagerstown 8/8/62. Served as acting PM at Williamsport 9/23–12/21/62. Furl. 10 days to appear as witness at court-martial in Hagerstown 3/10/63. Served as PM at Harpers Ferry 3/28/63. Ass. as AAG. to col. Dushane 7/20/63. RTD 11/29/63. Prom. maj. 1/21/64. WIA leg at Bethesda Church 5/27/64 and in neck at Weldon Railroad 8/18/64. Noted as AWOL 12/2–13/64. Requested court of inquiry to investigate case 12/20/64. Prom. bvt. ltc. for gallant and meritorious service during the Appomattox campaign 4/9/65. Prom. bvt. col. for faithful and gallant service. MO 5/31/65. Married Ellen Cecillia Carver at Hagerstown 10/27/43. Ten children born between 1844 and 1864. One son served in Mobley's co. Member of Masons, Odd Fellows, and GAR. Wife died in 1900. Mobley died of paralysis at Hagerstown 4/4/1906.

MORRISON, WILLIAM D. Born in Baltimore 1/16/27. 6'0", light complexion, dark hair, blue eyes. Farmer. Appt. cpt. of Co. D, 7th Md. Inf. Regt., at Baltimore

8/26/62. Detailed to bring recruits to the army from summer of 1863 until spring 1864. Furl. 8 days to visit relatives 11/1/63. Detached duty at Elmira, N.Y., at POW camp 7–8/64. Requested promotion to field grade with regt. in letter to Md. governor from Elmira 10/17/64. Suffered smashed right knee in train accident en route to Elmira from Baltimore at Troy, Pa., 12/20/64. Submitted letter of resignation for disability and chronic diarrhea at Elmira 1/15/65: "I wish those who are doing the duty to hold the position." Resignation accepted 1/17/65. Married Pauline DeWaele Tharp at Easton, Md., 3/3/68. Three children. After the war, Morrison lived in Md., Kan., Ill., and Texas. Wife died 9/11/1909. He died at Angleton, Tex. 11/6/1913.

RADCLIFF, WILLIAM D. Born in Liberty, Frederick Co., 12/28/39. 1860 cen.: res. Hagerstown, Washington Co.; son of William and Elizabeth Radcliff; father a butcher; $4,000/$500; four other children. 5'7", light complexion, dark hair, blue eyes. Clerk. Appt. 2lt. of Co. I, 7th Md. Inf. Regt., at Hagerstown 8/12/62. Prom. 1lt. 9/5/62 and cpt. 12/23/64. Furl. 6 days to visit Hagerstown to help parents move to Ill. and to procure uniform 3/27/63. Furl. 20 days to visit Springfield, Ill., to visit sick father 1/27/64. Examined in court of inquiry in the case of AWOL of Maj. Mobley 12/64. MO 5/31/65. Lived after the war in Ill., Kan., South Dakota, and Neb. Married Hannah Benson in Omaha, Neb., 9/22/87. He died in Omaha of arterios schloresis 11/9/1913. Buried in Forest Lawn Cemetery.

REIFSNIDER, CHARLES T. 1860 cen.: res. Frederick city; age 20; law student; born in Md.; lived in boardinghouse. Appt. 2lt. of Co. F, 7th Md. Inf. Regt., 8/12/62. Prom. 1lt. 9/2/62. Resigned for physical disability 10/22/62. NFR.

RINEHART, DANIEL. Born c. 1825. Brother of William H. Rinehart, famous sculptor. Appt. cpt. of Co. F, 7th Md. Inf. Regt., 8/28/62. WIA at Laurel Hill 5/8/64. Suffered attack of jaundice at City Point 8/27/64. Disch. for asthma and chronic diarrhea 11/28/64. Postwar farmer in Union Bridge, Carroll Co. Married Margaret Hyder before the war. She died 5/13/60. Five children. Married Rebecca L. Norris 3/7/65. One child. Rinehart died of heart disease 9/23/86. Second wife died at Union Bridge 6/28/1920.

ROBINSON, JOSEPH. 1860 cen.: res. Shawsville, Harford Co., age 25; teacher; born in Md.; son of Mary Robinson, farmer, born in Md.; $2,000/$500; five other children. Appt. 2lt. of Co. H, 7th Md. Inf. Regt., at Baltimore 9/4/62. Furl. 8 days to attend to business at home 1/29/63. Disch. for rheumatism 1/1/64. Postwar dentist in Baltimore. Married at Chestnut Hill, Harford Co., 5/18/69. Robinson died of consumption in Harford Co. 8/31/73.

SMITH, HENRY C. Born in Baltimore c. 1833. 1860 Baltimore city dir. shows res. at 115 Raborg. Carpenter. 5'10", fair complexion, brown hair, gray eyes. Appt. 2lt. of Co. F, 10th Md. Inf. Regt., at Baltimore 7/16/63. MO 1/29/64 but continued to serve in army as recruiter after this date. Trans. to Co. K, 7th Md. Inf. Regt., at Baltimore 2/16/64. Prom. 1lt. of that co. 3/2/64. Slightly WIA in neck at Petersburg 10/64. Furl. 15 days to visit sick wife in Baltimore 10/17/64. MO 5/31/65. Died in Baltimore 1/25/1913.

SMITH, JOHN K. Enl. at Middletown 8/13/62. Appt. 1lt. of Co. G, 7th Md. Inf. Regt., 9/12/62. Resigned to return to medical practice 12/23/62. Resignation accepted 1/11/63. Smith regarded himself "incompetent to discharge the duties of my position as a military man." NFR.

SUTER, CHARLES M. 1860 cen.: res. Hagerstown, Washington Co.; age 20; cabinetmaker; born in Hagerstown, Md.; son of William and Melinda Suter, cabinetmaker; ———/$200; both parents from Md.; five other children and one white servant. 5'7", fair complexion, light hair, blue eyes. Enl. as pvt. in Co. I, 7th Md. Inf. Regt., at Hagerstown 8/14/62. Prom. sgt. 9/5/62. Appt. 1lt. 12/19/64. Furl. 15 days to visit "blind and enfeebled" mother in Hagerstown 3/12/65. WIA at Five Forks 4/1/65. MO 5/31/65. Postwar merchant in Hagerstown. Married Laura V. Witzenbacher in Hagerstown 1/22/74. Six children. Suter died 1/8/1909. Wife died 11/10/1919.

TOWER, LAWRENCE. Born at Oriskany Falls, N.Y., 10/16/45. Son of Fayette B. Tower and Ann Regina Phelps. Father born in N.Y. and mother in Vermont. Farmer at Waterville, N.Y., before the war. 5'9", fair complexion, brown hair, brown eyes. Enl. as pvt. in Co. H, 7th Md. Inf. Regt., at Hagerstown 9/20/62. Prom. 1sg. of Co. G 4/10/63. Appt. 1lt. 9/30/63 and cpt. 1/21/64. Suspended from pay and rank for three months by general court-martial 4/16/65. MO 5/31/65. Postwar coal merchant in New York City. Married Anna Maria Hodgkins in Brooklyn 10/19/70. One child. He died in Brooklyn of chronic nephritis 6/4/1913. Wife died 12/30/1917.

TYLER, GEORGE L. Appt. 2lt. of Co. F, 7th Md. Inf. Regt., 8/20/62. Prom. 1lt. of Co. F 1/2/63 and appt. 1lt./adj. 5/1/63. WIA in right thigh at the Wilderness 5/5/64. Tendered resignation for disability from Frederick 10/25/64. Resignation accepted 11/3/64. Prom. bvt. cpt. for gallant and meritorious service at the Wilderness 3/13/65. NFR.

WEBSTER, JOSEPH P. Born at Bel Air, Harford Co., 9/26/35. Occupation farmer. 5'11", light complexion, brown hair, gray eyes. Enl. as pvt. in Co. C, 7th

Md. Inf. Regt., at Bel Air 8/18/62. Appt. 2lt. 9/4/62. Prom. 1lt. 9/9/62. Disch. for ruptured veins in stomach and testicles 1/1/64. Married Laura C. Mitchell at St. John's Protestant Episcopal Church in Havre de Grace 1/7/74. No children. She apparently died before Webster. He died in Baltimore 8/13/1915.

WEISE, ARTHUR JAMES. Born c. 1838. Appt. as 2lt. of Co. A, 7th Md. Inf. Regt., at Hagerstown 8/8/62. Prom. 1lt. 1/21/64. Tendered resignation to return to Hagerstown to take care of mother and three sisters after death of father and to take care of family business 10/6/64. Resignation accepted 10/10/64. Weise died in East Orange, N.J., 1/7/1921.

WHEELER, HENRY W. 1860 cen.: res. 14th Ward, Baltimore; age 21; clerk; born in Md.; son of Elizabeth Wheeler, who ran boardinghouse; ———/$600; father died in 1857. 1860 Baltimore city dir. shows Wheeler as salesman living at 17 South Howard St. 5'8", fair complexion, dark hair, hazel eyes. Enl. as pvt. in Co. B, 10th Md. Inf. Regt., at Baltimore 6/23/63. Elected 2lt. of Co. E 7/10/63. MO 1/29/64. Appt. cpt. of Co. K, 7th Md. Inf. Regt., at Baltimore 4/4/64. MO 5/31/65. Died of chronic diarrhea and typhoid fever at home in Baltimore 6/30/65.

WHITTLE, SAMUEL N. Born c. 1843. Res. Towsontown, Baltimore Co. Enl. as sgt. in Co. D, 7th Md. Inf. Regt., at Baltimore 8/14/62. Prom. sgm. 9/10/62. Noted as AWOL 12/30/62. Appt. 2lt. of Co. F 11/9/63. Prom. 1lt. 12/12/64. Stabbed while on guard duty during elections at Towsontown 4/6/64. Furl. 15 days to visit sick mother 2/23/65. MO 5/31/65. Postwar plasterer. Died before 9/92.

Union Officers of the 8th Maryland Infantry Regiment

ANDREWS, WILLIAM E. Born in Md. c. 1833. Appt. 1lt. of Co. F, 8th Md. Inf. Regt., at Baltimore 9/11/62. Andrews attempted to resign twice from military service claiming his own incompetence and poor handwriting. A board met to examine Andrews 1/9/64 yet apparently denied his request to resign as he was prom. cpt. of Co. F 7/1/64. Furl. 15 days to visit sick wife in Baltimore 1/11/65. MO 5/31/65. Married Margaret R. Sibley at Laurel, Md., 10/22/54. Andrews died of paralysis at Wilmington, Del., 8/31/95. Buried at Mt. Carmel Cemetery in Baltimore. Wife died 7/19/1909.

BARTLESON, HENRY C. Born in Radnor, Delaware Co., Pa. 1/23/44. 1860 cen.: res. Pleasantville, Harford Co.; age 16; farmer and student; born in Pa.; son of Mark and Mary Bartleson, both born in Pa., farmer; $8,000/$2,000; three other children and one white female servant. 5'10", fair complexion, light hair, gray eyes. Enl. as pvt. in Co. C, 8th Md. Inf. Regt., at Baltimore 8/18/62. Prom. corp. (date unknown) and sgt. 10/22/62. Prom. 1sg. 6/17/63. Appt. 1lt. of Co. G 7/24/64 and cpt. 12/26/64. Furl. 10 days to visit sick father 1/12/65. MO 5/31/65. Postwar resident of Harford Co., Philadelphia, and Lansdowne, Pa. Physician in Lansdowne in 1907. Married Clara Virginia Thompson at St. Matthews Protestant Episcopal Church in Philadelphia 11/28/72. Two children. Bartleson died at Lansdowne 1/29/1922. Wife died 2/27/1934.

BOWIE, WALLACE A. Born 1843. Son of Hyde Ray Bowie and Mary Wallace. Clerk. Fair complexion, dark hair, gray eyes. Enl. as pvt. in Co. B, 8th Md. Inf. Regt., at Baltimore 8/21/62. Prom. sgm. 8/29/62. Appt. 2lt. of Co. H 1/3/63. Disch. for ETS 11/12/63. Appt. acting 3rd asst. eng., U.S.N. 3/28/64. Served on board USS *Kearsage*. Continued in the service after the war but stricken with yellow fever in Panama. Resigned in 1868. Later resident of San Francisco. Married Libbie West. Six children. Died 7/21/1914.

BOYER, BENJAMIN R. Born in Chester Co., Pa., 9/28/31. Iron worker. 5'10", fair complexion, sandy hair, blue eyes. Enl. as 1sg. of Co. A, 8th Md. Inf. Regt., at Baltimore 8/13/62. Appt. 2lt. of Co. A 12/13/62. Acting RQM 8/1/63. Abs. furl. 12/8/63 through 1/27/64. Noted as AWOL 1/27/64 but this was changed to abs. sick 12/28/63 through 4/8/64. Furl. 20 days for chronic diarrhea 9/19/64. Prom. 1lt. of Co. A but never mustered 5/9/65. MO 5/31/65. Postwar resident of North East, Cecil Co., 1865 until death 11/1/1907.

BRAYS, WILLIAM J. Enl. as pvt. in Co. I (nine-month drafted men and substitutes), 8th Md. Inf. Regt., at Camp Bradford 12/28/62. Appt. 2lt. of same co. 3/19/63. Disch. for ETS 12/29/63.

BRIDE, JAMES. Born c. 1837 in Cork, Ireland. Son of John H. and Elizabeth Bride. Parents married at St. Nicholas Protestant Episcopal Church in Cork 7/2/36. Moved to United States and lived in Calif. 1850–59, where father made a living as miner and painter. Returned to Baltimore in 1859. 1860 Baltimore city dir. shows res. at 139 West Madison St. James Bride was a cheese and fish dealer at the Lexington Market. Appt. 2lt. of Co. D, 8th Md. Inf. Regt., at Baltimore 9/4/62. Prom. 1lt. 9/11/62 and cpt. 11/13/63. KIA at Laurel Hill while leading charge with regt. flag 5/8/64. Bride's mother died 7/17/66 and his father filed for pension for the loss of his son. The older Bride had been employed with the Baltimore tax collector's office in 1861 but lost his job because he refused to support the Confederacy. He then served as a "regulator" in 1861–62 and worked with the U.S. Christian Commission in 1864. The government refused to grant him a pension.

BROADFOOT, JOSEPH O. 1860 cen.: res. 3rd Ward, Baltimore; age 26; iron molder; born in Baltimore; single and lived with employer. 1860 Baltimore city dir. shows res. at 44 North Liberty St. 6'2", fair complexion. Enl. as pvt. in Co. C, 8th Md. Inf. Regt., at Baltimore 8/18/62. Detailed commissary sgt. 8/13/62. AWOL 2/18/63 and reduced to ranks by court-martial 6/14/63. Prom. sgt. 8/1/63 and RQM sgt. 2/24/64. Prom. 1lt. of Co. B 10/6/64. Adm. Annapolis GH with spinal injury 12/31/64. RTD 1/11/65. Declared AWOL 12/30/64 and after RTD 1/11/65 tried by military commission 1/27/65. The commission found that Broadfoot should have returned to duty with the utmost speed by the "regularily established U.S. Mail Route via Washington, D.C.," rather than by boat to Norfolk. It recommended that he be tried by court-martial for disobedience of orders and AWOL. Court-martial restored Broadfoot to duty but sentenced him to be cashiered 3/21/65. This sentence was later reversed and Broadfoot's absence was corrected to read on account of illness 11/30/1900. Postwar iron molder in Baltimore. Filed for pension in 1897. Married Marr L. Sanner. One child. NFR.

CASSARD, LOUIS R. Born c. 1840. Clerk. 1860 Baltimore city dir. shows res. at 243 North Lexington St. 5'11", fair complexion, light hair, blue eyes. Appt. 2lt. of Co. A, 8th Md. Inf. Regt., at Baltimore 8/9/62. Prom. 1lt. 8/15/62 and cpt. 9/1/63. He wrote letter to PM of Baltimore stating: "A notification of my being drafted having reached me. I have the honor to state that I am now in the service of the United States" 12/9/63. Tried to resign 1/7/64 but letter never left bde. headquarters. Furl. 15 days to visit sick brother in Baltimore 1/16/65. Prom. bvt. maj. for gallant and meritorious service at Five Forks 4/1/65. Served as acting bde. inspector 4/22/65. MO 5/31/65. Postwar merchant in Baltimore. Married Elizabeth H. Kensett in Baltimore Co. 11/7/68. Two children. Cassard died of kidney failure in Baltimore 4/22/94. Wife died 2/6/1912.

CHANEY, LOUIS. Appt. 2lt. of Co. G, 8th Md. Inf. Regt., at Baltimore 9/15/62. Prom. 1lt. 10/28/62. Listed as AWOL 3/16/63. Dismissed from the service 9/30/63. NFR.

CLAYTON, THEODORE. Served as 1lt./QM. of 1st Md. Light Artillery. Resigned 7/18/62. Appt. cpt. of Co. C, Purnell Legion Cavalry, at Baltimore 9/19/62. Trans. as cpt. to Co. I, 8th Md. Inf. Regt., 11/17/64. Tendered resignation because of dissatisfaction at having his co. transferred from cavalry to infantry 12/10/64. Resignation accepted 12/17/64. NFR.

COLE, WILLIAM P. Born in Md. c. 1836. Son of William P. Cole, Baltimore manufacturer of hats. 1860 Baltimore city dir. shows office at 273 West Baltimore St. and res. at 138 North High St. 5′8″, light complexion, light hair, blue eyes. Stonemason. Enl. as pvt. in Co. I (nine-month drafted men and substitutes), 8th Md. Inf. Regt., at Camp Bradford 10/30/62. Appt. 1lt. of Co. I 3/19/63. Served as acting adj. 10/8/63. Disch. for ETS 12/29/63. Wrote to governor for captain's commission in 100-day regt. 6/9/64. Appt. 2lt. of Co. I, 11th Md. Inf. Regt. (100 days), 6/15/64. MO 10/1/64. Postwar resident of Washington, D.C. Married Mary E. Crowther in Baltimore Co. 12/29/59. Three children. Cole died of chronic rheumatism and heart disease in Washington, D.C., 10/8/97. Buried at Hamstead, Md. Wife died 1/20/1901.

COOKE, WILLIAM H. Born c. 1842. Apprentice stone cutter to Alex Packie at Monument and Davis Sts. in Baltimore. Enl. as pvt. in Co. C, 8th Md. Inf. Regt., at Baltimore 8/18/62. Prom. corp. 9/10/62 and sgt. 1–2/63. Prom. 1sg. 7–8/64. Appt. 1lt. 5/9/65. MO 5/31/65. Postwar stonecutter and clerk in Baltimore post office. Married to Margaret A. James. No children. She died in Baltimore 1/6/95. Cooke died 1/23/1912.

DIXON, CHARLES T. Born c. 1837. Appt. cpt. of Co. E, 8th Md. Inf. Regt., at Hagerstown 9/21/62. Disch. for physical disability and AWOL 6/15/64. The latter reason was amended 2/10/75 when Dixon received a pension for injuries stemming from a sunstroke at Rappahannock Station in 8/63 and other ailments, including disease of the kidneys and malarial fever. Married Joanna Montgomery at the Methodist Episcopal Church in Frederick 8/14/60. Seven children. Dixon died of pneumonia in Pittsburgh, Pa., 11/8/1909. His wife died in Saluvia, Pa., 3/10/1918.

FAY, JAMES. Born c. 1834. 1860 Baltimore city dir. shows Fay as a plumber at 16 South Sharp St. Appt. 2lt. of Co. B, 8th Md. Inf. Regt., at Baltimore 8/29/62. Prom. 1lt. 4/14/63. WIA at Weldon Railroad 8/18/64. DOW at field hospital 8/28/64. Married Elizabeth McMahon at St. Vincent de Paul Roman Catholic Church in Baltimore 11/18/56. One child. Wife received a pension in 1864 but failed to claim it after 9/4/1903.

FEILEN, AUGUSTUS M. Born in Prussia c. 1824. Merchant. 5′10″, ruddy complexion, brown hair, blue eyes. Enl. as pvt. in Co. D, 8th Md. Inf. Regt., at Baltimore 2/26/64. Later prom. to sgt. Appt. 2lt. 9/12/64. MO 5/31/65. NFR.

FURLONG, McKENDREE C. Born c. 1843. Enl. as pvt. in Co. K (nine-month drafted men and substitutes), 8th Md. Inf. Regt., at Camp Bradford 10/28/62.

Prom. 2lt. 3/29/63. Tendered resignation for ETS at Camp Bradford 8/8/63: "After having served five months as a private, I was commissioned by the Governor of Maryland as 2nd Lieut of Co 'K' 8th Regt. Md. Vols, & accepted the commission under the impression that I would not be held longer than the nine months for which I was drafted, otherwise I would have respectfully declined the Commission & with cheerfulness have served out my time as a private." Resignation accepted 9/26/63. NFR.

GAMBLE, GEORGE. Born c. 1840. Tavern keeper in Baltimore. 1860 Baltimore city dir. shows Gamble as an iron finisher with res. at 186 McHenry St. Appt. 2lt. of Co. F, 8th Md. Inf. Regt., at Baltimore 8/13/62. Submitted letter of resignation for disability at Williamsport 9/25/62. Disch. 9/30/62. Gamble received a pension for a ruptured testicle, which he claimed occurred when he ordered a soldier to stop firing on cows from the train en route from Baltimore to Hagerstown via Harrisburg 9/62. The soldier, George Smith, told Gamble that he would shoot the officer at the first battle and then attacked him. Gamble was injured in his "privates" during this assault on the train. He submitted his resignation and received a pension until 7/7/64, when he was informed that he was ineligible because he had not served over 90 days in the army. In a postwar investigation, a special agent noted that Gamble was a faro dealer. He was shot by Gabriel D. Clark although no arrest was made. Gamble married Sarah Gordon 5/15/95. He died 6/11/1911.

GARDNER, RICHARD F. Born in Md. c. 1823. 1860 Baltimore city dir. shows Gardner as a tailor with res. at 29 East Baltimore St. Appt. 1lt/rqm. of the 3rd Md. Inf. Regt. at Baltimore 9/12/61. Resigned because of injuries received when he fell from a horse 5/7/62. Appt. cpt. of Co. G, 8th Md. Inf. Regt., at Baltimore 10/28/62. Tendered resignation because of dysentery 2/16/63. Resignation accepted 2/24/63. Married Eliza A. Zell in Baltimore 9/10/47. Gardner died of pneumonia 1/10/93. Buried in Baltimore Cemetery. His wife died in 1899.

GARMHAUSER, FREDERICK C. Born c. 1841. Son of John and Elizabeth Garmhauser. Appt. 2lt. of Co. G, 8th Md. Inf. Regt., at Baltimore 10/28/62. Garmhauser was ordered to be placed under arrest by the commander of Camp Tyler in Baltimore for unknown reason 9/25/63. Prom. 1lt. 4/2/64. WIA in neck and into the back at Harris Farm 5/19/64. Prom. cpt. 7/12/64. Adm. to Annapolis GH 11/14/64 and disch. for ulcers on the legs, which he contracted while at a field hospital in Petersburg 8/23/64. Disch. 11/24/64. Married Lizzi Chaney 8/18/63. Five children. Garmhauser abandoned his wife and went to live in Harrisburg, Pa., with another woman 1/77 but never divorced his wife. A pension was paid to both Garmerhauser and his wife. Wife died 10/9/1903 and Garm-hauser died c. 1904–1905.

GOLDSBOROUGH, EDWARD Y. Born in Frederick city 12/11/39. Son of Ed-ward Y. Goldsborough and Margaret Schley. Occupation lawyer. 5'6", fair com-plexion, brown hair, gray eyes. Appt. 1lt. of Co. E, 8th Md. Inf. Regt., 9/21/62. Detailed as judge advocate to court-martial 11/17/62. Furl. 8 days to attend court in Frederick 2/10/63. Detailed to court-martial duty 3/25/63. Wrote letter to Gen. Banks requesting staff appt. on Banks's staff in the Department of the South 5/18/63. Served as acting adj. 8/18/63. Tendered resignation 12/17/63 after hav-ing been elected state's attorney for Frederick Co. 11/4/63. Resignation accepted 12/21/63. Goldsborough served as volunteer ADC to Brig. Gen. E. B. Tyler dur-ing the Battle of Monocacy 7/9/64. Postwar lawyer in Frederick Co. Golds-borough led the effort in 1902 to receive compensation from U.S. Congress for ransom that Frederick city paid C.S. forces during summer 1864 campaign. Married Amy Ralston Auld in Protestant Episcopal Church in Painesville, Ohio, 6/10/74. One son. Goldsborough died of cerebral hemorrhage in Frederick 1/19/1915. Buried in Mt. Olivet Cemetery. Wife died 10/19/1921.

GRAESER, BERNARD N. Born in Erfurt, Germany, 2/13/36. 5'9", light com-plexion, light hair, gray eyes. Clerk and merchant. Immigrated to the United States in 1840. Lived in Ft. Hamilton, N.Y., and Baltimore. Enl. as pvt. in Co. H (nine-month drafted men and substitutes), 8th Md. Inf. Regt., at Baltimore 12/5/62. Appt. 1lt. 1/3/63. Tendered letter of resignation at Rappahannock Sta-tion 9/8/63 because his company had been discharged for ETS. MO 11/1/63. Postwar residences include New York, Ill., Mich., and Iowa. Married May A. Hicks at Milford, Ill., 6/6/70. She died in Des Moines, Iowa, 7/20/1904. Married Christina Bezler Haller at Bethany, Mo., 1909. Second wife had divorced her first husband in 1905. Graeser died in Des Moines 9/18/1920. Wife died 1/5/1928.

GROSS, RICHARD L. Born c. 1838. Appt. 2lt. of Co. C, 8th Md. Inf. Regt., at Baltimore 9/3/62. Tendered resignation because of chronic rheumatism 12/11/62. Resignation accepted 1/14/63. Enl. as pvt. in Co. C, 8th Md. Inf. Regt., at Cumberland 2/29/64. WIA in left forefinger at the Wilderness 5/5/64. Trans. to Co. D, 1st Md. Inf. Regt. MO 7/2/65. Married Caroline Hunkle at Cumberland 2/23/60. Four children. Gross applied for a pension 11/22/80. That same day, he was thrown from his horse, suffered a fractured skull, and died. His wife received the pension and died 11/6/1915.

HEATH, STEPHEN P. Born c. 1836. Enl. as pvt. in Co. I (nine-months drafted men and substitutes), 8th Md. Inf. Regt., at Camp Bradford 11/5/62. Appt. cpt.

3/19/63. Disch. 4/16/64. Appt. cpt. of Co. K, 5th Md. Inf. Regt., from civil life at Richmond 3/22/65. Prom. ltc. 8/10/65. Commandant of POW camp at Newport News, Va. MO 9/1/65. Died in Baltimore 1/21/1923.

HERRING, JAMES H. Born in Frederick Co. 12/31/38. Miller. 5'9", ruddy complexion, auburn hair, gray eyes. Enl. as pvt. in Co. B, Purnell Legion Cavalry, at Baltimore 8/19/62. Prom. corp. 9/1/62, sgt. 11/1/63, and 1sg. 10/25/64. Co. B, Purnell Legion Cavalry, trans. to 8th Md. Inf. Regt. and designated as Co. I 11/17/64. Appt. 1lt. of Co. H 12/23/64. Furl. 15 days to visit sick father in Md. 2/15/65. MO 5/31/65. Postwar resident of Baltimore, MO., and Ark. Married Susan S. Repp at Warrensburg, Johnson Co., MO., 10/9/67. Seven children. One son died in U.S. Army service during Spanish-American War. Herring died of Bright's disease in Johnson Co., Mo., 7/24/1911. Wife died 7/26/1929.

HOSMER, JAMES RAY. Born in New York City 12/4/34. Son of Oliver Ellsworth Hosmer and Nancy Hawes. 1860 cen.: res. 11th Ward, Baltimore; age 26; lawyer; born in N.Y.; wife and one child; lived with Augustus J. Albert, merchant; $275,000/$265,000. Hosmer's res. at enl. was 81 West Monument St. Att. Columbia University. Served as sgt. of Co. G, Md. Guard, in 1860. Appt. 2lt. of Co. D, 8th Md. Inf. Regt., at Baltimore 9/11/62. Appt. AQM 9/18/62. Detailed as member of court-martial in Baltimore 2/15/63. Tendered resignation 5/16/63 upon receipt of appt. as cpt./AQM of U.S. Volunteers 5/12/63. Resigned 12/13/64. Postwar resident of Baltimore, Chicago, New York City, London, Paris, Boston, Guatemala, and Honduras. Served as secretary to U.S. consul general in Central America 3/87–12/90. Volunteered for military service during Spanish-American War and appt. cpt./AQM of U.S. Volunteers 5/12/98. Served in Va. and Cuba. Disch. 5/12/99. Married Martha Jane Albert (daughter of Augustus) in Baltimore 12/21/58. One child. Wife died 1/3/67. Married Esther Bayard in New York City 9/71. Two children. Second wife died in Plainfield, N.J., 4/23/88. Married Isabella Findlay in New York City 4/9/1904. Member of the GAR, SAR, and Society of Colonial Wars. Hosmer died of arteriosclerosis at Harbor View in Brooklyn, 10/16/1923. Buried at Greenwood Cemetery in New York City. Third wife died c. 1939.

HULLETT, DAVID F. Born in Baltimore 7/14/38. Son of James Hullett. Carpenter. 1860 Baltimore city dir. shows res. at 240 Franklin St. Appt. 1lt. of Co. B, 8th Md. Inf. Regt., at Baltimore 8/29/62. Prom. cpt. of Co. H (nine-month drafted men and substitutes) 1/3/63. Furl. 10 days to go to Alexandria, Va., to visit sick wife 4/17/63. Disch. for ETS 11/5/63. Married Rebecca Gillen in Baltimore 11/2/65 (this appears to be in conflict with his request for leave). Seven children. Hullett died of nephritis in Baltimore 5/6/1905. Buried in Western Cemetery. Wife died 9/11/1915.

IRELAN, CHARLES DAVIS. 1860 cen.: res. 14th Ward, Baltimore; age 26; clerk; born in Md.; single; lived with a policeman. 1860 Baltimore city dir. shows res. at 35 Pine St. Appt. cpt. of Co. A, 5th Md. Inf. Regt., at Baltimore 9/21/61. Applied for furlough to visit North East, Cecil Co., but disapproved. Irelan left anyway 2/6/62. Arrested and charged with disobedience of orders 2/8/62. Tendered resignation 3/11/62. Resignation accepted 3/13/62. Appt. cpt. of Co. A, 8th Md. Inf. Regt., at Baltimore 8/13/62. Requested furl. to visit sick family in Cecil Co. 3/27/63. Tendered resignation at Harpers Ferry because of "excessive corpulency" and inability to march 4/22/63. Resignation accepted 4/27/63. Married after the war. Irelan died of diabetes in Baltimore 2/12/79. His wife died in Washington, D.C., 5/14/1926.

JANNEY, JOSEPH J. Born in New Lisbon, Ohio, 1/9/41. Occupation merchant. 5'7", light complexion, light hair, blue eyes. Enl. as sgt. in Co. C, Purnell Legion Cavalry, at Baltimore 9/8/62. Prom. 1sg. 1–2/63. Appt. 2lt. 11/8/64. Co. C trans. to Co. I, 8th Md. Inf. Regt., 11/17/64. Janney resigned because of this transfer 12/17/64. Postwar resident of Washington, D.C., Harford Co., and Baltimore. Married Anna M. Townshend in a Quaker ceremony at Mt. Washington, Md., 10/15/68. Two children. She died 2/26/91. Janney died in Baltimore 11/30/1920.

JOHANNES, JOHN G. 1860 cen.: res. 18th Ward, Baltimore; age 36; jeweler; born in Md.; wife and three children; $1,200/$6,000; one mulatto servant. 1860 Baltimore city dir. shows shop at Wine Alley between Charles and Light Sts., res. 469 West Fayette St. Served in Baltimore City Guard before the war. Appt. ltc. of Purnell Legion Reg. Inf. at Ft. McHenry 9/30/61. Tendered resignation at Baltimore 4/15/62: "I cannot remain in the Regiment under present circumstances—subalterns in the Staff are incessantly undermining and subverting all my efforts to establish proper discipline and my feeling as an officer and a man will not allow me to remain in the organization." Resignation accepted 4/20/62. Appt. 2lt. of Co. D, 8th Md. Inf. Regt., at Baltimore 8/13/62. Prom. cpt. 9/4/62. Prom. ltc. 9/8/62. Examined by board of Veteran Reserve Corps for appointment because of chronic diarrhea and rheumatism 4/24/65. Found "indifferent" for capacity of a commission, knowledge of tactics, discipline, and service; "fair" in knowledge of regulations; and "bad" concerning his knowledge of the Articles of War. Johannes was not recommended for a commission in the Veteran Reserve Corps and remained with the 8th Md. He was later charged with striking an enlisted man with a stick several times while being escorted to the guardhouse and found guilty 8/15/64. The court sentenced Johannes to a public reprimand in general orders by the divisional commander. WIA in hips by shell at Dabney's Mill 2/6/65. Nearly unhorsed but saved by pocket Bible. Disch. to accept colonelcy of the 11th Md. Inf. Regt. (one year) at Ft. Delaware 3/3/65. MO 6/15/65. Postwar jewelry manufacturer and resident in N.Y., Kan., and Washington, D.C. Married Mary P. Waters in Baltimore 4/10/45. Three children. Received pension for eye disease caused by explosion of ammunition he was destroying on Maryland Heights 7/1/63. Died of heart failure in Washington, D.C., 1/27/1904. Buried at Arlington National Cemetery. Wife died 9/7/1910.

JOHNSON, BOWIE F. Born c. 1842. Son of Reverdy Johnson, a state and U.S. senator from Md. and also U.S. attorney general and U.S. minister to England. Entered Georgetown College in 1856 and member of class of 1863. 5'8", dark complexion, dark hair, brown eyes. Appt. 2lt. of Co. F, 8th Md. Inf. Regt., 9/11/62. Served as ADC to Brig. Gen. Kenly 11–12/62 through 5–6/63. Prom. 1lt. of Co. C 9/1/63. Ordered to staff of Brig. Gen. Morrell at Indianapolis draft rendezvous 2/10/64. Disch. 12/14/64. Johnson enl. as substitute for Isaac Scull in Co. H, 4th N.J. Inf. Regt., at Camden, N.J., 1/16/65. MO 7/9/65. Postwar farmer in Oakland, Garrett Co., Md. Married Virginia M. Thayer at Oakland 10/31/72. Four children. Johnson died of apoplexy at Oakland 9/29/93. Buried in Odd Fellows Cemetery. Wife died in Washington, D.C., 1/1919.

KENNARD, LEWIS E. 1860 cen.: res. 18th Ward, Baltimore; age 21; iron finisher; born in Md.; lived with brother. Enl. as corp. in Co. F, 8th Md. Inf. Regt., at Baltimore 8/18/62. Prom. sgt. 11/18/62 and 1sg. 7/1/63. Appt. 1lt. of Co. E 7/7/64. Detailed AACS at division hospital 9–10/64 through 3–4/65. Furl. 15 days to administer estate in Baltimore 1/13/65. Furl. 20 days to visit sick family in Baltimore 4/26/65. MO 5/31/65. NFR.

LARRABEE, WILLIAM F. Born c. 1834. Son of Ephraim Larrabee, an importer and dealer in leather, shoe fittings, and medicines. Baltimore city dir. shows shop at 24 South Calvert St. and res. at 33 Calhoun St. Appt. 2lt. of Co. C, 8th Md. Inf. Regt., at Baltimore 8/11/62. Prom. cpt. 9/3/62. Detailed to general court-martial duty 11/17/62. Tendered resignation because "circumstances have occurred in his domestic relations which imperatively demand his presence at home" 1/5/63. Larrabee concluded, "It is perhaps, not improper here to state that he greatly regrets the necessity of this step and that he will hereafter as heretofore as a private Citizen earnestly sustain the government in its efforts to put down this rebellion." Resignation accepted 1/9/63. NFR.

LATCHFORD, THOMAS. Born c. 1837. Son of John D. Latchford and Jane Gainen. Res. Beltsville, Prince Georges Co. Enl. as pvt. in Co. K (nine-month drafted men and substitutes), 8th Md. Inf. Regt., at Camp Bradford 10/31/62. Appt. 1lt. 3/19/63. Disch. for ETS 3/11/64. Applied for appt. in U.S. Colored Troops 3/20/64. Appeared before board of examiners 5/25/64. Appt. 1lt. in Co. K, 28th U.S. Colored Troops 8/28/64. Appt. adj. 9/1/64. Prom. cpt. of Co. E 11/18/64. Served as AAAG, 3rd Bde., 3rd Div., 9th Army Corps, 11/4/64. Applied for RA commission at Corpus Christi 9/24/65. Denied on the grounds that no vacancies existed. MO 11/8/65. Appt. as 2lt. of 11th U.S. Inf. Regt. 4/6/66. Trans. to 20th U.S. Inf. Regt. 9/21/66. Prom. 1lt. 11/2/66. Served as RQM 8/20/68 to 12/31/70. Ass. to recruiting duty in Baltimore 1/71. Married Louise J. A. M. Mentz at St. Joseph's Roman Catholic Church in Baton Rouge, La., 4/4/69. One child. Latchford died of consumption at Laurel, Md., 7/12/73.

LEONARD, WILLIAM H. Born in Baltimore c. 1838. Son of William M. Leonard and Sarah Matilda. Enl. as 1sg. of Co. B, 8th Md. Inf. Regt., at Baltimore 8/19/62. Appt. 1lt. of Co. A 4/12/64. Furl. 6 days to go to Baltimore to obtain uniform 4/19/64. Served as acting adj. 6/1/64 through 8/15/64. Appt. 1lt./adj. 12/14/64. Furl. 15 days to visit sick wife in Baltimore 12/15/64. Furl. 10 days upon death of daughter 2/25/65. Suffered from neuralgia in the face contracted at Hatcher's Run 2/6/65. Prom. bvt. cpt. for gallant and meritorious service at Five Forks 4/1/65. MO 5/31/65. Postwar clerk of custom house and record office. Also operated conveyance business in Baltimore. Married Jane R. Merson at the Union Square Methodist Episcopal Church in Baltimore 4/8/61. Eight children. Wife died 1/4/84. Leonard died of consumption in Baltimore 7/27/91. Buried at Loudoun Park Cemetery, Baltimore.

McCULLOH, GEORGE WILLIAM. Born in Frostburg, Md., 4/17/36. Clerk. 5'11", fair complexion. Appt. 2lt. of Co. C, 2nd Reg. Potomac Home Brigade Inf., at Frostburg 8/14/61. Tendered resignation to accept another commission at Patterson Creek, W.Va. 3/31/62. Resignation accepted 4/8/62. Enl. as 1sg. of Co. C, 8th Md. Inf. Regt., at Baltimore 8/21/62. Appt. 2lt. 4/8/63. Injured by magazine explosion at Maryland Heights 6/30/63. Burned on the head, hands, and face. Abs. sick in Washington, D.C., until 8/4/63. Noted as AWOL from Campbell Hospital in Washington, D.C., 8/17/63 but appears to have been issued surgeons' certificates at Hancock, Md., 8/15/63 and 9/23/63. McCulloh was dismissed from the service for AWOL 2/24/64. Married Sarah Jane Beddeau in Clayton Co., Iowa, 1/31/54. Eight children, five survived. McCulloh died in Huntingdon, W.Va., 6/13/1916. His wife died 12/15/1926.

MOFFETT, EDWIN W. Born c. 1840. Son of William H. Moffett. Clerk. 1860 Baltimore city dir. shows res. at 64 North Front St. 5'6", fair complexion, brown hair, blue eyes. Edwin's brother William H. Moffett, Jr., served in Alexander's

Btry. throughout the war. Edwin Moffett enl. as 1sg. of Co. F, 8th Md. Inf. Regt., at Baltimore 8/22/62. Appt. 1lt. of Co. E 4/12/64. Furl. 10 days to obtain uniform in Baltimore 4/19/64. Prom. cpt. 7/7/64. WIA slightly at Weldon Railroad 8/21/64. Furl. 10 days to visit sick mother in Baltimore 1/2/65 and sick father 3/15/65. MO 5/31/65. Postwar resident of Baltimore and member of GAR. NFR.

MURRAY, ALEXANDER. Born c. 1838. Appt. 2lt. of Co. C, 8th Md. Inf. Regt., at Camp Bradford 8/15/62. Prom. 1lt. 9/3/62 and cpt. 1/9/63. Injured when thrown by horse at Williamsport in the fall of 1863. Noted as AWOL 11/10/63. Sentenced to forfeit half of all pay and allowances 11/1/63 through 1/21/64 by court-martial 2/6/64. WIA right ankle by minié ball at the Wilderness 5/5/64. Prom. bvt. maj. for gallant and meritorious service at Five Forks 4/1/65. MO 5/31/65. Postwar resident of Leesburg, Va. Died 4/15/95.

NORMAN, WILLIAM BUCKNER. Born in Baltimore 8/7/37. Son of Michael S. Norman and Rachel Jones. 1860 Baltimore city dir. shows that Norman was a stock and bill broker in his father's firm, office at 62 Second St. and res. at 61 McCullough St. Att. Princeton College. Appt. 2lt. of Co. A, 8th Md. Inf. Regt., at Baltimore 8/11/62. Appt. 1lt./adj. 8/13/62. Abs. sick leave 8/29/63. Detailed to bde. staff as ADC/AAAG 6/1/64 and 12/14/64. Appt. 1lt. of Co. A 12/14/64. MO 5/31/65. Postwar auctioneer and antique dealer and resident of Baltimore, Chicago, and New York City. Married Mary J. Milstead at the Church of the Transfiguration in New York City 6/8/83. Wife had previously been married twice before and had one child from first marriage. Norman died of pulmonary edema in New York City 8/12/1906. Wife died 3/3/1923.

PURNELL, WASHINGTON IRVING. Born c. 1842. Student in 1861. Son of J. F. Purnell of Snow Hill, Md. Appt. 2lt. of Co. C, Purnell Legion Cavalry, 9/19/62. Prom. 1lt. 3/26/64. WIA in left side and lower back at Weldon Railroad 8/18/64. Co. C trans. to Co. H, 8th Md. Inf. Regt., 11/17/64. Prom. cpt. 1/4/65. Detailed as acting asst. commissary of musters for 2nd Div., 5th Army Corps 2/22/65. Prom. bvt. maj. for gallant and meritorious service at Five Forks 4/1/65. MO 5/31/65. Postwar lawyer in Iowa and Dallas, Tex. Married Laura V. Giles at St. Peter's Protestant Episcopal Church in Baltimore 11/30/67. Three children. Wife divorced Purnell for cruelty 6/5/96. Purnell died in Dallas from sunstroke 8/4/96.

RIDDLE, BEAL D. 1860 cen.: res. 18th Ward, Baltimore; age 31; molder; born in Md.; wife; ———/$200. 1860 Baltimore city dir. shows res. at 454 West Lombard St. Appt. cpt. of Co. F, 8th Md. Inf. Regt., at Baltimore 9/11/62. Noted as AWOL 11/18–12/28/62. Tried for AWOL and sentenced to forfeit pay and allowances 3–4/63. Noted as AWOL again 6/2–10/63. Abs. sick from chronic diarrhea and remittent fever from 8/18/64 until the end of the war. Disch. 5/15/65. Postwar molder in Baltimore. Married Isabella Hume in Baltimore 11/30/59. Two children. A pension investigator noted that Riddle was continually drunk. Riddle died of cirrhosis of the liver in Baltimore 12/13/98. Buried in Baltimore Cemetery. Wife died 1/16/1911.

RIZER, EUGENE J. Born in Somerset Co., Pa., 2/15/42. Law student in 1861. 6'0", florid complexion, light hair, gray eyes. Enl. as pvt. in Co. F, 11th Pa. Inf. Regt. (three months), at Harrisburg, Pa., 4/20/61. MO 7/31/61. Appt. 2lt. of Co. D, 8th Md. Inf. Regt., at Baltimore 8/12/62. Prom. 1lt. 9/4/62 and cpt. 9/11/62. Noted as AWOL 6/30/63. Rizer had a surgeon's certificate for typhoid fever 8/17/63. Dismissed from the service 9/23/63 although dismissal revoked and Rizer restored to duty 3/8/64 (AWOL record was later determined to be erroneous 6/22/94). No vacancy existed in the 8th Md. for Rizer to fill. Enl. as pvt. in Co. G, 11th Md. Inf. Regt. (100 days), at Baltimore 6/10/64. Reenl. as 1sg. of Co. B, 11th Md. Inf. Regt. (one year), at Monrovia, Frederick Co., 9/22/64. Appt. 2lt. of Co. C 12/28/64. MO 6/15/65. Postwar lawyer and editor of the *Farm Independent News*. Lived in various locations in Pa., Iowa, Chicago, and Col. Married Sallie S. Earnest. Seven children. She died 6/7/88. Married Effie J. McDougall in Chicago 10/28/97. Rizer died in Proctor, Logan Co., Colo. 9/23/1913.

RODERICK, WILLIAM W. Born in Middletown, Frederick Co., 10/5/37. Printer. 5'8", light complexion, brown hair, blue eyes. Appt. 2lt. of Co. E, 8th Md. Inf. Regt., at Hagerstown 9/21/62. Requested leave to attend court in Frederick Co. 1/23/63. Thrown from a horse at Winchester and injured his left side 8/1/63. Detailed to receive recruits at Annapolis 7/25/63. Requested leave to visit sick wife and to vote in elections in Frederick Co. 10/31/63. Detailed at draft rendezvous at Mason's Island, Washington, D.C., 11–12/63 through 1–2/64. Tendered resignation in Washington, D.C., to attend to sick wife 1/11/64. Resignation accepted 3/7/64. Postwar Washington, D.C., policeman. Married Amanda Ellen Yates in Middletown 2/14/60. No children. His wife died in 1902. Roderick lived in the National Soldiers Home in Tenn. after 1908. He died there of cerebral hemorrhage 8/14/1917.

SCHLENNIG, FRITZ. Born in Hesse, Germany, c. 1832. 5'7", fair complexion, light hair, blue eyes. Enl. as pvt. in Co. H (nine-month drafted men and substitutes), 8th Md. Inf. Regt., in Baltimore 12/5/62. Schlennig had been drafted 11/14/62. Prom. corp. 1–2/63, sgt. 3–4/63, and 1sg. 5–6/63. Disch. 8/7/63. Schlennig was accepted as a substitute 12/1/63. He enl. as pvt. in Co. G, 8th

Md. Inf. Regt., at Baltimore 12/14/63. Prom. sgt. 4/13/64 and sgm. 7/21/64. Appt. 2lt. 9/18/64. Furl. 15 days to visit sick brother who arrived in Baltimore from Germany and was sick 1/26/65. Furl. 6 days to visit sick sister in Baltimore 5/15/65. Prom. 1lt. 5/9/65 but not mustered. MO 5/31/65. NFR.

SHEALEY, GEORGE W. Born in Towsontown 10/19/44. Occupation farmer. 5'5", light complexion, light hair, gray eyes. Enl. as pvt. in Co. C, Purnell Legion Cavalry, at Baltimore 11/11/62. Suffered ruptured abdomen from accident on horse at Wilmington, Del., 9–10/63. Appt. 1lt. 1/7/64. Co. C trans. to Co. I, 8th Md. Inf. Regt., 11/17/64. Furl. 15 days to visit sick mother in Baltimore 2/16/65. Prom. bvt. cpt. for gallant and meritorious service at Five Forks 4/1/65. Prom. cpt. 5/15/65. MO 5/31/65. Postwar resident of Md., Ohio, Iowa, Kan., and Calif. Married Lydia E. McCawen at Logan, Ohio, 11/21/67. No mention of children. Wife died before Shealey. Adm. National Home for Disabled Volunteer Soldiers in Sawtelle, Calif., 1916. Died of cancer of the stomach 3/31/1923.

SHRIVER, GEORGE W. Born in Westminster, Md., c. 1835. Printer. Son of Francis Shriver. 5'7", light complexion, light hair, gray eyes. Enl. as sgt. in Co. K, 1st D.C. Vols., at Washington, D.C. 10/19/61. Disch. 9/3/62. Enl. as pvt. in Co. K (nine-month drafted men and substitutes), 8th Md. Inf. Regt., at Camp Bradford 11/8/62. Appt. cpt. 3/19/63. Detailed to take charge of drafted men at Camp Tyler in Baltimore 9/28/63. Ass. as PM of Camp Distribution in Baltimore 12/28/63. Relieved of duty and ordered to report to PM 8th Army Corps 2/12/64. Disch. for ETS 3/11/64. Enl. as pvt. in Co. E, 12th Md. Inf. Regt. (100 days), at Baltimore 6/30/64. Appt. cpt. 7/28/64. MO 11/6/64. NFR.

SIMON, FREDERICK W. Born in Baltimore 1838. Att. Mt. Zion School. Moved to St. Louis, Mo., before the war. 1860 cen.: res. 12th Ward, Baltimore; age 20; clerk; born in Md.; son of Charles and Johanna M. Simon; parents born in Germany, merchant; $10,000/$20,000; two other children and three servants. Appt. 2lt. of Co. B, 8th Md. Inf. Regt., at Baltimore 8/13/62. Prom. cpt. 8/29/62. Detailed to Annapolis to receive drafted men 7/25/63. RTD 4/28/64. WIA in left leg at Laurel Hill 5/8/64. RTD 10/14/64. Appt. inspector of 2nd Bde., 2nd Div., 5th Army Corps, 10/26/64. WIA in right arm at Five Forks 4/1/65. Prom. bvt. maj. for gallant and meritorious service at Five Forks 4/1/65. MO 5/31/65. Postwar dry goods merchant in Baltimore. Married Florence T. Hooper in High Street Methodist Episcopal Church in Baltimore 11/16/69. Simon died in Baltimore of Bright's disease 10/6/93. Buried in Greenmount Cemetery. Wife died 5/30/1902.

SIMPERS, JOHN W. 1860 cen.: res. North East, Cecil Co.; age 34; constable; born in Md.; $500/$100; wife and three children; Wife born in New Brunswick, Canada. Appt. 2lt. of Co. A, 8th Md. Inf. Regt., at Baltimore 8/15/62. Submitted resignation at Camp Convalescent for rheumatism and heart pain 11/27/62. Resignation accepted 12/3/62. Married Mary Ann Crawford, date unknown. She died 6/10/54. Married Mary A. K. Boucher at Elkton, Md., 9/4/55. Wife's date of death unknown. Simpers died 2/15/1908.

STERLING, THOMAS J. Born in Baltimore c. 1840. Enl. as pvt. in Co. D, 8th Md. Inf. Regt., at Baltimore 8/20/62. Prom. sgt. 1/11/63 and 1sg. 3–4/64. Appt. 1lt. 4/19/64. Furl. 6 days to obtain uniform at Baltimore 4/19/64. WIA in right thigh at the Wilderness 5/5/64. Disch. for disability 7/23/64. Married Christina Rausch in Baltimore 9/6/64. Sterling died of apoplexy in Baltimore 2/16/99. Buried in Western Cemetery. His wife died at York, Pa., 6/4/1923.

SWAIN, JOHN H. BERTRAM. Born in Prince Georges Co. c. 1830. Clerk. Son of Colman B. Swain and Elizabeth Baden. 5'11", dark complexion, brown hair, blue eyes. Enl. as corp. in Co. B, 8th Md. Inf. Regt., at Baltimore 8/16/62. Adm. GH in Washington, D.C., for diarrhea 9/16/63. RTD 10/14/63. Prom. sgt. 12/20/63 and sgm. 9/12/64. Appt. 1lt. of Co. G 12/23/64. Furl. 20 days to visit sick father in Md. 4/26/65. Prom. cpt. but not mustered 5/9/65. MO 5/31/65. Married Martha Ann Rawlings at St. Paul's Protestant Episcopal Church in Nottingham, Prince Georges Co., 12/21/69. Swain's wife was 16 at the time of the wedding. Nine children. Swain died of rheumatism and heart disease in Duley, Prince Georges Co., 2/5/1904. His wife died 5/20/1929.

TROXELL, JACOB LUTHER. 1860 cen.: res. Allegheny Co.; age 19, apprentice wagonmaker; born in Md.; son of John and Christina Troxell; parents born in Va., gatekeeper; $1,200/$300. 5'9", fair complexion, dark hair, blue eyes. Enl. as pvt. in Co. C, 8th Md. Inf. Regt., at Camp Bradford 8/14/62. Prom. sgt. 10/22/62. Appt. 2lt. 9/6/64. KIA at Dabney's Mill 2/6/65.

WINGATE, CHRISTOPHER L. Born c. 1837. Enl. as sgt. in Co. A, 8th Md. Inf. Regt., at Baltimore 8/13/62. Prom. 1sg. 1/3/63. Appt. 1lt. of Co. F 7/24/64. Furl. 10 days to visit sick mother in Cecil Co. 1/11/65. Prom. bvt. cpt. for gallant and meritorious service at White Oak Road 3/31/65. MO 5/31/65. Married 12/17/67. Seven children. Wingate died of consumption at Elkton 6/25/79. Wife's date of death unknown. GAR post in North East named for Wingate.

YOUNG, JOHN C. Born c. 1823. 1860 Baltimore city dir. shows Young as a shoemaker with res. at 22 North Schroeder St. Enl. as pvt. in Co. D, 8th Md. Inf. Regt., at Baltimore 8/30/62. Prom. sgt. 1/11/63 and color sgt. 6/3/63. WIA in left thigh at the Wilderness 5/5/64. Appt. 2lt. 6/27/64. Prom. 1lt. 9/1/64. Abs. sick 1–4/65. Had surgeon's certificate for chronic diarrhea and remittent fever. Disch. for disability 5/15/65. Postwar shoemaker in Baltimore. Not known if he married. Young died 9/4/88.

Bibliography

Primary Sources

Manuscripts

Ammen, Samuel Z. Newspaper clippings assembled as "Maryland Troops in the Confederate Army from Original Sources." Original in possession of Elden E. Billings. Copy furnished by Ross M. Kimmel.

David Callan, Vero Beach, Florida
Genealogical Records and Letter to Author, August 24, 1990.

Catholic University of America, Washington, D.C.
Ford, Anna LeCompte. Papers.
Lee, Thomas Sim. Papers.

Civil War Library and Museum, Philadelphia, Pennsylvania
Membership application files, Military Order of the Loyal Legion of the United States.

Tom Clemens, Keedysville, Maryland
Erick Davis Collection, including G. G. Guillette Letter.

Duke University, Durham, North Carolina
Browing, Amos G. Scrapbook.
Johnson, Bradley T. Papers.
Munford-Ellis Family. Papers.
Purviance-Courtney Family. Papers.
Rodgers, Robert Smith. Papers.
Shell, Helen L. and Mary Virginia. Papers.
Weston, George H. Diaries.

Emory University, Atlanta, Georgia
John D. Babb Family. Papers.

Fort Ward Museum, Alexandria, Virginia
B. F. Cooling File on 1864 Summer Campaign.
Defending Washington, D.C., 1861–65, File.

Frederick County Historical Society, Frederick, Maryland
    Engelbrecht, Jacob. Diary.
    Steiner, John A. Diary.
Margaret K. Fresco, St. Marys County, Maryland
    Genealogical Records, Correspondence, and Interview, November 9, 1990.
Georgetown University, Washington, D.C.
    Alumni Records on various individuals.
George Washington University, Washington, D.C.
    Jennings Wood Collection of Confederate Imprints.
Jefferson County Museum, Charles Town, West Virginia
    Manuscript Biography of Major James Breathed.
Library of Congress, Washington, D.C.
    Gillette, James J. Papers.
    Gist Family Collection.
    Hatton, John William Ford. Memoir.
    Imboden, John D. Papers.
    Keidel Family Papers and War Record of Herman F. Keidel.
    Kirkley, Joseph William. Papers.
    Miscellaneous Manuscripts Collection.
    More, E. J. Collection. Letter of Emanuel Lookingbeal.
    Oliphant, Benjamin F. and Catherine. Papers.
    Scott, John White. Papers.
    Ward Family Papers.
Maryland Historical Society, Baltimore, Maryland
    Allard, Thomas B. Papers.
    Ball, Thomas S. Correspondence.
    Baltimore Battery Record Book.
    Booth, George W. Collection.
    Bowie, Lucy Leigh. Collection. Somerville Sollers Letters, Diary of Walter
        Bowie, and Letter of Mrs. Mary Beatty.
    Carroll, Robert Goodloe Harper. Papers.
    Civil War Collection.
    Clarke, J. Lyle. Papers.
    Daneker, William H. Correspondence.
    Dielman-Hayward File.
    Dukehart, Graham. Letters.
    Frisbee, Robert R. Letters.
    Gilmor, Harry. Papers.
    Gist Family Papers.
    Grand Army of the Republic, Department of Maryland. Annual Reports,
        1904–28.

Howard, Charles. Papers.
Kenly, John R. Papers.
Kimball, George Washington. Papers.
Lemmon Papers.
Lighter, William H. Papers.
Lomax-Early Papers.
Maryland Guard Constitution and Membership Roster.
Maryland Guard Record Book.
Maryland Volunteers, 2nd Regiment Records.
Matthews, Thomas L. Diary.
McHenry, James. Papers. Wilson Miles Cary Diary.
Mead, William L. Letters.
Miscellaneous Confederate Papers.
Moffett, Edwin W. Papers.
Murray, William H. Letters.
Ninth Regiment Record Book, Company B, June–December, 1863.
Phelps, Colonel Charles E. Reminiscences.
Sollers, Somerville. Papers.
Taylor, Benjamin Franklin. Papers.
Thompson, Winfield Scott. Papers.
Walker, Noah Dixon. Papers.
Minnesota Historical Society, St. Paul, Minnesota
    Bowie, Washington. Memoirs.
Museum of the Confederacy, Richmond, Virginia
    Bond, Frank A. "Personal Reminiscences of the Great War Between the
        States."
    C.S.A. Roll of Honour.
    Herbert, James R. Diary.
New-York Historical Society, New York, New York
    Bigelow, John. Letters.
North Carolina State Archives, Raleigh, North Carolina
    Conrad, John Thomas. Papers.
Historical Society of Pennsylvania, Philadelphia, Pennsylvania
    Civil War Papers, Records of the 2nd Regiment, Eastern Shore Infantry.
William A. Tidwell Collection, Fairfax, Virginia
    Emack, George M. Papers.
United States Army Military History Institute, Carlisle Barracks, Pennsylvania
    Civil War Miscellaneous Collection
        Eichelberger, Grayson M. Memoirs.
        Gardener, Elijah N. Papers.
        Lynch, Private Christopher Goodhand. Papers.

Stone, John H. Diary.
White, John Goldsborough. Newspaper Clipping.
"Experiences of Lieut. John Sachs as a Prisoner of War, 1863–1865."
Civil War Times Illustrated Collection
 Gillette, James J. Papers.
 McIlhenny, William A. Diary.
 Scott, David J. Letter.
Harrisburg Civil War Round Table Collection
 Coco, Gregory A. Collection. William A. McIlhenny Diary and Edwin
  Selvage Papers.
 Faehtz, Ernest F. M. Papers.
 Flegeal Family Papers.
Lewis Leigh Collection
 Boone, Jermingham. Letter, Book 24.
 Lieutenant "Hanford." Confederate memoir, Book 32.
 Wantz, David K. Letter, Book 42.
Pennsylvania Save the Flags Collection
 Moore, B. Franklin. Letter.
University of Maryland, College Park, Maryland
 Fish, William. Letter.
 Fowler, Edwin C. Letters.
University of Virginia, Charlottesville, Virginia
 Fleming, Malcolm. Letter.
 Hands, Washington. Notebook.
 Hotchkiss, Jedediah. Papers.
 Johnson, Claudia. Diary.
University of Washington, Seattle, Washington
 Crittenden Family Papers. Churchill Crittenden Letters.
Virginia Historical Society, Richmond, Virginia
 Byrd Family Papers. R. E. Byrd Affadavit.
 C.S. War Department, Conscription Bureau Enrolling Book, 1863–64.
Virginia Military Institute, Lexington, Virginia
 Alumni Records.
Wake Forest University Library, Wake Forest, North Carolina
 Confederate Broadside Poetry Collection.

Newspapers

Baltimore *American and Commercial Advertiser*
Baltimore *Sun*

New York *Times*
Richmond *Daily Dispatch*
Richmond *Daily Enquirer*
Richmond *Daily Examiner*
Richmond *Daily Whig*
Richmond *Enquirer* (Semiweekly)
Washington *Evening Star*
Washington *National Tribune*

City Directories

Boyd, William H. *Boyd's Washington and Georgetown Directory*. Washington, D.C., 1860.
Williams, C. S. *Williams' Frederick Directory, City Guide, and Business Mirror, Volume I, 1859–'60*. Frederick, 1859.
Woods, John W. *Woods' Baltimore City Directory, Containing a Corrected Engraved Map of the City*. Baltimore, 1860.

Published Primary Sources

Addresses Delivered at the Dedication of the Monument Erected in Loudoun Park Cemetery to Captain Wm. H. Murray and His Soldiers Who Fell in the Confederate War. Baltimore, 1875.
Anderson, George M., ed. "A Captured Confederate Officer: Nine Letters from Captain James Anderson to His Family." *Maryland Historical Magazine*, LXXVI (1981), 62–69.
Baldwin, Helene L., Michael Allen Mudge, and Keith W. Schlegel, eds. *The McKaig Family Journal: A Confederate Family of Cumberland*. Baltimore, 1984.
Barr, Paul E., Jr., and Michael P. Musick, eds. "'They Are Coming': Testimony at the Court of Inquiry on Imboden's Capture of Charles Town." *Magazine of the Jefferson County Historical Society*, LIV (December, 1988), 15–53.
Basler, Roy P., ed. *The Collected Works of Abraham Lincoln*. 8 vols. New Brunswick, 1953.
Baylor, George. *Bull Run to Bull Run; or Four Years in the Army of Northern Virginia*. 1900. Reprint. Washington, D.C., 1983.
Beauchamp, Virginia Walcott. *A Private War: Letters and Diaries of Madge Preston, 1862–1867*. New Brunswick, 1987.
Beirne, Rosamond Randall, ed. "Three War Letters." *Maryland Historical Magazine*, XL (1945), 290–94.

Blackford, William W. *War Years with Jeb Stuart.* New York, 1945.

Booth, George Wilson. *Illustrated Souvenir of the Maryland Line Confederate Soldiers Home, Pikesville, Maryland.* N.p., 1894.

————. *Personal Reminiscences of a Maryland Soldier in the War Between the States, 1861–1865.* 1898. Reprint. Gaithersburg, 1986.

Bowley, Freeman S. *A Boy Lieutenant.* Philadelphia, 1906.

Brown, George W. *Baltimore and the Nineteenth of April, 1861.* Baltimore, 1881.

Buchanan, W. Jefferson. *Maryland's Hope: Her Trials and Interests in Connexion with the War.* Richmond, 1864.

Camper, Charles, and J. W. Kirkley. *Historical Record of the First Maryland Infantry.* 1871. Reprint. Baltimore, 1990.

Casler, John O. *Four Years in the Stonewall Brigade.* Edited by James I. Robertson, Jr. Dayton, 1971.

Clemens, Thomas G., ed. "The 'Diary' of John H. Stone First Lieutenant, Company B, 2d Maryland Infantry, C.S.A." *Maryland Historical Magazine,* LXXXV (1990), 108–43.

Dennett, George M. *History of the Ninth U.S.C. Troops.* Philadelphia, 1866.

Douglas, Henry Kyd. *I Rode with Stonewall: The War Experiences of the Youngest Member of Jackson's Staff.* Chapel Hill, 1940.

Drickamer, Lee C., and Karen D. Drickamer, eds. *Fort Lyon to Harper's Ferry: On the Border of North and South with 'Rambling Jour,' The Civil War Letters and Newspaper Dispatches of Charles H. Moulton (34th Mass. Vol. Inf.).* Shippensburg, 1987.

Durkin, Joseph T., ed. *John Dooley, Confederate Soldier: His War Journal.* Ithaca, 1945.

Fielding, Geoffrey W., ed. "Gilmor's Field Report of His Raid in Baltimore County." *Maryland Historical Magazine,* XLVII (1952), 234–39.

Fraser, George C., ed. *A Petition Regarding the Conditions in the C.S.M. Prison at Columbia, S.C.* Lawrence, Kans., 1962.

Gill, John. *Reminiscences of Four Years as a Private Soldier in the Confederate Army, 1861–1865.* Baltimore, 1904.

Gilmor, Harry. *Four Years in the Saddle.* 1866. Reprint. Baltimore, 1987.

Goldsborough, Edward Y. *The Appeal of Frederick City to the Congress of the United States.* Frederick, 1989.

————. *Early's Great Raid.* N.p., 1898.

Goldsborough, W. W. *The Maryland Line in the Confederate Army.* 1869, 1900. Reprint. Port Washington, 1972.

Goodhart, Briscoe. *History of the Independent Loudoun Virginia Rangers, 1862–65.* Washington, D.C., 1896.

Grimsley, Daniel A. *Battles in Culpeper County, Virginia, 1861–1865.* 1900. Reprint. Orange, n.d.

Hayden, Horace Edwin. "The First Maryland Cavalry, C.S.A." *Southern Historical Society Papers*, V (1878), 251–53.

———. "The Maryland Line." *Southern Historical Society Papers*, IX (1881), 254–57.

Howard, McHenry. *Recollections of a Maryland Confederate Soldier and Staff Officer Under Johnston, Jackson, and Lee*. 1914. Reprint. Edited by James I. Robertson, Jr. Dayton, 1975.

James, William H. "A Baltimore Volunteer of 1864." *Maryland Historical Magazine*, XXXVI (1941), 22–33.

Johnson, Bradley T. *Maryland*. Vol. II of *Confederate Military History*, ed. Clement A. Evans. 1899. Reprint. Wilmington, 1987.

———. "The Maryland Line in the Confederate Army." *Southern Historical Society Papers*, XI (1883), 21–26.

———. "Memoir of First Maryland Regiment." *Southern Historical Society Papers*, IX, X (1881), 344–53, 481–88, 46–56, 97–109, 145–53, 214–23.

———. "My Ride Around Baltimore in Eighteen Hundred and Sixty-Four." *Southern Historical Society Papers*, XXX (1902), 215–25.

Jones, John B. *A Rebel War Clerk's Diary at the Confederate States Capital*. 2 vols. Philadelphia, 1866.

Keifer, Joseph Warren. *Slavery and Four Years of War: A Political History of Slavery in the United States*. Vol. II. New York, 1900.

Kelly, Tom, ed. *The Personal Memoirs of Jonathan Thomas Scharf of the First Maryland Artillery*. Baltimore, 1992.

Lancaster, Mary H., and Dallas M. Lancaster, eds. *The Civil War Diary of Anne S. Frobel of Wilton Hall in Virginia*. Birmingham, 1986.

Lewis, H. H. Walker. "The Schizophrenic Diary of Colonel Phelps." *Maryland Historical Magazine*, LXXVI (1981), 383–85.

Lucas, Thomas O. *A Diary of Four Months' Prison Life of First Maryland Regiment at Lynchburg and Richmond by a Sergeant of the First Maryland, a Prisoner*. Baltimore, 1862.

Marks, Bayley Ellen, and Mark Norton Schatz, eds. *Between North and South: A Maryland Journalist Views the Civil War*. Rutherford, 1976.

Matchett, William B. *Maryland and the Glorious Old Third in the War for the Union: Reimisciences [sic] in the Life of Her "Militant" Chaplain and Major Kramer, by His Esteemed Friend and Co-Laborer*. Washington, D.C., 1882.

McDonald, Archie P., ed. *Make Me a Map of the Valley: The Civil War Journal of Stonewall Jackson's Topographer*. Dallas, 1973.

McDonald, Hunter, ed. *A Diary with Reminiscences of the War and Refugee Life in the Shenandoah Valley, 1860–1865*. Nashville, 1934.

McGee, Charles M., Jr., and Ernest M. Lander, Jr. *A Rebel Came Home: The Diary and Letters of Floride Clemson, 1863–1866*. Rev. ed. Columbia, 1989.

McKim, Randolph H. *A Soldier's Recollections: Leaves from the Diary of a Young Confederate*. New York, 1910.

"Memoir of Jane Claudia Johnson." *Southern Historical Society Papers*, XXIX (1901), 33–45.

Mettam, Henry C. "Civil War Memoirs of the First Maryland Cavalry, C.S.A." Edited by Samuel H. Miller. *Maryland Historical Magazine*, LVIII (1963), 139–45.

Moore, Frank, ed. *The Rebellion Record: A Diary of American Events with Documents, Narratives, Illustrative Incidents, Poetry, Etc.* 12 vols. 1864. Reprint. New York, 1977.

Murray, J. Ogden. *The Immortal Six Hundred: A Story of Cruelty to Confederate Prisoners of War*. Roanoke, 1911.

The Murray Confederate Association, Confederate Relief Bazaar Association. 1885.

Newcomer, C. Armour. *Cole's Cavalry; or, Three Years in the Saddle in the Shenandoah Valley*. Baltimore, 1895.

"Noah Dixon Walker to His Father Noah Walker." *Maryland Historical Magazine*, XXX (1935), 363–65.

Paca, Edmund C., ed. "'Tim's Black Book': The Civil War Diary of Edward Tilghman Paca, Jr., CSA." *Maryland Historical Magazine*, LXXXIX (1994), 453–66.

Pember, Phoebe Yates. *A Southern Woman's Story: Life in Confederate Richmond*. Edited by Bell I. Wiley. St. Simons Island, 1959.

Philpott, G. B. "A Maryland Boy in the Confederate Army." *Confederate Veteran*, XXIV (1916), 312–15, 361–63.

Racine, J. Polk. *Recollections of a Veteran; or, Four Years in Dixie*. Elkton, 1894.

Reed, William Howell. *Hospital Life in the Army of the Potomac*. Boston, 1881.

Rich, Edward R. *Comrades Four*. New York, 1907.

Schilling, Edward. "My Three Years in the Volunteer Army of the United States of America." *Journal of the Alleghenies*, XX (1984), 3–11.

Scott, John. *Partisan Life with Col. John S. Mosby*. New York, 1867.

Shane, John H. *The First Regiment Eastern Shore Maryland Infantry at Gettysburg, July, 1863*. Baltimore, 1895.

Slingluff, Fielder C. "The Burning of Chambersburg." *Southern Historical Society Papers*, XXXVII (1909), 152–63.

Smith, Tunstall, ed. *Richard Snowden Andrews: A Memoir*. Baltimore, 1910.

Stern, Philip Van Doren, ed. *The Life and Writings of Abraham Lincoln*. New York, 1940.

Stiverson, Gregory A., ed. *"In Readiness to Do Every Duty Assigned": The Frederick Militia and John Brown's Raid on Harper's Ferry, October 17–18, 1859*. Annapolis, 1991.

Stonebraker, Joseph R. *A Rebel of '61*. New York, 1899.

Swank, Walbrook D., ed. *Courier for Lee and Jackson, 1861–1865: Memoirs*. Shippensburg, 1993.

"Three Civil War Letters of James H. Rigby, A Maryland Federal Artillery Officer." *Maryland Historical Magazine*, LVII (1962), 155–60.

Tocqueville, Alexis de. *Democracy in America*. Translated by Henry Reeve. 2 vols. New York, 1961.

Trundle, Joseph H. "Gettysburg Described in Two Letters from a Maryland Confederate." *Maryland Historical Magazine*, LIV (1959), 210–12.

Western Reserve Historical Society. *The James E. Taylor Sketchbook*. Cleveland, 1989.

Wild, Frederick W. *Memoirs and History of Capt. F. W. Alexander's Baltimore Battery*. Baltimore, 1912.

Worsham, John H. *One of Jackson's Foot Cavalry*. New York, 1912.

Public Documents

Maryland State Archives, Annapolis, Maryland
   Adjutant General's Papers, 1862, 1864.
   Adjutant General's Records, Civil War Returns of Military Units.
   Civil War Papers, 1862, 1864–65.
   Commission Applications, 1862–65.
   Discharges, Resignations, and Removals, 1862–63.
   Documents Accompanying the Governor's Message to the Legislature of Maryland.
      Annapolis, 1865.
   Executive Papers, 1863–65.
   Maryland Guard Register.
   Militia Appointments, 1853–62.
   Muster Rolls (Officers), 1862–63.
   Purnell Legion Order Book.
   Voter Registration Record, 1865.

Special Collections

Cushing, Robert H. Collection, 1861–65.
Green, John F. "Recollections of Maryland Guard Company B 21st Virginia."
Hopkins, Mrs. John H. Collection.
   Letters and Other Memorabilia of the United Daughters of the Confederacy, Howard County.
   Letters of Charles Ketterwell.
Jenkins, W. Kennedy. Letter.

McParlin Family Papers.

Mercer Family Papers.

West Collection (Letters of Martin L. Clem and William H. Renner).

White, M. P. Collection.

Wilson, George W. "Outline of Experiences with the 1st Maryland Battery."

National Archives, Washington, D.C.

Record Group 15, Records of the Veterans Administration.

Organization Index to Pension Files of Veterans Who Served Between 1861 and 1900. T289.

Pension Applications of Maryland Union Officers.

Record Group 29, Records of the Bureau of the Census.

Eighth Census of Maryland, 1860 (various counties and Baltimore city).

Record Group 94, Records of the Adjutant General's Office.

Case Files of Investigations by Levi C. Turner and Lafayette C. Baker, 1861–66. M797.

Compiled Service Records of Volunteer Union Soldiers Who Served in Organizations from the State of Maryland. M384.

1865 Officers' Reports of Various Divisions (uninventoried records).

Letters Received by the Office of the Adjutant General (Main Series), 1861–70.

Letters Received by the Secretary of War (Main Series), 1800–1870.

Letters Received, Volunteer Service Division.

Muster Rolls, Regimental Returns, Civil War Volunteer Organizations from Maryland.

Pardon Petitions and Related Papers Submitted in Response to President Andrew Johnson's Amnesty Proclamation of May 29, 1865. M1003.

Records of the Volunteer Service Branch.

Regimental Order Books and Papers, 1st Maryland Infantry Regiment (U.S.); 4th Maryland Infantry (U.S.); 7th Maryland Infantry Regiment (U.S.); 8th Maryland Infantry Regiment (U.S.).

Record Group 107, Records of the Office of the Secretary of War.

Applications for Appointment in the Regular Army, 1854–61: Maryland.

Letters Received from the President, Departments, and War Department Bureaus, 1862–70. M494.

Record Group 109, War Department Collection of Confederate Records.

Compiled Service Records of Confederate Generals and Staff Officers, and Nonregimental Enlisted Men. M258.

Compiled Service Records of Confederate Soldiers (various states).

Entry 65, Post Returns of Confederate Commands.

Entry 143, Departmental Records.

Entry 189, Intercepted Letters, Baltimore, Maryland.

Entry 199, Records of Confederates in Union Prisons, Station Rolls, "Maryland Duplicates."

Inspection Reports and Related Records Received by the Inspection Branch in the Confederate Adjutant and Inspector General's Office. M935.

Letters and Telegrams Sent by the Confederate Adjutant and Inspector General, 1861–65. M627.

Letters Received by the Confederate Adjutant and Inspector General, 1861–65. M474.

Letters Received by the Confederate Secretary of War, 1861–65. M437.

Muster and Pay Rolls for Maryland Units.

Orders and Circulars Issued by Minor Commands, 1861–65.

Orders and Circulars Issued by the Army of the Potomac and the Army and Department of Northern Virginia, C.S.A., 1861–65. M921.

Records of Virginia Forces, 1861. M998.

Unfiled Papers and Slips Belonging in the Confederate Compiled Service Records. M347.

Uninventoried Records, "CSA Printed and Written Reports, Secretary of War Court of Inquiry—Fall of New Orleans."

Union Provost Marshal's File of Papers Relating to Individual Civilians. M345.

Union Provost Marshal's File of Papers Relating to Two or More Civilians. M416.

Record Group 110, Records of the Provost Marshal General's Bureau (Civil War).

Entry 3646. Descriptive Lists, Men Who Deserted from Maryland Regiments.

Historical Reports of State Acting Assistant Provost Marshals General and District Provost Marshals, 1865. M1163.

Record Group 153, Records of the Judge Advocate General's Office.

Letters-Received File.

Proceedings of Military Commissions.

Record Group 217, Civil War State Claims, Maryland.

Returns for U.S. Maryland Volunteer Regiments.

Record Group 393, Records of U.S. Army Continental Commands, Part II, Progression 239 (Maryland Brigade).

Entry 3786. Letters and Endorsements Sent and Orders Received, June, 1863–March, 1864.

Entry 3787. Letters Sent, June, 1864–June, 1865.

Entry 3788. Register of Letters Received and Endorsements Sent, July, 1864–June, 1865.

Entry 3789. Register of Letters Received, February, 1863–April, 1864.

Entry 3790. Register of Letters Received, January–May, 1865.

Entry 3791. Register of Letters Received (Supplemental), 1864–65.

Entry 3792. Special Orders, June, 1863–June, 1865.

Entry 3793. Orders Received, March–April, 1864.

Entry 3794. Orders Received, May, 1864–June, 1865.

Entry 3795. Journal of Operations, June–October, 1863.

Entry 3796. Letters Sent and Letters and Orders Received by the Commissary of Subsistence, May–July, 1863.

Part II.

Entry 3980. Miscellaneous Letters, Reports, and Lists Received, 1861–65.

Uninventoried Records.

Maryland Slave Claims Commission.

C.S. War Department. *Regulations for the Army of the Confederate States*. 1863. Reprint. Harrisburg, 1980.

Fallon, John T. *List of Synonyms of Organizations in the Volunteer Service of the United States During the Years 1861, '62, '63, '64, and '65*. Washington, D.C., 1885.

U.S. Army Public Information Division. *The Medal of Honor of the United States*. Washington, D.C., 1948.

U.S. Census Bureau. *Agriculture in the United States in 1860; Compiled from the Original Returns of the Eighth Census*. Washington, D.C., 1864.

———. *Manufactures of the United States in 1860; Compiled from the Original Returns of the Eighth Census*. Washington, D.C., 1865.

———. *Population of the United States in 1860; Compiled from the Original Returns of the Eighth Census*. Washington, D.C., 1864.

U.S. Congress. House. *Reports of the Select Committee of Five on Alleged Hostile Organization Against the Government Within the District of Columbia*. H.R. 79, 36th Cong., 2nd Sess., 1861.

U.S. Department of the Army. FM 22-100. *Military Leadership*. Washington, D.C., 1983.

U.S. War Department. *General Court Martial Orders, Adjutant General's Office, 1865*. Washington, D.C., 1865.

———. *Official Army Register of the Volunteer Force of the United States Army for the Years 1861, '62, '63, '64, '65*. Part III. Washington, D.C., 1865.

———. *Revised Regulations for the Army of the United States, 1861*. 1861. Reprint. Harrisburg, 1980.

———. *The War of the Rebellion: A Compilation of the Official Records of the Union and Confederate Armies*. 128 vols. Washington, D.C., 1880–1901.

SECONDARY SOURCES

Books

Adams, Michael C. C. *Our Masters the Rebels: A Speculation on Union Military Failure in the East, 1861–1865*. Cambridge, Mass., 1978.

Allardice, Bruce S. *More Generals in Gray*. Baton Rouge, 1995.

Alotta, Robert I. *Civil War Justice: Union Army Executions Under Lincoln*. Shippensburg, 1989.

Anderson, Fred. *A People's Army: Massachusetts Soldiers and Society in the Seven Years' War*. Chapel Hill, 1984.

Apps, Walter E., Jr. *Maryland Mortalities from the Baltimore Sun Almanac*. Silver Spring, 1983.

Ash, Stephen V. *Middle Tennessee Society Transformed, 1860–1870: War and Peace in the Upper South*. Baton Rouge, 1988.

————. *When the Yankees Came: Conflict and Class in the Occupied South, 1861–1865*. Chapel Hill, 1995.

Ayers, Edward L. *Vengeance and Justice: Crime and Punishment in the 19th-Century American South*. New York, 1984.

Ayers, Edward L., and John C. Willis, eds. *The Edge of the South: Life in Nineteenth-Century Virginia*. Charlottesville, 1991.

Bailey, Fred Arthur. *Class and Tennessee's Confederate Generation*. Chapel Hill, 1987.

Baker, Jean H. *Ambivalent Americans: The Know-Nothing Party in Maryland*. Baltimore, 1977.

————. *The Politics of Continuity: Maryland Political Parties from 1858 to 1870*. Baltimore, 1973.

Balkoski, Joseph M. *The Maryland National Guard: A History of Maryland's Military Forces, 1634–1991*. Baltimore, 1991.

Barton, Michael. *Goodmen: The Character of Civil War Soldiers*. University Park, 1981.

Baruch, Mildred C., and Ellen J. Beckman. *Civil War Union Monuments*. Washington, D.C., 1978.

Barnes, John C. *Somerset County Maryland 1860 Census*. San Diego, 1988.

Beitzell, Edwin W. *Point Lookout Prison Camp for Confederates*. N.p., 1972.

Benton, Josiah Henry. *Voting in the Field: A Forgotten Chapter of the Civil War*. Boston, 1915.

Beringer, Richard H., Herman Hattaway, Archer Jones, and William N. Still, Jr. *Why the South Lost the Civil War*. Athens, 1986.

The Biographical Cyclopedia of Representative Men of Maryland and the District of Columbia. 2 vols. Baltimore, 1879.

Blakely, Arch Frederic. General John H. Winder C.S.A. Gainesville, 1990.

Bowie, Effie Gwynn. Across the Years in Prince George's County: A Genealogical and Biographical History of Some Prince George's County, Maryland, and Allied Families. Richmond, 1947.

Bradford, James C. Anne Arundel County, Maryland: A Bicentennial History, 1649–1977. Annapolis, 1977.

Brewer, James H. Fitzgerald. History of the 175th Infantry (Fifth Maryland). Baltimore, 1955.

Brice, Marshal M. Conquest of a Valley. Charlottesville, 1965.

Brown, Dee. The Galvanized Yankees. Urbana, 1963.

Brown, Louis A. The Salisbury Prison: A Case Study of Confederate Military Prisons, 1861–1865. Wendell, 1980.

Brown, Mary Ross. An Illustrated Genealogy of the Counties of Maryland and the District of Columbia as a Guide to Locating Records. Baltimore, 1967.

Browne, Gary Lawson. Baltimore in the Nation, 1789–1861. Chapel Hill, 1980.

Brugger, Robert J. Maryland: A Middle Temperament, 1634–1980. Baltimore, 1988.

Buel, C. C., and R. U. Johnson, eds. Battles and Leaders of the Civil War. 4 vols. 1887–88. Reprint. New York, 1956.

Carroll County Public Library. Carroll County, Maryland, 1860 Census. Westminster, 1990.

Catton, Bruce. The Army of the Potomac. 3 vols. New York, 1951–53.

Clark, Charles Branch. Politics in Maryland During the Civil War. Chestertown, 1952.

Click, Patricia C. The Spirit of the Times: Amusements in Nineteenth-Century Baltimore, Norfolk, and Richmond. Charlottesville, 1989.

Coffman, Edward M. The Old Army: A Portrait of the American Army in Peacetime, 1784–1898. New York, 1986.

Colleary, Shirley E., Harvey L. Lineback, and David Roberts. The 1860 Census of St. Mary's County, Maryland. N.p., 1982.

Cooling, B. F. Jubal Early's Raid on Washington, 1864. Baltimore, 1989.

Cottom, Robert I., Jr., and Mary Ellen, Hayward. Maryland in the Civil War: A House Divided. Baltimore, 1994.

Coulter, E. Merton. The Civil War and Readjustment in Kentucky. 1926. Reprint. Gloucester, 1966.

Craven, Avery O. Soil Exhaustion as a Factor in the Agricultural History of Virginia and Maryland, 1606–1860. 1925. Reprint. Gloucester, 1965.

Crofts, Daniel W. Reluctant Confederates: Upper South Unionists in the Secession Crisis. Chapel Hill, 1989.

Cunliffe, Marcus. Soldiers and Civilians: The Martial Spirit in America, 1775–1865. Boston, 1968.

Cunz, Dieter. *The Maryland Germans: A History.* Princeton, 1948.

Cuthbert, Norma, ed. *Lincoln and the Baltimore Plot, 1861.* San Marino, 1949.

Daniel, Larry J. *Soldiering in the Army of Tennessee: A Portrait of Life in a Confederate Army.* Chapel Hill, 1991.

Davis, William C. *Orphan Brigade: The Kentucky Confederates Who Couldn't Go Home.* Baton Rouge, 1983.

Dearing, Mary R. *Veterans in Politics: The Story of the G.A.R.* Baton Rouge, 1952.

Delauter, Roger U., Jr. *McNeill's Rangers.* Lynchburg, 1986.

———. *Winchester in the Civil War.* Lynchburg, 1992.

Denton, Lawrence M. *A Southern Star for Maryland: Maryland and the Secession Crisis, 1860–1861.* Baltimore, 1995.

Divine, John E. *35th Battalion Virginia Cavalry.* Lynchburg, 1985.

Driver, Robert J., Jr. *1st Virginia Cavalry.* Lynchburg, 1991.

Dupuy, Trevor D. *Attrition: Forecasting Battle Casualties and Equipment Losses in Modern War.* Fairfax, 1990.

Dyer, Frederick H. *A Compendium of the War of the Rebellion.* 3 vols. 1908. Reprint. Dayton, 1978.

Dyer, Gustavus W., and John Trotwood Moore, eds. *The Tennessee Civil War Veterans Questionnaires.* 5 vols. Easley, 1985.

Ellis, Helen M., comp. *The National Tribune: A Guide to Selected Materials of Civil War Interest.* N.p., 1968.

Emory, Frederic. *Queen Anne's County, Maryland: Its Early History and Development.* Baltimore, 1950.

Evitts, William J. *A Matter of Allegiances: Maryland from 1850 to 1861.* Baltimore, 1974.

Farquhar, Roger Brooke. *Historic Montgomery County, Maryland, Old Homes and History.* Baltimore, 1952.

Faust, Patricia, et al. *Historical Times Illustrated Encyclopedia of the Civil War.* New York, 1986.

Fellman, Michael. *Inside War: The Guerrilla Conflict in Missouri During the American Civil War.* New York, 1989.

Fields, Barbara Jeanne. *Slavery and Freedom on the Middle Ground: Maryland During the Nineteenth Century.* New Haven, 1985.

Fogel, Robert William, and Stanley L. Engerman. *Time on the Cross: The Economics of American Negro Slavery.* Boston, 1974.

———. *Time on the Cross: Evidence and Methods, A Supplement.* Boston, 1974.

Fox, William F. *Regimental Losses in the American Civil War, 1861–1865.* Albany, 1889.

Frank, Joseph Allen, and George A. Reaves. *"Seeing the Elephant": Raw Recruits at the Battle of Shiloh.* Westport, 1989.

Frederickson, George M. *The Inner Civil War: Northern Intellectuals and the Crisis of the Union*. New York, 1965.

Freehling, William W. *The Road to Disunion: Secessionists at Bay, 1776–1854*. New York, 1990.

Freeman, Douglas Southall. *Lee's Lieutenants: A Study in Command*. 3 vols. New York, 1942–44.

Fresco, Margaret K. *Doctors of St. Mary's County, 1634–1900*. N.p., 1992.

———. *Marriages and Deaths, St. Mary's County, Maryland, 1634–1900*. N.p., 1982.

Frye, Dennis. *12th Virginia Cavalry*. Lynchburg, 1988.

Gallagher, Gary W., ed. *Antietam: Essays on the 1862 Maryland Campaign*. Kent, 1989.

———. *Struggle for the Shenandoah. Essays on the 1864 Valley Campaign*. Kent, 1991.

Gary, Keith O. *Answering the Call: The Organization and Recruiting of the Potomac Home Brigade Maryland Volunteers Summer and Fall 1861*. Bowie, 1996.

Genealogy and Biography of Leading Families of the City of Baltimore and Baltimore County, Maryland. New York, 1897.

Gerster, Patrick, and Nicholas Cords, eds. *Myth and Southern History*. Chicago, 1974.

Glatthaar, Joseph T. *Forged in Battle: The Civil War Alliance of Black Soldiers and White Officers*. New York, 1990.

Griffith, Paddy. *Battle Tactics of the Civil War*. New Haven, 1989.

Grunder, Charles S., and Brandon H. Beck. *The Second Battle of Winchester, June 12–15, 1863*. Lynchburg, 1989.

Hagerman, Edward. *The American Civil War and the Origins of Modern Warfare*. Bloomington, 1988.

Hale, Laura Virginia. *Four Valiant Years in Lower Shenandoah Valley, 1861–1865*. Strasburg, 1968.

Hall, Clayton Colman, ed. *Baltimore: Its History and Its People*. 3 vols. New York, 1912.

Hamersly, Thomas H. S. *Complete Regular Army Register of the United States: For One Hundred Years (1779 to 1879)*. Washington, D.C., 1880.

Harvey, Katherine A. *The Best-Dressed Miners: Life and Labor in the Maryland Coal Region*. Ithaca, 1969.

Hartzler, Daniel D. *A Band of Brothers: Photographic Epilogue to Marylanders in the Confederacy*. N.p., 1992.

———. *Marylanders in the Confederacy*. Silver Spring, 1986.

Haselberger, Fritz. *2nd Maryland Cavalry Battalion C.S.A.: Roster and Losses Arranged by Name-Date-Place-Time*. N.p., 1992.

Heitman, Francis B. *Historical Register of the United States Army from Its Organization September 29, 1789, to September 29, 1889*. Washington, D.C., 1890.

Henry, Guy V. *Military Record of Civilian Appointments in the United States Army*. Vol. I. New York, 1870.

Hess, Earl J. *Liberty, Virtue, and Progress: Northerners and Their War for the Union*. New York, 1988.

Hewett, Janet B., ed. *The Roster of Confederate Soldiers, 1861–1865*. 8 vols. Wilmington, 1995.

————. *Supplement to the Official Records of the Union and Confederate Armies*. Wilmington, 1995–.

Holland, Celia M. *Old Homes and Families of Howard County, Maryland*. N.p., 1987.

Hopkins, Joseph G. E., ed. *Concise Dictionary of American Biography*. New York, 1964.

Howard, George. *The Monumental City: Its Past History and Present Resources*. 1873. Expanded ed. Baltimore, 1889.

Hunt, Roger D., and Jack R. Brown. *Brevet Brigadier Generals in Blue*. Gaithersburg, 1990.

Huntsberry, Thomas V., and Joanne M. Huntsberry. *Maryland in the Civil War*. 2 vols. Baltimore, 1985.

Jackson, Ronald Vern. *Maryland 1860 Census Index Except the City of Baltimore*. North Salt Lake City, 1988.

————. *Maryland 1890 Veterans*. Salt Lake City, 1990.

Jimerson, Randall C. *The Private Civil War: Popular Thought During the Sectional Conflict*. Baton Rouge, 1994.

Jones, Barbara, and Avlyn Conley. *Index to 1860 Census of Anne Arundel Co., Maryland*. N.p., 1986.

Jones, Virgil Carrington. *Gray Ghosts and Rebel Raiders*. New York, 1956.

Joslyn, Muriel. *The Biographical Register of the Immortal 600*. Shippensburg, 1992.

————. *Immortal Captives: The Story of the Six Hundred Confederate Officers and the United States Prisoner of War Policy*. Shippensburg, 1996.

Karsten, Peter, ed. *The Military in America: From the Colonial Period to the Present*. Rev. ed. New York, 1986.

Keegan, John. *The Face of Battle*. New York, 1976.

Keller, S. Roger. *Events of the Civil War in Washington County, Maryland*. Shippensburg, 1995.

Kirby, Walter J., and Lanetta W. Parks. *Roll Call: The Civil War in Kent County*. Silver Spring, 1985.

Klapthor, Margaret Brown, and Paul Dennis Brown. *The History of Charles County, Maryland*. La Plata, 1958.

Klein, Frederic Shriver, ed. *Just South of Gettysburg: Carroll County, Maryland, in the Civil War.* Westminster, 1963.

Krick, Robert K. *Lee's Colonels: A Biographical Register of the Field Officers of the Army of Northern Virginia.* 2nd rev. ed. Dayton, 1984.

————. *Stonewall Jackson at Cedar Mountain.* Chapel Hill, 1990.

Laurie, Bruce. *Working People of Philadelphia, 1800–1850.* Philadelphia, 1980.

LeFurgy, William G. *The Records of a City: A Guide to the Baltimore City Archives.* Baltimore, 1984.

Linderman, Gerald F. *Embattled Courage: The Experience of Combat in the American Civil War.* New York, 1987.

Lord, Francis A. *They Fought for the Union.* Harrisburg, 1960.

Manakee, Harold R. *Maryland in the Civil War.* Baltimore, 1961.

Marshall, John A. *American Bastille: A History of the Illegal Arrests and Imprisonment of American Citizens During the Late Civil War.* Philadelphia, 1870.

Maryland Historic Trust. *Inventory of Historic Sites in Calvert County, Charles County, and St. Mary's County.* Annapolis, 1980.

Massey, Mary Elizabeth. *Refugee Life in the Confederacy.* Baton Rouge, 1964.

Matter, William D. *If It Takes All Summer: The Battle of Spotsylvania.* Chapel Hill, 1988.

MacMaster, Richard K., and Ray Eldon Hiebert. *A Grateful Remembrance: The Story of Montgomery County, Maryland.* Rockville, 1976.

McIntire, Robert Harry. *Annapolis, Maryland, Families.* Baltimore, 1979.

McMurray, Richard M. *Two Great Rebel Armies: An Essay in Confederate Military History.* Chapel Hill, 1989.

McPherson, James M. *Battle Cry of Freedom: The Civil War Era.* New York, 1988.

————. *What They Fought For, 1861–1865.* Baton Rouge, 1994.

McWhiney, Grady, and Perry D. Jamieson. *Attack and Die: Civil War Military Tactics and the Southern Heritage.* University, Ala., 1982.

————. *Cracker Culture: Celtic Ways in the Old South.* Tuscaloosa, 1988.

Miller, William J., ed. *The Peninsula Campaign of 1862: Yorktown to the Seven Days.* Vol. I. Campbell, 1993.

Mitchell, Mary. *Divided Town.* Barre, 1968.

Mitchell, Reid. *Civil War Soldiers: Their Expectations and Experiences.* New York, 1988.

————. *The Vacant Chair: The Northern Soldier Leaves Home.* New York, 1993.

Molisani, Jackie. *1860 Census of Dorchester County, Maryland.* Silver Spring, 1984.

Moore, Albert B. *Conscription and Conflict in the Confederacy.* New York, 1963.

Murfin, James V. *The Gleam of Bayonets: The Battle of Antietam and the Maryland Campaign of 1862.* Cranbury, N.J., 1965.

Musick, Michael P. *6th Virginia Cavalry.* Lynchburg, 1990.

Neely, Mark E., Jr., Harold Holzer, and Gabor S. Boritt. *The Confederate Image: Prints of the Lost Cause*. Chapel Hill, 1987.

Nevins, Allan. *The War for the Union*. 4 vols. New York, 1959–71.

Newman, Harry Wright. *Maryland and the Confederacy*. Annapolis, 1976.

Nye, William Sturtevant. *Here Come the Rebels!* Baton Rouge, 1965.

Parrish, William E. *Turbulent Partnership: Missouri and the Union, 1861–1865*. Columbia, 1963.

Paul, William A. B. *Despot's Heel on Talbot*. N.p., 1966.

Pogue, Robert E. T. *Yesterday in Old St. Mary's County*. New York, 1968.

Portrait and Biographical Records of Harford and Cecil Counties, Maryland. New York, 1897.

Rable, George C. *Civil Wars: Women and the Crisis of Southern Nationalism*. Urbana, 1989.

Reamy, Bill, and Martha Reamy. *1860 Census of Baltimore City*. 2 vols. Westminster, 1987 and 1989.

Record, Milton A. *Guide Book and Descriptive Manual of Battleflags in the Flag Room of the State House at Annapolis, Md*. N.p., 1965.

Riley, Janet Wilson. *1860 Census of Talbot County, Maryland*. Silver Spring, 1985.

Robertson, James I., Jr. *Soldiers Blue and Gray*. Columbia, 1988.

———. *The Stonewall Brigade*. Baton Rouge, 1963.

Rorabaugh, W. J. *The Alcoholic Republic: An American Tradition*. New York, 1979.

Royster, Charles. *A Revolutionary People at War: The Continental Army and American Character, 1775–1783*. Chapel Hill, 1979.

Ruby, James S., ed. *Blue and Gray: Georgetown University and the Civil War*. Washington, D.C., 1961.

Ruffner, Kevin C. *44th Virginia Infantry*. Lynchburg, 1987.

Sarkesian, Sam C., ed. *Combat Effectiveness: Cohesion, Stress, and the Volunteer Army*. Beverly Hills, 1980.

Saum, Lewis O. *The Popular Mood of Pre–Civil War America*. Westport, 1980.

Scharf, J. Thomas. *The Chronicles of Baltimore*. Baltimore, 1874.

———. *History of Baltimore City and County*. Philadelphia, 1881.

———. *History of Maryland from the Earliest Period to the Present Day*. 3 vols. 1879. Reprint. Hatboro, 1967.

———. *History of Western Maryland*. 2 vols. Baltimore, 1968.

Shannon, Fred A. *The Organization and Administration of the Union Army*. 2 vols. Cleveland, 1928.

Sifaskis, Stewart. *Compendium of the Confederate Armies: Kentucky, Maryland, Missouri, the Confederate Units and Indian Units*. New York, 1995.

Simpson, Lewis P. *Mind and the American Civil War: A Meditation on Lost Causes*. Baton Rouge, 1989.

Smith, Edward Conrad. *The Borderland in the Civil War*. 1927. Reprint. Freeport, 1969.

Soderburg, Susan Cooke. *Lest We Forget: A Guide to Civil War Monuments in Maryland*. Shippensburg, 1995.

Sommers, Richard J. *Richmond Redeemed: The Seige at Petersburg*. New York, 1981.

Stein, Charles Francis, Jr. *Origin and History of Howard County, Maryland*. Baltimore, 1972.

Stott, Richard B. *Workers in the Metropolis: Class, Ethnicity, and Youth in Antebellum New York City*. Ithaca, 1990.

Stutler, Boyd B. *West Virginia in the Civil War*. 2nd ed. Charleston, 1966.

Tabb, Nancy Crockett. *1860 Census of Somerset County, Maryland*. Decorah, 1985.

Talbert, Bart Rhett. *Maryland: The South's First Casualty*. Berryville, 1995.

Tanner, Robert G. *Stonewall in the Valley: Thomas J. "Stonewall" Jackson's Shenandoah Valley Campaign, Spring 1862*. New York, 1976.

Taylor, William R. *Cavalier and Yankee: The Old South and American National Character*. New York, 1961.

Thomas, Emory. *The Confederate Nation*. Baton Rouge, 1978.

Thomas, James W., and T. J. C. Williams. *History of Allegany County, Maryland*. 2 vols. Hagerstown, 1923.

Tidwell, William A., James O. Hall, and David Winfred Gaddy. *Come Retribution: The Confederate Secret Service and the Assassination of Lincoln*. Jackson, 1988.

Toomey, Daniel Carroll. *The Civil War in Maryland*. Baltimore, 1983.

————. *Marylanders at Gettysburg*. Linthicum, 1994.

Townshend, George Alfred. *Katy of Catoctin or the Chain-Breakers*. Cambridge, Md., 1959.

Tyrrell, Ian R. *Sobering Up: From Temperance to Prohibition in Antebellum America, 1800–1860*. Westport, 1979.

Vinovskis, Maris A., ed. *Toward a Social History of the American Civil War*. New York, 1990.

Wagandt, Charles Lewis. *The Mighty Revolution: Negro Emancipation in Maryland, 1862–1864*. Baltimore, 1964.

Wallace, Lee A., Jr. *A Guide to Virginia Military Organizations, 1861–1865*. 2nd ed. Lynchburg, 1986.

War History of the "National Rifles," Company A, Third Battalion, District of Columbia Volunteers of 1861. Wilmington, 1887.

Warfield, J. D. *The Founders of Anne Arundel and Howard Counties, Maryland*. Baltimore, 1967.

Warner, Ezra J. *Generals in Blue: Lives of the Union Commanders*. Baton Rouge, 1964.

————. *Generals in Gray: Lives of the Confederate Commanders*. Baton Rouge, 1959.

Weinert, Richard P., Jr. *The Confederate Regular Army*. Shippensburg, 1991.

Wert, Jeffrey D. *Mosby's Rangers*. New York, 1990.

Whyte, James H. "Divided Loyalties in Washington During the Civil War." In *Records of the Columbia Historical Society of Washington, D.C., 1960–1962*, 103–22. Edited by Frances Coleman Rosenberger. Washington, D.C., 1963.

Widenour, Ralph W., Jr. *Confederate Monuments: Enduring Symbols of the South and the War Between the States*. N.p., 1982.

Wiley, Bell I. *The Life of Billy Yank: The Common Soldier of the Union*. 1980. Reprint. Baton Rouge, 1994.

————. *The Life of Johnny Reb: The Common Soldier of the Confederacy*. 1980. Reprint. Baton Rouge, 1994.

————. *They Who Fought Here*. New York, 1959.

Wiley, Peter Booth. *Yankees in the Land of the Gods: Commodore Perry and the Opening of Japan*. New York, 1990.

Williams, Hermann Warner, Jr. *The Civil War: The Artists' Record*. Meriden, 1961.

Williams, T. C. J., and Folger McKinsey. *History of Frederick County, Maryland*. 2 vols. 1910. Reprint. Baltimore, 1967.

————. *A History of Washington County, Maryland*. Baltimore, 1968.

Wilmer, L. Allison, J. H. Jarrett, and George W. F. Vernon. *History and Roster of Maryland Volunteers, War of 1861–65*. 2 vols. 1898. Reprint. Westminster, 1987 and 1990.

Wise, Jennings Cropper. *The Long Arm of Lee: The History of the Artillery of the Army of Northern Virginia*. New York, 1959.

Wright, William C. *The Secession Movement in the Middle Atlantic States*. Rutherford, 1973.

Wyatt-Brown, Bertram. *Honor and Violence in the Old South*. New York, 1986.

————. *Yankee Saints and Southern Sinners*. Baton Rouge, 1985.

Articles

Bailey, Fred A. "Class and Tennessee's Confederate Generation." *Journal of Southern History*, LI (1985), 31–60.

Bakeless, John. "Catching Harry Gilmor." *Civil War Times Illustrated*, X (January, 1971), 34–40.

Blassingame, John W. "The Recruitment of Negro Troops in Maryland." *Maryland Historical Magazine* LVIII (1963), 20–29.

Bowers, Douglas. "Ideology and Political Parties in Maryland, 1851–1856." *Maryland Historical Magazine*, LXIV (1969), 197–217.

Clark, Charles B. "Baltimore and the Attack on the Sixth Massachusetts Regiment, April 19, 1861." *Maryland Historical Magazine*, LVI (1961), 39–71.

———. "Recruitment of Union Troops in Maryland, 1861–1865." *Maryland Historical Magazine*, LIII (1958), 153–76.

———. "Suppression and Control of Maryland, 1861–1865: A Study of Federal-State Relations During Civil Conflict." *Maryland Historical Magazine*, LIV (1959), 241–71.

Clark, Ella E., ed. "Life on the C&O Canal." *Maryland Historical Magazine*, LV (1960), 88–122.

Clemmer, Gregg. "Duty Above and Beyond the Call. . . ." *Maryland Line*, XIII (May, 1993), 2.

Coffman, Edward M. "The New American Military History." *Military Affairs*, XLVIII (1984), 1–5.

"Confederate Association in Maryland." *Confederate Veteran*, I (1893), 71.

Cooling, Benjamin Franklin. "Toward a More Useable Past: A Modest Plea for a Newer Typology of Military History." *Military Affairs*, LII (1988), 29–31.

Cottrell, E. C. "The Fight at Fort Gregg." *Confederate Veteran*, VII (1899), 308.

Cunz, Dieter. "The Maryland Germans in the Civil War." *Maryland Historical Magazine*, XXXVI (1941), 394–419.

Curl, Donald Walter."The Baltimore Convention of the Constitutional Union Party." *Maryland Historical Magazine*, LXVII (1972), 254–77.

Della, M. Ray, Jr. "An Analysis of Baltimore's Population in the 1850's." *Maryland Historical Magazine*, LXVIII (1973), 20–35.

Donald, David. "The Confederate as a Fighting Man." *Journal of Southern History*, XXV (1959), 178–93.

Dorsey, Frank. "Last Days of the First Maryland Cavalry." *Confederate Veteran*, XXVII (1919), 254–55.

Duncan, Richard R. "Marylanders and the Invasion of 1862." *Civil War History*, X (1964), 141–48.

———. "Maryland's Reaction to Early's Raid in 1864: A Summer of Bitterness." *Maryland Historical Magazine*, LXIV (1969), 248–79.

Echterncamp, Jorg. "Emerging Ethnicity: The German Experience in Antebellum Baltimore." *Maryland Historical Magazine*, LXXXVI (1991), 1–22.

Eckhardt, C. F. "A Problem of Rank." *Civil War Times Illustrated*, XXIX (January–February, 1991), 52–54.

Ellenberger, Matthew. "Whigs in the Streets? Baltimore Republicanism in the Spring of 1861." *Maryland Historical Magazine*, LXXXVI (1991), 23–38.

Ernst, Kathleen. "Accompanied by Cries of 'Go It Boys! Maryland Whip Maryland!' Two 1st Maryland Infantries Clashed." *America's Civil War*, VII (July, 1994), 10–16.

Forbes, Charles P. "A 'Minute' Regarding Major Harry Gilmor." *Maryland Historical Magazine*, LXXXIX (1994), 469.

Frasure, Carl M. "Union Sentiment in Maryland, 1859–1861." *Maryland Historical Magazine*, XXIV (1929), 210–24.

Gaede, Frederick. "Military Prisoners in the Baltimore City Jail, 1864." *Maryland Historical Magazine*, LXXXIX (1994), 467–68.

Garonzik, Joseph. "The Racial and Ethnic Make-up of Baltimore's Neighborhoods, 1850–70." *Maryland Historical Magazine*, LXXI (1976), 392–402.

Garrett, Jane N. "Philadelphia and Baltimore, 1790–1840: A Study of Intra-Regional Unity." *Maryland Historical Magazine*, LV (1960), 1–13.

Greeman, Betty Dix. "The Democratic Convention of 1860: Prelude to Secession." *Maryland Historical Magazine*, LXVII (1972), 225–53.

Green, Fletcher M. "A People at War: Hagerstown, Maryland, June 15–August 31, 1863." *Maryland Historical Magazine*, XL (1945), 251–60.

Greenberg, Amy Sophia. "Mayhem in Mobtown: Firefighting in Antebellum Baltimore." *Maryland Historical Magazine*, XC (1995), 164–79.

Hall, James O. "Marylanders in the Civil War: The Death of Walter Bowie." *Maryland Line*, X (October, 1989), 2–3.

Hartzler, Daniel D. "Maryland Confederate Harry Gilmor, Part II." *Company of Military Historians*, XLVI (Spring, 1994), 21–25.

Haselberger, Fritz, and Mark Haselberger. "The Battle of Greenland Gap." *West Virginia History*, XXVIII (1967), 285–304.

"History of Confederates in Maryland." *Confederate Veteran*, X (1902), 166.

Hollyday, Frederic B. M., ed. "Running the Blockade: Henry Hollyday Joins the Confederacy." *Maryland Historical Magazine*, XLI (1946), 1–10.

Hollyday, Lamar. "Maryland Troops in the Confederate Service." *Southern Historical Society Papers*, III (1877), 130–39.

Howard, Charles McHenry. "Baltimore and the Crisis of 1861." *Maryland Historical Magazine*, XLI (1946), 257–81.

Hurst, Harold W. "The Northernmost Southern Town: A Sketch of Pre–Civil War Annapolis." *Maryland Historical Magazine* LXXVI (1981), 240–49.

Karsten, Peter. "The 'New' American Military History: A Map of the Territory, Explored and Unexplored." *American Quarterly*, XXXVI (1984), 389–418.

Kimmel, Ross M. "Enlisted Uniforms of the Maryland Confederate Infantry: A Case Study, Part I." *Military Collector and Historian*, XLI (1989), 98–108.

———. "Enlisted Uniforms of the Maryland Confederate Infantry: A Case Study, Part II." *Military Collector and Historian*, XLI (1989), 183–88.

Kohn, Richard H. "The Social History of the American Soldier: A Review and Prospectus for Research." *American Historical Review*, LXXXVI (1981), 553–67.

Nesenhöner, Stefan. "Maintaining the Center: John Pendleton Kennedy, the Border States, and the Secession Crisis." *Maryland Historical Magazine*, LXXXIX (1994), 412–26.

Peters, Winfield. "First Battle of Manassas." *Southern Historical Society Papers*, XXXIV (1906), 170–78.

Powell, John W. "How to Pick Out Bad Officers." *Civil War Times Illustrated*, XXX (1991), 46–49.

Pinkett, Harold T. "A Brother's Fight for Freedom." *Maryland Historical Magazine*, LXXXV (1991), 39–50.

Robertson, James I., Jr., ed. "A Federal Surgeon at Sharpsburg." *Civil War History*, IV (1960), 134–51.

———. "The War in Words." *Civil War Times Illustrated*, XVI (1977), 48.

Ruffner, Kevin Conley. "Civil War Letters of a Washington Rebel." *Washington History: Magazine of the Historical Society of Washington, D.C.*, IV (1992–93), 56–71.

———. "Lost in the Lost Cause: The 1st Maryland Infantry Regiment (C.S.)." *Maryland Historical Magazine*, XC (1995), 424–45.

———. "A Maryland Refugee in Virginia, 1863." *Maryland Historical Magazine*, LXXXIX (1994), 447–52.

———. "'More Trouble Than a Brigade': Harry Gilmor's 2d Maryland Cavalry in the Shenandoah Valley." *Maryland Historical Magazine*, LXXXIX (1994), 388–411.

Sanderlin, Walter S. "A House Divided—The Conflict of Loyalties on the Chesapeake and Ohio Canal, 1861–1865." *Maryland Historical Magazine*, XLI (1946), 257–81.

Schoeberlein, Robert W. "A Fair to Remember: Maryland Women in Aid of the Union." *Maryland Historical Magazine*, XC (1995), 466–88.

Schreier, E. Philip III. "Marylanders in the Civil War: William Worthington Goldsborough." *Maryland Line*, X (March, 1990), 2–4.

"Second Regiment, Maryland Volunteer Infantry." *Maryland Historical Magazine*, XII (1917), 41–45.

Semmes, Raphael. "Vignettes of Maryland History from the Society's Collections of Broadsides." *Maryland Historical Magazine*, XL (1945), 24–53.

Smith, W. Wayne. "Jacksonian Democracy on the Chesapeake: Class, Kinship and Politics." *Maryland Historical Magazine*, LXIII (1968), 55–67.

Stagg, J. C. A. "Enlisted Men in the United States Army, 1812–1815: A Preliminary Survey." *William and Mary Quarterly*, XLIII (1986), 615–45.

Steuart, Richard D. "Henry A. Steuart—Rebel Spy." *Confederate Veteran*, XVI (1908), 332–34.

Stonebraker, John R. "Munford's Marylanders Never Surrendered to Foe." *Southern Historical Society Papers*, XXXVII (1910), 309–12.

Swart, Stanley L. "The Military Examination Board in the Civil War: A Case Study." *Civil War History*, XVI (1970), 227–45.

Tidwell, William A. "Charles County: Confederate Cauldron." *Maryland Historical Magazine*, XCI (1996), 16–27.

Toomey, Daniel Carroll. "Murdered—A Yankee Marylander, Captain Thomas H. Watkins." *Maryland Line*, X (December, 1989), 2–3.

Towers, Frank, ed. "Military Waif: A Sidelight on the Baltimore Riot of 19 April 1861." *Maryland Historical Magazine*, LXXXIX (1994), 427–46.

"Union Soldier Slave Owners." *Confederate Veteran*, VII (1889), 408.

Vinovskis, Maris A. "Have Social Historians Lost the Civil War? Some Preliminary Demographic Speculations." *Journal of American History*, LXXVI (1989), 34–58.

Wagandt, Charles L. "Election by Sword and Ballot: The Emancipationist Victory of 1863." *Maryland Historical Magazine*, LIX (1964), 143–64.

Weedle, Kevin J. "Ethnic Discrimination in Minnesota Volunteer Regiments During the Civil War." *Civil War History*, XXXV (1989), 239–59.

Wiser, Vivian. "Improving Maryland's Agriculture, 1840–1860." *Maryland Historical Magazine*, LXIV (1969), 105–32.

Wooster, Ralph A. "The Membership of the Maryland Legislature of 1861." *Maryland Historical Magazine*, LVI (1961), 94–102.

Theses, Dissertations, and Unpublished Papers

Arisumi, Mark T. "The Irish as Southern Democrats: The Political Persuasions of the Catholic Irish Immigrants in Baltimore, 1850–1865." M.A. thesis, University of Maryland, 1988.

Callette, Millard Les. "A Study of the Recruitment of the Union Army in Maryland." M.A. thesis, Johns Hopkins University, 1954.

Duncan, Richard R. "The Social and Economic Impact of the Civil War on Maryland." Ph.D. dissertation, Ohio State University, 1963.

McCauley, Donald J. "The Limits of Change in the Tobacco South: An Economic and Social Analysis of Prince George's County, Maryland, 1840–1860." M.A. thesis, University of Maryland, n.d.

McDonald, Lawrence H. "Prelude to Emancipation: The Failure of the Great Reaction in Maryland, 1831–1860." Ph.D. dissertation, University of Maryland, 1974.

Priest, John M. "Lieutenants and Captains in the Army of the Potomac: The

Creation of a Professional Army." Paper presented at the 1990 conference of the Civil War Society, Crystal City, Arlington, Va., August 23, 1990.

Quinn, Edward. "Recruitment and Enlistment in Maryland During the Civil War." M.A. thesis, Catholic University of America, 1943.

Ridgway, Whitman. "A Social Analysis of Maryland Community Elites: A Study of the Distribution of Power in Baltimore City, Frederick County, and Talbot County." Ph.D. dissertation, University of Pennsylvania, 1973.

Rommel, William M. "A History of the First Maryland Confederate Infantry Regiment, 1861–1862." M.A. thesis, University of Maryland, 1979.

Schoeberlein, Robert. "Baltimore in 1861: A Case Study of Southern Unionism." M.A. thesis, University of Maryland, Baltimore County, 1994.

Index

Abercrombie, Ralph, 282n
Abolitionism, 57–58
Addison, Joseph T., 250, 354
Adreon, Harrison, 74, 234, 273, 275–76, 278, 285–86, 354–55
Albaugh, Maurice, 70, 333
Albert, Augustus J., 67
Albert, Augustus James, Jr., 67n
Allard, Thomas B., 271
Allen, William H., 65, 219, 355
American party. See Know-Nothing party
Anderson, Ephraim F., 240, 250, 364
Andrews, Richard Snowden, 46, 47, 55n, 84–85, 100, 122, 135, 141–42, 295
Andrews, William E., 69–70, 374
Antietam, battle of, 241–42
Appomattox Court House, 210, 278
Armacost, James T., 333
Armacost, Lewis, 333
Army of Northern Virginia. See Confederate Army of Northern Virginia
Army of the Potomac. See Union Army of the Potomac
Arnold, Amelia F., 232
Artillery batteries. See Confederate artillery batteries; Union artillery batteries
Ashby, Turner, 77, 108, 131, 190
Ayres, Romeyn B., 278

Baer, James S., 224, 334
Bailey, Fred A., 6
Baker, Jean H., 2, 3, 27, 57

Baker, John J., 334
Ball, John K., 268–69, 364–65
Baltimore, Maryland: industrial development of, 2, 22; federal occupation of, 3, 34–38, 40, 60; and Maryland Brigade soldiers (U.S.), 12, 61, 63, 74, 263, 278–79, 288; politics in, 19, 25–28, 30, 52; growth of, 22; free blacks in, 23, 25; and social turmoil of 1850s, 25; police in, 27, 61; and secession crisis, 29, 33, 39; and Lincoln, 32; riots in, 34–35, 56, 60; Maryland Line officers (C.S.) from, 41, 43, 287; militia forces of, 52, 54; Union recruitment in, 60–61; Front Royal battle reaction, 245; reputation of, 261, 288–89
Baltimore American, 264
Baltimore and Ohio Railroad, 21, 22, 38, 40, 52, 198, 202–204
Baltimore City Guard Battalion, 56, 70
Baltimore Light Artillery Association, 285n
Bamberger, William W., 278
Bank Riots of 1835, p. 52
Bankard, Charles H., 272
Bankerd, Josiah, 355
Banks, Nathaniel P., 61, 106, 266
Barber, John G., 355
Barber, Joseph W., 295
Barrett, Gregory, Jr., 72–73, 251–52, 263, 279, 355
Barry, Edmund, 54, 109, 112, 295–96

Bartleson, Henry C., 374–75

Batteries. *See* Confederate artillery batteries; Union artillery batteries

Bayley, James P., 296

Bazin, Casimer, 334

Beachum, F. Stanley, 365

Beall, Ellen O., 130

Bean, Hezekiah Henry, 108–109, 296

Bean, William Bennett, 122, 128–29, 296

Beatty, Edward, 35, 55n, 140–41, 296

Beatty, Edward W., 35

Beauregard, Pierre G. T., 93

Bell, John, 30

Bennett, David T., 365

Billheimer, Henry M., 232

Birchell, John, 195

Bishop, John L., 356

Blackford, John C., 198–99

Blackford, William Willis, 198n

Blackiston, Henry Curtis, 126, 127, 296

Blacks. *See* Free blacks; Slaves and slavery; United States Colored Troops (USCT)

Blair, Charles W., 102, 297

Blair, Montgomery, 214

Blumenburg, Leopold, 71

Bolling, John, 96

Bond, Francis A., 37–38, 123, 188, 297

Bonn, Samuel G., 55n, 142, 297

Booth, George Wilson, 4, 35, 52, 89–90, 107, 113, 113n, 126, 142–43, 297–98

Border states: Maryland as one of, 2, 6, 29–30, 33, 287; role of, 6; and elections of 1860, pp. 29–30; family division in, 48; and secession crisis, 49; and Maryland Brigade (U.S.), 262

Boteler, A. R., 200

Bouldin, Richard E., 365

Bounty and Furlough Act, 98–99, 101

Bowen, William, 232

Bowerman, Richard N., 226, 227, 277, 286

Bowie, Wallace A., 74, 375

Bowie, Walter, 127–28n

Boyd, Isaac L., 265, 356

Boyer, Benjamin R., 375

Boyle, John H., 265

Bradford, Augustus, 119, 214, 258

Bradshaw, John J., 334

Bragonier, Alphreod C., 221–22, 365

Bragonier, Charles A., 193

Brashears, William G., 334

Brays, William J., 375

Breckinridge, John C., 30

Brewer, Henry Wilmot, 298

Brewer, Valentine G., 365–66

Bride, James, 235, 240, 375–76

Brighthaupt, George A., 298

Broadfoot, Joseph O., 228, 376

Broadfoot, William J., 81, 298

Brockenbrough, John Bowyer, 122, 298–99

Brooks, Henry P., 229

Brouner, Richard R., 221, 228–29, 366

Brown, David, 130

Brown, George W., 36, 299

Brown, John, 28–29, 43, 51, 52, 72

Brown, John W., 356

Brown, Ridgely, 123–24, 139, 184, 192, 201, 299

Brown, William Dawson, 123, 132–33, 135, 138, 188, 299

Browne, Gary Lawson, 3

Buchanan, W. Jefferson, 96–97, 132–33

Burke, Francis W., 40, 299

Burke, John Redmond, 193–94, 195n, 300

Burke, Nicholas, 40, 193, 195–96, 300

Burke, Redmond, 194

Burnham, William H., 366

Burnside, Ambrose Everett, 266

Burroughs, Somerset B., 144, 300

Burrows, Hillary T., 366–67

Bussey, James Thomas, 182, 300–301

Butler, Benjamin, 38, 38n, 40, 60

Byus, William R., 301

Callan, Christopher Charles, 41, 136–38, 182, 301

Calmes, Fielding Helms, 200, 200n
Cameron, Simon, 60
Camp Dimmock, 122
Camp Howard, 185
Camp Maryland, 185, 206
Camp Parole, 250
Camper, Charles, 245, 335
Carl, Louis Adolph, 229, 356
Carr, Wilson, 96
Carroll, Charles, 335
Carroll, Robert G. H., 133
Cassard, Louis R., 240–41, 376
Catton, Bruce, 5, 267n
Cavalry. *See* Confederate cavalry; Union
   cavalry
Chambers, Ezekiel F., 31–32
Chambersburg raid, 128–29, 206
Chaney, Louis, 376
Chapman, Nathaniel, 150, 301–302
Chase, John H., 335
Chenoweth, Ferdinand, 267, 356–57
Chesapeake and Ohio Canal, 21, 38
Chevalier, as military model, 1–2, 4, 288,
   289
Chew, Walter Scott, 302
Childs, Jesse D., 265, 335
Chilton, R. H., 117
Civilians: soldiers employed as, 115; vio-
   lence toward, 124, 128–30, 270;
   women, 130–34; and Gilmor's men,
   196–97; and Confederate cavalry
   units, 201
Clark, Charles Branch, 3
Clark, James Louis, 207, 302
Clarke, J. Lyle, 82, 82n
Clayton, Theodore, 222–23, 376
Coal mining, 21–22
Cochran, James B., 268, 367
Cold Harbor, battle of, 209, 211
Cole, Henry A., 62
Cole, William P., 377
Colegate, Charles E., 217, 335–36
Colklesser, William H., 243, 367
Collier, Frank M., 227, 336

Coloney, Josiah B., 75, 236–37, 271, 336
Compromise of 1850, pp. 19, 25
Confederacy: Maryland's failure to join,
   40, 79; and invasion of Maryland, 63,
   118–19; and Maryland Line, 100, 112;
   Maryland's support of, 260–61; and
   Richmond evacuation, 278
Confederate Army of Northern Virginia:
   officers in, 7, 283; and railroads, 38,
   38n; in Maryland, 63, 117–19, 122,
   187; conscription for, 101; recruitment
   for, 118; counterterror measures of,
   127–28; Second Corps of, 181. *See also*
   Confederate Maryland Line
Confederate artillery batteries: Maryland
   exiles in, 7, 10, 11; 3rd Maryland Battery, 12; Chesapeake Artillery, 44, 123;
   Maryland Flying Artillery, 84; commanders' duties, 86; 1st Maryland Battery, 100, 122, 185–87, 282, 284; Baltimore Light Artillery, 108, 122–23;
   Rockbridge Artillery, 122; 2nd Maryland Battery, 184; 4th Maryland Battery, 186; consolidation of Maryland
   batteries, 187
Confederate cavalry: Maryland exiles in,
   7, 10, 11; Howard County Dragoons,
   37, 84, 85; Charles County Volunteer
   Cavalry, 85; 1st Maryland Cavalry Battalion, 123–24, 126, 127, 142, 184,
   187–89, 192, 207–208, 210, 284,
   285n; 2nd Maryland Cavalry Battalion, 127, 142, 179, 184, 189, 206,
   207–209, 280n, 284; Winder Rangers,
   137; 12th Virginia Cavalry Regiment,
   190, 193, 200
Confederate infantry: Maryland exiles in,
   7, 10, 11; 1st Maryland Infantry, 79,
   81–85, 92, 94, 98–103, 105–20, 122,
   141, 179, 183, 186, 245, 282, 284; 2nd
   Maryland Infantry Battalion, 124, 143,
   179–82, 184, 209–10, 280, 280n, 284
Confederate Maryland Line: and Chevalier model, 4, 289; composition of, 12;

and First Manassas battle, 92–93; and
Gettysburg, 181; reconstitution of,
184; transfers to, 184–86; split of, 186;
battle record of, 210–11; casualties of,
280–81; administration of, 283–84
—officers of: general description of, 40–
47, 132, 287–88; family relationships
of, 47–48, 50–51, 132; secession crisis
views of, 49–50; and slavery, 49–40,
51, 55, 287; prewar military experiences of, 52, 54, 89; militia service of,
54; as prisoners, 78, 142–47, 281; election of, 80–81, 94–95, 102, 180, 282;
enlistment terms for, 81, 98–99, 101,
186; company commanders of, 86–91,
96; duties of, 87–91, 150; appointments of, away from companies, 89–
91, 182; promotions of, 103, 181, 182;
dissatisfaction of, 113n, 282; and 1st
Maryland Infantry disbandment, 117,
120, 122, 179, 183, 284; desertions of,
135–36, 282; losses of 141–42, 182,
281; devotion of, to cause, 147–48;
leadership of, 179, 209, 283, 286
—enlisted men of: 96–97, 104; recruit-
ment of, 100–101, 109, 185, 206
Conner, Charles A., 367
Conrad, Robert Y., 201
Conscription acts, 101, 186
Constitution of 1851, pp. 21, 25
Constitutional reform, 19–20, 22
Constitutional Union party, 30
Contee, Charles Snowden, 85, 135, 141,
185, 302–303
Cooke, Adolphus, 303
Cooke, William H., 377
Cooper, James, 213–15, 216, 217
Cooper, Samuel, 190, 193
Costello, Thomas, 303
Crane, James Parran, 180, 183, 303
Crawford, William J., 229, 357
Creager, Noble Harwood, 367–68
Crittenden, Churchill, 145
Crittenden Compromise, 32

Cromwell, William H., 368
Cross, Alexander, 113, 116, 304
Cross, E. W., 203
Cross Keys, battle of, 108–109, 211
Crouch, David, 286, 357
Cullimore, William H., 336
Cunliffe, Marcus, 1–2, 4, 288, 289
Cushing, John, Jr., 55n, 113, 304

Dabney, Frederick Y., 42, 85, 304
Dabney's Mills, battle of, 236, 239
Dahlgren, Ulric, 204
Daneker, William H., 276
Davis, Benjamin F., 247
Davis, Henry Winter, 29, 71, 119
Davis, James A., 136, 304
Davis, Jefferson, 83, 93, 97, 135, 138, 188
Davis, T. Sturgis, 193, 200–201, 205
Davis, Thomas H., 357
Davis, William H., 250, 357
Dayhoff, Joshua T., 219, 368
Deas, George, 81, 98–99
Deitz, Charles Aloysius, 336–37
Delisle, William, 205n
Della, M. Ray, Jr., 23
Dement, William Fendley, 47, 48, 85,
186–87, 304–305
Democratic party: and elections of 1847,
pp. 19–20; in Maryland, 19, 22, 26;
and immigrants, 23, 27; and elections
of 1852, pp. 25, 27; and Know-Noth-
ing party, 26; reform spirit of, 28; and
elections of 1860, p. 30; and Confeder-
ate Maryland Line, 287
Deppish, Edward Christian, 111, 115, 305
Devallin, Henry, 272
Deveney, John, 357
Devilbliss, Isaiah, 368
Devinney, Benjamin F., 305
Digges, Eugene, 46–47, 134, 145, 198,
305
Ditty, Cyrus Irving, 210, 305–306
Divinney, Benjamin F., 134–35
Dix, John A., 61, 116, 262

Dixon, Charles T., 377
Dooley, William, 201
Dorsey, Edward Rutland, 55n, 82, 82n, 83, 84, 89, 103, 104, 306
Dorsey, Frank, 210
Dorsey, Gustavus Warfield, 188–89, 207, 306
Dorsey, Samuel Worthington, 84
Dorsey, William H. B., 38n, 102, 126, 306
Douglas, Henry Kyd, 3, 51, 131
Douglas, Stephen A., 30
Douglass, Frederick, 21
Downing, Samuel W., 257
Dudrow, Charles Edwin, 337
Dukehart, Graham, 241, 244, 270, 274–75, 277
Dulaney, Bladen T. F., 70, 231–32, 337
Dulany, Richard H., 205
Dunphy, Richard G., 368
Dushane, Nathan T., 225, 230, 251n, 256, 277
Dutton, Norris B., 337
Duvall, Ferdinand C., 306–307

Early, Jubal A., 127–29, 202, 203, 206–208
Eastern Shore: 19–21, 25, 30, 31, 33, 41, 57, 62, 63, 282n
Easton, William Thomas, 358
Edelin, Charles Columbus, 93, 99, 99–100n, 103, 109, 135–36, 307
Edelin, William H. H., 109, 307
Edwards, Joseph, 265
Eichelberger, Grayson M., 72
Elections: of 1847, pp. 19–20; of 1852, pp. 25, 27; of 1855, pp. 26–27; of 1856, p. 27; violence of, 27–28; of 1859, p. 28; of 1860, pp. 29–30, 59; of 1864, pp. 263–64; Maryland Brigade (U.S.) voting patterns in, 263–64
Ellers, John T., 358
Elliott, Joseph, 358
Elzey, Arnold, 83–84, 92–93, 103, 185, 186, 204, 206

Emack, George M., 77, 128, 131, 133, 188, 207, 307
Emancipation Proclamation, 58
Engelbrecht, Jacob, 59
Evans, Thomas R., 337–38
Evitts, William J., 2, 3
Ewell, Richard S., 108, 184, 187

Faehtz, Ernest F. M., 71
Fay, James, 377
Federal government, 3, 34–38, 40, 60, 213–14
Federalist party, 19
Feilen, Augustus M., 377
Fellman, Michael, 6
Fields, Barbara Jeanne, 3
Fillmore, Millard, 27
Finigan, James, 307–308
Five Forks, battle of, 239, 278
Flag presentations, 212, 212n
Fleagel, Amos, 59
Forney, George W., 308
Forrest, David Crawford, 308
Forrest, Joseph, 44, 123, 308
Fox, William F., 280n
Franklin, James Shaw, 127, 147, 308
Franklin, William B., 206
Fredericksburg, battle of, 261
Free blacks: of Maryland, 2; role of, 3; as soldiers, 7, 10, 58; of Eastern Shore, 20; in western Maryland, 21; whites' fear of, 21, 28–29, 58; in Baltimore, 23, 25
Freeman, Douglas Southall, 5
Front Royal, battle of, 105–107, 239, 244–46, 248, 281
Fugitive Slave Act, 25
Furlong, McKendree C., 222, 377–78

Gaines Mill, battle of, 211
Gaither, George Ridgely, Jr., 37, 38n, 84, 85, 123
Gale, John, 309
Gallaher, John H., 338

Gamble, George, 270–71, 378
Gardner, Richard F., 378
Garmhauser, Frederick C., 378–79
Garrett, John W., 38
George, William E., 106–107, 229–30, 257, 338
German-speaking settlers, 5, 16, 22, 23, 71
Gettysburg, battle of, 121, 131, 181, 184, 192–93, 211
Giles, William F., Jr., 131
Gillette, James J., 215–16, 242, 253, 262, 266–67, 270, 276
Gillingham, Christopher R., 248, 267, 338–39
Gillingham, Edward E., 257–58, 339
Gillingham, Henry Raborg, 218–19, 339–40
Gilmor, Harry: writings of, 4, 191n, 205; and Chambersburg, 128, 206; and women, 131–32; and Keidel, 145; and cavalry consolidation, 188; partisan ranger unit of, 190–92, 199–200; recruitment efforts of, 192–95, 200; and discipline of troops, 196–98, 202–206, 205n, 209; battle record of, 198–99, 206; promotion of, 207; wounding of, 208; and Cole's Cavalry, 274; and Abercrombie, 282n
Gilmor, Meredith, 309
Gilmor, Richard Tilghman, 309–10
Gilmor, Robert, III, 191
Gist, Richard I., 238
Glenn, W. Y., 193
Goldsborough, Charles E., 48
Goldsborough, Edward Y., 74, 262, 274, 379
Goldsborough, William Worthington: writings of, 4; family relationships of, 47, 48; and 1st Maryland Infantry, 84, 102, 113; and Edelin, 99–100n; imprisonment of, 145, 182–83; and 2nd Maryland Infantry, 181; biographical sketch of, 310

Goodman, John, 129–30, 310
Gorrell, Skipworth C., 242, 368
Gorsuch, Robert McIntire, 230, 238, 358
Grady, John, 271
Graeser, Bernard N., 222, 379
Grant, Ulysses S., 278
Grason, John, 47, 123, 310
Green, Hanson T. C., 247
Green, John Kirkwood, 243, 368–69
Green, Thomas J., 310–11
Griffin, Joseph, 311
Griffin, William Hunter, 122, 145, 311
Griffith, Frank, 311
Griffith, George, 119
Griffith, Thomas, II, 123, 312
Groshon, John F., 102, 113, 312
Gross, Richard L., 379
Guerrilla warfare, 189, 273
Guillette, Gilbert G., 121–22, 133, 312
Gwynn, Andrew Jackson, 77, 141, 180, 312

Hack, Henry C., 218, 340
Hagan, Peter Augustus, 250, 369
Haggerty, John B., 340
Hands, Washington, 112
Hanover Junction, 184–86
Harkins, Joseph A., 268, 369
Harkins, Nathan, 268
Harn, Thomas W., 369
Harpers Ferry: Brown's seizure of, 28–29, 43, 51, 52; Virginia troops' garrison in, 38, 38n; and Johnson, 79; Confederate troops mustered in, 81; and 1st Maryland Infantry, 107; Maryland Brigade (U.S.) officers injured in, 243; and Jackson, 246–47; and 9th Maryland Infantry, 247
Harrison, John Spencer, 313
Harrisonburg, battle of, 108, 124
Hartigan, John, 145
Hatcher's Run, battle of, 143, 236
Haugh, Henry, 225, 340
Heard, John W., 119

Heath, Levi Theodore, 65, 230–31, 340–41

Heath, Stephen P., 379–80

Heine, Peter Bernard Wilhelm, 71, 232–33, 341

Henry, John C., 282n

Henry, Thomas, 341

Henry House Hill, 92, 93

Herbert, James R., 42, 45–46, 85, 103, 111, 124, 130, 180–82, 313

Hergesheimer, Robert H., 260–61, 275, 276, 369

Herring, James H., 261, 380

Hicks, Thomas H., 31, 36, 37, 39, 56–57, 60, 119

Hill, William Isaac, 313

Hilleary, William T., 220–21, 341–42

Hobbs, Nathan Chew, 313–14

Hodges, Charles W., 140, 314

Holbrook, Thomas H., 81, 314

Hooker, Joseph, 266

Horine, William Henry Harrison, 369–70

Hosmer, James Ray, 67, 69, 75, 380

Hough, William Dickinson, 55n, 113, 314

Howard, Clara Randolph, 114

Howard, George, 84, 95–96, 114, 134, 145, 314–15

Howard, John, 370

Howard, McHenry, 4, 49–50, 79, 85–86, 96

Howard, William Key, 107, 315

Hudson, Adam, 231

Hullett, David F., 380–81

Husband, Albert S., 225, 358–59

Hutchins, Sarah, 132

Huxford, David C., 217, 342

Hyde, Edward, 243, 359

Hyland, John G., 315

Imboden, John D., 195, 197–200, 204–205, 247

Immigrants, 2, 5, 16, 23, 25, 26, 27, 41, 65, 71

Independent Greys Battalion, 53

Independent Maryland Line, 85

Industrial development, 2, 21–22

Infantry. *See* Confederate infantry; Union infantry

Ingle, Frank, 193

Irelan, Charles Davis, 219, 381

Isaacs, John W., 230, 359

Jackson, Thomas J. "Stonewall," 93, 105–107, 123, 244, 246

Jacobs Bill, 29

Jamieson, Perry, 288

Janney, Joseph J., 222–23, 381

Jenkins, Albert G., 192

Johannes, John G., 56, 66–67, 70–71, 74–75n, 231, 243, 271, 381–82

Johnson, Bowie F., 69, 73, 74, 274, 382

Johnson, Bradley T.: views of, on Confederate Marylanders, 4–5, 288; and federal occupation of Baltimore, 37; and secession crisis, 39; family relationships of, 47; and Virginia blockade, 78–79; and 1st Maryland Infantry, 83–84, 102, 113; and Maryland Line (C.S.) support, 85, 100, 110, 112–13, 117–18, 183, 185–86, 283–84; and battle of First Manassas, 93; on enlistment terms, 98–99, 104, 110–11; promotion of, 103; and Front Royal battle, 105–106; and Cross Keys battle, 108–109; and Point Lookout prison camp, 127; and Chambersburg raid, 128–29; and Digges, 134; officers' deaths, 139–40; and Moorefield battle, 142–43, 206; and 2nd Maryland Infantry, 144, 180–81; and disbandment of Confederate regiment, 282; and postwar interest in Maryland Line (C.S.), 289n

Johnson, Jane Claudia, 79–80, 113

Johnson, Margaret A., 237–38

Johnson, Otis, 118, 315

Johnson, Reverdy, 73

Johnson, Thomas Scott Jesup, 70, 229–30, 237–38, 342

Johnston, Joseph E., 82, 92, 93

Jones, John B., 121

Junior officers. *See* Confederate Maryland Line; Union Maryland Brigade; and names of specific officers

Kane, George P., 37, 61, 185

Kane, Thomas L., 108

Kealhofer, Mary Louisa, 131

Kearny, Philip, 232

Keener, David S., 278

Keidel, Herman F., 145–47, 198

Kemp, Thomas Edwin, 359

Kemp, William H., 315–16

Kenly, John R., regiments, 60–61, 63, 212, 215, 217–18, 231, 245–46, 251n

Kennard, Lewis E., 382

Kennedy, Anthony, 54

Kennedy, John Pendleton, 14, 25

Kidd, Mary Jane, 72

Kilpatrick, Hugh Judson, 204

King, Richard, 264

Knobelock, Simon, 342–43

Knodle, Charles S., 370

Knoppel, John Joseph, 224, 343

Know-Nothing party, 26–28, 30, 52, 73, 288

Koogle, Jacob, 236, 370

Kugler, George W., 343

Kuhnes, William, 271

Larrabee, William F., 220, 382

Latchford, Thomas, 382–83

Laurel Hill, battle of, 235, 239–41

Lawrence, Stephen Demett, 316

Lawrenson, Emma, 212

Lecompte, Thomas P., 316

Lee, Eva, 132

Lee, Robert E.: and Confederate Maryland Line, 117–18, 186; and Goodman, 129–30; and Gilmor, 192, 197–98, 204, 206; and Early, 202

Lemmon, Robert, 80–81, 88, 96, 124–25

Leonard, William H., 231, 383

Letcher, John, 80, 82, 85, 96

Lewis, John Wesley, 343

Libby Prison, 77, 248, 249

Lightner, Isaiah, 370–71

Ligon, Thomas W., 27

Lincoln, Abraham, 30, 32, 36–37, 38, 59, 60, 63, 137, 214, 220, 232, 263, 277

Linderman, Gerald F., 5, 95

Lomax, Lunsford L., 187–89, 207–208

Lutts, John J., 114, 316

Lyeth, John McF., 245, 265, 343

Lyon, Lemuel Z., 343–44

Mace, Oscar A., 227, 359–60

Makechney, John, 371

Manassas battles, 92–94, 113, 211, 215

Mansfield, James T., 344

Marriott, Joseph G. W., 318

Marshall, Charles, 197

Marshall, J. W., 115

Marshall, John Prevost, 109, 120, 318

Maryland: as border state, 2, 6, 29–30, 33, 287; militarism in, 2; politics of, 2–3, 14; and secession crisis, 3, 29–33, 39–40, 56–57; slavery in, 3, 57–58, 263; occupied, 4; and sectionalism, 14, 33; control of, by Army of the Potomac (U.S.), 34, 40; Washington D.C.'s proximity to, 36–37, 38; militia forces of, 37, 52–54, 60, 74, 74–75n; lack of support for Confederates in, 40, 79; Confederate invasion of, 63, 117–19; southern sentiment against, 120–22, 121n; and officer appointments, 213–14; Confederate sentiment of, 260–61; Union loyalty of, 260–63; soldier votes in, 263–64; prewar uncertainty of, 287. *See also* Baltimore, Maryland; Eastern Shore; Northern Maryland; Southern Maryland; Western Maryland

Maryland Brigade. *See* Union Maryland Brigade

Maryland Guard Battalion, 53, 82

Maryland Line. *See* Confederate Maryland Line

Maryland Regiments: 5th Maryland Regiment, 52; 53rd Maryland Regiment, 52, 53; Kenly's organization of, 60–61. *See also* Confederate and Union headings

Mason-Dixon line, 2, 29

McAleer, Joseph L., 149, 183, 316

McAllister, John A., 371

McCarroll, William J., 316

McCausland, John, 128, 142–43, 206

McClellan, George B., 232, 262, 263, 266–67, 267n, 277

McConnell, John C., 60–61, 214, 217, 344

McCoy, Henry, 114, 316–17

McCracken, John H., 240–41

McCulloh, George William, 243, 383

McCullough, Samuel Thomas, 51–52, 127, 147, 149, 317

McKaig, William Wallace, Jr., 203n, 317

McKim, Randolph H., 3, 40–41, 88, 93, 96

McKim, William Duncan, 96

McKnew, Mason E., 138, 144, 317–18

McMorris, John, 371

McNeill, Jesse C., 208

McNulty, John R., 318

McNulty, Joseph, 344

McNulty, Thomas, 227, 344

McPherson, James M., 5

McWhiney, Grady, 288

Meade, George G., 267

Meade, Robert B., 228, 360

Melton, Samuel W., 204

Mercer, Virgil T., 274, 345

Militia forces, 37, 52–54, 60, 74, 74–75n

Millender, John Henry, 244, 360

Mills, Thomas Allen, 360

Mitchell, Hugh, 318–19

Mitchell, Reid, 5

Mobley, Edward M., 57, 251, 371

Moffett, Edwin W., 269, 277, 383–84

Moffett, William H., Jr., 242–43

Monocacy, battle of, 265

Moorefield, battle of, 142–43, 206–207

Morris, Robert A., 345

Morrison, William D., 219, 371–72

Mosby, John S., 190, 208, 273

Moulton, Charles A., 226

Mullan, James, 319

Munford, Thomas T., 210

Murray, Alexander, 243, 384

Murray, Clapham, 47, 93, 319

Murray, William H.: family relationships of, 47; prewar military experience of, 54; and company elections, 80–81, 94–95; as commander, 82, 82n, 91, 94; and First Manassas battle, 92–94; and 1st Maryland Infantry, 102; promotion of, 103; and Front Royal battle, 106–107, 245; recruitment efforts of, 109; and conduct of war, 125; death of, 139, 181, 284; respect of, for fellow soldiers, 139, 284; and 2nd Maryland Infantry, 180; respect of soldiers for, 284, 286; biographical sketch of, 319

Murray Confederate Association, 284, 285n

Nativism, 25–26, 30

Neely, Robert, 345

Nicholas, John S., 47

Nicholas, Wilson Carey, 37, 41, 46, 47, 80, 103, 108, 138, 319–20

Nicholson, Edward E., 70, 219, 360–61

Nicodemus, William J. L., 225–26

Noonan, Robert C., 124

Norman, William Buckner, 69, 243, 384

Northern Central Railroad, 56

Northern Maryland, 21, 33

O'Brien, Edmund, 320

Ocker, Thomas, 238–39

Officers. *See* Confederate Maryland Line; Union Maryland Brigade; and names of specific officers

O'Neill, Charles Z., 237, 361
O'Neill, Deborah, 237
O'Neill, John, 111
Orem, Joseph Bailey, 218, 225–26, 345–46
Orphan Brigade, 284
Overland campaign, 239

Palfrey, E. A., 192
Partisan Ranger Act, 189–90
Partisan units, 189–91, 199–201, 206, 208
Pember, Phoebe Yates, 122
Pennington, W. C., 53
Pennsylvania Bucktails, 108
Perry, Matthew C., 71
Petersburg, Virginia, 210, 211, 239, 278
Phelps, Charles E., 240, 250
Philpot, G. Blanchard, 77
Pikesville Forest Rangers, 37
Pittman, Alexander McK., 42, 116, 136, 320
Placide, Paul D., 361
Plater, John Edward, 123, 135, 320–21
Point Lookout prison camp, 127
Politics: of Maryland, 2–3, 14; in southern Maryland, 16, 19; in Baltimore, 19, 25–28, 30, 52; in Eastern Shore region, 21. *See also* specific political parties
Polk, John W., 321
Pope, John, 270
Post, John Eager Howard, 107
Price, Frank S., 81, 98, 321
Prohibition, 25–26
Protestants, 23, 26, 45
Pue, Edward H. D., 141, 321
Pue, James A. Ventress (or Ventris), 123, 145, 322
Purnell, George Washington, 62–63, 322
Purnell, Washington Irving, 384

Quaker, as military model, 1, 2, 288
Quinn, Joseph P., 136, 322

Radcliff, William D., 372
Railroads, 21, 22, 34, 37, 38, 38n, 56
Randall, James Ryder, 35–36
Randolph, George, 112
Ransom, Robert, 207
Rasin, William Independence, 42–43, 47, 78, 322–23
Rattie, Patrick, 138
Ray, Richard M., 258
Reckerd, John William, 361
Redwood, Allen C., 289n
Reed, Isaac, 242
Reed, Seth G., 346
Reed, William, 198
Reese, John, 268, 346
Reifsnider, Charles T., 372
Republican party, 30
Reynolds, Alfred D., 235, 346–47
Reynolds, Robert W., 347
Richardson, Charles H., 247
Richardson, William H., 323
Richmond, Virginia: Maryland's proximity to, 6; defense of, 40; Maryland refugees in, 111; contempt for Marylanders in, 120–21, 121n; Confederate evacuation, 278
Riddle, Beal D., 384–85
Rifleman, as military model, 1, 2, 4, 288, 289
Rigsby, James H., 241–42
Rimby, Jacob, 362
Rinehart, Daniel, 73, 372
Rinehart, William H., 73
Rizer, Eugene J., 227–28, 385
Roberts, Benjamin G., 323
Roberts, Joseph Kent, Jr., 47, 323
Robertson, James I., Jr., 5
Robertson, Michael Stone, 82, 102, 108, 125, 148–49, 324
Robinson, Joseph, 372
Roderick, William W., 220, 385
Rodgers, R. S., 201
Roman Catholic Church, 14, 26, 45, 287
Ross, David M., 205, 324

Rosser, Thomas L., 201
Rousselot, C. A., 324
Ruhl, Henry, 347
Ruths, George, 362

Sachs, John, 249
Saville, Thomas, 224–25, 245, 347–48
Schlennig, Fritz, 385–86
Schley, Benjamin H., 61, 256, 348
Schley, Mrs. Benjamin H., 260
Schley, John, 362
Schwartze, Augustus F., 324
Scott, John, 137
Scott, Sir Walter, 2, 289
Scott, Winfield, 25, 38
Secession crisis, 3, 29–33, 34, 39–40, 49–50, 56–57
Sectionalism, 14, 33
Seddon, James A., 190–92, 195
Selvage, Edwin, 113
Seven Days' battles, 109
Seward, William Henry, 277
Sharpsburg campaign, 113, 120
Shealey, George W., 243, 386
Shearer, George E., 193–94, 194n, 196–97, 197n
Shearer, George M. E., 80, 102, 194n, 324
Shellman, George Krebs, 102, 324–25
Shenandoah Valley: and Moorefield battle, 143, 207; and 2nd Maryland Infantry, 180; and Maryland Line (C.S.), recruits, 185; and Gilmor, 199, 205, 206, 208; reputation of, 201, 204; guerrilla warfare in, 273
Shenandoah Valley campaign: and enlistment terms, 99; Front Royal battle, 105–106; and 1st Maryland Infantry, 108, 109; and 1st Maryland Cavalry Battalion, 123
Sheppard, William Ludwell, 289n
Sheridan, Philip, 208
Shriver, F. A., 59
Shriver, George W., 386

Sigel, Franz, 253
Simon, Frederick W., 386
Simpers, John W., 387
Simpson, Benjamin L., 247–48
Slaves and slavery: in Maryland generally, 3, 57–58, 263; role of, in Civil War, 3; in southern Maryland, 17–18; in Eastern Shore region, 20, 57; in western Maryland, 21, 22; in Baltimore, 23, 29; and Compromise of 1850, p. 25; and Democratic party, 26, 30; and Know-Nothing party, 26, 28; Maryland Line (C.S.) officers' attitude toward, 49–50, 51, 55, 55n, 287; and Maryland Brigade (U.S.), 57–58, 149, 249, 288
Slingluff, Fielder Cross, 47, 142, 325
Smith, Frances M., 235–36, 239, 348
Smith, George, 221, 245, 270–71, 348
Smith, Henry C., 373
Smith, John K., 220, 373
Smith, John Louis, 81–82, 103, 113, 325
Smith, Robert Carter, 54, 102, 188, 248–49, 325–26
Smith, Robert S., 348
Smith, Thomas Jefferson, 326
Smith, Thomas Washington, 109, 112, 326
Smoot, William Sidney, 348–49
Smyth, William, 41, 326
Snow, Alonzo, 63
Snowden, Nicholas N., 38, 85, 108, 326
Sollers, Somerville, 94, 120, 209–10
Southern Maryland: decline of, 16–20; politics in, 16, 19–26; and Washington D.C., 16–17; slavery in, 17–18; daily life in, 18–19; and elections of 1860, p. 30; and secession crisis, 31, 33; Maryland Line (C.S.) officers from, 41, 287; Maryland Brigade (U.S.) officers from, 63, 74
Stanton, David Leroy, 252–53, 349
Starkweather, Norris G., 349
Stephenson's Depot, battle of, 247
Sterling, Thomas J., 387

Steuart, George H.: and 1st Maryland Infantry, 83–84, 93–94, 102, 116; Booth as adjutant for, 90; and Maryland Line (C.S.), support, 100–101, 183, 283–84; promotion of, 103; and Tormey, 117; and Bond, 123; and Crane, 180; and 2nd Maryland Infantry, 181
Steuart, Henry A., 78
Stewart, Joseph H., 81, 115, 326–27
Stewart, Septimus H., 90, 113, 327
Stewart, Thomas Richard, 185, 327
Stiffler, John Nelson, 349
Stone, John H., 95, 124–27, 130, 134, 148, 327
Stonebraker, Joseph H., 349–50
Stonestreet, Joseph Harris, 328
Stuart, J. E. B., 191, 192, 194, 204
Sudler, John Emory, 328
Sudsberg, Joseph M., 256
Suter, Charles M., 373
Suter, John H., 72, 362–63
Suter, Martin, 75, 363
Swain, John H. Bertram, 387
Swann, Thomas, 27

Tarr, Frederick Crey, 246, 350
Taylor, Richard, 123
Taylor, William, 235, 249–50, 350
Taylor, William H., 350
Taylor, William R., 288
Taylor, Zachary, 73
Thom, J. Pembroke, 125
Thomas, Francis J., 82–83
Thomas, George, 130–31, 328
Thomas, William P., 328
Thompson, George W., 271, 351
Tobacco, 2, 14, 16, 17
Tocqueville, Alexis de, 2, 280, 283
Tolson, Thomas Hill, 47, 130, 140, 143, 148, 187, 209, 328–29
Tormey, Frank A., 117, 329
Torsch, John W., 43, 182, 185, 210, 280, 329–30
Tower, Lawrence, 65, 373

Trimble, Isaac R., 37
Troxell, Jacob Luther, 387
Tucker, John A., 244, 363
Turnbull, S. Graeme (or Graham), 330
Tyler, George L., 219, 373

Union Army of the Potomac: officers of, 7, 244, 252, 283; control of Maryland by, 34, 40; morale within, 244; and McClellan, 266; victory parade of, 278. See also Union Maryland Brigade
Union artillery batteries: Maryland regiments of, 7, 9–10; Alexander's Baltimore Battery, 63; and Purnell Legion, 63; 2nd New York Artillery, 257; 1st Maryland Light Artillery, 258
Union cavalry: Maryland regiments of, 7, 9; Cole's Cavalry, 62, 247, 273–74; Purnell Legion, 62–63, 71, 214, 222, 255, 283; 1st Maryland Cavalry Regiment, 63, 218, 247, 272; 13th New York Cavalry Regiment, 257; 3rd Maryland Cavalry Regiment, 258
Union infantry: Maryland regiments of, 7, 8–9; 1st Maryland Infantry, 61, 106, 212, 215, 217–18, 224, 235, 239, 244–46, 255–56, 263, 264, 270n, 272–73, 280–81n, 281, 283; 2nd Maryland Infantry Regiment, 61, 264; 3rd Maryland Infantry Regiment, 61–62, 216, 217, 255, 264; 5th Maryland Infantry Regiment, 61, 247, 248, 249, 255–56, 261, 264; Baltimore Light Infantry, 61, 216; German Rifles, 61, 215, 216; Potomac Home Brigade Infantry, 62, 216, 246–47; and Purnell Legion, 62–63, 71, 222; 6th Maryland Infantry, 63, 247, 261, 281n; 9th Maryland Infantry Regiment, 199, 247–48; 4th Maryland Infantry Regiment, 215, 234, 240, 254; 8th Maryland Infantry, 222, 255, 278, 283; 34th Massachusetts Infantry Regiment, 248; 7th Maryland Infantry, 251–52; 2nd Regiment Eastern Shore

Infantry, 255; 11th Maryland Infantry, 255, 258

Union Maryland Brigade: composition of, 12; and slavery, 57–58, 149, 249, 288; recruitment for, 60–61, 62, 212–13, 255–57; consolidation of regiments of, 216, 255, 282–83; and Maryland's loyalty to Union cause, 260–63; and spring campaign of 1865, p. 278; administration of, 283
—officers of: general description of, 12, 61–67, 69–75, 288; enlistment terms of, 213, 222, 258, 272–73; elections of, 214; removal and resignation of, 216–23, 281–82; conduct of, 223–33, 257, 270–74; casualties of, 234–42, 246, 255, 280–81; Medals of Honor awarded to, 235–36; as prisoners, 244–50, 281; assignments of, outside of unit, 250–51, 251n; replacement system for, 252–55, 282; promotions within, 252–55, 253n, 283; morale of, 256, 265–66, 283; voting patterns of, 263–64; home front service of, 264–65; furloughs for, 267–68; discipline of, 270–72, 281–82; benefits of military life to, 274–76; and Veteran Reserve Corps service, 274; desertions of, 282n; leadership of, 286; and Rifleman model, 289
—enlisted men of: 252–54, 269, 270–71, 283, 289

Union Rifles, 56, 60
Union V Corps, 239, 251
Unionism, 27, 32
Unionsverein, 71
United States Colored Troops (USCT), 7, 10, 58

Veidt, Henry Jacob Julius, 217, 351
Veteran Reserve Corps, 274
Veterans' groups, 274, 284, 285n, 289n
Vink, John E., 351
Violence: in elections, 27–28; and Balti-more, 34–36, 288; toward civilians, 124, 128–29, 270

Virginia: Maryland officers fighting in, 10, 85; and Harpers Ferry capture, 38; as locus of war, 40; Maryland Brigade (U.S.) officers from, 65; Confederate Marylanders in, 76; running blockade of, 76–79, 144; Maryland Line (C.S.) units in, 186
Virginia State Reserves, 113
Volunteer Ununiformed Corps, 37
Von Hagen, Sigismund, 363

Wagoner, George, 195
Walker, Joseph E., 351–52
Walker, Noah Dixon, 48–49
Walker, William, 42
Waltemeyer, Charles, 352
Waltemeyer, Francis G. F., 61, 69, 352
Walter, Edward H., 116, 330
Walters, James D., 330
Wantz, David K., 226
Ward, Francis Xavier, 35, 36, 43, 107, 115, 330
Warren, Gouverneur K., 221, 239–40, 279
Washington, D.C.: security of, 3, 6, 34, 36–38; and southern Maryland's economy, 16–17; and Baltimore, 22; Maryland Brigade (U.S.) soldiers from, 63; and Virginia blockade, 76
Watkins, Thomas H., 265
Watson, Hugh, 352
Watson, Robert, 286, 363
Webster, Edwin H., 228–29
Webster, Joseph P., 373–74
Weise, Arthur James, 219–20, 374
Weldon Railroad, battle of, 235, 239, 242, 281n, 285
Wellmore, Henry, 81, 116, 135, 331
Wells, John B., 331
Welsh, Milton, 331
Welsh, Warner Griffith, 144–45n, 331
West, Edward L., 91

Western Maryland: Maryland Brigade (U.S.) soldiers from, 12, 61, 62, 63, 74, 288; political strength of, 19; and constitution of 1851, p. 21; industrial development of, 21–22; Democratic party in, 22; Whig party in, 22, 25; and elections of 1860, p. 30; and secession crisis, 33, 39; Maryland Line (C.S.) officers from, 41, 287
Weston, George H., 104
Weston, J. Alden, 82n, 111
Wharry, Robert N., 251, 352–53
Wheeler, Henry W., 374
Whig party, 19–26
Whites: in southern Maryland, 16; in Eastern Shore region, 20; and free black population, 21, 28–29, 58; in western Maryland, 21; immigrant populations as proportion of, 23
Whitson, David, 271
Whittle, Samuel N., 265, 374
Wilderness, battle of, 239
Wiley, Bell Irvin, 5, 91
Wilhelm, Elizabeth Kone, 74
Wilhelm, Henry, 74, 363–64
Wilhelm, James T., 122, 331–32
Wilhelm, Peter B., 74

Williams, Anthony C., 364
Williams, Edward, 353
Williams, Seth, 232–33
Williamson, George, 96
Wilson, Isaac, 236, 353
Wilson, James Hebb, 332
Wilson, John W., 56, 60, 75, 224, 230–31, 235, 236, 251, 256, 353–54
Wilson, Robert A., 236, 354
Winchester, Virginia, 107, 196, 201, 203, 245; battle of Second Winchester, 211
Winder, Charles S., 83
Winder, John H., 114, 121, 137
Wingate, Christopher L., 387
Wise, Charles Bennett, 332
Wood, Francis G., 49–50
Woodson, Charles H., 208
Woolcot, John W., 63
Wright, Charles Wesley, 246, 354
Wrightson, William C., 332

Young, George W., 271
Young, John C., 388
Young Men's Christian Association of Baltimore, 36

Zollinger, William P., 144, 332–33